Seeing Society

Perspectives on Social Life

Second Edition

3-8
9-16
121-123
17-18
49-58

PAUL B. BREZINA
CHARLES SELENGUT
ROBERT A. WEYER

County College of Morris

ALLYN AND BACON
Boston London Toronto Sydney Tokyo Singapore

To our children, the next generation:
Emily, Katherine, Philip
Nora, Suzanne, Erica, Daniel
Jonathan, Meg

A Division of Simon & Schuster, Inc.
160 Gould Street
Needham Heights, MA 02194

Series Editor: Karen Hanson
Editorial Assistant: Sarah L. Dunbar
Production Administrator: Deborah Brown
Editorial-Production Service: P. M. Gordon Associates
Cover Administrator: Suzanne Harbison
Composition Buyer: Linda Cox
Manufacturing Buyer: Megan Cochran

Library of Congress Cataloging-in-Publication Data

Seeing society: perspectives on social life / [edited by] Paul B. Brezina, Charles Selengut, Robert A. Weyer.—2nd ed.
p. cm.
Includes bibliographical references.
ISBN 0–205–14348–2
1. Sociology. I. Brezina, Paul B. II. Selengut, Charles. III. Weyer, Robert A.
HM51.S376 1994
301—dc20 93-9936
CIP

Printed in the United States of America
10 9 8 7 6 5 4 3 2 98 97 96 95

Contents

Preface ix

Acknowledgments xiii

General Introduction xv

Part One The Field and Its Methods

I Sociological Perspectives 1

1 Invitation to Sociology 3
Peter L. Berger

2 The Sociological Imagination 9
C. Wright Mills

II Methods and Styles of Social Research 17

3 Knowing About Things 19
Jonathan Turner

4 Chartering and Bartering: Elite Education and Social Reproduction 22
Caroline Hodges Persell and Peter W. Cookson, Jr.

5 I Q and Heredity: Suspicion of Fraud Beclouds Classic Experiment 41
Nicholas Wade

Part Two Core Concepts

III Culture 49

6 Queer Customs 51
Clyde Kluckhohn

7 The Sounds of Silence 59
Edward Hall and Mildred Hall

8 Iran's White Revolution and Its Outcome for Iranian Women 70
Hamid R. Kusha

IV Socialization 77

9 Backyard Versus Little League Baseball: The Impoverishment of Children's Games 79
Edward C. Devereux

10 Police Accounts of Normal Force 95
Jennifer Hunt

11 The Social Psychology of George Herbert Mead 107
Bernard N. Meltzer

V Social Structure and Groups 121

12 Institutions and Social Roles 125
Hans Gerth and C. Wright Mills

13 The Nudist Management of Respectability 128
Martin S. Weinberg

14 Presentation of Self in Everyday Life 140
Erving Goffman

VI Sociology of Deviance 151

15 Notes on the Sociology of Deviance 153
Kai Erikson

16 On Being Sane in Insane Places 162
D. L. Rosenhan

17 A Case of a Psychotic Navaho Indian Male 181
Donald P. Jewell

Part Three Social Inequality

VII Social Differentiation and Stratification 191

18 Principles of Social Stratification 193
Kingsley Davis and Wilbert E. Moore

19 Karl Marx's Theory of Alienation 200
Erich Fromm

20 Tracked to Fail 210
Sheila Tobias

VIII Sociology of Gender and Age 217

21 Blowing the Whistle on the "Mommy Track" 221
Barbara Ehrenreich and Deirdre English

22 Understanding Sexual Violence 226
Diana Scully

23 A Generation at Risk: When the Baby Boomers Reach Golden Pond 234
Robert N. Butler

IX Racial and Ethnic Relations 245

24 Assimilation in America: Theory and Reality 247
Milton M. Gordon

25 Cognitive Styles and Multicultural Populations 258
James A. Anderson

26 A New Pool of Talent 267
Phillip Hoose

Part Four Major Institutions

X The Family 277

27 The Shape of the American Family in the Year 2000 279
Andrew Cherlin and Frank F. Furstenberg, Jr.

28 Commuter Marriage 288
Naomi Gersel and Harriet Gross

29 Differential Socialization and Role Stereotypes in Japanese Families 296
John W. Conner

XI Religion **303**

30 Divided We Fall: America's Two Civil Religions 305
Robert Wuthnow

31 Secularization, Revival, and Cult Formation 313
Rodney Stark and William Sims Bainbridge

XII Organizations and Economic Life **321**

32 New Worlds of Computer-Mediated Work 323
Shoshana Zuboff

33 The Funeral Home as a Work System: A Sociological Analysis 329
Jerome J. Salomone

34 Ethical Dimensions of the Challenger Disaster 339
Russell Boisjoly, Ellen Foster Curtis, and Eugene Mellican

XIII Education **357**

35 Democratic Faith and Education 359
John Dewey

36 Should Social Background Count? 364
Charles Selengut

37 From Idealism to Pragmatic Detachment: The Academic Performance of College Athletes 368
Peter Adler and Patricia A. Adler

38 The Case Against IQ Tests: The Concept of Intelligence 380
Jerome Kagan

XIV Politics and Power **385**

39 On Power 387
Robert Bierstedt

40 Medicalized Killing 394
Robert Jay Lifton

41 America: What Went Wrong? 400
Donald L. Barlett and James B. Steel

Part Five Cultural Change and Social Issues

XV Population and Health **407**

42 Lifestyle: It's in the Cards 409
Jeffrey P. Rosenfeld and Susan Rodin

43 The Social Meaning of AIDS 414
Peter Conrad

XVI Community and Urban Life **425**

44 Community and Society 427
Ferdinand Töennies

45 Homelessness: Reducing the Distance 435
Kim Hopper

XVII Collective Behavior **447**

46 The Crowd 449
Gustave LeBon

47 The Razor Blade in the Apple: The Social Construction of Urban Legends 452
Joel Best and Gerald T. Horiuchi

48 Violence: Out of Hand in the Stands 468
Bil Gilbert and Lisa Twyman

XVIII Social Change **481**

49 The McDonaldization of Society 483
George Ritzer

50 The Soviet Upheaval and Western Sovietology 492
Bruce Parrott

51 The Psychology of Hitlerism 497
Harold D. Lasswell

References **507**

Preface

THE PURPOSE OF this book is to help make the teaching of sociology more rewarding and the learning of sociology more enjoyable and valuable. We have selected articles with great care, keeping in mind the needs of both instructors and students. For instructors, we have chosen articles that will not only inform and stimulate students, but also illustrate the scope and diversity of sociology. Classic statements concerning the nature of social life are balanced with contemporary selections which examine salient sociological issues and controversies. For students, we realize that the introductory course is usually their first exposure to "seeing" themselves and their surroundings in a new and different light. Sociological concepts and perspectives are often elusive and difficult to "pin down" and understand. The goal of this book is to provide a link between textbook terminology and actual sociological studies and analysis. We have selected articles which serve to clarify core concepts and perspectives and to highlight current sociological issues.

The second edition has been extensively changed and updated. We have selected twenty-three new articles concerning a diverse range of topics and issues including police work, prep schools, the shuttle disaster, nudists, insanity, alienation, sexual violence, the Holocaust, and changes in Iran and the Soviet Union. Since the majority of the articles are from sociological works and academic sociological journals, we have done some thoughtful editing in order to tailor the readings to undergraduate courses but without sacrificing the substance and quality of the material. An introduction is provided to each chapter that focuses on the major perspectives, concepts, and issues involved in the chapter. We demonstrate how each article relates to the central sociological theme of the chapter topic. Also, we provide discussion questions at the end of each selection in order to aid student comprehension of the material. These readings are explicitly designed to pique student interest in social behavior and to develop analytical and critical thinking.

This anthology is designed to complement introductory sociology textbooks, but it may also stand alone. It is intended to expand classroom discussion of the major issues in sociology. Currently, there are two basic types of anthologies available for sociology courses. One type is the "relevant" reader which is composed of nonsociological, journalistic articles from popular periodicals and magazines. We have used this type of reader in our courses and have found the material to be too light and inadequate for developing an appreciation of the sociological perspective. Rather, these types of anthologies function to confuse students about the nature of sociology. Sociology is not journalism. A second type of anthology is composed of unedited, high level journal articles and is oriented to upper level sociology students. These anthologies are useful in elective and graduate courses, but contain material that is simply too abstract or technical for undergraduate students to fully comprehend. This book focuses on the middle ground between these two types of anthologies. We balance the classic statements of the discipline with contemporary articles designed to stimulate student interest concerning current issues and events.

In this regard there are a number of key features which we feel make this book unique:

a. The book is avowedly *international* and *comparative* in its approach and scope. Selections are not limited to the American scene. Studies included are based on data from Sweden, Israel, China, Iran, France, Japan, Italy, Great Britain, Latin America, Saudi Arabia, the former Soviet Union, and Mormon and Navaho cultures. Our goal is to enable students to intuitively grasp and comprehend other cultures, world views, and national systems.

b. The book is *issue-oriented.* It presents material on some of the major controversies and issues of our era. Articles focus on such topics as sexual violence, cults, aging, the Holocaust, alienation, educational tracking, mental illness, the shuttle disaster, AIDS, heart disease, the homeless, crowd violence, and inequality (class, gender, age, race, ethnic). Both students and instructors can use selected articles as a basis for discussing the social and political ramifications of these contemporary issues.

c. The book is *student-oriented.* While we include theoretical perspectives, the prime objective is to include selections that relate theory to the world of everyday life and individual identity. Selections include emphasis on leisure and work, big time college sports, urban myths and legends, Little League baseball, and body language.

d. We stress the *academic* nature of sociology. We have avoided the "journalistic route" and have generally stayed within the parameters of sociological literature. Selections are included from major sociological works and from a variety of academic journals such as the *American Sociological Review, Social Problems, American Quarterly, Social Policy, Sociology of Education, Journal of Business Ethics, Journal of Psychological Anthropology, Harvard Business Review, Urban Life, Human Organization, Journal of American Culture, Political Quarterly, International Journal of Health Services, Science, The Antioch Review, New England Journal of Human Services,* and *American Demographics.* Some of the selections are challenging for the introductory student, but we have carefully edited the material in order to make the material more readable and understandable.

e. The book is *contemporary* in its approach. Although we provide coverage of the more classical statements concerning social life (John Dewey, Clyde Kluckhohn, Ferdinand Töennies, C. Wright Mills, Erving Goffman), the majority of the selections were published within the last decade. Also, we have selected articles that examine major events of our time including the shuttle disaster, changes in Iran, and the breakup of the Soviet Union.

We ask you, the student, to take an active part in these readings and do more than just read the words. We ask you to explore the meanings of the ideas raised in the selections and relate them to the world in which you live. We want you to understand what sociology is, to see how sociologists go about their work, and to comprehend the theories and perspectives which serve as guidelines in the study and analysis of social life.

P.B.B.

Acknowledgments

WE WISH TO thank a number of colleagues, staff, and students for their support and assistance in the publication of this book. We would like to thank our colleagues at the County College of Morris for their suggestions of potential articles and their helpful advice concerning the editing process. We are grateful to Arlene Cervenka, our department secretary, for her patience and competence in helping us with the various stages of this project. We are grateful to the late Terrence West, our former division dean, who steadfastly supported this project.

We wish to thank Evelyn Entwisle, our division secretary, for her encouragement concerning this project. Also, we appreciate the feedback of our students on potential selections for this book.

We would like to thank Karen Hanson, sociology editor at Allyn and Bacon, for her continuing support and timely advice concerning the project.

We also would like to thank Sarah L. Dunbar, editorial assistant at Allyn and Bacon, for her tireless aid in pulling together this project. We wish to thank our reviewers: Shelley Tenenbaum, Clark University; David F. Gordon, SUNY-Geneseo; Robert Rothman, University of Delaware; and Ronald Wohlstein, Eastern Illinois University, for their helpful input to the various stages of the book.

Finally, we wish to acknowledge a special debt to our colleague, William G. DiComo, who was instrumental in initiating this project many years ago. We also wish to thank Cynthia Chazen, sales representative for Allyn and Bacon for her insight and advice on this book.

General Introduction

SEEING SOCIETY: PERSPECTIVES ON SOCIAL LIFE takes the classical tradition in sociology seriously. Our basic objectives in this book are to introduce college students to sociological concepts and principles and to demonstrate how social organization affects personal behavior and identity. Our guiding principle has been to include selections that show how people are shaped by the consequences of biography, history, and social organization. In this regard, we follow the French sociologist Emile Durkheim in seeing the human person as *homo duplex,* a product of the unique interaction between the individual and culture.

This book is based upon the belief that the contemporary world is emerging as a multinational, multi-ethnic social system necessitating interaction and mutual understanding among members of different societies. Consequently, the selections reflect an emphasis on cross-cultural and comparative sociology. Such materials help students to better appreciate general sociological principles and develop empathic understanding for the great variety of contemporary cultural forms and national systems. Our objective is to help students develop authentic insights into the "inner life" and meanings used in different cultures. For this reason, we include selections that explore the ongoing relationship between a culture's beliefs and values and its normative structure.

We see sociology not only as a scientific enterprise but also as a humanistic search for educated self-discovery. As teachers of sociology, therefore, we can only concur with Max Weber who said,"The important task of the good teacher is to inform the student about inconvenient facts." This book contains concepts, theories, and cross-cultural materials which challenge students to view their own cultures and backgrounds in a comparative sociological fashion. For example, in discussions of family and courtship, we contrast traditional patterns with newly emerging understandings of divorce and singlehood; and in discussions of religion we offer material on established groups as well as insights on developing religious sensibilities and forms.

The book is divided into five parts: The Field and Its Methods, Core Concepts, Social Inequality, Major Institutions, and Cultural Change and Social Issues. Each of these can serve as a teaching unit, centered as it is on a major area of sociological interest. Our approach is to begin with the theoretical and methodological background of the discipline presented in Part One, The Field and Its Methods, before going on to an in-depth study of central sociological principles presented in Part Two, Core Concepts. Parts Three and Four, Social Inequality and Major Institutions, examine continuing sociological research on social institutions and structured social inequality. Having developed the basic sociological perspective, we proceed to Part Five, Cultural Change and Social Issues. This section focuses on current social issues and the nature and meaning of social change.

Sociology has much to teach in that it provides students with the means to understand human behavior. Sociology offers no fixed answers, no ultimate truth, no unquestionable guidelines but it provides an interpretive framework and a perspective with which the multiplicity of cultures and behaviors, present in modern societies, can be understood and, hopefully, appreciated. The experience of sociological learning, we believe, will help clarify the ambiguities of choice and enhance informed decision-making.

I

Sociological Perspectives

WHAT TO FOCUS ON:

1. What is unique about the sociological study of human interaction and group life?
2. What special methodological procedures are utilized in sociological research to ensure objectivity?

SOCIOLOGY IS THE SCIENTIFIC STUDY of human behavior in social settings. Sociology focuses on the structure of social interaction and patterns of group behavior. The sociological perspective stresses the importance of society and history in shaping behavior, beliefs, and feelings. Behavior from the sociological point of view must be viewed in its own specific social context if that behavior is to be understood correctly. For example, meat-eating or peer group dating—normal and appropriate behavior in North American society—would be viewed as serious breaches of proper behavior in a religious Hindu family in India. The sociologist therefore, studies the beliefs, norms, and values of the surrounding society to discover those social forces that influence individual behavior and moral concern.

Another central aspect of the sociological perspective is its emphasis on "objectivity" in theory formation, data collection, and research reporting. Sociologists, in the words of the German sociologist Max Weber, must strive to be "value-neutral," i.e., distinguish clearly in their work between empirical facts and moral convictions grounded in a particular set of social or religious values. While sometimes difficult to achieve in a specific case, the goal of the sociological enterprise is to insure that sociological research continually discovers or uncovers new information which will help to develop an objective understanding of how human beings interact in social settings.

The selection by Peter Berger "Invitation to Sociology" calls special attention to the unique perspective sociology brings to the study of social life. Berger tells us that sociology enables us to see the usual and ordinary in new and exciting ways. Sociologists do not necessarily travel to exotic places but the sociological perspective can bring about its own unique form of "culture shock". For Berger, sociological analysis can portray the familiar in ways people never imagined and also present what is distant and foreign in ways understandable in terms of one's own culture.

C. Wright Mills in his now classic statement on "The Sociological Imagination" describes the intricate connection between personal biography and social history. Mills shows how the events of a particular era—political, social, or economic—can affect the behavior, values, and outlook of people living in that time-period. The individual, as Mills puts it, can only "understand his experiences and gauge his own fate by locating himself within his own period." For Mills, it is essential to distinguish between "troubles" which are personal difficulties not caused by social change and "issues" which are social problems arising from societal transformation or economic upheaval. Mills demonstrates how, in the sociological imagination, war or widespread unemployment, for example, are not only political or economic events but conditions which have enormous consequences for social relations and personality development.

Article 1

Invitation to Sociology

PETER L. BERGER

THE SOCIOLOGIST, then, is someone concerned with understanding society in a disciplined way. The nature of this discipline is scientific. This means that what the sociologist finds and says about the social phenomena he studies occurs within a certain rather strictly defined frame of reference. One of the main characteristics of this scientific frame of reference is that operations are bound by certain rules of evidence. As a scientist, the sociologist tries to be objective, to control his personal preferences and prejudices, to perceive clearly rather than to judge normatively. This restraint, of course, does not embrace the totality of the sociologist's existence as a human being, but is limited to his operations *qua* sociologist. Nor does the sociologist claim that his frame of reference is the only one within which society can be looked at. For that matter, very few scientists in any field would claim today that one should look at the world only scientifically. The botanist looking at a daffodil has no reason to dispute the right of the poet to look at the same object in a very different manner. There are many ways of playing. The point is not that one denies other people's games but that one is clear about the rules of one's own. The game of the sociologist, then, uses scientific rules. As a result, the sociologist must be clear in his own mind as to the meaning of these rules. That is, he must concern himself with methodological questions. Methodology does not constitute his goal.

The latter, let us recall once more, is the attempt to understand society. Methodology helps in reaching this goal. In order to understand society, or that segment of it that he is studying at the moment, the sociologist will use a variety of means. Among these are statistical techniques. Statistics can be very useful in answering certain sociological questions. But statistics does not constitute sociology. As a scientist, the sociologist will have to be concerned with the exact significance of the terms he is using. That is, he will have to be careful about terminology. This does not have to mean that he must invent a new language of his own, but it does mean that he cannot naively use the language of everyday discourse. Finally, the interest of the sociologist is primarily theoretical. That is, he is interested in understanding for its own sake. He may be aware of or even concerned with the practical applicability and consequences of his findings, but at that point he leaves the sociological frame of reference as such and moves into realms of values, beliefs and ideas that he shares with other men who are not sociologists.

We dare say that this conception of the sociologist would meet with very wide consensus within the discipline today. But we would like to go a little bit further here and ask a somewhat more personal (and therefore, no doubt, more controversial) question. We would like to ask not only what it is that the sociologist is doing but also what it is that drives him to it. Or, to use the phrase Max Weber used in a similar connection, we want to inquire a little into the nature of the sociologist's demon. In doing so, we shall evoke an image that is not so much ideal—typical in the above sense but more confessional in the sense of personal commitment. Again, we are not interested in excommunicating anyone. The game of sociology goes on in a spacious playground. We are just describing a little more closely those we would like to tempt to join our game.

We would say then that the sociologist (that is, the one we would really like to invite to our game) is a person intensively, endlessly, shamelessly interested in the doings of men. His natural habitat is all the human gathering places of the world, wherever men come together. The sociologist may be interested in many other things. But his consuming interest remains in the world of men, their institutions, their history, their passions. And since he is interested in men, nothing that men do can be altogether tedious for him. He will naturally be interested in the events that engage men's ultimate beliefs, their moments of tragedy and grandeur and ecstasy. But he will also be fascinated by the commonplace, the everyday. He will know reverence, but this reverence will not prevent him from wanting to see and to understand. He may sometimes feel revulsion or contempt. But this also will not deter him from wanting to have his questions answered. The sociologist, in his quest for understanding, moves through the world of men without respect for the usual lines of demarcation. Nobility and degradation, power and obscurity, intelligence and folly—these are equally *interesting* to him, however unequal they may be in his personal values or tastes. Thus his questions may lead him to all possible levels of society, the best and the least known places, the most respected and the most despised. And, if he is a good sociologist, he will find himself in all these places because his own questions have so taken possession of him that he has little choice but to seek for answers.

It would be possible to say the same things in a lower key. We could say that the sociologist, but for the grace of his academic title, is the man who must listen to gossip despite himself, who is tempted to look through keyholes, to read other people's mail, to open closed cabinets. Before some otherwise unoccupied psychologist sets out now to construct an aptitude test for sociologists on the basis of sublimated voyeurism, let us quickly say that we are speaking merely by way of analogy. Perhaps some little boys consumed with curiosity to watch their maiden aunts in the bathroom later become inveterate sociologists. This is quite uninteresting. What interests us is the curiosity that grips any sociologist in front of a closed door behind which there are human voices. If he is a good sociologist, he will want to open that door, to understand these voices. Behind each closed door he will anticipate some new facet of human life not yet perceived and understood.

The sociologist will occupy himself with matters that others regard as too sacred or as too distasteful for dispassionate investigation. He will find rewarding the company of priests or of prostitutes, depending not on his personal preferences but on the questions he happens to be asking at the moment. He will also concern himself with matters that others may find much too boring. He will be interested in the human interaction that goes with warfare or with great intellectual discoveries, but also in the relations between people employed in a restaurant or between a group of little girls playing with their dolls. His main focus of attention is not the ultimate significance of what men do, but the action in itself, as another example of the infinite richness of human conduct. So much for image of our playmate.

In these journeys through the world of men the sociologist will inevitably encounter other professional Peeping Toms. Sometimes these will resent his presence, feeling that he is poaching on their preserves. In some places the sociologist will meet up with the economist, in others with the political scientist, in yet others with the psychologist or the ethnologist. Yet chances are that the questions that have brought him to these same places are different from the ones that propelled his fellow-trespassers. The sociologist's questions always remain essentially the same: "What are people doing with each other here?" "What are their relationships to each other?" "How are these relationships organized in institutions?" "What are the collective ideas that move men and institutions?" In trying to answer these questions in specific instances, the sociologist will, of course, have to deal with economic or political matters, but he will do so in a way rather different from that of the economist or the political scientist. The scene that he contemplates is the same human scene that these other scientists concern themselves with. But the sociologist's angle of vision is different. When this is understood, it becomes clear that it makes little sense to try to stake out a special enclave within which the sociologist will carry on business in his own right. Like Wesley the sociologist will have to confess that his parish is the world. But unlike some latter-day Wesleyans he will gladly share this parish with others. There is, however, one traveler whose path the sociologist will cross more often than anyone else's on his journeys. This is the historian. Indeed, as soon as the sociologist turns from the present to the past, his preoccupations are very hard indeed to distinguish from those of the historian. However, we shall leave this relationship to a later part of our considerations.

Suffice it to say here that the sociological journey will be much impoverished unless it is punctuated frequently by conversation with that other particular traveler.

Any intellectual activity derives excitement from the moment it becomes a trail of discovery. In some fields of learning this is the discovery of worlds previously unthought and unthinkable. This is the excitement of the astronomer or to the nuclear physicist on the antipodal boundaries of the realities that man is capable of conceiving. But it can also be the excitement of bacteriology or geology. In a different way it can be the excitement of the linguist discovering new realms of human expression or of the anthropologist exploring human customs in faraway countries. In such discovery, when undertaken with passion, a widening of awareness, sometimes a veritable transformation of consciousness, occurs. The universe turns out to be much more wonder-full than one had ever dreamed. The excitement of sociology is usually of a different sort. Sometimes, it is true, the sociologist penetrates into worlds that had previously been quite unknown to him—for instance, the world of crime, or the world of some bizarre religious sect or the world fashioned by the exclusive concerns of some group such as medical specialists or military leaders or advertising executives. However, much of the time the sociologist moves in sectors of experience that are familiar to him and to most people in his society. He investigates communities, institutions and activities that one can read about every day in the newspapers. Yet there is another excitement of discovery beckoning in his investigations. It is not the excitement of coming upon the totally unfamiliar, but rather the excitement of finding the familiar becoming transformed in its meaning. The fascination of sociology lies in the fact that its perspective makes us see in a new light the very world in which we have lived all our lives. This also constitutes a transformation of consciousness. Moreover, this transformation is more relevant existentially than that of many other intellectual disciplines, because it is more difficult to segregate in some special compartment of the mind. The astronomer does not live in the remote galaxies, and the nuclear physicist can, outside his laboratory, eat and laugh and marry and vote without thinking about the insides of the atom. The geologist looks at rocks only at appropriate times, and the linguist speaks English with his wife. The sociologist lives in society, on the job and off it. His own life, inevitably is part of his subject matter. Men being what they are, sociologists too manage to segregate their professional insights from their everyday affairs. But it is a rather difficult feat to perform in good faith.

The sociologist moves in the common world of men, close to what most of them would call real. The categories he employs in his analyses are only refinements of the categories by which other men live—power, class, status, race, ethnicity. As a result, there is a deceptive simplicity and obviousness about some sociological investigations. One reads them, nods at the familiar scene, remarks that one has heard all this before and don't people have better things to do than to waste their time on truisms—until one is suddenly brought up against an insight that radically questions everything one had previously assumed about this familiar scene. This is the point at which one begins to sense the excitement of sociology.

Let us take a specific example. Imagine a sociology class in a Southern college where almost all the students are white Southerners. Imagine a lecture on the subject of the racial system of the South. The lecturer is talking here of matters that have been familiar to his students from the time of their infancy. Indeed, it may be that they are much more familiar with the minutiae of this system than he is. They are quite bored as a result. It seems to them that he is only using more pretentious words to describe what they already know. Thus he may use the term "caste," one commonly used now by American sociologists to describe the Southern racial system. But in explaining the term he shifts to traditional Hindu society, to make it clearer. He then goes on to analyze the magical beliefs inherent in caste taboos, the social dynamics of commensalism and connubium, the economic interests concealed within the system, the way in which religious beliefs relate to the taboos the effects of the caste system upon the industrial development of the society and vice versa—all in India. But suddenly India is not very far away at all. The lecture then goes back to its Southern theme. The familiar now seems not quite so familiar any more. Questions are raised that are new, perhaps raised angrily, but raised all the same. And at least some of the students have begun to understand that there are functions involved in this business of race that they have not read about in the newspapers (at least not those in their hometowns) and that their parents have not told them—partly, at least, because neither the newspapers nor the parents knew about them.

It can be said that the first wisdom of sociology is this—things are not what they seem. This too is a deceptively simple statement. It ceases to be simple after a while. Social reality turns out to have many layers of meaning. The discovery of each new layer changes the perception of the whole.

Anthropologists use the term "culture shock" to describe the impact of a totally new culture upon a newcomer. In an extreme instance such shock will be experienced by the Western explorer who is told, halfway through dinner, that he is eating the nice old lady he had been chatting with the previous day—a shock with predictable physiological if not moral consequences. Most explorers no longer encounter cannibalism in their travels today. However, the first encounters with polygamy or with puberty rites or even with the way some nations drive their automobiles can be quite a shock to an American visitor. With the shock may go not only disapproval or disgust but a sense of excitement that things can *really* be that different from what they are at home. To some extent at least, this is the excitement of any first travel abroad. The experience of sociological discovery could be described as "culture shock" minus geographical displacement. In other words, the sociologist travels at home—with shocking results. He is unlikely to find that he is eating a nice old lady for dinner. But the discovery, for instance, that his own church has considerable money invested in the missile industry or that a few blocks from his home there are people who engage in cultic orgies may not be drastically different in emotional impact. Yet we would not want to imply that sociological discoveries are always or even usually outrageous to moral sentiment. Not at all. What they have in common with exploration in distant lands, however, is the sudden illumination of new and unsuspected facets of human existence in society. This is the excitement and, as we shall try to show later, the humanistic justification of sociology.

People who like to avoid shocking discoveries, who prefer to believe that society is just what they were taught in Sunday School, who like the safety of the rules and the maxims of what Alfred Schuetz has called the "world-taken-for-granted," should stay away from sociology. People who feel no temptation before closed doors, who have no curiosity about human beings, who are content to admire scenery without wondering about the people who live in those houses on the other side of that river, should probably also stay away from sociology. They will find it unpleasant or, at any rate, unrewarding. People who are interested in human beings only if they can change, convert or reform them should also be warned, for they will find sociology much less useful than they hoped. And people whose interest is mainly in their own conceptual constructions will do just as well to turn to the study of little white mice. Sociology will be satisfying, in the long run, only to those who can think of nothing more entrancing than to watch men and to understand things human.

It may now be clear that we have, albeit deliberately, understated the case in the title of this chapter. To be sure, sociology is an individual pastime in the sense that it interests some men and bores others. Some like to observe human beings, others to experiment with mice. The world is big enough to hold all kinds and there is no logical priority for one interest as against another. But the word "pastime" is weak in describing what we mean. Sociology is more like a passion. The sociological perspective is more like a demon that possesses one, that drives one compellingly, again and again, to the questions that are its own. An introduction to sociology is, therefore, an invitation to a very special kind of passion. No passion is without its dangers. The sociologist who sells his wares should make sure that he clearly pronounces a *caveat emptor* quite early in the transaction.

DISCUSSION QUESTIONS

1. What basic questions do sociologists ask?
2. What is meant by "culture shock"?

Article 2

The Sociological Imagination

C. WRIGHT MILLS

NOWADAYS MEN OFTEN feel that their private lives are a series of traps. They sense that within their everyday worlds, they cannot overcome their troubles, and in this feeling, they are often quite correct: What ordinary men are directly aware of and what they try to do are bounded by the private orbits in which they live; their visions and their powers are limited to the close-up scenes of job, family, neighborhood; in other millieux, they move vicariously and remain spectators. And the more aware they become, however vaguely, of ambitions and of threats which transcend their immediate locales, the more trapped they seem to feel.

Underlying this sense of being trapped are seemingly impersonal changes in the very structure of continent-wide societies. The facts of contemporary history are also facts about the success and the failure of individual men and women. When a society is industrialized, a peasant becomes a worker; a feudal lord is liquidated or becomes a businessman. When classes rise or fall, a man is employed or unemployed; when the rate of investment goes up or down, a man takes new heart or goes broke. When wars happen, an insurance salesman becomes a rocket launcher; a store clerk, a radar man; a wife lives alone; a child grows up without a father.

Neither the life of an individual nor the history of a society can be understood without understanding both.

Yet men do not usually define the troubles they endure in terms of historical change and institutional contradiction. The well-being they enjoy, they do not usually impute to the big ups and downs of the societies in which they live. Seldom aware of the intricate connection between the patterns of their own lives and the course of world history, ordinary men do not usually know what this connection means for the kinds of men they are becoming and for the kinds of history-making in which they might take part. They do not possess the quality of mind essential to grasp the interplay of man and society, of biography and history, of self and world. They cannot cope with their personal troubles in such ways as to control the structural transformations that usually lie behind them.

Surely it is no wonder. In what period have so many men been so totally exposed at so fast a pace to such earthquakes of change? That Americans have not known such catastrophic changes as have the men and women of other societies is due to historical facts that are now quickly becoming "merely history." The history that now affects every man is world history. Within this scene and this period, in the course of a single generation, one-sixth of mankind is transformed from all that is feudal and backward into all that is modern, advanced, and fearful. Political colonies are freed; new and less visible forms of imperialism installed. Revolutions occur; men feel the intimate grip of new kinds of authority. Totalitarian societies rise, and are smashed to bits—or succeed fabulously. After two centuries of ascendancy, capitalism is shown up as only one way to make society into an industrial apparatus. After two centuries of hope, even formal democracy is restricted to a quite small portion of mankind. Everywhere in the underdeveloped world, ancient ways of life are broken up and vague expectations become urgent demands. Everywhere in the overdeveloped world, the means of authority and of violence become total in scope and bureaucratic in form. Humanity itself now lies before us, the super-nation at either pole concentrating its most co-ordinated and massive efforts upon the preparation of World War Three.

The very shaping of history now outpaces the ability of men to orient themselves in accordance with cherished values. And which values? Even when they do not panic, men often sense that older ways of feeling and thinking have collapsed and that newer beginnings are ambiguous to the point of moral stasis. Is it any wonder that ordinary men feel they cannot cope with the larger worlds with which they are so suddenly confronted? That they cannot understand the meaning of their epoch for their own lives? That—in defense of selfhood—they become morally insensible, trying to remain altogether private men? Is it any wonder that they come to be possessed by a sense of the trap?

It is not only information that they need—in this Age of Fact, information often dominates their attention and overwhelms their capacities to assimilate it. It is not only the skills of reason that they need—although their struggles to acquire these often exhaust their limited moral energy.

What they need, and what they feel they need, is a quality of mind that will help them to use information and to develop reason in order to achieve lucid summations of what is going on in the world and of what may be happening within themselves. It is this quality, I am going to contend, that journalists and scholars, artists and publics, scientists and editors are coming to expect of what may be called the sociological imagination.

1

The sociological imagination enables its possessor to understand the larger historical scene in terms of its meaning for the inner life and the external career of a variety of individuals. It enables him to take into account how individuals, in the welter of their daily experience, often become falsely conscious of their social positions. Within that welter, the framework of modern society is sought, and within that framework the psychologies of a variety of men and women are formulated. By such means the personal uneasiness of individuals is focused upon explicit troubles and the indifference of publics is transformed into involvement with public issues.

The first fruit of this imagination—and the first lesson of the social science that embodies it—is the idea that the individual can understand his own experience and gauge his own fate only by locating himself within his period, that he can know his own chances in life only by becoming aware of those of all individuals in his circumstances. In many ways it is a terrible lesson; in many ways a magnificent one. We do not know the limits of man's capacities for supreme effort or willing degradation, for agony or glee, for pleasurable brutality or the sweetness of reason. But in our time we have come to know that the limits of "human nature" are frighteningly broad. We have come to know that every individual lives, from one generation to the next, in some society; that he lives out a biography, and that he lives it out within some historical sequence. By the fact of his living he contributes, however minutely, to the shaping of this society and to the course of its history, even as he is made by society and by its historical push and shove.

The sociological imagination enables us to grasp history and biography and the relations between the two within society. That is its task and its promise. To recognize this task and this promise is the mark of the classic social analyst. It is characteristic of Herbert Spencer—turgid, polysyllabic, comprehensive; of E. A. Ross—graceful, muckraking, upright; of Auguste Comte and Emile Durkheim; of the intricate and subtle Karl Mannheim. It is the quality of all that is intellectually excellent in Karl Marx, it is the clue to Thorstein Veblen's brilliant and ironic insight, to Joseph Schumpeter's many-sided constructions of reality; it is the basis of the psychological sweep of W. E. H. Lecky no less than of the profundity and clarity of Max Weber. And it is the signal of what is best in contemporary studies of man and society.

No social study that does not come back to the problems of biography, of history and of their intersections within a society has completed its intellectual journey. Whatever the specific problems of the classic social analysts, however limited or however broad the features of social reality they have examined, those who have been imaginatively aware of the promise of their work have consistently asked three sorts of questions:

(1) What is the structure of this particular society as a whole? What are its essential components, and how are they related to one another? How does it differ from other varieties of social order? Within it, what is the meaning of any particular feature for its continuance and for its change?

(2) Where does this society stand in human history? What are the mechanics by which it is changing? What is its place within and its meaning for the development of humanity as a whole? How does any particular feature we are examining affect, and how is it affected by, the historical period in which it moves? And this period—what are its essential features? How does it differ from other periods? What are its characteristic ways of history-making?

(3) What varieties of men and women now prevail in this society and in this period? And what varieties are coming to prevail? In what ways are they selected and formed, liberated and repressed, made sensitive and blunted? What kinds of "humane nature" are revealed in the conduct and character we observe in this society in this period? And what is the meaning for "human nature" of each and every feature of the society we are examining?

Whether the point of interest is a great power state or a minor literary mood, a family, a prison, a creed—these are the kinds of questions the best social analysts have asked. They are the intellectual pivots of classic studies of man in society—and they are the questions inevitably raised by any mind possessing the sociological imagination. For that imagination is the capacity to shift from one perspective to another—from the political to the psychological; from examination of a single family to comparative assessment of the national budgets of the world; from the theological school to the military establishment; from considerations of an oil industry to studies of contemporary poetry. It is the capacity to range from the most impersonal and remote transformations to the most intimate features of the human self—and to see the relations between the two. Back of its use there is always the urge to know the social and historical meaning of the individual in the society and the period in which he has his quality and his being.

That, in brief, is why it is by means of the sociological imagination that men now hope to grasp what is going on in the world, and to understand what is happening in themselves as minute points of the intersections of biography and history within society. In large part, contemporary man's self-conscious view of himself as at least an outsider, if not a permanent stranger, rests upon an absorbed realization of social relativity and of the transformative power of history. The sociological imagination is the most fruitful form of this self-consciousness. By its use men whose mentalities have swept only a series of limited orbits often come to feel as if suddenly awakened in a house with which they had only supposed themselves to be familiar. Correctly or incorrectly, they often come to feel that they can now provide themselves with adequate summations, cohesive assessments, comprehensive orientations. Older decisions that once appeared sound now seem to them products of a mind unaccountably dense. Their capacity for astonishment is made lively again. They acquire a new way of thinking, they experience a transvaluation of values: in a word, by their reflection and by their sensibility, they realize the cultural meaning of the social sciences.

2

Perhaps the most fruitful distinction with which the sociological imagination works is between "the personal troubles of milieu" and "the public issues of social structure." This distinction is an essential tool of the sociological imagination and a feature of all classic work in social science.

Troubles occur within the character of the individual and within the range of his immediate relations with others; they have to do with his self and with those limited areas of social life of which he is directly and personally aware. Accordingly, the statement and the resolution of troubles properly lie within the individual as a biographical entity and within the scope of his immediate milieu—the social setting that is directly open to his personal experience and to some extent his willful activity. A trouble is a private matter: values cherished by an individual are felt by him to be threatened.

Issues have to do with matters that transcend these local environments of the individual and the range of his inner life. They have to do with the organization of many such milieux into the institutions of a historical society as a whole, with the ways in which various milieux overlap and interpenetrate to form the larger structure of social and historical life. An issue is a public matter: some value cherished by publics is felt to be threatened. Often there is a debate about what that value really is and about what it is that really threatens it. This debate is often without focus if only because it is the very nature of an issue, unlike even widespread trouble, that it cannot very well be defined in terms of the immediate and everyday environments of ordinary men. An issue, in fact, often involves a crisis in institutional arrangements, and often too it involves what Marxists call "contradictions" or "antagonisms."

Examples of trouble a issues

In these terms, consider unemployment. When in a city of 100,000, only one man is unemployed, that is his personal trouble, and for its relief we properly look to the character of the man, his skills, and his immediate opportunities. But when in a nature of 50 million employees, 15 million men are unemployed, that is an issue, and we may not hope to find its solution within the range of opportunities open to any one individual. The very structure of opportunities has collapsed. Both the correct statement of the problem and the range of possible solutions require us to consider the economic and political institutions of the society, and not merely the personal situation and character of a scatter of individuals.

Consider war. The personal problem of war, when it occurs, may be how to survive it or how to die in it with honor; how to make money out of it; how to climb into the higher safety of the military apparatus; or how to contribute to the war's termination. In short, according to one's values, to find a set of milieux and within it to survive the war or make one's death in it meaningful. But the structural issues of war have to do with its causes; with what types of men it throws up into command; with its effects upon economic and political, family and religious institutions, with the unorganized irresponsibility of a world of nation-status.

Consider marriage. Inside a marriage a man and a woman may experience personal troubles, but when the divorce rate during the first four years of marriage is 250 out of every 1,000 attempts, this is an indication of a structural issue having to do with the institutions of marriage and the family and other institutions that bear upon them.

Or consider the metropolis—the horrible, beautiful, ugly, magnificent sprawl of the great city. For many upper-class people, the personal solution to "the problem of the city" is to have an apartment with private garage under it in the heart of the city, and forty miles out, a house by Henry Hill, garden by Garrett Eckbo, on a hundred acres of private land. In these two controlled environments—with a small staff at each end and a private helicopter connection—most people could solve many of the problems of personal milieux caused by the facts of the city. But all this, however splendid, does not solve the public issues that the structural fact of the city poses. What should be done with this wonderful monstrosity? Break it all up into scattered units, combining residence and work? Refurbish it as it stands? Or, after evacuation, dynamite it and build new cities according to new plans in new places? What should those plans be? And who is to decide and to accomplish whatever choice is made? These are structural issues; to confront them and to solve them requires us to consider political and economic issues that affect innumerable milieux.

Insofar as an economy is so arranged that slumps occur, the problem of unemployment becomes incapable of personal solution. Insofar as war is inherent in the nation-state system and in the uneven industrialization of the world, the ordinary individual in his restricted milieu will be powerless—with or without psychiatric aid—to solve the troubles this system or lack of system imposes upon him. Insofar as the family as an institution turns women into darling little slaves and men into their chief providers and unweaned dependents, the problem of a satisfactory marriage remains incapable of purely private solution. Insofar as the overdeveloped megalopolis and the overdeveloped automobile are built-in features of the overdeveloped society, the issues of urban living will not be solved by personal ingenuity and private wealth.

What we experience in various and specific milieux, I have noted, is often caused by structural changes. Accordingly, to understand the changes of many personal milieux we are required to look beyond them. And the number and variety of such structural changes increases as the institutions within which we live become more embracing and more intricately connected with one another. To be aware of the idea of social structure and to use it with sensibility is to be capable of tracing such linkages among a great variety of milieux. To be able to do that is to possess the sociological imagination.

3

What are the major issues for publics and the key troubles of private individuals in our time? To formulate issues and troubles, we must ask what values are cherished yet threatened, and what values are cherished and supported, by the characterizing trends of our period. In the case both of threat and of support we must ask what salient contradictions of structure may be involved.

When people cherish some set of values and do not feel any threat to them, they experience *well-being.* When they cherish values but *do* feel them to be threatened, they experience a crisis—either as a personal trouble or as a public issue. And if all their values seem involved, they feel the total threat of panic.

But suppose people are neither aware of any cherished values nor experience any threat? That is the experience of *indifference,* which, if it seems to involve all their values, becomes apathy. Suppose, finally, they are unaware of any cherished values, but still are very much aware of a threat? That is the experience of *uneasiness,* of anxiety, which, if it is total enough, becomes a deadly unspecified malaise.

Ours is a time of uneasiness and indifference—not yet formulated in such ways as to permit the work of reason and the play of sensibility. Instead of troubles—defined in terms of values and threats—there is often the misery of vague uneasiness; instead of explicit issues there is often merely the beat feeling that all is somehow not right. Neither the values threatened nor whatever threatens them has been stated; in short, they have not been carried to the point of decision. Much less have they been formulated as problems of social science.

In the thirties there was little doubt—except among certain deluded business circles that there was an economic issue which was also a pack of personal troubles. In these arguments about "the crisis of capitalism," the formulations of Marx and the many unacknowledged re-formulations of his work probably set the leading terms of the issue, and some men came to understand their personal troubles in these terms. The values threatened were plain to see and cherished by all; the structural contradictions that threatened them also seemed plain. Both were widely and deeply experienced. It was a political age.

But the values threatened in the era after World War Two are often neither widely acknowledged as values nor widely felt to be threatened. Much private uneasiness goes unformulated; much public malaise and many decisions of enormous structural relevance never become public issues. For those who accept such inherited values as reason and freedom, it is the uneasiness itself that is the trouble; it is the indifference itself that is the issue. And it is this condition, of uneasiness and indifference, that is the signal feature of our period.

All this is so striking that it is often interpreted by observers as a shift in the very kinds of problems that need now to be formulated. We are frequently told that the problems of our decade, or even the crises of our period, have shifted from the external realm of economics and now have to do with the quality of individual life—in fact with the question of whether there is soon going to be anything that can properly be called individual life. Not child labor but comic books, not poverty but mass leisure, are at the center of concern. Many great public issues as well as many private troubles are described in terms of "the psychiatric"—often, it seems, in a pathetic attempt to avoid the large issues and problems of modern society. Often this statement seems to rest upon a provincial narrowing of interest to the Western societies, or even to the United States—thus ignoring two-thirds of mankind; often, too, it arbitrarily divorces the individual life from the larger institutions within which that life is enacted, and which on occasion bear upon it more grievously than do the intimate environments of childhood.

Problems of leisure, for example, cannot even be stated without considering problems of work. Family troubles over comic books cannot be formulated as problems without considering the plight of the contemporary family in its new relations with the newer institutions of the social structure. Neither leisure nor its debilitation uses can be understood as problems without recognition of the extent to which malaise and indifference now form the social and personal climate of contemporary American society. In this climate, no problems of "the private life" can be stated and solved without recognition of the crisis of ambition that is part of the very career of men at work in the incorporated economy.

It is true, as psychoanalysts continually point out, that people do often have "the increasing sense of being moved by obscure forces within themselves which they are unable to define." But it is *not* true, as Ernest Jones asserted, that "man's chief enemy and danger is his own unruly nature and the dark forces pent up within him." On the contrary: "Man's chief danger" today lies in the unruly forces of contemporary society itself, with its alienating methods of production, its enveloping techniques of political domination, its international anarchy—in a word, its pervasive transformations of the very "nature" of man and the conditions and aims of his life.

It is now the social scientist's foremost political and intellectual task—for here the two coincide—to make clear the elements of contemporary uneasiness and indifference. It is the central demand made upon him by other cultural workmen—by physical scientists and artists, by the intellectual community in general. It is because of this task and these demands, I believe, that the social sciences are becoming the common denominator of our cultural period, and the sociological imagination our most needed quality of *mind.*

DISCUSSION QUESTIONS

1. How does Mills distinguish between "troubles" and "issues"?
2. How does the "sociological imagination" help to explain the existence of social problems?

II

Methods and Styles of Social Research

WHAT TO FOCUS ON:

1. How is the theoretical base of a science influenced by its methods of data collecting?
2. What are the consequences of unethical data collection and analysis?

THE INTRODUCTORY STUDENT may perceive sociological methods as a topic overloaded with minute details, technical concepts, or irrelevant statistics. This perception may be the result of an unclear understanding of the role of methodology within the discipline of sociology. Methodology *is* important to scientific discipline. All sciences establish a knowledge base which includes: theoretical positions, boundaries of interests, conceptual tools, analytical issues and a means of data collection. Each science, therefore, develops methods of research uniquely their own. However, they share a concern for valid and reliable procedures.

Many views regarding methodology center around ideas of collecting information and helping science be objective and unbiased. Methodological procedures are the means with which theory is connected to reality. They help a science demonstrate what it knows and what it seeks to discover. Consequently, methodology refers to the procedures science uses to: 1) formulate research questions, 2) operationalize concepts, 3) collect data, 4) establish its data as valid, and 5) to provide statistical testing for theoretical positions. It is important for the student to know the functions played by the "details and statistics" for the discipline of sociology. The articles in this chapter help to define and discuss the methodological issues relevant to sociology.

Jonathan Turner provides an overall discussion of the uses of science and particularly of the connection between theory and methods. This work is important because it demonstrates that both theory and methods are essential to the other. Without either, what can a science know or seek to discover? Specifically, Turner notes: "If we do not have methods and statistics, we cannot have confidence in our theories. . . . " This material provides a significant base for the following two articles.

The work by Persell and Cookson provides an excellent example of the research process. Beginning with specific research and theoretical questions—what role does education play in status attainment and elite reproduction? The authors demonstrate methods used to answer these questions. The resulting data are analyzed in a sociological discussion that leads one to wonder if good grades are all that is necessary for admission to elite schools. This article takes the student from the beginning of the research process to its conclusion and demonstrates the unique understanding of social life provided by sociological study.

Finally, in the Nicholas Wade piece we find an examination of the role of ethics in research. Here is an example of how researchers can bend, fold, and mutilate the data, or how statistics can say whatever we want them to say. Consequently, the person doing the research is an important factor in the methodological procedure. However, Wade also demonstrates how such fraudulent practices can be found out. The beauty of science and its methodological interests is that those doing research have a means to check themselves and others. When a piece of data doesn't support what is previously established, both the earlier material, as well as the most recent, can be re-examined.

These three articles should help the student explore the means through which a science establishes itself, analyzes its data and examines its validity and reliability.

Article 3

Knowing about Things

JONATHAN TURNER

THE GOAL OF ALL SCIENCE is to produce theory. Since the word "theory" has such unsavory connotations, perhaps I should clarify just what theory is. Theory is *not* wild-eyed speculation. It can, initially, involve creative speculation but in the end theory is formal and rather sedate. Theory is *not* pie-in-the-sky ideas. True, it is abstract but the purpose of theory is to help us explain real events in the actual world. Theory is *not* dull or hard to understand. Students often think that it is because it is often removed from everyday events and the concrete world.

What, then, is theory? Theory is nothing more or less than formal statements that tell us how and why events in the world occur. Scientific theory has a special characteristic. It is designed to be proven *wrong*. Yes, wrong. The whole idea is to make statements that tell us how and why events occur and then try to show them to be wrong. This is done by collecting information or data on empirical events to see if things do indeed work as the theory says they should.[1] If a theory stands intact after repeated assaults, then it is considered plausible and is accepted for the time being as the explanation of the way things are. A theory is actually never proven; it can only be disproven. Tomorrow, someone might collect data to show that it is wrong, forcing us to reject or revise the theory. Yet, when theories stand the test of time—that is, repeated efforts to disprove them—then they become provisionally accepted as truth, as the way things are.

This is the way all science works. It is not an efficient process, but it is the way we keep our theories tied to real events. We hold theories skeptically and constantly check them against the facts.

Just how is theory checked? This is done by following some general procedures, often termed "scientific method." The general idea behind the methods of science is to develop unbiased procedures for collecting data and then to specify clearly the procedures we have used, so that others can come along and check up on us and verify that we were honest and didn't make any dumb mistakes. Without data that we can trust, or have confidence in, we do not know if the data really do bear on the theory we are testing.

The reason sociologists are concerned with methodology is that they, like all scientists, want to be sure that the procedures, or methods, used in collecting information are not biased, inappropriate, or faulty.[2] Otherwise, we cannot be sure that our data are any good and we cannot test our theory with it.

The use of statistics is simply a way of manipulating data once we have it in hand for interpretation. Without statistics, our capacity to interpret the world would be very limited. We would miss much and make lots of mistakes just because we could not get at the facts in sufficient detail.

Science, then, involves a constant interplay among theory, methods (data collection), and analysis (statistics in our case). If we relied only on our intuition, we could create theories that were "confirmed" simply by selective perception. We need to subject our hunches to a more rigorous scrutiny than that. Only by so doing can we begin to understand the social world and how it operates. . . .

But there is a broader issue to consider, besides merely getting a job. If we want to realize our humanism—and this motive is what gets most of us started in sociology—we need to be skilled at gathering and interpreting information about situations we want to change and people we want to help. We also need to understand *why* and *how* the situations operate. And we need to be able to anticipate the consequences of any changes we initiate and to collect accurate information on these changes. We cannot rely on intuition and our personal ideologies in these matters. We need formal theory that has withstood efforts to disprove it to tell us how and why things operate, and we need to use this theory in ascertaining what needs to be done to improve a situation. We will also need to collect accurate information and analyze it carefully to know just what exists in a situation and just what the consequences of our theoretically informed actions are.

If we have no theory, we have no framework to understand and interpret the social world. Hence, we do not know what we have done or what to expect. If we do not have methods and statistics, we cannot have confidence in our theories, since they have not been tested, and we cannot know exactly what in a situation needs to be changed. We can use our familiarity with a situation and our creative intuition to bring to bear relevant theories and to develop ways of gathering information. But our intuition cannot substitute for formal theory, carefully constructed methods, and detailed statistical analysis. Those who think it can are more likely to hurt than help people, despite their voiced concern for a more humane world.

NOTES

1. For the most authoritative account of this argument, read Karl R. Popper, *The Logic of Scientific Inquiry* (New York: Basic Books, 1959). For a readable analysis of the interplay between theory and empirical data, see Bernard P. Cohen's *Developing Sociological Knowledge: Theory and Method* (Englewood Cliffs, N.J.: Prentice-Hall, 1980).

2. See Earl Babbie's *The Practice of Social Research* (Belmont, Calif.: Wadsworth, 1979) for a readable discussion of methods in sociology. Also, see volumes in Prentice-Hall's "Methods and Theories in the Social Sciences." In particular, I recommend Neil J. Smelser's *Comparative Methods in the Social Sciences,* H. W. Smith's *Strategies of Social Research,* Leonard Schatzman and Anselm Strauss's *Field Research,* James A. Davis's *Elementary Survey Analysis,* and Carol H. Weis's *Evaluation Research.* All are very readable and in paperback. Still the best book on the general issues surrounding research is Abraham Kaplan, *The Conduct Inquiry* (Scranton, Penn.: Chandler, 1964).

DISCUSSION QUESTIONS

1. How does Turner show that theory and methods are related to each other?
2. Using the material by Turner, show how methodology helps science establish its knowledge base.

Article 4

Chartering and Bartering

Elite Education and Social Reproduction

CAROLINE HODGES PERSELL AND PETER W. COOKSON, JR.

THE CONTINUATION OF POWER and privilege has been the subject of intense sociological debate. One recurring question is whether the system of mobility is open or whether relationships of power and privilege are reproduced from one generation to the next. If reproduction occurs, is it the reproduction of certain powerful and privileged families or groups (cf. Robinson, 1984)? Or, does it involve the reproduction of a structure of power and privilege which allows for replacement of some members with new recruits while preserving the structure?

From *Social Problems,* Vol. 33, No. 2, Dec. 1985, pp. 114–126.

We wish to thank E. Digby Baltzell, Steven Brint, Kevin Dougherty, Eliot Freidson, Kathleen Gerson, David Greenberg, Wolf Heydebrand, Herbert Menzel, John Meyer, Karen Miller, Richard R. Peterson, Edwin Schur, Susan Shapiro, Beth Stevens, and a number of anonymous reviewers for their thoughtful reactions to this paper. Needless to say, they cannot be held responsible for the way we have utilized their comments. Correspondence to Persell, Department of Sociology, New York University, 269 Mercer Street, New York, NY 10003.

The role of education in these processes has been the subject of much dispute. Researchers in the status attainment tradition stress the importance for mobility of the knowledge and skills acquired through education thereby emphasizing the meritocratic and open basis for mobility (e.g., Alexander and Ecklane, 1975; Alexander et al., 1975; Blau and Duncan, 1967; Haller and Portes, 1973; Otto and Haller, 1970; Kerckhoff, 1984; Sewell et al., 1969, 1970; Wilson and Portes, 1975). On the other hand, theorists such as Bowles and Gintis (1976) suggest education inculcates certain non-cognitive personality traits which serve to reproduce the social relations within a class structure; thus they put more emphasis on non-meritocratic features in the educational process.

Collins (1979) also deals with non-meritocratic aspects when he suggests that educational institutions develop and fortify status groups, and that differently valued educational credentials protect desired market positions such as those of the professions. In a related vein, Meyer (1977) notes that certain organizational "charters" serve as "selection criteria" in an educational or occupational marketplace. Meyer defines "charter" as "the social definition of the products of [an] organization" (Meyer, 1970:577). Charters do not need to be recognized formally or legally to operate in social life. If they exist, they would create structural limitations within a presumably open market by making some people eligible for certain sets of rights that are denied to other people.

Social observers have long noted that one particular set of schools is central to the reproduction and solidarity of a national upper class, specifically elite secondary boarding schools (Baltzell, 1958, 1964; Domhoff, 1967, 1970, 1983; Mills, 1956). As well as preparing their students for socially desirable colleges and universities, traditionally such schools have been thought to build social networks among upper class scions from various regions, leading to adult business deals and marriages. Although less than one percent of the American population attends such schools, that one percent represents a strategic segment of American life that is seldom directly studied. Recently, Useem and Karabel (1984) reported that graduates of 14 elite boarding schools were much more likely than non-graduates to become part of the "inner circle" of Fortune 500 business leaders. This evidence suggests that elite schools may play a role in class reproduction.

Few researchers have gained direct access to these schools to study social processes bearing on social reproduction. The research reported here represents the first systematic study of elite secondary boarding schools and their social relations with another important institution, namely colleges and universities.

The results of this research illustrate Collins' view that stratification involves networks of "persons making bargains and threats . . . [and that] the key resource of powerful individuals is their ability to impress and manipulate a network of social contacts" (1979:26). If such were the case, we would expect to find that upper class institutions actively develop social networks for the purpose of advancing the interests of their constituencies.

By focusing on the processes of social reproduction rather than individual attributes or the results of intergenerational mobility, our research differs from the approaches taken in both the status attainment and status allocation literature. Status attainment models focus on individual attributes and achievements, and allocation models examine structural supports or barriers to social mobility; yet neither approach explores the underlying processes. Status attainment models assume the existence of a relatively open contest system, while reproduction and allocation models stress that selection criteria and structural barriers create inequalities, limiting opportunities for one group while favoring another (Kerckhoff, 1976, 1984). Neither attainment nor allocation models show how class reproduction, selection criteria, or structural opportunities and impediments operate in practice.

Considerable evidence supports the view that structural limitations operate in the labor market (e.g., Beck et al., 1978; Bibb and Form, 1977; Stolzenberg, 1975) but, with the exception of tracking, little evidence has been found that similar structural limitations exist in education. Tracking systems create structural impediments in an open model of educational attainment (Oakes, 1985; Persell, 1977; Rosenbaum, 1976, 1980), although not all research supports this conclusion (e.g., Alexander et al., 1978; Heyns, 1974).

In this paper we suggest that there is an additional structural limitation in the key transition from high school to college. We explore the possibility that special organizational "charters" exist for certain secondary schools and that a process of "bartering" occurs between representatives of selected secondary schools and some college admissions officers. These processes have not been clearly identified by prior research on education and stratification, although there has been some previous research which leads in this direction.

Networks and the Transmission of Privilege

We believe it is worth investigating whether certain secondary schools have special organizational charters, at least in relation to certain colleges. If they do, the question arises, how do organizational charters operate? Network analysts suggest that "the pattern of ties in a network provides significant opportunities and constraints because it affects the relative access of people and institutions to such resources as information, wealth and power" (Wellman, 1981:3). Furthermore, "because of their structural location, members of a social system differ greatly in their access to these resources" (Wellman, 1981:30). Moreover, network analysts have suggested that class-structured networks work to preserve upper class ideology, consciousness, and life style (see for example Laumann, 1966:132–36).

We expect that colleges and secondary schools have much closer ties than has previously been documented. Close networks of personal relationships between officials at certain private schools and some elite colleges transform what is for many students a relatively standardized, bureaucratic procedure into a process of negotiation. As a result, they are able to communicate more vital information about their respective needs, giving selected secondary school students an inside track to gaining acceptance to desired colleges. We call this process "bartering."

Sample and Data

Baltzell (1958, 1964) noted the importance of elite secondary boarding schools for upper class solidarity. However, he was careful to distinguish between those boarding schools that were truly socially elite and those that had historically served somewhat less affluent and less powerful families. He indicates that there is a core group of eastern Protestant schools that "set the pace and bore the brunt of criticism received by private schools for their so-called 'snobbish,' 'undemocratic' and even 'un-American' values" (Baltzell, 1958:307–08). These 16 schools are: Phillips (Andover) Academy (MA), Phillips Exeter Academy (NH), St. Paul's School (NH), St. Mark's School (MA), Groton School (MA), St. George's School (RI), Kent School (CT), The Taft School (CT), The Hotchkiss School (CT), Choate Rosemary Hall (CT), Middlesex School (MA), Deerfield Academy (MA), The Lawrenceville School (NJ), The Hill School (PA), The Episcopal High School (VA), and Woodberry Forest School (VA). We refer to the schools on Baltzell's list as the "select 16."[1]

In 1982 and 1983, we visited a representative sample of 12 of the select 16 schools. These 12 schools reflect the geographic distribution of the select 16 schools. In this time period we also visited 30 other "leading" secondary boarding schools drawn from the 1981 *Handbook of Private Schools'* list of 289 "leading" secondary boarding schools. This sample is representative of leading secondary boarding schools nationally in location, religious affiliation, size, and the sex composition of the student body. These schools are organizationally similar to the select 16 schools in offering only a college preparatory curriculum, in being incorporated as non-profit organizations, in their faculty/student ratios, and in the percent of boarders who receive financial aid. They differ somewhat with respect to sex composition, average size, the sex of their heads, and number of advanced placement courses (see Table 1). However, the key difference between the select 16 schools and the other "leading" schools is that the former are more socially elite

TABLE 4.1 Comparison of Population and Two Samples of Boarding Schools[a]

	Total Population (N = 289)	Other Boarding School Sample (N = 30)	Select 16 Sample (N = 12)
Percent with College Preparatory Curriculum	100	100	100
Percent with No Religious Affiliation	65	70	67
Percent Incorporated, Not-for-profit	83	90	83
Average Faculty/Student Ratio	0.17	0.15	0.15
Average Percent of Boarders Aided	15	16	18
Percent of Schools which are All-Boys	28	17	33
Percent of Schools which are All-Girls	17	28	0
Percent Coeducational Schools	55	65	67
Percent with Male Heads	92	73	100
Average Number of Advanced Courses	3.5	4.8	6.7
Average Size	311	322	612

a. Computed from data published in the *Handbook of Private Schools* (1981).

than the latter. For instance, in one of the select 16 boarding schools in 1982, 40 percent of the current students' parents were listed in *Social Register*.[2]

All 42 schools were visited by one or both of the authors. Visits lasted between one and five days and included interviews with administrators, teachers and students. Most relevant to this study were the lengthy interviews with the schools' college advisors. These interviews explored all aspects of the college counseling process, including the nature and content of the advisors' relationships with admissions officers at various colleges. At a representative sample of six of the select 16 schools, and a representative sample of 13 of the other "leading" schools a questionnaire was administered to seniors during our visits.[3] The questionnaire contained more than 50 items and included questions on parental education, occupation, income, number of books in the home, family travel, educational legacies as well as many questions on boarding school life and how students felt about their experiences in school. Overall, student survey and school record data were collected on 687 seniors from the six select 16 schools and 658 seniors from other leading schools. Although not every piece of data was available for every student, we did obtain 578 complete cases from six select 16 schools and 457 cases from ten leading schools.[4] School record data included student grade point averages, Scholastic Aptitude Test (SAT) scores, class rank, names of colleges to which students applied, names of colleges to which students were accepted, and names of colleges students will attend. This material was supplied by the schools after the seniors graduated in the summer or fall of 1982 and 1983. With this population actual enrollment matches school reports with high reliability. The record data have been linked with questionnaire data from the seniors and with various characteristics of the college. The colleges students planned to attend, were coded as to academic selectivity, Ivy League, and other characteristics not analyzed here.[5]

Chartering

Historical evidence shows that the select 16 schools have had special charters in relation to Ivy League colleges in general, and Harvard, Yale, and Princeton in particular. In the 1930s and 1940s, two-thirds of all graduates of 12 of the select 16 boarding schools attended Harvard, Yale, or Princeton (Karabel, 1984). But, by 1973, this share had slipped noticeably to an average of 21 percent, although the rate of acceptance between schools ranged from 51 percent to 8 percent (Cookson and Persell, 1978: Table 4). In the last half century, then, the proportion of select 16 school graduates who attended Harvard, Yale, or Princeton dropped substantially.

This decrease was paralleled by an increase in the competition for admission to Ivy League colleges. According to several college advisors at select 16 boarding schools, 90 percent of all applicants to Harvard in the 1940s were accepted as were about half of those in the early 1950s. In 1982, the national acceptance rate for the eight Ivy League schools was 26 percent, although it was 20 percent or less at Harvard, Yale, and Princeton (*National College Data Bank,* 1984).

The pattern of Ivy League college admissions has changed during this time. Ivy League colleges have begun to admit more public school graduates. Before World

War II at Princeton, for example, about 80 percent of the entering freshmen came from private secondary schools (Blumberg and Paul, 1975:70). In 1982, 34 percent of the freshman class at Harvard, 40 percent of Yale freshmen, and 40 percent of Princeton freshmen were from nonpublic high schools (*National College Data Bank,* 1984).

This shift in college admissions policy, combined with increased financial aid and an inflationary trend in higher education that puts increased emphasis on which college one attends, contributes to the large number of applications to certain colleges nationally. Thus, while in the past decade the number of college age students has declined, the number of students applying to Ivy League colleges has increased (Mackay-Smith, 1985; Maeroff, 1984; Winerip, 1984).

In view of these historical changes, is there any evidence that the select 16 schools still retain special charters in relation to college admissions? When four pools of applications to the Ivy League colleges are compared, the acceptance rate is highest at select 16 schools, followed by a highly selective public high school, other leading boarding schools, and finally the entire national pool of applications (Table 2).[6]

While we do not have comparable background data on all the applicants from these various pools, we do know that the students in the highly selective public high school have among the highest academic qualifications in the country.[7] Their combined SAT scores, for example, average at least 150 points higher than those of students at the leading boarding schools. On that basis they might be expected to do considerably better than applicants from boarding schools: which they do at some colleges but not at Harvard, Yale or Princeton.

The most revealing insights into the operation of special charters, however, are provided by a comparison between select 16 boarding schools and other leading boarding schools—the most similar schools and the ones on which we have the most detailed data.

Students from select 16 schools apply to somewhat different colleges than do students from other leading boarding schools. Select 16 school students were much more likely to apply to one or more of the eight Ivy League and at least one of the other highly-selective colleges than were students from other leading boarding schools (Table 3). Among those who applied, select 16 students were more likely to be accepted than were students from other boarding schools, and if accepted, they were slightly more likely to attend.

Before we can conclude that these differences are due to a school charter, we need to control for parental SES[8] and student SAT scores.[9] This analysis is shown in Table 4. One striking finding here is the high rate of success enjoyed by boarding school students in general. At least one-third and as many as 92 percent of the students in each cell of Table 4 are accepted. Given that the average freshman combined SAT score is more than 1175 at these colleges and universities, it is particularly notable that such a large proportion of those with combined SAT scores of 1050 or less are accepted.

In general, high SAT scores increase chances of acceptance, but the relationship is somewhat attenuated under certain conditions. Students with low SAT scores are

TABLE 4.2 Percent of Applications That Were Accepted at Ivy League Colleges from Four Pools of Applications

College Name	Select 16 Boarding Schools[a] (1982–83)	Other Leading Boarding Schools[b] (1982–83)	Selective Public High School[c] (1984)	National Group of Applicants[d] (1982)
Brown University				
Percent Accepted	35	20	28	22
Number of Applications	95	45	114	11,854
Columbia University				
Percent Accepted	66	29	32	41
Number of Applications	35	7	170	3,650
Cornell University				
Percent Accepted	57	36	55	31
Number of Applications	65	25	112	17,927
Dartmouth				
Percent Accepted	41	21	41	22
Number of Applications	79	33	37	8,313
Harvard University				
Percent Accepted	38	28	20	17
Number of Applications	104	29	127	13,341
Princeton University				
Percent Accepted	40	28	18	18
Number of Applications	103	40	109	11,804
University of Pennsylvania				
Percent Accepted	45	32	33	36
Number of Applications	40	19	167	11,000
Yale University				
Percent Accepted	40	32	15	20
Number of Applications	92	25	124	11,023
Overall Percent Accepted	42	27	30	26
Total Number of Applications	613	223	960	88,912

a. Based on school record data on the applications of 578 seniors.
b. Based on school record data on the applications of 457 seniors.
c. Based on data published in the school newspaper.
d. Based on data published in the *National College DataBank* (1984).

more likely to be accepted at highly selective colleges if they have higher SES backgrounds, especially if they attend a select 16 school. These students seem to have relatively high "floors" placed under them, since two-thirds of those from select 16 schools and more than half of those from other schools were accepted by one of the most selective colleges.[10]

TABLE 4.3 Boarding School Students' College Application, Chances of Acceptance, and Plans to Attend

A. Percent of Boarding School Samples Who Applied		Ivy League Colleges	Highly Selective Colleges
Select 16 Boarding Schools	% =	61	87
	N =	(353)	(502)
Other Leading Boarding Schools	% =	28	61
	N =	(129)	(279)
B. Percent of Applicants Who Were Accepted		**Ivy League Colleges**	**Highly Selective Colleges**
Select 16 Boarding Schools	% =	54	84
	N =	(191)	(420)
Other Leading Boarding Schools	% =	36	64
	N =	(47)	(178)
C. Percent of Acceptees Who Plan to Attend		**Ivy League Colleges**	**Highly Selective Colleges**
Select 16 Boarding Schools	% =	79	81
	N =	(151)	(340)
Other Leading Boarding Schools	% =	53	77
	N =	(25)	(137)

The most successful ones of all are relatively low SES students with the highest SATs attending select 16 schools—92 percent of whom were accepted. Students from relatively modest backgrounds appear to receive a "knighting effect" by attending a select 16 school. Thus, select 16 schools provide mobility for some individuals from relatively less privileged backgrounds. To a considerable degree all students with high SATs, regardless of their SES, appear to be "turbocharged" by attending a select 16 school compared to their counterparts at other leading schools.

At every level of SATs and SES, students' chances of acceptance increase if they attend a select 16 school. Such a finding is consistent with the argument that a chartering effect continues to operate among elite educational institutions. The historical shifts toward admitting more public school students on the part of Ivy League colleges and the increased competition for entry, described above, have meant that more effort has been required on the part of select 16 schools to retain an advantage for their students. We believe that certain private boarding schools have buttressed their charters by an increasingly active bartering operation.

Bartering

Normally, we do not think of the college admissions process as an arena for bartering. It is assumed that colleges simply choose students according to their own criteria and needs. Few students and no high schools are thought to have any special

TABLE 4.4 Percent of Students Who Applied to the Most Highly Selective Colleges Who Were Accepted, with SAT Scores, SES, and School Type Held Constant[a]

		Student Combined SAT Scores					
		High (1580–1220)		Medium (1216–1060)		Low (1050–540)	
		Select 16 Schools	Other Leading Boarding Schools	Select 16 Schools	Other Leading Boarding Schools	Select 16 Schools	Other Leading Boarding Schools
Student Socio-economic Status							
High	% =	87	70	80	64	65	53
	N =	(93)	(33)	(73)	(36)	(34)	(30)
Medium	% =	89	71	85	76	44	35
	N =	(100)	(28)	(66)	(46)	(18)	(51)
Low	% =	92	72	78	69	55	33
	N =	(72)	(25)	(51)	(32)	(33)	(49)

a. Based on student questionnaires and school record data on 1035 seniors for whom complete data were available.

"leverage" in admissions decisions. Our research revealed, however, that select 16 schools—perhaps because of their perennial supply of academically able and affluent students—can negotiate admissions cases with colleges. The colleges are aware that select 16 schools attract excellent college prospects and devote considerable attention to maintaining close relationships with these schools, especially through the college admissions officers. Secondary school college advisors actively "market" their students within a context of tremendous parental pressure and increasing competition for admission to elite colleges.

Select 16 College Advisors and Ivy League Admissions Directors: The Old School Tie

Of the 11 select 16 school college advisors on whom data were available, 10 were graduates of Harvard, Yale, or Princeton. Of the 23 other leading boarding school college advisors on whom data were available, only three were Ivy League graduates, and none of them from Harvard, Yale, or Princeton. College advisors are overwhelmingly white men. At the select 16 schools only one (an acting director) was a woman, and at other schools five were women. Some college advisors have previously worked as college admissions officers. Their educational and social similarity to college admissions officers may facilitate the creation of social ties and the sharing of useful information. Research shows that the exchange of ideas most frequently occurs between people who share certain social attributes (Rogers and Kincaid, 1981).

College advisors at select 16 schools tend to have long tenures—15 or more years is not unusual. On the other hand, college advisors at other schools are more likely to have assumed the job recently. A college advisor at one select 16 school stressed the "importance of continuity on both sides of the relationship." Thus, it is not surprising that select 16 schools hold on to their college advisors.

Select 16 college advisors have close social relationships with each other and with elite college admissions officers that are cemented through numerous face-to-face meetings each year. All of the select 16 schools are on the east coast, whereas only 70 percent of the other leading boarding schools are in that region. However, even those leading boarding schools on the east coast lack the close relationships with colleges that characterize the select 16 schools. Thus, geography alone does not explain these relationships.

The college advisors at most of the boarding schools we studied have personally visited a number of colleges around the country. Boarding schools often provide college advisors with summer support for systematic visits, and a number of geographically removed colleges offer attractive incentives, or fully paid trips to their region (e.g., Southern California). These trips often take place during bitter New England winters, and include elegant food and lodging as well as a chance to see colleges and meet admissions officers.

However, the college advisors at select 16 schools are likely to have visited far more schools (several mentioned that they had personally visited 60 or 70 schools) than college advisors at other schools (some of whom had not visited any). They are also much more likely to visit regularly the most selective and prestigious colleges.[11]

Numerous college admissions officers also travel to these boarding schools to interview students and meet the college advisors. The select 16 schools have more college admissions officers visit than do other schools; more than 100 in any given academic year is not unusual. College advisors have drinks and dinner with selected admissions officers, who often stay overnight on campus. As one college advisor noted, "We get to establish a personal relationship with each other." Moreover, Ivy League colleges bring students from select 16 schools to their campus to visit for weekends.

By knowing each other personally, college advisors and admissions officers "develop a relationship of trust," so that they can evaluate the source as well as the content of phone calls and letters. We observed phone calls between college advisors and admissions officers when we were in their offices. Several college advisors mentioned, "It helps to know personally the individual you are speaking or writing to," and one college advisor at a select 16 school said, "I have built up a track record with the private colleges over the years."

Virtually all of the select 16 school college advisors indicated that in the spring—before colleges have finished making their admissions decisions—they take their application files and drive to elite colleges to discuss "their list." They often sit in on the admissions deliberations while they are there. In contrast, the other schools' college advisors generally did not make such trips. Such actions suggest the existence of strong social networks between select 16 school college advisors and elite college admissions officers.

How the System Works: "Fine Tuning" the Admissions Process

Bartering implies a reciprocal relationship, and select 16 schools and elite colleges have a well-developed system of information exchange. Both sides have learned to cooperate to their mutual benefit. College advisors try to provide admissions officers with as much information about their students as possible to help justify the acceptance of a particular applicant. Select 16 schools have institutionalized this process more than other schools. The most professional operation we found was in a select 16 school where about half the graduating class goes to Harvard, Yale or Princeton. There, the college advisor interviews the entire faculty on each member of the senior class. He tape records all their comments and has them transcribed. This produces a "huge confidential dossier which gives a very good sense of where each student is." In addition, housemasters and coaches write reports. Then the college advisor interviews each senior, dictating notes after each interview. After assimilating all of these comments on each student, the college advisor writes his letter of recommendation, which he is able to pack with corroborative details illustrating a candidate's strengths. The thoroughness, thought, and care that goes into this process insures that anything and everything positive that could be said about a student is included, thereby maximizing his or her chances for a favorable reception at a college.[12]

Information also flows from colleges to the secondary schools. By sitting in on the admissions process at colleges like Harvard, Princeton, and Yale, select 16 school college advisors say they "see the wealth and breadth of the applicant pool." They get a first-hand view of the competition their students face. They also obtain a sense of how a college "puts its class together," which helps them to learn strategies for putting forward their own applicants.

By observing and participating in the admissions process, select 16 school college advisors gain an insider's view of a college's selection process. This insider's knowledge is reflected in the specific figures select 16 advisors mentioned in our conversations with them. One select 16 school college advisor said that a student has a "two and one half as good a chance for admission to Harvard if his father went there than if he did not." Another said, "while 22 percent in general are admitted to Ivy League colleges, 45 percent of legacies are admitted to Ivy League colleges." In both cases, they mentioned a specific, quantified statement about how being a legacy affected their students' admissions probabilities.[13] Similarly, several select 16 school college advisors mentioned the percentages of the freshman class at Harvard and Yale that were from public and private schools, and one even mentioned how those percentages have changed since 1957. College advisors at other schools do not lace their conversations with as many specific figures nor do they belong to the special organization that some of the select 16 schools have formed to share information and strategies.

The special interest group these schools have formed is able to negotiate with the colleges to their students' advantage. For instance, the college advisors explained that select 16 school students face greater competition than the average high school student and carry a more rigorous course load.[14] Therefore, this group persuaded the colleges that their students stand by decile or quintile. Colleges may then put such students in a "not ranked" category or report the decile or quintile rank. No entering student from such a secondary school is clearly labeled as the bottom person in the class. To our knowledge, only select 16 schools have made this arrangement.

Armed with an insider's knowledge of a college's desires, select 16 school college advisors seek to present colleges with the most appropriate candidates. As one select 16 school college advisor said, "I try to shape up different applicant pools for different colleges," a process that has several components. First, college advisors try to screen out hopeless prospects, or as one tactfully phrased it, "I try to discourage unproductive leads." This is not always easy because, as one said, "Certain dreams die hard." College advisors in other schools were more likely to say that they never told students where they should or should not apply.

One select 16 school requires students to write a "trial college essay" that helps the college advisor ascertain "what kind of a student this is." From the essay he can tell how well students write, determine whether they follow through and do what they need to do on time, and learn something about their personal and family background. With faculty and student comments in hand, college advisors can begin to assemble their applicant pools. One thing they always want to learn is which college is a student's first choice, and why. This is useful information when bartering with colleges.

Some college advisors are quite frank when bartering, for example, the select 16 college advisor who stressed, "I am candid about a student to the colleges, something that is not true at a lot of schools where they take an advocacy position in relation to their students. . . . We don't sell damaged goods to the colleges." College advisors at other schools did not define their role as one of weeding out candidates prior to presenting them to colleges, although they may do this as well. It would seem then that part of the gate-keeping process of admission to college is occurring in select 16 secondary schools. College advisors, particularly those with long tenures at select 16 schools, seem quite aware of the importance of maintaining long-term credibility with colleges, since credibility influences how effectively they can work for their school in the future.

While the children of certain big donors (so-called "developmental cases") may be counseled with special care, in general the college advisors have organizational concerns that are more important than the fate of a particular student. Several select 16 school college advisors spoke with scorn about parents who see a rejection as the "first step in the negotiation." Such parents threaten to disrupt a delicate network of social relationships that link elite institutions over a considerable time span.

At the same time, college advisors try to do everything they can to help their students jump the admissions hurdle. One select 16 school college advisor said,

> I don't see our students as having an advantage (in college admissions). We have to make the situation unequal. We do this by writing full summary reports on the students, by reviewing the applicants with the colleges several times during the year, and by traveling to the top six colleges in the spring. . . . [Those visits] are an advocacy proceeding on the side of the students. The colleges make their best decisions on our students and those from [another select 16 school] because they have the most information on these students.

Another select 16 college advisor said, "We want to be sure they are reading the applications of our students fairly, and we lobby for our students." A third select 16 college advisor made a similar statement, "When I drove to the [Ivy League] colleges, I give them a reading on our applicants. I let them know if I think they are making a mistake. There is a lobbying component here."

Select 16 college advisors do not stop with simply asking elite college admissions officers to reconsider a decision, however. They try to barter, and the colleges show they are open to this possibility when the college admissions officer says, "Let's talk about your group." One select 16 college advisor said he stresses to colleges that if his school recommends someone and he or she is accepted, that student will come. While not all colleges heed this warranty, some do.

One select 16 college advisor said, "It is getting harder than it used to be to say to an admissions officer, 'take a chance on this one,' especially at Harvard which now has so many more applications." But it is significant that he did not say that it was impossible. If all else fails in a negotiation, a select 16 college advisor said, "we lobby for the college to make him their absolute first choice on the waiting list." Such a compromise represents a chance for both parties to save face.

Most public high school counselors are at a distinct disadvantage in the bartering process because they are not part of the interpersonal network, do not have strategic information, and are thus unable to lobby effectively for their students. One select 16 advisor told us about a counselor from the Midwest who came to an Ivy League college to sit in on the admissions committee decision for his truly outstanding candidate—SATs in the 700s, top in his class, class president, and star athlete. The select 16 college advisor was also there, lobbying on behalf of his candidate—a nice undistinguished fellow (in the words of his advisor, "A good kid,") with SATs in the 500s, middle of his class, average athlete, and no strong signs of leadership. After hearing both the counselors, the Ivy League college chose the candidate from the select 16 school. The outraged public school counselor walked out in disgust. Afterwards, the Ivy League college admissions officer said to the select 16 college advisor, "We may not be able to have these open meetings anymore." Even in the unusual case where a public school counselor did everything that a select 16 boarding school college advisor did, it was not enough to secure the applicant's admission. Despite the competitive environment that currently surrounds admission to elite colleges, the admissions officers apparently listen more closely to advisors from select 16 boarding schools than to public school counselors.

Conclusions and Implications

The graduates of certain private schools are at a distinct advantage when it comes to admission to highly selective colleges because of the special charters and highly developed social networks these schools possess. Of course, other factors are operating as well. Parental wealth (which is not fully tapped by a measure of SES based on education, occupation, and income), preference for the children of alumni, Advanced Placement (AP) coursework, sports ability especially in such scarce areas as ice hockey, crew or squash, and many other factors also influence the process of college admission. Elite boarding schools are part of a larger process whereby more privileged members of society transmit their advantages to their children. Attendance at a select 16 boarding school signals admissions committees that an applicant may have certain valuable educational and social characteristics.

Significantly, neither the families nor the secondary schools leave the college admissions process to chance or to formal bureaucratic procedures. Instead, they use personal connections to smooth the process, and there is reason to believe that these efforts affect the outcomes. The "knighting effect" of select 16 schools helps a few low SES, high SAT students gain admission to highly selective colleges, evidence of sponsored mobility for a few worthy youngsters of relatively humble origins. Our findings are consistent with Kamens' (1974) suggestion that certain schools make their students eligible for special social rights. Furthermore, the interaction between social background, SATs, and select 16 school attendance suggests that both individual ability and socially structured advantages operate in the school-college transition.

These results illustrate Collins' (1979) view that stratified systems are maintained through the manipulation of social contacts. They show one way the networks and stratification processes are interconnected. College access is only one aspect of the larger phenomenon of elite maintenance and reproduction. Elite boarding schools no doubt contribute as well to the social contacts and marriage markets of their graduates. What this instance shows is that reproduction is not a simple process. It involves family and group reproduction as well as some structural replacement with carefully screened new members. There is active personal intervention in what is publicly presented as a meritocratic and open competition. The internal processes and external networks described here operate to construct class privileges as well as to transmit class advantages, thereby helping to reproduce structured stratification within society.

If this example is generalizable, we would expect that economically and culturally advantaged groups might regularly find or create specially chartered organizations and brokers with well-developed networks to help them successfully traverse critical junctures in their social histories. Such key switching points include the transition from secondary school to college, admission to an elite graduate or professional school, obtaining the right job, finding a mentor, gaining a medical residency at a choice hospital (Hall, 1947, 1948, 1949) getting a book manuscript published (Coser et al., 1982), having one's paintings exhibited at an art gallery or museum, obtaining a theatrical agent, having one's business considered for venture capital or bank support (Rogers and Larsen, 1984), being offered membership in an exclusive social club, or being asked to serve on a corporate or other board of directors (Useem, 1984).

In all of these instances, many qualified individuals seek desired, but scarce, social and/or economic opportunities. Truly open competition for highly desired outcomes leaves privileged groups vulnerable. Because the socially desired positions are finite at any given moment, processes that give an advantage to the members of certain groups work to limit the opportunities of individuals from other groups.[15] In these ways, dominant groups enhance their chances, at the same time that a few worthy newcomers are advanced, a process which serves to reproduce and legitimate a structure of social inequality.

NOTES

1. Others besides Baltzell have developed lists of elite private schools including Baird (1977), Domhoff (1967, 1970, 1983), and McLachlan (1970).

2. We were not able to compute the percent of students in *Social Register* for every school because most schools do not publish the names of their students. Hence, we were not able to look their families up in *Social Register.* We do know that less than .000265 percent of American families are listed in *Social Register.* See Levine (1980) for an historical discussion of the social backgrounds of students at several of the select 16 schools.

3. We asked to give the student questionnaires at nine of the 12 select 16 schools and six of those nine schools agreed. At the other leading schools, we asked to give the questionnaires at 15 and 13 schools agreed.

4. Three leading schools did not supply the college data.

5. Following Astin et al. (1981:7), we measured selectivity with the average SAT scores of the entering freshmen.

6. The entire national applicant pool includes the relatively more successful subgroups within it. If they were excluded, the national acceptance rate would be even lower.

7. Students admitted to this selective public high school must be recommended by their junior high school to take a competitive entrance exam, where they must score very well. The school was among the top five in the nation with respect to the number of National Merit Scholarships won by its students, and each year a number of students in the school win Westinghouse science prizes. This school was selected for purposes of comparison here because academically it is considered to be among the very top public schools in the nation. However, it does not have the social prestige of the select 16 boarding schools.

8. SES was measured by combining father's education, father's occupation, and family income into a composite SES score. These SES scores were then standardized for this population, and each student received a single standardized SES score.

9. The combined verbal and mathematics scores were used.

10. We performed separate analyses for boys and girls to see if sex was related to admission to a highly selective college when type of boarding school, SATs, and SES were held constant, and generally it was not. Girls who attend either select 16 or other leading boarding schools do as well or better in admission to college as do their male counterparts,

with the single exception of girls at select 16 schools in the top third on their SATs and SES. In that particular group, 92 percent of the boys but only 77 percent of the girls were accepted at the most highly selective colleges. Since that is the only exception, boys and girls are discussed together in the text of the paper.

11. Our field visits and interviews with college advisors at two highly selective public high schools and three open admissions public high schools show that college advisors at even the most selective public high schools generally do not personally know the admissions officers at colleges, particularly at the most selective and Ivy League colleges, nor do they talk with them over the phone or in person prior to their admissions decisions.

12. Such a procedure requires considerable financial and personnel resources. Select 16 schools have more capital-intensive and professional office services supporting their college admissions endeavor than other schools. Most of them have word processors, considerable professional staff, and ample secretarial and clerical help.

13. We did not ask students what colleges their parents attended so we could not control for college legacy in our analysis. Future research on the admissions process should do so.

14. One way select 16 schools establish their reputations as rigorous schools is through the numbers of their students who succeed on the Advanced Placement (AP) Exams given by the College Entrance Examination Board. Compared to other secondary schools, select 16 schools offer larger numbers of advanced courses (Table 1), encourage more students to take them, coach students very effectively on how to take the test, and maintain contacts with the people who design and read AP exams so that they know what is expected and can guide students accordingly. (See Cookson and Persell, 1985, for more discussion of these processes.) Other schools are much less likely than select 16 ones to have teachers who have graded AP exams or to know people who have helped to write the tests.

15. See Parkin (1979) for a discussion of social closure as exclusion and usurpation.

REFERENCES

Alexander, Karl L., Martha Cook and Edward L. McDill (1978). "Curriculum tracking and educational stratification: some further evidence." *American Sociological Review* 43:47–66.

Alexander, Karl L. and Bruce K. Eckland (1975). "Contextualized effects in the high school attainment process." *American Sociological Review* 40:402–16.

——— (1977) "High school context and college selectivity: institutional constraints in educational stratification." *Social Forces* 56:166–88.

Alexander, Karl L., Bruce K. Eckland and Larry J. Griffin (1975). "The Wisconsin model of socioeconomic achievement: a replication." *American Journal of Sociology* 81:324–42.

Alexander, Karl L. and Edward L. McDill (1976). "Selection and allocation within schools: some causes and consequences of curriculum placement." *American Sociological Review* 41:963–80.

Astin, Alexander W., Margo R. King, and Gerald T. Richardson (1981). The American Freshman: National Norms for Fall 1981. Los Angeles: *Laboratory for Research in Higher Education,* University of California.

Averch, Harvey A., Steven A. Carroll, Theodore S. Donaldson, Herbert J. Kiesling, and John Pincus (1972). How Effective is Schooling? *A Critical Review and Synthesis of Research Findings.* Santa Monica, CA: The Rand Corporation.

Baird, Leonard L. (1977). The Elite Schools. Lexington, MA: Lexington Books.
Baltzell, E. Digby (1958). Philadelphia Gentlemen. New York: Free Press.
——— (1964) The Protestant Establishment. New York: Random House.
Beck, E. M., Patrick M. Horan, and Charles M. Tolbert II (1978). "Stratification in a dual economy." *American Sociological Review* 43:704–20.
Bibb, Robert C. and William Form (1977). "The effects of industrial, occupational and sex stratification on wages in blue-collar markets." *Social Forces* 55:974–96.
Blau, Peter and Otis D. Duncan (1967). The American Occupational Structure. New York: Wiley.
Blumberg, Paul M. and P. W. Paul (1975). "Continuities and discontinuities in upper-class marriages." *Journal of Marriage and the Family* 37:63–77.
Bowles, Samuel and Herbert Gintis (1976). Schooling in Capitalist America. New York: Basic Books.
Collins, Randall (1979). The Credential Society. New York: Academic Press.
Cookson, Peter Willis, Jr. (1981). "Private secondary boarding school and public suburban high school graduation: an analysis of college attendance plans." Unpublished Ph.D. dissertation, New York University.
Cookson, Peter W., Jr. and Caroline Hodges Persell (1978). "Social structure and educational programs: a comparison of elite boarding schools and public education in the United States." Paper presented at the annual meeting of the American Sociological Association, San Francisco.
——— (1985) Preparing for Power: America's Elite Boarding Schools. New York: Basic Books.
Coser, Lewis A., Charles Kadushin, and Walter W. Powell (1982). Books: The Culture & Commerce of Publishing. New York: Basic Books.
Domhoff, G. William (1967). Who Rules America? Englewood Cliffs: Prentice-Hall.
——— (1970) The Higher Circles. New York: Vintage.
——— (1983) Who Rules America Now? Englewood Cliffs: Prentice-Hall.
Falsey, Barbara and Barbara Heyns (1984). "The college channel: private and public schools reconsidered." *Sociology of Education* 57:111–22.
Hall, Oswald (1946). "The informal organization of the medical profession." *Canadian Journal of Economics and Political Science* 12:30–41.
——— (1948) "The stages of a medical career." *American Journal of Sociology* 53:327–36.
——— (1949) "Types of medical careers." *American Journal of Sociology* 55:243–53.
Haller, Archibald O. and Alejandro Portes (1973). "Status attainment processes." *Sociology of Education* 46:51–91.
Hammack, Floyd M. and Peter W. Cookson, Jr. (1980). "Colleges attended by graduates of elite secondary schools." *The Educational Forum* 44:483–90.
Handbook of Private Schools (1981). Boston: Porter, Sargent Publishers, Inc.
Heyns, Barbara (1974). "Social selection and stratification within schools." *American Journal of Sociology* 79:1434–51.
Jaffe, Abraham and Walter Adams (1970). "Academic and socio-economic factors related to entrance and retention at two- and four-year colleges in the late 1960s." New York: Bureau of Applied Social Research, Columbia University.
Jencks, Christopher, Marshall Smith, Henry Acland, Mary Jo Bane, David Cohen, Herbert Gintis, Barbara Heyns, and Stephan Michelson (1972). Inequality. New York: Basic Books.
Kamens, David (1974). "Colleges and elite formation: the ease of prestigious American colleges." *Sociology of Education* 47:354–78.

——— (1977) "Legitimating myths and educational organization: the relationship between organizational ideology and formal structure." *American Sociological Review* 42:208–19.

Karabel, Jerome (1984). "Status-group struggle, organizational interests, and the limits of institutional autonomy: the transformation of Harvard, Yale, and Princeton 1918–1940." *Theory and Society* 13:1–40.

Karen, David (1985). Who Gets into Harvard? Selection and Exclusion. Unpublished Ph.D. Dissertation, Department of Sociology, Harvard University.

Kerckhoff, Alan C. (1976). "The status attainment process: socialization or allocation?" *Social Forces* 55:368–81.

——— (1984) "The current state of social mobility research." *Sociological Quarterly* 25:139–53.

Klitgaard, Robert (1985). Choosing Elites. New York: Basic Books.

Laumann, Edward O. (1966). Prestige and Association in an Urban Community: An Analysis of an Urban Stratification System. Indianapolis: Bobbs-Merrill.

Levine, Steven B. (1980). "The rise of American boarding schools and the development of a national upper class." *Social Problems* 28:63–94.

Lewis, Lionel S. and Richard A. Wanner (1979). "Private schooling and the status attainment process." *Sociology of Education* 52:99–112.

Mackay-Smith, Anne (1985). "Admissions crunch: top colleges remain awash in applicants despite a smaller pool." Wall Street Journal (April 2):1,14.

Maeroff, Gene I. (1984). "Top Eastern colleges report unusual rise in applications." New York Times (February 21):A1,C10.

McLachlan, James (1970). American Boarding Schools: A Historical Study. New York: Charles Scribner's Sons.

Meyer, John (1970). "The charter: conditions of diffuse socialization in school." Pp. 564–78 in W. Richard Scott (ed.), Social Processes and Social Structure. New York: Holt, Rinehart.

——— (1977) "Education as an institution." *American Journal of Sociology* 83:55–77.

Mills, C. Wright (1956). The Power Elite. London: Oxford University Press.

National College Data Bank (1984). Princeton: Peterson's Guides, Inc.

Oakes, Jeannie (1985). Keeping Track: How Schools Structure Inequality. New Haven: Yale University Press.

Otto, Luther B. and Archibald O. Haller (1979). "Evidence for a social psychological view of the status attainment process: four studies compared." *Social Forces* 57:887–914.

Parkin, Frank (1979). Marxism and Class Theory: A Bourgeois Critique. New York: Columbia University Press.

Persell, Caroline Hodges (1977). Education and Inequality. New York: Free Press.

Robinson, Robert V. (1984). "Reproducing class relations in industrial capitalism." *American Sociological Review* 49:182–96.

Rogers, Everett M. and Judith K. Larsen (1984). Silicon Valley Fever: The Growth of High-Tech Culture. New York: Basic Books.

Rosenbaum, James E. (1976). Making Inequality: The Hidden Curriculum of High School Tracking. New York: Wiley.

——— (1980) "Track misperceptions and frustrated college plans: an analysis of the effects of tracks and track perceptions in the national longitudinal survey." *Sociology of Education* 53:74–88.

Sewell, William H., Archibald O. Haller, and Alejandro Portes (1969). "The educational and early occupational attainment process." *American Sociological Review* 34:82–91.

Sewell, William H., Archibald O. Haller, and George W. Ohlendorf (1970). "The educational and early occupational status achievement process: replication and revision." *American Sociological Review* 35:1014–27.

Social Register (1984). New York: Social Register Association.

Stolzenberg, Ross M. (1975). "Occupations, labor markets and the process of wage attainment." *American Sociological Review* 40:645–65.

Useem, Michael (1984). The Inner Circle: Large Corporations and the Rise of Business Political Activity in the U.S. and U.K. New York: Oxford University Press.

Wellman, Barry (1981). "Network analysis from method and metaphor to theory and substance." Working Paper Series 1B. Structural Analysis Programme, University of Toronto.

Wilson, Kenneth L. and Alejandro Portes (1975). "The educational attainment process: results from a national sample." *American Journal of Sociology* 81:343–63.

Winerip, Michael (1984). "Hot colleges and how they get that way." New York Times Magazine (November 18):68ff.

DISCUSSION QUESTIONS

1. What roles do high schools play in "chartering" elite criteria for status attainment?
2. For admission into elite schools, how important are networks of personal relations between high school counselors and college admission boards?

Article 5

IQ and Heredity

Suspicion of Fraud Beclouds Classic Experiment

NICHOLAS WADE

CHARGES OF SCIENTIFIC FRAUD, as yet unproved, have been made against an eminent English psychologist, the late Cyril Burt, whose work has featured prominently in the debate about racial differences and intelligence.

Burt is accused by his critics of having doctored or even invented his extensive and partly unique collection of IQ test data in order to support his theory that intelligence is determined primarily by heredity.

Should the accusation prove true, the forgery may rank with that of the Piltdown Man in that for years it remained undetected while occupying a pivotal place in a fierce scientific controversy.

Burt's work has been used not only in the United States, notably by hereditarians such as Arthur Jensen of the University of California and Richard Herrnstein of Harvard, but also in England where Burt wielded considerable influence over national educational policy. As a government adviser in the 1930s and 1940s, he was influential in setting up the three-tier system of British education. In accordance with Burt's views that intelligence is largely innate, children were irredeemably

From "IQ and Heredity: Suspicion of Fraud Beclouds Classic Experiment," by Nicholas Wade, *Science,* Vol. 194, Nov. 26, 1976, pp. 916–918.

assigned to one of the three educational levels on the basis of a test given at the age of 11.

Burt's conclusions have been under suspicion for several years because of internal inconsistencies in his data. What has sparked off accusations of outright fraud is an article in the London *Sunday Times*. The newspaper's medical correspondent, Oliver Gillie, reported his failure to find any evidence that Burt's two chief coauthors on his later papers, Miss Margaret Howard and Miss J. Conway, had ever existed.

Gillie could find no sign of Howard or Conway in the records of London University, the address given on their scientific papers, and none of 18 acquaintances of Burt could remember having ever met or heard of them. "It must be considered a possibility," Gillie concluded, "that Margaret Howard and J. Conway never existed, but were the fantasy of an aging professor who became increasingly lonely and deaf." Burt died in 1971 at the age of 88, having retired from the chair of psychology at University College, London, some 20 years earlier.

For those who were in any case skeptical of the notable fit between Burt's data and his theories, the failure to trace his collaborators has come as clinching evidence of fraud. Leon Kamin of Princeton University says of Burt's work, "It was a fraud linked to policy from the word go. The data were cooked in order for him to arrive at the conclusions he wanted." On the other side of the Atlantic Liam Hudson, professor of psychology at Edinburgh University, considers that the inconsistencies in Burt's data and the difficulty in tracking down his coauthors put the question of Burt's fraudulence "beyond argument." . . .

It was because of its central role in the debates touched off by the Jensen and Herrnstein arguments that Burt's work—apparently for the first time—came under serious critical review. The critic was Kamin, a psychologist who specializes in the conditioned reflex and who had never ventured into the IQ field until 1972 when a student urged him to read one of Burt's papers. "The immediate conclusion I came to after 10 minutes of reading was that Burt was a fraud," he says. Being an outsider to the field, Kamin spotted what no one inside had seen, that Burt's results are riddled with internal implausibilities and basic methodological oversights.

For example, the pearl of Burt's data collection is a survey of separated identical twins. Since the twins have the same genes, any difference in their intelligence should be due to environment alone, so that the correlation of their IQ scores in theory gives a pure measure of the influence of heredity on intelligence. This is a classical experiment in psychology, but one that is not often done because of the rarity of separated identical twins.

Burt published the first full report of his twins in 1955, when he had located 21 pairs, a second report in 1958 when the collection amounted to "over 30" pairs, and a final report in 1966 with 53 pairs. What Kamin noticed was that the correlation between the IQ scores of the separated twins was given as 0.771 for all three studies. For the correlation to remain unchanged through different sample sizes is improbable even at one occurrence, but the IQ correlation between identical twins reared together sticks at 0.944 through three different sample sizes, and there are many other such examples. For whatever reason, there is a strange imperturbability in the results Burt obtained from a changing data base.

Kamin also noticed that Burt often failed to record facts quite basic to the methodology of his surveys, such as the sexes of the children, the age at which they were tested, or even what particular test was applied. "The numbers left behind by Professor Burt," Kamin concluded in a lecture given in 1973, "are simply not worthy of serious scientific attention."

Kamin's views on IQ lie at the environmentalist pole of the debate, his position being that there is no way of proving that intelligence is inheritable. His opinions of Burt are not universally accepted. The suggestion of fraud "is so outrageous I find it hard to stay in my chair," said Herrnstein when asked his opinion of Kamin's criticisms. "Burt was a towering figure of 20th century psychology. I think it is a crime to cast such doubt over a man's career." But Burt's empirical legacy has probably been harmed beyond repair, and the man who delivered the coup de grace is none other than Jensen.

Jensen greatly admired Burt, came to know him in the last years of his life, and described Burt in an obituary as "one of the world's great psychologists." As a service to other psychologists, Jensen decided to make a compendium of all the data on kinship correlations which Burt had published in scattered form in numerous papers. On a visit to England in May, 1972 he gathered a full set of reprints from Burt's former housekeeper and started to tabulate all Burt's data. In so doing he came across the same curious consistencies noted by Kamin.

Any particular instance of an invariant correlation with a changing sample size, Jensen observed, "can be rationalized as being not too improbable. But 20 such instances unduly strain the laws of chance and can only mean error, at least in some of the cases." Burt's correlations "are useless for hypothesis testing," he concluded in an article which appeared in *Behavior Genetics* in 1974. As to the reason for the errors, Jensen speculated, "It is almost as if Burt regarded the actual data as merely an incidental backdrop for the illustration of the theoretical issues in quantitative genetics, which, to him, seemed always to hold the center of the stage."

It is greatly to Jensen's credit that he was prepared to read out of the scientific literature, as his article essentially does, data which had been an important buttress of his own controversial position. Moreover, Burt was a man to whom Jensen was linked both by belief and academic lineage (Jensen was a postgraduate student of H. J. Eysenck, who was a pupil of Burt's). As to the credit for discovering Burt's errors, Jensen's article was the first to be published (Kamin's appeared in his book *The Science and Politics of IQ,* also 1974), but Kamin was the first to comment on the errors, in lectures given around the country in 1972 and 1973. Jensen did not personally attend any of these lectures but acknowledges in a footnote that Kamin was the first to draw attention to the invariant correlation of the twin studies.

Even Eysenck, whom Burt considered his brightest pupil, has conceded that Burt's data are unusable. The problem described by Jensen, Eysenck said in a recent letter to the London *Sunday Times,* "makes it impossible to rely on these figures in the future."

Are the errors in Burt's papers the results of a deliberate attempt to deceive or simply the inattention to detail of an elderly and ailing man? Burt is not around to defend himself, but both Eysenck and Jensen believe that there are innocent explanations of what happened. Kamin, on the other hand, has come to suspect that Burt consistently invented data from his very first work published in 1909.

One event that has made the issue harder to resolve is the destruction of Burt's original data. After his death his housekeeper invited colleagues to his apartment to take their pick of the books and papers she could not place with libraries. Burt had half a dozen tea-chests full of papers and the housekeeper asked advice about them of two people who happened to be visiting the apartment, one of whom was Liam Hudson of Edinburgh University. Hudson, who is not one of Burt's academic allies, says that the tea-chests were full of raw test sheets, unfiled and impossible for anyone but Burt to make sense of. He told the housekeeper, he says, that she would be "perfectly justified in burning them." Asked if the tea-chests might not have contained data bearing on the disputed twin studies, Hudson replies, "What I was doing was walking around a gloomy house with a distraught housekeeper. Whether they contained anything of genuine significance I just don't know."

Most of Burt's data on IQ and kinship correlations were published after his retirement in 1950. According to Leslie Hearnshaw of Liverpool University, who is preparing a biography, Burt was hard up during this time and had to do a lot of hack work to make ends meet. He was suffering from a form of deafness known as Ménière's disease which made it hard for him to communicate. He wrote several papers on psychological research, in which he had long been interested. Philip Vernon, a collaborator of Burt's who is now at the University of Calgary, Alberta, says of Burt's state of mind that he was always a bit paranoiac. "He would train students brilliantly but once they turned against him he would turn on them with a vengeance. He was very helpful if one was with him, as long as one did not criticize the theories he built up in the 1910s and 1920s. Unfortunately, he never changed his theories."

Old, ailing, embattled in numerous controversies, it is quite possible that Burt was simply careless with his data and neglectful of accuracy. Jensen, for example, says that though he can't offer any explanation for the errors, "they seem to be too haphazard and not planned. If Burt was trying to fake the data a person with his statistical skills would have done a better job."

Eysenck's suggestion, somewhat more damaging to Burt, is that to avoid the chore of recalculating the correlations with the new data, Burt simply carried over the correlation figures from his earlier papers. Though quite inadmissible as a scientific procedure, a shortcut of this nature would fall a long way short of fraud since not done with intent to deceive.

A similar explanation is proposed by G. C. Drew, present occupant of Burt's chair of psychology. "As he got old he was remembering old figures that stuck in his mind from earlier papers." But Drew still sees the affair as purely a matter of carelessness. "Burt was totally convinced of the rightness of his views and he became exceedingly careless with the data," he says.

Reading Burt's final paper on the twin survey in the light of such suspicions, it is hard not to be struck by the patness with which crucial, yet hitherto unpublished, data are adduced to demolish each of his critics' arguments. The paper appeared in the *British Journal of Psychology* in 1966, when Burt was 83. The number of separated identical twin pairs had grown from "over 30" in 1958 to 53; making the study by far the largest of its kind. But the study was now revealed to possess a feature that made it even more unique and authoritative. The anti-hereditarians had been claiming that the high IQ correlations found between separated twins might have a lot to do with a correlation between their environments. This was a plausible argument—and one that is true of all the other twin studies—because adopted children are indeed usually placed in homes similar to their own. Though it was not mentioned in the earlier reports of 1955 and 1958, the 1966 paper now reveals the remarkable fact that the homes of Burt's twin pairs, as judged by the occupational categories of the parents and foster parents, are entirely uncorrelated. (The correlation, though Burt gives only the raw figures, is –0.4.) "These figures," Burt then proceeds to observe, "should dispose of one of the commonest explanations advanced by thoroughgoing environmentalists—namely, that the high correlations for the separated twins is due to the way the foster-parents were chosen."

Burt's figures were unlikely enough to have prompted an inquiry from at least one psychologist. Sandra Scarr-Salapatek of the University of California wrote in 1970 asking Burt for more information because the data "looked funny" to her. And Vernon says he thought at the time that the result was highly unlikely. "I could not stomach that, I could not believe that. I didn't know what he had done." Asked why no one had disputed Burt's result, Vernon says that "there were certainly grave doubts although nobody dared to put them into print, because Burt was enormously powerful." Burt's power seemed to have stemmed not so much from patronage—he was by then retired—as from the way he would use his formidable prose style and mastery of statistics to take out after his critics. "He would write a 50-page paper denouncing any criticisms," says Vernon.

Hearnshaw, Burt's biographer, believes that, for whatever reason, it is only Burt's later work that is flawed. Kamin, on the other hand, is coming increasingly to suspect that Burt concocted data from the very beginning of his research career. "He was doing it very flagrantly at the end of his life. Earlier he was more careful in covering his tracks," says Kamin. This intriguing hypothesis is based partly on what Kamin sees as a succession of implausible results which accord with Burt's apparent social biases, and partly on a "pattern of consistent obscurity" that runs through Burt's papers; he rarely gives primary data but refers the reader to unpublished reports, at least some of which Kamin has found to be as elusive as Howard and Conway.

These two authors, Kamin notes, appear frequently in the 1950s as contributors to Burt's journal, writing in a style that is "unmistakably Burtian," but their literary endeavors ceased almost immediately after Burt quit as editor. They and other reviewers with a similar style claim priority for Burt in various discoveries, demolish books written by his critics, and heap praise upon books written by Burt. "It is inconceivable that the writings of Howard and Conway should have been by anyone but Burt," Kamin says. He rejects the idea that the pseudonyms and other flaws can be attributed to senility. The twins, for example, many of whom Kamin suspects may never have existed, are referred to in passing in a paper of 1943 when Burt was at the height of his powers. "I suspect that everything the man did from 1909 is wholly fraudulent," Kamin suggests.

The flaws in Burt's work, whatever the reason for them, are obvious enough now that Kamin and Jensen have pointed them out. Yet Burt's work was never challenged during his lifetime. He was preeminent among his colleagues in England, being the first psychologist to receive a knighthood, and the American Psychological Association awarded him its Thorndike prize in 1971. At least from 1969 onward, his data occupied a central position in controversy, in a subject which is presumably no less rigorous than other disciplines. Why were the flaws not detected earlier? Why did journal editors and journal boards not require that he report his results in a more complete or accurate form?

"The sober fact is that scholarly penetration of the literature, and endless delving into primary sources, occurs only very rarely," suggests Hudson. "It reflects on us all that these figures should have been in the literature of a highly contentious and important area for more than a decade before anyone went back to examine them as Kamin did. It strikes me as very damaging to us as a profession that articles were coming from someone called Conway whom no one had ever heard of. That is not the way that a community of scholars should be working."

Kamin's interpretation is that Burt's data remained unchallenged because they confirmed what everyone wanted to believe. "Every professor knew that his child was brighter than the ditch-digger's child, so what was there to challenge?" The moral of the tale, according to Kamin, is "Caveat emptor! The people who buy social science should remember that those who have collected the data may have axes to grind."

Others see the episode as less far-reaching. Scarr-Salapatek, one of the early doubters of Burt's data, says that "people trusted Burt to be reporting accurately what he did, so I don't think it is surprising they accepted his data even if they were implausible." In fact, apart from the strange lack of environmental correlation in the twin study, Burt's results for the IQ correlations of his twins are well in line with those of other studies. This, and the fact that the data are published in such scattered form that the discrepancies are not readily apparent, are reasons why the flaws remained undetected, suggests Jensen.

As for the practical implication of removing Burt's data from the scientific literature, there is, naturally, a range of opinion. Kamin states that the data have played a "monumentally important role," particularly those to do with certain rare kinship correlations (such as between second cousins). Richard Lewontin of Harvard, an anti-hereditarian and eminent population geneticist, says that Burt's twin study "is the only large study which is methodologically correct, so its loss is no trivial problem for the heritability people. It is also not nice for them to have this mess in their backyard," he observes. But according to Jensen, all Burt's salient results have now been duplicated, and no one was led to any conclusions which they would not have reached even if Burt had never existed. "It is not like the Piltdown man which led people into error," Jensen says, adding that he does not mean to imply by the comparison that Burt's data too were forged. Scarr-Salapatek, on the other hand, thinks that subtraction of Burt's data "results in a downward estimate of heritability, though not a radical reassessment." The reassessment might require the hereditarians to reduce their estimate of the heritability of intelligence from 80 percent (Herrnstein, 1971) to nearer 60 percent, the figure arrived at by Christopher Jencks of Harvard without using Burt's data.

Burt's data are probably now unusable in any case, but it would still be of some historical interest to know whether the flaws resulted from systematic fraud, mere carelessness, or something in between. The facts so far available do not allow any of these explanations to be ruled out. The only sure evidence of error, the invariant correlations, is a curious mistake for a cunning forger to make. Perhaps, when old and ill, Burt was too proud to ask for help in doing the calculations and, as Eysenck suggests, carried over the results from earlier papers. That is probably the most plausible present explanation for those who like economy in hypotheses. The question is how well it stands up under such burdens to belief as the failure to locate Misses Howard and Conway, the implausibility of some of Burt's results, the apparent use of pseudonyms, and any other suspicions that may accumulate. Should it not, Burt would have much to answer for.

DISCUSSION QUESTIONS

1. As demonstrated by Wade, what role does the researcher play in carrying out the methodological process? How can the researcher affect the results of its study?
2. How did researchers begin to suspect fraud in the IQ material and what are some of the reasons given for such fraudulent data?

III

Culture

WHAT TO FOCUS ON:

1. Why is "culture" an important concept in the sociological analysis of human behavior and social interaction?
2. In what ways are people the product of both biology and culture?

CULTURE REFERS TO THE STANDARDIZED ways of thinking, feeling, and acting which a person acquires as a member of society. The way people greet each other, the guidelines governing dating and courtship, the material objects used in everyday life, the way holidays are celebrated, and the political forms we establish are all examples of culture. Culture, in summary, is the way of life which typifies a human collectivity. Culture is *normative,* it not only describes how life is lived but specifies how life ought to be lived, what rules and procedures are to be followed in the course of one's biography and social interactions. Culture thus has a coercive element and failure to comply with cultural norms and values can result in disapproval and subsequent social sanction.

While every human society must satisfy basic human needs—cultural universals—the form and manner for the fulfillment of these needs vary from culture to culture. Clyde Kluckhohn's article "Queer Customs," informs us about the enormous variability and diversity in the way cultures have gone about meeting basic human needs. Every culture, for example, establishes rules regarding sexual behavior. Some, however, set up a norm of celibacy before marriage while others encourage a type of promiscuity, Some cultures consider such foods as beef, pork, or fish appropriate—even desirable—for inclusion in the diet while others consider these foods taboo, inappropriate for human consumption. Kluckhohn's work demonstrates how human biological functioning is itself modified by cultural training. In this he emphasizes the dual nature—*homo duplex*—of the human person for we are all products of both biology and culture.

Edward and Mildred Hall describe how culture shows itself in body language. We learn not only a verbal language as part of our cultural inheritance but also a "silent language" showing us the proper way we are to move and interact with others. Hall and Hall explain how people come to take the particular body language of their culture for granted and misunderstand or even become annoyed with people of other cultures who move and act differently. The "hidden rules" of body language, the authors explain, sometimes make it difficult for people of different backgrounds to interact in a comfortable way. Misunderstandings of this type can even affect married couples who come from different cultural backgrounds.

Hamid R. Kusha's article "Iran's White Revolution and Its Outcome for Iranian Women" teaches us about the importance of cultural continuity. Kusha explains that the Shah failed in his attempts at Westernization because he did not respect Iran's cultural traditions and sensitivities. In his attempt to industrialize the country, the Shah sought to replace age-old Iranian values with modern Western beliefs: In so doing he lost the loyalty of the Iranian people.

Article 6

Queer Customs

CLYDE KLUCKHOHN

WHY DO THE CHINESE dislike milk and milk products? Why would the Japanese die willingly in a Banzai charge that seemed senseless to Americans? Why do some nations trace descent through the father, others through the mother, still others through both parents? Not because they were destined by God or fate to different habits, not because the weather is different in China and Japan and the United States. Sometimes shrewd common sense has an answer that is close to that of the anthropologist: "because they were brought up that way." By "culture" anthropology means the total life way of a people, the social legacy the individual acquires from his group. Or culture can be regarded as that part of the environment that is the creation of man.

This technical term has a wider meaning than the "culture" of history and literature. A humble cooking pot is as much a cultural product as is a Beethoven sonata. In ordinary speech a man of culture is a man who can speak languages other than his own, who is familiar with history, literature, philosophy, or the fine arts. In some cliques that definition is still narrower. The cultured person is one who can talk about James Joyce, Scarlatti, and Picasso. To the anthropologist, however, to be human is to be cultured. There is culture in general, and then there are the specific cultures such as Russian, American, British, Hottentot, Inca. The general abstract notion serves to remind us that we cannot explain acts solely in terms of the biological properties of the people concerned, their individual past experience, and the immediate situation. The past experience of other men in the form of culture enters into almost every event. Each specific culture constitutes a kind of blueprint for all of life's activities.

One of the interesting things about human beings is that they try to understand themselves and their own behavior. While this has been particularly true of Europeans in recent times, there is no group which has not developed a scheme or schemes to explain man's actions. To the insistent human query "why?" the most exciting illumination anthropology has to offer is that of the concept of culture. Its explanatory importance is comparable to categories such as evolution in biology, gravity in physics, disease in medicine. A good deal of human behavior can be understood, and indeed predicted, if we know a people's design for living. Many acts are neither accidental nor due to personal peculiarities nor caused by supernatural forces nor simply mysterious. Even those of us who pride ourselves on our individualism follow most of the time a pattern not of our own making. We brush our teeth on arising. We put on pants—not a loincloth or grass skirt. We eat three meals a day—not four or five or two. We sleep in a bed—not in a hammock or on a sheep pelt. I do not have to know the individual and his life history to be able to predict these and countless other regularities, including many in the thinking process, of all Americans who are not incarcerated in jails or hospitals for the insane.

To the American woman a system of plural wives seems "instinctively" abhorrent. She cannot understand how any woman can fail to be jealous and uncomfortable if she must share her husband with other women. She feels it "unnatural" to accept such a situation. On the other hand, a Koryak woman of Siberia, for example, would find it hard to understand how a woman could be so selfish and so undesirous of feminine companionship in the home as to wish to restrict her husband to one mate.

Some years ago I met in New York City a young man who did not speak a word of English and was obviously bewildered by American ways. By "blood" he was as American as you or I, for his parents had gone from Indiana to China as missionaries. Orphaned in infancy, he was reared by a Chinese family in a remote village. All who met him found him more Chinese than American. The facts of his blue eyes and light hair were less impressive than a Chinese style of gait, Chinese arm and hand movements, Chinese facial expression, and Chinese modes of thought. The biological heritage was American, but the cultural training had been Chinese. He returned to China. Another example of another kind: I once knew a trader's wife in Arizona who took a somewhat devilish interest in producing a cultural reaction. Guests who came her way were often served delicious sandwiches filled with a meat that seemed to be neither chicken nor tuna fish yet was reminiscent of both. To queries she gave no reply until each had eaten his fill. She then explained that what they had eaten was not chicken, not tuna fish, but the rich, white flesh of freshly killed rattlesnakes. The response was instantaneous—vomiting, often violent vomiting. A biological process is caught in a cultural web.

A highly intelligent teacher with long and successful experience in the public schools of Chicago was finishing her first year in an Indian school. When asked how her Navaho pupils compared in intelligence with Chicago youngsters, she replied, "Well, I just don't know. Sometimes the Indians seem just as bright. At other times they just act like dumb animals. The other night we had a dance in the high school. I saw a boy who is one of the best students in my English class standing off by himself. So I took him over to a pretty girl and told them to dance. But they just stood there with their heads down. They wouldn't even say anything." I inquired if she knew whether or not they were members of the same clan. "What difference would that make?"

"How would you feel about getting into bed with your brother?" The teacher walked off in a huff, but, actually, the two cases were quite comparable in principle. To the Indian the type of bodily contact involved in our social dancing has a directly sexual connotation. The incest taboos between members of the same clan are as severe as between true brothers and sisters. The shame of the Indians at the suggestion that a clan brother and sister should dance and the indignation of the white teacher at the idea that she should share a bed with an adult brother represent equally nonrational responses, culturally standardized unreason.

All this does not mean that there is no such thing as raw human nature. The very fact that certain of the same institutions are found in all known societies indicates that at bottom all human beings are very much alike. The files of the Cross-Cultural Survey at Yale University are organized according to categories such as "marriage ceremonies," "life crisis rites," "incest taboos." At least 75 of these categories are represented in every single one of the hundreds of cultures analyzed. This is hardly surprising. The members of all human groups have about the same biological equipment. All men undergo the same poignant life experiences such as birth, helplessness, illness, old age, and death. The biological potentialities of the species are the blocks with which cultures are built. Some patterns of every culture crystallize around focuses provided by the inevitables of biology: the difference between the sexes, the presence of persons of different ages, the varying physical strength and skill of individuals. The facts of nature also limit culture forms. No culture provides patterns for jumping over trees or for eating iron ore.

There is thus no "either-or" between nature and that special form of nurture called culture. Culture determinism is as one-sided as biological determinism. The two factors are interdependent. Culture arises out of human nature, and its forms are restricted both by man's biology and by natural laws. It is equally true that culture channels biological processes vomiting, weeping, fainting, sneezing, the daily habits of food intake and waste elimination. When a man eats, he is reacting to an internal "drive," namely, hunger contractions consequent upon the lowering of blood sugar, but his precise reaction to these internal stimuli cannot be predicted by physiological knowledge alone. Whether a healthy adult feels hungry twice, three times, or four times a day and the hours at which this feeling recurs is a question of culture. *What* he eats is of course limited by availability, but is also partly regulated by culture. It is a biological fact that some types of berries are poisonous; it is a cultural fact that, a few generations ago, most Americans considered tomatoes to be poisonous and refused to eat them. Such selective, discriminative use of the environment is characteristically cultural. In a still more general sense, too, the process of eating is channeled by culture. Whether a man eats to live, lives to eat, or merely eats and lives is only in part an individual matter, for there are also cultural trends. Emotions are physiological events. Certain situations will evoke fear in people from any culture. But sensations of pleasure, anger, and lust may be stimulated by cultural cues that would leave unmoved someone who has been reared in a different social tradition.

Except in the case of newborn babies and of individuals born with clear-cut structural or functional abnormalities we can observe innate endowments only as modified by cultural training. In a hospital in New Mexico where Zuni Indian, Navaho Indian, and white American babies are born, it is possible to classify the newly arrived infants as unusually active, average, and quiet. Some babies from each "racial" group will fall into each category, though a higher proportion of the white babies will fall into the unusually active class. But if a Navaho baby, a Zuni baby, and a white baby—all classified as unusually active at birth—are again observed at the age of two years, the Zuni baby will no longer seem given to quick and restless activity—*as compared with the white child*—though he may seem so as compared with the other Zunis of the same age. The Navaho child is likely to fall in between as contrasted with the Zuni and the white, though he will probably still seem more active than the average Navaho youngster.

It was remarked by many observers in the Japanese relocation centers that Japanese who were born and brought up in this country, especially those who were reared apart from any large colony of Japanese, resemble in behavior their white neighbors much more closely than they do their own parents who were educated in Japan.

I have said "culture channels biological processes." It is more accurate to say "the biological functioning of individuals is modified if they have been trained in certain ways and not in others." Culture is not a disembodied force. It is created and transmitted by people. However, culture, like well-known concepts of the physical sciences, is a convenient abstraction. One never sees gravity. One sees bodies falling in regular ways. One never sees an electromagnetic field. Yet certain happenings that can be seen may be given a neat abstract formulation by assuming that the electromagnetic field exists. Similarly, one never sees culture as such. What is seen are regularities in the behavior or artifacts of a group that has adhered to a common tradition. The regularities in style and technique of ancient Inca tapestries or stone axes from Melanesian islands are due to the existence of mental blueprints for the group.

Culture is a way of thinking, feeling, believing. It is the group's knowledge stored up (in memories of men; in books and objects) for future use. We study the products of this "mental" activity: the overt behavior, the speech and gestures and activities of people, and the tangible results of these things such as tools, houses, cornfields, and what not. It has been customary in lists of "culture traits" to include such things as watches or lawbooks. This is a convenient way of thinking about them, but in the solution of any important problem we must remember that they, in themselves, are nothing but metals, paper, and ink. What is important is that some men know how to make them, others set a value on them, are unhappy without them, direct their activities in relation to them, or disregard them.

It is only a helpful shorthand when we say "The cultural patterns of the Zulu were resistant to Christianization." In the directly observable world of course, it was individual Zulus who resisted. Nevertheless, if we do not forget that we are speaking at a high level of abstraction, it is justifiable to speak of culture as a cause. One may compare the practice of saying "syphilis caused the extinction of the native population of the island." Was it "syphilis" or "syphilis germs" or "human beings who were carriers of syphilis"?

"Culture," then is "a theory." But if a theory is not contradicted by any relevant fact and if it helps us to understand a mass of otherwise chaotic facts, it is useful. Darwin's contribution was much less the accumulation of new knowledge than the creation of a theory which put in order data already known. An accumulation of facts, however large, is no more a science than a pile of bricks is a house. Anthropology's demonstration that the most weird set of customs has consistency and an order is comparable to modern psychiatry's showing that there is meaning and purpose in the apparently incoherent talk of the insane. In fact, the inability of the older psychologies and philosophies to account for the strange behavior of madmen and heathens was the principal factor that forced psychiatry and anthropology to develop theories of unconscious and of culture.

Since culture is an abstraction, it is important not to confuse culture with society. A "society" refers to a group of people who interact more with each other than they do with other individuals—who cooperate with each other for the attainment of certain ends. You can see and indeed count the individuals who make up a society. A "culture" refers to the distinctive ways of life of such a group of people. Not all social events are culturally patterned. New types of circumstances arise frequently.

A culture constitutes a storehouse of the pooled learning of the group. A rabbit starts life with some innate responses. He can learn from his own experience and perhaps from observing other rabbits. A human infant is born with fewer instincts and greater plasticity. His main task is to learn the answers that persons he will never see, persons long dead, have worked out. Once he has learned the formulas supplied by the culture of his group, most of his behavior becomes almost as automatic and unthinking as if it were instinctive. There is a tremendous amount of intelligence behind the making of a radio, but not much is required to learn to turn it on.

The members of all human societies face some of the unavoidable dilemmas, posed by biology and other facts of the human situation. This is why the basic categories of all cultures are so similar. Human culture without language is unthinkable. No culture fails to provide for aesthetic expression and aesthetic delight. Every culture supplies standardized orientations toward the deeper problems, such as death. Every culture is designed to perpetuate the group and its solidarity, to meet the demands of individuals for an orderly way of life and for satisfaction of biological needs.

However, the variations of these basic themes are numberless. Some languages are built up out of twenty basic sounds, others out of forty. Nose plugs were considered beautiful by the predynastic Egyptians but are not by the modern French. Puberty is a biological fact. But one culture ignores it, another prescribes informal instructions about sex but no ceremony, a third has impressive rites for girls only, a fourth for boys and girls. In this culture, the first menstruation is welcomed as a happy, natural event; in that culture the atmosphere is full of dread and supernatural threat. Each culture dissects nature according to its own system of categories. The Navaho Indians apply the same word to the color of robin's egg and to that of grass. A psychologist once assumed that this meant a difference in the sense organs, that Navahos didn't have the physiological equipment to distinguish "green" from "blue." However, when he showed them objects of the two colors and asked them if they were exactly the same colors, they looked at him with astonishment. His dream of discovering a new type of color blindness was shattered.

Every culture must deal with the sexual instinct. Some, however, seek to deny all sexual expression before marriage, whereas a Polynesian adolescent who was not promiscuous would be distinctly abnormal. Some cultures enforce lifelong monogamy, others, like our own, tolerate serial monogamy; in still other cultures, two or more women may be joined to one man or several men to a single woman. Homosexuality has been a permitted pattern in the Greco-Roman world and in various primitive tribes. Large portions of the population of Tibet, and of Christendom at some places and periods, have practiced complete celibacy. To us marriage is first and foremost an arrangement between two individuals. In many more societies marriage is merely one facet of a complicated set of reciprocities, economic and otherwise, between two families or two clans.

The essence of the cultural process is selectivity. The selection is only exceptionally conscious and rational. Cultures are like Topsy. They just grew. Once, however, a way of handling a situation becomes institutionalized, there is ordinarily great resistance to chance or deviation. When we speak of "our sacred beliefs," we mean of course that they are beyond criticism and that the person who suggests modification or abandonment must be punished. No person is emotionally indifferent to his culture. Certain cultural premises may become totally out of accord with a new factual situation. Leaders may recognize this and reject the old ways in theory. Yet their emotional loyalty continues in the face of reason because of the intimate conditionings of early childhood.

A culture is learned by individuals as the result of belonging to some particular group, and it constitutes that part of learned behavior which is shared with others. It is our social legacy, as contrasted with our organic heredity. It is one of the important factors which permits us to live together in an organized society, giving us ready-made solutions to our problems, helping us to predict the behavior of others, and permitting others to know what to expect of us.

Culture regulates our lives at every turn. From the moment we are born until we die there is, whether we are conscious of it or not, constant pressure upon us to follow certain types of behavior that other men have created for us. Some paths we follow willingly, others we follow because we know no other way, still others we deviate from or go back to most unwillingly. Mothers of small children know how unnaturally most of this comes to us—how little regard we have, until we are "culturalized," for the "proper" place, time, and manner for certain acts such as eating, excreting, sleeping, getting dirty, and making loud noises. But by more or less adhering to a system of related designs for carrying out all the acts of living, a group of men and women feel themselves linked together by a powerful chain of sentiments. Ruth Benedict gave an almost complete definition of the concept when she said, "Culture is that which binds men together."

It is true any culture is a set of techniques for adjusting both to the external environment and to other men. However, cultures create problems as well as solve them. If the lore of a people states that frogs are dangerous creatures, or that it is not safe to go about at night because of witches or ghosts, threats are posed which do not arise out of the inexorable facts of the external world. Cultures produce needs as well as provide a means of fulfilling them. There exists for every group culturally defined, acquired drives that may be more powerful in ordinary daily life than the biologically inborn drives. Many Americans, for example, will work harder for "success" than they will for sexual satisfaction.

Most groups elaborate certain aspects of their culture far beyond maximum utility or survival value. In other words, not all culture promotes physical survival. At times, indeed, it does exactly the opposite. Aspects of culture which once were adaptive may persist long after they have ceased to be useful. An analysis of any culture will disclose many features which cannot possibly be construed as adaptations to the total environment in which the group now finds itself. However, it is altogether likely that these apparently useless features represent survivals, with modifications through time, of cultural forms once useful.

Any cultural practice must be functional or it will disappear before long. That is, it must somehow contribute to the survival of the society or to the adjustment of the individual. However, many cultural functions are not manifest but latent. A cowboy will walk three miles to catch a horse which he then rides one mile to the store. From the point of view of manifest function this is positively irrational. But the act has the latent function of maintaining the cowboy's prestige in the terms of his own subculture. One can instance the buttons on the sleeve of a man's coat, our absurd English spelling, the use of capital letters, and a host of other apparently nonfunctional customs. They serve mainly the latent function of assisting individuals to maintain their security by preserving continuity with the past and by making certain sectors of life familiar and predictable.

Every culture is a precipitate of history. In more than one sense history is a sieve. Each culture embraces those aspects of the past which, usually in altered form and with altered meanings, live on in the present. Discoveries and inventions, both material and ideological, are constantly being made available to a group through its historical contacts with other peoples or being created by its own members. However, only those that fit the total immediate situation in meeting the group's needs for survival or in promoting the psychological adjustment of individuals will become part of the culture. The process of culture building may be regarded as an addition to man's innate biological capacities, an addition providing instruments which enlarge, or may even substitute for, biological functions, and to a degree compensating for biological limitations—as in ensuring that death does not always result in the loss to humanity of what the deceased has learned.

Culture is like a map. Just as a map isn't the territory but an abstract representation of a particular area, so also a culture is an abstract description of trends toward uniformity in the words, deeds, and artifacts of human group. If a map is accurate and you can read it, you won't get lost; if you know a culture you will know your way around in the life of a society.

DISCUSSION QUESTIONS

1. What does Kluckhohn mean by the statement, "culture is like a map"? Do you agree?
2. Does culture affect biological processes?

Article 7
The Sounds of Silence

EDWARD HALL AND MILDRED HALL

BOB LEAVES HIS APARTMENT at 8:15 A.M. and stops at the corner drugstore for breakfast. Before he can speak, the counterman says, "The usual?" Bob nods yes. While he savors his Danish, a fat man pushes onto the adjoining stool and overflows into his space. Bob scowls and the man pulls himself in as much as he can. Bob has sent two messages without speaking a syllable.

Henry has an appointment to meet Arthur at 11 o'clock; he arrives at 11:30. Their conversation is friendly, but Arthur retains a lingering hostility. Henry has unconsciously communicated that he doesn't think the appointment is very important or that Arthur is a person who needs to be treated with respect.

George is talking to Charley's wife at a party. Their conversation is entirely trivial, yet Charley glares at them suspiciously. Their physical proximity and the movements of their eyes reveal that they are powerfully attracted to each other.

Jose Ybarra and Sir Edmund Jones are at the same party and it is important for them to establish a cordial relationship for business reasons. Each is trying to be warm and friendly, yet they will part with mutual distrust and their business transaction will probably fall through. Jose, in Latin fashion, moved closer and closer to Sir Edmund as they spoke, and this movement was miscommunicated as pushiness to Sir Edmund, who kept backing away from this intimacy, and this was miscommunicated to Jose as coldness. The silent languages of Latin and English cultures are more difficult to learn than their spoken languages.

In each of these cases, we see the subtle power of nonverbal communication. The only language used throughout most of the history of humanity (in evolutionary terms, vocal communication is relatively recent), it is the first form of communication you learn. You use this preverbal language, consciously and unconsciously, every day to tell other people how you feel about yourself and them. This language includes your posture, gestures, facial expressions, costume, the way you walk, even your treatment of time and space and material things. All people communicate on several different levels at the same time but are usually aware of only the verbal dialogue and don't realize that they respond to nonverbal messages. But when a person says one thing and really believes something else, the discrepancy between the two can usually be sensed. Nonverbal-communication systems are much less subject to the conscious deception that often occurs in verbal systems. When we find ourselves thinking, "I don't know what it is about him, but he doesn't seem sincere," it's usually this lack of congruity between a person's words and his behavior that makes us anxious and uncomfortable.

Few of us realize how much we all depend on body movement in our conversation or are aware of the hidden rules that govern listening behavior. But we know instantly whether or not the person we're talking to is "tuned in" and we're very sensitive to any breach in listening etiquette. In white middle-class American culture, when someone wants to show he is listening to someone else, he looks either at the other person's face or, specifically, at his eyes, shifting his gaze from one eye to the other.

If you observe a person conversing, you'll notice that he indicates he's listening by nodding his head. He also makes little "Hmm" noises. If he agrees with what's being said, he may give a vigorous nod. To show pleasure or affirmation, he smiles; if he has some reservations, he looks skeptical by raising an eyebrow or pulling down the corners of his mouth. If a participant wants to terminate the conversation, he may start shifting his body position, stretching his legs, crossing or uncrossing them, bobbing his foot or diverting his gaze from the speaker. The more he fidgets, the more the speaker becomes aware that he has lost his audience. As a last measure, the listener may look at his watch to indicate the imminent end of the conversation.

Talking and listening are so intricately intertwined that a person cannot do one without the other. Even when one is alone and talking to oneself, there is part of the brain that speaks while another part listens. In all conversations, the listener is positively or negatively reinforcing the speaker all the time. He may even guide the conversation without knowing it, by laughing or frowning or dismissing the argument with a wave of his hand.

The language of the eyes—another age-old way of exchanging feelings—is both subtle and complex. Not only do men and women use their eyes differently but there are class, generation, regional, ethnic and national cultural differences. Americans often complain about the way foreigners stare at people or hold a glance too long. Most Americans look away from someone who is using his eyes in an unfamiliar way because it makes them selfconscious. If a man looks at another man's wife in a certain way, he's asking for trouble, as indicated earlier. But he might not be ill mannered or seeking to challenge the husband. He might be a European in this country who hasn't learned our visual mores. Many American women visiting France or Italy are acutely embarrassed because, for the first time in their lives, men really look at them—their eyes, hair, nose, lips, breasts, hips, legs, thighs, knees, ankles, feet, clothes, hairdo, even their walk. These same women, once they become used to being looked at, often return to the United States and are overcome with the feeling that "No one ever really looks at me anymore."

Analyzing the mass of data on the eyes, it is possible to sort out at least three ways in which the eyes are used to communicate: dominance *vs.* submission, involvement *vs.* detachment and positive *vs.* negative attitude. In addition, there are three levels of consciousness and control, which can be categorized as follows: (1) conscious use of the eyes to communicate, such as the flirting blink and the intimate nose-wrinkling squint; (2) the very extensive category of unconscious but learned behavior governing where the eyes are directed and when (this unwritten set of rules dictates how and under what circumstances the sexes, as well as people of all status categories, look at each other); and (3) the response of the eye itself, which is completely outside both awareness and control-changes in the cast (the sparkle) of the eye and the pupillary reflex.

The eye is unlike any other organ of the body, for it is an extension of the brain. The unconscious pupillary reflex and the cast of the eye have been known by people of Middle Eastern origin for years—although most are unaware of their knowledge. Depending on the context, Arabs and others look either directly at the eyes or deeply *into* the eyes of their interlocutor. We became aware of this in the Middle East several years ago while looking at jewelry. The merchant suddenly started to push a particular bracelet at a customer and said, "You buy this one." What interested us was that the bracelet was not the one that had been consciously selected by the purchaser. But the merchant, watching the pupils of the eyes, knew what the purchaser really wanted to buy. Whether he specifically knew *how* he knew is debatable.

A psychologist at the University of Chicago, Eckhard Hess, was the first to conduct systematic studies of the pupillary reflex. His wife remarked one evening, while watching him reading in bed, that he must be very interested in the text because his pupils were dilated. Following up on this, Hess slipped some pictures of nudes into a stack of photographs that he gave to his male assistant. Not looking at the photographs but watching his assistant's pupils, Hess was able to tell precisely when the assistant came to the nudes. In further experiments, Hess retouched the eyes in a photograph of a woman. In one print he made the pupils small, in another, large; nothing else was changed. Subjects who were given the photographs found the woman with the dilated pupils much more attractive. Any man who has had the experience of seeing a woman look at him as her pupils widen with reflex speed knows that she's flashing him a message.

The eye-sparkle phenomenon frequently turns up in our interviews of couples in love. It's apparently one of the first reliable clues in the other person that love is genuine. To date, there is no scientific data to explain eye sparkle; no investigation of the pupil, the cornea or even the white sclera of the eye shows how the sparkle originates. Yet we all know it when we see it.

One common situation for most people involves the use of the eyes in the street and in public. Although eye behavior follows a definite set of rules, the rules vary according to the place, the needs and feelings of the people, and their ethnic background. For urban whites, once they're within definite recognition distance (16–32 feet for people with average eyesight) there is mutual avoidance of eye contact—unless they want something specific: a pickup, a handout or information of some kind. In the West and in small towns generally, however, people are much more likely to look at and greet one another, even if they're strangers.

It's permissible to look at people if they're beyond recognition distance; but once inside this sacred zone, you can only steal a glance at strangers. You *must* greet friends, however; to fail to do so is insulting. Yet, to stare too fixedly even at them is considered rude and hostile. Of course, all of these rules are variable.

A great many blacks, for example, greet each other in public even if they don't know each other. To blacks, most eye behavior of whites has the effect of giving the impression that they aren't there, but this is due to white avoidance of eye contact with *anyone* in the street.

Another very basic difference between people of different ethnic backgrounds is their sense of territoriality and how they handle space. This is the silent communication, or miscommunication, that caused friction between Mr. Ybarra and Sir Edmund Jones in our earlier example. We know from research that everyone has around himself an invisible bubble of space that contracts and expands depending on several factors: his emotional state, the activity he's performing at the time and his cultural background. This bubble is a kind of mobile territory that he will defend against intrusion. If he is accustomed to close personal distance between himself and others, his bubble will be smaller than that of someone who's accustomed to greater personal distance. People of North European heritage—English, Scandinavian, Swiss and German—tend to avoid contact. Those whose heritage is Italian, French, Spanish, Russian, Latin American or Middle Eastern like close personal contact.

People are very sensitive to any intrusion into their spatial bubble. If someone stands too close to you, your first instinct is to back up. If that's not possible, you lean away and pull yourself in, tensing your muscles. If the intruder doesn't respond to these body signals, you may then try to protect yourself, using a briefcase, umbrella or raincoat. Women—especially when traveling alone—often plant their pocketbook in such a way that no one can get very close to them. As a last resort, you may move to another spot and position yourself behind a desk or chair that provides screening. Everyone tries to adjust the space around himself in a way that's comfortable for him; most often, he does this unconsciously.

Emotions also have a direct effect on the size of a person's territory. When you're angry or under stress, your bubble expands and you require more space. New York psychiatrist Augustus Kinzel found a difference in what he calls Body-Buffer Zones between violent and nonviolent prison inmates. Dr. Kinzel conducted experiments in which each prisoner was placed in the center of a small room and then Dr. Kinzel slowly walked toward him. Nonviolent prisoners allowed him to come quite close, while prisoners with a history of violent behavior couldn't tolerate his proximity and reacted with some vehemence.

Apparently, people under stress experience other people as looming larger and closer than they actually are. Studies of schizophrenic patients have indicated that they sometimes have a distorted perception of space, and several psychiatrists have reported patients who experience their body boundaries as filling up an entire room. For these patients, anyone who comes into the room is actually inside their body, and such an intrusion may trigger a violent outburst.

Unfortunately, there is little detailed information about normal people who live in highly congested urban areas. We do know, of course, that the noise, pollution, dirt, crowding and confusion of our cities induce feelings of stress in most of us, and stress leads to a need for greater space. The man who's packed into a subway, jostled in the street, crowded into an elevator and forced to work all day in a bull pen or in a small office without auditory or visual privacy is going to be very stressed at the end of his day. He needs places that provide relief from constant overstimulation of his nervous system. Stress from overcrowding is cumulative and people can tolerate more crowding early in the day than later; note the increased bad temper during the evening rush hour as compared with the morning melee. Certainly one factor in people's desire to commute by car is the need for privacy and relief from crowding (except, often, from other cars); it may be the only time of the day when nobody can intrude.

In crowded public places, we tense our muscles and hold ourselves stiff, and thereby communicate to others our desire not to intrude on their space and above all, not to touch them. We also avoid eye contact, and the total effect is that of someone who has "tuned out." Walking along the street, our bubble expands slightly as we move in a stream of strangers, taking care not to bump into them. In the office, at meetings, in restaurants, our bubble keeps changing as it adjusts to the activity at hand.

Most white middle-class Americans use four main distances in their business and social relations: intimate, personal, social and public. Each of these distances has a near and a far phase and is accompanied by changes in the volume of the voice. Intimate distance varies from direct physical contact with another person to a distance of six to eighteen inches and is used for our most private activities—caressing another person or making love. At this distance, you are overwhelmed by sensory inputs from the other person—heat from the body, tactile stimulation from the skin, the fragrance of perfume, even the sound of breathing—all of which literally envelop you. Even at the far phase, you're still within easy touching distance. In general, the use of intimate distance in public between adults is frowned on. It's also much too close for strangers, except under conditions of extreme crowding.

In the second zone—personal distance—the close phase is one and a half to two and a half feet; it's at this distance that wives usually stand from their husbands in public. If another woman moves into this zone, the wife will most likely be disturbed. The far phase—two and a half to four feet—is the distance used to "keep someone at arm's length" and is the most common spacing used by people in conversation.

The third zone—social distance—is employed during business transactions or exchanges with clerk or repairman. People who work together tend to use close social distance—four to seven feet. This is also the distance for conversations at social gatherings. To stand at this distance from someone who is seated has a dominating effect (e.g., teacher to pupil, boss to secretary). The far phase of the third zone—seven to twelve feet—is where people stand when someone says, "Stand back so I can look at you." This distance lends a formal tone to business or social discourse. In an executive office, the desk serves to keep people at this distance.

The fourth zone—public distance—is used by teachers in classrooms or speakers at public gatherings. At its farthest phase—25 feet and beyond—it is used for important public figures. Violations of this distance can lead to serious complications. During his 1970 U.S. visit, the president of France, Georges Pompidou, was harassed by pickets in Chicago, who were permitted to get within touching distance. Since pickets in France are kept behind barricades a block or more away, the president was outraged by this insult to his person, and President Nixon was obliged to communicate his concern as well as offer his personal apologies.

It is interesting to note how American pitchmen and panhandlers exploit the unwritten, unspoken conventions of eye distance. Both take advantage of the fact that once explicit eye contact is established, it is rude to look away, because to do so means to brusquely dismiss the other person and his needs. Once having caught the eye of his mark, the panhandler then locks on not letting go until he moves through the public zone, the social zone, the personal zone and, finally, into the intimate sphere, where people are most vulnerable.

Touch also is an important part of the constant stream of communication that takes place between people. A light touch, a firm touch, a blow, a caress are all communications. In an effort to break down the barriers among people, there's been a recent upsurge in group-encounter activities, in which strangers are encouraged to touch one another. In special situations such as these, the rules for not touching are broken with group approval and people gradually lose some of their inhibitions.

Although most people don't realize it, space is perceived and distances are set not by vision alone but with all the senses. Auditory space is perceived with the ears, thermal space with the skin, kinesthetic space with the muscles of the body and olfactory space with the nose. And, once again, it's one's culture that determines how his senses are programmed—which sensory information ranks highest and lowest. The important thing to remember is that culture is very persistent. In this country, we've noted the existence of culture patterns that determine distance between people in the third and fourth generations of some families, despite their prolonged contact with people of very different cultural heritages.

Whenever there is great cultural distance between two people, there are bound to be problems arising from differences in behavior and expectations. An example is the American couple who consulted a psychiatrist about their marital problems. The husband was from New England and had been brought up by reserved parents who taught him to control his emotions and to respect the need for privacy. His wife was from an Italian family and had been brought up in close contact with all the members of her large family, who were extremely warm, volatile and demonstrative.

When the husband came home after a hard day at the office, dragging his feet and longing for peace and quiet, his wife would rush to him and smother him. Clasping his hands, rubbing his brow, crooning over his weary head, she never left him alone. But when the wife was upset or anxious about her day, the husband's response was to withdraw completely and leave her alone. No comforting, no affectionate embrace, no attention—just solitude. The woman became convinced her husband didn't love her and, in desperation, she consulted a psychiatrist. Their problem wasn't basically psychological but cultural.

Why has man developed all these different ways of communicating messages without words? One reason is that people don't like to spell out certain kinds of messages. We prefer to find other ways of showing our feelings. This is especially true in relationships as sensitive as courtship. Men don't like to be rejected and most women don't want to turn a man down bluntly. Instead, we work out subtle ways of encouraging or discouraging each other that save face and avoid confrontations.

How a person handles space in dating others is an obvious and very sensitive indicator of how he or she feels about the other person. On a first date, if a woman sits or stands so close to a man that he is acutely conscious of her physical presence—inside the intimate distance zone—the man usually construes it to mean that she is encouraging him. However, before the man starts moving in on the woman, he should be sure what message she's really sending; otherwise, he risks bruising his ego. What is close to someone of North European background may be neutral or distant to someone of Italian heritage. Also, women sometimes use space as a way of misleading a man and there are few things that put men off more than women who communicate contradictory messages—such as women who cuddle up and then act insulted when a man takes the next step.

How does a woman communicate interest in a man? In addition to such familiar gambits as smiling at him, she may glance shyly at him, blush and then look away. Or she may give him a real come-on look and move in very close when he approaches. She may touch his arm and ask for a light. As she leans forward to light her cigarette, she may brush him lightly, enveloping him in her perfume. She'll probably continue to smile at him and she may use what ethologists call preening gestures—touching the back of her hair, thrusting her breasts forward, tilt in her hips as she stands or crossing her legs if she's seated, perhaps even exposing one thigh or putting a hand on her thigh and stroking it. She may also stroke her wrists as she converses or show the palm of her hand as a way of gaining his attention. Her skin may be unusually flushed or quite pale, her eyes brighter, the pupils larger.

If a man sees a woman whom he wants to attract, he tries to present himself by his posture and stance as someone who is self-assured. He moves briskly and confidently. When he catches the eye of the woman, he may hold her glance a little longer than normal. If he gets an encouraging smile, he'll move in close and engage her in small talk. As they converse, his glance shifts over her face and body. He, too, may make preening gestures—straightening his tie, smoothing his hair or shooting his cuffs.

How do people learn body language? The same way they learn spoken language—by observing and imitating people around them as they're growing up. Little girls imitate their mothers or an older female. Little boys imitate their fathers or a respected uncle or a character on television. In this way, they learn the gender signals appropriate for their sex. Regional, class, and ethnic patterns of body behavior are also learned in childhood and persist throughout life.

Such patterns of masculine and feminine body behavior vary widely from one culture to another. In America, for example, women stand with their thighs together. Many walk with their pelvis tipped slightly forward and their upper arms close to their body. When they sit, they cross their legs at the knee or, if they are well past middle age, they may cross their ankles. American men hold their arms away from their body, often swinging them as they walk. They stand with their legs apart (an extreme example is the cowboy, with legs apart and thumbs tucked into his belt). When they sit, they put their feet on the floor with legs apart and, in some parts of the country, they cross their legs by putting one ankle on the other knee.

Leg behavior indicates sex, status and personality. It also indicates whether or not one is at ease or is showing respect or disrespect for the other person. Young Latin-American males avoid crossing their legs. In their world of *machismo,* the preferred position for young males when with one another (if there is no older dominant male present to whom they must show respect) is to sit on the base of their spine with the leg muscles relaxed and their feet wide apart. Their respect position is like our military equivalent; spine straight, heels and ankles together—almost identical to that displayed by properly brought up young women in New England in the early part of this century.

American women who sit with their legs spread apart in the presence of males are *not* normally signaling a come-on they are simply (and often unconsciously) sitting like men. Middle-class women in the presence of other women to whom they are very close may on occasion throw themselves down on a soft chair or sofa and let themselves go. This is a signal that nothing serious will be taken up. Males, on the other hand, lean back and prop their legs up on the nearest object.

The way we walk, similarly, indicates status, respect, mood and ethnic or cultural affiliation. The many variants of the female walk are too well known to go into here, except to say that a man would have to be blind not to be turned on by the way some women walk—a fact that made Mae West rich before scientists ever studied these matters. To white Americans, some French middle-class males walk in a way that is both humorous and suspect. There is a bounce and looseness to the French walk, as though the parts of the body were somehow unrelated. Jacques Tati, the French movie actor, walks this way; so does the great mime, Marcel Marceau.

Blacks and whites in America—with the exception of middle- and upper-middle-class professionals of both groups—move and walk very differently from each other. To the blacks, whites often seem incredibly stiff, almost mechanical in their movements. Black males, on the other hand, have a looseness and coordination that frequently makes whites a little uneasy; it's too different, too integrated, too alive, too male. Norman Mailer has said that squares walk from the shoulders, like bears, but blacks and hippies walk from the hips, like cats.

All over the world, people walk not only in their own characteristic way but have walks that communicate the nature of their involvement with whatever it is they're doing. The purposeful walk of North Europeans is an important component of proper behavior on the job. Any male who has been in the military knows how essential it is to walk properly (which makes for a continuing source of tension between blacks and whites in the Service). The quick shuffle of servants in the Far East in the old days was a show of respect. On the island of Truk, when we last visited, the inhabitants even had a name for the respectful walk that one used when in the presence of a chief or when walking past a chief's house. The term was *sufan,* which meant to be humble and respectful.

The notion that people communicate volumes by their gestures, facial expressions, posture and walk is not new; actors, dancers, writers and psychiatrists have long been aware of it. Only in recent years, however, have scientists begun to make systematic observations of body motions. Ray L. Birdwhistell of the University of Pennsylvania is one of the pioneers in body-motion research and coined the term kinesics to describe this field. He developed an elaborate notation system to record both facial and body movements, using an approach similar to that of the linguist, who studies the basic elements of speech. Birdwhistell and other kinesicists such as Albert Sheflen, Adam Kendon and William Condon take movies of people interacting. They run the film over and over again, often at reduced speed for frame-by-frame analysis, so that they can observe even the slightest body movements not perceptible at normal interaction speeds. These movements are then recorded in notebooks for later analysis.

To appreciate the importance of nonverbal-communication systems, consider the unskilled inner-city black looking for a job. His handling of time and space alone is sufficiently different from the white middle-class pattern to create great misunderstandings on both sides. The black is told to appear for a job interview at a certain time. He arrives late. The white interviewer concludes from his tardy arrival that the black is irresponsible and not really interested in the job. What the interviewer doesn't know is that the black time system (often referred to by blacks as C.P.T.—colored people's time) isn't the same as that of whites. In the words of a black student who had been told to make an appointment to see his professor: "Man, you *must* be putting me on. I never had an appointment in my life."

The black job applicant, having arrived late for his interview, may further antagonize the white interviewer by his posture and his eye behavior. Perhaps he slouches and avoids looking at the interviewer; to him, this is playing it cool. To the interviewer, however, he may well look shifty and sound uninterested. The interviewer has failed to notice the actual signs of interest and eagerness in the black's behavior, such as the subtle shift in the quality of the voice—a gentle and tentative excitement—an almost imperceptible change in the cast of the eyes and a relaxing of the jaw muscles.

Moreover, correct reading of black-white behavior is continually complicated by the fact that both groups are comprised of individuals—some of whom try to accommodate and some of whom make it a point of pride *not* to accommodate. At present, this means that many Americans, when thrown into contact with one another, are in the precarious position of not knowing which pattern applies. Once identified and analyzed, nonverbal-communication systems can be taught, like a foreign language. Without this training, we respond to nonverbal communications in terms of our own culture; we read everyone's behavior as if it were our own, and thus we often misunderstand it.

Several years ago in New York City, there was a program for sending children from predominantly black and Puerto Rican low-income neighborhoods to summer school in a white upper class neighborhood on the East Side. One morning, a group of young black and Puerto Rican boys raced down the street, shouting and screaming and overturning garbage cans on their way to school. A doorman from an apartment building nearby chased them and cornered one of them inside a building. The boy drew a knife and attacked the doorman. This tragedy would not have occurred if the doorman had been familiar with the behavior of boys from low-income neighborhoods, where such antics are routine and socially acceptable and where pursuit would be expected to invite a violent response.

The language of behavior is extremely complex. Most of us are lucky to have under control one subcultural system—the one that reflects our sex, class, generation and geographic region within the United States. Because of its complexity, efforts to isolate bits of nonverbal communication and generalize from them are in vain; you don't become an instant expert on people's behavior by watching them at cocktail parties. Body language isn't something that's independent of the person, something that can be donned and doffed like a suit of clothes.

Our research and that of our colleagues has shown that, far from being a superficial form of communication that can be consciously manipulated, nonverbal-communication systems are interwoven into the fabric of the personality and, as sociologist Erving Goffman has demonstrated, into society itself. They are the warp and woof of daily interactions with others and they influence how one expresses oneself, how one experiences oneself as a man or a woman.

Nonverbal communications signal to members of your own group what kind of person you are, how you feel about others, how you'll fit into and work in a group, whether you're assured or anxious, the degree to which you feel comfortable with standards of your own culture, as well as deeply significant feelings about the self, including the state of your own psyche. For most of us, it's difficult to accept the reality of another's behavioral system. And, of course, none of us will ever become fully knowledgeable of the importance of every non-verbal signal. But as long as each of us realizes the power of these signals, this society's diversity can be a source of great strength rather than a further—and subtly powerful—source of division.

DISCUSSION QUESTIONS

1. Does knowledge of a culture's body language help us to interact in that culture? Why?
2. Compare and contrast personal distance and social distance.

Article 8

Iran's White Revolution and Its Outcome for Iranian Women

HAMID R. KUSHA

SOCIOLOGIST KINGSLEY DAVIS suggested that the more industrialized a nation becomes, the larger will be the number of women who enter the labor force. Industrialization creates more job opportunities in general and increased opportunities for women to earn income outside the home. In this sense the two-earner system reflects a rise in the standard of living of industrialized nations. Consequently, many leaders of Third World nations have considered industrialization to be an important step in their own development programs. These programs, however, have not produced the desired results, especially with regard to the situation of women in the labor force. The question addressed here is this: If some events produce positive results in one part of the world, does this mean that a program designed to encourage the same events will produce the same results in other parts of the world? Put another way, do you think that Iran's modernization has had the same effects on male and female relationships as America's Industrial Revolution? By focusing on Iran's industrialization under the late Shah, Muhammad Reza Pahlavi, we will explore this question.

From "Iran's White Revolution: Outcome for Iranian Women," by Hamid R. Kusha, *Sociology: A Global Perspective,* Joan Ferrante (ed.). Wadsworth, Belmont, California, 1992. Reprinted by permission.

During his 37-year reign (1941–1979), the Shah tried to imitate the Western models of modernization by using Iran's oil income to industrialize the country. Although he had some successes, he had many more failures because, among other things, he failed to consider Iran's cultural traditions and sensitivities. The Shah initiated his modernization plans through a program called the White Revolution. On January 9, 1963, the Shah declared six principles of this "Revolution" and subsequently added six more. These twelve were: (1) land reform, (2) nationalization of forests and pastures, (3) public sale of state-owned factories to finance the land reform, (4) profit sharing in industry by the workers and owners, (5) reform of electoral law to include women, (6) creation of the Literacy Corps, (7) creation of the Health Corps, (8) creation of the Reconstruction and Development Corps, (9) establishment of the rural Courts of Justice, (10) nationalization of the waterways, (11) national reconstruction, and (12) educational and administrative revolution (Richards 1975, pp. 20–21).

Because industrialization required a cheap female labor force in addition to a male labor force, women's role in Iranian society had to be altered because their participation in the industrial labor force necessitated some level of formal schooling and involvement outside the household. This required that certain participatory rights for women be recognized and that these rights be protected. This was achieved through the enactment of the Family Protection Law by the Iranian Parliament, which gave Iranian women some protection against abuses at home and in the workplace. Under certain specified circumstances (for example, if a woman could show her economic independence), women were given custodial rights to their offspring upon divorce, a right that had belonged to men prior to the law's enactment. In addition, they were given the right to vote, to travel, to hold office, and to be elected to office.

These reforms took a long time to implement, but by 1979 the Shah could boast of having created a modern Iran. His success, however, was shallow and mostly short-lived, especially with respect to Iranian women. The Shah saw himself as liberating women from the chains of tradition and backwardness. Yet many Iranian women participated in the mass demonstrations against the Shah and in support of the late Ayatollah Khomeini, a man who gave only lip service to Iranian women's desires for equality with men, democracy, and participatory rights. Once he assumed power, Khomeini dismissed these ideals and maintained that women should be obedient to their husbands and to the demands of the new state. In light of Khomeini's restrictive policies toward women, you may wonder why Iranian women opposed the late Shah and his modernization efforts. The answer is simple: to succeed, any program of social change must be sensitive to that society's social and cultural norms. In other words, if you show no appreciation of my cultural norms or of my likes and dislikes, I will resist your agenda for change, no matter what your intention. Accordingly, the partial success and the many failures of the Shah's modernization efforts were a product of five basic factors.

First, the Shah failed to consider Iran's cultural traditions and sensitivities. Iran has a long history (25 centuries) of cultural traditions that pertain to respect for authority, the family, and the elderly, as well as sophisticated and elaborate norms about conversing with others and treating guests, friends, and relatives. These traditions have deep roots in Iranian society and bestow pride and a strong sense of identity on Iranians of all walks of life. Cultural traditions do not die easily, but rather linger on long after new traditions are introduced. The Shah's modernization efforts were intended to replace Iran's long-cherished traditions with those of the West and especially those of the United States. The Shah personally admired American culture and the American way of life for a number of reasons. He owed his reign to the Republican administration of President Eisenhower, who allowed the Central Intelligence Agency to carry out a coup d'état in Iran in August 1953 that toppled Iran's democratic government under Premier Dr. Musaddiq. Because of the coup, many Iranians considered the Shah a puppet of the United States; the Shah saw himself as a friend of the United States. Reportedly, he had told a number of Western diplomats and journalists that his ultimate goal was to make Iran a "Little America." The White Revolution was one step in that direction. Many educated Iranians resented what they saw as the Shah's aim to make Iran dependent upon the United States, while the noneducated viewed his actions as un-Islamic. This was quite a negative image, an image that intensified when Iran's Ayatollahs (the highest religious authorities in Shia Islam) turned against him.[1,2]

Second, the Shah neglected the agricultural sector of the economy in order to develop the industrial sector. Until recent times Iran's economy was based on agriculture. In agricultural societies women till the land, attend the livestock, and play an important role in the village economy. Also, in agricultural societies women have traditionally held certain rights with regard to the land, the water, and the harvests. Prior to modernization Iranian women were no exception. Because the Shah's declared aim was to industrialize Iran through the White Revolution, he had to acquire capital, technology, and trained manpower. This policy weakened Iran's agricultural economy because more and more resources were directed toward industry rather than agriculture.

One way to industrialize Iran was to modernize Iranian agriculture. Another more immediate way was to neglect labor-intensive agriculture and concentrate on capital-intensive industries. The Shah's planners chose the second strategy, with the hope that the cheap labor force for the industries would come from the much neglected agricultural sector. It soon became apparent that the Shah's White Revolution would inevitably have devastating effects on Iran's agriculture and that a large, cheap labor force would leave the villages and emigrate to the cities. The dislocation deprived Iranian women of a way of life that recognized certain rights for them in the village community. Moreover, many of these uneducated women were not and, in fact, could not be absorbed into the new industries. The dislocation of village life led to slum dwellings and the creation of shanty towns (*Halabi-abads*) around Tehran and other large industrial cities including Esfahan, Tabriz, Arak, and Qazvin. This dislocated populace greatly resented the social impasse created by the White Revolution. On the one hand, a return to the traditional village community was impossible because that way of life no longer existed; on the other hand, the urban way of life required education, job opportunities, and new social norms, all of which were alien to the slum dwellers. It was from the rank and file of these poor slum dwellers that Khomeini recruited a large number of his followers to fight the Shah and destroy his dream of making Iran a "Little America."

Third, the Shah did not receive the support of all the Ayatollahs. In Iran the state has historically played an important role as an agent of change. A state is a structured frame of relationships that affects citizens' lives through its bureaucratic actions; it has the means—the police, the army, the secret service, and so on—to enforce citizen rights and responsibilities. For the last 25 centuries Iran has been governed by men who have called themselves Shah (king). The strong ones have called themselves Shahinshah (literally, the Shah of the Shahs or the king of the kings). In general, these Shahs have always been dictators, and the state has functioned to carry out their wishes and commands. As a result, Iran's official religion and Iran's Ayatollahs, to some extent, have been at the service of the Shahs. They have functioned as powerful legitimizers of the Shahs'[3] deeds and actions, provided that the Shahs have not committed "unreligious" acts. The late Shah was accused by some Ayatollahs (including Khomeini) of having committed un-Islamic acts. What is and what is not "un-Islamic" is something that Iran's Ayatollahs have traditionally decided upon. The much celebrated Ayatollah Khomeini is one such figure who characterized the White Revolution and especially the Family Protection Law as un-Islamic.

Fourth, the Shah failed to consider the overall impact of Iran's long and powerful religious traditions. Iranians adhere to Islam, a religion that is practiced by some 700 to 900 million adherents all over the world. It shares many of the Judaic and Christian beliefs pertaining to the existence of a universal God, the creation, the existence of life after death, and the final day of judgment. As in Judaism and Christianity, the family is a very important institution in Islam because it is the first social setting in which the society's religious traditions and values are defined. One of the most sensitive traditions in Islam is the relationship between man and woman. In Islam's Holy Text, the Qur'an (Koran), woman is given an esteemed position and is regarded as man's spiritual equal. However, other parts of the Qur'an demand that women be obedient to men. Furthermore, certain privileges are denied women (to a certain degree) and are accorded to men (for example, the witness of two women equals that of one man; daughters receive one-third of the amount of inheritance given to sons; women are not allowed judgeship). Although interpreters of the Qur'an have cautioned that its declarations are subject to the passage of time and to prevailing social conditions, many instances of strict and literal interpretation have more often than not been detrimental to women's rights. Not surprisingly, the issue of equality between men and women in many Islamic countries, including Iran, has stirred much controversy among those tradition-bound segments. Any change in traditional family structure (such as that brought on by urbanization) is seen by many men as threatening to their authority in the family. (This is, of course, the position of those Iranian men who do not consider women their equals; other Iranian men have no problem in accepting women as their equals. One of the most effective ways to deny equality between the sexes has been to hide behind religion.)

Although the Family Protection Law addressed the issue of inequality and therefore allowed some level of public debate to take place on this sensitive issue, the law was problematic because the Shah attempted to give some measure of economic independence to women and yet not compromise male authority. Thus the law did not recognize women's rights to their fullest extent because the Shah did not want to offend Iran's powerful Ayatollahs. He was also careful not to totally uproot Iran's traditions. The Shah wanted to change women's roles and still have the support of the people. In the end, he managed to antagonize both the Iranian women and the Ayatollahs.[4]

Comparing Article 1105 of the Family Protection Law and Article 1 of the Amendatory Bill to the Law of the Land Reform shows the contradictions the Shah created. Article 1105 of the Family Protection Law stated: "In the course of relations between the married couple, the affairs of the household is characteristically under the auspices of the husband" (cited in Rad and Asi 1974, p. 4). Article 1 of the Amendatory Bill to the Law of the Land Reform declared: "The head of the family is one who is responsible for the income of the family" (cited in Rad and Asi 1974, p. 4). As noted previously, in the village community, Iranian women played an important economic role. But they never demanded to be recognized as the head of the family because it was against the cultural norms of these communities. Also, even if women had demanded to be recognized as such, they lacked the economic means to do so because in the villages their earnings were appropriated by men. Once dislocated and cut off from the village economy, if they were absorbed into the labor market, women could demand some equality with men because market economy allows some measure of economic independence for women as wage earners.

Finally, the Shah did not believe in real equality between the sexes. In several interviews he granted to journalists Barbara Walters and Oriana Fallaci, he elaborated on certain pseudoscientific theories of why a woman is not a man's equal. In this respect the Shah was no different from Khomeini and his lieutenants, who have argued unabashedly that women are deficient in rationality (*naghis ul-aql*). Under the Shah, educated Iranian women held posts in the government, in the cabinet, in the parliament, and in the Shah's court. However, these positions were of a window-dressing type and entailed no independent decision-making power. This was only natural given that the Shah was a dictator and his regime was a one-man show.

In conclusion, it may be argued that the White Revolution was not a total failure. For women, the Family Protection Law was a positive step toward toppling a number of Iran's traditional norms governing the relationship between men and women. By implementing a number of reform measures in education, employment, and family and social relations, this law opened an avenue for Iranian women to participate in social affairs. However, because the Shah was a dictator and because he was negatively viewed as an American puppet, he never acquired mass popular support. He never delegated real authority to the circle of educated men and women officials of his court, army, and government bureaucracy. Once the cosmetic nature of these rights under the Shah and his White Revolution was exposed, the Shah's government could no longer contain the demands of the educated, progressive, and politically conscious Iranian women who agitated for equality. As it became clear that true democratic rights were beyond the Shah's desire and ability to grant, the avant-garde of these politically active women became revolutionaries.

NOTES

1. There are several spellings for Shia, Shi'a, Shi'i, and Shiite. Among Islam scholars Shi'a is considered correct. On television the term Shiite is heard most often. Among Western writers Shia is seen most often.

2. Throughout Iran's long history religion has played an important role in shaping Iranian cultural heritages. Religion is an institution that has historically been dominated by men who have interpreted Islam's laws, ordinances, and edicts for their own benefit. To give an example, these men have consistently argued that women should not be involved in society's affairs because such participation will corrupt them. One manifestation of this argument has been the absence of Iranian women from Iran's spheres of politics and economics. Women are kept socially and economically disadvantaged by men who have all the powerful positions in society. This underprivileged position of women is then justified on the basis of different theories.

3. During the Safavid Dynasty (1501–1722), the Qajar Dynasty (1797–1896), and the Pahlavi Dynasty (1921–1979) reigns in Iran, the Shia divines acted as a powerful legitimizer of the state. However, there are historical occasions in which Iran's powerful Ayatollahs (for example, Shirazi, Modarres, Taleqani and Khomeini) protested the state's "un-Islamic" deeds.

4. Khomeini was incensed by the Shah's Family Protection Law and by his granting prosecutorial immunity to American military advisors. This meant, in essence, that American military advisors could commit any crime in Iran but not stand trial in that country. No sovereign nation would grant such privileges to any foreign power unless it were a colony of that power. Khomeini characterized the law as un-Islamic and the granting of immunity as equivalent to selling Iran's sovereignty to the Americans.

REFERENCES

Jazani, Bijan. 1980. *Capitalism and Revolution in Iran.* New York: Zed Press.

Keyhan International. "Women's Status in Islam." May 2, 1984.

McIntosh, Mary. 1978. "The State and Oppression of Women." Pp. 254–89 in *Feminism and Materialism,* edited by A. Kuhn and A. Wolpe. London: Routledge & Kegan Paul.

Rad, Forough and Azar Asi. 1974. *Setam Keshidegi-e Zan dar Iran* (The Oppression of Women in Iran). New York: Famous Publications.

Richards, Helmut. 1975. "The White Revolution: Kulaks to Rescue." *Merip Reports* 9(40):20–22.

Tabari, Azar. 1982. "Islam and the Struggle for Emancipation of Iranian Women." Pp. 5–25 in *In the Shadow of Islam: The Women's Movement in Iran,* compiled by A. Tabari and N. Yeganeh. London: Zed Press.

DISCUSSION QUESTIONS

1. Why did Iranian women oppose the Shah?
2. What is the role of religion in Iranian culture?

IV

Socialization

WHAT TO FOCUS ON:

1. What are some of the socialization functions of childhood play? How does a child learn to experience the meaning of society through play activities?
2. How are police officers socialized in regard to the use of force? Does the informal world of police work legitimate the use of excessive force?

COMPARED WITH OTHER ANIMAL YOUNG, human infants are more helpless neonately and have a longer period of dependency. The relative helplessness of the human infant is due to both biological and social factors. Humans do not enter the world with the biological characteristics that allow them to easily adapt to their surroundings. Rather our biological resources must be given time to develop. Humans are also born into a social and cultural system that preceded their existence. Humans do not automatically absorb the norms and values of their cultural system. The experience of society must be learned. Socialization refers to the process whereby an individual learns the values, norms, and appropriate behaviors of his/her society. Socialization is an essential component of human development. Humans do not develop normally without interaction and contact with others. Human development does not merely reflect the gradual unfolding of our biological potential, but rather is dependent on a learned process of social development called socialization.

Although our culture has become increasingly "child-centered," sometimes it is difficult for a child to be a child. In the first article, Edward C. Devereux examines the impact of adults on the culture of children's games. Many theorists (Piaget,

Lewin, Parsons and Bales, Kohlberg) have analyzed the developmental functions of self-organized children's games. In our culture, informal and spontaneous games have become increasingly formalized and structured. This process has affected the whole culture of childhood. Devereux suggests that we need to keep in mind "not what the boy is doing to the ball, but what the ball is doing to the boy!"

Socialization occurs in occupational structure. The process of socialization changes people. For example, in the military a recruit is transformed during boot camp into a soldier. Both explicit and implicit patterns of socialization occur in occupational training. In the second article, Jennifer Hunt examines both the formal and informal training of rookie police officers with regard to the use of force. The Rodney King incident which triggered the Los Angeles riots in 1992 involved what many believe to be the use of excessive force. Hunt's article illustrates the process of how the application of excessive force may be legitimated by police during real life situations.

The final selection examines George Herbert Mead's social psychological theory of the formation of the self. Bernard N. Meltzer provides an excellent overview of Mead's ideas. For Mead, socialization involves a process whereby the self emerges out of society. The human mind is unique in both its potential to create and use symbolic language and its capacity to comment to itself about one's own behavior. Since humans are capable of using symbols, we engage in an "imaginative rehearsal" in our mind concerning possible social action. Social order is possible due to the process of "symbolic interaction" whereby we interpret the intentions of the acts of others and then make our own response on the basis of that intention. Mead's work offers rich insight into the complex relationship between self and society.

Article 9

Backyard Versus Little League Baseball

The Impoverishment of Children's Games

EDWARD C. DEVEREUX

In this paper I shall focus on some consequences of young children's participation in highly competitive, adult-organized and promoted athletic programs such as Little League baseball, football, Pee Wee hockey, and interscholastic sports. My critique of Little League baseball and other such major sports programs for children will be based not so much upon what participation in such activities *does* for the children as upon what it does *not* do for them. I will argue that "Little Leaguism" is threatening to wipe out the spontaneous culture of free play and games among American children, and that it is therefore robbing our children not just of their childish fun but also of some of their most valuable learning experiences.

From "Backyard Versus Little League Baseball: The Impoverishment of Children's Games," by Edward Devereux, *Social Problems in Athletes,* University of Illinois Press, Champaign, 1977, pp. 38–41, 43–46, 52–54.

On the Impoverishment of Children's Games in America

One way to gain insight about what is happening to contemporary America is to look at ourselves in cross-cultural and historical perspective. I recently spent two months in Japan, carrying out a survey among Japanese schoolchildren. I spent as much time as I could observing children in informal play settings such as parks, neighborhood playgrounds, schoolyards, apartment courtyards, and city streets. What struck me most forcefully was the observation that Japanese children seemed to spend very little time just "hanging around"; whenever two or more children found themselves together, they seemed to move very quickly into some kind of self-organized but rule-oriented play. Though I made no formal inventory, I was impressed with the great variety and richness of the games I observed. Although the Japanese also have Little League baseball, most of the games I observed were carried out wholly without adult instigation or supervision.

On one occasion my wife and I observed a group of a dozen kindergarten children playing ring games in a public park. I had no doubt that these children were brought to the park by some teacher or adult supervisor, and I kept waiting for some adult to appear to structure the next game for them. But during the forty-five minutes we remained in the vicinity no adult ever approached or spoke to the children. Evidently the game repertory, the motivation to play, and the ability to organize and pace their own activities were well rooted in the children's own heads.

Later I went to Israel on another research project, and again I spent as much time as I could observing the informal play activities of the Israeli children. Here also I was impressed with the enormous variety of spontaneous games and play activities. On this, we also have some impressive research documentation in the work of the Israeli psychologist Rivka Eifermann (1971a). In her study, a team of 150 observers recorded the play activities of 14,000 Israeli school children, in kibbutzim, moshavim, and cities, in schoolyards, playgrounds, and streets, over a two-year period. One result of this research was the compilation of an encyclopedia of over 2,000 games the children were observed to be playing, including many bewildering variants on such well-known games as soccer, tag, and hop scotch, as well as hundreds of less well-known games, also in endless variations (Eifermann 1971b). Most of these games were being played wholly without adult instigation or supervision.

Still more impressive is the monumental evidence compiled by Iona and Peter Opie, in their monograph on *Children's Games in Street and Playground* (1969), regarding the richness of spontaneous games among English children. These authors were able to identify, describe, and classify more than 2,500 different games which possess these common elements: they are played spontaneously by English children without any adult leadership or instigation; they require no equipment whatever—not even a ball; and they are transmitted almost entirely in the oral culture of the children themselves. Most of them have been passed along among children for generations without ever having their "rules" written down, at least until the Opies turned their hands to the task. Indeed, these authors observed that children's games tend to suffer a rapid decline in interest and popularity when adults took an interest in them and began to promote them.

All this challenges us to raise the question: What has happened to the culture of children's games in America? Looking back to my own childhood some fifty years ago, I can recall literally dozens of games which we played regularly and with enthusiasm—puss in the corner, red rover, capture the flag, one-o-cat, statues, stealing sticks, blind man's buff, croquet, leap frog, duck on the rock, prisoner's base, and many, many more. No doubt some of these are still around, in vestigial form; but my impression is that I rarely see these, or other games like them, being played spontaneously by children. Those which are played seem to be adult-instigated and supervised, in schools, camps, or other organized play settings, or in party settings in homes. And even here, our game culture has become sadly impoverished. Ask any group of children what they did at a birthday party, and nine out of ten will say they pinned the tail on the donkey. Halloween? Bob for apples and tricks or treats! What ever happened to the tricks, incidentally? We have institutionalized and sterilized Halloween, and thereby killed most of its creativity and fun. It appears that our game culture has declined in richness and vitality from lack of use and from excessive adult supervision and control. "Come on, children, we're all going to play a game now!" "Do we *have* to?" You can almost hear the groans.

On these trends, there is also some research evidence in a fascinating study by Sutton-Smith and Rosenberg (1971). These authors compare game preferences of American children as documented in four different research studies spanning a period from the late 1890's to the late 1950's. Even though these four studies are not strictly comparable, certain general trends are impressively clear. The great variety of once-popular indoor and backyard skill games, such as croquet and quoits, have all declined in interest, to be replaced by the ubiquitous ping-pong. Leader games, such as Simon says, statues, and follow the leader, are now of little interest for boys. Chasing games, like tag, are now acceptable only to very little children. Central-person parlor games, such as hide the thimble, forfeits, and twenty questions, have mostly disappeared, as have the endless varieties of ring games, such as drop the handkerchief and London Bridge, and the team guessing and acting games like charades. Individual games of skill—remember mumblede peg?—are withering away. Virtually all of the undifferentiated team games, such as hare and hound, prisoner's base, etc., have either disappeared or declined in interest as boys have devoted more of their attention to a few major sports. And even here, the authors conclude, the range of choice has narrowed significantly: ". . . trends would indicate that boys are spending more and more time on fewer sports. Bowling, basketball, and football improve in rank positions, but all other sports decline. . . . This would appear to be further evidence of the increasing circumscription of the boy's play role."

How can we account for this apparently very real constriction in the game culture of American children? How do American children really spend their spare time? I am tempted to say that they are all out there on the baseball and football fields, or in the hockey rinks, participating according to season in the sports programs organized for them by schools and other adult sponsoring agencies. In fact, as we all know, several hundred thousand of them are doing just that—for example, as members of the now more than 40,000 Little League baseball teams. There can be no doubt that such team activities capture a very large share of these children's time and attention. In one study reported by Skubic (1956), for example, 81 out of 96 Little League players in the Santa Maria area "reported that half to most of their leisure time during the whole year is spent on baseball."

But even conceding that a very large absolute number of children now participate in such organized sports, the fact remains that the vast majority of children in the eight-to-twelve age range are not. What do they do instead? A great deal of unstructured, non-rule-oriented play: bike riding, for example, still ranks very high with both boys and girls. In American homes, toys, hobby kits, and various proprietary games such as Monopoly still find wide acceptance among children. Just hanging around and talking, or very informal horseplay with friends, now occupies a very large share of the typical preadolescent's time. Finally, and by far the most important, there is television watching, to which this age group now devotes some twenty hours per week.

The availability of a mass television audience has had a lot to do with the extraordinary ascendancy of Big Leaguism in America, and, perhaps indirectly, of Little Leaguism as well. By focusing the attention of millions of viewers on a handful of major sports, and on the heroic teams and individual stars within them, we have converted ourselves to a nation of spectators. For most of us, sports are something to be watched, not played—at least not by amateurs.

Personally, I doubt that very many children in the eight-to-twelve age range are television sports addicts, though some undoubtedly are. But children surely perceive where their father's interests are focused, and by the age of ten or twelve they are well aware of the extraordinary payoff of success in major sports in America. They see how the star athletes are rewarded in college and high school sports, and how pleased their fathers are at any athletic achievements of their own. I suspect that Little Leaguism for elementary school children is fostered more by the parents than by the children themselves, though for some it falls on well-cultivated ground. Here is a chance to play at something really important that parents and adults generally seem to take very seriously.

Even for children who have no special interest or competence in any major sport (probably a majority of all children), or for those who are actually alienated by the whole subculture of organized, competitive sports, the model is still present and highly salient. Against the heroic, if perhaps somewhat myopic, standards of Big League or Little League sports, who would dare propose a simple game of puss in the corner, capture the flag, or red rover? Kid stuff, unworthy of the time and attention of any red-blooded American boy past the age of seven or eight!

On the Educational Functions of Play and Games

Why should we care about what has been happening to the recreational and spare-time activities of our children? In approaching an answer to this question, I would like to say just a bit about the functions of games and informal play activities in childhood and comment specifically about the kinds of learning which may occur in spontaneous, self-organized children's games. I will then go on to assess how organized, adult-sponsored competitive sports stack up against this model.

But before turning to sociological or psychological analysis, let me try to give you some notion of the appeal and fun of games as they may appear to the children themselves. On this I can do no better than to quote a few passages from the Opies' account of play and games among English children:

> Play is unrestricted; games have rules. Play may merely be the enactment of a dream, but in each game there is a contest. Yet it will be noticed that when children play a game in the street they are often extraordinarily naïve or, according to viewpoint, highly civilized. They seldom need an umpire, they rarely trouble to keep scores, little significance is attached to who wins or loses, they do not require the stimulus of prizes, it does not seem to worry them if a game is not finished. Indeed, children like games in which there is a sizeable element of luck, so that individual abilities cannot be directly compared. They like games which restart almost automatically, so that everybody is given a new chance. They like games which move in stages, in which each stage, the choosing of leaders, the picking-up of sides, the determining of which side shall start, are almost games in themselves. In fact children's games often seem laborious to adults who, if invited to join in, may find themselves becoming impatient and wanting to speed them up. Adults do not always see, when subjected to lengthy preliminaries, that many of the games, particularly those of young children, are more akin to ceremonies than competitions. (1969: 2)

This last point, incidentally, exactly describes my own experiences as an observer on the Ithaca school playgrounds. At first I was distressed that children could "waste" as much as half their lunch period on the preliminaries before a game was actually begun; but ultimately I came to realize that, from the children's point of view, these all were considered as part of the game itself. Much of the fun and learning occurs during these ritualized but self-organized preliminaries.

But let me quote a bit more from the Opies' perceptive account:

> Just as the shy man reveals himself by his formalities, so does the child disclose his unsureness of his place in the world by welcoming games with set procedures, in which his relationships with his fellows are clearly established. In games a child can exert himself without having to explain himself, he can be a good player without having to think whether he is a popular person, he can find himself being a useful partner to someone of whom he is ordinarily afraid. He can be confident, too, in particular games, that it is his place to issue commands, to inflict pain, to steal people's possessions, to pretend to be dead, to hurl a ball actually at someone, to pounce on someone, or to kiss someone he has caught. In ordinary life either he never knows these experiences or, by attempting them, makes himself an outcast.
>
> It appears to us that when a child plays a game he creates a situation which is under his control, and yet it is one of which he does not know the outcome. In the confines of a game there can be all the excitement and uncertainty of an adventure, yet the young player can comprehend the whole, can recognize his place in the scheme, and, in contrast to the confusion of real life, can tell what is right action. He can, too, extend his environment, or feel that he is doing so, and gain knowledge of sensations beyond ordinary experience. . . . As long as the action of the game is of a child's own making, he is ready, even anxious, to sample the perils of which

> this world has such plentiful supply. In the security of a game he makes acquaintance with insecurity; he is able to rationalize absurdities, reconcile himself to not getting his own way, "assimilate reality" (Piaget), act heroically without being in danger. The thrill of a chase is accentuated by viewing the chaser not as a boy in short trousers, but as a bull. It is not a classmate's back he rides upon, but a knight's fine charger. It is not a party of other boys his side skirmishes with, but Indians, robbers, men from Mars. And, always provided that the environment is of his own choosing, he—or she—is even prepared to meet the "things that happen in the dark," playing games that would seem strange amusement if it were thought they were being taken literally: murder in the dark, ghosties in the garret, moonlight, starlight, bogey won't come out tonight. And yet, within the context of the game, these alarms are taken literally. (1969: 3–4)

So much for the appeal of games for children. But what can be said about the functions of games for child development?

It has long been recognized that children's games and play activities represent miniature and playful models of a wide variety of cultural and social activities and concerns. To take a familiar example, the activities of little girls revolving about dolls and playing house undoubtedly serve some function in the process of anticipatory socialization to future roles as mothers and housekeepers. Similarly, in the games of boys, such elemental social themes as leading and following, of capturing and rescuing, chasing and eluding, attacking and defending, concealing and searching, are endlessly recombined in games of varying complexity in what Sutton-Smith (1971) has called a syntax of play. For example, the chase-and-elude themes of tag are combined with the capture-and-rescue elements of relievo in the more complex game of prisoner's base. When the chase-and-elude themes of tag are combined with the attack-and-defend themes of dodge ball, we have the more complex game represented in football.

As Roberts and Sutton-Smith (1962) have pointed out, games of different types represent microcosmic social structures in which various different styles of competing, winning, or losing are subtly encoded. Through their participation in a wide variety of different game types, in which the various elements of skill, chance, and strategy are variously recombined in gradually increasing complexity, children find an opportunity to experiment with different success styles and gain experience in a variety of cognitive and emotional processes which cannot yet be learned in full-scale cultural participation.

I would stress, at this point, that for game experiences to serve their socialization functions effectively, it is essential that children engage in a wide variety of different types of games, and at varying levels of complexity appropriate to their stage of development. If the American game culture is becoming overly constricted, will our coping styles and success strategies as adults also become constricted? Could it be, as some journalists have speculated, that America's inability to cope with the realities of world politics stems in part from the fact that our president, a football addict, is committed to a narrow-gauge game plan and success style which is grossly inadequate to deal with those of opponents who are skilled in such sophisticated games as chess and go?

Another feature of spontaneous games renders them especially effective in serving as "buffered learning experiences" for our children: the models they embody are miniaturized and rendered relatively safe by the recreational context in which they typically occur. As Lewin (1944) noted, games tend to occur on a "plane of unreality," which renders them especially well suited as contexts in which to toy with potentially dangerous psychological and emotional problems. Thus Phillips (1960) has observed that many children's games provide a miniature and relatively safe context for gaining useful experience in the mastery of anxiety. Consider in this connection the titillating joys of peek-a-boo, the universally popular game in which infants toy with the anxieties associated with mother absence, and the happy resolution achieved in the discovery that one can bring her back by uncovering one's eyes. In playful games, older children deliberately project themselves into situations involving risk, uncertainty, and insecurity, and the tensions generated by the conflicting valences of hope and fear. Particularly where some element of chance is involved, failure is less invidious and hence more easily bearable. Similarly, in games involving mock combat, aggression may be safely expressed because, as Menninger (1942: 175) pointed out, "one can hurt people without really hurting them"—and, of course, without too much danger of being really hurt in return.

I must stress in particular the point that children's games are effective as expressive models for gaining experience in the mastery of dangerous emotions very largely because of their miniature scale and their playful context. They are rendered safe by remaining on a plane of unreality, in which "reality consequences" do not have to be faced. I would like to go on to argue that "child's play," far from being a frivolous waste of time as it is so often pictured in our task-oriented, puritan culture, may in fact represent an optimum setting for children's learning.

To gain some perspective on this matter, consider what psychologists are saying about the kinds of conditions in which optimum learning may occur. In designing their famous computer-typewriter-teaching-machine, or "automatic reflexive environment," O. K. Moore and A. R. Anderson (1969) were careful to take into account what they believe to be the essential features of a really good learning environment: it should permit free and safe exploration; it should be self-pacing; it should be "agent-responsive"; it should provide immediate and directly relevant feedback; it should be "productive," that is, so structured that a wide variety of ramifying principles and interconnections can be learned; it should be "autotelic" or self-rewarding, i.e., related directly to the child's own spontaneous interests and motivations; and, finally, it should be responsive to the child's own initiatives in a way which will permit him to take a "reflexive view of himself." Otherwise put, the environment should be such that the child may alternate in the roles of active agent and patient, and at times may step back and view the whole setting from the viewpoint of an umpire.

If we take these principles seriously, it is easy to see why many children do not learn very much in traditionally structured school settings. In such traditional schools, the pupils are patients and the teacher is the active agent. The principles which are to be learned are explained, perhaps even demonstrated, by the teacher, rather than being discovered by the children themselves. Learning is defined as work, which implies that the children, left to follow their own motivations and interests freely, would rather be doing something else. The pacing of activities is rigidly controlled by the teacher, the school schedules, or the tyranny of the lesson plan. And the evaluative feedback, coming from the teacher rather than from the materials themselves, is often delayed, irrelevant, and peculiarly invidious.

These principles, so widely violated in the regular educational settings in which children are supposed to be learning, are all admirably incorporated in a spontaneous, self-organized and self-paced game of backyard baseball, and in many other children's games and play activities. Little League baseball—and other adult-organized and supervised sports—do a pretty good job of bankrupting most of the features of this, and other, learning models.

But before continuing with this line of argument, I would call your attention to another eminent child psychologist's observations about the functions of spontaneous, self-organized children's games. In his classic study of the moral development of children, Jean Piaget (1932) noted that social rules, for the young child, originally appear as part of the external situation, defined and enforced by powerful adults. At an early stage of "moral realism," the child conforms because he must, to avoid punishment and to maintain the needed goodwill of his parents. But he feels no internalized moral commitment to these rules; he had no share in defining them, they often seem arbitrary or unnecessary, and they are often imposed in an arbitrary and punitive fashion. Piaget argued that children's experiences in informal games and play activities with their own age mates play an essential role in moving them beyond this stage of moral realism. In an informal game of marbles, for example, where there is no rule book and no adult rule-imposer or enforcer, and where the players know the rules only vaguely or have differences of opinion about what they really are, the children must finally face up to the realization that some kinds of rules really are necessary. They must decide for themselves what kinds of rules are fair, in order to keep the game going, and interesting, and fun for all; they must participate in establishing the rules and must learn how to enforce them. Experiences like this, Piaget theorized, play a vital role in helping the child grow to a more mature stage of moral development based on the principles of cooperation and consent.

Along somewhat similar lines, Parsons and Bales (1955) have argued that the enormous power differentials between adults and children present serious obstacles to certain kinds of essential learning. For example, adult authority usually appears to young children to be heavily ascriptive in character; authority flows from the fact that one is a parent, a teacher, a coach, or simply an adult, possessed of awesome powers to punish or reward. But the relevance of this power is not always obvious. Within the peer group, where differences in power are on a much smaller scale, leadership is much more likely to be based on relevant, universalistic criteria. A child leader is accepted and followed only to the extent that he effectively expresses the children's own values and helps them to work or play together in self-satisfying ways. It is largely within the framework of informally organized peer groups, these authors reason, that the child learns to conceive of social relationships as being patterned on relevant, universalistic principles in which people must get along in common subjection to general rules.

Kohlberg (1964) has pointed to yet another feature of unstructured children's play for the processes of moral development. If rules are rigidly fixed once and for all by parents, teachers, coaches, or rule books, the child may learn them and perhaps accept them, but he will not gain much experience in the development of mature moral judgment. According to Kohlberg, it is only with some real experience with dissonance, as when the rules are ambiguous or when there is some cross-pressure or opinion difference about which rules should apply, that children learn to understand how certain more general moral principles must be formulated to help them decide for themselves what they should do. Much of my own recent research has tended to support the notion that informal peer group experiences and their accompanying dissonance contribute to the development of moral autonomy in children (Devereux 1970) and that authoritarian control by adults has precisely the opposite effect (Devereux 1972).

Backyard versus Little League Baseball, Viewed as Learning Settings

In the light of what has been said thus far, I shall now comment on what I see as some crucial differences between an informal and spontaneous version of backyard baseball and the organized and adult-controlled Little League version of the same game. Let me grant at once that the latter form of the game is obviously much better equipped, better coached, and probably also a good deal safer. No doubt Little League children really do get better training in the official rules and strategies of our national sport, and better experience in the complex physical skills of ball handling, fielding, and so on. If the purpose of the game is to serve as an anticipatory socialization setting for developing future high school, college, and professional ball players, the Little League sport is clearly the winner.

But if we look at the matter in a more general educational perspective, it appears that those gains are not achieved without serious cost. In educational terms, the crucial question must always be not what the boy is doing to the ball, but what the ball is doing to the boy. In Little League baseball this is often not the case. Almost inevitably, in a highly organized, competitive sport, the focus is on winning and the eye is on the ball. How often does the well-intentioned volunteer coach from the phys ed department really think about what kind of total experience his boys are having, including those who have warmed the bench all afternoon, or who were not selected for League competition?

Of that, more shortly. But first let me describe a typical variant of backyard baseball, as played in my own neighborhood some fifty years ago. We called it one-o-cat. There were no teams. With a minimum of five kids you could start up a game, though it was better with seven or eight; once the game got started, usually a few more kids would wander over to join in. Often these were kids of the wrong age or sex, but no matter: it was more fun with more kids, and the child population was a bit sparse back then. One base—usually a tree, or somebody's sweater or cap.

Home plate, usually a flat stone. Two batters, a catcher, a pitcher, a first baseman. If other kids were available, you had some fielders, too. If someone had a catcher's mitt, we'd use a hard ball; otherwise a softball, tennis ball, or anything else. If someone had a face mask, the catcher would play right behind the batter; otherwise, way back. There was no umpire to call balls and strikes, so the pitcher was disciplined mostly by shouts of "put it over!" Fouls were balls that went to the right of the tree marking first base or to the left of a shrub on the other side; in other yards or fields, different foul markers would have to be agreed upon.

The rules of the game, as we vaguely understood or invented them, were fairly simple. Pitched balls not swung at didn't count either as balls or strikes. Three swings without a hit and you were out. In principle you could go on hitting fouls indefinitely, but after a while the other kids would complain and make you swing at a wild one. A caught fly put you out. A good hit could get you to the tree and back for a home run; a lesser hit could leave you stranded at first, to be hit in, maybe, by the other batter. Or you could be put out either at first base or at the home plate in the usual fashion. Since there were no fixed base lines, when a runner was caught between the first baseman and the catcher, a wild chase all over the yard frequently ensued. When you went out, you retired to right field and everybody moved up one notch, catcher to batter, pitcher to catcher, first baseman to pitcher, left fielder to first, etc. There were no teams and nobody really bothered to keep score, since the personnel of the game usually changed during the session anyway, as some kids had to go do their chores or as others joined in. The object seemed to be to stay at bat as long as you could, but during the afternoon every kid would have plenty of opportunities to play in every position, and no one was ever on the bench. If a few more kids showed up, the game was magically transformed to two-o-cat, now with three rotating batters and a second base somewhere near where third would have been; the runners now had to make the full triangular circuit in order to complete their run.

Maybe we didn't learn to be expert baseball players, but we did have a lot of fun. Moreover, in an indirect and incidental way, we learned a lot of other kinds of things which are probably more important for children between the ages of eight and twelve. Precisely because there was no official rule book and no adult or even other child designated as rule enforcer, we somehow had to improvise the whole thing; this entailed endless hassles about whether a ball was fair or foul, whether a runner was safe or out, or more generally, simply about what was fair. We gradually learned to understand the invisible boundary conditions of our relationships to each other. Don't be a poor sport or the other kids won't want you to play with them. Don't push your point so hard that the kid with the only catcher's mitt will quit the game. Pitch a bit more gently to the littler kids so they can have some fun, too; besides, you realize that you must keep them in the game because numbers are important. Learn how to get a game started and somehow keep it going, as long as the fun lasts. How to pace it. When to quit for a while to get a round of cokes or just to sit under a tree for a bit. How to recognize the subtle boundaries indicating that the game is really over—not an easy thing, since there are no innings, no winners or losers—and slide over into some other activity. "Let's play tag"—"Not it!"

Perhaps after supper, a game of catch with your father, who might try to give you a few very non-professional pointers. Perhaps, for a few, excited accounts to the family of your success at bat that day and momentary dreams of later glory in the big leagues. But mostly on to the endless variety of other games, pastimes, and interests which could so engage a young boy on a summer afternoon or evening.

In terms of the learning models proposed by Roberts, Sutton-Smith, Moore, Piaget, Parsons, Kohlberg, and many others, it was all there. It was fun; the scale was small, and the risks were minimal; we felt free and relatively safe (at least psychologically); it was spontaneous, autotelic, and agent responsive; it was self-pacing and the feedback was continuous and relevant. The game was so structured that it required us to use our utmost ingenuity to discover and understand the hidden rules behind the rules—the general principles which make games fair, fun, and interesting, and which had to govern our complex relationships with each other; the recognition of the subtle differences in skills, including social skills, which gave added respect and informal authority to some; the ability to handle poor sports, incompetents, cry-babies, little kids, and girls, when the easy out of excluding them from the game entirely was somehow impractical. How to handle it when your own anger or frustrations welled up dangerously close to the point of tears. Although the formal structure of the game was based on a model of competition and physical skill, many of its most important lessons were in the social-emotional sector—how to keep the group sufficiently cohesive to get on with the play, and how to handle the tensions which arose within and between us.

All these are things which were happening to the boys when left to themselves in this informal game situation. And it seems to me that they are far more important than what was happening to the ball. By now the ball is lost, anyway, somewhere in the bushes over by left field. Perhaps someone will find it tomorrow. And besides, it's too hot for baseball now, and the kids have all gone skinny-dipping in the little pond down the road.

How does Little League baseball stack up against this model? Rather badly, in my opinion. The scale is no longer miniature and safe, what with scoreboards, coaches, umpires, parents, and a grandstand full of spectators all looking at you and evaluating your every move with a single, myopic criterion: Perform! Win! The risks of failure are large and wounding, and in the pyramidal structure of League competition, only a few can be winners; everybody else must be some kind of loser.

In Little League ball, the spontaneity is largely killed by schedules, rules, and adult supervision—a fixed time and place for each game, a set number of innings, a commitment to a whole season's schedule at the expense of alternative activities. Self-pacing? Obviously not. Fun? Yes, in a hard sort of way; but please, no fooling around or goofing off out there in right field; keep your eyes on the ball! Instant feedback? Yes, loud and clear from all sides, if you make a mistake; but mostly from adults, in terms of their criteria of proper baseball performance.

The major problem with Little League baseball, as I see it, is that the whole structure of the game is rigidly fixed once and for all. It's all there in the rule books and in the organization of the League and the game itself. It is all handed to the children, ready-made, together with the diamonds, bats, and uniforms. It is all so carefully supervised by adults, who are the teachers, coaches, rule-enforcers, decision-makers, and principal rewarders and punishers, that there's almost nothing left for the children to do but play the game. Almost all the opportunities for incidental learning which occur in spontaneous self-organized and self-governed children's games have somehow been sacrificed on the altar of safety (physical only) and competence (in baseball only).

Competition and Little Leaguism in Contemporary America

No doubt there are some who will argue that ours is a tough, competitive society and that somehow, during the educational process, children must be readied for the rigorous competition of real life they will face later on. It is certainly true that competition has played a central role in American society, and for generations there were many, like Theodore Roosevelt, who thought of it as the backbone of American character and achievement. But at what cost to other values? More than thirty years ago the psychoanalyst Karen Horney, in her classic analysis of *The Neurotic Personality of Our Time* (1937), saw fit to devote an entire chapter to "neurotic competitiveness." But while Horney saw the problem clearly enough, most psychologists and educators of that generation did not. It is interesting to note that among the twenty-three experimental studies of competition reported by Murphy, Murphy, and Newcomb (1937), the focus is almost invariably upon the effects of competition on the performance of some task; not one of these studies dealt with any measures of the effects of competition upon the subjects themselves!

But there undoubtedly are effects, among them the apparent inability of American children, reared in a competitive style, to know when *not* to compete. This point was neatly demonstrated in an experiment by Madsen and Shapira (1970). An apparatus was so arranged that no child could get any reward without cooperating with the other children. Mexican children (and, in another study by Shapira and Madsen [1969], Israeli kibbutz children) were quick to fall into a cooperative plan, to everybody's mutual advantage, but the American children continued to compete even after it became quite obvious that no one could win anything.

The time has surely come to reassess the heavy stress we have placed on competition in our educational system, and in our culture generally. In this connection it is interesting to note that recent movements toward educational reform call for a drastic reduction in the role of competition. More generally, the new counterculture flourishing on our college campuses is strongly anticompetitive in basic orientation. Somehow a whole generation of fathers, still deeply involved in major sports and other facets of the old American dream, has managed to rear a generation of sons, a very substantial segment of whom will have no part of it.

What can be said, more specifically, of the effects of Little League competition on children? I shall not take space here to consider such measured physiological side-effects as the famous Little League elbow, or the evidences of measured galvanic skin responses of young boys before and after competition (Skubic 1955), or the reported losses of sleep and appetite before or following competition (Skubic 1956). I have no reason to doubt that first-rate child athletes, like the adult athletes studied by Ogilvie and Tutko (1971), really are better built, better coordinated, and have fairly well integrated, if somewhat aggressive, personalities, in comparison with less athletic peers. But the crucial question must be whether participation in Little League sports helps make them that way, or whether the reported differences are a result of the selection processes involved. In the adult study cited above, the authors believe that most observed differences result from the selection processes rather than from the character-molding experiences of athletic competition. Hale's (1956) finding that the Little League players who made it to the Williamsport national competition had more, darker, and curlier pubic hair than non-playing age mates almost certainly reflects a selective factor rather than a consequence of ball playing.

Similarly, in Seymour's (1956) study, it is clear that the major reported differences between the Little Leaguers and their class mates, documenting the superiority of the League players, all existed before the season began. On all the self-rating scales used in this study, moreover, the nonparticipants actually improved more than the participants, ending ahead of the participants in their post-season self-ratings of their feelings about "me and my school" and "me and my home." The nonparticipants also gained somewhat more than the participants in the teacher ratings on social consciousness, emotional adjustment, and responsibility. On the sociometric ratings, as expected, the athletes were the sociometric stars in their classrooms both before and after the season. The author does note, however, that on the post-season sociometric test, the Little League boys were somewhat less accepting of their peers, as measured by ratings they extended to others, than they had been before the season started. Perhaps these results represent a gentle forecast of the Ogilvie-Tutko description of adult athletes: "Most athletes indicate low interest in receiving support and concern from others, low need to take care of others and low need for affiliation. Such a personality seems necessary to achieve victory over others" (1971: 61–62).

If some processes of selection are at work in sifting out the children who get to play in League or interscholastic competition (as they quite obviously are), and if both the adult and peer cultures shower these children with special attention and kudos (as they surely do), then responsible educators must have some concern about all the other children who are losers or nonparticipants in this one-dimensional competition. How sure are we that the values and character traits selected and carefully reinforced in Little League sports are really the best for wholesome child development? In a culture as fanatically dedicated to excellence in competitive sports as we have become in modern America, are we needlessly and cruelly punishing the children who are physically smaller or less mature, or less well coordinated or aggressive, who can't compete successfully and perhaps don't even want to? Many will no doubt turn into fine and productive adults—but only after a childhood in which they were never able to live up to the myopic values of the peer culture, or to the expectations of their sport-addicted fathers.

Don't misunderstand me. I am certainly not coming out against baseball as such, though for the reasons indicated I believe that the informal, backyard variants have far more learning values for children than the formally organized, adult-supervised version. My most fundamental opposition to Little League baseball is based not so much on what it does by way of either harm or good to the players, as it is on what Little League*ism* is doing to the whole culture of childhood, to participants and nonparticipants alike, and to the schools, families, neighborhoods, and communities where Little Leaguism has taken root.

Look first at what has happened to organized sports in high schools, and the picture is perhaps clearer. In a high school of 2,000 students, only a relative handful get to participate even on the squads of any of the major teams. All the rest are consigned to the role of frenzied spectators at interscholastic meets, or, still worse, in many sport-minded communities, to being nonparticipant nonspectators, perceived by adults and peers alike as odd-balls or pariahs. As Coleman (1961) showed, this group may in fact include some of the best students, but they get precious little reward for their academic efforts. The kids who do go out in earnest for a high school sport find that, to compete at all effectively against our fanatic standards of excellence, they have to make it almost a full-time job both in season and out, at the expense of virtually all other extracurricular and leisure activities. In one way, you're damned if you don't participate; in another way, you're damned if you do.

In Little League and other variations of organized interscholastic sports, we now see clear indications of the invasion of this sports culture into the much more precious and vulnerable world of little children. Like the bad currency in Gresham's famous law, it is an inferior product which ends up driving out the good. Because of its peculiar fascination, more for the parents than for the children themselves, it nearly monopolizes the field and drives almost to bankruptcy the natural and spontaneous culture of play and games among American children.

Let me close with yet another quotation from the Opies' fascinating monograph:

> In the long run, nothing extinguishes self-organized play more effectively than does action to promote it. It is not only natural but beneficial that there should be a gulf between the generations in their choice of recreation. Those people are happiest who can most rely on their own resources; and it is to be wondered whether middle-class children in the United States will ever reach maturity "whose playtime has become almost as completely organized and supervised as their study" (Carl Withers). If children's games are tamed and made part of school curricula, if wastelands are turned into playing-fields for the benefit of those who conform and ape their elders, if children are given the idea that they cannot enjoy themselves without being provided with the "proper" equipment, we need blame only ourselves when we produce a generation who have lost their dignity, who are ever dissatisfied, and who descend for their sport to the easy excitement of rioting, or pilfering, or vandalism. (1969: 16)

A final word to physical education professionals is in order. My rather limited contacts with physical education teachers have persuaded me that many (perhaps most) of you are really on my side on the matter of promoting competitive sports among young children. The problem, as I see it, stems not from the physical education programs in our elementary schools and from those who teach in these settings. It stems far more from the parents and from the common culture in our sports-ridden communities.

What can you do about it? Not too much, I'm afraid. But I can think of at least three things I would hope that you might try. First, in training students who will work with young children, urge them to keep in mind that "It's not what the boy is doing to the ball, but what the ball is doing to the boy!" Or, to reverse the old cliché: "Keep your eye on the boy!"

Second, physical education instructors, as experts in this area, are in a strategic position to influence public opinion on this important matter. I hope that you, in your contacts with parents, teachers, school administrators, and community leaders generally, will continually stress the important role of spontaneous play and of unsupervised, self-organized games for young children, and the very real costs involved when we push our children into competitive sports too early.

Finally, I hope that physical education instructors who work with children will do whatever they can to reintroduce some of the wonderful traditional games which earlier generations of children found so rewarding, and which, in my opinion, are far more appropriate for the elementary school ages. The instant success of capture the flag, introduced to one of our schools by a student volunteer, indicates that perhaps it can be done. The kids simply didn't know what they had been missing.

But once a game has been taught and is beginning to catch on with the children, I'm afraid the rest of my message really is: "Get lost!" Let the kids handle it themselves.

REFERENCES

Coleman, J. (1961) *The Adolescent Society.* Glencoe, Ill.: Free Press.

Devereux, E. C. (1970) "The Role of Peer Group Experience in Moral Development." In Hill, J. P., ed. *Minnesota Symposia on Child Psychology* 4:94–140. Minneapolis: University of Minnesota Press.

——— (1972) "Authority and Moral Development among American and West German Children." *Journal of Comparative Family Studies* 3:99–124.

Eifermann, Rivka R. (1971a) "Social Play in Childhood." In Herron, R. E., and Sutton-Smith, B., eds. *Child's Play.* New York: John Wiley and Sons, Pp. 270–297.

——— (1971b) *Determinants of Children's Game Styles.* Jerusalem: Israel Academy of Sciences and Humanities.

Hale, C. J. (1956) "Physiological Maturity of Little League Baseball Players." *Research Quarterly* 27:276–282.

Herron, R. E., and Sutton-Smith, B., eds. (1971) *Child's Play.* New York: John Wiley and Sons.

Horney, Karen. (1937) *The Neurotic Personality of Our Time.* New York: W. W. Norton.

Kohlberg, L. (1964) "Development of Moral Character and Moral Ideology." In Hoffman, M. L., and Hoffman, L. W., eds. *Review of Child Development Research* 1:383–431. New York: Russell Sage Foundation.

Lewin, Kurt, et al. (1944) "Level of Aspiration." In Hunt, J. M., ed. *Personality and Behavior Disorders.* New York: Ronald Press.

Madsen, M. C., and Shapira, A. (1970) "Cooperative and Competitive Behavior of Urban Afro-American, Anglo-American, Mexican-American and Mexican Village Children." *Developmental Psychology* 3:16–20.

Menninger, K. (1942) *Love against Hate.* New York: Harcourt.

Moore, O. K., and Anderson, A. R. (1969) "Some Principles for the Design of Clarifying Educational Environments." In Goslin, D., ed. *Handbook of Socialization Theory and Research.* New York: Rand McNally. Pp. 571–613.

Murphy, G.; Murphy, L. B.; and Newcomb, R. M. (1937) *Experimental Social Psychology.* New York: Harper Bros.

Ogilvie, B. C., and Tutko, T. A. (1971) "If You Want to Build Character, Try Something Else." *Psychology Today* 5:60–63.

Opie, Iona, and Opie, Peter. (1969) *Children's Games in Street and Playground.* Oxford: Clarendon Press.

Parsons, R., and Bales, R. F. (1955) *Family, Socialization and Interaction Process.* Glencoe, Ill.: Free Press.

Piaget, Jean. (1932) *The Moral Judgment of the Child.* New York: Harcourt.

Phillips, R. H. (1960) "The Nature and Function of Children's Formal Games." *Psychoanalytic Quarterly* 29:200–207.

Roberts, J. M., and Sutton-Smith, B. (1962) "Child Training and Game Involvement." *Ethnology* 1:166–185.

Seymour, E. W. (1956) "Comparative Study of Certain Behavior Characteristics of Participants and Non-participants in Little League Baseball." *Research Quarterly* 27:338–346.

Shapira, A., and Madsen, M. C. (1969) "Cooperative and Competitive Behavior of Kibbutz and Urban Children in Israel." *Child Development* 40:609–617.

Skubic, E. (1955) "Emotional Responses of Boys to Little League and Middle League Competitive Baseball." *Research Quarterly* 26:342–352.

——— (1956) "Studies of Little League and Middle League Baseball." *Research Quarterly* 27:97–110.

Sutton-Smith, B. (1971) "A Syntax for Play and Games." In Herron, R. E., and Sutton-Smith, B., eds. *Child's Play.* New York: John Wiley and Sons. Pp. 298–307.

———, and Rosenberg, B. G. (1971) "Sixty Years of Historical Change in the Game Preferences of American Children." In Herron, R. E., and Sutton-Smith, B., eds. *Child's Play.* New York: John Wiley and Sons. Pp. 18–50.

DISCUSSION QUESTIONS

1. What has accounted for the constriction and formalization of children's games?
2. Compare and contrast the developmental functions of informal children's games with adult-sponsored sports.

Article 10

Police Accounts of Normal Force

JENNIFER HUNT

THE POLICE ARE REQUIRED to handle a variety of peace-keeping and law enforcement tasks including settling disputes, removing drunks from the street, aiding the sick, controlling crowds, and pursuing criminals. What unifies these diverse activities is the possibility that their resolution might require the use of force. Indeed, the capacity to use force stands at the core of the police mandate (Bittner, 1980).

Although force not accountable in legal terms is technically labelled excessive by the courts and the public, the police perceive many forms of illegal force as normal. Normal force involves coercive acts that specific "cops" on specific occasions formulate as necessary, appropriate, reasonable, or understandable. Although not always legitimized or admired, normal force is depicted as a necessary or natural response of normal police to particular situational exigencies.

Most officers are expected to use both legal and normal force as a matter of course in policing the streets. In contrast, excessive force or brutality exceeds even working police notions of normal force. These are acts of coercion that cannot be explained by the routine police accounting practices ordinarily used to justify or excuse force. Brutality is viewed as illegal, illegitimate, and often immoral violence,

From "Police Accounts of Normal Force," by Jennifer Hunt. *Urban Life,* Vol. 13, No. 4, Jan. 1985. Reprinted by permission of Sage Publications, Inc.

but the police draw the lines in extremely different ways and at different points than do either the court system or the public.

These processes of assessing and accounting for the use of force, with special reference to the critical distinction between normal and excessive force as drawn by the police, will be explored in what follows. The study begins by examining how rookie police learn on the street to use and account for force in a manner that contradicts what they were taught at the academy. It then considers "normal force" and the accounting processes whereby police discriminatively judge when and how much force is appropriate in specific situations and incidents. It concludes with a discussion of excessive force and peer reactions to those who use it frequently.

The article is based on approximately eighteen months of participant observation in a major urban police department referred to as the Metro City P.D. I attended the police academy with male and female recruits and later rode with individual officers in one-person cars on evening and night shifts in high crime districts.[1] The female officers described in this research were among the first 100 women assigned to the ranks of uniformed patrol as a result of a discrimination suit filed by the Justice Department and a policewoman plaintiff.

Learning to Use Normal Force

The police phrase "it's not done on the street the way that it's taught at the academy" underscores the perceived contradiction between the formal world of the police academy and the informal world of the street. This contradiction permeates the police officer's construction of his world, particularly his view of the rational and moral use of force.

In the formal world of the police academy, the recruit learns to account for force by reference to legality. He or she is issued the regulation instruments and trained to use them to subdue, control, and restrain a suspect. If threatened with great bodily harm, the officer learns that he can justifiably use deadly force and fire his revolver. Yet the recruit is taught that he cannot use his baton, jack, or gun, unnecessarily to torture, maim, or kill a suspect.

When recruits leave the formal world of the academy and are assigned to patrol a district, they are introduced to an informal world in which police recognize normal as well as legal and brutal force. Through observation and instruction, rookies gradually learn to apply force and account for its use in terms familiar to the street cop. First, rookies learn to adjust their arsenals to conform to street standards. They are encouraged to buy the more powerful weapons worn by veteran colleagues as these colleagues point out the inadequacy of a wooden baton or compare their convoy jacks to vibrators. They quickly discover that their department-issued equipment marks them as new recruits. At any rate, within a few weeks, most rookies have dispensed with the wooden baton and convoy jack and substituted them with the more powerful plastic nightstick and flat headed slapjack.[2]

Through experience and informal instruction, the rookie also learns the street use of these weapons. In school, for example, recruits are taught to avoid hitting a person on the head or neck because it could cause lethal damage. On the street, in contrast, police conclude that they must hit wherever it causes the most damage in order to incapacitate the suspect before they themselves are harmed. New officers also learn that they will earn the respect of their veteran coworkers not by observing legal niceties in using force, but by being "aggressive" and using whatever force is necessary in a given situation.

Peer approval helps neutralize the guilt and confusion that rookies often experience when they begin to use force to assert their authority. One female officer, for example, learned she was the object of a brutality suit while listening to the news on television. At first, she felt so mortified that she hesitated to go to work and face her peers. In fact, male colleagues greeted her with a standing ovation and commented, "You can use our urinal now." In their view, any aggressive police officer regularly using normal force might eventually face a brutality suit or civilian complaint. Such accusations confirm the officer's status as a "street cop" rather than an "inside man" who doesn't engage in "real police work."[3]

Whereas male rookies are assumed to be competent dispensers of force unless proven otherwise, women are believed to be physically weak, naturally passive, and emotionally vulnerable.[4] Women officers are assumed to be reluctant to use physical force and are viewed as incompetent "street cops" until they prove otherwise. As a result, women rookies encounter special problems in learning to use normal force in the process of becoming recognized as "real street cops." It becomes crucial for women officers to create or exploit opportunities to display their physical abilities in order to overcome sexual bias and obtain full acceptance from coworkers. As a result, women rookies are encouraged informally to act more aggressively and to display more machismo than male rookies.

For a street cop, it is often a graver error to use too little force and develop a "shaky" reputation than it is to use too much force and be told to calm down. Thus officers, particularly rookies, who do not back up their partners in appropriate ways or who hesitate to use force in circumstances where it is deemed necessary are informally instructed regarding their aberrant ways. If the problematic incident is relatively insignificant and his general reputation is good, a rookie who "freezes" one time is given a second chance before becoming generally known as an untrustworthy partner. However, such incidents become the subject of degrading gossip, gossip that pressures the officer either to use force as expected or risk isolation. Such talk also informs rookies about the general boundaries of legal and normal force.

For example, a female rookie was accused of "freezing" in an incident that came to be referred to as a "Mexican standoff." A pedestrian had complained that "something funny is going on in the drugstore." The officer walked into the pharmacy where she found an armed man committing a robbery. Although he turned his weapon on her when she entered the premises, she still pulled out her gun and pointed it at him. When he ordered her to drop it, claiming that his partner was behind her with a revolver at her head, she refused and told him to drop his.[5] He refused, and the stalemate continued until a sergeant entered the drugstore and ordered the suspect to drop his gun.

Initially, the female officer thought she had acted appropriately and even heroically. She soon discovered, however, that her hesitation to shoot had brought into question her competence with some of her fellow officers. Although many veterans claimed that "she had a lot a balls" to take her gun out at all when the suspect already had a gun on her, most contended "she shoulda shot him." Other policemen confirmed that she committed a "rookie mistake"; she had failed to notice a "lookout" standing outside the store and hence had been unprepared for an armed confrontation. Her sergeant and lieutenant, moreover, even insisted that she had acted in a cowardly manner, despite her reputation as a "gung-ho cop," and cited the incident as evidence of the general inadequacy of policewomen.

In the weeks that followed, this officer became increasingly depressed and angry. She was particularly outraged when she learned that she would not receive a commendation, although such awards were commonly made for "gun pinches" of this nature. Several months later, the officer vehemently expressed the wish that she had killed the suspect and vowed that next time she would "shoot first and ask questions later." The negative sanctions of supervisors and colleagues clearly encouraged her to adopt an attitude favorable to using force with less restraint in future situations.

Reprimand, gossip, and avoidance constitute the primary means by which police try to change or control the behavior of coworkers perceived as unreliable or cowardly. Formal accusations, however, are discouraged regardless of the seriousness of the misconduct. One male rookie, for example, earned a reputation for cowardice after he allegedly had to be "dragged" out of the car during an "assist officer." Even then, he apparently refused to help the officers in trouble. Although no formal charges were filed, everyone in the district was warned to avoid working with this officer.

Indeed, to initiate formal charges against a coworker may discredit the accuser. In one incident a male rookie, although discouraged by veteran officers and even his district captain, filed charges of cowardice against a female rookie. The rookie gained the support of two supervisors and succeeded in having the case heard before the Board of Inquiry. During the trial he claimed the woman officer failed to aid him in arresting a man who presented physical resistance and had a knife on his person. In rebuttal, the woman testified that she perceived no need to participate in a physical confrontation because she saw no knife and the policeman was hitting the suspect. In spite of conflicting testimony, she was found guilty of "Neglect of Duty." Although most veterans thought the woman was "flaky" and doubted her competence, they also felt the male rookie had exaggerated his story. Moreover, they were outraged that he filed formal charges and he quickly found himself ostracized.

At the same time that male and female rookies are commended for using force under appropriate circumstances, they are reprimanded if their participation in force is viewed as excessive or inappropriate. In this way, rookies are instructed that although many acts of coercion are accepted and even demanded, not everything goes. They thereby learn to distinguish between normal and brutal force. In the following incident, for example, a policewoman describes how she instructed a less experienced officer that her behavior was unreasonable and should be checked.

Here, the new officer is chastised for misreading interactional cues and overreacting to minor affronts when treating a crazy person involved in a minor dispute as if he were a serious felon.[6]

> But like I said, when I first heard about it (another fight) I'd wondered if Mary had provoked it any because we'd gone on a disturbance and it was a drunk black guy who called to complain that the kid who lived upstairs keeps walking through his apartment. The kid to me looks wacky. He's talking crazy. He's saying they shoulda sent men. What are you women going to do. Going on and on. And to me it was a bullshit job. But Mary turns around and says, "We don't have to take that from him. Let's lock him up." I said, "Mary forget it." And the kid has numchuck sticks on him and when he turned his back . . . he had them in his back pocket. So, as he's pulling away saying you're scared, like a little kid, I turned around and said, "I've got your sticks." And I go away. Mary . . . so Mary was . . . I looked at her and she was so disappointed in me . . . like I'd turned chicken on her. So I tried to explain to her, I said "Mary, all we have is disorderly conduct. That's a summary offense. That's bullshit." I said, "Did you want to get hurt for a summary offense?" I said, "The guy was drunk who called to complain. It wasn't even a legit complaint." I said, "It's just . . . You've got to use discretion. If you think I'm chicken think of the times when a 'man with a gun' comes over the air and I'm the first car there." I said, "When it's worth it, I'll do anything. When it's not worth it, I back off." And I think she tries to temper herself some because Collette and her, they finally had a talk about why they hated each other. And Collette said to her, "I think you're too physical. I think you look for fights." And I think maybe Mary hearing it twice, once from me and once from Collette, might start to think that maybe she does provoke. Instead of going up . . . I always go up to them friendly and then if they act shitty I get shitty.

In summary, when rookies leave the academy, they begin to familiarize themselves with street weapons and to gain some sense of what kinds of behavior constitute too little or too much force. They also begin to develop an understanding of street standards for using and judging appropriate necessary force. By listening to and observing colleagues at work and by experiencing a variety of problematic interactions with the public, newcomers become cognizant of the occasions and circumstances in which to use various degrees and kinds of force. But at the same time, they are learning not only when and how to use force, but also a series of accounting practices to justify and to legitimate as "normal" (and sometimes to condemn) these acts of coercion. Normal force is thus the product of the police officers' accounting practices for describing what happened in ways that prefigure or anticipate the conclusion that it was in some sense justified or excusable and hence "normal." It is to a consideration of the ways in which officers learn to provide such accounts for normal force that I now turn.

Accounting for Normal Force

Police routinely normalize the use of force by two types of accounts: excuses and justifications. Excuses deny full responsibility for an act of force but acknowledge its inappropriateness. Acts of force become excusable when they are depicted as the natural outcome of strong, even uncontrollable emotions normally arising in certain routine sorts of police activities. Through such accounts, officers excuse force by asserting that it is a "natural," "human" reaction to certain extreme, emotionally trying situations. Justifications accept responsibility for the coercive act in question but deny that the act was wrongful or blameworthy (Scott and Lyman, 1968; Emerson, 1969: 142–171). Police justify force through two analytically distinct kinds of accounts: situational and abstract. In the former, the officer represents force as a response in some specific situation needed to restore immediate control or to reestablish the local order of power in the face of a threat to police authority. In contrast, abstract accounts justify force as a morally appropriate response to certain categories of crime and criminals who symbolize a threat to the moral order. As an account, abstract justification does not highlight processes of interactional provocation and threats to immediate control, but rather legitimatizes force as a means of obtaining some higher moral purpose, particularly the punishment of heinous offenders.

None of these accounts are mutually exclusive, and are often combined in justifying and excusing the use of force in any specific instance. For example, police consider it justifiable to use force to regain control of someone who has challenged an officer's authority. However, an officer may also excuse his behavior as an "overreaction," claiming he "snapped out" and lost control, and hence used more force or different kinds of force than were required to regain control. Mixed accounts involving situational and abstract justifications of force are also frequent: force may be depicted as necessary to regain control when an officer is physically assaulted; but at the same time it may also be justified as punishment appropriate to the kind of morally unworthy person who would challenge an officer's authority.

Excuses and Normal Force

Excuses are accounts in which police deny full responsibility for an act but recognize its inappropriateness. Excuses therefore constitute socially approved vocabularies for relieving responsibility when conduct is questionable. Police most often excuse morally problematic force by referring to emotional or physiological states that are precipitated by some circumstances of routine patrol work. These circumstances include shootouts, violent fights, pursuits, and instances in which a police office mistakenly comes close to killing an unarmed person.

Policework in these circumstances can generate intense excitement in which the officer experiences the "combat high" and "adrenaline rush" familiar to the combat soldier.[7] Foot and car pursuits not only bring on feelings of danger and excitement from the chase, but also a challenge to official authority. As one patrolman commented about a suspect: "Yeh, he got tuned up (beaten) . . . you always tune them up after a car chase." Another officer normalized the use of force after a pursuit in these terms:

> It's my feeling that violence inevitably occurs after a pursuit. . . . The adrenaline . . . and the insult involved when someone flees increases with every foot of the pursuit. I know the two or three times that I felt I lost control of myself

> . . . was when someone would run on me. The further I had to chase the guy the madder I got. . . . The funny thing is the reason for the pursuit could have been for something as minor as a traffic violation or a kid you're chasing who just turned on a fire hydrant. It always ends in violence. You feel obligated to hit or kick the guy just for running.

Police officers also excuse force when it follows an experience of helplessness and confusion that has culminated in a temporary loss of emotional control. This emotional combination occurs most frequently when an officer comes to the brink of using lethal force, drawing a gun and perhaps firing, only to learn there were no "real" grounds for this action. The officer may then "snap out" and hit the suspect.[8] In one such incident, for example, two policemen picked up a complainant who positively identified a suspect as a man who just tried to shoot him. Just as the officers approached the suspect, he suddenly reached for his back pocket for what the officers assumed to be a gun. One officer was close enough to jump the suspect before he pulled his hand from his pocket. As it turned out, the suspect had no weapon, having dropped it several feet away. Although he was unarmed and under control, the suspect was punched and kicked out of anger and frustration by the officer who had almost shot him.[9]

Note that in both these circumstances—pursuit and near-miss mistaken shootings—officers would concede that the ensuing force is inappropriate and unjustifiable when considered abstractly. But although abstractly wrong, the use of force on such occasions is presented as a normal, human reaction to an extreme situation. Although not every officer might react violently in such circumstances, it is understandable and expected that some will.

Situational Justifications

Officers also justify force as normal by reference to interactional situations in which an officer's authority is physically or symbolically threatened. In such accounts, the use of force is justified instrumentally—as a means of regaining immediate control in a situation where that control has become tenuous. Here, the officer depicts his primary intent for using force as a need to reestablish immediate control in a problematic encounter, and only incidentally as hurting or punishing the offender.

Few officers will hesitate to assault a suspect who physically threatens or attacks them. In one case, an officer was punched in the face by a prisoner he had just apprehended for allegedly attempting to shoot a friend. The incident occurred in the stationhouse and several policemen observed the exchange. Immediately, one officer hit the prisoner in the jaw and the rest immediately joined the brawl. . . .

Abstract Justifications

Police also justify the use of extreme force against certain categories of morally reprehensible persons. In this case, force is not presented as an instrumental means to regain control that has been symbolically or physically threatened. Instead, it is justified as an appropriate response to particularly heinous offenders. Categories of such offenders include: cop haters who have gained notoriety as persistent police antagonists; cop killers or any person who has attempted seriously to harm a police officer (Westley, 1970:131); sexual deviants who prey on children and "moral women";[10] child abusers; and junkies and other "scum" who inhabit the street. The more morally reprehensible the act is judged, the more likely the police are to depict any violence directed toward its perpetrator as justifiable. Thus a man who exposes himself to children in a playground is less likely to experience police assault than one who rapes or sexually molests a child.

"Clean" criminals, such as high level mafioso, white-collar criminals, and professional burglars, are rarely subject to abstract force. Nor are perpetrators of violent and nonviolent street crimes who prey on adult males, prostitutes, and other categories of persons who belong on the street.[14] Similarly, the "psycho" or demented person is perceived as so mentally deranged that he is not responsible for his acts and hence does not merit abstract, punitive force (Van Maanen, 1978:233–4).

Police justify abstract force by involving a higher moral purpose that legitimatizes the violation of commonly recognized standards.[15] In one case, for example, a nun was raped by a 17-year-old male adolescent. When the police apprehended the suspect, he was severely beaten and his penis put in an electrical outlet to teach him a lesson. The story of the event was told to me by a police officer who, despite the fact that he rarely supported the use of extra-legal force, depicted this treatment as legitimate. Indeed, when I asked if he would have participated had he been present, he responded, "I'm Catholic. I would have participated."

Excessive Force and Peer Responses

Although police routinely excuse and justify many incidents where they or their coworkers have used extreme force against a citizen or suspect, this does not mean that on any and every occasion the officer using such force is exonerated. Indeed, the concept of normal force is useful because it suggests that there are specific circumstances under which police officers will not condone the use of force by themselves or colleagues as reasonable and acceptable. Thus, officer-recognized conceptions of normal force are subject to restrictions of the following kinds:

(1) Police recognize and honor some rough equation between the behavior of the suspect and the harmfulness of the force to which it is subject. There are limits, therefore, to the degree of force that is acceptable in particular circumstances. In the following incident, for example, an officer reflects on a situation in which a "symbolic assailant" (Skolnick, 1975:45) was mistakenly subject to more force than he "deserved" and almost killed:

> One time Bill Johnson and I, I have more respect for him than any other policeman. . . . He and I, we weren't particularly brutal. If the guy deserved it, he got it. It's generally the attitude that does it. We had a particularly rude drunk one day. He was

> really rude and spit on you and he did all this stuff and we even had to cuff him lying down on the hard stretcher, like you would do an epileptic. . . . We were really mad at this guy. So, what you normally do with drunks is you take them to the district cell. . . . So we were really mad. We said let's just give him one or two shots . . . slamming on the brakes and having him roll. But we didn't use our heads. He's screaming and hollering "You lousy cops" and we slammed on the brakes and we didn't use our heads and we heard the stretcher go nnnnnnBam and then nothing. We heard nothing and we realized we had put this man in with his head to the front so when we slammed on the brakes this stretcher. . . . I guess it can roll four foot. Well, it was his head that had hit the front of it and we heard no sounds and my God, I've never been so scared. Me and Bill we thought we killed him. So I'm saying "Bill, what are we gonna do? How are we gonna explain this one." The guy's still saying nothing. So, we went to Madison Street and parked. It's a really lonely area. And we unlocked the wagon and peeked in. We know he's in there. We were so scared and we look in and there's not a sound and we see blood coming in front of the wagon and think "Oh my God we killed this man. What am I gonna do? What am I gonna tell my family?" And to make a long story short, he was just knocked out. But boy was I scared. From then on we learned, feet first.

(2) Although it is considered normal and natural to become emotional and angry in highly charged, taut encounters, officers nonetheless prefer to minimize the harmful consequences of the use of force. As a result, officers usually acknowledge that emotional reactions that might lead to extreme force should be controlled and limited by coworkers if at all possible. In the following account, for example, an officer justified the use of force as a legitimate means to regain situational control when physically challenged. Nonetheless, he expressed gratitude to his partner for stopping him from doing serious harm when he "snapped out" and lost control:

> Well, I wasn't sure if she was a girl until I put my hand on her shoulder and realized it was a woman's shoulder. I was trying to stop her. But it happened when she suddenly kicked me in the balls. Then everything inside of me exploded and I grabbed her and pushed her against the car and started pressing her backwards and kept pressing her backwards. All of a sudden something clicked inside of me because I noticed her eyes changed and her body caved in and she looked frightened because she knew that I was gonna kill her. And I stopped. I think I stopped because Susan was on the scene. She must have said something. But anyway she (Susan) told me later that I should calm down. And I snapped at her and told her to mind her own business because she didn't know what happened. The girl kicked me in the balls. But she was right about it. I mean it was getting to me. I'd never hit a woman before.

Conclusion

The organization of policework reflects a poignant moral dilemma: for a variety of reasons, society mandates to the police the right to use force but provides little direction as to its proper use in specific, "real life" situations. Thus, the police, as officers of the law, must be prepared to use force under circumstances in which its rationale is often morally, legally, and practically ambiguous. This fact explains some otherwise puzzling aspects of police training and socialization.

The police academy provides a semblance of socialization for its recruits by teaching formal rules for using force. It is a semblance of socialization because it treats the use of force as capable of rationalization within the moral and legal conventions of the civilian world. The academy also, paradoxically, trains recruits in the use of tools of violence with potential for going far beyond the limitations of action imposed by those conventions. Consequently, the full socialization of a police officer moves from its idealizations to the practicalities of the street. This movement involves several phases: (1) a decisive, practical separation from the formal world established within the academy; (2) the cultivation of a working distinction between what is formally permissible and what is practically and informally required of the "street cop"; and (3) the demonstration of competence in using and accounting for routine street practices that are morally and legally problematic for those not working the street.

The original dilemma surrounding the use of force persists throughout the socialization process, but is increasingly dealt with by employing accounts provided by the police community that reduce and neutralize the moral tension. The experienced "street cop" becomes an expert at using techniques of neutralization (Sykes and Matza, 1957) to characterize the use of force on the streets, at judging its use by others, and at evaluating the necessity for using force by standards those techniques provide. Use of these techniques also reinforces the radical separation of the formal and informal worlds of policework, duplicating within the context of the organization itself the distinction between members and outsiders. This guarantees that members will be able to distinguish between those who can and cannot be trusted to use force and to understand the conditions under which its use is reasonable.

As accounts neutralizing the use of force, justifications and excuses both serve—though each in a different way—to manage the tension inherent in situations fraught with moral insecurity. They conventionalize but do not reform situations that are inherently charged and morally ambiguous. In this way they simultaneously preserve the self-image of police as agents of the conventional order, provide ways in which individual officers can resolve their personal doubts as to the moral status of their action and those of their colleagues, and reinforce the solidarity of the police community.

NOTES

1. Nonetheless masculine pronouns are generally used to refer to the police in this article, because the Metro P.D. remained dominated by men numerically, in style and in tone.

My fieldwork experience is discussed in detail in a forthcoming paper (Hunt, 1984).

2. Some officers also substitute a large heavy duty flashlight for the nightstick. If used correctly, the flashlight can inflict more damage than the baton and is less likely to break when applied to the head or other parts of the body.

3. For a discussion of the cultural distinction between "inside men" who handle desk and administrative tasks and "real cops" who work outside on the street, see Hunt (1984).

4. As the Metro City Police Commissioner commented in an interview: "In general, they (women) are physically weaker than males. . . . I believe they would be inclined to let their emotions all too frequently overrule their good judgment . . . there are periods in their life when they are psychologically unbalanced because of physical problems that are occurring within them."

5. The woman officer later explained that she did not obey the suspect's command because she saw no reflection of the partner in the suspect's glasses and therefore assumed he was lying.

6. Patrol officers do not view demented people as responsible for their acts and therefore do not hold them strictly culpable when they challenge an officer's authority (see Van Maanen, 178:231). In dealing with such persons, coercion other than that narrowly required for control and self-protection tends to be viewed as inappropriate and unjustifiable.

7. The combat high is a state of controlled exhilaration in which the officer experiences a heightened awareness of the world around him. Officers report that perception, smell, and hearing seem acute; one seems to stand outside oneself and the world appears extraordinarily vivid and clear. At the same time, officers insist that they are able to think rationally and instantly translate thoughts into action; when experienced, fear is not incapacitating but instead enhances the ability to act.

8. This police experience of fear and helplessness, leading to a violent outburst, may be analogized to a parent's reaction on seeing his child almost die in an accident. Imagine a scene in which a father is walking with his six-year-old son. Suddenly, the boy runs into the street to get a red ball on the pavement. The father watches a car slam on the brakes and miss the boy by two inches. He grabs his son and smacks him on the face before he takes him in his arms and holds him.

9. Rubinstein (1973: 304–305) describes a similar instance of police use of force.

10. According to Van Maanen (1978: 224), such persons tend to be labeled "assholes." The "asshole," who symbolically challenges an officer's control and thereby defies his definition of a situation, provokes the officer's wrath and becomes a likely candidate for street justice (Van Maanen, 1978: 24).

11. Note that this account employs both the justifications of reestablishing real and symbolic control, and the excuse of emotionally snapping out in response to this symbolic challenge and to the resulting pursuit.

12. Again, such affronts are with different frequency and have different impact depending upon gender. Although policemen are occasionally subjected to sexual insults by women and teenage girls, this kind of harassment is more commonly experienced by women and thus constitutes a special type of affront to the female officer.

13. For a discussion of the significance of "the moral woman," see Hunt (1984).

14. The categories of persons who merit violence are not unique to the police. Prisoners, criminals, and hospital personnel appear to draw similar distinctions between morally unworthy persons; on the latter, see Sudnow (1967: 105).

15. Abstract force constitutes what Emerson (1969: 149) calls a "principled justification":

> Here one depicts the act as an attempt to realize some absolute moral or social value that has precedence over the value violated by the act.

REFERENCES

Bittner, E. (1980) The Functions of the Police in Modern Society. Cambridge, MA: Oelgeschlager, Gunn & Hain.

Blumberg, M. (1983) The Use of Firearms by Police Officers: The Impact of Individuals, Communities, and Race. Ph.D. dissertation. School of Criminal Justice, State University of New York at Albany.

Emerson, R. M. (1969) Judging Delinquents: Context and Process in Juvenile Court. Chicago: Aldine.

Friedrich, R. (1980) "Police use of force: Individuals, situations, and organizations." *The Annals* 452: 82–97.

Fyfe, J. J. (1983) "Police shootings: Environment, license and individuals." *Presented at the Annual Meeting of the Amer. Society of Criminology.*

Hunt, J. (forthcoming) "The development of rapport through the negotiation of gender in field work among police." Human Organization.

Lee, J. A. (1981) "Some structural aspects of police deviance in relation to minority groups," in C. D. Shearing (ed.) Organizational Police Deviance. Toronto: Butterworths.

Niederhoffer, A. (1967) Behind the Shield: The Police in Urban Society. Garden City, NY: Anchor-Doubleday.

Reiss, A. J. (1970) "Police brutality—answers to key questions," in A. Niederhoffer and A. S. Blumberg (eds.) The Ambivalent Force: Perspectives on the Police. Toronto: Xerox College Publishing.

Rubinstein, J. (1973) City Police. New York: Ballentine.

Scott, M. B. and S. M. Lyman (1968) "Accounts." *Amer. Soc. Rev.* 33: 46–62.

Skolnick, J. (1975) Justice Without Trial. New York: John Wiley.

Sudnow, D. (1967) Passing On: The Social Organization of Dying. Englewood Cliffs, NJ: Prentice-Hall.

Sykes, G. M. and D. Matza (1957) "Techniques of neutralization: A theory of delinquency." *Amer. Soc. Rev.* 22: 664–70.

Van Maanen, J. (1978) "The asshole," in P. K. Manning and J. Van Maanen (eds.) Policing: A View From the Street. Santa Monica, CA: Goodyear.

Waegel, W. B. (1984) "The use of deadly force by police: The effect of statutory change." *Crime and Delinquency* 30: 121–140.

Westley, W. A. (1970) Violence and the Police: A Sociological Study of Law, Custom and Morality. Cambridge, MA: MIT.

DISCUSSION QUESTIONS

1. What is normal force? What are the differences between legal and normal force?
2. How are police officers socialized to learn about the general boundaries of both legal and normal force?

Article 11

The Social Psychology of George Herbert Mead

BERNARD N. MELTZER

A. Preliminary Remarks

WHILE MEAD'S SYSTEM of Social Psychology is given its fullest exposition in *Mind, Self and Society,* each of three other books (as well as a few articles) rounds out the complete picture.

It should be pointed out at this juncture that Mead himself published no full-length systematic statement of his theory. All four of the books bearing his authorship are posthumously collected and edited works. They comprise a loose accumulation of his lecture notes, fragmentary manuscripts, and tentative drafts of unpublished essays. Since the chief aim of his editors has been completeness—rather than organization—the books consist, in considerable part, of alternative formulations, highly repetitive materials, and sketchily developed ideas.

Nevertheless, a brief description of these volumes is in order, since they constitute the major source-materials concerning Mead's social psychology.

Philosophy of the Present (1932) contains the Paul Carus Foundation lectures delivered by Mead in 1930, a year before his death. These lectures present a philosophy of history from the pragmatist's point of view. Moreover, this volume presents his ideas on the analogous developments of social experience and of scientific hypotheses.

From *The Social Psychology of George Herbert Mead,* by Bernard N. Meltzer, Center for Sociological Research, Western Michigan University. Reprinted by permission of the author.

Mind, Self and Society (1934) is chiefly a collection of lectures delivered to his classes in Social Psychology at the University of Chicago.

Movements of Thought in the 19th Century (1936) is largely a collection of lectures delivered to his classes in the History of Ideas.

Philosophy of the Act (1938), according to Paul Schilpp, represents a fairly *systematic* statement of the philosophy of pragmatism. This "systematic" statement I found (as did G. S. Lee) to be made up of essays and miscellaneous fragments, which are technical and repetitious, obscure and difficult.

A final observation regarding the content of these books should be made: Mead's orientation is generally *philosophical.* Rather than marshalling his own empirical evidence, he uses the findings of various sciences and employs frequent apt and insightful illustrations from everyday life. These illustrations usually are not used to prove points, but rather to serve as data to be analyzed in terms of his scheme.

Before launching upon a presentation of Mead's social-psychological theories, it might be wise to explain his designation of his viewpoint as that of "Social Behaviorism." By this term Mead means to refer to the description of behavior at the distinctively human level. Thus, for social behaviorism, the basic datum is the social act. As we shall see, the study of social acts entails concern with the covert aspects of behavior. Further, the concept of the "social act" implies that human conduct and experience has a fundamental social dimension—that the social context is an inescapable element in distinctively human actions.

Like Watsonian radial behaviorism, Mead's social behaviorism starts with the observable actions of individuals; but *unlike* the former, social behaviorism conceives behavior in broad enough terms to include *covert* activity. This inclusion is deemed necessary to understanding the distinctive character of human conduct, which Mead considers a qualitatively different emergent from infrahuman behavior. Watson's behaviorism, on the other hand, reduces human behavior to the very same mechanisms as are found on the infrahuman level. As a corollary, Watson sees the social dimension of human behavior as merely a sort of external influence upon the individual. Mead, by contrast, views generically human behavior as *social* behavior, human acts as *social* acts. For Mead, both the content and the very existence of distinctively human behavior are accountable only on a social basis. (These distinctions should become more clear in the course of this report.)

It can readily be inferred from this brief explanation of Mead's usage of the term "social behaviorism" that, before we can explore the nature and function of the mind—which Mead considers a uniquely human attribute—supporting theories of society, and of self—another uniquely human attribute—require elaboration. Hence, the natural, logical order of Mead's thinking seems to have been society, self, and mind—rather than "Mind, Self, and Society."

B. Content of Mead's Social Psychology

1. Society

According to Mead, all group life is essentially a matter of cooperative behavior. Mead makes a distinction, however, between infrahuman society and human society.

Insects—whose society most closely approximates the complexity of human social life—act together in certain ways because of their biological makeup. Thus, their cooperative behavior is physiologically determined. This is shown by many facts, among which is the fact of the fixity, the stability, of the relationships of insect-society members to one another. Insects, according to the evidence, go on for countless generations without any difference in their patterns of association. This picture of infrahuman society remains essentially valid as one ascends the scale of animal life, until we arrive at the human level.

In the case of human association, the situation is fundamentally different. Human cooperation is not brought about by mere physiological factors. The very diversity of the patterns of human group life makes it quite clear that human cooperative life cannot be explained in the same terms as the cooperative life of insects and the lower animals. The fact that human patterns are not stabilized and cannot be explained in biological terms led Mead to seek another basis of explanation of human association. Such cooperation can only be brought about by some process wherein: (a) each acting individual ascertains the *intention* of the acts of others, and then (b) makes his own response on the basis of that intention. What this means is that, in order for human beings to cooperate, there must be present some sort of mechanism whereby each acting individual: (a) can come to understand the lines of action of others, and (b) can guide his own behavior to fit in with those lines of action. Human behavior is not a matter of responding directly to the activities of others. Rather, it involves responding to the *intentions* of others, i.e., to the future, intended behavior of others—not merely to their present actions.

We can better understand the character of this distinctively human mode of interaction between individuals by contrasting it with the infrahuman "conversation of gestures." For example when a mother hen clucks, her chicks will respond by running to her. This does not imply however, that the hen clucks *in order* to guide the chicks, i.e., with the *intention* of guiding them. Clucking is a natural sign or signal—rather than a significant (meaningful) symbol—as it is not meaningful to the hen. That is, the hen (according to Mead) does not take the role, or viewpoint, of the chicks toward its own gesture and respond to it, in imagination, as they do. The hen does not envision the response of the chicks to her clucking. Thus, hens and chicks do not share the same experience.

Let us take another illustration by Mead: Two hostile dogs, in the pre-fight stage, may go through elaborate conversation of gestures (snarling, growling, baring fangs, walking stiffleggedly around one another, etc.). The dogs are adjusting themselves to one another by responding to one another's gestures. (A gesture is that portion of an act which represents the entire act; it is the initial, overt phase of the act, which epitomizes it, e.g., shaking one's fist at someone.) Now, in the case of the dogs the response to a gesture is dictated by preestablished tendencies to respond in certain ways. Each gesture leads to a direct, immediate, automatic, and unreflecting response by the recipient of the gesture (the other dog). Neither dog responds to the *intention* of the gestures. Further, each dog does not make his gestures with the intent of eliciting certain responses in the other dog. Thus, animal interaction is devoid of conscious, deliberate meaning.

To summarize: Gestures, at the nonhuman or nonlinguistic level, do not carry the connotation of conscious meaning or intent, but serve merely as cues for the appropriate responses of others. Gestural communication takes place immediately, without any interruption of the act, without the mediation of a definition or meaning. Each organism adjusts "instinctively" to the other; it does not stop and figure out which response it will give. Its behavior is, largely, a series of direct automatic responses to stimuli.

Human beings, on the other hand, respond to one another on the basis of intentions or meanings of gestures. This renders the gesture *symbolic,* i.e., the gesture becomes a symbol to be interpreted; it becomes something which, in the imaginations of the participants, stands for the entire act.

Thus, individual A begins to act, i.e., makes a gesture: for example, he draws back an arm. Individual B (who perceives the gesture) completes, or fills in, the act in his imagination; i.e., B imaginatively projects the gesture into the future: "He will strike me." In other words, B perceives what the gesture stands for, thus getting its meaning. In contrast to the direct responses of the chicks and the dogs, the human being inserts an interpretation between the gesture of another and his response to it. Human behavior involves responses to *interpreted* stimuli.[1]

We see, then, that people respond to one another on the basis of imaginative activity. In order to engage in concerted behavior, however, each participating individual must be able to attach the same meaning to the same gesture. Unless interacting individuals interpret gestures similarly, unless they fill out the imagined portion in the same way, there can be no cooperative action. This is another way of saying what has by now become a truism in sociology and social psychology: Human society rests upon a basis of *consensus,* i.e., the sharing of meanings in the form of common understandings and expectations.

In the case of the human being, each person has the ability to respond to his own gestures; and thus, it is possible to have the same meaning for the gestures as other persons. (For example: As I say "chair," I present to myself the same image as to my hearer; moreover, the same image as when someone else says "chair.") This ability to stimulate oneself as one stimulates another, and to respond to oneself as another does, Mead ascribes largely to man's vocal-auditory mechanism. (The ability to hear oneself implies at least the potentiality for responding to oneself.) When a gesture has a shared, common meaning, when it is—in other words—a *linguistic* element, we can designate it as a "significant symbol." (Take the words, "Open the window": the pattern of action symbolized by these words must be in the mind of the speaker as well as the listener. Each must respond, in imagination, to the words in the same way. The speaker must have an image of the listener responding to his words by opening the window, and the listener must have an image of his opening the window.)

The imaginative completion of an act—which Mead calls "meaning" and which represents mental activity—necessarily takes place through *role-taking.* To complete imaginatively the total act which a gesture stands for, the individual must put himself in the position of the other person, must identify with him. The earliest beginnings of role-taking occur when an already established act of another individual is stopped short of completion, thereby requiring the observing individual to fill in, or complete, the activity imaginatively. (For example, a crying infant may have an image of its mother coming to stop its crying.)

As Mead points out, then, the relation of human beings to one another arises from the developed ability of the human being to respond to his own gestures. This ability enables different human beings to respond in the same way to the same gesture, thereby sharing one another's experience.

This latter point is of great importance. Behavior is viewed as "social" not simply when it is a response to others, but rather when it has incorporated in it the behavior of others. The human being responds to himself as other persons respond to him, and in so doing he imaginatively shares the conduct of others. That is, in imagining their response he shares that response.[2]

2. Self

To state that the human being can respond to his own gestures necessarily implies that he possesses a *self.* In referring to the human being as having a self, Mead simply means that such an individual may act socially toward himself, just as toward others. He may praise, blame, or encourage himself; he may become disgusted with himself, may seek to punish himself, and so forth. Thus, the human being may become the object of his own actions. The self is formed in the same way as other objects—through the "definitions" made by others.

The mechanism whereby the individual becomes able to view himself as an object is that of role-taking, involving the process of communication, especially by vocal gestures or speech. (Such communication necessarily involves role-taking.) It is only by taking the role of others that the individual can come to see himself as an object. The standpoint of others provides a platform for getting outside oneself and thus viewing oneself. The development of the self is concurrent with the development of the ability to take roles.

The crucial importance of language in this process must be underscored. It is through language (significant symbols) that the child acquires the meanings and definitions of those around him. By learning the symbols of his groups, he comes to internalize their definitions of events or things, including their definitions of his own conduct.

It is quite evident that, rather than assuming the existence of selves and explaining society thereby, Mead starts out from the prior existence of society as the context within which selves arise. This view contrasts with the nominalistic position of the social contract theorists and of various individualistic psychologies.

Genesis of the Self. The relationship between role-playing and various stages in the development of the self is described below:

1. *Preparatory Stage* (not explicitly named by Mead, but inferable from various fragmentary essays). This stage is one of meaningless imitation by the infant (for example, "reading" the newspaper). The child does certain things that

others near it do without any understanding of what he is doing. Such imitation, however, implies that the child is incipiently taking the roles of those around it, i.e., is on the verge of putting itself in the position of others and acting like them.

2. *Play Stage.* In this stage the actual playing of roles occurs. The child plays mother, teacher, storekeeper, postman, streetcar conductor, Mr. Jones, etc. What is of central importance in such play-acting is that it places the child in the position where it is able to act back toward itself in such roles as "mother" or "teacher." In this stage, then, the child first begins to form a self, that is, to direct activity toward itself—and it does so by taking the roles of others. This is clearly indicated by use of the third person in referring to oneself instead of the first person: "John wants . . .," "John is a bad boy."

   However, in this stage the young child's configuration of roles is unstable; the child passes from one role to another in unorganized, inconsistent fashion. He has, as yet, no unitary standpoint from which to view himself, and hence, he has no unified conception of himself. In other words, the child forms a number of separate and discrete objects of itself, depending on the roles in which it acts toward itself.

3. *Game Stage.* This is the "completing" stage of the self. In time, the child finds himself in situations wherein he must take a number of roles simultaneously. That is, he must respond to the expectations of several people at the same time. This sort of situation is exemplified by the game of baseball—to use Mead's own illustration. Each player must visualize the intentions and expectations of several other players. In such situations the child must take the roles of groups of individuals as over against particular roles. The child becomes enabled to do this by abstracting a "composite" role out of the concrete roles of particular persons. In the course of his association with others, then, he builds up a *generalized other,* a generalized role or standpoint from which he views himself and his behavior. This generalized other represents, then, the set of standpoints which are common to the group.

   Having achieved this generalized standpoint, the individual can conduct himself in an organized, consistent manner. He can view himself from a consistent standpoint. This means, then, that the individual can transcend the local and present expectations and definitions with which he comes in contact. An illustration of this point would be the Englishman who "dresses for dinner" in the wilds of Africa. Thus, through having a generalized other, the individual becomes emancipated from the pressures of the peculiarities of the immediate situation. He can act with a certain amount of consistency in a variety of situations because he acts in accordance with a generalized set of expectations and definitions that he has internalized.

The "I" and the "Me." The self is essentially a social process within the individual involving two analytically distinguishable phases: The "I" and the "Me."

The "I" is the impulsive tendency of the individual. It is the initial, spontaneous, unorganized aspect of human experience. Thus, it represents the undirected tendencies of the individual.

The "Me" represents the incorporated other within the individual. Thus, it comprises the organized set of attitudes and definitions, understandings and expectations—or simply meanings—common to the group. In any given situation the "Me" comprises the generalized other and, often, some particular other.

Every act begins in the form of an "I" and usually ends in the form of the "Me." For the "I" represents the initiation of the act prior to its coming under control of the definitions or expectations of others (the "Me"). The "I" thus gives *propulsion* while the "Me" gives *direction* to the act. Human behavior, then, can be viewed as a perpetual series of initiations of acts by the "I" and of acting-back-upon the act (that is, guidance of the act) by the "Me." The act is a resultant of this interplay.

The "I," being spontaneous and propulsive, offers the potentiality for new, creative activity. The "Me," being regulatory, disposes the individual to both goal-directed activity and conformity. In the operation of these aspects of the self, we have the basis for, on the one hand, social control and, on the other, novelty and innovation. We are thus provided with a basis for understanding the mutuality of the relationship between the individual and society.[3]

Implications of Selfhood. Some of the major implications of selfhood in human behavior are as follows:

1. The possession of a self makes of the individual a society in miniature. That is, he may engage in interaction with himself just as two or more different individuals might. In the course of this interaction, he can come to view himself in a new way, thereby bringing about changes in himself.
2. The ability to act toward oneself makes possible an inner experience which need not reach overt expression. That is, the individual, by virtue of having a self, is thereby endowed with the possibility of having a mental life: He can make indications to himself—which constitutes *mind.*
3. The individual with a self is thereby enabled to direct and control his behavior. Instead of being subject to all impulses and stimuli directly playing upon him, the individual can check, guide, and organize his behavior. He is, then, *not* a mere passive agent.

All three of these implications of selfhood may be summarized by the statement that the self and the mind (mental activity) are twin emergents in the social process.

3. Mind

Development of Mind. As in the instance of his consideration of the self, Mead rejects individualistic psychologies, in which the social process (society, social interaction) is viewed as presupposing, and being a product of, mind. In direct contrast is his view that mind presupposes, and is a product of, the social process. Mind is seen by Mead as developing correlatively with the self, constituting (in a very important sense) the self in action.

Mead's hypothesis regarding mind (as regarding the self) is that the mental emerges out of the organic life of man through communication. The mind is present only at certain points in human behavior, viz, when significant symbols are being used by the individual. This view dispenses with the substantive notion of mind as existing as a box-like container in the head, or as some kind of fixed, ever-present entity. Mind is seen as a *process,* which manifests itself whenever the individual is interacting with himself by using significant symbols.

Mead begins his discussion of the mind with a consideration of the relation of the organism to its environment. He points out that the central principle in all organic behavior is that of continuous adjustment, or adaptation, to an environing field. We cannot regard the environment as having a fixed character for all organisms, as being the same for all organisms. All behavior involves selective attention and perception. The organism accepts certain events in its field, or vicinity, as stimuli and rejects or overlooks certain others as irrelevant to its needs. (For example, an animal battling for life ignores food.) Bombarded constantly by stimuli, the organism selects those stimuli or aspects of its field which pertain to, are functional to, the acts in which the organism is engaged. Thus, the organism has a hand in determining the nature of its environment. What this means, then, is that Mead, along with Dewey, regards all life as ongoing activity, and views stimuli—not as initiators of activity—but as elements selected by the organism in the furtherance of that activity.

Perception is thus an activity that involves selective attention to certain aspects of a situation, rather than a mere matter of something coming into the individual's nervous system and leaving an impression. Visual perception, e.g., is more than a matter of just opening one's eyes and responding to what falls on the retina.

The determination of the environment by the biologic individual (infrahumans and the unsocialized infant) is not a cognitive relationship. It is selective, but does not involve consciousness, in the sense of reflective intelligence. At the distinctively human level, on the other hand, there is a hesitancy, an inhibition of overt conduct, which is *not* involved in the selective attention of animal behavior. In this period of inhibition, mind is present.

For human behavior involves inhibiting an act and trying out the varying approaches in imagination. In contrast, as we have seen, the acts of the biologic individual are relatively immediate, direct, and made up of innate or habitual ways of reacting. In other words, the unsocialized organism lacks consciousness of meaning. This being the case, the organism has no means for the abstract analysis of its field when new situations are met, and hence no means for the reorganization of action-tendencies in the light of that analysis.[4]

Minded behavior (in Mead's sense) arises around problems. It represents, to repeat an important point, a temporary inhibition of action wherein the individual is attempting to prevision the future. It consists of presenting to oneself, tentatively and in advance of overt behavior, the different possibilities or alternatives of future action with reference to a given situation. The future is, thus, present in terms of images of prospective lines of action from which the individual can make a selection. The mental process is, then, one of delaying, organizing, and selecting a response to the stimuli of the environment. This implies that the individual *constructs* his act, rather than responding in predetermined ways. Mind makes it possible for the individual purposively to control and organize his responses. Needless to say, this view contradicts the stimulus-response conception of human behavior.

When the act of an animal is checked, it may engage in overt trial and error or random activity. In the case of blocked human acts, the trial and error may be carried on covertly, implicitly. Consequences can be imaginatively "tried out" in advance. This is what is primarily meant by "mind," "reflective thinking," or "abstract thinking."

What this involves is the ability to indicate elements of the field or situation, abstract from the situation, and recombine them so that procedures can be considered in advance of their execution. Thus, to quote a well-known example, the intelligence of the detective as over against the intelligence of the bloodhound lies in the capacity of the former to isolate and indicate (to himself and to others) what the particular characters are which will call out the response of apprehending the fugitive criminal.

The mind is social in both origin and function. It arises in the social process of communication. Through association with the members of his groups, the individual comes to internalize the definitions transmitted to him through linguistic symbols, learns to assume the perspectives of others, and thereby acquires the ability to think. When the mind has risen in this process, it operates to maintain and adjust the individual in his society; and it enables the society to persist. The persistence of a human society depends, as we have seen, upon consensus; and consensus necessarily entails minded behavior.

The mind is social in function in the sense that the individual continually indicates to himself in the role of others and controls his activity with reference to the definitions provided by others. In order to carry on thought, he must have some standpoint from which to converse with himself. He gets this standpoint by importing into himself the roles of others.

By "taking the role of the other," as I earlier pointed out, we can see ourselves as others see us, and arouse in ourselves the responses that we call out in others. It is this conversation with ourselves, between the representation of the other (in the form of the "Me") and our impulses (in the form of the "I") that constitutes mind. Thus, what the individual actually does in minded behavior is to carry on an internal conversation. By addressing himself from the standpoint of the generalized other, the individual has a universe of discourse, a system of common symbols and meanings, with which to address himself. These are presupposed as the context for minded behavior.

Mead holds, then, that mental activity is a peculiar type of activity that goes on in the experience of the person. The activity is that of the person responding to himself, of indicating things to himself.

To repeat, mind originates in the social process, in association with others. There is little doubt that human beings lived together in groups before mind ever evolved. But there emerged, because of certain biological developments, the point where human beings were able to respond to their own acts and gestures. It was at this point that mind, or minded behavior, emerged. Similarly, mind comes into existence for the individual at the point where the individual is capable of responding to his own behavior, i.e., where he can designate things to himself.

Summarizing this brief treatment of mind, mental activity, or reflective thinking, we may say that it is a matter of making indications of meanings to oneself as to others. This is another way of saying that mind is the process of using significant symbols. For thinking goes on when an individual uses a symbol to call out in himself the responses which others would make. Mind, then, is symbolic behavior.[5] As such, mind is an emergent from nonsymbolic behavior and is fundamentally irreducible to the stimulus-response mechanisms which characterize the latter form of behavior.

It should be evident that Mead avoids both the behavioristic fallacy of reduction and the individualistic fallacy of taking for granted the phenomenon that is to be explained.

Objects. Returning to Mead's discussion of the organism-in-environment, we can now give more explicit attention to his treatment of *objects.* As we have seen, we cannot regard the environment as having a fixed character for all organisms. The environment is a function of the animal's own character, being greatly determined by the makeup of the animal. Each animal largely selects its own environment. It selects out the stimuli toward which it acts, its makeup and ongoing activity determining the kinds of stimuli it will select. Further, the qualities which are possessed by the objects toward which the animal acts arise from the kind of experiences that the animal has with the objects. (To illustrate, grass is not the same phenomenon for a cat and for a cow.) The environment and its qualities, then, are always functional to the structure of the animal.

As one passes on to the human level, the relation of the individual to the world becomes markedly more complicated. This is so because the human being is capable of forming objects. Animals, lacking symbols, see stimuli, such as patches of color—not objects. An object has to be detached, pointed out, "imaged" to oneself. The human being's environment is constituted largely by objects.

Now, let us look at the relation of the individual to objects. An object represents a plan of action. That is, an object doesn't exist for the individual in some pre-established form. Perception of any object has telescoped in it a series of experiences which one would have if he carried out the plan of action toward that object. The object has no qualities for the individual, aside from those which would result from his carrying out a plan of action. In this respect, the object is constituted by one's activities with reference to it. (For example, chalk is the sum of qualities which are perceived as a result of one's actions: a hard, smooth, white writing implement.)

The objects which constitute the "effective environment," the individual's experienced environment, are established by the individual's activities. To the extent that his activity varies, his environment varies. In other words, objects change as activities toward them change. (Chalk, for instance, may become a missile.)

Objects, which are constituted by the activities of the human individual, are largely *shared* objects. They stand for common patterns of activity of individuals. This is true, Mead points out, by virtue of the fact that objects arise, and are present in experience, only in the process of being indicated to oneself (and, hence, explicitly or implicitly, to others). In other words, the perspective from which one indicates an object implicates definitions by others. Needless to say, these definitions involve language, or significant symbols. The individual acquires a commonality of perspective with others by learning the symbols by which they designate aspects of the world.[6]

4. The Act

All human activity other than reflex and habitual action is built up in the process of its execution; i.e., behavior is constructed as it goes along, for decisions must be made at several points. The significance of this fact is that people act—rather than merely react.

For Mead, the unit of study is "the act," which comprises both overt and covert aspects of human action. Within the act, all the separated categories of the traditional, orthodox psychologies find a place. Attention, perception, imagination, reasoning, emotion, and so forth, are seen as parts of the act—rather than as more or less extrinsic influences upon it. Human behavior presents itself in the form of acts, rather than of concatenations of minute responses.

The act, then, encompasses the total process involved in human activity. It is viewed as a complete span of action: Its initial point is an impulse and its terminal point some objective which gives release to the impulse. In between, the individual is in the process of constructing, organizing his behavior. It is during this period that the act undergoes its most significant phase of development. In the case of human behavior, this period is marked by the play of images of possible goals or lines of action upon the impulse, thus directing the activity to its consummation.

In pointing out that the act begins with an impulse, Mead means that organisms experience disturbances of equilibrium. In the case of the lower animals, their biological makeup channelizes the impulse toward appropriate goals. In the case of the human being, the mere presence of an impulse leads to nothing but mere random, unorganized activity. This is most clearly—but definitely not exclusively—seen in the instance of the behavior of infants. Until the defining actions of others set up goals for it, the human infant's behavior is unchannelized. It is the function of images to direct, organize and construct this activity. The presence in behavior of images implies, of course, a process of indicating to oneself, or mind.

The act may have a short span (e.g., attending a particular class meeting, or starting a new page of notes) or may involve the major portion of a person's life (e.g., trying to achieve a successful career). Moreover, acts are parts of an interlacing of previous acts, are built up, one upon another. This is in contradistinction to the view that behavior is a series of discrete stimulus-response bonds. Conceiving human behavior in terms of acts, we become aware of the necessity for viewing any particular act within its psychosocial context.[7]

Using the concept of the act, Mead sets up classes of acts—the automatic act, the blocked act, the incomplete act, and the retrospective act—and analyzes them in terms of his frame of reference. Space does not permit presentation of these intriguing analyses.

C. Summary

At several points in this report the reader must have been aware of the extremely close interwoven character of Mead's various concepts. In the discussions of society, or self, and of mind, certain ideas seemed to require frequent (and, perhaps, repetitious) statement. A brief summary of Mead's position may help to reveal more meaningfully the way in which his key concepts interlock and logically imply one another.

The human individual is born into a society characterized by *symbolic interaction.* The use of *significant symbols* by those around him enables him to pass from the conversation of gestures—which involves direct, unmeaningful response to the overt acts of others—to the occasional *taking of the roles* of others. This role-taking enables him to share the perspectives of others. Concurrent with role-taking, the *self* develops, i.e., the capacity to act toward oneself. Action toward oneself comes to take the form of viewing oneself from the standpoint, or perspective, of the *generalized other* (the composite representative of others, of society, within the individual), which implies defining one's behavior in terms of the expectations of others. In the process of such viewing of oneself, the individual must carry on symbolic interaction with himself, involving an internal conversation between his impulsive aspect (the "I") and the incorporated perspectives of others (the "Me"). The *mind,* or mental activity, is present in behavior whenever such symbolic interaction goes on—whether the individual is merely "thinking" (in the everyday sense of the word) or is also interacting with another individual. (In both cases the individual must indicate things to himself.) Mental activity necessarily involves *meanings,* which usually attach to and define, *objects.* The meaning of an object or event is simply an image of the pattern of action which defines the object or event. That is, the completion in one's imagination of an act, or the mental picture of the actions and experiences symbolized by an object, defines the act or the object. In the unit of study that Mead calls "the act," all of the foregoing processes are usually entailed. The concluding point to be made in this summary is the same as the point with which I began: Mead's concepts intertwine and mutually imply one another. To drive home this important point, I must emphasize that human society (characterized by symbolic interaction) both precedes the rise of individual selves and minds, and is maintained by the rise of individual selves and minds. This means, then, that symbolic interaction is both the medium for the development of human beings and the process by which human beings associate as human beings.

Finally, it should be clearly evident by now that any distinctively human act necessarily involves: symbolic interaction, role-taking, meaning, mind, and self. Where one of these concepts is involved, the others are, also, necessarily involved. Here we see, unmistakably, the organic unity of Mead's position.

NOTES

1. The foregoing distinctions can also be expressed in terms of the differences between "signs," or "signals," and symbols. A sign stands for something else because of the fact that it is present at approximately the same time and place with that "something else." A symbol, on the other hand, stands for something else because its users have agreed to let it stand for that "something else." Thus, signs are directly and intrinsically linked with present or proximate situations; while symbols, having arbitrary and conventional, rather than intrinsic, meanings, transcend the immediate situation. (We shall return to this important point in our discussion of "mind.") Only symbols, of course, involve interpretation, self-stimulation and shared meaning.

2. To anyone who has taken even one course in sociology it is probably superfluous to stress the importance of symbols, particularly language, in the acquisition of all other elements of culture. The process of socialization is essentially a process of symbolic interaction.

3. At first glance, Mead's "I" and "Me" may appear to bear a close affinity with Freud's concepts of Id, Ego, and Superego. The resemblance is, for the most part, more apparent than real. While the Superego is held to be harshly frustrating and repressive of the instinctual, libidinous, and aggressive Id, the "Me" is held to provide necessary direction—often of a *gratifying* nature—to the otherwise undirected impulses constituting the "I." Putting the matter in figurative terms: Freud views the Id and the Superego as locked in combat upon the battleground of the Ego; Mead sees the "I" and "Me" engaged in close collaboration. This difference in perspective may derive from different preoccupations: Freud was primarily concerned with tension, anxiety, and "abnormal" behavior; Mead was primarily concerned with behavior generically.

It is true, on the other hand, that the Id, Ego, and Superego—particularly as modified by such neoFreudians as Karen Horney, Erich Fromm, and H. S. Sullivan—converge at a few points with the "I" and "Me." This is especially evident in the emphasis of both the Superego and "Me" concepts upon the internalization of the norms of significant others through the process of identification, or role-taking.

Incidentally, it should be noted that both sets of concepts refer to processes of behavior, *not* to concrete entities or structures. See, also, the discussion of "mind" which follows.

4. The reader should recognize here, in a new guise, our earlier distinction between signs and symbols. Signs have "intrinsic" meanings which induce direct reactions; symbols have arbitrary meanings which require interpretations by the actor prior to his response or action. The former, it will be recalled, are "tied to" the immediate situation, while the latter "transcend" the immediate situation. Thus, symbols may refer to past or future events, to hypothetical situations, to nonexistent or imaginary objects, and so forth.

5. A growing number of linguists, semanticists, and students of speech disorders are becoming aware of the central role of symbols in the *content,* as well as the process of thought. Edward Sapir and Benjamin Whorf have formulated "the principle of linguistic relativity," which holds that the structure of a language influences the manner in which the users of the language will perceive, comprehend, and act toward reality. Wendell Johnson, in the field of semantics, and Kurt Goldstein, in the study of aphasia, are representative investigators who have recognized the way in which symbols structure perception and thought. Mead's theory clearly foreshadows these developments.

6. The contrast between this view of learning and the neo-behavioristic "learning theory" of Clark Hull and other psychologists should be clearly evident. Basically, learning theorists attempt to reduce human learning to the mechanisms found in infrahuman learning.

This is reflected in their tendency to ignore the role of linguistic symbols in human behavior, their conceptualization of human activity in terms of stimulus-response couplets, and their view of learning as equivalent with conditioning. (For an excellent critique of learning theory from the symbolic interactionist standpoint, see: Manford H. Kuhn, "Kinsey's View of Human Behavior," *Social Problems,* 1 (April 1954), pp. 119–125.

7. The reader may have noted that this discussion makes no explicit reference to the problem of motivation. Mead had little to say regarding motives. Adherents to his general orientation have tended either to regard motives as implicit in the concept of *object* ("a plan of action") or to consider them "mere" verbal labels offered in supposed explanation of the actions of oneself or of others.

In my judgment, a conception of motivation can be formulated that is both useful and consistent with Mead's theories. Motivation can refer to "a process of defining (symbolically, of course) the goal of an act." Thus, while both human and infrahuman behavior may be viewed as goal-directed, only human behavior would be considered "motivated." Just as "motive" would be restricted to the human level, "drive" might serve a comparable function on the infrahuman level.

This would not imply that motives lie back of, or "cause," human acts. Rather, human acts are in constant process of construction, and the goal-definitions by individuals undergo constant reformulation. I mean to designate by "motive," however, the definition the individual makes, *at any given time,* of the objectives of his own specific acts. Such definitions, obviously, would be socially derived.

DISCUSSION QUESTIONS

1. Describe the genesis of the self. How does each stage contribute to the process of socialization?
2. According to Mead, human behavior is not a matter of responding directly to the activities of others. Rather, it involves responding to the intentions of others. What does this mean? What is social cooperation based on?

V

Social Structure and Groups

WHAT TO FOCUS ON:

1. How does the structure of group life produce power and morality in social relations?
2. By what means can the individual use social structured arrangements to present its sense of "self"?

It is often assumed that human interaction is spontaneous and subject to the free will of the individuals involved. Yet, for sociologists, nothing could be further from the truth. Sociology sees human interaction occurring within a context of inter-relationships of values, norms, roles, and statuses appropriate to a given situation. As such, social life is organized through these relationships: This organization is referred to as *social structure.*

Some simple examples are needed to demonstrate this concept. Do we greet our parents in the same way we greet our friends or fellow students, or our professors or bosses at work? Are there different topics of conversation more appropriate with one of these groups than the other? For instance, with whom are we more likely to talk about sex—parents, friends, bosses, etc.? The difference in our interaction and response is not solely due to the individual's personality and free will, but a consequence of role relationships, their different statuses and the values and norms of the situation. Therefore, we can say that human interaction takes place within a social structure. One of the results of this organization is that behavior becomes patterned and predictable. Students act in ways different from professors, children different from parents, and workers from bosses.

An additional point for the sociologist is that we come to rely upon this structure as providing for regularity of behavior, therefore creating a sense of normality. The idea of a "normal" family involves more than just the mother, father, and children. Also included in this conception are valuative and normative structures regarding emotional ties, role conceptions of what moms and dads do and expectations of children's behavior. The intriguing nature of social structure is that we may not always recognize its existence until its boundaries are violated. Why do we get upset over spouse or child abuse? What values and norms of family life are being violated?

Therefore, for sociologists, social structure becomes an important concept, reflecting the organization of culture's values and norms, and providing regularity in social behavior. The articles in this chapter demonstrate the importance of structure, but also show its complex intricacies and nuances we often take for granted.

Hans Gerth and C. Wright Mills demonstrate that the relationship between the person and one's social groups lies in the "role." The role is the means of maintaining social institutions and yet is also a means for the development of personal identity. The roles we play are related to the historical circumstance of the society. This article links the person, social institutions, and historical society together through this notion of the role.

Such structural arrangements are identified through the study of group life. The Weinberg article examines the concept of morality within a group often perceived as having little morality—nudists. Through this material we see group life among nudists as highly constrained by various rules and procedures which allow nudity to be exhibited without the usual attendant sexual connotations. To the outsider, images of people interacting in total nudity includes activity of a sexual nature. However, Weinberg demonstrates that group life among nudists indicates a highly organized morality that separates sexuality from nudity. How much of sex is free will and instinctual if it can be constrained by a group's structure of morality?

Erving Goffman's conceptualization of "the presentation of self" focuses upon the performance of the individual within a complex social setting. Can a social actor stage an impression in a way that elicits a certain response? Goffman's discussion maintains that the individual can create a performance much like that in theater. Such a creation is not merely the result of complete spontaneity, but as in the theater, the actor is provided with the basis for the performance through scenery, props, scripts, and direction. In real life, our role performance is created within the context of social structure. Goffman's material is significant in understanding the intimate link between individuality and group expectations.

Article 12

Institutions and Social Roles

HANS GERTH AND C. WRIGHT MILLS

OUT OF THE METAPHORS OF POETS and philosophers, who have likened man's conduct to that of the stage actor, sociologists have fashioned analytical tools. Long-used phrases readily come to mind: "playing a role" in the "great theater of public life," to move "in the limelight," the "theater of war," the "stage is all set." More technically, the concept "role" refers to units of conduct (1) which by their recurrence stand out as regularities and (2) which are oriented to the conduct of other actors. These recurrent interactions form patterns of mutually oriented conduct.

By definition, roles are interpersonal, that is, oriented to the conduct and expectations of others. These others, who expect things of us, are also playing roles: we expect them to act in certain ways and to refrain from acting and feeling in other ways. Interpersonal situations are thus built up and sets of roles held in line by mutual expectation, approbation, and disfavor.

Much of our social conduct, as we know from direct experience, is enacted in order to meet the expectations of others. In this sense, our enemies often control us as much as our friends. The father of a patriarchal family is expected by his wife and children to act in certain ways when confronted with given situations, and he in turn expects them to act in certain regular ways. Being acquainted with these simple facts about patriarchal families we expect regularities of conduct from each of their members, and having experienced family situations, we expect, with some degree of probability, that each of these members will experience his place and his self in a certain way.

Man as a person is an historical creation, and can most readily be understood in terms of the roles which he enacts and incorporates. These roles are limited by the kind of social institutions in which he happens to be born and in which he matures into an adult. His memory, his sense of time and space, his perception, his motives, his conception of his self . . . his psychological functions are shaped and steered by the specific configuration of roles which he incorporates from his society.

Perhaps the most important of these features of man is his image of his self, his idea of what kind of person he is. This experience of self is a crucially interpersonal one. Its basic organization is reflected from surrounding persons to whose approbation and criticism one pays attention.

What we think of ourselves is decisively influenced by what others think of us. Their attitudes of approval and of disapproval guide us in learning to play the roles we are assigned or which we assume. By internalizing these attitudes of others toward us and our conduct we not only gain new roles, but in time an image of ourselves. Of course, man's "looking-glass self" may be a true or a distorted reflection of his actual self. Yet those from whom a man continually seeks approval are important determinants of what kind of man he is becoming. If a young lawyer begins to feel satisfaction from the approval of the boss of the local political machine, if the labels which this boss uses to describe his behavior matter a lot to the lawyer, he is being steered into new roles and into a new image of his self by the party machine and its boss. Their values may in time become his own and he will apply them not only to other men but to his own actions as well.[1] The self, Harry Stack Sullivan once said, is made up of the reflected appraisals of others.[2]

The concept of role does not of course imply a one person-one role equation. One person may play many different roles, and each of these roles may be a segment of the different institutions and interpersonal situations in which the person moves. A corporation executive acts differently in his office than in his child's nursery. An adolescent girl enacts a different role when she is at a party composed of members of her own clique than when she is at her family's breakfast table. . . .

The roles allowed and expected, the self-images which they entail, and the consequences of these roles and images on the persons we are with are firmly embedded in a social context. Inner psychological changes and the institutional controls of a society are thus interlinked.

An institution is an organization of roles, which means that the roles carry different degrees of authority, so that one of the roles—we may call it the "head" role—is understood and accepted by the members of the other roles as guaranteeing the relative permanence of the total conduct pattern. An *institution* is thus (1) an organization of roles, (2) one or more of which is understood to serve the maintenance of the total set of roles. . . .

By choosing the social role as a major concept we are able to reconstruct the inner experience of the person as well as the institutions which make up an historical social structure. For man as a *person* (from the Latin *persona,* meaning "mask") is composed of the specific roles which he enacts and of the effects of enacting these roles upon his self. And society as a *social structure* is composed of roles as segments variously combined in its total circle of institutions. The organization of roles is important in building up a particular social structure; it also has psychological implications for the persons who act out the social structure.

Most of the various interpersonal situations in which we are involved exist within institutions, which make up a social structure and changes of social structure make up the main course of human history. In order to understand men's conduct and experience we must reconstruct the historical social structures in which they play roles and acquire selves. For such regularity of conduct, and of the motives for this conduct, as we may find will rest upon the historical regularities of these social structures, rather than upon any suprahistorical, biological elements assumed to be innate and constant within the organism. From the sociological point of view, man as a person is a social-historical creation. If his view of his self and of his motives is intimately connected with the roles which are available to him and which he incorporates, then we may not expect to learn much that is very concrete about individual men unless we investigate a number of his specific roles in a number of varied social-historical settings.

Rather than constant elements within a physiological organism, the sociologist rests his primary model of explanation upon the interpersonal situations, and in the last analysis, the social structures within which persons live out their lives.

NOTES

1. The mechanism by which persons thus internalize roles and the attitudes of others is language. Language is composed of gestures, normally verbal, which call forth similar responses in two individuals. Without such gestures man could not incorporate the attitudes of others and could not so easily make these attitudes a condition of his own learning and enactment of roles of his own image of self.

2. "Conceptions of Modern Psychiatry," *Psychiatry,* Vol. III, No. 1 (February 1949), pp. 10–11. Compare also C. H. Cooley's *Human Nature and the Social Order* (rev. ed.; New York: Scribner's, 1922). The tradition is well documented by Fay B. Karpf, *American Social Psychology* (New York: McGraw-Hill, 1932).

DISCUSSION QUESTIONS

1. What is the significance of "role" in connecting the individual with the group?
2. What is a social institution and what is its significance to social structure?

Article 13

The Nudist Management of Respectability

MARTIN S. WEINBERG

PUBLIC NUDITY IS TABOO in our society. Yet there is a group who breach this moral rule. They call themselves "social nudists."

A number of questions may be asked about these people. For example, how can they see their behavior as morally appropriate? Have they constructed their own morality? If so, what characterizes this morality and what are its consequences?[1]

This article will attempt to answer these questions through a study of social interaction in nudist camps. The data come from three sources: two summers of participant observation in nudist camps; 101 interviews with nudists in the Chicago area; and 617 mailed questionnaires completed by nudists in the United States and Canada.[2]

The Construction of Situated Moral Meanings: The Nudist Morality

The construction of morality in nudist camps is based on the official interpretations that camps provide regarding the moral meanings of public heterosexual nudity. These are (1) that nudity and sexuality are unrelated, (2) that there is nothing

From "The Nudist Management of Respectability," by Martin S. Weinberg. *Sex Research: Studies from the Kinsey Institute,* Oxford University Press, New York, 1976, pp. 217–232. Reprinted by permission.

shameful about the human body, (3) that nudity promotes a feeling of freedom and natural pleasure, and (4) that nude exposure to the sun promotes physical, mental, and spiritual well-being.

This official perspective is sustained in nudist camps to an extraordinary degree, illustrating the extent to which adult socialization can affect traditional moral meanings. (This is especially true with regard to the first two points of the nudist perspective, which will be our primary concern since these are its "deviant" aspects.) The assumption in the larger society that nudity and sexuality are related, and the resulting emphasis on covering the sexual organs, make the nudist perspective a specifically situated morality. My field work, interview, and questionnaire research show that nudists routinely use a special system of rules to create, sustain, and enforce this situated morality.

Strategies for Sustaining a Situated Morality

The first strategy used by the nudist camp to anesthetize any relationship between nudity and sexuality[3] involves a system of organizational precautions regarding who can come into the camp. Most camps, for example, regard unmarried people, especially single men, as a threat to the nudist morality. They suspect that singles may indeed see nudity as something sexual. Thus, most camps either exclude unmarried people (especially men), or allow only a small quota of them. Camps that do allow single men may charge them up to 35 per cent more than they charge families. (This is intended to discourage single men, but since the cost is still relatively low compared with other resorts, this measure is not very effective. It seems to do little more than create resentment among the singles, and by giving formal organizational backing to the definition that singles are not especially desirable, it may contribute to the segregation of single and married members in nudist camps.)

Certification by the camp owner is another requirement for admission to camp grounds, and three letters of recommendation regarding the applicant's character are sometimes required. These regulations help preclude people whom members regard as a threat to the nudist morality.

> [The camp owner] invited us over to see if we were *desirable* people. Then after we did this, he invited us to camp on probation; then they voted us into camp. [Q: Could you tell me what you mean by desirable people?] Well, not people who are inclined to drink, or people who go there for a peep show. Then they don't want you there. They feel you out in conversation. They want people for mental and physical health reasons.
>
> Whom to admit [is the biggest problem of the camp]. [Q][4] Because the world is so full of people whose attitudes on nudity are hopelessly warped. [Q: Has this always been the biggest problem in camp?] Yes. Every time anybody comes, a decision has to be made. [Q] . . . The lady sitting at the gate decides about admittance. The director decides on membership.

A limit is sometimes set on the number of trial visits a non-member may make to camp. In addition, there is usually a limit on how long a person can remain clothed. This is a strategy to mark guests who may not sincerely accept the nudist perspective.

The second strategy for sustaining the nudist morality involves norms of interpersonal behavior. These norms are as follows:

No Staring. This rule controls overt signs of overinvolvement. As the publisher of one nudist magazine said, "They all look up to the heavens and never look below." Such studied inattention is most exaggerated among women, who usually show no recognition that the male is unclothed. Women also recount that they had expected men to look at their nude bodies, only to find, when they finally did get up the courage to undress, that no one seemed to notice. As one woman states: "I got so mad because my husband wanted me to undress in front of other men that I just pulled my clothes right off thinking everyone would look at me." She was amazed (and somewhat disappointed) when no one did.

The following statements illustrate the constraints that result:

> [Q: Have you ever observed or heard about anyone staring at someone's body while at camp?] I've heard stories, particularly about men that stare. Since I heard these stories, I tried not to, and have even done away with my sunglasses after someone said, half-joking, that I hide behind sunglasses to stare. Toward the end of the summer I stopped wearing sunglasses. And you know what, it was a child who told me this.
>
> [Q: Would you stare. . . ?] Probably not, cause you can get in trouble and get thrown out. If I thought I could stare unobserved I might. They might not throw you out, but it wouldn't do you any good. [Q] The girl might tell others and they might not want to talk to me. . . . [Q] They disapprove by not talking to you, ignoring you, etc.
>
> [Someone who stares] wouldn't belong there. [Q] If he does that he is just going to camp to see the opposite sex. [Q] He is just coming to stare. [Q] You go there to swim and relax.
>
> I try very hard to look at them from the jaw up—even more than you would normally.[5]

No Sex Talk. Sex talk, or telling "dirty jokes," is uncommon in camp. The owner of a large camp in the Midwest stated: "It is usually expected that members of a nudist camp will not talk about sex, politics, or religion." Or as one single male explained: "It is taboo to make sexual remarks here." During my field work, it was rare to hear "sexual" joking such as one hears at most other types of resort. Interview respondents who mentioned that they had talked about sex qualified this by explaining that such talk was restricted to close friends, was of a "scientific nature," or, if a joke, was of a "cute sort."

Asked what they would think of someone who breached this rule, respondents indicated that such behavior would cast doubt on the situated morality of the nudist camp:

> One would expect to hear less of that at camp than at other places. [Q] Because you expect that the members are screened in their attitude for nudism—and this isn't one who prefers sexual jokes.

I've never heard anyone swear or tell a dirty joke out there.

No. Not at camp. You're not supposed to. You bend over backwards not to.

They probably don't belong there. They're there to see what they can find to observe. [Q] Well, their mind isn't on being a nudist, but to see so and so nude.

No Body Contact. Although the extent to which this is enforced varies from camp to camp, there is at least some degree of informal enforcement in nearly every camp. Nudists mention that they are particularly careful not to brush against anyone or have any body contact for fear of how it might be interpreted:

I stay clear of the opposite sex. They're so sensitive, they imagine things.

People don't get too close to you. Even when they talk. They sit close to you, but they don't get close enough to touch you.

We have a minimum of contact. There are more restrictions [at a nudist camp]. [Q] Just a feeling I had. I would openly show my affection more readily someplace else.

And when asked to conceptualize a breach of this rule, the following response is typical:

They are in the wrong place. [Q] That's not part of nudism. [Q] I think they are there for some sort of sex thrill. They are certainly not there to enjoy the sun.

Also, in photographs taken for nudist magazines, the subjects usually have only limited body contact. One female nudist explained: "We don't want anyone to think we're immoral." Outsiders' interpretations, then, can also constitute a threat.

Associated with the body contact taboo is a prohibition of nude dancing. Nudists cite this as a separate rule. This rule is often talked about by members in a way that indicates organizational strain—that is, the rule itself makes evident that a strategy is in operation to sustain their situated morality.

This reflects a contradiction in our beliefs. But it's self-protection. One incident and we'd be closed.

No Alcoholic Beverages in American Camps. This rule guards against breakdowns in inhibition, and even respondents who admitted that they had "snuck a beer" before going to bed went on to say that they fully favor the rule.

Yes. We have [drunk at camp]. We keep a can of beer in the refrigerator since we're out of the main area. We're not young people or carousers. . . . I still most generally approve of it as a camp rule and would disapprove of anyone going to extremes. [Q] For common-sense reasons. People who overindulge lose their inhibitions, and there is no denying that the atmosphere of a nudist camp makes one bend over backwards to keep people who are so inclined from going beyond the bounds of propriety.

Anyone who drinks in camp is jeopardizing their membership and they shouldn't. Anyone who drinks in camp could get reckless. [Q] Well, when guys and girls drink they're a lot bolder—they might get fresh with someone else's girl. That's why it isn't permitted, I guess.

Rules Regarding Photography. Photography in a nudist camp is controlled by the camp management. Unless the photographer works for a nudist magazine, his (or her) moral perspective is sometimes suspect. One photographer's remark to a woman that led to his being so typed was, "Do you think you could open your legs a little more?"

Aside from a general restriction on the use of cameras, when cameras are allowed, it is expected that no pictures will be taken without the subject's permission. Members blame the misuse of cameras especially on single men. As one nudist said: "You always see the singles poppin' around out of nowhere snappin' pictures." In general, control is maintained, and any infractions that take place are not blatant or obvious. Overindulgence in picture-taking communicates an overinvolvement in the subjects' nudity and casts doubt on the assumption that nudity and sexuality are unrelated.

> Photographers dressed only in cameras and light exposure meters. I don't like them. I think they only go out for pictures. Their motives should be questioned.

Photographers for nudist magazines recognize the signs that strain the situated morality that characterizes nudist camps. As one such photographer commented:

> I never let a girl look straight at the camera. It looks too suggestive. I always have her look off to the side.

Similarly, a nudist model showed the writer a pin-up magazine to point out how a model could make a nude picture "sexy"—through the use of various stagings, props, and expressions—and in contrast, how the nudist model eliminates these techniques to make her pictures "natural." Although it may be questionable that a nudist model completely eliminates a sexual perspective for the non-nudist, the model discussed how she attempts to do this.

> It depends on the way you look. Your eyes and your smile can make you look sexy. The way they're looking at you. Here, she's on a bed. It wouldn't be sexy if she were on a beach with kids running around. They always have some clothes on too. See how she's "looking sexy"? Like an "oh dear!" look. A different look can change the whole picture.
>
> Now here's a decent pose. . . . Outdoors makes it "nature." Here she's giving you "the eye," or is undressing. It's cheesecake. It depends on the expression on her face. Having nature behind it makes it better. Don't smile like "come on honey!" It's that look and the lace thing she has on. . . . Like when you half-close your eyes, like "oh baby," a Marilyn Monroe look. Art is when you don't look like you're hiding it halfway.

The element of trust plays a particularly strong role in socializing women to the nudist perspective. Consider this in the following statements made by another model for nudist magazines. She and her husband had been indoctrinated in the nudist ideology by friends. At the time of the interview, however, the couple had not yet been to camp, although they had posed indoors for nudist magazines.

> [Three months ago, before I was married] I never knew a man had any pubic hairs. I was shocked when I was married. . . . I wouldn't think of getting undressed in front of my husband. I wouldn't make love with a light on, or in the daytime.

With regard to being a nudist model, this woman commented:

> None of the pictures are sexually seductive. [Q] The pose, the look—you can have a pose that's completely nothing, till you get a look that's not too hard to do. [Q: How do you do that?] I've never tried. By putting on a certain air about a person; a picture that couldn't be submitted to a nudist magazine—using _______ [the nudist photographer's] language. . . . [Q: Will your parents see your pictures in the magazine?] Possibly. I don't really care. . . . My mother might take it all right. But they've been married twenty years and she's never seen my dad undressed.[6]

No Accentuation of the Body. Accentuating the body is regarded as incongruent with the nudist morality. Thus, a woman who had shaved her pubic hair was labeled "disgusting" by other members. There was a similar reaction to women who sat in a blatantly "unladylike" manner.

> I'd think she was inviting remarks. [Q] I don't know. It seems strange to think of it. It's strange you ask it. Out there, they're not unconscious about their posture. Most women there are very circumspect even though in the nude.
>
> For a girl, . . . [sitting with your legs open] is just not feminine or ladylike. The hair doesn't always cover it. [Q] Men get away with so many things. But, it would look dirty for a girl, like she was waiting for something. When I'm in a secluded area I've spread my legs to sun, but I kept an eye open and if anyone came I'd close my legs and sit up a little. It's just not ladylike.
>
> You can lay on your back or side, or with your knees under your chin. But not with your legs spread apart. It would look to other people like you're there for other reasons. [Q: What other reasons?] . . . To stare and get an eyeful. . . . not to enjoy the sun and people.

No Unnatural Attempts at Covering the Body. "Unnatural attempts" at covering the body are ridiculed since they call into question the assumption that there is no shame in exposing any area of the body. If such behavior occurs early in one's nudist career, however, members usually have more compassion, assuming that the person just has not yet fully assimilated the new morality.

It is how members interpret the behavior, however, rather than the behavior per se, that determines whether covering up is disapproved.

> If they're cold or sunburned, it's understandable. If it's because they don't agree with the philosophy, they don't belong there.
>
> I would feel their motives for becoming nudists were not well founded. That they were not true nudists, not idealistic enough.

A third strategy that is sometimes employed to sustain the nudist reality is the use of communal toilets. Not all the camps have communal toilets, but the large camp where I did most of my field work did have such a facility, which was marked, "Little Girls Room and Little Boys Too." Although the stalls had three-quarter-length doors, this combined facility still helped to provide an element of consistency; as the owner said, "If you are not ashamed of any part of your body or any of its natural functions, men and women do not need separate toilets." Thus, even the physical ecology of the nudist camp was designed to be consistent with the nudist morality. For some, however, communal toilets were going too far.

> I think they should be separated. For myself it's all right. But there are varied opinions, and for the satisfaction of all, I think they should separate them. There are niceties of life we often like to maintain, and for some people this is embarrassing. . . . [Q] You know, in a bowel movement it always isn't silent.

The Routinization of Nudity

In the nudist camp, nudity becomes routinized; its attention-provoking quality recedes, and nudity becomes a taken-for-granted state of affairs. Thus, when asked questions about staring ("While at camp, have you ever stared at anyone's body? Do you think you would stare at anyone's body?"), nudists indicate that nudity generally does not invoke their attention.

> Nudists don't care what bodies are like. They're out there for themselves. It's a matter-of-fact thing. After a while you feel like you're sitting with a full suit of clothes on.
>
> To nudists the body becomes so matter-of-fact, whether clothed or unclothed, when you make it an undue point of interest it becomes an abnormal thing.
>
> [Q: What would you think of someone staring?] I would feel bad and let down. [Q] I have it set up on a high standard. I have never seen it happen. . . . [Q] Because it's not done there. It's above that; you don't stare. . . . If I saw it happen, I'd be startled. There's no inclination to do that. Why would they?
>
> There are two types—male and female. I couldn't see why they were staring. I wouldn't understand it.

In fact, these questions about staring elicit from nudists a frame of possibilities in which what is relevant to staring is ordinarily not nudity itself. Rather, what evokes attention is something unusual, something the observer seldom sees and thus is not routinized to.[7]

> There was a red-haired man. He had red pubic hair. I had never seen this before. . . . He didn't see me. If anyone did, I would turn the other way.
>
> Well, once I was staring at a pregnant woman. It was the first time I ever saw this. I was curious, her stomach stretched, the shape. . . . I also have stared at extremely obese people, cripples. All this is due to curiosity, just a novel sight. [Q] . . . I was discreet. [Q] I didn't look at them when their eyes were fixed in a direction so they could tell I was.
>
> [Q: While at camp have you ever stared at someone's body?] Yes. [Q] A little girl. She has a birthmark on her back, at the base of her spine.
>
> [Q: Do you think you would ever stare at someone's body while at camp?] No. I don't like that. I think it's silly. . . . What people are is not their fault if they are deformed.
>
> I don't think it would be very nice, very polite. [Q] I can't see anything to stare at, whether it's a scar or anything else. [Q] It just isn't done.
>
> I've looked, but not stared. I'm careful about that, because you could get in bad about that. [Q] Get thrown out by the owner. I was curious when I once had a

> perfect view of a girl's sex organs, because her legs were spread when she was sitting on a chair. I sat in the chair across from her in perfect view of her organs. [Q] For about ten or fifteen minutes. [Q] Nobody noticed. [Q] It's not often you get that opportunity."[8]
>
> [Q: How would you feel if you were alone in a secluded area of camp sunning yourself, and then noticed that other nudists were staring at your body?] I would think I had some mud on me. [Q] . . . I would just ask them why they were staring at me. Probably I was getting sunburn and they wanted to tell me to turn over, or maybe I had a speck of mud on me. [Q] These are the only two reasons I can think of why they were staring.

In the nudist camp, the arousal of attention by nudity is usually regarded as *unnatural.* Thus, staring is unnatural, especially after a period of grace in which to adjust to the new meanings.

> If he did it when he was first there, I'd figure he's normal. If he kept it up I'd stay away from him, or suggest to the owner that he be thrown out. [Q] At first it's a new experience, so he might be staring. [Q] He wouldn't know how to react to it. [Q] The first time seeing nudes of the opposite sex. [Q] I'd think if he kept staring, that he's thinking of something, like grabbing someone, running to the bushes and raping them. [Q] Maybe he's mentally unbalanced.
>
> He just sat there watching the women. You can forgive it the first time, because of curiosity. But not every weekend. [Q] The owner asked him to leave.
>
> These women made comments on some men's shapes. They said, "He has a hairy body or ugly bones," or "Boy his wife must like him because he's hung big." That was embarrassing. . . . I thought they were terrible. [Q] Because I realized they were walking around looking. I can't see that.

Organizations and the Constitution of Normality

The rules-in-use of an organization *and the reality they sustain* form the basis on which behaviors are interpreted as "unnatural."[9] Overinvolvement in nudity, for example, is interpreted by nudists as unnatural (and not simply immoral). Similarly, erotic stimuli or responses, which breach the nudist morality, are defined as unnatural.

> They let one single in. He acted peculiar. . . . He got up and had a big erection. I didn't know what he'd do at night. He might molest a child or anybody. . . . My husband went and told the owner.
>
> I told you about this one on the sundeck with her legs spread. She made no bones about closing up. Maybe it was an error, but I doubt it. It wasn't a normal position. Normally you wouldn't lay like this. It's like standing on your head. She had sufficient time and there were people around.
>
> She sat there with her legs like they were straddling a horse. I don't know how else to describe it. [Q] She was just sitting on the ground. [Q] I think she's a dirty pig. [Q] If you sit that way, everyone don't want to know what she had for breakfast. [Q] It's just the wrong way to sit. You keep your legs together even with clothes on.
>
> [Q: Do you think it is possible for a person to be modest in a nudist camp?] I think so. [Q] If a person acts natural. . . . An immodest person would be an exhibitionist, and you find them in nudism too. . . . Most people's conduct is all right.

When behaviors are constituted as *unnatural,* attempts to understand them are usually suspended, and reciprocity of perspectives is called into question. (The "reciprocity of perspectives" involves the assumption that if one changed places with the other, one would, for all practical purposes, see the world as the other sees it.[10])

> [Q: What would you think of a man who had an erection at camp?] Maybe they can't control themselves. [Q] Better watch out for him. [Q] I would tell the camp director to keep an eye on him. And the children would question that. [Q: What would you tell them?] I'd tell them the man is sick or something.
>
> [Q: What would you think of a Peeping Tom—a non-nudist trespasser?] They should be reported and sent out. [Q] I think they shouldn't be there. They're sick. [Q] Mentally. [Q] Because anyone who wants to look at someone else's body; well, is a Peeping Tom, is sick in the first place. He looks at you differently than a normal person would. [Q] With ideas of sex.
>
> [A trespasser] . . . is sick. He probably uses this as a source of sexual stimulation.

Such occurrences call into question the taken-for-granted character of nudity in the nudist camp and the situated morality that is officially set forth.

Inhibiting Breakdowns in the Nudist Morality

Organized nudism promulgates a nonsexual perspective toward nudity, and breakdowns in that perspective are inhibited by (1) controlling erotic actions and (2) controlling erotic reactions. Nudity is partitioned off from other forms of "immodesty" (e.g., verbal immodesty, erotic overtures). In this way, a person can learn more easily to attribute a new meaning to nudity.[11] When behaviors occur that reflect other forms of "immodesty," however, nudists often fear a voiding of the nonsexual meaning that they impose on nudity.

> This woman with a sexy walk would shake her hips and try to arouse the men. . . . [Q] These men went to the camp director to complain that the woman had purposely tried to arouse them. The camp director told this woman to leave.

Nudists are sensitive to the possibility of a breakdown in the nudist morality. Thus, they have a low threshold for interpreting acts as "sexual."

> Playing badminton, this teenager was hitting the birdie up and down and she said, "What do you think of that?" I said, "Kind of sexy." ________ [the president of the camp] said I shouldn't talk like that, but I was only kidding.

Note the following description of "mauling":

> I don't like to see a man and a girl mauling each other in the nude before others. . . . [Q: Did you ever see this at camp?] I saw it once. . . . [Q: What do you mean by mauling?] Just, well, I never saw him put his hands on her breast, but he was running his hands along her arms.

This sensitivity to "sexual" signs also sensitizes nudists to the possibility that certain of their own acts, although not intended as "sexual," might nonetheless be interpreted that way.

> Sometimes you're resting and you spread your legs unknowingly. [Q] My husband just told me not to sit that way. [Q] I put my legs together.

Since "immodesty" is defined as an unnatural manner of behavior, such behaviors are easily interpreted as being motivated by "dishonorable" intent. When the individual is thought to be in physical control of the "immodest" behavior and to know the behavior's meaning within the nudist scheme of interpretation, sexual intentions are assigned. Referring to a quotation that was presented earlier, one man said that a woman who was lying with her legs spread may have been doing so unintentionally, "but I doubt it. [Q] It wasn't a normal position. Normally you wouldn't lay like this. It's like standing on your head."

Erotic reactions, as well as erotic actions, are controlled in camp. Thus, even when erotic stimuli come into play, erotic responses may be inhibited.

> When lying on the grass already hiding my penis, I got erotic thoughts. And then one realizes it can't happen here. With fear there isn't much erection.
>
> Yes, once I started to have an erection. Once. [Q] A friend told me how he was invited by some young lady to go to bed. [Q] I started to picture the situation and I felt the erection coming on; so I immediately jumped in the pool. It went away.
>
> I was once in the woods alone and ran into a woman. I felt myself getting excited. A secluded spot in the bushes which was an ideal place for procreation. [Q] Nothing happened, though.

When breaches of the nudist morality do occur, other nudists' sense of modesty may inhibit sanctioning. The immediate breach may go unsanctioned. The observers may feign inattention or withdraw from the scene. The occurrence is usually communicated, however, via the grapevine, and it may reach the camp director.

> We were shooting a series of pictures and my wife was getting out of her clothes. ________ [the photographer] had an erection but went ahead like nothing was happening. [Q] It was over kind of fast. . . . [Q] Nothing. We tried to avoid the issue. . . . Later we went to see ________ [the camp director] and ________ [the photographer] denied it.
>
> [If a man had an erection] people would probably pretend they didn't see it.
>
> [Q: What do you think of someone this happens to?] They should try to get rid of it fast. It don't look nice. Nudists are prudists. They are more prudish. Because they take their clothes off they are more careful. [Q] They become more prudish than people with clothes. They won't let anything out of the way happen.

As indicated in the remark, "nudists are prudists," nudists may at times become aware of the fragility of their situated moral meanings.

> At ________ [camp], this family had a small boy no more than ten years old who had an erection. Mrs. ________ [the owner's wife] saw him and told his parents

that they should keep him in check, and tell him what had happened to him and to watch himself. This was silly, for such a little kid who didn't know what happened.

Deviance and Multiple Realities

There are basic social processes that underlie responses to deviance. Collectivities control thresholds of response to various behaviors, determining the relevance, meaning, and importance of the behavior. In the nudist camp, as pointed out previously, erotic overtures and erotic responses are regarded as unnatural, and reciprocity of perspectives is called into question by such behaviors.

> We thought this single was all right, until others clued us in that he had brought girls up to camp. [Then we recalled that] . . . he was kind of weird. The way he'd look at you. He had glassy eyes, like he could see through you.[12]

Such a response to deviance in the nudist camp is a result of effective socialization to the new system of moral meanings. The deviant's behavior, on the other hand, can be construed as reflecting an ineffective socialization to the new system of meanings.

> I think it's impossible [to have an erection in a nudist camp]. [Q] In a nudist camp you must have some physical contact and a desire to have one.
>
> He isn't thinking like a nudist. [Q] The body is wholesome, not . . . a sex object. He'd have to do that—think of sex.
>
> Sex isn't supposed to be in your mind, as far as the body. He doesn't belong there. [Q] If you go in thinking about sex, naturally it's going to happen. . . . You're not supposed to think about going to bed with anyone, not even your wife.

As these quotes illustrate, the unnaturalness or deviance of a behavior is ordinarily determined by relating it to an institutionalized scheme of interpretation. Occurrences that are "not understandable" in the reality of one collectivity may, however, be quite understandable in the reality of another collectivity.[13] Thus, what are "deviant" occurrences in nudist camps probably would be regarded by members of the clothed society as natural and understandable rather than unnatural and difficult to understand.

Finally, a group of people may subscribe to different and conflicting interpretive schemes. Thus, the low threshold of nudists to anything "sexual" is a function of their marginality; the fact that they have not completely suspended the moral meanings of the clothed society is what leads them to constitute many events as "sexual" in purpose.

NOTES

1. In my previous papers, I have dealt with other questions that are commonly asked about nudists. How persons become nudists is discussed in my "Becoming a Nudist,"

Psychiatry, XXIX (February, 1966), 15–24. A report on the nudist way of life and social structure can be found in my article in *Human Organization,* XXVI (Fall, 1967), 91–99.

2. Approximately one hundred camps were represented in the interviews and questionnaires. Interviews were conducted in the homes of nudists during the off season. Arrangements for the interviews were initially made with these nudists during the first summer of participant observation; selection of respondents was limited to those living within a one-hundred-mile radius of Chicago. The questionnaires were sent to all members of the National Nudist Council. The different techniques of data collection provided a test of convergent validation.

3. For a discussion of the essence of such relationships, see Alfred Schutz, *Collected Papers: The Problem of Social Reality,* Maurice Natanson, ed. (The Hague: Nijhoff, 1962), I, 287 ff.

4. [Q] is used to signify a neutral probe by the interviewer that follows the course of the last reply, such as "Could you tell me some more about that?" or "How is that?" or "What do you mean?" Other questions by the interviewer are given in full.

5. The King and Queen contest, which takes place at conventions, allows for a patterned evasion of the staring rule. Applicants stand before the crowd in front of the royal platform, and applause is used for selecting the winners. Photography is also allowed during the contest, and no one is permitted to enter the contest unless willing to be photographed. The major reason for this is that this is a major camp event, and contest pictures are used in nudist magazines. At the same time, the large number of photographs taken by lay photographers (that is, not working for the magazines), makes many nudists uncomfortable by calling into question a nonsexual definition of the situation.

6. I was amazed at how many young female nudists described a similar pattern of extreme clothing modesty among their parents and in their own married life. Included in this group was another nudist model, one of the most photographed of nudist models. Perhaps there are some fruitful data here for cognitive-dissonance psychologists.

7. Cf. Schutz, *op. cit.,* p. 74

8. For some respondents, the female genitals, because of their hidden character, never become a routinized part of camp nudity; thus their visible exposure does not lose an attention-provoking quality.

9. Compare Harold Garfinkel, "A Conception of, and Experiments with, 'Trust' as a Condition of Stable Concerted Actions," in O. J. Harvey, ed., *Motivation and Social Interaction* (New York: Ronald, 1963).

10. See: Schutz, *op. cit.,* I, 11, for his definition of reciprocity of perspectives.

11. This corresponds with the findings of learning-theory psychologists.

12. For a study of the process of doublethink, see James L. Wilkins, "Doublethink: A Study of Erasure of the Social Past," unpublished doctoral dissertation, Northwestern University, 1964.

13. Cf. Schutz, *op. cit.,* pp. 229 ff.

DISCUSSION QUESTIONS

1. What characterizes the morality of nudists?
2. Through what procedures do nudist camps maintain their morality?

Article 14
Presentation of Self in Everyday Life

ERVING GOFFMAN

PERFORMANCES

Belief in the Part One Is Playing

WHEN AN INDIVIDUAL plays a part he implicitly requests his observers to take seriously the impression that is fostered before them. They are asked to believe that the character they see actually possesses the attributes he appears to possess, that the task he performs will have the consequences that are implicitly claimed for it, and that, in general, matters are what they appear to be. In line with this, there is the popular view that the individual offers his performance and puts on his show "for the benefit of other people." It will be convenient to begin a consideration of performances by turning the question around and looking at the individual's own belief in the impression of reality that he attempts to engender in those among whom he finds himself.

At one extreme, one finds that the performer can be fully taken in by his own act; he can be sincerely convinced that the impression of reality which he stages is the real reality. When his audience is also convinced in this way about the show he puts on—and this seems to be the typical case—then for the moment at least, only the sociologist or the socially disgruntled will have any doubts about the "realness" of what is presented.

At the other extreme, we find that the performer may not be taken in at all by his own routine. This possibility is understandable, since no one is in quite as good an observational position to see through the act as the person who puts it on. Coupled with this, the performer may be moved to guide the conviction of his audience only as a means to other ends, having no ultimate concern in the conception that they have of him or of the situation. When the individual has no belief in his own act and no ultimate concern with the beliefs of his audience, we may call him cynical, reserving the term "sincere" for individuals who believe in the impression fostered by their own performance. It should be understood that the cynic, with all his professional disinvolvement, may obtain unprofessional pleasures from his masquerade, experiencing a kind of gleeful spiritual aggression from the fact that he can toy at will with something his audience must take seriously.[1]

It is not assumed, of course, that all cynical performers are interested in deluding their audiences for purposes of what is called "self-interest" or private gain. A cynical individual may delude his audience for what he considers to be their own good, or for the good of the community, etc. For illustrations of this we need not appeal to sadly enlightened showmen such as Marcus Aurelius or Hsun Tzu. We know that in service occupations practitioners who may otherwise be sincere are sometimes forced to delude their customers because their customers show such a heartfelt demand for it. Doctors who are led into giving placebos, filling station attendants who resignedly check and recheck tire pressures for anxious women motorists, shoe clerks who sell a shoe that fits but tell the customer it is the size she wants to hear—these are cynical performers whose audiences will not allow them to be sincere. Similarly, it seems that sympathetic patients in mental wards will sometimes feign bizarre symptoms so that student nurses will not be subjected to a disappointingly sane performance.[2] So also, when inferiors extend their most lavish reception for visiting superiors, the selfish desire to win favor may not be the chief motive; the inferior may be tactfully attempting to put the superior at ease by simulating the kind of world the superior is thought to take for granted.

I have suggested two extremes: an individual may be taken in by his own act or be cynical about it. These extremes are something a little more than just the ends of a continuum. Each provides the individual with a position which has its own particular securities and defenses, so there will be a tendency for those who have traveled close to one of these poles to complete the voyage. . . .

Front

I have been using the term "performance" to refer to all the activity of an individual which occurs during a period marked by his continuous presence before a particular set of observers and which has some influence on the observers. It will be convenient to label as "front" that part of the individual's performance which regularly functions in a general and fixed fashion to define the situation for those who observe the performance. Front, then, is the expressive equipment of a standard kind intentionally or unwittingly employed by the individual during his performance. For preliminary purposes, it will be convenient to distinguish and label what seem to be the standard parts of front.

First, there is the "setting," involving furniture, decor, physical layout, and other background items which supply the scenery and stage props for the spate of human action played out before, within, or upon it. A setting tends to stay put, geographically speaking, so that those who would use a particular setting as part of their performance cannot begin their act until they have brought themselves to the appropriate place and must terminate their performance when they leave it. It is only in exceptional circumstances that the setting follows along with the performers; we see this in the funeral cortege, the civic parade, and the dream-like processions that kings and queens are made of. In the main, these exceptions seem to offer some kind of extra protection for performers who are, or who have momentarily become, highly sacred. These worthies are to be distinguished, of course, from quite profane performers of the peddler class who move their place of work between performances, often being forced to do so. In the matter of having one fixed place for one's setting, a ruler may be too sacred, a peddler too profane. . . .

If we take the term "setting" to refer to the scenic parts of expressive equipment, one may take the term "personal front" to refer to the other items of expressive equipment, the items that we most intimately identify with the performer himself and that we naturally expect will follow the performer wherever he goes. As part of personal front we may include: insignia of office or rank; clothing; sex, age, and racial characteristics; size and looks; posture; speech patterns; facial expressions; bodily gestures; and the like. Some of these vehicles for conveying signs, such as racial characteristics, are relatively fixed and over a span of time do not vary for the individual from one situation to another. On the other hand, some of these sign vehicles are relatively mobile or transitory, such as facial expression, and can vary during a performance from one moment to the next.

It is sometimes convenient to divide the stimuli which make up personal front into "appearance" and "manner," according to the function performed by the information that these stimuli convey. "Appearance" may be taken to refer to those stimuli which function at the time to tell us of the performer's social statuses. These stimuli also tell us of the individual's temporary ritual state, that is, whether he is engaging in formal social activity, work, or informal recreation, whether or not he is celebrating a new phase in the season cycle or in his life-cycle. "Manner" may be taken to refer to those stimuli which function at the time to warn us of the interaction role the performer will expect to play in the oncoming situation. Thus a haughty, aggressive manner may give the impression that the performer expects to be the one who will initiate the verbal interaction and direct its course. A meek, apologetic manner may give the impression that the performer expects to follow the lead of others, or at least that he can be led to do so. . . .

Dramatic Realization

While in the presence of others, the individual typically infuses his activity with signs which dramatically highlight and portray confirmatory facts that might otherwise remain unapparent or obscure. For if the individual's activity is to become significant to others, he must mobilize his activity so that it will express *during the interaction* what he wishes to convey. In fact, the performer may be required not only to express his claimed capacities during the interaction but also to do so during a split second in the interaction. Thus, if a baseball umpire is to give the impression that he is sure of his judgment, he must forgo the moment of thought which might make him sure of his judgment; he must give an instantaneous decision so that the audience will be sure that he is sure of his judgment.[3]

It may be noted that in the case of some statuses dramatization presents no problem, since some of the acts which are instrumentally essential for the completion of the core task of the status are at the same time wonderfully adapted, from the point of view of communication, as means of vividly conveying the qualities and attributes claimed by the performer. The roles of prizefighters, surgeons, violinists, and policemen are cases in point. These activities allow for so much dramatic self-expression that exemplary practitioners—whether real or fictional—become famous and are given a special place in the commercially organized fantasies of the nation.

In many cases, however, dramatization of one's work does constitute a problem. An illustration of this may be cited from a hospital study where the medical nursing staff is shown to have a problem that the surgical nursing staff does not have:

> The things which a nurse does for postoperative patients on the surgical floor are frequently of recognizable importance, even to patients who are strangers to hospital activities. For example, the patient sees his nurse changing bandages, swinging orthopedic frames into place, and can realize that these are purposeful activities. Even if she cannot be at his side, he can respect her purposeful activities.
>
> Medical nursing is also highly skilled work. . . . The physician's diagnosis must rest upon careful observation of symptoms over time where the surgeon's are in larger part dependent on visible things. The lack of visibility creates problems on the medical staff. A patient will see his nurse stop at the next bed and chat for a moment or two with the patient there. He doesn't know that she is observing the shallowness of the breathing and color and tone of the skin. He thinks she is just visiting. So, alas, does his family who may thereupon decide that these nurses aren't very impressive. If the nurse spends more time at the next bed than at his own, the patient may feel slighted. . . . The nurses are "wasting time" unless they are darting about doing some visible thing such as administering hypodermics.[4]

Similarly, the proprietor of a service establishment may find it difficult to dramatize what is actually being done for clients because the clients cannot "see" the overhead costs of the service rendered them. Undertakers must therefore charge a great deal for their highly visible product—a coffin that has been transformed into a casket—because many of the other costs of conducting a funeral are ones that cannot be readily dramatized.[5] Merchants, too, find that they must charge high prices for things that look intrinsically expensive in order to compensate the establishment for expensive things like insurance, slack periods, etc., that never appear before the customer's eyes.

The problem of dramatizing one's work involves more than merely making invisible costs visible. The work that must be done by those who fill certain statuses is often so poorly designed as an expression of a desired meaning, that if the incumbent would dramatize the character of his role, he must divert an appreciable amount of his energy to do so. And this activity diverted to communication will often require different attributes from the ones which are being dramatized. Thus to furnish a house so that it will express simple, quiet dignity, the householder may have to race to auction sales, haggle with antique dealers, and doggedly canvass all the local shops for proper wallpaper and curtain materials. To give a radio talk that will sound genuinely informal, spontaneous, and relaxed, the speaker may have to design his script with painstaking care, testing one phrase after another, in order to follow the content, language, rhythm, and pace of everyday talk.[6] Similarly, a *Vogue* model, by her clothing, stance, and facial expression, is able expressively to portray a cultivated understanding of the book she poses in her hand; but those who trouble to express themselves so appropriately will have very little time left over for reading. As Sartre suggested: "The attentive pupil who wishes to *be* attentive, his eyes riveted on the teacher, his ears open wide, so exhausts himself in playing the attentive role that he ends up by no longer hearing anything."[7] And so individuals often find themselves with the dilemma of expression *versus* action. Those who have the time and talent to perform a task well may not, because of this, have the time or talent to make it apparent that they are performing well. It may be said that some organizations resolve this dilemma by officially delegating the dramatic function to a specialist who will spend his time expressing the meaning of the task and spend no time actually doing it. . . .

Idealization

The notion that a performance presents an idealized view of the situation *is,* of course, quite common. Cooley's view may be taken as an illustration:

> If we never tried to seem a little better than we are, how could we improve or "train ourselves from the outside inward?" And the same impulse to show the world a better or idealized aspect of ourselves finds an organized expression in the various professions and classes, each of which has to some extent a cant or pose, which its members assume unconsciously, for the most part, but which has the effect of a conspiracy to work upon the credulity of the rest of the world. There is a cant not only of theology and of philanthropy, but also of law, medicine, teaching, even of science—perhaps especially of science, just now, since the more a particular kind of merit is recognized and admired, the more it is likely to be assumed by the unworthy.[8]

Thus, when the individual presents himself before others, his performance will tend to incorporate and exemplify the officially accredited values of the society, more so, in fact, than does his behavior as a whole.

To the degree that a performance highlights the common official values of the society in which it occurs, we may look upon it, in the manner of Durkheim and Radcliffe-Brown, as a ceremony—as an expressive rejuvenation and reaffirmation of the moral values of the community. Furthermore, insofar as the expressive bias of performances comes to be accepted as reality, then that which is accepted at the moment as reality will have some of the characteristics of a celebration. To stay in one's room away from the place where the party is given, or away from where the practitioner attends his client, is to stay away from where reality is being performed. The world, in truth, is a wedding. . . .

In spite of our willingness to appreciate the expressive requirements of these several kinds of situations, we tend to see these situations as special cases; we tend to blind ourselves to the fact that everyday secular performances in our own Anglo-American society must often pass a strict test of aptness, fitness, propriety, and decorum. Perhaps this blindness is partly due to the fact that as performers we are often more conscious of the standards which we might have applied to our activity but have not than of the standards we unthinkingly apply. In any case, as students we must be ready to examine the dissonance created by a misspelled word or by a slip that is not quite concealed by a skirt; and we must be ready to appreciate why a nearsighted plumber, to protect the impression of rough strength that is *de rigueur* in his profession, feels it necessary to sweep his spectacles into his pocket when the housewife's approach changes his work into a performance, or why a television repairman is advised by his public relations counsels that the screws he fails to put back into the set should be kept alongside his own so that the unreplaced parts will not give an improper impression. In other words, we must be prepared to see that the impression of reality fostered by a performance is a delicate, fragile thing that can be shattered by very minor mishaps.

The expressive coherence that is required in performances points out a crucial discrepancy between our all-too-human selves and our socialized selves. As human beings we are presumably creatures of variable impulse with moods and energies that change from one moment to the next. As characters put on for an audience, however, we must not be subject to ups and downs. As Durkheim suggested, we do not allow our higher social activity "to follow in the trail of our bodily states, as our sensations and our general bodily consciousness do."[9] A certain bureaucratization of the spirit is expected so that we can be relied upon to give a perfectly homogeneous performance at every appointed time.

Misrepresentation

As members of an audience it is natural for us to feel that the impression the performer seeks to give may be true or false, genuine or spurious, valid or "phony." So common is this doubt that, as suggested, we often give special attention to features of the performance that cannot be readily manipulated, thus enabling ourselves to judge the reliability of the more misrepresentable cues in the performance. (Scientific police work and projective testing are extreme examples of the application of this tendency.) And if we grudgingly allow certain symbols of status to establish a performer's right to a given treatment, we are always ready to pounce on chinks in his symbolic armor in order to discredit his pretensions.

When we think of those who present a false front or "only" a front, of those who dissemble, deceive, and defraud, we think of a discrepancy between fostered appearances and reality. We also think of the precarious position in which these performers place themselves, for at any moment in their performance an event may occur to catch them out and baldly contradict what they have openly avowed, bringing them immediate humiliation and sometimes permanent loss of reputation. We often feel that it is just these terrible eventualities, which arise from being caught out *flagrante delicto* in a patent act of misrepresentation, that an honest performer is able to avoid. This commonsense view has limited analytical utility.

Sometimes when we ask whether a fostered impression is true or false, we really mean to ask whether or not the performer is authorized to give the performance in question and are not primarily concerned with the actual performance itself. When we discover that someone with whom we have dealings is an imposter and out-and-out fraud, we are discovering that he did not have the right to play the part he played, that he was not an accredited incumbent of the relevant status. We assume that the imposter's performance, in addition to the fact that it misrepresents him, will be at fault in other ways, but often his masquerade is discovered before we can detect any other differences between the false performance and the legitimate one which it simulates. Paradoxically, the more closely the imposter's performance approximates to the real thing, the more intensely we may be threatened, for a competent performance by someone who proves to be an imposter may weaken in our minds the moral connection between legitimate authorization to play a part and the capacity to play it. . . .

The Role of Expression Is Conveying Impressions of Self

Underlying all social interaction there seems to be a fundamental dialectic. When one individual enters the presence of others, he will want to discover the facts of the situation. Were he to possess this information, he could know, and make allowances for, what will come to happen and he could give the others present as much of their due as is consistent with his enlightened self-interest. To uncover fully the factual nature of the situation, it would be necessary for the individual to know all the relevant social data about the others. It would also be necessary for the individual to know the actual outcome or end product of the activity of the others during the interaction, as well as their innermost feelings concerning him. Full information of this order is rarely available; in its absence, the individual tends to employ substitutes—cues, tests, hints, expressive gestures, status symbols, etc.—as predictive devices. In short, since the reality that the individual is concerned with is unperceivable at the moment, appearances must be relied upon in its stead. And, paradoxically, the more the individual is concerned with the reality that is not available to perception, the more must he concentrate his attention on appearances.

The individual tends to treat the others present on the basis of the impression they give now about the past and the future. It is here that communicative acts are translated into moral ones. The impressions that the others give tend to be treated as claims and promises they have implicitly made, and claims and promises tend to have a moral character. In his mind the individual says: "I am using these impressions of you as a way of checking up on you and your activity, and you ought not to lead me astray." The peculiar thing about this is that the individual tends to take this stand even though he expects the others to be unconscious of many of their expressive behaviors and even though he may expect to exploit the others on the basis of the information he gleans about them. Since the sources of impression used by the observing individual involve a multitude of standards pertaining to politeness and decorum, pertaining both to social intercourse and task-performance, we can appreciate afresh how daily life is enmeshed in moral lines of discrimination. . . .

We come now to the basic dialectic. In their capacity as performers, individuals will be concerned with maintaining the impression that they are living up to the many standards by which they and their products are judged. Because these standards are so numerous and so pervasive, the individuals who are performers dwell more than we might think in a moral world. But, *qua* performers, individuals are concerned not with the moral issue of realizing these standards, but with the amoral issue of engineering a convincing impression that these standards are being realized. Our activity, then, is largely concerned with moral matters, but as performers we do not have a moral concern with them. As performers we are merchants of morality. Our day is given over to intimate contact with the goods we display and our minds are filled with intimate understandings of them; but it may well be that the more attention we give to these goods, then the more distant we feel from them and from those who are believing enough to buy them. To use a different imagery, the very obligation and profitability of appearing always in a steady moral light, of being a socialized character, forces one to be the sort of person who is practiced in the ways of the stage.

Staging and the Self

The general notion that we make a presentation of ourselves to others is hardly novel; what ought to be stressed in conclusion is that the very structure of the self can be seen in terms of how we arrange for such performances in our Anglo-American society.

In this report, the individual was divided by implication into two basic parts: he was viewed as a *performer,* a harried fabricator of impressions involved in the all-too-human task of staging a performance; he was viewed as a *character,* a figure, typically a fine one, whose spirit, strength, and other sterling qualities the performance was designed to evoke. The attributes of a performer and the attributes of a character are of a different order, quite basically so, yet both sets have their meaning in terms of the show that must go on.

First, character. In our society the character one performs and one's self are somewhat equated, and this self-as-character is usually seen as something housed within the body of its possessor, especially the upper parts thereof, being a nodule, somehow, in the psychobiology of personality. I suggest that this view is an implied part of what we are all trying to present, but provides, just because of this, a bad analysis of the presentation. In this report the performed self was seen as some kind of image, usually creditable, which the individual on stage and in character effectively attempts to induce others to hold in regard to him. While this image is entertained *concerning* the individual, so that a self is imputed to him, this self itself does not derive from its possessor, but from the whole scene of his action, being generated by that attribute of local events which renders them interpretable by witnesses. A correctly staged and performed scene leads the audience to impute a self to a performed character, but this imputation—this self—is a *product* of a scene that comes off, and is not a *cause* of it. The self, then, as a performed character, is not an organic thing that has a specific location, whose fundamental fate is to be born, to mature, and to die; it is a dramatic effect arising diffusely from a scene that is presented, and the characteristic issue, the crucial concern, is whether it will be credited or discredited.

In analyzing the self then we are drawn from its possessor, from the person who will profit or lose most by it, for he and his body merely provide the peg on which something of collaborative manufacture will be hung for a time. And the means for producing and maintaining selves do not reside inside the peg; in fact these means are often bolted down in social establishments. There will be a back region with its tools for shaping the body, and a front region with its fixed props. There will be a team of persons whose activity on stage in conjunction with available props will constitute the scene from which the performed character's self will emerge, and another team, the audience, whose interpretive activity will be necessary for this emergence. The self is a product of all these arrangements, and in all of its parts bears the marks of this genesis.

The whole machinery of self-production is cumbersome, of course, and sometimes breaks down, exposing its separate components: back region control; team collusion; audience tact; and so forth. But, well-oiled, impressions will flow from it fast enough to put us in the grips of one of our types of reality—the performance will come off and the firm self accorded each performed character will appear to emanate intrinsically from its performer.

Let us turn now from the individual as character performed to the individual as performer. He has a capacity to learn, this being exercised in the task of training for a part. He is given to having fantasies and dreams, some that pleasurably unfold a triumphant performance, others full of anxiety and dread that nervously deal with vital discreditings in a public front region. He often manifests a gregarious desire for teammates and audiences, a tactful considerateness for their concerns; and he has a capacity for deeply felt shame, leading him to minimize the chances he takes of exposure.

These attributes of the individual *qua* performer are not merely a depicted effect of particular performances; they are psychobiological in nature, and yet they seem to arise out of intimate interaction with the contingencies of staging performances.

And now a final comment. In developing the conceptual framework employed in this report, some language of the stage was used. I spoke of performers and audiences; of routines and parts; of performances coming off or falling flat; of cues, stage settings and backstage; of dramaturgical needs, dramaturgical skills, and dramaturgical strategies. Now it should be admitted that this attempt to press a mere analogy so far was in part a rhetoric and a maneuver.

The claim that all the world's a stage is sufficiently commonplace for readers to be familiar with its limitations and tolerant of its presentation, knowing that at any time they will easily be able to demonstrate to themselves that it is not to be taken too seriously. An action staged in a theater is a relatively contrived illusion and an admitted one; unlike ordinary life, nothing real or actual can happen to the performed characters—although at another level of course something real and actual can happen to the reputation of performers *qua* professionals whose everyday job is to put on theatrical performances.

And so here the language and mask of the stage will be dropped. Scaffolds, after all, are to build other things with, and should be erected with an eye to taking them down. This report is not concerned with aspects of theater that creep into everyday life. It is concerned with the structure of social encounters—the structure of those entities in social life that come into being whenever persons enter one another's immediate physical presence. The key factor in this structure is the maintenance of a single definition of the situation, this definition having to be expressed, and this expression sustained in the face of a multitude of potential disruptions.

A character staged in a theater is not in some ways real, nor does it have the same kind of real consequences as does the thoroughly contrived character performed by a confidence man; but the *successful* staging of either of these types of false figures involves use of *real* techniques—the same techniques by which everyday persons sustain their real social situations. Those who conduct face to face interaction on a theater's stage must meet the key requirement of real situations; they must expressively sustain a definition of the situation: but this they do in circumstances that have facilitated their developing an apt terminology for the interactional tasks that all of us share.

NOTES

1. Perhaps the real crime of the confidence man is not that he takes money from his victims but that he robs all of us of the belief that middle-class manners and appearance can be sustained only by middle-class people. A disabused professional can be cynically hostile to the service relation his clients expect him to extend to them; the confidence man is in a position to hold the whole "legit" world in this contempt.

2. See Harold Taxel, "Authority Structure in a Mental Hospital Ward" (unpublished Masters' thesis, Dept. of Sociology, University of Chicago, 1953): p. 4. Harry Stack Sullivan has suggested that the tact of institutionalized performers can operate in the other direction, resulting in a kind of *noblesse-oblige* sanity. See his "Socio-Psychiatric Research," *American Journal of Psychiatry,* X, pp. 987–88.

"A study of 'social recoveries' in one of our large mental hospitals some years ago taught me that patients were often released from care because they had learned not to manifest symptoms to the environing persons; in other words, had integrated enough of the personal environment to realize the prejudice opposed to their delusions. It seemed almost as if they grew wise enough to be tolerant of the imbecility surrounding them, having finally discovered that it was stupidity and not malice. They could then secure satisfaction from contact with others, while discharging a part of their cravings by psychotic means."

3. See Babe Pinelli, as told to Joe King, *Mr. Ump* (Philadelphia: Westminster Press, 1953), p. 75.

4. Edith Lentz, "A Comparison of Medical and Surgical Floors" (Mimeo: New York State School of Industrial and Labor Relations, Cornell University, 1954), pp. 2–3.

5. Material on the burial business used throughout this report is taken from Robert W. Habenstein, "The American Funeral Director" (unpublished Ph.D. dissertation, Department of Sociology, University of Chicago, 1954). I owe much to Mr. Habenstein's analysis of a funeral as a performance.

6. John Hilton, "Calculated Spontaneity," *Oxford Book of English Talk* (Oxford: Clarendon Press, 1953), pp. 399–404.

7. Jean-Paul Sartre, *Being and Nothingness,* tran. by Hazel E. Barnes (New York: Philosophical Library, 1956).

8. Charles H. Cooley, *Human Nature and the Social Order* (New York: Scribners, 1922), pp. 352–53.

9. Emile Durkheim, *The Elementary Forms of the Religious Life,* trans. J. W. Swain (London: Allen & Unwin, 1926), p. 272.

DISCUSSION QUESTIONS

1. For Goffman, what is the difference between "cynical" and "sincere" role performances?
2. According to Goffman, why is the individual faced with the "dilemma of expression versus action"?

VI

Sociology of Deviance

WHAT TO FOCUS ON:

1. In what ways does deviant behavior reflect the normative structure and cultural standards of a given society?
2. Can psychiatrists consistently distinguish between sanity and insanity? Why or why not?

SOCIOLOGY FOCUSES on the patterns and regularities of social conduct. Societies exhibit norms which set guidelines for appropriate behavior. Norms are both the basis for social order and deviance. The potential for deviance exists in all societies because norms can make behavior proper and correct but also can define that behavior as improper and deviant. The key component in the sociology of deviance is the social reaction of the group. Since norms are socially constructed, deviance is not something naturally inherent in any social act, but can only be understood in relation to the norms and values of a given society.

Crime and deviance do not mean the same thing. Crime is behavior that violates the statutes of criminal law and is sanctioned by legal authority. Deviance is behavior that violates community standards and is determined by the social reaction of the group. There is a strong correlation between crime and deviance as in the cases of rape and child abuse. However, many crimes such as traffic offenses and white collar crime are not necessarily viewed as deviant by society. Also, individuals may be viewed as deviant although they have not violated criminal law.

What exactly is deviance? The focus is not merely on the deviant act or on the deviant individual per se, but on how and why the act and the individual are deemed deviant by the larger society. Understanding deviance rests on examining the dynamics of societal reaction to particular individuals and forms of behavior. Deviance is behavior that surpasses the tolerance limit of a given community. Deviants are those individuals who conflict with the norms and values of a community and who generate the attention of social control agents.

At first glance deviance appears to be a major threat to social order. Kai Erikson's discussion of deviance points out the necessity of deviance for *preservation* of social order. Drawing upon Emile Durkheim's analysis of deviance, Erikson examines the relative functions of deviance for community life. One way a society recognizes the boundaries of acceptable behavior is through societal reaction to deviance.

Can psychiatrists clearly differentiate the sane from the insane? In the second article, D. L. Rosenhan examines how eight sane pseudopatients are diagnosed and labeled as being insane by mental health professionals. The article raises some salient questions for the sociology of deviance. By what criteria are individuals defined and labeled as being mentally ill? What are the social and psychological consequences of being diagnosed as mentally ill? Is the label mental illness a permanent attribute of one's character?

The final selection examines the cultural component of deviance. Patterns of social behavior reflect cultural standards of "normal" and "abnormal" conduct. Donald P. Jewell's discussion of the experiences of Bill, a Navaho Indian, illustrates that what is regarded as being either sane or psychotic is a cultural creation.

Article 15

Notes on the Sociology of Deviance

KAI ERIKSON

IT IS GENERAL PRACTICE in sociology to regard deviant behavior as an alien element in society. Deviance is considered a vagrant form of human activity, moving outside the more orderly currents of social life. And since this type of aberration could only occur (in theory) if something were wrong within the social organization itself, deviant behavior is described almost as if it were leakage from machinery in poor condition: it is an accidental result of disorder and anomie, a symptom of internal breakdown.

The purpose of the following remarks will be to review this conventional outlook and to argue that it provides too narrow a framework for the study of deviant behavior. Deviation, we will suggest, recalling Durkheim's classic statement on the subject, can often be understood as a normal product of stable institutions, a vital resource which is guarded and preserved by forces found in all human organizations.[1]

From "Notes on the Sociology of Deviance," by Kai Erikson, *Social Problems,* Vol. 9, No. 4, Spring 1962, pp. 307–314.

I

According to current theory, deviant behavior is most likely to occur when the sanctions governing conduct in any given setting seem to be contradictory.[2] This would be the case, for example, if the work rules posted by a company required one course of action from its employees and the longer-range policies of the company required quite another. Any situation marked by this kind of ambiguity, of course, can pose a serious dilemma for the individual: if he is careful to observe one set of demands imposed upon him, he runs the immediate risk of violating some other, and thus may find himself caught in a deviant stance no matter how earnestly he tries to avoid it. In this limited sense, deviance can be regarded as a "normal" human response to "abnormal" social conditions, and the sociologist is therefore invited to assume that some sort of pathology exists within the social structure whenever deviant behavior makes an appearance.

This general approach is clearly more concerned with the *etiology* of deviant behavior than with its continuing social *history*—and as a result it often draws sociological attention away from an important area of inquiry. It may be safe to assume that naive acts of deviance, such as first criminal offenses, are provoked by strains in the local situation. But this is only the beginning of a much longer story, for deviant activities can generate a good deal of momentum once they are set into motion: they develop forms of organization, persist over time, and sometimes remain intact long after the strains which originally produced them have disappeared. In this respect, deviant activities are often absorbed into the main tissue of society and derive support from the same forces which stabilize other forms of social life. There are persons in society, for example, who make career commitments to deviant styles of conduct, impelled by some inner need for continuity rather than by any urgencies in the immediate social setting. There are groups in society which actively encourage new deviant trends, often prolonging them beyond the point where they represent an adaptation to strain. These sources of support (for deviant behavior) are difficult to visualize when we use terms like "strain," "anomie," or "breakdown" in discussions of the problem. Such terms may help us to explain how the social structure creates fresh deviant potential, but they do not help us explain how that potential is later shaped into durable, persisting social patterns.[3] The individual's need for self-continuity and the group's offer of support are altogether normal processes, even if they are sometimes found in deviant situations; and thus the study of deviant behavior is as much a study of social organization as it is a study of *dis*organization and anomie.

II

From a sociological standpoint, deviance can be defined as conduct which is generally thought to require the attention of social control agencies—that is, conduct about which "something should be done." Deviance is not a property *inherent* in certain forms of behavior; it is a property *conferred upon these* forms by the audiences which directly or indirectly witness them. Sociologically, then, the critical variable in the study of deviance is the social *audience* rather than the individual *person,* since it is the audience which eventually decides whether or not any given action or actions will become a visible case of deviation.

This definition may seem a little indirect, but it has the advantage of bringing a neglected sociological issue into proper focus. When a community acts to control the behavior of one of its members, it is engaged in a very intricate process of selection. Even a determined miscreant conforms in most of his daily behavior—using the correct spoon at mealtime, taking good care of his mother, or otherwise observing the mores of his society—and if the community elects to bring sanctions against him for the occasions when he does act offensively, it is responding to a few deviant details set within a vast context of proper conduct. Thus a person may be jailed or hospitalized for a few scattered moments of misbehavior, defined as a full-time deviant despite the fact that he had supplied the community with countless other indications that he was a decent, moral citizen. The screening device which sifts these telling details out of the individual's overall performance, then, is a sensitive instrument of social control. It is important to note that this screen takes a number of factors into account which are not directly related to the deviant act itself: it is concerned with the actor's social class, his past record as an offender, the amount of remorse he manages to convey, and many similar concerns which take hold in the shifting moods of the community. This is why the community often overlooks behavior which seems technically deviant (like certain kinds of white collar graft) or takes sharp exception to behavior which seems essentially harmless (like certain kinds of sexual impropriety). It is an easily demonstrated fact, for example, that working class boys who steal cars are far more likely to go to prison than upper class boys who commit the same or even more serious crimes, suggesting that from the point of view of the community lower class offenders are somehow more deviant. To this extent, the community screen is perhaps a more relevant subject for sociological research than the actual behavior which is filtered through it.

Once the problem is phrased in this way, we can ask: how does a community decide what forms of conduct should be singled out for this kind of attention? And why, having made this choice, does it create special institutions to deal with the persons who enact them? The standard answer to this question is that society sets up the machinery of control in order to protect itself against the "harmful" effects of deviance, in much the same way that an organism mobilizes its resources to combat an invasion of germs. At times, however, this classroom convention only seems to make the problem more complicated. In the first place, as Durkheim pointed out some years ago, it is by no means clear that all acts considered deviant in a culture are in fact (or even in principle) harmful to group life.[4] And in the second place, specialists in crime and mental health have long suggested that deviance can play an important role in keeping the social order intact—again a point we owe originally to Durkheim.[5] This has serious implications for sociological theory in general.

III

In recent years, sociological theory has become more and more concerned with the concept "social system"—an organization of society's component parts into a form which sustains internal equilibrium, resists change, and is boundary maintaining. Now this concept has many abstract dimensions, but it is generally used to describe those forces in the social order which promote a high level of uniformity among human actors and a high degree of symmetry within human institutions. In this sense, the concept is normatively oriented since it directs the observer's attention toward those centers in social space where the core values of society are figuratively located. The main organizational principle of a system, then, is essentially a centripetal one: it draws the behavior of actors toward the nucleus of the system, bringing it within range of basic norms. Any conduct which is neither attracted toward this nerve center by the rewards of conformity nor compelled toward it by other social pressures is considered "out of control," which is to say, deviant.

This basic model has provided the theme for most contemporary thinking about deviance, and as a result little attention has been given to the notion that systems operate to maintain boundaries. Generally speaking, boundaries are controls which limit the fluctuation of a system's component parts so that the whole retains a defined range of activity—a unique pattern of constancy and stability—within the larger environment.[6] The range of human behavior is potentially so great that any *social* system must make clear statements about the nature and location of its boundaries, placing limits on the flow of behavior so that it circulates within a given cultural area. Thus boundaries are a crucial point of reference for persons living within any system, a prominent concept in the group's special language and tradition. A juvenile gang may define its boundaries by the amount of territory it defends, a professional society by the range of subjects it discusses, a fraternal order by the variety of members it accepts. But in each case, members share the same idea as to where the group begins and ends in social space and know what kinds of experience "belong" within this domain.

For all its apparent abstractness, a social system is organized around the movements of persons joined together in regular social relations. The only material found in a system for marking boundaries, then, is the behavior of its participants; and the form of behavior which best performs this function would seem to be deviant almost by definition, since it is the most extreme variety of conduct to be found within the experience of the group. In this respect, transactions taking place between deviant persons on the one side and agencies of control on the other are boundary maintaining mechanisms. They mark the outside limits of the area in which the norm has jurisdiction, and in this way assert how much diversity and variability can be contained within the system before it begins to lose its distinct structure, its unique shape.

A social norm is rarely expressed as a firm rule or official code. It is an abstract synthesis of the many separate times a community has stated its sentiments on a given issue. Thus the norm has a history much like that of an article of common law:

it is an accumulation of decisions made by the community over a long period of time which gradually gathers enough moral influence to serve as a precedent for future decisions. Like an article of common law, the norm retains its validity only if it is regularly used as a basis for judgment. Each time the community censures some act of deviance, then, it sharpens the authority of the violated norm and re-establishes the boundaries of the group.

One of the most interesting features of control institutions, in this regard, is the amount of publicity they have always attracted. In an earlier day, correction of deviant offenders took place in the public market and gave the crowd a chance to display its interest in a direct, active way. In our own day, the guilty are no longer paraded in public places, but instead we are confronted by a heavy flow of newspaper and radio reports which offer much the same kind of entertainment. Why are these reports considered "newsworthy" and why do they rate the extraordinary attention they receive? Perhaps they satisfy a number of psychological perversities among the mass audience, as many commentators have suggested, but at the same time they constitute our main source of information about the normative outlines of society. They are lessons through which we teach one another what the norms mean and how far they extend. In a figurative sense, at least, morality and immorality meet at the public scaffold, and it is during this meeting that the community declares where the line between them should be drawn.

Human groups need to regulate the routine affairs of everyday life, and to this end the norms provide an important focus for behavior. But human groups also need to describe and anticipate those areas of being which lie beyond the immediate borders of the group—the unseen dangers which in any culture and in any age seem to threaten the security of group life. The universal folklore depicting demons, devils, witches and evil spirits may be one way to give form to these otherwise formless dangers, but the visible deviant is another kind of reminder. As a trespasser against the norm, he represents those forces excluded by the group's boundaries: he informs us, as it were, what evil looks like, what shapes the devil can assume. In doing so, he shows us the difference between kinds of experience which belong within the group and kinds of experience which belong outside it.

Thus deviance cannot be dismissed as behavior which *disrupts* stability in society, but is itself, in controlled quantities, an important condition for *preserving* stability.

IV

This raises a serious theoretical question. If we grant that deviant behavior often performs a valuable service in society, can we then assume that society as a whole actively tries to promote this resource? Can we assume, in other words, that some kind of active recruitment process is going on to assure society of a steady volume of deviance? Sociology has not yet developed a conceptual language in which this sort of question can be discussed without a great deal of circularity, but one observation can be made which gives the question an interesting perspective—

namely, that deviant activities often seem to derive support from the very agencies designed to suppress them. Indeed, the institutions devised by human society for guarding against deviance sometimes seem so poorly equipped for this task that we might well ask why this is considered their "real" function at all.

It is by now a thoroughly familiar argument that many of the institutions built to inhibit deviance actually operate in such a way as to perpetuate it. For one thing, prisons, hospitals, and other agencies of control provide aid and protection for large numbers of deviant persons. But beyond this, such institutions gather marginal people into tightly segregated groups, give them an opportunity to teach one another the skills and attitudes of a deviant career, and even drive them into using these skills by reinforcing their sense of alienation from the rest of society.[7] This process is found not only in the institutions which actually confine the deviant, but in the general community as well.

The community's decision to bring deviant sanctions against an individual is not a simple act to censure. It is a sharp rite of transition, at once moving him out of his normal position in society and transferring him into a distinct deviant role.[8] The ceremonies which accomplish this change of status, usually, have three related phases. They arrange a formal *confrontation* between the deviant suspect and representatives of his community (as in the criminal trial or psychiatric case conference); they announce some *judgment* about the nature of his deviancy (a "verdict" or "diagnosis," for example); and they perform an act of social *placement,* assigning him to a special deviant role (like that of "prisoner" or "patient") for some period of time. Such ceremonies tend to be events of wide public interest and ordinarily take place in a dramatic, ritualized setting.[9] Perhaps the most obvious example of a commitment ceremony is the criminal trial, with its elaborate ritual and formality, but more modest equivalents can be found almost anywhere that procedures are set up for judging whether or not someone is officially deviant.

An important feature of these ceremonies in our culture is that they are almost irreversible. Most provisional roles conferred by society—like those of the student or citizen soldier, for instance—include some kind of terminal ceremony to mark the individual's movement back out of the role once its temporary advantages have been exhausted. But the roles allotted to the deviant seldom make allowance for this type of passage. He is ushered into the special position by a decisive and dramatic ceremony, yet is retired from it with hardly a word of public notice. As a result, the deviant often returns home with no proper license to resume a normal life in the community. From a ritual point of view, nothing has happened to cancel out the stigmas imposed upon him by earlier commitment ceremonies: the original verdict or diagnosis is still formally in effect. Partly for this reason, the community is apt to place the returning deviant on some form of probation within the group, suspicious that he will return to deviant activity upon a moment's provocation.

A circularity is thus set into motion which has all the earmarks of a "self-fulfilling prophecy," to use Merton's fine phrase. On the one hand, it seems obvious that the apprehensions of the community help destroy whatever chances the deviant might otherwise have for a successful return to society. Yet, on the other hand, everyday experience seems to show that these apprehensions are altogether reasonable, for it is a well-known and highly publicized fact that most ex-convicts return to prison and that a large proportion of mental patients require additional treatment after once having been discharged. The community's feeling that deviant persons cannot change, then, may be based on a faulty premise, but it is repeated so frequently and with such conviction that it eventually creates the facts which "prove" it correct. If the returned deviant encounters this feeling of distrust often enough, it is understandable that he too may begin to wonder if the original verdict or diagnosis is still in effect—and respond to this uncertainty by resuming deviant activity. In some respects, this solution may be the only way for the individual and his community to agree what forms of behavior are appropriate for him.

Moreover, this prophecy is found in the official policies of even the most advanced agencies of control. Police departments could not operate with any real effectiveness if they did not regard ex-convicts as an almost permanent population of offenders, a constant pool of suspects. Nor could psychiatric clinics do a responsible job if they did not view former patients as a group unusually susceptible to mental illness. Thus the prophecy gains currency at many levels within the social order, not only in the poorly informed attitudes of the community at large, but in the best informed theories of most control agencies as well.

In one form or another, this problem has been known to Western culture for many hundreds of years, and this simple fact is a very important one for sociology. For if the culture has supported a steady flow of deviant behavior throughout long periods of historical evolution, then the rules which apply to any form of functionalist thinking would suggest the strong forces must be at work to keep this flow intact. This may not be reason enough to assert that deviant behavior is altogether "functional"—in any of the many senses of that term—but it should make us reluctant to assume that the agencies of control are somehow organized to prevent deviant acts from occurring or to "cure" deviant offenders of their misbehavior.[10]

This in turn might suggest that our present models of the social system, with their clear emphasis on harmony and symmetry in social relations, only do a partial job of representing reality. Perhaps two different (and often conflicting) currents are found within any well-functioning system: those forces which promote a high over-all degree of conformity among human actors, and those forces which encourage some degree of diversity so that actors can be deployed throughout social space to mark the system's boundaries. In such a scheme, deviant behavior would appear as a variation on normative themes, a vital form of activity which outlines the area within which social life as such takes place.

As Georg Simmel wrote some years ago:

> An absolutely centripetal and harmonious group, a pure "unification," not only is empirically unreal, it could show no real life process. . . . Just as the universe needs "love and hate," that is, attractive and repulsive forces, in order to have any form at all, so society, too, in order to attain a determinate shape, needs some quantitative ratio of harmony and disharmony of association and competition, of favorable and

> unfavorable tendencies. . . . Society, as we know it, is the result of both categories of interaction, which thus both manifest themselves as wholly positive.[11]

V

In summary, two new lines of inquiry seem to be indicated by the argument presented above.

First, this paper attempts to focus our attention on an old but still vital sociological question: how does a social structure communicate its "needs" or impose its "patterns" on human actors? In the present case, how does a social structure enlist actors to engage in deviant activity? Ordinarily, the fact that deviant behavior is more common in some sectors of society than in others is explained by declaring that something called "anomie" or "disorganization" prevails at these sensitive spots. Deviance leaks out where the social machinery is defective; it occurs where the social structure *fails* to communicate its needs to human actors. But if we consider the possibility that deviant persons are responding to the same social forces that elicit conformity from others, then we are engaged in another order of inquiry altogether. Perhaps the stability of some social units is maintained only if juvenile offenders are recruited to balance an adult majority; perhaps some families can remain intact only if one of their members becomes a visible deviant or is committed to a hospital or prison. If this supposition proves to be a useful one, sociologists should be interested in discovering how a social unit manages to differentiate the roles of its members and how certain persons are "chosen" to play the more deviant parts.

Second, it is evident that cultures vary in the way they regulate traffic moving back and forth from their deviant boundaries. Perhaps we could begin with the hypothesis that the traffic pattern known in our own culture has a marked puritan cast: a defined portion of the population, largely drawn from young adult groups and from the lower economic classes, is stabilized in deviant roles and generally expected to remain there for indefinite periods of time. To this extent, puritan attitudes about predestination and reprobation would seem to have retained a significant place in modern criminal law and public opinion. In other areas of the world, however, different traffic patterns are known. There are societies in which deviance is considered a natural pursuit for the young, an activity which they can easily abandon when they move through defined ceremonies into adulthood. There are societies which give license to large groups of persons to engage in deviant behavior for certain seasons or on certain days of the year. And there are societies in which special groups are formed to act in ways "contrary" to the normal expectations of the culture. Each of these patterns regulates deviant traffic differently, yet all of them provide some institutionalized means for an actor to give up a deviant "career" without permanent stigma. The problem for sociological theory in general might be to learn whether or not these varying patterns are functionally equivalent in some meaningful sense; the problem for applied sociology might be to see if we have anything to learn from those cultures which permit re-entry into normal social life to persons who have spent a period of "service" on society's boundaries.

NOTES

1. Emile Durkheim, *The Rules of Sociological Method* (translated by S. A. Solovay and J. H. Mueller), Glencoe: The Free Press, 1958.

2. The best known statements of this general position, of course, are by Robert K. Merton and Talcott Parsons. Merton, *Social Theory and Social Structures* (revised edition), Glencoe: The Free Press, 1957; and Parsons, *The Social System,* Glencoe: The Free Press, 1951.

3. Cf. Daniel Glaser and Kent Rice, "Crime, Age, and Employment," *American Sociological Review,* 24 (1959), pp. 679–686.

4. Emile Durkheim, *The Division of Labor in Society* (translated by George Simpson), Glencoe: The Free Press, 1952. See particularly Chapter 2, Book 1.

5. Emile Durkheim, *The Rules of Sociological Method, op. cit.*

6. Cf. Talcott Parsons, *The Social System, op. cit.*

7. For a good description of this process in the modern prison, see Gresham Sykes, *The Society of Captives,* Princeton: Princeton University Press, 1958. For views of two different types of mental hospital settings, see Erving Goffman, "The Characteristics of Total Institutions," *Symposium on Preventive and Social Psychiatry.* Washington, D.C.: Walter Reed Army Institute of Research, 1957; and Kai Erikson, "Patient Role and Social Uncertainty: A Dilemma of the Mentally Ill," *Psychiatry,* 20 (1957), pp. 263–274.

8. Talcott Parsons, *op. cit.,* has given the classical description of how this role transfer works in the case of medical patients.

9. Cf. Harold Garfinkel, "Successful Degradation Ceremonies," *American Journal of Sociology,* 61 (1956), pp. 420–424.

10. Albert K. Cohen, for example, speaking for most sociologists, seems to take the question for granted: "It would seem that the control of deviant behavior is, by definition, a culture goal." In "The Study of Social Disorganization and Deviant Behavior," Merton, *et al.,* editors, *Sociology Today.* New York: Basic Books, 1959, p. 465.

11. Georg Simmel, *Conflict* (translated by Kurt H. Wolff), Glencoe: The Free Press, 1955, pp. 15–16.

DISCUSSION QUESTIONS

1. How does deviant behavior help to shape the boundaries of acceptable behavior in a given society?
2. According to Erikson, deviance provides a valuable service in preserving the stability of society. What are the social functions of deviance?

Article 16

On Being Sane in Insane Places

D. L. ROSENHAN

IF SANITY AND INSANITY exist, how shall we know them?

The question is neither capricious nor itself insane. However much we may be personally convinced that we can tell the normal from the abnormal, the evidence is simply not compelling. It is commonplace, for example, to read about murder trials wherein eminent psychiatrists for the defense are contradicted by equally eminent psychiatrists for the prosecution on the matter of the defendant's sanity. More generally, there are a great deal of conflicting data on the reliability, utility, and meaning of such terms as "sanity," "insanity," "mental illness," and "schizophrenia" (*1*). Finally, as early as 1934, Benedict suggested that normality and abnormality are not universal (*2*). What is viewed as normal in one culture may be seen as quite aberrant in another. Thus, notions of normality and abnormality may not be quite as accurate as people believe they are.

To raise questions regarding normality and abnormality is in no way to question the fact that some behaviors are deviant or odd. Murder is deviant. So, too, are hallucinations. Nor does raising such questions deny the existence of the personal anguish that is often associated with "mental illness." Anxiety and depression exist.

From "On Being Sane in Insane Places," D. L. Rosenhan, *Science,* 179, 1973, pp. 250–258. Reprinted with permission.

Psychological suffering exists. But normality and abnormality, sanity and insanity, and the diagnoses that flow from them may be less substantive than many believe them to be.

At its heart, the question of whether the sane can be distinguished from the insane (and whether degrees of insanity can be distinguished from each other) is a simple matter: do the salient characteristics that lead to diagnoses reside in the patients themselves or in the environments and contexts in which observers find them? From Bleuler, through Kretchmer, through the formulators of the recently revised *Diagnostic and Statistical Manual* of the American Psychiatric Association, the belief has been strong that patients present symptoms, that those symptoms can be categorized, and, implicitly, that the sane are distinguishable from the insane. More recently, however, this belief has been questioned. Based in part on theoretical and anthropological considerations, but also on philosophical, legal, and therapeutic ones, the view has grown that psychological categorization of mental illness is useless at best and downright harmful, misleading, and pejorative at worst. Psychiatric diagnoses, in this view, are in the minds of the observers and are not valid summaries of characteristics displayed by the observed (*3–5*).

Gains can be made in deciding which of these is more nearly accurate by getting normal people (that is, people who do not have, and have never suffered, symptoms of serious psychiatric disorders) admitted to psychiatric hospitals and then determining whether they were discovered to be sane and, if so, how. If the sanity of such pseudopatients were always detected, there would be prima facie evidence that a sane individual can be distinguished from the insane context in which he is found. Normality (and presumably abnormality) is distinct enough that it can be recognized wherever it occurs, for it is carried within the person. If, on the other hand, the sanity of the pseudopatients were never discovered, serious difficulties would arise for those who support traditional modes of psychiatric diagnosis. Given that the hospital staff was not incompetent, that the pseudopatient had been behaving as sanely as he had been outside of the hospital, and that it had never been previously suggested that he belonged in a psychiatric hospital, such an unlikely outcome would support the view that psychiatric diagnosis betrays little about the patient but much about the environment in which an observer finds him.

This article describes such an experiment. Eight sane people gained secret admission to 12 different hospitals (*6*). Their diagnostic experiences constitute the data of the first part of this article; the remainder is devoted to a description of their experiences in psychiatric institutions. Too few psychiatrists and psychologists, even those who have worked in such hospitals, know what the experience is like. They rarely talk about it with former patients, perhaps because they distrust information coming from the previously insane. Those who have worked in psychiatric hospitals are likely to have adapted so thoroughly to the settings that they are insensitive to the impact of that experience. And while there have been occasional reports of researchers who submitted themselves to psychiatric hospitalization (*7*), these researchers have commonly remained in the hospitals for short periods of time, often with the knowledge of the hospital staff. It is difficult to know the extent to which they were treated like patients or like research colleagues. Nevertheless, their reports about the inside of the psychiatric hospital have been valuable. This article extends those efforts.

Pseudopatients and Their Settings

The eight pseudopatients were a varied group. One was a psychology graduate student in his 20's. The remaining seven were older and "established." Among them were three psychologists, a pediatrician, a psychiatrist, a painter, and a housewife. Three pseudopatients were women, five were men. All of them employed pseudonyms, lest their alleged diagnoses embarrass them later. Those who were in mental health professions alleged another occupation in order to avoid the special attentions that might be accorded by staff, as a matter of courtesy or caution, to ailing colleagues (*8*). With the exception of myself (I was the first pseudopatient and my presence was known to the hospital administrator and chief psychologist and, so far as I can tell, to them alone), the presence of pseudopatients and the nature of the research program were not known to the hospital staffs (*9*).

The settings were similarly varied. In order to generalize the findings, admission into a variety of hospitals was sought. The 12 hospitals in the sample were located in five different states on the East and West coasts. Some were old and shabby, some were quite new. Some were research-oriented, others not. Some had good staff-patient ratios, others were quite understaffed. Only one was a strictly private hospital. All of the others were supported by state or federal funds or, in one instance, by university funds.

After calling the hospital for an appointment, the pseudopatient arrived at the admissions office complaining that he had been hearing voices. Asked what the voices said, he replied that they were often unclear, but as far as he could tell they said "empty," "hollow," and "thud." The voices were unfamiliar and were of the same sex as the pseudopatient. The choice of these symptoms was occasioned by their apparent similarity to existential symptoms. Such symptoms are alleged to arise from painful concerns about the perceived meaninglessness of one's life. It is as if the hallucinating person were saying, "My life is empty and hollow." The choice of these symptoms was also determined by the *absence* of a single report of existential psychoses in the literature.

Beyond alleging the symptoms and falsifying name, vocation, and employment, no further alterations of person, history, or circumstances were made. The significant events of the pseudopatient's life history were presented as they had actually occurred. Relationships with parents and siblings, with spouse and children, with people at work and in school, consistent with the aforementioned exceptions, were described as they were or had been. Frustrations and upsets were described along with joys and satisfactions. These facts are important to remember. If anything, they strongly biased the subsequent results in favor of detecting sanity, since none of their histories or current behaviors were seriously pathological in any way.

Immediately upon admission to the psychiatric ward, the pseudopatient ceased simulating *any* symptoms of abnormality. In some cases, there was a brief period of mild nervousness and anxiety, since none of the pseudopatients really believed that they would be admitted so easily. Indeed, their shared fear was that they would be immediately exposed as frauds and greatly embarrassed. Moreover, many of them had never visited a psychiatric ward; even those who had, nevertheless had some genuine fears about what might happen to them. Their nervousness, then, was quite appropriate to the novelty of the hospital setting, and it abated rapidly.

Apart from that short-lived nervousness, the pseudopatient behaved on the ward as he "normally" behaved. The pseudopatient spoke to patients and staff as he might ordinarily. Because there is uncommonly little to do on a psychiatric ward, he attempted to engage others in conversation. When asked by staff how he was feeling, he indicated that he was fine, that he no longer experienced symptoms. He responded to instructions from attendants, to calls for medication (which was not swallowed), and to dining-hall instructions. Beyond such activities as were available to him on the admissions ward, he spent his time writing down his observations about the ward, its patients, and the staff. Initially, these notes were written "secretly," but as it soon became clear that no one much cared, they were subsequently written on standard tablets of paper in such public places as the dayroom. No secret was made of these activities.

The pseudopatient, very much as a true psychiatric patient, entered a hospital with no foreknowledge of when he would be discharged. Each was told that he would have to get out by his own devices, essentially by convincing the staff that he was sane. The psychological stresses associated with hospitalization were considerable, and all but one of the pseudopatients desired to be discharged almost immediately after being admitted. They were, therefore, motivated not only to behave sanely, but to be paragons of cooperation. That their behavior was in no way disruptive is confirmed by nursing reports, which have been obtained on most of the patients. These reports uniformly indicate that the patients were "friendly," "cooperative," and "exhibited no abnormal indications."

The Normal Are Not Detectably Sane

Despite their public "show" of sanity, the pseudopatients were never detected. Admitted, except in one case, with a diagnosis of schizophrenia (*10*), each was discharged with a diagnosis of schizophrenia "in remission." The label "in remission" should in no way be discussed as a formality, for at no time during any hospitalization had any question been raised about the pseudopatient's simulation. Nor are there any indications in the hospital records that the pseudopatient's status was suspect. Rather, the evidence is strong that, once labeled schizophrenic, the pseudopatient was stuck with that label. If the pseudopatient was to be discharged, he must naturally be "in remission"; but he was not sane, nor in the institution's view, had he ever been sane.

The uniform failure to recognize sanity cannot be attributed to the quality of the hospitals, for, although there were considerable variations among them, several are considered excellent. Nor can it be alleged that there was simply not enough time to observe the pseudopatients. Lengths of hospitalization ranged from 7 to 52 days, with an average of 19 days. The pseudopatients were not, in fact, carefully observed, but this failure clearly speaks more to traditions within psychiatric hospitals than to lack of opportunity.

Finally, it cannot be said that the failure to recognize the pseudopatients' sanity was due to the fact that they were not behaving sanely. While there was clearly some tension present in all of them, their daily visitors could detect no serious behavioral consequences—nor, indeed, could other patients. It was quite common for the patients to "detect" the pseudopatients' sanity. During the first three hospitalizations, when accurate counts were kept, 35 of a total of 118 patients on the admissions ward voiced their suspicions, some vigorously. "You're not crazy. You're a journalist, or a professor [referring to the continual note-taking]. You're checking up on the hospital." While most of the patients were reassured by the pseudopatient's insistence that he had been sick before he came in but was fine now, some continued to believe that the pseudopatient was sane throughout his hospitalization (*11*). The fact that the patients often recognized normality when staff did not raises important questions.

Failure to detect sanity during the course of hospitalization may be due to the fact that physicians operate with strong bias toward what statisticians call the type 2 error (*5*). This is to say that physicians are more inclined to call a healthy person sick (a false positive, type 2) than a sick person healthy (a false negative, type 1). The reasons for this are not hard to find: it is clearly more dangerous to misdiagnose illness than health. Better to err on the side of caution, to suspect illness even among the healthy.

But what holds for medicine does not hold equally well for psychiatry. Medical illnesses, while unfortunate, are not commonly pejorative. Psychiatric diagnoses, on the contrary, carry with them personal, legal, and social stigmas (*12*). It was therefore important to see whether the tendency toward diagnosing the sane insane could be reversed. The following experiment was arranged at a research and teaching hospital whose staff had heard these findings but doubted that such an error could occur in their hospital. The staff was informed that at some time during the following 3 months, one or more pseudopatients would attempt to be admitted into the psychiatric hospital. Each staff member was asked to rate each patient who presented himself at admissions or on the ward according to the likelihood that the patient was a pseudopatient. A 10-point scale was used, with a 1 and 2 reflecting high confidence that the patient was a pseudopatient.

Judgments were obtained on 193 patients who were admitted for psychiatric treatment. All staff who had had sustained contact with or primary responsibility for the patient—attendants, nurses, psychiatrists, physicians, and psychologists—were asked to make judgments. Forty-one patients were alleged, with high confidence, to be pseudopatients by at least one member of the staff. Twenty-three were considered suspect by at least one psychiatrist. Nineteen were suspected by one psychiatrist *and* one other staff member. Actually, no genuine pseudopatient (at least from my group) presented himself during this period.

The experiment is instructive. It indicates that the tendency to designate sane people as insane can be reversed when the stakes (in this case, prestige and diagnostic acumen) are high. But what can be said of the 19 people who were suspected of being "sane" by one psychiatrist and another staff member? Were these people truly "sane," or was it rather the case that in the course of avoiding the type 2 error the staff tended to make errors of the first sort—calling the crazy "sane"? There is no way of knowing. But one thing is certain: any diagnostic process that lends itself so readily to massive errors of this sort cannot be a very reliable one.

The Stickiness of Psychodiagnostic Labels

Beyond the tendency to call the healthy sick—a tendency that accounts better for diagnostic behavior on admission than it does for such behavior after a lengthy period of exposure—the data speak to the massive role of labeling in psychiatric assessment. Having once been labeled as schizophrenic, there is nothing the pseudopatient can do to overcome the tag. The tag profoundly colors others' perceptions of him and his behavior.

From one viewpoint, these data are hardly surprising, for it has long been known that elements are given meaning by the context in which they occur. Gestalt psychology made this point vigorously, and Asch (*13*) demonstrated that there are "central" personality traits (such as "warm" versus "cold") which are so powerful that they markedly color the meaning of other information in forming an impression of a given personality (*14*). "Insane," "schizophrenic," "manic-depressive," and "crazy" are probably among the most powerful of such central traits. Once a person is designated abnormal, all of his other behaviors and characteristics are colored by that label. Indeed, the label is so powerful that many of the pseudopatients' normal behaviors were overlooked entirely or profoundly misinterpreted. Some examples may clarify this issue.

Earlier I indicated that there were no changes in the pseudopatient's history and current status beyond those of name, employment, and, where necessary, vocation. Otherwise, a veridical description of personal history and circumstances was offered. Those circumstances were not psychotic. How were they made consonant with the diagnosis of psychosis? Or were those diagnoses modified in such a way as to bring them into accord with the circumstances of the pseudopatient's life, as described by him?

As far as I can determine, diagnoses were in no way affected by the relative health of the circumstances of a pseudopatient's life. Rather, the reverse occurred: the perception of his circumstances was shaped entirely by the diagnosis. A clear example of such translation is found in the case of a pseudopatient who had a close relationship with his mother but was rather remote from his father during his early childhood. During adolescence and beyond, however, his father became a close friend, while his relationship with his mother cooled. His present relationship with his wife was characteristically close and warm. Apart from occasional angry exchanges, friction was minimal. The children had rarely been spanked. Surely there is nothing especially pathological about such a history. Indeed, many readers may see a similar pattern in their own experiences, with no markedly deleterious consequences. Observe, however, how such a history was translated in the psychopathological context, this from the case summary prepared after the patient was discharged.

> This white 39-year-old male . . . manifests a long history of considerable ambivalence in close relationships, which begins in early childhood. A warm relationship with his mother cools during his adolescence. A distant relationship to his father is described as becoming very intense. Affective stability is absent. His attempts to control emotionality with his wife and children are punctuated by angry outbursts and, in the case of the children, spankings. And while he says that he has several good friends, one senses considerable ambivalence embedded in those relationships also. . . .

The facts of the case were unintentionally distorted by the staff to achieve consistency with a popular theory of the dynamics of a schizophrenic reaction (*15*). Nothing of an ambivalent nature had been described in relations with parents, spouse, or friends. To the extent that ambivalence could be inferred, it was probably not greater than is found in all human relationships. It is true the pseudopatient's relationships with his parents changed over time, but in the ordinary context that would hardly be remarkable—indeed, it might very well be expected. Clearly, the meaning ascribed to his verbalizations (that is, ambivalence, affective instability) was determined by the diagnosis: schizophrenia. An entirely different meaning would have been ascribed if it were known that the man was "normal."

All pseudopatients took extensive notes publicly. Under ordinary circumstances, such behavior would have raised questions in the minds of observers, as, in fact, it did among patients. Indeed, it seemed so certain that the notes would elicit suspicion that elaborate precautions were taken to remove them from the ward each day. But the precautions proved needless. The closest any staff member came to questioning these notes occurred when one pseudopatient asked his physician what kind of medication he was receiving and began to write down the response. "You needn't write it," he was told gently. "If you have trouble remembering, just ask me again."

If no questions were asked of the pseudopatients, how was their writing interpreted? Nursing records for three patients indicate that the writing was seen as an aspect of their pathological behavior. "Patient engages in writing behavior" was the daily nursing comment on one of the pseudopatients who was never questioned about his writing. Given that the patient is in the hospital, he must be psychologically disturbed. And given that he is disturbed, continuous writing must be a behavioral manifestation of that disturbance, perhaps a subset of the compulsive behaviors that are sometimes correlated with schizophrenia.

One tacit characteristic of psychiatric diagnosis is that it locates the sources of aberration within the individual and only rarely within the complex of stimuli that surrounds him. Consequently, behaviors that are stimulated by the environment are commonly misattributed to the patient's disorder. For example, one kindly nurse found a pseudopatient pacing the long hospital corridors. "Nervous, Mr. X?" she asked. "No, bored," he said.

The notes kept by pseudopatients are full of patient behaviors that were misinterpreted by well-intentioned staff. Often enough, a patient would go "berserk" because he had, wittingly or unwittingly, been mistreated by, say, an attendant. A nurse coming upon the scene would rarely inquire even cursorily into the environmental stimuli of the patient's behavior. Rather, she assumed that his upset derived from his pathology, not from his present interactions with other staff members. Occasionally, the patient's family (especially when they had recently visited) or other patients had stimulated the outburst. But never were the staff found to assume that one of themselves or the structure of the hospital had anything to do with a patient's behavior. One psychiatrist pointed to a group of patients who were sitting outside the cafeteria entrance half an hour before lunchtime. To a group of young residents he indicated that such behavior was characteristic of the oral-acquisitive nature of the syndrome. It seemed not to occur to him that there were very few things to anticipate in a psychiatric hospital besides eating.

A psychiatric label has a life and an influence of its own. Once the impression has been formed that the patient is schizophrenic, the expectation is that he will continue to be schizophrenic. When a sufficient amount of time has passed, during which the patient has done nothing bizarre, he is considered to be in remission and available for discharge. But the label endures beyond discharge, with the unconfirmed expectation that he will behave as a schizophrenic again. Such labels, conferred by mental health professionals, are as influential on the patient as they are on his relatives and friends, and it should not surprise anyone that the diagnosis acts on all of them as a self-fulfilling prophecy. Eventually, the patient himself accepts the diagnosis, with all of its surplus meanings and expectations, and behaves accordingly (*5*).

The inferences to be made from these matters are quite simple. Much as Zigler and Phillips have demonstrated that there is enormous overlap in the symptoms presented by patients who have been variously diagnosed (*16*), so there is enormous overlap in the behaviors of the sane and the insane. The sane are not "sane" all of the time. We lose our tempers "for no good reason." We are occasionally depressed or anxious, again for no good reason. And we may find it difficult to get along with one or another person—again for no reason that we can specify. Similarly, the insane are not always insane. Indeed, it was the impression of the pseudopatients while living with them that they were sane for long periods of time—that the bizarre behaviors upon which their diagnoses were allegedly predicated constituted only a small fraction of their total behavior. If it makes no sense to label ourselves permanently depressed on the basis of an occasional depression, then it takes better evidence than is presently available to label all patients insane or schizophrenic on the basis of bizarre behaviors or cognitions. It seems more useful, as Mischel (*17*) has pointed out, to limit our discussions to *behaviors,* the stimuli that provoke them, and their correlates.

It is not known why powerful impressions of personality traits, such as "crazy" or "insane," arise. Conceivably, when the origins of and stimuli that give rise to a behavior are remote or unknown, or when the behavior strikes us as immutable, trait labels regarding the *behaver* arise. When, on the other hand, the origins and stimuli are known and available, discourse is limited to the behavior itself. Thus, I may hallucinate because I am sleeping, or I may hallucinate because I have ingested a peculiar drug. These are termed sleep-induced hallucinations, or dreams, and drug-induced hallucinations, respectively. But when the stimuli to my hallucinations are unknown, that is called craziness, or schizophrenia—as if that inference were somehow as illuminating as the others.

The Experience of Psychiatric Hospitalization

The term "mental illness" is of recent origin. It was coined by people who were humane in their inclinations and who wanted very much to raise the station of (and the public's sympathies toward) the psychologically disturbed from that of witches and "crazies" to one that was akin to the physically ill. And they were at least partially successful, for the treatment of the mentally ill *has* improved considerably over the years. But while treatment has improved, it is doubtful that people really regard the mentally ill in the same way that they view the physically ill. A broken leg is something one recovers from, but mental illness allegedly endures forever (*18*). A broken leg does not threaten the observer, but a crazy schizophrenic? There is by now a host of evidence that attitudes toward the mentally ill are characterized by fear, hostility, aloofness, suspicion, and dread (*19*). The mentally ill are society's lepers.

That such attitudes infect the general population is perhaps not surprising, only upsetting. But that they affect the professionals—attendants, nurses, physicians, psychologists, and social workers—who treat and deal with the mentally ill is more disconcerting, both because such attitudes are self-evidently pernicious and because they are unwitting. Most mental health professionals would insist that they are sympathetic toward the mentally ill, that they are neither avoidant nor hostile. But it is more likely that an exquisite ambivalence characterizes their relations with psychiatric patients, such that their avowed impulses are only part of their entire attitude. Negative attitudes are there too and can easily be detected. Such attitudes should not surprise us. They are the natural offspring of the labels patients wear and the places in which they are found.

Consider the structure of the typical psychiatric hospital. Staff and patients are strictly segregated. Staff have their own living space, including their dining facilities, bathrooms, and assembly places. The glassed quarters that contain the professional staff, which the pseudopatients came to call "the cage," sit out on every dayroom. The staff emerges primarily for caretaking purposes—to give medication, to conduct a therapy or group meeting, to instruct or reprimand a patient. Otherwise, staff keep to themselves, almost as if the disorder that afflicts their charges is somehow catching.

So much is patient-staff segregation the rule that, for four public hospitals in which an attempt was made to measure the degree to which staff and patients mingle, it was necessary to use "time out of the staff cage" as the operational measure. While it was not the case that all time spent out of the cage was spent mingling with patients (attendants, for example, would occasionally emerge to watch television in the dayroom), it was the only way in which one could gather reliable data on time for measuring.

The average amount of time spent by attendants outside of the cage was 11.3 percent (range, 3 to 52 percent). This figure does not represent only time spent mingling with patients, but also includes time spent on such chores as folding laundry, supervising patients while they shave, directing ward clean-up, and sending patients to off-ward activities. It was the relatively rare attendant who spent time talking with patients or playing games with them. It proved impossible to obtain a "percent mingling time" for nurses, since the amount of time they spent out of the cage was too brief. Rather, we counted instances of emergence from the cage. On the average, daytime nurses emerged from the cage 11.5 times per shift, including instances when they left the ward entirely (range, 4 to 39 times). Late afternoon and night nurses were even less available, emerging on the average 9.4 times per shift (range, 4 to 41 times). Data on early morning nurses, who arrived usually after midnight and departed at 8 a.m., are not available because patients were asleep during most of this period.

Physicians, especially psychiatrists, were even less available. They were rarely seen on the wards. Quite commonly, they would be seen only when they arrived and departed, with the remaining time being spent in their offices or in the cage. On the average, physicians emerged on the ward 6.7 times per day (range, 1 to 17 times). It proved difficult to make an accurate estimate in this regard, since physicians often maintained hours that allowed them to come and go at different times.

The hierarchical organization of the psychiatric hospital has been commented on before (*20*), but the latent meaning of that kind of organization is worth noting again. Those with the most power have least to do with patients, and those with the least power are most involved with them. Recall, however, that the acquisition of role-appropriate behaviors occurs mainly through the observation of others, with the most powerful having the most influence. Consequently, it is understandable that attendants not only spend more time with patients than do any other members of the staff—that is required by their station in the hierarchy—but also, insofar as they learn from their superiors' behavior, spend as little time with patients as they can. Attendants are seen mainly in the cage, which is where the models, the action, and the power are.

I turn now to a different set of studies, these dealing with staff response to patient-initiated contact. It has long been known that the amount of time a person spends with you can be an index of your significance to him. If he initiates and maintains eye contact, there is reason to believe that he is considering your requests and needs. If he pauses to chat or actually stops and talks, there is added reason to infer that he is individuating you. In four hospitals, the pseudopatient approached the staff member with a request which took the following form: "Pardon me, Mr. [or Dr. or Mrs.] X, could you tell me when I will be eligible for grounds privileges?" (or ". . . when I will be presented at the staff meeting?" or ". . . when I am likely to be discharged?"). While the content of the question varied according to the appropriateness of the target and the pseudopatient's (apparent) current needs the form was always a courteous and relevant request for information. Care was taken never to approach a particular member of the staff more than once a day, lest the staff member become suspicious or irritated. In examining these data, remember that the behavior of the pseudopatients was neither bizarre nor disruptive. One could indeed engage in good conversation with them.

The data for these experiments are shown in Table 1, separately for physicians (column 1) and for nurses and attendants (column 2). Minor differences between these four institutions were overwhelmed by the degree to which staff avoided continuing contacts that patients had initiated. By far, their most common response consisted of either a brief response to the question, offered while they were "on the move" and with head averted, or no response at all.

The encounter frequently took the following bizarre form: (pseudopatient) "Pardon me, Dr. X. Could you tell me when I am eligible for grounds privileges?" (physician) "Good morning, Dave. How are you today?" (Moves off without waiting for a response.)

It is instructive to compare these data with data recently obtained at Stanford University. It has been alleged that large and eminent universities are characterized by faculty who are so busy that they have no time for students. For this comparison, a young lady approached individual faculty members who seemed to be walking purposefully to some meeting or teaching engagement and asked them the following six questions.

1) "Pardon me, could you direct me to Encina Hall?" (at the medical school: ". . . to the Clinical Research Center?").

2) "Do you know where Fish Annex is?" (there is no Fish Annex at Stanford).

3) "Do you teach here?"

4) "How does one apply for admission to the college?" (at the medical school: ". . . to the medical school?").

5) "Is it difficult to get in?"

6) "Is there financial aid?"

Without exception, as can be seen in Table 1 (column 3), all of the questions were answered. No matter how rushed they were, all respondents not only maintained eye contact, but stopped to talk. Indeed, many of the respondents went out of their way to direct or take the questioner to the office she was seeking, to try to locate "Fish Annex," or to discuss with her the possibilities of being admitted to the university.

Similar data, also shown in Table 1 (columns 4, 5, and 6), were obtained in the hospital. Here too, the young lady came prepared with six questions. After the first question, however, she remarked to 18 of her respondents (column 4), "I'm looking for a psychiatrist," and to 15 others (column 5), "I'm looking for an internist." Ten other respondents received no inserted comment (column 6). The general degree of cooperative responses is considerably higher for these university groups than it was for pseudopatients in psychiatric hospitals. Even so, differences are apparent within the medical school setting. Once having indicated that she was looking for a psychiatrist, the degree of cooperation elicited was less than when she sought an internist.

TABLE 16.1 Self-initiated contact by pseudopatients with psychiatrists and nurses and attendants, compared to contact with other groups

	Psychiatric hospitals		University campus (nonmedical)	University medical center		
				Physicians		
Contact	(1) Psychiatrists	(2) Nurses and attendants	(3) Faculty	(4) "Looking for a psychiatrist"	(5) "Looking for an internist"	(6) No additional comment
Responses						
Moves on, head averted (%)	71	88	0	0	0	0
Makes eye contact (%)	23	10	0	11	0	0
Pauses and chats (%)	2	2	0	11	0	10
Stops and talks (%)	4	0.5	100	78	100	90
Mean number of questions answered (out of 6)		*	6	3.8	4.8	4.5
Respondents (No.)	13	47	14	18	15	10
Attempts (No.)	185	1283	14	18	15	

*Not applicable.

Powerlessness and Depersonalization

Eye contact and verbal contact reflect concern and individuation; their absence, avoidance and depersonalization. The data I have presented do not do justice to the rich daily encounters that grew up around matters of depersonalization and avoidance. I have records of patients who were beaten by staff for the sin of having initiated verbal contact. During my own experience, for example, one patient was beaten in the presence of other patients for having approached an attendant and told him, "I like you." Occasionally, punishment meted out to patients for misdemeanors seemed so excessive that it could not be justified by the most radical interpretations of psychiatric canon. Nevertheless, they appeared to go unquestioned. Tempers were often short. A patient who had not heard a call for medication would be roundly excoriated, and the morning attendants would often wake patients with, "Come on, you m—f—s, out of bed!"

Neither anecdotal nor "hard" data can convey the overwhelming sense of powerlessness which invades the individual as he is continually exposed to the depersonalization of the psychiatric hospital. It hardly matters *which* psychiatric hospital—the excellent public ones and the very plush private hospital were better than the rural and shabby ones in this regard, but, again, the features that psychiatric hospitals had in common overwhelmed by far their apparent differences.

Powerlessness was evident everywhere. The patient is deprived of many of his legal rights by dint of his psychiatric commitment (*21*). He is shorn of credibility by virtue of his psychiatric label. His freedom of movement is restricted. He cannot initiate contact with the staff, but may only respond to such overtures as they make. Personal privacy is minimal. Patient quarters and possessions can be entered and examined by any staff member, for whatever reason. His personal history and anguish are available to any staff member (often including the "grey lady" and "candy striper" volunteer) who chooses to read his folder, regardless of their therapeutic relationship to him. His personal hygiene and waste evacuation are often monitored. The water closets may have no doors.

At times, depersonalization reached such proportions that pseudopatients had the sense that they were invisible, or at least unworthy of account. Upon being admitted, I and other pseudopatients took the initial physical examinations in a semipublic room, where staff members went about their own business as if we were not there.

On the ward, attendants delivered verbal and occasionally serious physical abuse to patients in the presence of other observing patients, some of whom (the pseudopatients) were writing it all down. Abusive behavior, on the other hand, terminated quite abruptly when other staff members were known to be coming. Staff are credible witnesses. Patients are not.

A nurse unbuttoned her uniform to adjust her brassiere in the presence of an entire ward of viewing men. One did not have the sense that she was being seductive. Rather, she didn't notice us. A group of staff persons might point to a patient in the dayroom and discuss him animatedly, as if he were not there.

One illuminating instance of depersonalization and invisibility occurred with regard to medications. All told, the pseudopatients were administered nearly 2100 pills, including Elavil, Stelazine, Compazine, and Thorazine, to name but a few. (That such a variety of medications should have been administered to patients presenting identical symptoms is itself worthy of note.) Only two were swallowed. The rest were either pocketed or deposited in the toilet. The pseudopatients were not alone in this. Although I have no precise records on how many patients rejected their medications, the pseudopatients frequently found the medications of other patients in the toilet before they deposited their own. As long as they were cooperative, their behavior and the pseudopatients' own in this matter, as in other important matters, went unnoticed throughout.

Reactions to such depersonalization among pseudopatients were intense. Although they had come to the hospital as participant observers and were fully aware that they did not "belong," they nevertheless found themselves caught up in and fighting the process of depersonalization. Some examples: a graduate student in psychology asked his wife to bring his textbooks to the hospital so he could "catch up on his homework"—this despite the elaborate precautions taken to conceal his professional association. The same student, who had trained for quite some time to get into the hospital, and who had looked forward to the experience, "remembered" some drag races that he had wanted to see on the weekend and insisted that he be discharged by that time. Another pseudopatient attempted a romance with a nurse. Subsequently, he informed the staff that he was applying for admission to graduate school in psychology and was very likely to be admitted, since a graduate professor was one of his regular hospital visitors. The same person began to engage in psychotherapy with other patients—all of this as a way of becoming a person in an impersonal environment.

The Sources of Depersonalization

What are the origins of depersonalization? I have already mentioned two. First are attitudes held by all of us toward the mentally ill—including those who treat them—attitudes characterized by fear, distrust, and horrible expectations on the one hand, and benevolent intentions on the other. Our ambivalence leads, in this instance as in others, to avoidance.

Second, and not entirely separate, the hierarchical structure of the psychiatric hospital facilitates depersonalization. Those who are at the top have least to do with patients, and their behavior inspires the rest of the staff. Average daily contact with psychiatrists, psychologists, residents, and physicians combined ranged from 3.9 to 25.1 minutes, with an overall mean of 6.8 (six pseudopatients over a total of 129 days of hospitalization). Included in this average are time spent in the admissions interview, ward meetings in the presence of a senior staff member, group and individual psychotherapy contacts, case presentation conferences, and discharge meetings. Clearly, patients do not spend much time in interpersonal contact with doctoral staff. And doctoral staff serve as models for nurses and attendants.

There are probably other sources. Psychiatric installations are presently in serious financial straits. Staff shortages are pervasive, staff time at a premium.

Something has to give, and that something is patient contact. Yet, while financial stresses are realities, too much can be made of them. I have the impression that the psychological forces that result in depersonalization are much stronger than the fiscal ones and that the addition of more staff would not correspondingly improve patient care in this regard. The incidence of staff meetings and the enormous amount of record-keeping on patients, for example, have not been as substantially reduced as has patient contact. Priorities exist, even during hard times. Patient contact is not a significant priority in the traditional psychiatric hospital, and fiscal pressures do not account for this. Avoidance and depersonalization may.

Heavy reliance upon psychotropic medication tacitly contributes to depersonalization by convincing staff that treatment is indeed being conducted and that further patient contact may not be necessary. Even here, however, caution needs to be exercised in understanding the role of psychotropic drugs. If patients were powerful rather than powerless, if they were viewed as interesting individuals rather than diagnostic entities, if they were socially significant rather than social lepers, if their anguish truly and wholly compelled our sympathies and concerns, would we not *seek* contact with them, despite the availability of medications? Perhaps for the pleasure of it all?

The Consequences of Labeling and Depersonalization

Whenever the ratio of what is known to what needs to be known approaches zero, we tend to invent "knowledge" and assume that we understand more than we actually do. We seem unable to acknowledge that we simply don't know. The needs for diagnosis and remediation of behavioral and emotional problems are enormous. But rather than acknowledge that we are just embarking on understanding, we continue to label patients "schizophrenic," "manic-depressive," and "insane," as if in those words we had captured the essence of understanding. The facts of the matter are that we have known for a long time that diagnoses are often not useful or reliable, but we have nevertheless continued to use them. We now know that we cannot distinguish insanity from sanity. It is depressing to consider how that information will be used.

Not merely depressing, but frightening. How many people, one wonders, are sane but not recognized as such in our psychiatric institutions? How many have been needlessly stripped of their privileges of citizenship, from the right to vote and drive to that of handling their own accounts? How many have feigned insanity in order to avoid the criminal consequences of their behavior, and, conversely, how many would rather stand trial than live interminably in a psychiatric hospital—but are wrongly thought to be mentally ill? How many have been stigmatized by well-intentioned, but nevertheless erroneous, diagnoses? On the last point, recall again that a "type 2 error" in psychiatric diagnosis does not have the same consequences it does in medical diagnosis. A diagnosis of cancer that has been found to be in error is cause for celebration. But psychiatric diagnoses are rarely found to be in error. The label sticks, a mark of inadequacy forever.

Finally, how many patients might be "sane" outside the psychiatric hospital but seem insane in it—not because craziness resides in them, as it were, but because they are responding to a bizarre setting, one that may be unique to institutions which harbor nether people? Goffman (*4*) calls the process of socialization to such institutions "mortification"—an apt metaphor that includes the processes of depersonalization that have been described here. And while it is impossible to know whether the pseudopatients' responses to these processes are characteristic of all inmates—they were, after all, not real patients—it is difficult to believe that these processes of socialization to a psychiatric hospital provide useful attitudes or habits of response for living in the "real world."

Summary and Conclusions

It is clear that we cannot distinguish the sane from the insane in psychiatric hospitals. The hospital itself imposes a special environment in which the meanings of behavior can easily be misunderstood. The consequences to patients hospitalized in such an environment—the powerlessness, depersonalization, segregation, mortification, and self-labeling—seem undoubtedly countertherapeutic.

I do not, even now, understand this problem well enough to perceive solutions. But two matters seem to have some promise. The first concerns the proliferation of community mental health facilities, of crisis intervention centers, of the human potential movement, and of behavior therapies that, for all of their own problems, tend to avoid psychiatric labels, to focus on specific problems and behaviors, and to retain the individual in a relatively nonpejorative environment. Clearly, to the extent that we refrain from sending the distressed to insane places, our impressions of them are less likely to be distorted. (The risk of distorted perceptions, it seems to me, is always present, since we are much more sensitive to an individual's behaviors and verbalizations than we are to the subtle contextual stimuli that often promote them. At issue here is a matter of magnitude. And, as I have shown, the magnitude of distortion is exceedingly high in the extreme context that is a psychiatric hospital.)

The second matter that might prove promising speaks to the need to increase the sensitivity of mental health workers and researchers to the *Catch 22* position of psychiatric patients. Simply reading materials in this area will be of help to some such workers and researchers. For others, directly experiencing the impact of psychiatric hospitalization will be of enormous use. Clearly, further research into the social psychology of such total institutions will both facilitate treatment and deepen understanding.

I and the other pseudopatients in the psychiatric setting had distinctly negative reactions. We do not pretend to describe the subjective experiences of true patients. Theirs may be different from ours, particularly with the passage of time and the necessary process of adaptation to one's environment. But we can and do speak to the relatively more objective indices of treatment within the hospital. It could be a mistake, and a very unfortunate one, to consider that what happened to us derived from malice or stupidity on the part of the staff. Quite the contrary, our overwhelming impression of them was of people who really cared, who were committed and who were uncommonly intelligent. Where they failed, as they sometimes did painfully, it would be more accurate to attribute those failures to the environment in which they, too, found themselves than to personal callousness. Their perceptions and behavior were controlled by the situation, rather than being motivated by a malicious disposition. In a more benign environment, one that was less attached to global diagnosis, their behaviors and judgments might have been more benign and effective.

REFERENCES AND NOTES

1. P. Ash, *J. Abnorm. Soc. Psychol.* 44, 272 (1949); A. T. Beck, *Amer. J. Psychiat.* 119, 210 (1962); A. T. Boisen, *Psychiatry* 2, 233 (1938); N. Kreitman, *J. Ment. Sci.* 107, 876 (1961); N. Kreitman, P. Sainsbury, J. Morrisey, J. Towers, J. Scrivener, *ibid.*, p. 887; H. O. Schmitt and C. P. Fonda, *J. Abnorm. Soc. Psychol.* 52, 262 (1956); W. Seeman, *J. Nerv. Ment. Dis.* 118, 541 (1953). For an analysis of these artifacts and summaries of the disputes, see J. Zubin, *Annu. Rev. Psychol.* 18, 373 (1967); L. Phillips and J. G. Draguns, *ibid.* 22, 447 (1971).

2. R. Benedict, *J. Gen. Psychol.* 10, 59 (1934).

3. See in this regard H. Becker, *Outsiders: Studies in the Sociology of Deviance* (Free Press, New York, 1963); B. M. Braginsky, D. D. Braginsky, K. Ring, *Methods of Madness: The Mental Hospital as a Last Resort* (Holt, Rinehart & Winston, New York, 1969); G. M. Crocetti and P. V. Lemkau, *Amer. Sociol. Rev.* 30, 577 (1965); E. Goffman, *Behavior in Public Places* (Free Press, New York, 1964); R. D. Laing, *The Divided Self: A Study of Sanity and Madness* (Quadrangle, Chicago, 1960); D. L. Phillips, *Amer. Sociol. Rev.* 28, 963 (1963); T. R. Sarbin, *Psychol. Today* 6, 18 (1972); E. Schur, *Amer. J. Sociol.* 75, 309 (1969); T. Szasz, *Law, Liberty and Psychiatry* (Macmillan, New York, 1963); *The Myth of Mental Illness: Foundations of a Theory of Mental Illness* (Hoeber-Harper, New York, 1963). For a critique of some of these views, see W. R. Gove, *Amer. Sociol. Rev.* 35, 873 (1970).

4. E. Goffman, *Asylums* (Doubleday, Garden City, N.Y., 1961).

5. T. J. Scheff, *Being Mentally Ill: A Sociological Theory* (Aldine, Chicago, 1966).

6. Data from a ninth pseudopatient are not incorporated in this report because, although his sanity went undetected, he falsified aspects of his personal history, including his marital status and parental relationships. His experimental behaviors therefore were not identical to those of the other pseudopatients.

7. A. Barry, *Bellevue Is a State of Mind* (Harcourt Brace Jovanovich, New York, 1971); J. Belknap, *Human Problems of a State Mental Hospital* (McGraw-Hill, New York, 1956); W. Caudill, F. C. Redlich, H. R. Gilmore, E. B. Brody, *Amer. J. Orthopsychiat.* 22, 314 (1952); A. R. Goldman, R. H. Bohr, T. A. Steinberg, *Prof. Psychol.* 1, 427 (1970); unauthored, *Roche Report* 1 (No. 13), 8 (1971).

8. Beyond the personal difficulties that the pseudopatient is likely to experience in the hospital, there are legal and social ones that, combined, require considerable attention before entry. For example, once admitted to a psychiatric institution, it is difficult, if not impossible, to be discharged on short notice, state law to the contrary notwithstanding. I was not sensitive

to these difficulties at the outset of the project, nor to the personal and situational emergencies that can arise, but later a writ of habeas corpus was prepared for each of the entering pseudopatients and an attorney was kept "on call" during every hospitalization. I am grateful to John Kaplan and Robert Bartels for legal advice and assistance in these matters.

9. However distasteful such concealment is, it was a necessary first step to examining these questions. Without concealment, there would have been no way to know how valid these experiences were; nor was there any way of knowing whether whatever detections occurred were a tribute to the diagnostic acumen of the staff or to the hospital's rumor network. Obviously, since my concerns are general ones that cut across individual hospitals and staffs, I have respected their anonymity and have eliminated clues that might lead to their identification.

10. Interestingly, of the 12 admissions, 11 were diagnosed as schizophrenic and one, with the identical symptomatology, as manic-depressive psychosis. This diagnosis has a more favorable prognosis, and it was given by the only private hospital in our sample. On the relations between social class and psychiatric diagnosis, see A. deB. Hollingshead and F. C. Redlich, *Social Class and Mental Illness: A Community Study* (Wiley, New York, 1958).

11. It is possible, of course, that patients have quite broad latitudes in diagnosis and therefore are inclined to call many people sane, even those whose behavior is patently aberrant. However, although we have no hard data on this matter, it was our distinct impression that this was not the case. In many instances, patients not only singled us out for attention, but came to imitate our behaviors and styles.

12. J. Cumming and E. Cumming, *Community Ment. Health* 1, 135 (1965); A. Farina and K. Ring, *J. Abnorm. Psychol.* 70, 47 (1965); H. E. Freeman and O. G. Simmons, *The Mental Health Patient Comes Home* (Wiley, New York, 1963); W. J. Johannsen, *Ment. Hygiene* 53, 218 (1969); A. S. Linsky, *Soc. Psychiat.* 5, 166 (1970).

13. S. E. Asch, *J. Abnorm. Soc. Psychol.* 41, 258 (1946); *Social Psychology* (Prentice-Hall, New York, 1952).

14. See also I. N. Mensh and J. Wishner, *J. Personality* 16, 188 (1947); J. Wishner, *Psychol. Rev.* 67, 96 (1960); J. S. Bruner and R. Tagiuri, in *Handbook of Social Psychology,* G. Lindzey, Ed. (Addison-Wesley, Cambridge, Mass., 1954), vol. 2, pp. 634–654; J. S. Bruner, D. Shapiro, R. Tagiuri, in *Person Perception and Interpersonal Behavior,* R. Tagiuri and L. Petrullo, Eds. (Stanford Univ. Press, Stanford, Calif., 1958), pp. 277–288.

15. For an example of a similar self-fulfilling prophecy, in this instance dealing with the "central" trait of intelligence, see R. Rosenthal and L. Jacobson, *Pygmalion in the Classroom* (Holt, Rinehart & Winston, New York, 1968).

16. E. Zigler and L. Phillips, *J. Abnorm. Soc. Psychol.* 63, 69 (1961). See also R. K. Freudenberg and J. P. Robertson, *A.M.A. Arch. Neurol. Psychiatr.* 76, 14 (1956).

17. W. Mischel, *Personality and Assessment* (Wiley, New York, 1968).

18. The most recent and unfortunate instance of this tenet is that of Senator Thomas Eagleton.

19. T. R. Sarbin and J. C. Mancuso, *J. Clin. Consult. Psychol.* 35, 159 (1970); T. R. Sarbin, *ibid.* 31, 447 (1967); J. C. Nunnally, Jr., *Popular Conceptions of Mental Health* (Holt, Rinehart & Winston, New York, 1961).

20. A. H. Stanton and M. S. Schwartz, *The Mental Hospital: A Study of Institutional Participation in Psychiatric Illness and Treatment* (Basic, New York, 1954).

21. D. B. Wexler and S. E. Scoville, *Ariz. Law Rev.* 13, 1 (1971).

22. I thank W. Mischel, E. Orne, and M. S. Rosenhan for comments on an earlier draft of this manuscript.

DISCUSSION QUESTIONS

1. Why are labels of mental illness so difficult to overcome? Why are the mentally ill generally more stigmatized than the physically ill?
2. What are some of the consequences of powerlessness and depersonalization for patients in psychiatric hospitals?

—Article 17—

A Case of a Psychotic Navaho Indian Male

DONALD P. JEWELL

Introduction

INCREASED PSYCHOLOGICAL and ethnological rapprochement has resulted in a greater understanding of American subgroups and the processes of acculturation. Examples of this integrated approach are to be seen in Barnouw's study of Chippewa Indian acculturation[1] and, on the individual level, Devereux's psychotherapy of an alcoholic Sioux.[2]

Sometimes identified as the "culture-personality" orientation, this approach has reached a degree of clarification which justifies consistent designation. It is suggested here that it be defined as ethnopsychological. It is an approach which, as Kluckhohn has shown, has about a century of development.[3] Ethnopsychology has generally concerned itself with the definition of general normal personality characteristics of other cultures, only occasionally with the neurotic individual, and rarely with the psychotic.

From "A Case of a Psychotic Navaho Indian Male," by Donald P. Jewell, *Human Organization,* Vol. 11, No. 1, 1952, pp. 32–36. Reproduced by permission of The Society for Applied Anthropology.

Note: This study was undertaken during the writer's internship in Clinical Psychology at Patton State Hospital, Patton, California. The writer wishes to gratefully acknowledge the supervision of this study by Mr. William Walcott, Clinical Psychologist and Supervisor of Interns. This study was made possible by the interest and cooperation of Dr. Otto L. Gericke, Superintendent of the hospital.

Purpose of This Study

The writer had the opportunity recently to make a rather extensive observation of a Navaho Indian institutionalized as a psychotic in a California state mental hospital. By drawing from the literature of Navaho ethnopsychology and the writer's own experience among the Navaho people, it was hoped that the dynamics of the patient's maladjustment would be revealed. It was also anticipated that some sort of psychotherapy would evolve.

This report is a summary of those endeavors to understand and assist the Navaho patient. Cultural and linguistic obstacles prohibited an ideal approach, but enough was accomplished to permit considerable insight into the patient's behavior. There were features about the patient's personality which would not fit harmoniously with concepts of psychiatric symptomatology derived from European culture, those concepts dealing particularly with the dynamics of the patient's diagnosis of catatonic schizophrenia. The unique characteristics of this individual's personality leads, in fact, to the question as to what extent he should be considered psychotic, and whether that consideration should be viewed from Navaho or Anglo perspective.

During his many interviews with the patient, some of them with the aid of a Navaho interpreter, the writer developed an increasing awareness that to call the patient psychotic was an arbitrary matter. When this Navaho is referred to as psychotic, then, it is merely because he carried such a diagnosis during his 18 months of hospitalization as a mental patient.

Orientation

Considerable literary attention has been given to the general psychological characteristics of Navaho Indians.[4] These have related psychological findings to ethnological contexts, and so offer a background against which the atypical Navaho individual may be examined.

On the behavioral level, the Navahos are in many ways unique, not only with respect to white people, but other Indian tribes as well. One of their most characteristic traits may be seen in crisis situations. Kluckhohn and Leighton describe it as a passive resistance, the individual masking his fear by quiet unmovingness, an appearance of stoicism. If forced into action, the response is a mechanical, apparently uncomprehending behavior.[5]

Another form of withdrawal is often expressed in periods of depression, apparently a morbid preoccupation with health.[6]

These being salient aspects of the typical Navaho personality, the question now arises as to how those traits would be characterized on the psychotic level. Under prolonged psychological stress, what would develop from the stoicism and moods of morbid preoccupation?

In an endeavor to answer this question a survey was made of those mental hospitals which would most likely be caring for Navaho patients. The Bureau of Indian Affairs' policy is not to concentrate Indian patients, but to subsidize their care in whatever hospital they may have been committed. It is thus possible that a few

Navahos may be hospitalized some distance from their reservation area of New Mexico, Utah, and Arizona, and have not been located in this survey. It is felt, however, that a survey of those mental hospitals in the Southwest only would be adequate to show general trends. The findings are summarized in the following table.

Elimination of the organic psychoses leaves one manic, one depressive, and 10 schizophrenics. Of the schizophrenics, seven are catatonic. This is an unusually high incidence of catatonic schizophrenia and seems to indicate that Navahos are predisposed toward that particular psychosis. This immediately suggests that the above described stoicism has been carried to pathological extremes, and possibly that the stoicism is actually a transient form of catatonia. It was with this problem in mind that the Navaho patient discussed in this report was studied.

The Patient

The patient was a 26-year-old Navaho male. For purposes of anonymity he will be referred to as Bill. He came to the writer's attention through a survey of Indian patients at the hospital. He was the only Navaho of 13 Indian patients scattered throughout the various wards and cottages, and of the 4,000 general patient population.

The outlook for examination and therapy seemed at first quite discouraging. The patient was in a cottage ordinarily reserved for the most regressed patients. Unlike most of the others in this cottage, however, he was not there because of repeated failure of such routine therapies as shock treatment, occupational therapy,

TABLE 17.1

Diagnosis	Number	Sex and Age
Psychosis with syphillis of the C.N.C.	2	1f: 47; 1m: 31
Psychosis with cerebral arteriosclerosis	1	1f: 62
Psychosis due to trauma (organic)	1	1m: 47
Epilepsy	8	6m: 20, 24, 29, 33, 37, 39; 2f: 20, 32
Schizophrenia, simple type	1	1m: 25
Schizophrenia, mixed type	1	1f: 26
Schizophrenia, hebephrenic type	1	1f: 30
Schizophrenia, catatonic type	7	4m: 26, 28, 28, 36; 3f: 20, 30, 38
Depressed state	1	1f: 37
Manic depressive psychosis, manic type	1	1m: 42

Legend: f: female; m: male
Summary of survey of Navaho Indian mental patients hospitalized in southwestern United States, excluding mental defectives. (Acknowledgement of the hospitals cooperating in this survey must be regretfully omitted due to the need to protect the identity of the patients.)

etc. It was unusual for a patient in his condition, who had been at the hospital for eight months, not to have received at least electric shock treatment.

A preliminary period was spent at the cottage, observing Bill's behavior. He was very withdrawn. Most of his day was spent in inactive sitting or sleeping. He would rouse himself only for eating or attending to other personal needs. He would assist with floor waxing, dishwashing, or other activities the attendants might require of him, but in a perfunctory and apathetic manner. His behavior was not patently catatonic, but certainly suggestive of it.

Most of the attendants reported never having heard Bill speak. A few, however, indicated that Bill would occasionally approach them and, in almost unintelligible English, ask if he could go home.

Shortly thereafter Bill was brought to the writer's office where he was greeted in Navaho. Bill responded in that language, glancing briefly at the writer before returning his gaze to the floor.

This closer inspection of Bill revealed occipital flattening, resulting from the cradle board as a child, and the pierced ear lobes of a conservative Navaho. During this first interview he complained about the close haircuts he received at the hospital, further evidence that he belonged to the old-fashioned, "long hair" conservatives of the reservation.

The interview proceeded very slowly, but gradually a system of communication began to evolve. By utilizing mutually understood Navaho and English words, by means of pantomime, and with the aid of penciled sketches, the system became increasingly refined during the following interviews.

Bill was seen three hours a week for three months. The writer then took an eight months' leave of absence from the hospital, during which time he spent several months in Bill's home area near Shiprock, New Mexico.

While in the Shiprock area, the writer endeavored to locate Bill's family to advise them of the patient's circumstances. Bill had previously drawn a map indicating the approximate location of his family's *hogans* (dwellings), but it proved impossible to find them. The *hogans* were located about five miles from the nearest road, and even if a horse and interpreter had been available the chances of locating the specific *hogans* were slight. The situation was complicated by the fact that the family did not have American names and the writer did not know their Navaho names. Missionaries and Bureau of Indian Affairs personnel were consequently given the problem of finding the family but several months elapsed before they were equipped with sufficient information to do so.

Although he could not communicate with Bill's family the writer succeeded in talking with several Navahos who had known Bill, and in obtaining ecological and further case history material.

Shortly after the writer's return to the hospital, a Navaho interpreter was brought in from the Sherman Institute, a large Indian school not far from the hospital. Interviews with the patient through the interpreter corroborated the case history material obtained, and further satisfied the writer in his clinical evaluation of the patient. Both of these areas are separately discussed in the following text.

Case History

The gathering of Bill's history extended over a period of 11 months and was obtained piecemeal from a variety of sources. In summarizing, however, this material will be integrated for greater coherency.

Bill was born in a part of the reservation noted for being both very conservative and poverty-stricken. Only 50 miles away is the markedly contrasting community of Shiprock, considered to be one of the most acculturated Navaho communities. It is also prospering from recently developed uranium operations in the region.

During his early years Bill saw very little of Shiprock and was reared in the traditional Navaho way. He was born during an eclipse (it is not known whether of the sun or moon) and was thus destined to take part in a periodic ceremony identified to the writer as the "Breath of Life" sing. The first of this series of ceremonies was held while he was still an infant, the second about six years ago. During the ceremony he inhales the breath of a great deity and is thus assured of continued good health in the respiratory and vocal organs.

Bill lived with his immediate family until he was six years of age. He had only one younger sister at that time, although the family was later to include seven living siblings. He did not become well acquainted with his family, however, as he was given to his grandfather when he was six years old. The grandfather, a widower, lived several miles deeper into the reservation and required Bill's assistance as a sheepherder.

Bill worked for his grandfather as a sheepherder until he was 17, except for one interruption when, at the age of 15, he spent 50 days in the Shiprock hospital with a back ailment. Bill reports that the old man never talked to him.

At his grandfather's death Bill went to work for the railroad in Colorado. This was cut short by an illness which confined him to the Navaho Medical Center in Fort Defiance, Arizona. The illness was diagnosed as tuberculosis, pulmonary, moderately advanced. He was in the hospital for eight months and was discharged in the summer of 1944.

Bill returned to railroad employment and worked in Utah, Oregon, and Nebraska. He was always part of Navaho crews and thus never exposed to acculturative influences. His father and a younger brother were also part of these crews.

Bill returned home for a brief visit in 1949, accompanied by his brother and father. He had saved $1,022. Subsequently, he went to Phoenix, Arizona, to pick cotton, a job that had been found for him by the employment agency at Shiprock. This was his first trip from home without a family member.

The employment at Phoenix did not last long and in December, 1949, on the advice of an Indian friend he went to Barstow, California, seeking railroad employment. At the section camp there his attempt to find work was unsuccessful, and after three days he started by bus back to Phoenix.

On this return trip he stopped for dinner at Colton. A white man he met there promised to obtain railroad employment for him. The stranger said that he required funds for this effort and in some way relieved Bill of his savings which had now dwindled to $725.

Bill returned home penniless, pawned some jewelry, borrowed some money, and returned to Colton to try to find the man who had taken his savings. He also looked for Navahos who might have information about employment. The many hours of waiting around the bus station searching for his man apparently caused suspicion, for he was arrested for vagrancy.

In jail he met some Navahos with whom he went to Barstow after his release. But in Barstow he was still unable to find employment and after six days he was completely out of funds. He started walking toward Phoenix and was picked up by a man driving a truck. This man gave Bill one day's employment which allowed for funds for a return to Barstow and another attempt to find work.

He managed to raise a little money doing odd jobs about the section camp near Barstow, and then returned to San Bernardino on the first lap of his return to Phoenix and home. It occurred to him that if he could get to a hospital, the officials there would send him to a reservation hospital, from whence he would be sent home. This was logical thinking: on the reservations, the hospitals, schools, and trading posts are the major source of assistance in all sorts of troubles.

As this idea occurred to Bill, he noticed a woman dressed in white whom he took to be a nurse. He approached her and endeavored to explain that he was sick, but his endeavors were misinterpreted and he was taken to jail.

At the county jail Bill was apparently mistaken for a Mexican since a Mexican interpreter had tried to interview him. When the interview failed he was transferred to the psychopathic ward. Interviewed by the medical examiner there, he reportedly demonstrated an anguished appearance and repeated, "Me sick." He was diagnosed as schizophrenia, catatonic type, and delivered to the state mental hospital.

Upon admission to the hospital, Bill was first taken to be a Filipino. The psychiatric admission note indicated that he was, " . . . confused, dull, and preoccupied. He has a look of anguish and appears to be hallucinating. . . . He repeats, 'I don't know.'" He was diagnosed as dementia praecox, which was later specified as hebephrenic type.

Several months later the psychiatrist on Bill's cottage tested him for *cerea flexibilitas* (waxy flexibility) and, finding it to be present, altered the diagnosis to catatonic type.

Eight months after his admittance he was discovered by the writer.

Psychological Aspects

Concomitant with gathering the case history material presented above, endeavors were made to evaluate the patient's intelligence and personality. The lack of culturally-biased examining techniques made this extremely difficult.

Bill's performance on the various tests that were administered led to a conclusion that his probable I.Q. was in the vicinity of 80. This had to take into consideration the patient's slowness. At best, a Navaho refuses to be put under pressure of time, and to what extent Bill's slowness was cultural rather than psychotically pathological was a question of primary concern.

Bill's apathetic and withdrawn behavior has already been described. For diagnostic purposes, however, this syndrome is confused by cultural factors. It is common for Navahos, with their morbid fear of hospitals, to demonstrate just such a withdrawal patterning.[7] It is not known whether or not this would reach a stage of *cerea flexibilitas* or how long this behavior will persist. Accordingly it was concluded that Bill's apparent catatonia should not be accepted as a symptom of schizophrenia until underlying signs of schizophrenic processes could be detected.

During the first interview Bill was given the Draw-A-Person Test. The figure he drew was indistinct and without facial features and clearly reflected his withdrawal.

On the seventh interview the test was again given. Compared with the earlier attempt, the second drawing clearly reflected an improvement. It probably indicated the therapeutic benefits derived from the extensive individual treatment the patient was receiving.

The second drawing filled the paper, the facial features were portrayed, the arms were extended, and the drawing generally implied those signs which are held to indicate good contact with reality.

Although Bill's second drawing seems to infer considerable personality change, no changes could be observed in his behavior. He continued to appear apathetic and withdrawn. On several occasions he indicated his reluctance to talk because, "me no good this place," pointing to his chest. This suggested the characteristic organ cathexes of schizophrenia. However, the patient's thinking behind this statement was made clear during the later interviews through an interpreter.

Bill was concerned about the fact that he had not completed the second series of "Breath of Life" ceremony. This matter had gone too long unattended, and he assumed that he must conserve his vocal energies until they could be supplemented by the breath of the deity. He expressed a great need to return home to pursue the ceremony.

In continued endeavor to detect schizophrenic underlay of his apparent catatonia, Bill was given a series of tests, none of which revealed responses normally associated with schizophrenia.

During the early course of the interviews with Bill, although not satisfied that the patient was not psychotic, the writer recommended that the best therapeutic environment for him would be his own home. This recommendation was not acted upon, partly because no one knew where his home was, or how he could be supervised there, but chiefly because he continued to appear catatonic.

Later, as the writer became convinced that the catatonia—if such it could be termed—was not symptomatic of underlying schizophrenia, efforts were renewed to release the patient. The outcome of these endeavors are summarized in the following section.

Outcome

As mentioned earlier, the final interviews with Bill were carried on with the aid of a Navaho interpreter. Bill conversed quite freely with the other Navahos and expressed gratitude at being able to talk to someone in his own language. The conversations did not add much to the history and understanding previously gained, but did offer an opportunity to inquire for the presence of hallucinations, delusions, and more subtle clues of schizophrenic thinking. Unless Bill's anxiety regarding the uncompleted "Breath of Life" ceremony could be considered bizarre nothing of significance was elicited.

The interpreter's reaction to the interviews represented their most significant outcome. He was a professional interpreter, with vast experience in interviewing Navaho youths in strange environments. He expressed a strong conviction that Bill's behavior and attitudes were not unusual under the circumstances.

The interpreter communicated his feeling to the superintendent of the Sherman Institute who took an immediate and active interest in the case. After several interviews with Bill, satisfied that he could observe nothing about Bill's behavior which could be considered atypical under the circumstances, the superintendent offered to accept him into the flexible program of the Sherman Institute.

Bill was accordingly released under custody of the superintendent and careful plans were made to assure his adjustment at the school. At first, he was quartered in the school hospital, but allowed to participate in the school's social and recreational activities. He was employed with the animal husbandry and gardening program.

The writer's last visit to the Sherman Institute disclosed that Bill's adjustment had been quite rapid. He had put on weight and after about two weeks announced that he "felt right at home, now."

It had been difficult at first, because in spite of all precautions the students had learned something of Bill's past hospitalization. To the Navahos the hospital symbolizes death, and death is particularly abhorrent to them as they have no clearly structured concepts of an afterlife. The students consequently shied away from Bill a little when he arrived, but he has since found acceptance.

He will go back to the reservation in the spring, at the close of the school year, and attend to the unfinished business of the "Breath of Life" ceremony.

Concluding Discussion

In the course of this Navaho's commitment and 18 months of hospitalization, he was routinely examined by several psychiatrists, all of whom concurred with the diagnosis of schizophrenia. Without verbal communication with the patient, diagnosis was necessarily derived from observation of his overt behavior. Diagnosis was apparently confident as the patient was not referred to staff clinic or for psychological testing, the normal procedure with questionable cases.

Most of the psychiatrists' diagnostic observations were based on information received from the attendants of Bill's cottage, who reported the patient's withdrawn and apathetic behavior. Upon closer examination the patient would demonstrate *cerea flexibilitas.* Because of these factors the patient was assumed to be catatonic and hence schizophrenic.

Actually, many of the classic symptoms of catatonia were not present in this patient. He was not markedly stuporous or mute; he was clean in his personal habits and would eat willingly; he tended to doze as he sat rather than stare fixedly into space as does the typical catatonic. The writer, too, examined Bill for *cerea flexibilitas,* but learned later that the patient held grotesque positions because he thought it was expected of him,

With the assumption, however, that the patient's overt behavior could be interpreted as symptomatic of catatonic schizophrenia, it remains to be explained why testing and closer observation did not reveal the underlying ego disintegration which should be expected.

General personality traits of the Navaho people, as briefly reviewed earlier in this paper, could possibly infer a potential for schizophrenic disintegration. Navahos do not have the imaginative activity and the inner control which is so important to adjustment in the Anglo world. The scales are balanced, however, by a defense of rigidity and constriction. In a threatening situation they strive to maintain ego structure by psychic withdrawal.

The few tests that were applicable in examining Bill did not permit a very intensive examination of the dynamics of his withdrawal, but all indications were that he continued to maintain ego strength. He could account for his acts rationally, he performed very well with conceptualization, he maintained orientation for time and place, and could hold in mind simultaneously various aspects of situations or problems. His visuo-motor performance exhibited no signs of distorted perspective. Many of his expressions could be considered naive, but hardly bizarre.

The apparent incongruity between the patient's overt behavior and underlying personality dynamics, although not fully understood psychologically, should not be considered as psychotic manifestation. Culturally derived, it can probably be explained as a defense mechanism characterized by an extreme and sustained withdrawal.

To what extent Bill's case may be typical of other Navaho patients diagnosed as catatonic schizophrenia cannot, of course, be proposed. It would be necessary to know if those patients were similarly diagnosed on the basis of overt behavior alone.

It is also unknown to what degree Bill may personify on-reservation Navaho youth. Superficially at least, his history appears quite typical. His lack of school, his years as a sheepherder for his grandfather, his attack of tuberculosis, and his railroad employment, are circumstances and events common to many Navahos. His grandfather's apparent lack of affection implies an almost feral existence for the growing boy, but even this situation is not unusual. It is, in fact, difficult to discern some way in which this patient could be atypical as evaluated against his cultural background. Except for his possible low intelligence, he appears to represent a typical Navaho youth, a fact heavy with implication when his 18 months of hospitalization as a mental patient is considered.

The previously cited survey of hospitalized Navaho mental patients shows an amazingly small percentage of the total Navaho population (which is about 65,000). This is probably because few Navahos are currently coming in very close contact with Anglo structure.

Of the catatonic schizophrenics, it would be of value to know more about the details of their admission. If they were referred from the reservation it probably meant that they were considered psychotic within the Navaho milieu; if, on the other hand, they were referred by agencies off the reservation (as was Bill), it would imply an evaluation derived from Anglo perspective. This will become a more poignant problem with increasing off-reservation movement of the Navaho people.

In addition to what this study may imply with respect to the Navaho Indians, it is hoped also that it may illustrate the need to consider the influence of cultural environment in any study of individual personality. The psychiatric approach usually concerns itself with the abnormal personality, and evaluates the individual according to concepts of what constitutes the normal personality. Too often these concepts are preconceived and stereotyped, giving very little consideration to the individual's cultural frame of reference. This factor naturally varies in proportion to the degree of the individual's acculturation.

The cultural factor seems to be particularly important in reconciling overt behavior with covert personality dynamics. This is often a difficult reconciliation even with the patients of the general American cultural patterning, and becomes increasingly more difficult the farther removed the individual is from acculturation.

The need to consider emotional maladjustment with respect to cultural factors has long been recognized. It has, however, been somewhat of an academic acknowledgment which demands greater practical application on the clinical level.

NOTES

1. Barnouw, V., "Acculturation and Personality Among the Wisconsin Chippewa," *American Anthropologist,* Memoir Number 72, Vol. 52, 1950.
2. Devereux, G., *Reality and Dream,* International Universities Press, Inc., 1950.
3. Kluckhohn, C., "The Influence of Psychiatry on Anthropology in America During the Past One Hundred Years," eds. J. K. Hall, C. Zilboorg, and E. A. Bunker, *One Hundred Years of American Psychiatry,* Columbia University Press, 1947, pp. 589–617.
4. Henry, W., "The Thematic Apperception Technique in the Study of Culture-Personality Relations," *Genetic Psychology Monographs,* Vol 35, 1947, pp. 3–135; Kluckhohn, C., and Leighton, D., *Children of the People,* Harvard University Press, 1948.
5. Kluckhohn and Leighton, *ibid.,* p. 108.
6. *Ibid.,* p. 110.
7. *Ibid.,* pp. 108–109.

DISCUSSION QUESTIONS

1. What is the "Breath of Life" ceremony? In what ways did the "Breath of Life" ceremony influence Bill's overt behavior?
2. Should mental health officials consider the cultural environment as a factor in evaluating one's mental health? Why or why not?

VII

Social Differentiation and Stratification

WHAT TO FOCUS ON:

1. How do stratification systems affect the individual's sense of involvement in the larger society, as well as future possibilities?
2. Using the material by Fromm, and Davis and Moore, what are the different views regarding the activity of work?

MUCH OF THE SOCIOLOGICAL discussion presented in the preceding chapters relates to the means by which the individual becomes a part of the group. Culture, social structure, and socialization all deal with the connecting relationships between groups and the individuals that comprise them. While social stratification is also oriented to the group, it does so in a different manner. From the standpoint of a definition, we can say that social stratification refers to the ways in which a group's wealth, power, resources and opportunities are distributed to its members. Groups, referred to as classes, form on the basis of the amount of distribution common to their members. Such phrases as *upper, middle* and *working class,* and *the poor,* refer to groups of individuals or families who share a particular amount of wealth, power and opportunity. However, in addition to the fact that groups are socially organized in this way, they are also restricted in the way that they can participate and interact with others. Therefore, we become differentiated (*upper class* is different from *working class*) through the process of *stratification.* Consequently, while the process of stratification includes some individuals, it also excludes individuals. The result is a sociological arena that is filled with a dynamic tension between these two points—inclusion and exclusion.

Such a sociological topic has a long tradition of controversy concerning this unequal distribution. The issue has been to understand the dynamics of stratification. Do capitalist societies have different rules than non-capitalist ones? What prevents wealth, power, resources and opportunities from being evenly distributed throughout the group? What are the chances of moving from one class to another? Such questions are only the beginning of any sociological attempt to understand and explain this phenomena. The articles for this chapter present different positions which attempt a general interpretation regarding this subject.

The article by Kingsley Davis and Wilbert E. Moore is a classic statement of the functional position of social stratification. Here we see the idea of a relationship between inequalities related to the nature of work and corresponding inequalities of distribution. Stratification becomes a function of work. According to Davis and Moore, it also serves a functional role of motivating individuals to enter jobs that are more arduous, socially responsible and require lengthy training. Is stratification a functional necessity and an inevitability?

Erich Fromm provides an excellent explanation of Marx's view of labor in industrial capitalism. While the material aspects of labor were important to Marx, he was also concerned about the consequences such labor had on human beings. Material aspects aside, Fromm explains Marx's theme of capitalist alienation of labor. Is work the source of our satisfaction and contribution to society, or does labor turn us into passive objects of others? Who controls the labor process? Marx's answers to these questions are unique and often ignored by the members of capitalist systems.

Some sociologists have problems with the functional explanation of stratification. These sociologists argue that it creates the image of a meritocracy—those at the top merit being there because they have more training or their job is more significant to the group. The Tobias article examines how the educational system affects future stratification opportunities. She demonstrates a relationship between standardized performance testing with the student's placement in different "tracks" (curricula with different educational goals) and the resulting likelihood of future opportunities. A pivotal part of this relationship is the controversy of the validity of the standardized performance-based tests—do these tests reflect innate abilities, can poor performance be improved through educational programs, and do the tests reflect the needed skills and information actually present in social reality? Tobias argues that the tests create an impression which legitimates tracking some students to succeed and others to fail.

Article 18

Principles of Social Stratification

KINGSLEY DAVIS AND WILBERT E. MOORE

IN A PREVIOUS PAPER some concepts for handling the phenomena of social equality were presented.[1] In the present paper a further step in stratification theory is undertaken—an attempt to show the relationship between stratification and the rest of the social order.[2] Starting from the proposition that no society is "classless," or unstratified, an effort is made to explain, in functional terms, the universal necessity which calls forth stratification in any social system. Next, an attempt is made to explain the roughly uniform distribution of prestige as between the major types of positions in every society. Since, however, there occur between one society and another great differences in the degree and kind of stratification, some attention is also given to the varieties of social inequality and the variable factors that give rise to them.

Clearly, the present task requires two different lines of analysis—one to understand the universal, the other to understand the variable features of stratification. Naturally each line of inquiry aids the other and is indispensable, and in the treatment that follows the two will be interwoven, although, because of space limitations, the emphasis will be on the universals.

From "Principles of Social Stratification," by Kingsley Davis and Wilbert E. Moore, *American Sociological Review,* Vol. 10, April 1945, pp. 242–249. Reprinted by permission of the publisher.

Throughout, it will be necessary to keep in mind one thing—namely, that the discussion relates to the system of positions, not to the individuals occupying those positions. It is one thing to ask why different positions carry different degrees of prestige; and quite another to ask how certain individuals get into those positions. Although, as the argument will try to show, both questions are related, it is essential to keep them separate in our thinking. Most of the literature on stratification has tried to answer the second question (particularly with regard to the ease or difficulty of mobility between strata) without tackling the first. The first question, however, is logically prior and, in the case of any particular individual or group, factually prior.

The Functional Necessity of Stratification

Curiously, however, the main functional necessity explaining the universal presence of stratification is precisely the requirement faced by any society of placing and motivating individuals in the social structure. As a functioning mechanism a society must somehow distribute its members in social positions and induce them to perform the duties of these positions. It must thus concern itself with motivation at two different levels: to instill in the proper individuals the desire to fill certain positions, and, once in these positions, the desire to perform the duties attached to them. Even though the social order may be relatively static in form, there is a continuous process of metabolism as new individuals are born into it, shift with age, and die off. Their absorption into the positional system must somehow be arranged and motivated. This is true whether the system is competitive or non-competitive. A competitive system gives greater importance to the motivation to perform the duties of the positions; but in any system both types of motivation are required.

If the duties associated with the various positions were all equally pleasant to the human organism, all equally important to societal survival, and all equally in need of the same ability or talent, it would make no difference who got into which positions, and the problem of social placement would be greatly reduced. But actually it does make a great deal of difference who gets into which positions, not only because some positions are inherently more agreeable than others, but also because some require special talents or training and some are functionally more important than others. Also, it is essential that the duties of the positions be performed with the diligence that their importance requires. Inevitably, then, a society must have, first, some kind of rewards that it can use as inducements, and, second, some way of distributing these rewards differentially according to positions. The rewards and their distribution become a part of the social order, and thus give rise to stratification.

One may ask what kinds of rewards a society has at its disposal in distributing its personnel and securing essential services. It has, first of all, the things that contribute to sustenance and comfort. It has, second, the things that contribute to humor and diversion. And it has, finally, the things that contribute to self-respect and ego expansion. The last, because of the peculiarly social character of the self, is largely a function of the opinion of others, but it nonetheless ranks in importance with the first two. In any social system all three kinds of rewards must be dispensed differentially according to positions.

In a sense the rewards are "built into" the position. They consist in the "rights" associated with the position, plus what may be called its accompaniments or perquisites. Often the rights, and sometimes the accompaniments, are functionally related to the duties of the position. (Rights as viewed by the incumbent are usually duties as viewed by other members of the community.) However, there may be a host of subsidiary rights and perquisites that are not essential to the function of the position and have only an indirect and symbolic connection with its duties, but which still may be of considerable importance in inducing people to seek the positions and fulfill the essential duties.

If the rights and perquisites of different positions in a society must be unequal, then the society must be stratified, because that is precisely what stratification means. Social inequality is thus an unconsciously evolved device by which societies insure that the most important positions are conscientiously filled by the most qualified persons. Hence every society, no matter how simple or complex, must differentiate persons in terms of both prestige and esteem, and must therefore possess a certain amount of institutionalized inequality.

It does not follow that the amount or type of inequality need be the same in all societies. This is largely a function of factors that will be discussed presently.

The Two Determinants of Positional Rank

Granting the general function that inequality subserves, one can specify the two factors that determine the relative rank of different positions. In general those positions convey the best reward, and hence have the highest rank, which (a) have the greatest importance for the society and (b) require the greatest training or talent. The first factor concerns function and is a matter of relative significance; the second concerns means and is a matter of scarcity.

Differential functional importance. Actually a society does not need to reward positions in proportion to their functional importance. It merely needs to give sufficient reward to them to insure that they will be filled competently. In other words, it must see that less essential positions do not compete successfully with more essential ones. If a position is easily filled, it need not be heavily rewarded, even though important. On the other hand, if it is important but hard to fill, the reward must be high enough to get it filled anyway. Functional importance is therefore a necessary but not a sufficient cause of rank being assigned to a position.[3]

Differential scarcity of personnel. Practically all positions, no matter how acquired, require some form of skill or capacity for performance. This is implicit in the very notion of position, which implies that the incumbent must, by virtue of his incumbency, accomplish certain things.

There are, ultimately, only two ways in which a person's qualifications come about: through inherent capacity or through training. Obviously, in concrete activities both are always necessary, but from a practical standpoint the scarcity may lie primarily in one or the other, as well as in both. Some positions require innate talents of such high degree that the persons who fill them are bound to be rare. In many cases, however, talent is fairly abundant in the population but the training process is so long, costly, and elaborate that relatively few can qualify. Modern medicine, for example, is within the mental capacity of most individuals, but a medical education is so burdensome and expensive that virtually none would undertake it if the position of the M.D. did not carry a reward commensurate with the sacrifice.

If the talents required for a position are abundant and the training easy, the method of acquiring the position may have little to do with its duties. There may be, in fact, a virtually accidental relationship. But if the skills required are scarce by reason of the rarity of talent or the costliness of training, the position, if functionally important, must have an attractive power that will draw the necessary skills in competition with other positions. This means, in effect, that the position must be high in the social scale—must command great prestige, high salary, ample leisure, and the like.

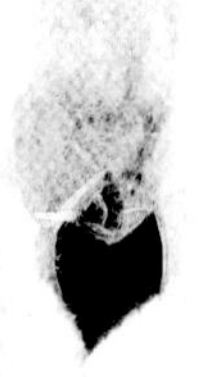

How variations are to be understood. Insofar as there is a difference between one system of stratification and another, it is attributable to whatever factors affect the two determinants of differential reward—namely, functional importance and scarcity of personnel. Positions important in one society may not be important in another, because the conditions faced by the societies, or their degree of internal development, may be different. The same conditions, in turn, may affect the question of scarcity; for in some societies the stage of development, or the external situation, may wholly obviate the necessity of certain kinds of skill or talent. Any particular system of stratification, then, can be understood as a product of the special conditions affecting the two aforementioned grounds of differential reward. . . .

Wealth, property, and labor. Every position that secures for its incumbent a livelihood is, by definition, economically rewarded. It therefore becomes convenient for the society to use unequal economic returns as a principal means of controlling the entrance of persons into positions and stimulating the performance of their duties. The amount of the economic return therefore becomes one of the main indices of social status.

It should be stressed, however, that a position does not bring power and prestige *because* it draws a high income. Rather, it draws a high income because it is functionally important and the available personnel is for one reason or another scarce. It is therefore superficial and erroneous to regard high income as the cause of a man's power and prestige, just as it is erroneous to think that a man's fever is the cause of his disease.[4]

The economic source of power and prestige is not income primarily, but the ownership of capital goods (including patents, good will, and professional reputation). Such ownership should be distinguished from the possession of consumers' goods, which is an index rather than a cause of social standing. In other words, the ownership of producers' goods is, properly speaking, a source of income like other positions, the income itself remaining an index. Even in situations where social values are widely commercialized and earnings are the readiest method of judging social position, income does not confer prestige on a position so much as it induces people to compete for the position. It is true that a man who has a high income as a result of one position may find this money helpful in climbing into another position as well, but this again reflects the effect of his initial, economically advantageous status, which exercises its influence through the medium of money.

In a system of private property in productive enterprise, an income above what an individual spends can give rise to possession of capital wealth. Presumably such possession is a reward for the proper management of one's finances originally and of the productive enterprise later. But as social differentiation becomes highly advanced and yet the institution of inheritance persists, the phenomenon of pure ownership, and reward for pure ownership, emerges. In such a case it is difficult to prove that the position is functionally important or that the scarcity involved is anything other than extrinsic and accidental. It is for this reason, doubtless, that the institution of private property in productive goods becomes more subject to criticism as social development proceeds toward industrialization. It is only this pure, that is, strictly legal and functionless ownership, however, that is open to attack; for some form of active ownership, whether private or public, is indispensable.

One kind of ownership of production goods consists in rights over the labor of others. The most extremely concentrated and exclusive of such rights are found in slavery, but the essential principle remains in serfdom, peonage, encomienda, and indenture. Naturally this kind of ownership has the greatest significance for stratification, because it necessarily entails an unequal relationship.

But property in capital goods inevitably introduces a compulsive element even into the nominally free contractual relationship. Indeed, in some respects the authority of the contractual employer is greater than that of the feudal landlord, inasmuch as the latter is more limited by traditional reciprocities. Even the classical economics recognized that competitors would fare unequally, but it did not pursue this fact to its necessary conclusion that, however it might be acquired, unequal control of goods and services must give unequal advantage to the parties to a contract.

Technical Knowledge. The function of finding means to single goals, without any concern with the choice between goals, is the exclusively technical sphere. The explanation of why positions requiring great technical skill receive fairly high rewards is easy to see, for it is the simplest case of rewards being so distributed as to draw talent and motivate training. Why they seldom if ever receive the highest rewards is also clear: the importance of technical knowledge from a societal point of view is never so great as the integration of goals, which takes place on the religious, political, and economic levels. Since the technological level is concerned solely with means, a purely technical position must ultimately be subordinate to other positions that are religious, political, or economic in character.

Nevertheless, the distinction between expert and layman in any social order is fundamental, and cannot be entirely reduced to other terms. Methods of recruitment, as well as of reward, sometimes lead to the erroneous interpretation that technical positions are economically determined. Actually, however, the acquisition of knowledge and skill cannot be accomplished by purchase, although the opportunity to learn may be. The control of the avenues of training may inhere as a sort of property right in certain families or classes, giving them power and prestige in consequence. Such a situation adds an artificial scarcity to the natural scarcity of skills and talents. On the other hand, it is possible for an opposite situation to arise. The rewards of technical position may be so great that a condition of excess supply is created, leading to at least temporary devaluation of the rewards. Thus "unemployment in the learned professions" may result in a debasement of the prestige of those positions. Such adjustments and readjustments are constantly occurring in the changing societies; and it is always well to bear in mind that the efficiency of a stratified structure may be affected by the modes of recruitment for positions. The social order itself, however, sets limits to the inflation or deflation of the prestige experts: an over-supply tends to debase the rewards and discourage recruitment or produce revolution, whereas an under-supply tends to increase the rewards or weaken the society in competition with other societies.

Particular systems of stratification show a wide range with respect to the exact position of technically competent persons. This range is perhaps most evident in the degree of specialization. Extreme division of labor tends to create many specialists without high prestige since the training is short and the required native capacity relatively small. On the other hand it also tends to accentuate the high position of the true experts—scientists, engineers, and administrators—by increasing their authority relative to other functionally important positions. But the idea of a technocratic social order or a government or priesthood of engineers or social scientists neglects the limitations of knowledge and skills as a basic for performing social functions. To the extent that the social structure is truly specialized the prestige of the technical person must also be circumscribed.

NOTES

1. Kingsley Davis, "A Conceptual Analysis of Stratification," *American Sociological Review.* 7: 309–321, June, 1942.

2. The writers regret (and beg indulgence) that the present essay, a condensation of a longer study, covers so much in such short space that adequate evidence and qualification cannot be given and that as a result what is actually very tentative is presented in an unfortunately dogmatic manner.

3. Unfortunately, functional importance is difficult to establish. To use the position's prestige to establish it, as is often unconsciously done, constitutes circular reasoning from our point of view. There are, however, two independent clues: (a) the degree to which a position is functionally unique, there being no other positions that can perform the same function satisfactorily; (b) the degree to which other positions are dependent on the one in question. Both clues are best exemplified in organized systems of positions built around one major function. Thus, in most complex societies the religious, political, economic, and

educational functions are handled by distinct structures not easily interchangeable. In addition, each structure possesses many different positions, some clearly dependent on, if not subordinate to, others. In sum, when an institutional nucleus becomes differentiated around one main function, and at the same time organizes a large portion of the population into its relationships, the *key* positions in it are of the highest functional importance. The absence of such specialization does not prove functional unimportance, for the whole society may be relatively unspecialized; but it is safe to assume that the more important functions receive the first and clearest structural differentiation.

4. The symbolic rather than intrinsic role of income in social stratification has been succinctly summarized by Talcott Parsons, "An Analytical Approach to the Theory of Social Stratification," *American Journal of Sociology.* 45: 841–862, May, 1940.

DISCUSSION QUESTIONS

1. According to Davis and Moore, what is the functional theory of social stratification?
2. Can you identify some work that Davis and Moore would say is functionally important? Why do you define it in this way? Can you think of arguments that lead to defining all work as functionally important?

Article 19

Karl Marx's Theory of Alienation

ERICH FROMM

MARX'S CENTRAL CRITICISM of capitalism is not the injustice in the distribution of wealth; it is the perversion of labor into forced, alienated, meaningless labor, hence the transformation of man into a "crippled monstrosity." Marx's concept of labor as an expression of man's individuality is succinctly expressed in his vision of the complete abolition of the lifelong submersion of a man in one occupation. Since the aim of human development is that of the development of the total, universal man, man must be emancipated from the crippling influence of specialization. In all previous societies, Marx writes, man has been "a hunter, a fisherman, a shepherd, or a critical critic, and must remain so if he does not want to lose his means of livelihood; while in communist society, where nobody has one exclusive sphere of activity but each can become accomplished in any branch he wishes, society regulates the general production and thus makes it possible for me to do one thing today and another tomorrow, to hunt in the morning, fish in the afternoon, rear cattle in the evening, criticize after dinner, just as I have a mind, without ever becoming hunter, fisherman, shepherd, or critic."[1]

There is no greater misunderstanding or misrepresentation of Marx than that which is to be found, implicitly or explicitly, in the thought of the Soviet Communists, the reformist socialists, and the capitalist opponents of socialism alike, all of whom assume that Marx wanted only the economic improvement of the working class, and that he wanted to abolish private property so that the worker would own what the capitalist now has. The truth is that for Marx the situation of a worker in a Russian "socialist" factory, a British state-owned factory, or an American factory such as General Motors, would appear essentially the same. This, Marx expresses very clearly in the following:

"An enforced *increase in wages* (disregarding the other difficulties, and especially that such an anomaly could only be maintained by force) would be nothing more than a *better renumeration of slaves* and would not restore, either to the worker or to the work, their human significance and worth.

"Even the *equality of incomes* which Proudhon demands would only change the relation of the present-day worker to his work into a relation of all men to work. Society would then be conceived as an abstract capitalist."[2]

The central theme of Marx is the transformation of alienated, meaningless labor into productive, free labor, not the better payment of alienated labor by a private or "abstract" state capitalism.

The concept of the active, productive man who grasps and embraces the objective world with his own powers cannot be fully understood without the concept of the *negation of productivity: alienation.* For Marx the history of mankind is a history of the increasing development of man, and at the same time of increasing alienation. His concept of socialism is the emancipation from alienation, the return of man to himself, his self-realization.

Alienation (or "estrangement") means, for Marx, that man does *not* experience himself as the acting agent in his grasp of the world, but that the world (nature, others, and he himself) remain alien to him. They stand above and against him as objects, even though they may be objects of his own creation. Alienation is essentially experiencing the world and oneself passively, receptively, as the subject separated from the object.

The whole concept of alienation found its first expression in Western thought in the Old Testament concept of idolatry.[3] The essence of what the prophets call "idolatry" is not that man worships many gods instead of only one. It is that the idols are the work of man's own hands—they are things, and man bows down and worships things; worships that which he has created himself. In doing so he transforms himself into a thing. He transfers to the things of his creation the attributes of his own life, and instead of experiencing himself as the creating person, he is in touch with himself only by the worship of the idol. He has become estranged from his own life forces, from the wealth of his own potentialities, and is in touch with himself only in the indirect way of submission to life frozen in the idols.[4]

The deadness and emptiness of the idol is expressed in the Old Testament: "Eyes they have and they do not see, ears they have and they do not hear," etc. The more man transfers his own powers to the idols, the poorer he himself becomes, and the more dependent on the idols, so that they permit him to redeem a small part of what was originally his. The idols can be a god-like figure, the state, the church, a person, possessions. Idolatry changes its objects; it is by no means to be found only in those forms in which the idol has a so-called religious meaning. Idolatry is always the worship of something into which man has put his own creative powers, and to which he now submits, instead of experiencing himself in his creative act. Among the many forms of alienation, the most frequent one is alienation in language. If I express a feeling with a word, let us say, if I say "I love you," the word is meant to be an indication of the reality which exists within myself, the power of my loving. The *word* "love" is meant to be a symbol of the *fact* love, but as soon as it is spoken it tends to assume a life of its own, it becomes a reality. I am under the illusion that the saying of the word is the equivalent of the experience, and soon I say the word and feel nothing, except the *thought* of love which the word expresses. The alienation of language shows the whole complexity of alienation. Language is one of the most precious human achievements; to avoid alienation by not speaking would be foolish—yet one must be always aware of the danger of the spoken word, that it threatens to substitute itself for the living experience. The same holds true for all other achievements of man; ideas, art, any kind of man-made objects. They are man's creations; they are valuable aids for life, yet each one of them is also a trap, a temptation to confuse life with things, experience with artifacts, feeling with surrender and submission.

The thinkers of the eighteenth and nineteenth centuries criticized their age for its increasing rigidity, emptiness, and deadness. In Goethe's thinking the very same concept of productivity that is central in Spinoza as well as in Hegel and Marx, was a cornerstone. "The divine," he says, "is effective in that which is alive, but not in that which is dead. It is in that which is becoming and evolving, but not in that which is completed and rigid. That is why *reason,* in its tendency toward the divine, deals only with that which is becoming, and which is alive, while the *intellect* deals with that which is completed and rigid, in order to use it."[5]

We find similar criticisms in Schiller and Fichte, and then in Hegel and in Marx, who makes a general criticism that in his time "truth is without passion, and passion is without truth."[6]

Essentially the whole existentialist philosophy, from Kierkegaard on, is, as Paul Tillich puts it, "an over one-hundred-years-old movement of rebellion against the dehumanization of man in industrial society." Actually, the concept of alienation is, in nontheistic language, the equivalent of what in theistic language would be called "sin": man's relinquishment of himself, of God within himself.

The thinker who coined the concept of alienation was Hegel. To him the history of man was at the same time the history of man's alienation (Entfremdung). "What the mind really strives for," he wrote in *The Philosophy of History,* "is the realization of its notion; but in doing so it hides that goal from its own vision and is proud and well satisfied in this alienation from its own essence."[7] For Marx, as for Hegel, the concept of alienation is based on the distinction between existence and essence, on the fact that man's existence is alienated from his essence, that in reality he is not what he potentially is, or, to put it differently, that *he is not what he ought to be, and that he ought to be that which he could be.*

For Marx the process of alienation is expressed in work and in the division of labor. Work is for him the active relatedness of man to nature, the creation of a new world, including the creation of man himself. (Intellectual activity is of course, for

Marx, always work, like manual or artistic activity.) But as private property and the division of labor develop, labor loses its character of being an expression of man's powers; labor and its products assume an existence separate from man, his will and his planning. "The object produced by labor, its product, now stands opposed to it as an *alien being,* as a *power independent* of the producer. The product of labor is labor which has been embodied in an object and turned into a physical thing; this product is an *objectification* of labor."[8] Labor is alienated because the work has ceased to be a part of the worker's nature and "consequently, he does not fulfill himself in his work but denies himself, has a feeling of misery rather than well-being, does not develop freely his mental and physical energies but is physically exhausted and mentally debased. The worker therefore feels himself at home only during his leisure time, whereas at work he feels homeless."[9] Thus, in the act of production the relationship of the worker to his own activity is experienced "as something alien and not belonging to him, activity as suffering (passivity), strength as powerlessness, creation as emasculation."[10] While man thus becomes alienated from himself, the product of labor becomes "an alien object which dominates him. This relationship is at the same time the relationship to the sensuous external world, to natural objects, as an alien and hostile world."[11] Marx stresses two points: 1) in the process of work, and especially of work under the conditions of capitalism, man is estranged from his own creative powers, and 2) the *objects* of his own work become alien beings, and eventually rule over him, become powers independent of the producer. "The laborer exists for the process of production, and not the process of production for the laborer."[12]

A misunderstanding of Marx on this point is widespread, even among socialists. It is believed that Marx spoke primarily of the *economic* exploitation of the worker, and the fact that his share of the product was not as large as it should be, or that the product should belong to him, instead of to a capitalist. But as I have shown before, the state as a capitalist, as in the Soviet Union, would not have been any more welcome to Marx than the private capitalist. He is not concerned primarily with the equalization of income. He is concerned with the liberation of man from a kind of work which destroys his individuality, which transforms him into a thing, and which makes him into the slave of things. Just as Kierkegaard was concerned with the salvation of the individual, so Marx was, and his criticism of capitalist society is directed not at its method of distribution of income, but its mode of production, its destruction of individuality and its enslavement of man—worker *and* capitalist—by things and circumstances of their own making.

Marx goes still further. In unalienated work man not only realizes himself as an individual, but also as a species-being. For Marx, as for Hegel and many other thinkers of the enlightenment, each individual represents the species, that is to say, humanity as a whole, the universality of man: the development of man leads to the unfolding of his whole humanity. In the process of work he "no longer reproduces himself merely intellectually, as in consciousness, but actively and in a real sense, and he sees his own reflection in a world which he has constructed. While, therefore, alienated labor takes away the object of production from man, it also takes away his *species life,* his real objectivity as a species-being, and changes his advantage over animals into a disadvantage in so far as his inorganic body, nature, is taken from him. Just as alienated labor transforms free and self-directed activity into a means, so it transforms the species life of man into a means of physical existence. Consciousness, which man has from his species, is transformed through alienation so that species life becomes only a means for him.[13]

As I indicated before, Marx assumed that the alienation of work, while existing throughout history, reaches its peak in capitalist society, and that the working class is the most alienated one. This assumption was based on the idea that the worker, having no part in the direction of the work, being "employed" as part of the machines he serves, is transformed into a thing in its dependence on capital. Hence, for Marx, "the emancipation of society from private property, from servitude, takes the political form of the *emancipation of workers;* not in the sense that only the latter's emancipation is involved, but because this emancipation includes the *emancipation of humanity as a whole.* For all human servitude is involved in the relation of the worker to production, and all types of servitude are only modifications or consequences in this relation."[14]

Again it must be emphasized that Marx's aim is not limited to the emancipation of the working class, but the emancipation of the human being through the restitution of the unalienated and hence free activity of all men, and a society in which man, and not the production of things, is the aim, in which man ceases to be "a crippled monstrosity, and becomes a fully developed human being."[15] Marx's concept of the alienated product of labor is expressed in one of the most fundamental points developed in *Capital,* in what he calls "the fetishism of commodities." Capitalist production transforms the relations of individuals into qualities of things themselves, and this transformation constitutes the nature of the commodity in capitalist production. "It cannot be otherwise in a mode of production in which the laborer exists to satisfy the need of self-expansion of existing values, instead of on the contrary, material wealth existing to satisfy the needs of development on the part of the laborer. As in religion man is governed by the products of his own brain, so in capitalist production he is governed by the products of his own hands."[16] "Machinery is adapted to the weakness of the human being in order to turn the weak human being into a machine."[17]

The alienation of work in man's production is much greater than it was when production was by handicraft and manufacture. "In handicrafts and manufacture, the workman makes use of a tool; in the factory the machine makes use of him. There the movements of the instrument of labor proceed from him; here it is the movement of the machines that he must follow. In manufacture, the workmen are parts of a living mechanism; in the factory we have a lifeless mechanism, independent of the workman, who becomes its mere living appendage."[18] It is of the utmost importance for the understanding of Marx to see how the concept of alienation was and remained the focal point in the thinking of the young Marx who wrote the *Economic and Philosophical Manuscripts,* and of the "old" Marx who wrote *Capital.* Aside from the examples already given, the following passages, one from the *Manuscripts,* the other from *Capital,* ought to make this continuity quite clear:

"This fact simply implies that the object produced by labor, its product, now stands opposed to it as an *alien being,* as a *power independent* of the producer. The product of labor is labor which has been embodied in an object and turned into a physical thing; this product is an *objectification* of labor. The performance of work is at the same time its objectification. The performance of work appears in the sphere of political economy as a *vitiation* of the worker, objectification as a *loss* and as *servitude to the object,* and appropriation as *alienation.*"[19]

This is what Marx wrote in *Capital*: "Within the capitalist system all methods for raising the social productiveness of labor are brought about at the cost of the individual laborer; all means for the development of production transform themselves into means of domination over, and exploitation of, the producers; they mutilate the laborer into a fragment of a man, degrade him to the level of an appendage of a machine, destroy every remnant of charm in his work and turn it into a hated toil; they estrange from him the intellectual potentialities of the labor process in the same proportion as science is incorporated in it as in independent power."[20]

Again the role of private property (of course not as property of objects of use, but as capital which hires labor) was already clearly seen in its alienating functioning by the young Marx: *"Private property,"* he wrote, "is therefore the product, the necessary result, of *alienated labor,* of the external relation to the worker to nature and to himself. *Private property* is thus derived from the analysis of the concept of *alienated labor;* that is, alienated man, alienated labor, alienated life, and estranged man."[21]

It is not only that the world of things becomes the ruler of man, but also that the *social and political circumstances* which he creates become his masters. "This consolidation of what we ourselves produce, which turns into an objective power above us, growing out of our control, thwarting our expectations, bringing to naught our calculations, is one of the chief factors in historical development up to now."[22] The alienated man, who believes that he has become the master of nature, has become the slave of things and of circumstances, the powerless appendage of a world which is at the same time the frozen expression of his own powers.

For Marx, alienation in the process of work, from the product of work and from circumstances, is inseparably connected with alienation from oneself, from one's fellow man and from nature. "A direct consequence of the alienation of man from the product of his labor, from his life activity and from his species life is that *man* is *alienated* from other men. When man confronts himself, he also confronts *other* men. What is true of man's relationship to his work, to the product of his work and to himself, is also true of his relationship to other men, to their labor and to the objects of their labor. In general, the statement that man is alienated from his species life means that each man is alienated from others and that each of the others is likewise alienated from human life."[23] The alienated man is not only alienated from other men; he is alienated from the essence of humanity, from his "species-being," both in his natural and spiritual qualities. This alienation from the human essence leads to an existential egotism, described by Marx as man's human essence becoming "a *means* for his *individual existence.* It [alienated labor] alienates from man his own body, external nature, his mental life and his *human* life."[24]

Marx's concept touches here the Kantian principle that man must always be an end in himself, and never a means to an end. But he amplifies this principle by stating that man's human essence must never become a means for individual existence. The contrast between Marx's view and Communist totalitarianism could hardly be expressed more radically; humanity in man, says Marx, must not even become a *means* to his individual existence; how much less could it be considered a means for the state, the class, or the nation.

Alienation leads to the perversion of all values. By making economy and its values—"gain, work, thrift, and sobriety"[25]—the supreme aim of life, man fails to develop the truly moral values, "the riches of a good conscience, of virtue, etc., but how can I be virtuous if I am not alive, and how can I have a good conscience if I am not aware of anything?"[26] In a state of alienation each sphere of life, the economic and the moral, is independent from the other, "each is concentrated on a specific area of alienated activity and is itself alienated from the other."[27]

Marx recognized what becomes of human needs in an alienated world, and he actually foresaw with amazing clarity the completion of this process as it is visible only today. While in a socialist perspective the main importance should be attributed "to the *wealth* of human needs, and consequently also to a *new mode of production* and to a new *object* of production," to "a new manifestation of *human* powers and a new enrichment of the human being,"[28] in the alienated world of capitalism needs are not expressions of man's latent powers, that is, they are not *human* needs; in capitalism "every man speculates upon creating a *new* need in another in order to force him to a new sacrifice, to place him in a new dependence, and to entice him into a new kind of pleasure and thereby into economic ruin. Everyone tries to establish over others an *alien* power in order to find there the satisfaction of his own egoistic need. With the mass of objects, therefore, there also increases the realm of alien entities to which man is subjected. Every new product is a new *potentiality* of mutual deceit and robbery. Man becomes increasingly poor as a man; he has increasing need of *money* in order to take possession of the hostile being. The power of his *money* diminishes directly with the growth of the quantity of production, i.e., his need increases with the increasing *power* of money. The need for money is therefore the real need created by the modern economy, and the only need which it creates. The *quantity* of money becomes increasingly its only important quality. Just as it reduces every entity to its abstraction, so it reduces itself in its own development to a *quantitative* entity. Excess and immoderation become its true standard. This is shown subjectively, partly in the fact that the expansion of production and of needs becomes an *ingenious* and always *calculating* subservience to inhuman, depraved, unnatural, and *imaginary* appetites. Private property does not know how to change crude need into *human* need; its *idealism* is *fantasy, caprice* and *fancy.* No eunuch flatters his tyrant more shamefully or seeks by more infamous means to stimulate his jaded appetite, in order to gain some favor, than does the eunuch of industry, the entrepreneur, in order to acquire a few silver coins or to charm the gold from the purse of his dearly beloved neighbor. (Every product is a bait by means of which the individual tries to entice the essence of the other person, his money. Every real or potential need is a weakness which will draw the bird into the lime. Universal exploitation of human communal life. As every imperfection of man is a bond with heaven, a point at which his heart is accessible to the priest, so every want is an opportunity for approaching one's neighbor with an air of friendship, and saying, 'Dear friend, I will give you what you need, but you know the *conditio sine qua non.* You know what ink you must use in signing yourself over to me. I shall swindle you while providing your enjoyment.') The entrepreneur accedes to the most depraved fancies of his neighbor, plays the role of pander between him and his needs, awakens unhealthy appetites in him, and watches for every weakness in order, later, to claim the remuneration for this labor of love."[29] The man who has thus become subject to his alienated needs is "a *mentally* and *physically dehumanized* being . . . the *self-conscious* and *self-acting commodity.*"[30] This commodity-man knows only one way of relating himself to the world outside, by having it and by consuming (using) it. The more alienated he is, the more the sense of having and using constitutes his relationship to the world. "The less you *are,* the less you express your life, the more you *have,* the greater is your *alienated* life and the greater is the saving of your alienated being."[31]

There is only one correction which history has made in Marx's concept of alienation; Marx believed that the working class was the most alienated class, hence that the emancipation from alienation would necessarily start with the liberation of the working class. Marx did not foresee the extent to which alienation was to become the fate of the vast majority of people, especially of the ever-increasing segment of the population which manipulate symbols and men, rather than machines. If anything, the clerk, salesman, the executive, are even more alienated today than the skilled manual worker. The latter's functioning still depends on the expression of certain personal qualities like skill, reliability, etc., and he is not forced to sell his "personality," his smiles, his opinions in the bargain; the symbol manipulators are hired not only for their skill, but for all those personality qualities which make them "attractive personality packages," easy to handle and to manipulate. They are the true "organization men"—more so than the skilled laborer—their idol being the corporation. But as far as consumption is concerned, there is no difference between manual workers and the members of the bureaucracy. They all crave for things, new things, to have and to use. They are the passive recipients, the consumers, chained and weakened by the very things which satisfy their synthetic needs. They are not related to the world productively, grasping it in its full reality and in this process becoming one with it; they worship things, the machines which produce the things—and in this alienated world they feel as strangers and quite alone. In spite of Marx's underestimating the role of the bureaucracy, his general description could nevertheless have been written today: "Production does not simply produce man as a *commodity,* the *commodity-man,* man in the role of *commodity;* it produces him in keeping with this role as a *spiritually* and physically *dehumanized* being—[the] immorality, deformity, and hebetation of the workers and the capitalists. Its product is the *self-conscious* and *self-acting commodity* . . . the human commodity."[32]

To what extent things and circumstances of our own making have become our masters, Marx could hardly have foreseen; yet nothing could prove his prophecy more drastically than the fact that the whole human race is today the prisoner of the nuclear weapons it has created, and to the political institutions which are equally of its own making. A frightened mankind waits anxiously to see whether it will be saved from the power of the things it has created, from the blind action of the bureaucracies it has appointed.

NOTES

1. *German Ideology,* 1.c. p. 22.
2. *E. P. MSS.*, p. 107.
3. The connection between alienation and idolatry has also been emphasized by Paul Tillich in *Der Mensch im Christentum und im Marxismus,* Düsseldorf, 1953, p. 14. Tillich also points out in another lecture, "Protestantische Vision," that the concept of alienation in substance is to be found also in Augustine's thinking. Löwith also has pointed out that what Marx fights against are not the gods, but the idols, [cf. *Von Hegel zu Nietzsche,* 1.c. p. 378].
4. This is, incidentally, also the psychology of the fanatic. He is empty, dead, depressed, but in order to compensate for the state of depression and inner deadness, he chooses this idol, be it the state, a party, an idea, the church, or God. He makes this idol into the absolute, and submits to it in an absolute way. In doing so his life attains meaning, and he finds excitement in the submission to the chosen idol. His excitement, however, does not stem from joy in productive relatedness; it is intense, yet cold excitement built upon inner deadness or, if one would want to put it symbolically, it is "burning ice."
5. Eckermann's conversation with Goethe, February 18, 1829, published in Leipzig, 1894, page 47. [My translation—E. F.]
6. *18th Brumaire of Louis Bonaparte.*
7. *The Philosophy of History,* translated by J. Sibree, The Colonial Press, New York, 1899.
8. *E. P. MSS.*, p. 95.
9. *E. P. MSS.*, p. 98.
10. *E. P. MSS.*, p. 99.
11. *E. P. MSS.*, p. 99.
12. *Capital I,* 1.c. p. 536
13. *E. P. MSS.*, p. 102–3.
14. *E. P. MSS.*, p. 107.
15. *Capital I,* 1.c. p. 396.
16. *Capital I,* 1.c. p. 680–1.
17. *E. P. MSS.*, p. 143.
18. *Capital I,* 1.c. p. 461–2.
19. *E. P. MSS.*, p. 95.
20. *Capital I,* 1.c. p. 708.
21. *E. P. MSS.*, p. 105–6.
22. *German Ideology,* 1.c. p. 23.
23. *E. P. MSS.*, p. 103.
24. *E. P. MSS.*, p. 103.
25. *E. P. MSS.*, p. 146.
26. *E. P. MSS.*, p. 146.
27. *E. P. MSS.*, p. 146.

28. *E. P. MSS.*, p. 140.
29. *E. P. MSS.*, pp. 140–2.
30. *E. P. MSS.*, p. 111.
31. *E. P. MSS.*, p. 144.
32. *E. P. MSS.*, p. 111.

DISCUSSION QUESTIONS

1. Why does Marx reject the notion that labor can be satisfied through better pay?
2. How can Marx's concept of alienation be applied to white collar bureaucracies and corporate work?

Article 20

Tracked to Fail

SHEILA TOBIAS

NO ONE WHO has ever read Aldous Huxley's anti-utopian novel, *Brave New World,* can forget the book's opening scene, a tour of the "Hatchery and Conditioning Centre." There human embryos in their first hours of existence are transformed into Alphas, Betas, Gammas, Deltas and Epsilons—the five social classes that collectively meet the economy's manpower needs. Arrested in their development, the Gamma, Delta and Epsilon embryos are programmed *in vitro* for a lower-class future. After "birth," whatever individuality remains with these preordained proletarians will be conditioned out of each child, until there is no one in this brave new world who does not grow up accepting and even loving his bleak servitude.

Huxley's totalitarian embryology may seem fanciful to us, but his real message was political, not technological. Huxley understood, as he wrote in the foreword to the 1946 edition of *Brave New World,* that any "science of human differences" would enable the authorities to assess the relative capacities of each of us and then assign everybody his or her appropriate place in society. Huxley's vision of the modern state, with its desire for social control, implies that the discovery that ability can be measured will suggest that it *should* be. Similarly, the knowledge that people can be sorted by ability will lead irresistibly to the belief that they ought to be.

Today, many educators contend that a "science of human differences" does exist in the form of standardized tests for intelligence and ability. And, as Huxley foresaw, the pressures have grown to put these discriminating instruments to use.

From "Tracked To Fail," by Sheila Tobias. *Psychology Today,* September, 1989, pp. 54–60. Reprinted by permission.

Education in this country is becoming a process of separating the "gifted" from the "average," the "intelligent" from the "slow"—one is tempted to say, the wheat from the chaff. From an early age, children are now ranked and sorted (a process known variably as tracking, ability grouping or screening) as they proceed through school. Those who test well are encouraged and expected to succeed and offered the most challenging work. Those who do not, get a watered-down curriculum that reflects the system's minimal expectations of them.

All this is a far cry from the vision of schooling that America's founding educators had in mind. Horace Mann, the father of American public education and the influential first secretary of the Massachusetts board of education from 1837 to 1848, thought public education would be "the great equalizer" in a nation of immigrants. For over a century now, Mann's egalitarian vision, translated into educational policy, has helped millions of immigrants to assimilate and to prosper here. But this vision is now threatened by a competing view of individual potential—and worth. We are becoming a society where test-taking skills are the prerequisites for a chance at getting a good education, and where hard work, hope and ambition are in danger of becoming nothing more than meaningless concepts.

A poor showing on tests was once a signal to all concerned—child, teacher, parents—that greater effort was needed to learn, or to teach, what was required. It didn't mean that a child *couldn't* learn. But the damaging assumption behind testing and tracking as they are now employed in many schools is that *only* those who test well are capable of learning what is needed to escape an adult life restricted to menial, dead-end jobs. This new message imparted by our schools is profoundly inegalitarian: that test-measured ability, not effort, is what counts. What many students are learning is that they are *not* equal to everybody else. Gammas, Deltas and Epsilons shouldn't even try to compete with Alphas. Alphas are better, *born* better, and it is impossible for others to catch up. What's tragic about this change is not just that it's unjust—but that it's untrue.

A Lifetime of Testing

In a private Los Angeles primary school, a 4-year-old is being taught to play a gamelike test he is going to have to pass to show that he is ready for kindergarten. This is the first in an endless series of evaluations that will determine who he is, what he can learn and how far he will go in school. Just before the test begins, the counselor hands him the red plastic cube he will use. But he doesn't need her cube. He has taken this test so often, as his parents drag him around for his preschool admission screenings, that when the time comes to play, he pulls his *own* bright red cube out of his pocket. Whether or not he is ready for this particular school, he is more than ready for the test.

Each year after this child's admission to kindergarten, he will take "norm-referenced tests" to show his overall achievement against those of his age group and "criterion-referenced tests," which examine the specific skills he is supposed to have learned in each grade. Even if he and his parents are not told his test scores (a practice that varies from school to school), ability-grouping in elementary school will soon let him know where he stands. "By the second or third grade," says Susan Harter, a psychology professor at the University of Denver who studies social development in children, "children know precisely where they stand on the 'smart or dumb' continuum, and since most children at this age want to succeed in school, this knowledge profoundly affects their self-esteem."

The point is that today "smart or dumb" determinations are made very early. "Those who come to school knowing how to read or who learn very quickly are pronounced bright," says Jeannie Oakes, author of *Keeping Track: How Schools Structure Inequality.* "Those for whom reading is still a puzzle at the end of the first grade are judged slow." And these early decisions stick. As children proceed through the elementary grades, more and more of their course work is grouped by ability. By ninth grade, 80% to 90% of students are in separate classes determined by whether they are judged to be "fast," "average" or "slow."

Magnifying Our Differences

Tracking in all its variants is rarely official policy, and the validity and fairness of standardized testing have long been under fire. Nevertheless, both tracking and testing are becoming more common. As a result, argues University of Cincinnati education professor Joel Spring (in unwitting resonance with Huxley), education in America has become a "sorting machine."

Moreover, the stunting effects of this machine may remain with students for a lifetime. "Adults can remember well into middle age whether they were 'sharks' or 'goldfish' in reading," says Bill Kelly, professor of education at Regis College in Denver. Students learn whether they have good verbal skills or mathematical ones. They learn whether or not they are musically or mechanically inclined, and so on. There are millions of adults who carry with them the conviction that they "can't do math" or play an instrument or write well. And it may all be the result of assessments made of them and internalized as children—long before they had any idea of what they wanted from life. Their sense of inadequacy may prevent them from exploring alternative careers or simply narrow their experiences.

Why are testing and tracking on the rise? Oakes, who has studied more than 13,000 junior- and senior-high-school students, their schools and their teachers, suggests that the answer has several components. They range from the focus on educational excellence during the last decade to widespread public confidence that testing is an accurate, appropriate way of gauging educational potential. Oakes also believes that testing and tracking comprise a not-so-subtle effort to resegregate desegregated schools. But they reflect as well a preference among teachers for "homogeneous groupings" of students, which are easier to teach than classes composed of students of varying abilities.

Whatever the motives, Oakes is convinced that the basic premise of the whole system is wrong. There is no way, she says, to determine accurately the potential of young or even older children by standardized tests. One key reason: Such examinations are always fine-tuned to point out differences, not similarities. They eliminate those items that everyone answers the same way—either right or wrong. Thus, small differences that may or may not measure ability in general are amplified to give the test makers what they want, namely ease of sorting. Test results, then, will make any group of individuals appear to be more different than they really are.

Benjamin Bloom, Distinguished Service Professor Emeritus of Education at the University of Chicago, agrees. "I find that many of the individual differences in school learning are man-made and accidental rather than fixed in the individual at the time of conception," he writes in his book *All Our Children Learning*. "When students are provided with unfavorable learning conditions, they become even more dissimilar." Bloom concedes that some longitudinal studies show that between grades 3 and 11, for example, children's rank in class remains virtually the same. But this is not because intelligence is fixed, he argues. It is the result of the unequal, unsupportive education the schools provide. So long as schools think there is little they can do about "learning ability," says Bloom, they will see their task as weeding out the poorer learners while encouraging the better learners to get as much education as they can.

Watered-Down Education

Research generated by Oakes and others supports Bloom, revealing that placement in a low track has a corroding impact on students' self esteem. Worse yet, because there are real differences not just in level but in the *content* of what is being taught, tracking may in fact contribute to academic failure.

Students in low-track courses are almost never exposed to what educators call "high-status knowledge," the kind that will be useful in colleges and universities. They do not read works of great literature in their English classes, Oakes's team found, and instead of critical-thinking skills and expository writing, low-track students are taught standard English usage and "functional literacy," which involves mainly filling out forms, job applications and the like. In mathematics, high-track students were exposed to numeration, computational systems, mathematical models, probability and statistics in high school. "In contrast," writes Oakes, "low-track classes focused grade after grade on basic computational skills and arithmetic facts" and sometimes on simple measurement skills and converting English to metric.

More generally, Oakes's team also found that high-track classes emphasize reasoning ability over simple memorization of disembodied facts. Low-track students, meanwhile, are taught by rote, with an emphasis on conformity. "Average" classes—the middle track—resembled those in the high track, but they are substantially "watered down."

Is this discriminatory system the only way to handle differences in ability among students? One innovative program is challenging that notion. Called "accelerated learning," it is the creation of Henry M. Levin, a professor of education and economics at Stanford University. Levin, an expert on worker-managed companies, decided to apply the principles of organizational psychology to an analysis of the crisis in education. He began with a two-year-study, during which he surveyed the literature on education and looked at hundreds of evaluations of at-risk students at elementary and middle schools. Fully one-third of all students, he estimated, were "educationally disadvantaged" in some way, were consigned to a low track and were falling farther and farther behind, in one or more areas. These children needed remedial help, but that help, Levin writes, treated "such students and their educators as educational discards, marginal to mainstream education." For them, the pace of instruction was slowed to a crawl and progressed by endless repetition. The whole system seemed designed to demoralize and fail everyone who was a part of it. As Levin told one reporter, "As soon as you begin to talk about kids needing remediation, you're talking about damaged merchandise. And as soon as you have done that, you have lost the game."

To try to change the game, Levin designed and is helping to implement the Accelerated Schools Program. Now being tested in California, Utah, Missouri and (this fall) Illinois, the project accepts that elementary school children who are having academic problems *do* need special assistance, but it departs radically from traditional tracking in every other respect. First, Accelerated Schools are expected to have all their students learning at grade level by the time they reach the sixth grade. In other words, the remedial track exists only to get students off it. Collectively, the teachers and administrators at each school are allowed to design their own curricula, but they must create a clear set of measurable (and that means testable) goals for students to meet each year they are in the program. Finally, it is expected that the curriculum, whatever its specifics, will be challenging and fast-paced and will emphasize abstract reasoning skills and a sophisticated command of English.

Levin's program reflects the current administration's view that business practice has much to contribute to schooling. Levin wants schools to find a better way to produce what might be called their product—that is, children willing and able to get the quality education they will need in life. To do this, he recognizes that schools must offer better performance incentives to students, teachers and administrators. "Everyone benefits from the esprit de corps," explains Levin, "and the freedom to experiment with curriculum and technique—which we also encourage—is an incentive for teachers." By insisting upon school and teacher autonomy, the regular attainment of measurable goals and the development of innovative, engaging curricula, Accelerated Schools also hope to erase the stigma associated with teaching or needing remediation. The early results of this six-year test program are encouraging: The Hoover Elementary School in Redwood City, CA, one of the first schools to embark on the project, is reporting a 22 percentile increase in sixth-grade reading scores, actually outperforming state criteria. Both Levin and Ken Hill, the district superintendent, caution that these results are preliminary and the improved scores could be due to many factors other than the Accelerated Schools Program. But regardless of the program's measurable impact, Hill sees real changes in the school. "Teachers are now working with the kids on science projects and developing a literature-based reading program. There's a positive climate, and all the kids are learners."

Another alternative to tracking is what Bloom calls "mastery learning." He believes that it is the rate of learning, not the capacity to learn, that differentiates students with "high" or "low" abilities. This is a critical distinction, for we are rapidly approaching the day when all but the most menial jobs will require relatively complex reasoning and technical skills.

In a mastery class, children are given as much time as they need to become competent at a certain skill or knowledge level. Teachers must take 10% to 15% more time with their classes and break the class down into small groups in which the fast learners help their peers along. In time, the slower students catch up both in the amount of knowledge acquired and in the rate at which they learn. Though slow students may start out as much as five times slower than their classmates, Bloom says, "in mastery classes, fast and slow students become equal in achievement and increasingly similar in their learning rates."

At present, fewer than 5% of the nation's schools are following either of these promising strategies, estimates Gary Fenstermacher, dean of the University of Arizona's College of Education. He is a firm believer that de-tracking in some form must be the educational wave of the future. "There are ethical and moral imperatives for us to do whatever we can to increase the equality of access to human knowledge and understanding," he says.

Second Class and Dropping Out

Until society responds to those ethical and moral imperatives, however, the educational system, with its testing, tracking and discriminatory labeling, will continue on its questionable course. Today, around 25% of America's teenagers—40% to 60% in inner-city schools—do not graduate from high school, according to Jacqueline P. Danzberger of the Institute for Educational Leadership in Washington, DC. Most of the attrition occurs by the third year of high school, and many educators believe increased testing is a contributing factor.

Norman Gold, former director of research for the District of Columbia's public school system, says school dropouts are linked to the raising of standards (with no compensatory programs) in the late 1970s and the end of "social promotions"—the habit of routinely allowing failing students to move to a higher grade. "Studies show," he says, "that the risk of dropping out goes up 50% if a child fails one school year." Neil Shorthouse, executive director of Atlanta's Cities in Schools, which enrolls 750 teenagers on the point of dropping out, agrees. "Most of these kids quit school," he says of his students, "because they repeatedly get the message that they are bad students, 'unteachables.' "

Ending social promotions was long overdue. What purpose is served by graduating high-school students who can't read, write or do simple arithmetic? But schools have done little to help these failing students catch up. The present system is continuing to produce a whole class of people, particularly inner-city blacks and Hispanics, who have little economic role in our society. High school, Gold observes, has become an obstacle course that a significant number of young people are unable to negotiate. "We expect them to fail. We have to have greater expectations, and equally great support."

These failing students are missing what John Ogbu, an educational anthropologist at the University of California, Berkeley, calls "effort optimism," the faith that hard work will bring real rewards in life. Ogbu's ethnographic studies of black and Hispanic schoolchildren in Stockton, CA, suggest that one reason today's inner-city children do poorly in tests is that "they do not bring to the test situation serious attitudes and do not persevere to maximize their scores." The fault lies neither with their intelligence, Ogbu argues, nor with the absence of the "quasi-academic training" that middle-class children experience at home. Rather, it is their lower caste status and the limited job prospects of their parents that lower their sights. Tracking formalizes this caste humiliation and leads to disillusionment about school and what school can do for their lives.

Who Is "Smart"? Who Will "Succeed"?

The consequences of increased testing and tracking are only now beginning to be felt. First there is personal trauma, both for students who do reasonably well but not as well as they would like, and for those who fail. "When a child is given to understand that his or her worth resides in what he or she achieves rather than in what he or she is, academic failure becomes a severe emotional trauma," David Elkind writes in *The Child and Society.*

But the most severe consequence may be what only dropouts are so far demonstrating—an overall decline in Ogbu's effort optimism. Its potential social effects extend well beyond the schoolroom. Intelligence and ability, says writer James Fallows, have become legally and socially acceptable grounds for discrimination, and both are measured by the testing and tracking system in our schools. Doing well in school has thus come to be the measure of who is intelligent and who has ability. Beyond that, Fallows writes, our culture increasingly accepts that "he who goes further in school will go further in life." Many of the best jobs and most prestigious professions are restricted to those with imposing academic and professional degrees, thus creating a monopoly on "positions of privilege."

At a time when our economy requires better-educated workers than ever before, can we afford to let abstract measures of ability curtail the educational aspirations and potential accomplishments of our children? Quite aside from questions of national prosperity, do we really want to become a culture whose fruits are not available to most of its citizens? Despite income disparities and more classism than many observers are willing to admit, there has always been the *belief* in America that success, the good life, is available to all who are willing to work for it. But with our current fixation on testing and tracking, and what Fallows calls credentialism, we may be abandoning that belief and, with it, the majority of our young people.

DISCUSSION QUESTIONS

1. What is the philosophical basis that supports "tracking"?
2. How has early childhood education become a "sorting machine"?

VIII
Sociology of Gender and Age

WHAT TO FOCUS ON:

1. What are the sociological and economic consequences of gender stratification?
2. Are we prepared to cope with the demographic reality of people living well into their 80s and 90s? What policies and support systems need to be implemented in order to make the process of aging a more productive and satisfying part of our lives?

IN THIS CHAPTER we focus on separate but related components of one's social identity, gender and age. Both components are influenced by cultural definitions and standards. In many societies gender and age are the primary basis for being assigned a special status.

Sociologists distinguish between biological sexual identity—male and female—and gender—masculinity and femininity—which refers to a culturally patterned mode of behavior associated with biological sex. Gender has been the basis for status inequality in many societies throughout human history. Socialization into gendered identities has encouraged both males and females to internalize the differential evaluation of gender. Various sociological studies demonstrate that what has been referred to as "the social construction of gender" begins very early—even in infancy, male and female babies are treated differently—and is reinforced throughout the life cycle by prevailing social attitudes, values, and institutions. Gender stratification referring to the differential ranking and evaluation of individuals on the basis of sex roles has resulted in widespread economic and social inequality for women.

Aging is a natural and inevitable biological fact. Physically we develop, mature, and decline over a life course. However, aging is more than a biological process. We do not categorize people solely on the basis of the biological characteristics of age. All societies create social definitions of age. We impose social distinctions on the young, the middle-aged, and the old. Age differentiation refers to the process by which people are placed into social roles on the basis of age. Societies construct sets of role expectations that people of certain age groups are expected to follow. Social judgments concerning appropriate behavior correspond with age-related norms. There is considerable cultural variation concerning age differentiation. In middle class American society, one may not enter matrimony until one is well into his or her twenties. In other societies, one may be expected to be married by fourteen or fifteen.

Gerontology is a field that studies aging as a physiological, psychological, and sociological experience. Aging affects one's physiological state and both the individual and the surrounding society have to cope with gradually diminishing physical functions. Psychologically, one's self-concept and personality may be affected by the experience of aging. Social gerontologists have demonstrated that aging is strongly influenced by social and historical factors. One's birth cohort locates an individual both in society and in history. People who were born during a certain time period share a common social and cultural history. For people raised during the depression this experience greatly influenced their concerns about money and security. Their attitudes about money and security (save, be thrifty) may vary with future generations because of their relationship to social and historical frameworks.

In the first selection, Barbara Ehrenreich and Deirdre English focus on the misconceptions concerning the "mommy track." Is there solid evidence to support the corporate assumption that women are more costly to employ than men? Do corporations penalize parenthood by consigning women with children to low paying, part-time work? Does parenthood result in a greater disadvantage for the female gender in terms of corporate promotions and success? The article raises some important questions about the juggling act that many women perform regarding parenthood, child care, and career.

Sexual violence is largely related to power and force rather than to sexuality per se. In the second article, Diana Scully examines the results of her study of convicted rapists which discusses the ideology of rape culture. Rapists draw upon cultural stereotypes about women in order to justify rape.

In the third article, "A Generation at Risk: When the Baby Boomers Reach Golden Pond," Robert N. Butler focuses on two trends and their effect on contemporary society. We face a new demographic reality of longer life and many of us can expect to live well into our 80s. Also, we face an increasing proportion of elderly people in the future due to the aging of the birth cohort of 76.4 million people born between 1946 and 1964 called the baby boomers. Dr. Butler is chairman of the department of geriatrics of the Mount Sinai Medical Center in New York City. He points out that we must exhibit foresight and mobilize our resources in order to cope with the challenges posed by a new demographic order. With well thought-out policies and programs, we can create institutional structures that will make for meaningful and productive aging. Future generations can say that "we knew how to age well."

Article 21

Blowing the Whistle on the "Mommy Track"

BARBARA EHRENREICH AND DEIRDRE ENGLISH

WHEN A FEMINIST HAS SOMETHING BAD TO SAY ABOUT WOMEN, the media listen. Three years ago it was Sylvia Hewlett, announcing in her book *A Lesser Life* that feminism had sold women out by neglecting to win child-care and maternity leaves. This year it's Felice Schwartz, the New York-based consultant who argues that women—or at least the mothers among us—have become a corporate liability. They cost too much to employ, she argues, and the solution is to put them on a special lower-paid, low-pressure career track—the now-notorious "mommy track."

The "mommy track" story rated prominent coverage in the *New York Times* and *USA Today,* a cover story in *Business Week,* and airtime on dozens of talk-shows. Schwartz, after all, seemed perfectly legitimate. She is the president of Catalyst, an organization that has been advising corporations on women's careers since 1962. She had published her controversial claims in no less a spot than the *Harvard Business Review* ("Management, Women and the New Facts of Life," January-February 1989). And her intentions, as she put it in a later op-ed piece, seemed thoroughly benign: "to urge employers to create policies that help mothers balance career and family responsibilities."

From "Blowing the Whistle on the 'Mommy Track,'" by Barbara Ehrenreich and Deirdre English, *Ms.,* Vol. 18, No. 1 & 2 (July/August), 1989, pp. 56 and 58.

Moreover, Schwartz's argument seemed to confirm what everybody already knew. Women haven't been climbing up the corporate ladder as fast as might once have been expected, and women with children are still, on average, groping around the bottom rungs. Only about 40 percent of top female executives have children, compared to 95 percent of their male peers. There have been dozens of articles about female dropouts: women who slink off the fast track, at age 30-something, to bear a strategically timed baby or two. In fact, the "mommy track"—meaning a lower-pressure, flexible, or part-time approach to work—was neither a term Schwartz used nor her invention. It was already, in an anecdotal sort of way, a well-worn issue.

Most of the controversy focused on Schwartz's wildly anachronistic "solution." Corporate employers, she advised, should distinguish between two categories of women: "career-primary" women, who won't interrupt their careers for children and hence belong on the fast track with the men, and "career-and-family" women, who should be shunted directly to the mommy track. Schwartz had no answers for the obvious questions: how is the employer supposed to sort the potential "breeders" from the strivers? Would such distinction even be legal? What about *fathers?* But in a sense, the damage had already been done. A respected feminist, writing in a respected journal, had made a case that most women can't pull their weight in the corporate world and should be paid accordingly.

Few people, though, actually read Schwartz's article. The first surprise is that it contains *no* evidence to support her principal claim, that "the cost of employing women in management is greater than the cost of employing men." Schwartz offers no data, no documentation at all—except for two unpublished studies by two *anonymous* corporations. Do these studies really support her claim? Were they methodologically sound? Do they even exist? There is no way to know.

Few media reports of the "mommy track" article bothered to mention the peculiar nature of Schwartz's "evidence." We, however, were moved to call the *Harvard Business Review* and inquire whether the article was representative of its normal editorial standard. Timothy Blodgett, the executive editor, defended the article as "an expression of opinion and judgment." When we suggested that such potentially damaging "opinions" might need a bit of bolstering, he responded by defending Schwartz: "She speaks with a tone of authority. That comes through."

(The conversation went downhill from there, with Blodgett stating sarcastically, "I'm sure your article in *Ms.* will be *very* objective." Couldn't fall much lower than the *Harvard Business Review,* we assured him.)

Are managerial women more costly to employ than men? As far as we could determine—with the help of the Business and Professional Women's Foundation and Women's Equity Action League—there is no *published* data on this point. A 1987 government study did show female managerial employees spending less time with each employer than males (5 years compared to 6.8 years), but there is no way of knowing what causes this turnover or what costs it incurs. And despite pregnancy, and despite women's generally greater responsibility for child-raising, they use up on the average only 5.1 sick days per year, compared to 4.9 for men.

The second surprise, given Schwartz's feminist credentials, is that the article is riddled with ancient sexist assumptions—for example, about the possibility of a more androgynous approach to child-raising *and* work. She starts with the unobjectionable statement that "maternity is biological rather than cultural." The same thing, after all, could be said of paternity. But, a moment later, we find her defining maternity as ". . . a continuum that begins with an awareness of the ticking of the biological clock, proceeds to the anticipation of motherhood, includes pregnancy, childbirth, physical recuperation, psychological adjustment, and continues on to nursing, bonding, and child-rearing."

Now, pregnancy, childbirth, and nursing do qualify as biological processes. But slipping child-rearing into the list, as if changing diapers and picking up socks were hormonally programmed activities, is an old masculinist trick. Child-raising is a *social* undertaking, which may involve nannies, aunts, grandparents, day-care workers, or, of course, *fathers.*

Equally strange for a "feminist" article is Schwartz's implicit assumption that employment, in the case of married women, is strictly optional, or at least that *mothers* don't need to be top-flight earners. The "career-and-family woman," she tells us, is "willing" and "satisfied" to forgo promotions and "stay at the middle level." What about the single mother, or the wife of a low-paid male? But Schwartz's out-of-date—and class-bound—assumption that every woman is supported by a male breadwinner fits in with her apparent nostalgia for the era of the feminine mystique. "Ironically," she writes, "although the feminist movement was an expression of women's quest for freedom from their home-based lives, *most women were remarkably free already* [emphasis added]."

But perhaps the oddest thing about the "mommy track" article—even as an "expression of opinion and judgment"—is that it is full of what we might charitably call ambivalence or, more bluntly, self-contradictions. Take the matter of the "glass ceiling," which symbolized all the barriers, both subtle and overt, that corporate women keep banging their heads against. At the outset, Schwartz dismisses the glass ceiling as a "misleading metaphor." Sexism, in short, is not the problem.

Nevertheless, within a few pages, she is describing the glass ceiling (not by that phrase, of course) like a veteran. "Male corporate culture," she tells us, sees both the career-primary and the career-and-family woman as "unacceptable." The woman with family responsibilities is likely to be seen as lacking commitment to the organization, while the woman who *is* fully committed to the organization is likely to be seen as "abrasive and unfeminine." She goes on to cite the corporate male's "confusion, competitiveness," and his "stereotypical language and sexist . . . behavior," concluding that "with notable exceptions, men are still more comfortable with other men."

And we're supposed to blame *women* for their lack of progress in the corporate world?

Even on her premier point, that women are more costly to employ, Schwartz loops around and rebuts herself. Near the end of her article, she urges corporations to conduct their own studies of the costs of employing women—the two anonymous studies were apparently not definitive after all—and asserts confidently ("of course I believe") that the benefits will end up outweighing the costs. In a more recent New

York *Times* article, she puts it even more baldly: "The costs of employing women pale beside the payoffs."

Could it be that both Felice Schwartz and the editors of the *Harvard Business Review* are ignorant of that most basic financial management concept, the cost-benefit analysis? If the "payoffs" outweigh the costs of employing women—runny noses and maternity leaves included—then the net cost may indeed be *lower* than the cost of employing men.

In sum, the notorious "mommy track" article is a tortured muddle of feminist perceptions and sexist assumptions, good intentions and dangerous suggestions—unsupported by any acceptable evidence at all. It should never have been taken seriously, not by the media and not by the nation's most prestigious academic business publication. The fact that it was suggests that something serious *is* afoot: a backlash against America's high-status, better paid women, and potentially against all women workers.

We should have seen it coming. For the past 15 years upwardly mobile, managerial women have done everything possible to fit into an often hostile corporate world. They dressed up as nonthreatening corporate clones. They put in 70-hour work weeks; and of course, they postponed childbearing. Thanks in part to their commitment to the work world, the birthrate dropped by 16 percent since 1970. But now many of these women are ready to start families. This should hardly be surprising; after all, 90 percent of American women do become mothers.

But while corporate women were busily making adjustments and concessions, the larger corporate world was not. The "fast track," with its macho camaraderie and toxic work load, remains the only track to success. As a result, success is indeed usually incompatible with motherhood—as well as with any engaged and active form of fatherhood. The corporate culture strongly discourages *men* from taking parental leave even if offered. And how many families can afford to have both earners on the mommy track?

Today there's an additional factor on the scene—the corporate women who *have* made it. Many of them are reliable advocates for the supports that working parents need. But you don't have to hang out with the skirted-suit crowd for long to discover that others of them are impatient with, and sometimes even actively resentful of, younger women who are trying to combine career and family. Recall that 60 percent of top female executives are themselves childless. Others are of the "if I did it, so can you" school of thought. Felice Schwartz may herself belong in this unsisterly category. In a telling anecdote in her original article, she describes her own problems with an executive employee seeking maternity leave, and the "somewhat awkward conversations" that ensued.

Sooner or later, corporations will have to yield to the pressure for paid parental leave, flextime, and child care, if only because they've become dependent on female talent. The danger is that employers—no doubt quoting Felice Schwartz for legitimation—will insist that the price for such options be reduced pay and withheld promotions, i.e., consignment to the mommy track. Such a policy would place a penalty on parenthood, and the ultimate victims—especially if the policy trickles down to the already low-paid female majority—will of course be children.

Bumping women—or just fertile women, or married women, or whomever—off the fast track may sound smart to cost-conscious CEOs, but eventually it is the corporate culture itself that needs to slow down to a human pace. No one, male or female, works at peak productivity for 70 hours a week, year after year, without sabbaticals or leaves. Think of it this way. If the price of success were exposure to a toxic chemical, would we argue that only women should be protected? Work loads that are incompatible with family life are themselves a kind of toxin—to men as well as women, and ultimately to businesses as well as families.

DISCUSSION QUESTIONS

1. What is the "mommy track?" From a corporate perspective, what is the difference between "career-primary" women and "career and family" women?
2. Is there solid empirical data to support the claim that women are more expensive to employ than men?

Article 22

Understanding Sexual Violence

DIANA SCULLY

SEXUALLY VIOLENT MEN need not search far for cultural language that supports the premise that women are responsible for, or at least provoke, rape. In addition to common cultural stereotypes, the fields of psychiatry and criminology, particularly the subfield of victimology, have traditionally provided justifications for rape, often by portraying raped women as the victims of their own seduction. Through this ideological filter, criminal attacks are made to appear as if they were consensual sexual encounters. For example:

> Considering the amount of illicit intercourse, rape of women is very rare, indeed. Flirtation and provocative conduct, i.e., tacit (if not actual) consent, is generally the prelude to intercourse. (Hollander 1924, 130)

Since women are expected to be coy about their sexual availability, refusal to comply with a man's sexual demands lacks meaning, and rape appears normal. The fact that violence and, often, a weapon are used to accomplish the rape is not considered. As an example, one psychiatrist has argued:

From *Understanding Sexual Violence: A Study of Convicted Rapists* by Diana Scully, Routledge, Chapman and Hall, Inc., New York, 1990, pp. 103–112.

> The conscious or unconscious biological and psychological attraction between man and woman does not exist only on the part of the offender toward the woman but, also, on her part toward him, which in many instances may, to some extent, be the impetus for his sexual attack. Often a women [sic] unconsciously wishes to be taken by force—consider the theft of the bride in Peer Gynt. (Abrahamsen 1960, 161)

Like Peer Gynt, deniers attempted to demonstrate that their victims were willing and, in some cases, enthusiastic participants. In these accounts, the rape became more dependent upon the victim's behavior than upon the man's own actions.

An extreme view of the victim was presented by 31 percent of the deniers. Not only willing, she was the aggressor, a seductress who lured the man, unsuspecting, into sexual action. Typical was a denier convicted of his first rape and accompanying crimes of burglary, sodomy, and abduction. According to the records, he had broken into the victim's house and raped her at knife point. While he admitted to the breaking and entry, which he claimed was for altruistic purposes ("to pay for the prenatal care of a friend's girlfriend"), he also argued that when the victim discovered him, he had tried to leave but she had asked him to stay. Telling him she cheated on her husband, she had voluntarily removed her clothes and seduced him. She was, according to him, an exemplary sex partner who "enjoyed it very much and asked for oral sex." "Can I have it now?" he reported her as saying. He claimed they had spent hours in bed, after which the victim had told him he was good looking and asked to see him again. "Who would believe I'd meet a fellow like this?" he claimed she said.

In addition to this extreme group, 25 percent of deniers said their victims were willing and had made some sexual advances. An additional 9 percent said the victims were willing to have sex for money or drugs. In two of these three cases, the victims had been either an acquaintance or picked up, which the rapists said led them to expect sex.

Women Mean Yes When They Say No

Despite these claims of victim willingness, it is significant that 34 percent of deniers described their victims as unwilling, at least initially, indicating either that the women had resisted or that they had said no. Despite this, and even though according to the records weapons had been present in 64 percent of these cases, deniers justified their behavior by arguing either that the victims had not resisted enough or that their no had really meant yes. For example, one denier was serving time for rape when he was convicted of attempting to rape a prison nurse. He insisted that the rape of the nurse had been completed, and said of his victim, "She semi-struggled but deep down inside I think she felt it was a fantasy come true." The nurse, according to him, had asked a question about his rape conviction, which he interpreted as teasing. "It was like she was saying 'rape me.'" Further, he claimed that she had helped him along with oral sex and "from her actions, she was enjoying it." In another case, a 34-year-old man convicted of abducting and raping a 15-year-old teenager at knife point as she walked on the beach claimed what he had done was not rape because he believed women like to be overpowered before sex, but to dominate after it begins.

> A man's body is like a Coke bottle, shake it up, put your thumb over the opening and feel the tension. When you take a woman out, woo her, then she says, "no, I'm a nice girl," you have to use force. All men do this. She said "no" but it was a societal "no," she wanted to be coaxed. All women say "no" when they mean "yes" but it's a societal "no" so they won't have to feel responsible later.

Claims that the victim didn't resist or, if she did, did not resist enough, were also used by 24 percent of admitters to explain why, during the incident, they thought the victim was willing and that what they were doing was not rape. According to these men, it was not until sometime after the crimes that they redefined their acts. For example, an admitter who used a bayonet to threaten his victim, an employee of the store he had been robbing, stated:

> At the time I didn't think it was rape. I just asked her nicely and she didn't resist. I never considered prison. I just felt like I had met a friend. It took about five years of reading and going to school to change my mind about whether it was rape. I became familiar with the subtlety of violence. But at the time, I believed that as long as I didn't hurt anyone it wasn't wrong. At the time, I didn't think I would go to prison, I thought I would beat it.

Another typical case involved a gang rape in which the victim was abducted at knife point as she walked home about midnight. According to two of the rapists (both of whom were interviewed), at the time they had thought the victim had willingly accepted a ride from the third rapist (who was not interviewed). They claimed that the victim did not resist, and one of the men reported her as saying she would do anything if they would take her home. In this man's view, "She acted like she enjoyed it, but maybe she was just acting. She wasn't crying, she was engaging in it." He reported that she had been friendly to the man who abducted her, and, claiming not to have a home phone, she gave him her office number—a smart tactic which she used eventually to catch the three. In retrospect, this young man had decided, "She was scared and just relaxed and enjoyed it to avoid getting hurt." Note, however, that while he had redefined the act as rape, he continued to believe she enjoyed it.

Men who claimed to have been unaware that they were raping viewed sexual aggression as a man's prerogative at the time of the rape. Thus, they regarded their acts as little more than minor wrongdoing, even though most possessed or used weapons. Lack of resistance, despite weapons, became for them consent. As long as the victim survived without major physical injury, from their perspective, a rape had not taken place. Confiding that he used to believe women were "electrified by my touch," one young man explained that since he did not cause physical injury, he told himself it was what she wanted. Indeed, even U.S. courts have often taken the position that physical injury is a necessary ingredient for a rape conviction.

Women Eventually "Relax and Enjoy It"

It is clear that whatever else they may believe, sexually violent men believe the cultural stereotype that, once the rape began, their victims relaxed and enjoyed it. Indeed, 69 percent of deniers justified their behavior by claiming not only that their victims were willing but that they enjoyed themselves—in some cases, to an immense degree. Several men even boasted that they had made their victims' fantasies come true. Additionally, while the majority of admitters used adjectives such as "dirty," "humiliated," and "disgusted" to describe how they thought rape made women feel, 20 percent still believed that their victims, in particular, had enjoyed themselves. For example, one denier who, according to his records, had posed as a salesman to gain entry to the victim's house, claimed that the victim agreed to have sex with him for drugs. He bragged that the opportunity to have sex with him produced "a glow, because she was really into oral stuff and fascinated by the idea of sex with me. She felt satisfied, fulfilled, wanted me to stay, but I didn't want her."

In another case, a denier who had broken into his victim's house but who insisted the victim was his lover and let him in voluntarily, declared, "She felt good, kept kissing me and wanted me to stay the night. She felt proud after sex with me." Another denier, who hid in the victim's closet and later attacked her while she slept, argued that while she was scared at first, "once we got into it, she was okay." He continued to believe that what he did was not rape because "she enjoyed it and it was like she consented." Finally, more realism from a participant in a group rape and abduction who claimed the victim was a hired prostitute: he conceded that "by her movements she seemed to enjoy it, she seemed pleased, but it may have been because she was alive and going home."

Central to the usefulness of this justification was the denier's ability to produce a reason for the contradiction obviated by the fact that his victim had charged him with rape. Although 13 percent of men had no ready explanation, the majority suggested that their victims had not acted completely of their own volition in the matter. Primarily, two arguments were advanced: 28 percent claimed that someone else, such as a boyfriend, husband, or parent, had forced the victim to report or had done so themselves; an additional 28 percent maintained that the victim was forced to report rape as a cover-up for her own behavior or to avoid personal consequences. To further buttress these claims, 22 percent of deniers asserted that their victims had experienced a change of heart and admitted to culpability, and one man insisted that his victim had gone insane and been institutionalized as a result of her guilt over his conviction.

Contrary to the way that sexually violent men construct reality, the research is quite clear in showing that the extreme opposite is actually true. For example, one study found that not 1 out of 93 adult women rape victims gave a positive response to the question, "How did it feel sexually?" (Holmstrom and Burgess 1978a). In fact, a number of studies have shown that far from enjoyment, rape victims experience adverse psychological consequences, in some cases extreme, prompting some to move, change jobs, or drop out of school (see Burgess and Holmstrom 1974; Kilpatrick et al. 1979; Ruch et al. 1980; Shore 1979). Further, the trauma of rape is so severe that it disrupts sexual functioning, in terms of both frequency and satisfaction, for the overwhelming majority of women, at least during the period immediately following the rape and, in fewer cases, for an extended period of time (Burgess and Holmstrom 1979; Feldman-Sommers et al. 1979). Indeed, from the victim's perspective, rape is a life-altering experience that leaves an emotional residue that may never completely disappear. And even women who have not been victimized know that because they are women, they are rapable. This fear and the threat of rape causes many women to limit their activities in ways that men never have to consider. No, women do not enjoy sexual violence (for a discussion of women's experiences, see Stanko 1985).

Nice Girls Don't Get Raped

Perception of fault in rape is also affected by the belief that "nice girls don't get raped." Thus, any behavior on the part of the victim that is perceived as violating gender role expectations is perceived as contributing to the commission of the act. For example, in one study, hitchhike rape was defined as a victim-precipitated offense by male researchers (Nelson and Amir 1975). The victim's personal life also is used to discredit her and to present her as the legitimate object of sexual attack. Ultimately, a woman's sexual background can be used to deny her legal protection, as one criminologist makes clear when he states:

> The victim could be held unworthy of being protected by the law, either not being a female "of previous chaste character" or succumbing to false pretenses which would not deceive "a man of ordinary intelligence and caution." (von Hentig 1940, 307)

Echoing similar beliefs, it is significant that while they were not asked for the information, a large number of the men succeeded in interjecting something about the victim's sexual reputation into the interview. Once again, deniers, 69 percent, were more likely than admitters, 22 percent, to justify their sexual violence by claiming that the victim was known to be a prostitute, or a "loose" woman, or to have had a lot of affairs, or to have had a child out of wedlock, allegations they assumed would cast her in an unfavourable light. For example, a denier who abducted his victim at knife point from the street stated:

> To be honest, we [his family] knew she was a damn whore and whether she screwed 1 or 50 guys didn't matter.

In another case, a denier who claimed to have known his victim by reputation stated:

> If you wanted drugs or a quick piece of ass, she would do it. In court she said she was a virgin, but I could tell during sex [rape] that she was very experienced.

When other types of discrediting biographical information were added to these sexual slurs, a total of 78 percent of the deniers used their victims' alleged reputations to substantiate their accounts. Most frequently, they referred to the victim's emotional state or alleged drug use. For example, one denier claimed his victim was known to be loose and, additionally, had turned state's evidence against her husband to put him in prison and save herself from a burglary conviction. Further, he asserted that she had met her current boyfriend, who was himself in and out of prison, in a drug rehabilitation center where they were both clients.

Evoking the stereotype that women provoke rape by the way they dress, a description of the victim as seductively attired appeared in the accounts of 22 percent of deniers and 17 percent of admitters, even though they were not asked for this information. Typically, these descriptions were used to substantiate their claims about their victims' reputations. Some men went to extremes to paint a tarnished picture of the victim, describing her as dressed in tight black clothes and without a bra; in one case, the victim was portrayed as sexually provocative in dress and carriage. Not only did she wear short skirts, but she was observed to "spread her legs while getting out of cars."

The intent of these discrediting statements is clear. The men were attempting to justify or excuse their own behavior by arguing that the women were "legitimate" victims who got what they deserved. In the men's view, a woman's lack of a pedestal gave them rights she was deprived of. For example, one denier stated that all of his victims had been prostitutes. Referring to them as "dirty sluts," he argued that anything he did to them was justified. The fact that the records showed they were not prostitutes is less the issue than his belief that prostitutes have no rights.

Such statements also reflect an effort to establish a reputational basis for claiming that the victim was guilty of false accusation and perjured herself in court. Not all of the men attempted to assassinate their victims' reputations with equal vengeance. Numerous times they would make subtle and offhand remarks like, "She was a waitress and you know how they are." Nevertheless, the intent was the same—to cast doubt on the victims' integrity or virtue and to make their own behavior appear more appropriate or reasonable. Their attempts to discredit and present a negative image of their victims take on greater meaning because, as the next section will demonstrate, they expended an equal effort to present themselves in what they thought was a favorable light.

Macho Man Image

In addition to the trivialization of their actions, a number of deniers also attempted to present themselves in a light that made it improbable that they would "need" to rape. For example, they used the argument that they had wives or girlfriends to demonstrate that there had been no reason for them to rape.

One-third of deniers expressed an extreme form of self-aggrandizement. Through their exaggerated pronouncements and extreme show of macho, these men seemed to capture the essence of what all deniers were claiming. The content of their bragging was primarily, though not exclusively, sexual and was an effort to emphasize information that augmented their view of self as nonrapists.

To demonstrate that they did not need to rape, it was not sufficient for these men to produce a single wife or girlfriend. Instead, they claimed to have an excessive amount of sexual opportunity. Typical of this bragging, one man claimed to have 20 women providing him with sex while he was in prison and even more while he was on the outside, and another argued that at his trial, five women had testified to the fact that he didn't need to rape. To substantiate claims of victim willingness, these men made extravagant statements about their attractiveness and desirability to women. The victim, in these cases, was presented as just one of many women who had sought the man's sexual favor. For example, one denier, reciting a list of women he claimed wanted divorces because of him, stated, "I don't think a woman has ever said no to me," and then confided his belief that he was in prison "because of my desirability, women are attracted to me."

To reinforce their contentions that their victims had enjoyed themselves, these men claimed to have superior sexual capacity and technique. For example, an older rapist stated with disdain, "Most men don't know how to satisfy a woman," and described his own sexual partners as "out of their heads with enjoyment." It was not enough for these men to present themselves as just normal. Instead, they claimed to be multitalented superachievers, better at almost everything than anyone else. As one man put it, "I'm better at sex, sports, you name it—there just are too many things." And another denier, who believed "I'm better than the other guys in prison," claimed that he had retained "the best lawyer in the state" to free him. He vowed to get his victim to retract her charges, because "not only have I been cheated but the whole community is cheated because I'm in prison."

Finally, a few deniers even bragged about raping, though they did not view it as such. The message seemed to be that women found sex with them so rewarding that, despite recurrent acts of force, this was their first rape charge! Said one young man:

> If I thought a broad was dominant, I had to use strength. If she was passive, I'd still use strength, but not as much. Strength means pushing her on. I was a good actor—among the best! She would feel my palm on her head pushing her down if she played games. If I can show her the beauty of it, that's strength. Rape is force.

DISCUSSION QUESTIONS

1. What are some of the stereotypes about women that support the belief that women are somewhat responsible for being raped? How do rapists justify rape?
2. What are some of the psychological and sociological consequences of rape? How does rape affect an individual's life?

Article 23

A Generation at Risk

When the Baby Boomers Reach Golden Pond

ROBERT N. BUTLER

THE TIME IS NOW to build into our personal and corporate behavior the realities of a long life ending not in the 60s and 70s but in the 80s and 90s. More and more of us are reaching these years. This is where some revolutionary trends of modern life are taking us as predecessors, successors, and members of the baby-boom generation.

We are relatively unprepared. Yes, we do worry about pensions and Social Security income and the costs of Medicare. Only beginning to sting are long-term care expenses and associated taxes affecting corporate, government, individual, and family budgets. These costs are harbingers of a complex future that we must begin to plan for systematically, starting now.

The 20th century has seen average life expectancy in this country move from under 50 to over 70. Our society has become incredibly efficient at bringing children into maturity. Today's infant has a 50-50 chance of living more than the biblical three score and 10.

From "A Generation At Risk: When the Baby Boomers Reach Golden Pond," by Robert N. Butler, *The Conference Board,* 1988. Reprinted by permission of the publisher and author.

Converging with this expansion of average life expectancy is a second great trend: the aging of that enormous cohort of 76.4 million persons born in the 1946–1964 period. This baby-boom cohort will continue to stress our institutions: The schools were among the first to feel their impact, then the job market; next will be pension plans, Social Security, medical and social care, and other institutions concerned with later life.

The baby boomers constitute a generation at risk. The critical years of their retirement will start about 2010. By 2030, there will be over 50 million retirees, twice today's 65-and-over population. Where 1 in 9 Americans are elderly today, the ratio a half century hence may be 1 in 5, assuming that fertility stays at about the replacement level.

If baby boomers have fewer children per family than their predecessors, this expectation will have profound socioeconomic consequences. The ratio of Americans of typical working age to Americans 65-and-over will reach 2 to 1 as baby-boom retirements increase, considerably under today's 3 to 1. However, the total number of dependents—under 18 and over 65—per 100 working-age Americans will actually be fewer in 2030 than in 1970 or 1960. (See table.) Presumably, workers will spend less on children and will have more for the elderly.

I disagree with warnings that generational conflict will occur when younger workers are forced to support ever growing numbers of elderly. Not only does this line of argument ignore the decline projected in children per household, which will reduce the overall dependency costs of the baby boomers, it overlooks as well the income transfers that go on from elders to the young.

According to A.J. Jaffe in *The New York Statistician* for November-December 1982, the total dependency ratio in today's population is about 1 to 1, and in 2050 "about half of the total population will still be supporting the other half. . . . The change in the dependency burden is the shift from more younger to more older persons." Jaffe believes that the cost of raising and educating the child population about equals total retirement benefits. "It is evading the issue, if not outright misuse of statistics, only to compare the working force and the over 65," he says. . . .

On a scale no other birth cohort has confronted, the baby boomers will confront a double challenge. First, as they approach and enter retirement, they will have to balance their own needs with those of parents and even grandparents. This is illustrated by the 68-year-old daughter who oversees the care, at home or in an institution, of an 87-year-old mother while dealing with her own need for chronic care and that of her 72-year-old husband on a slender retirement income.

Second, as the baby boomers reach the oldest ages, they will have fewer family members to turn to for the same kind of help they gave in earlier years. Not only are more people living to the ages of highest sickness rates but family structure is changing: fewer children, more divorce, and more social isolation, especially because of widowhood. Given the continued emphasis on mobility and living independently, the elders of tomorrow may have to turn to strangers, particularly paid employees of social-service and health-care organizations.

This double challenge will grow rapidly as the population of the most frail elders increases: now one-third of all elders, they will comprise 40% in only 10 years. The challenge will spread faster among older women, blacks, and Hispanics, since these groups of elderly are growing faster than the total 65-and-over population. For older women, the challenge will be particularly intense; they outlive men and typically are the mainstays of long-term care within the family.

The age distribution of the U.S. population seems to me to be far less a matter for concern than is the future of the economy. Whatever economic complications the baby boom causes for itself through low fertility could be compensated for by a more productive economy, one that utilizes the able elderly. Excluding them from roles in wealth production would represent an immense failure of heart and imagination. The longevity revolution will test our economy's capacity to use the added labor potential.

To minimize dependency and maximize productivity, our society will have to spur institutional change. Age discrimination . . . serves to maximize dependency and minimize productivity among the elderly. In our personal and corporate lives, we must continue to break down barriers of myth and prejudice.

We will need organized approaches through government and the private sector to improve income maintenance and support systems. This means well-directed investment in biomedical, sociobehavioral and productivity-related gerontological research. We must originate, refine, and routinize programs to help preserve (and recover) health and productivity at any phase of the adult life cycle. Surely this is one of the best ways to reduce the dependency costs of the generation at risk.

Extending the Work Span

How shall we finance the added years of life? Assuming a life span of 85 years, we can imagine the working portion as about half, counting 20 years for retirement and 25 for maturation and education. A 40-year work span could easily accommodate two or more careers.

We could add to savings by extending the work span—by delaying retirement, by taking less leisure time during the working years, and banking the income, and by investing more in public and private pension programs. A delayed-retirement strategy implies a full-employment economy. Will our society have jobs for everyone as the baby boomers move toward old age? If we are evolving into a society that needs fewer people in the conventional work force, how will individuals build up reserves for retirement? Will automation drastically alter the education-work-retirement proportions of the life span?

These questions must be answered if we are serious about reducing risks for the baby-boom generation and its children. Likewise, we must ask hard questions about the solidity and efficiency of retirement-income programs, including Social Security, private pensions, and individual retirement accounts. Major evaluations should be made of the use of tax breaks to encourage people to plan for their own retirement. Should the goal be to encourage those who can to save more, allowing income to escape Federal taxation? Or should the goal be to assure an adequate basic income in retirement for all (for example, through higher Social Security benefits based on higher taxes and more income transferring)? Do we need a better balance between these goals than now exists?

Unfortunately, planning for population aging tends to occur in relatively narrow contexts, in response to perceived institutional crises. The recent deliberations of the National Commission on Social Security Reform extended gingerly into some of the issues of health and productivity. But the approach was to shore up the Social Security financing, and this necessarily limited the explorations. Nonetheless, the Commission's recommendations offer an entree into some of the practical issues of planning for population aging.

The bipartisan panel dealt with short- and long-range problems. A deficit of somewhere between $150 billion and $200 billion in Social Security revenue was projected for the 1983–89 period. The panel recommended that this could be made up by a combination of taxes and benefit cuts. Some of these proposed actions would also reduce deficits expected after 2020, when the baby-boom retirees would reach a peak. However, an unresolved issue was how to meet fully the long-range gap.

Republican appointees on the Commission endorsed a gradual rise in the age of full entitlement, or indexing of that age to improvements in average life expectancy. They argued that postponing the age to 68 would be sufficient to keep the program sound through the mid-21st century.

Democratic appointees called the proposed age change a benefit cut for young workers confronting higher taxes over the proposed longer period until retirement.

TABLE 23.1 Age Distribution of the U.S. Population

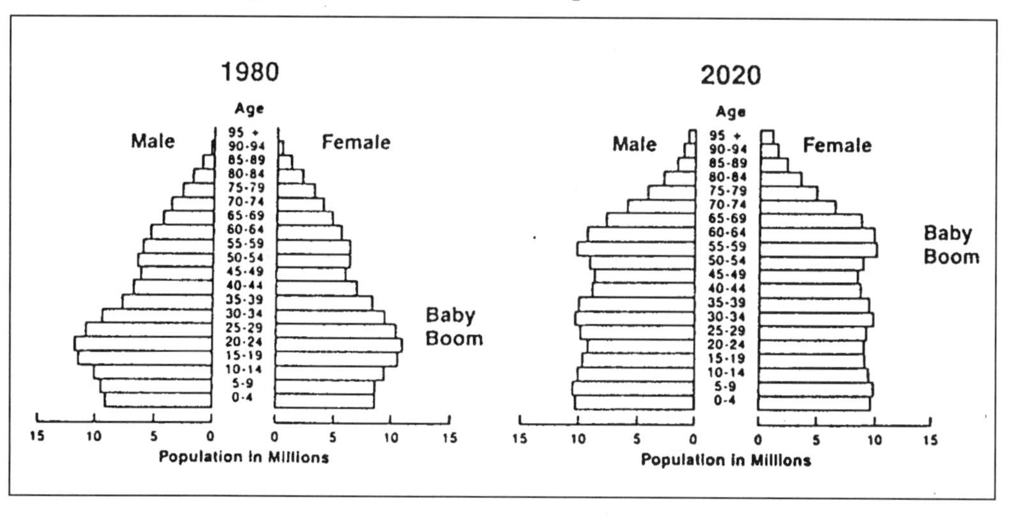

The size of the baby-boom generation in 1980, and the projected size in 2020, compared with the rest of the population. The ratio of working-age Americans to those 65+ will decline 2:1 as baby-boom retirements increase, considerably under today's 3:1 (Source: The Social Security Administration).

Such a step was unnecessary now, they argued, since the long-range deficit might well be made up through economic growth or additional tax increases.

The consensus recommendation of the Commission, however, omitted any call for an age change and instead advocated a policy of encouraging retirement at age 66, 67, or 68 by raising benefits by 8% for each year of delay. Congress was divided on the issue and in the end prescribed a gradual rise to age 67 by the early 21st century. This provision is in the law signed by President Reagan.

Neither the Commission nor Congress directly raised the question of whether the United States spends enough on its Social Security program. Other advanced countries—with proportions of elderly the U.S. has yet to experience—seem able to manage a greater investment. Some devote twice the proportion of gross national product to benefits comparable to those offered under our Social Security system.

A major intent of proposals to raise the full benefits age is clear: each year of delay means the individual will put more money into the system and will take less out of it. Attempts to assure the system's soundness are praiseworthy, but we must consider some implications. Will jobs be available? Will they be open to older workers? Will employers or the government be willing to retrain them? Will they be healthy enough and willing to work? Or will they see delayed retirement as an unprofitable trade of healthy years for sick years?

Corporations in various fields have demonstrated ways of keeping older workers on the job, encouraging their re-entry into the work force, and developing part-time arrangements to meet retirees' needs for supplementary cash, as well as their own needs for their skills and for flexible scheduling. *Young Programs for Older Workers,* published by Work in America Institute in 1980, provides case studies of such programs.

Wm. Wrigley Jr. Company has a long-standing practice of phased retirement for employees at age 65: The first year the employee takes a month off without pay, the second year, two months, and the third year, three months. For each year he works from age 65 to 70, the employee adds 8% to his base pension; $100 of pension income at age 65 thus becomes $147 at age 70. The term "phased retirement," or "flexible retirement," describes any program that allows the employee to gradually change the proportion of leisure time to work time, whether in the form of shorter days, shorter weeks, or months off.

There are various other arrangements to accommodate older workers. IBM fosters second careers to help individuals adjust to technologic and business changes and, when retirement is imminent, to develop new interests and skills. Tektronix Inc. employs a medical placement specialist to redesign jobs for better efficiency and improved job satisfaction on the part of workers who have physical limitations. A carpenter with a back injury can still saw and use the lathe but can't bend to trim moldings; that part of his job is eliminated and, instead, he is given part of another job, say, driving a truck and delivering supplies. The Toro Company has a program that uses part-timers in two ways: Some do regular part-time work and others are on call for overload periods.

Surveys show that many retirees want to work, that many workers in their 50s intend to extend their working careers, and that business recognition of older-worker productivity is increasing. Employment agencies for older workers have developed to serve these parties. In Los Angeles, a Second Careers Program—a nonprofit organization administered by the Los Angeles Voluntary Action Center—has been assisting companies since 1975 to begin or enlarge pre-retirement and retirement programs and to identify opportunities for volunteer and paid second-career jobs. Mature Temps, formed by the Colonial Penn Group, provides jobs for people over age 50 through 14 offices around the country.

A lot more has to be done to provide options in employment and retirement for older workers. Robert W. Feagles, senior vice president of The Travelers Insurance Company, which two years ago eliminated mandatory retirement, points out that our society has built a system allowing more people to enjoy retirement but, at the same time, limits choices for older people. "In reality," he says, "most people over 65, whatever they may wish to do, face two stark alternatives: either full-time work or full-time retirement, with few options in between." Most private pension systems define retirement so strictly that even a short interval of paid work threatens loss of benefits. Social Security is a prime example of the earnings test.

We have to differentiate the expectations and conditions of tomorrow's older workers from those of today and yesterday. The fact is that two-thirds of Social Security retirements occur before age 65. These individuals have actuarially reduced monthly benefits for the rest of their lives. Some early retirements are for reasons of health. Some of these persons are disabled but do not qualify for

TABLE 23.2 Younger and Older Dependents

Year	Number under 18 per 100 Aged 18–64	Number 65+ per 100 Aged 18–64	Total
1930	58.9	9.1	68.0
1940	48.9	11.0	59.9
1950	51.0	13.4	64.4
1960	65.1	16.8	81.9
1970	61.4	17.7	79.1
1980	47.2	18.6	65.8
1990	43.5	20.0	63.5
2000	43.2	19.9	63.1
2010	39.2	20.2	59.4
2020	41.2	26.0	67.2
2030	42.0	31.8	73.8
2040	41.2	30.6	71.8
2050	41.7	30.2	71.9

Projections of the numbers of "dependents" in the U.S. population, young and old (derived from U.S. Census figures by Herman B. Brotman, a consulting gerontologist). The table shows that while the proportion of those over 65 will steadily increase the relative numbers of those under 18 is generally decreasing. Thus, the total "burden" on the working-age population of both young and old would not be unreasonable. In fact, the proportion of dependents may have been higher in 1960 and 1970.

disability insurance and, through it, Medicare coverage. The disability definition of Social Security has been criticized as unduly severe: an individual must be unable to perform in any job no matter where it is in the nation; older workers cannot be expected to move thousands of miles just to find a job they are able to do. (The commissioners who proposed a change in the full benefits age also suggested provisions to assist sick early retirees; this group confronts reduced benefits at a time of above-average sickness costs—and no eligibility for Medicare until age 65.)

The One-Hoss-Shay Issue

The Commission also considered the notion that people should be able to have longer work lives because improvements in longevity have been accompanied by improvements in health. In June 1982, as director of the National Institute on Aging, I discussed the point at the panel's request, along with Dr. Jacob Feldman of the National Center for Health Statistics.

The Commission wanted comments on a hypothesis set forth by Dr. James Fries of Stanford University that the natural limit of the human life span is about 85 years. Fries's policy-relevant point is that the period of morbidity in later life is shortening; people are likely to stay healthy longer, deteriorating much like the "one hoss shay" in the poem, almost all at once. If true, the trend might provide support for raising the Social Security full-benefit age beyond 65. In addition, the hypothesis offers the comforting prospect of moderation in the spiraling costs of Medicare and Medicaid as sickness diminishes in late life.

Trend data from the National Health Interview Survey do not support the Fries hypothesis. Sickness and disability rates by age bracket appear to have held steady over the last decade. Conceivably, this could change. However, applying current rates to the growing elderly population, we project a heavier load of sickness and disability in the 21st century.

Policymakers cannot reasonably ignore this projection, even though some anecdotal evidence suggests that the elders of today are in better health than their forebears. Some surely are. But some reach old age already sick, their lives preserved by medical care. Some live to the oldest ages despite great handicaps. And some maintain good health almost to the very end of life. How this mixed picture relates to ability to work is not precisely clear, since we lack objective criteria for assessing various physical and psychological factors in relation to different kinds of work. . . .

The activity limitations—joint stiffness, visual and hearing impairment, cardiovascular problems, and other handicaps—need not be so serious as to prevent employment. Policies could be adopted to promote employment of such people. The working day or week could be adjusted. Work environments and tasks might be modified. . . .

Ways of making such changes for all kinds of jobs are being, and surely will be, researched and tested. The willingness of public and private sectors to pay their fair share for the accommodations would be an important issue. We are already seeing controversy between government and corporate interests over the recent law requiring job-based health insurance to supplant Medicare as the primary coverage for older workers. The companies oppose the law since private insurance costs more for older workers than for younger workers.

But we must also plan for persons with serious functional limitations who require considerable social support, including medical, hospital, nursing home, and at-home services. We must keep in mind that this group constitutes a sizable minority, but a minority nonetheless, of the elderly population. At any one time, only 1 person in 20 of the general elderly population is in a nursing home; the proportion after age 80 is 1 in 5. This is an important point in considering needs for both institutional and community-based services. According to some estimates, a population double the 1.3 million nursing-home residents is in need of long-term care services in the community. If true, the market for major long-term care services is probably about 4 million of the nation's 26 million elderly.

Because mortality and sickness rates accelerate markedly after age 75, the size of this population has implications for the development of health and social services. It is growing fast—over 9 million today, probably 14 million by 2000. The fastest growing segment of the entire U.S. population is the group aged 85 and older. In 1980, there were 2.6 million, or 1.1% of the U.S. population at this age. In 2020, there will be 7.6 million, or 2.5%.

Between 1980 and 2020, the 75-and-over population with activity limitations due to chronic conditions will increase 2.5 times, to 10.7 million. The number of short-stay hospitalizations will rise to 104.6 million days from 45.8 million. Instead of 1.1 million in nursing homes, there will be 2.7 million. The number of physician visits will double. Personal expenditure for health care will more than double for the aged, while it rises by 50% for the entire U.S. population. Nursing-home expenditures will be in the forefront.

The Geriatrics Gap

Geriatric researchers seek ways to prevent a slow decline in various body systems and to help the patient adjust to changed conditions. They also study a variety of special problems of the elderly. The reactions of the older person to drugs, infection, pain, heart attacks, and other conditions may be different from the reactions of younger adults. For example, mental confusion, not chest pain, may be symptomatic of a heart attack in the older person. So-called senility, or senile dementia, may be reversible once the cause of confusion and memory loss is traced to a treatable cause, such as infection, malnutrition, alcoholism, drug abuse, or depression. Geriatric practice must be concerned with educating patients and families on the true nature of illness in old age, lest misconceptions like "it's just old age" delay treatment beyond the time when it can be most effective.

Unfortunately, the field of geriatrics is underdeveloped in this country. Scientific research into the processes of aging did not expand until recently, and some new conclusions are beginning to appear. Several studies have been done that show far less deterioration in information-processing and problem-solving abilities than investigators in the 1930s had thought.

Some of the most significant conclusions from recent gerontologic research are cautionary. First, what sometimes looks like psychological deterioration due to aging may in fact be more the result of a poor socioeconomic background or little education. For example, a 60-year-old born in 1910 may have greater ability than a 60-year-old born in 1880 simply because he has had a better education.

The enactment of Medicare in 1965 was not accompanied by major investments in research, manpower for service and for research, or by the organization and funding of geriatric services. Medicare was, and is, a benefit package based on what young adults need. It emphasizes short-term or acute care.

The Medicare nursing-home benefit, called "extended care" at first, was basically for convalescence after hospitalization. Because costs could not be forecast reliably, Congress omitted long-term care from the Medicare law. Administrative definitions of reimbursable illness costs exclude coverage of what is disparagingly called "custodial services," some of which are essential to the survival or functioning of patients who are not likely to get "better." For want of home care and other mundane assistance, sound geriatric principles cannot be applied, and some patients become expensive institutional cases.

The only large-scale program of long-term care benefits is found in Medicaid, the Federally aided program of state benefits for the poor. Medicaid money accounts for about half the annual $22 billion spent on nursing-home care. (The other half comes directly from patients or families.) The program's growth is threatening many state treasuries. Unless costs can be moderated, taxes will increase and the increases will cut into profits and wages. This is one reason why some forward-looking business groups are examining long-term care issues and their responsibilities for assisting in resolving them.

Private insurance has eschewed coverage of nursing-home and home-maker services. Reimbursement arrangements under conventional health insurance policies are ill suited to geriatric practice. Only grudgingly do they recognize time spent hearing out, examining, and counseling a patient, or the use of experts in medicine, nursing, and social work as a diagnostic and treatment team. The team approach, a cornerstone of geriatrics, disintegrates at the billing office and dies at the bank. A breakthrough in insurance coverage, through private or public approaches, or a combination of them, is sorely needed.

In addition, we will have to somehow meet the demand for more geriatric physicians—a prospect that now seems unlikely since only a small number of the nation's 127 medical schools have professors of geriatrics or required courses in geriatrics.

Organizing for Productive Aging

How may we organize our thinking for action in the interests of today's elderly and the generation at risk? Plans under way at the Mount Sinai Medical Center in New York City may provide one model.

In 1982, the Medical Center established the nation's first medical school department of geriatrics. The Gerald and May Ellen Ritter Foundation funded the department and the Brookdale Foundation supported the chair in geriatrics that I occupy. The department has six faculty members and eight postgraduate fellows. Wholehearted support by the trustees and administration assured substantial room for mandatory instruction in geriatrics in a crowded medical curriculum. A biomedical research program was authorized. Plans for inpatient and outpatient services for geriatric patients and their families were completed. In addition to providing the community with home care and a wellness clinic, the department is creating a geriatric assessment and referral unit to assist physicians, patients, and families in defining and carrying out programs of care. Special clinics will be devoted to patients with senile dementia, menopausal problems, incontinence, and mobility limitations.

Students and medical residents will be exposed to the well and ill elderly in the community at the hospital and at the Jewish Home and Hospital for Aged. The latter, a nationally recognized long-term care institution, will become a teaching nursing home—a counterpart of the teaching hospital.

To conduct policy-related research and analysis and to raise public and professional awareness of population aging, the department is creating an Institute for Studies of Health and Aging. Applying a broad conception of health, the Institute plans to organize these divisions as funds become available:

> The Center for Productive Aging, to study and offer consultation services on issues involved in enhancing the contributions of the older population to the economy and to family and civic life. The center will advise on such topics as: personnel policies and programs for long-term health and productivity; objective criteria for personal and corporate decisions on work and retirement, and adaptation of the elderly to work tasks and environments.
>
> The Center for Long-Term Care Systems, to focus particularly on long-term care insurance. The center will provide advice and information to corporations, labor unions, health-care organizations, senior citizen groups, and others concerned about long-term care and geriatrics.
>
> The Leadership Forum on Population Aging, to air the issues of population aging in seminars and other formats of practical use to public and private decision-makers. An Aging Information Service will serve the public and mass media as well as private clients.
>
> The Center for International Aging Studies, to bring policy specialists and social and health-care professionals together to examine population-aging issues of international significance. A program of regular exchange between U.S. and foreign teachers and practitioners is contemplated to accelerate the diffusion of geriatric knowledge and skills.
>
> The National Reference Center on Geriatric Education, to promote the development of geriatric training by collecting and disseminating innovative curricula and teaching materials and by advising schools on how to get started.

With well-conceived policies, later life will be a time of options. Even if impaired in some way, we will have opportunities to be productive; we will maintain our vigor for as long as possible, and we will not easily lose our personal autonomy. Supportive programs will exist, staffed by perceptive and humane practitioners, paid for by some contributory method that protects us against impoverishment and affirms our dignity. We will be proud of these accomplishments and leave them to our children. They will say we knew how to age well.

DISCUSSION QUESTIONS

1. Why are the baby boomers a generation at risk? What are the two main challenges that this birth cohort will face?
2. What policies should the government and the private sector develop and implement in order to minimize dependency and maximize productivity of our older population?

IX
Racial and Ethnic Relations

WHAT TO FOCUS ON:

1. Does American society encourage the assimilation of minority groups?
2. What special problems do minority groups face in contemporary America?

AMERICAN SOCIETY is composed of a wide variety of ethnic, racial, and religious groups. Frequently, these groups are bearers of a distinct cultural, religious, or linguistic heritage and lifestyle. A central issue for a pluralistic society such as ours is how the various subgroups can be organized into a cohesive culture. Are we a nation of separate communities each with its own behavioral style and values or is the expectation that all Americans share a common culture and lifestyle? In sociological terms, is assimilation or cultural pluralism the American ideal?

These issues have been raised since the founding of the republic and are still current concerns. Milton M. Gordon in the selection "Assimilation in America: Theory and Reality" presents a penetrating historical and sociological analysis of minority group life in America. Gordon sees three approaches, cultural pluralism, Anglo-conformity, and melting pot theory as competing modes for the integration of minority peoples in the American mosaic. Gordon's work shows how different historical eras have stressed one approach over others. Overall, Gordon acknowledges the reality of widespread assimilation but he points out subtle distinctions in the assimilation process between behavioral and structural forms.

Some contemporary authors have questioned whether assimilation is indeed the fate of all American minority groups. In the article, "Cognitive Styles and Multicultural Populations," James A. Anderson demonstrates that American society is indeed pluralistic and that it is necessary for educational institutions to accept this cultural and cognitive diversity in order that they may more effectively serve minority populations. Anderson carefully contrasts what he refers to as the "holistic" style of minority populations with the "analytical" thinking representative of the dominant majority culture. Anderson advocates that schools adopt a multicultural approach so that both holistic and analytical styles are fully accommodated in American educational institutions.

Phillip Hoose's work highlights the way a society's false preconceptions about a minority group leads to discrimination. Hoose's essay tells about the emergence of a new group of black swimmers who engage in the highest levels of competition. Until recently, coaches assumed, incorrectly, that blacks were physiologically unsuited for competitive swimming. Hoose shows that this was a "racial myth" and, given the opportunity, blacks perform as well as other groups in swimming tournaments.

Article 24

Assimilation in America

Theory and Reality

MILTON M. GORDON

THREE IDEOLOGIES or conceptual models have competed for attention on the American scene as explanations of the way in which a nation, in the beginning largely white, Anglo-Saxon and Protestant, has absorbed over 41 million immigrants and their descendants from variegated sources and welded them into the contemporary American people. These ideologies are Anglo-conformity, the melting pot, and cultural pluralism. They have served at various times, and often simultaneously, as explanations of what has happened—descriptive models—and of what should happen—goal models. Not infrequently they have been used in such a fashion that it is difficult to tell which of these two usages the writer has had in mind. In fact, one of the more remarkable omissions in the history of American intellectual thought is the relative lack of close analytical attention given to the theory of immigrant adjustment in the United States by its social scientists. . . .

Anglo-Conformity

"Anglo-conformity"[1] is a broad term used to cover a variety of viewpoints about assimilation and immigration; they all assume the desirability of maintaining English institutions (as modified by the American Revolution), the English language,

From "Assimilation in America: Theory and Reality," by Milton M. Gordon, Ethnic Groups in American Life, *Daedalus, Journal of the American Academy of Arts and Sciences,* Vol. 90, No. 2, Spring 1961. Reprinted by permission of the publisher.

and English-oriented cultural patterns as dominant and standard in American life. However, bound up with this assumption are related attitudes. These may range from discredited notions about race and "Nordic" and "Aryan" racial superiority, together with the nativist political programs and exclusionist immigration policies which such notions entail, through an intermediate position of favoring immigration from northern and western Europe on amorphous, unreflective grounds ("They are more like us"), to a lack of opposition to any source of immigration, as long as these immigrants and their descendants duly adopt the standard Anglo-Saxon cultural patterns. There is by no means any necessary equation between Anglo-conformity and racists attitudes.

It is quite likely that "Anglo-conformity" in its more moderate aspects, however explicit its formulation, has been the most prevalent ideology of assimilation goals in America throughout the nation's history. As far back as colonial times, Benjamin Franklin recorded concern about the clannishness of the Germans in Pennsylvania, their slowness in learning English, and the establishment of their own native-language press.[2] Others of the founding fathers had similar reservations about large-scale immigration from Europe. In the context of their times they were unable to foresee the role such immigration was to play in creating the later greatness of the nation. They were not all men of unthinking prejudices. The disestablishment of religion and the separation of church and state (so that no religious group—whether New England Congregationalists, Virginian Anglicans, or even all Protestants combined—could call upon the federal government for special favors or support, and so that man's religious conscience should be free) were cardinal points of the new national policy they fostered. "The Government of the United States," George Washington had written to the Jewish congregation of Newport during his first term as president, "gives to bigotry no sanction, to persecution no assistance."

Political differences with ancestral England had just been written in blood; but there is no reason to suppose that these men looked upon their fledgling country as an impartial melting pot for the merging of the various cultures of Europe, or as a new "nation of nations," or as anything but a society in which, with important political modifications, Anglo-Saxon speech and institutional forms would be standard. Indeed, their newly won victory for democracy and republicanism made them especially anxious that these still precarious fruits of revolution should not be threatened by a large influx of European peoples whose life experiences had accustomed them to the bonds of despotic monarchy. Thus, although they explicitly conceived of the new United States of America as a haven for those unfortunates of Europe who were persecuted and oppressed, they had characteristic reservations about the effects of too free a policy. "My opinion, with respect to immigration," Washington wrote to John Adams in 1794, "is that except of useful mechanics and some particular descriptions of men or professions, there is no need of encouragement, while the policy or advantage of its taking place in a body (I mean the settling of them in a body) may be much questioned; for, by so doing, they retain the language, habits and principles (good or bad) which they bring with them.[3] Thomas Jefferson, whose views on race and attitudes towards slavery were notably liberal and advanced for his time, had similar doubts concerning the effects of mass immigration on American institutions, while conceding that immigrants, "if they come of themselves . . . are entitled to all the rights of citizenship."[4]

The attitudes of Americans toward foreign immigration in the first three-quarters of the nineteenth century may correctly be described as ambiguous. On the one hand, immigrants were much desired, so as to swell the population and importance of states and territories, to man the farms of expanding prairie settlement, to work the mines, build the railroads and canals, and take their place in expanding industry. This was a period in which no federal legislation of any consequence prevented the entry of aliens, and such state legislation as existed attempted to bar on an individual basis only those who were likely to become a burden on the community, such as convicts and paupers. On the other hand, the arrival in an overwhelmingly Protestant society of large numbers of poverty-stricken Irish Catholics, who settled in groups in the slums of Eastern cities, roused dormant fears of "Popery" and Rome. Another source of anxiety was the substantial influx of Germans, who made their way to the cities and farms of the midwest and whose different language, separate communal life, and freer ideas on temperance and sabbath observance brought them into conflict with the Anglo-Saxon bearers of the Puritan and Evangelical traditions. Fear of foreign "radicals" and suspicion of the economic demands of the occasionally aroused workingmen added fuel to the nativist fires. In their extreme form these fears resulted in the Native-American movement of the 1830s and 1840s and the "American" or "Know-Nothing" party of the 1850s, with their anti-Catholic campaigns and their demands for restrictive laws on naturalization procedures and for keeping the foreign-born out of political office. While these movements scored local political success and their turbulences so rent the national social fabric that the patches are not yet entirely invisible, they failed to influence national legislative policy on immigration and immigrants; and their fulminations inevitably provoked the expected reactions from thoughtful observers.

The flood of newcomers to the westward expanding nation grew larger, reaching over one and two-thirds million between 1841 and 1850 and over two and one-half million in the decade before the Civil War. Throughout the entire period, quite apart from the excesses of the Know-Nothings, the predominant (though not exclusive) conception of what the ideal immigrant adjustment should be was probably summed up in a letter written in 1818 by John Quincy Adams, then Secretary of State, in answer to the inquiries of the Baron von Fürstenwaerther. If not the earliest, it is certainly the most elegant version of the sentiment, "If they don't like it here, they can go back where they came from." Adams declared:[5]

> They [immigrants to America] come to a life of independence, but to a life of labor—and, if they cannot accommodate themselves to the character, moral, political and physical, of this country with all its compensating balances of good and evil, the Atlantic is always open to them to return to the land of their nativity and their fathers. To one thing they must make up their minds, or they will be disappointed in every expectation of happiness as Americans. They must cast off the European skin, never to resume it. They must look forward to their posterity rather

> than backward to their ancestors; they must be sure that whatever their own feelings may be, those of their children will cling to the prejudices of this country.

The events that followed the Civil War created their own ambiguities in attitude toward the immigrant. A nation undergoing wholesale industrial expansion and not yet finished with the march of westward settlement could make good use of the never faltering waves of newcomers. But sporadic bursts of labor unrest, attributed to foreign radicals, the growth of Catholic institutions and the rise of Catholics to municipal political power, and the continuing association of immigrant settlement with urban slums revived familiar fears. The first federal selective law restricting immigration was passed in 1882, and Chinese immigration was cut off in the same year. The most significant development of all, barely recognized at first, was the change in the source of European migrants. Beginning in the 1880s, the countries of southern and eastern Europe began to be represented in substantial numbers for the first time, and in the next decade immigrants from these sources became numerically dominant. Now the notes of a new, or at least hitherto unemphasized, chord from the nativist lyre began to sound—the ugly chord, or dischord, of racism. Previously vague and romantic notions of Anglo-Saxon peoplehood, combined with general ethnocentrism, rudimentary wisps of genetics, selected tidbits of evolutionary theory, and naive assumptions from an early and crude imported anthropology produced the doctrine that the English, Germans, and others of the "old immigration" constituted a superior race of tall, blonde, blue-eyed "Nordics" or "Aryans," whereas the peoples of eastern and southern Europe made up the darker Alpines or Mediterraneans—both "inferior" breeds whose presence in America threatened, either by intermixture or supplementation, the traditional American stock and culture. The obvious corollary to this doctrine was to exclude the allegedly inferior breeds; but if the new type of immigrant could not be excluded, then everything must be done to instill Anglo-Saxon virtues in these benighted creatures. Thus, one educator writing in 1909 could state:[6]

> These southern and eastern Europeans are of a very different type from the north Europeans who preceded them. Illiterate, docile, lacking in self-reliance and initiative, and not possessing the Anglo-Teutonic conceptions of law, order, and government, their coming has served to dilute tremendously our national stock, and to corrupt our civic life. . . . Everywhere these people tend to settle in groups or settlements, and to set up here their national manners, customs, and observances. Our task is to break up these groups or settlements, to assimilate and amalgamate these people as a part of our American race, and to implant in their children, so far as can be done, the Anglo-Saxon conception of righteousness, law and order, and popular government, and to awaken in them a reverence for our democratic institutions and for those things in our national life which we as a people hold to be of abiding worth.

Anglo-conformity received its fullest expression in the so-called Americanization movement which gripped the nation during World War I. While "Americanization" in its various stages had more than one emphasis, it was essentially a consciously articulated movement to strip the immigrant of his native culture and attachments and make him over into an American along Anglo-Saxon lines—all this to be accomplished with great rapidity. To use an image of a later day, it was an attempt at "pressure-cooking assimilation." It has pre-war antecedents, but it was during the height of the world conflict that federal agencies, state governments, municipalities, and a host of private organizations joined in the effort to persuade the immigrant to learn English, take out naturalization papers, buy war bonds, forget his former origins and culture, and give himself over to patriotic hysteria.

The Melting Pot

While Anglo-conformity in various guises has probably been the most prevalent ideology of assimilation in the American historical experience, a competing viewpoint with more generous and idealistic overtones has had its adherents and exponents from the eighteenth century onward. Conditions in the virgin continent, it was clear, were modifying the institutions which the English colonists brought with them from their mother country. Arrivals from non-English homelands such as Germany, Sweden, and France were similarly exposed to this fresh environment. Was it not possible, then, to think of the evolving American society not as a slightly modified England but rather as a totally new blend, culturally and biologically, in which the stocks and folkways of Europe, figuratively speaking, were indiscriminately mixed in the political pot of the emerging nation and fused by the fires of American influence and interaction into a distinctly new type?

Such, at any rate, was the conception of the new society which motivated that eighteenth-century French-born writer and agriculturalist, J. Hector St. John Crèvecoeur, who, after many years of American residence, published his reflections and observations in *Letters from an American Farmer.*[7] Who, he asks, is the American?

> He is either an European, or the descendant of an European, hence that strange mixture of blood, which you will find in no other country. I could point out to you a family whose grandfather was an Englishman, whose wife was Dutch, whose son married a French woman, and whose present four sons have now four wives of different nations. *He* is an American, who leaving behind him all his ancient prejudices and manners, receives new ones from the new mode of life he has embraced, the new government he obeys, and the new rank he holds. He becomes an American by being received in the broad lap of our great *Alma Mater.* Here individuals of all nations are melted into a new race of men, whose labours and posterity will one day cause great changes in the world.

It remained for an English-Jewish writer with strong social convictions, moved by his observation of the role of the United States as a haven for the poor and oppressed of Europe, to give utterance to the broader view of the American melting pot in a way which attracted public attention. In 1908, Israel Zangwill's drama, *The Melting Pot,* was produced in this country and became a popular success. It is a play dominated by the dream of its protagonist, a young Russian-Jewish immigrant to America, a composer, whose goal is the completion of a vast "American" symphony which will express his deeply felt conception of his adopted country as a divinely appointed crucible in which all the ethnic divisions of mankind will divest themselves of their ancient animosities and differences and become fused into one group, signifying the brotherhood of man. In the process he falls in love with a beautiful and cultured Gentile girl. The play ends with the performance of the symphony and, after numerous vicissitudes and traditional family opposition from both sides, with the approaching marriage of David Quixano and his beloved. During the course of these developments, David, in the rhetoric of the time, delivers himself of such sentiments as these:[8]

> America is God's crucible, the great Melting Pot where all the races of Europe are melting and re-forming! Here you stand, good folk, think I, when I seem them at Ellis Island, here you stand in your fifty groups, with your fifty languages and histories and your fifty blood hatreds and rivalries. But you won't be long like that, brothers, for these are the fires of God you've come to—these are the fires of God. A fig for your feuds and vendettas! Germans and Frenchmen, Irishmen and Englishmen, Jews and Russians—into the Crucible with you all! God is making the American.

Here we have a conception of a melting pot which admits of no exceptions or qualifications with regard to the ethnic stocks which will fuse in the great crucible. Englishmen, Germans, Frenchmen, Slavs, Greeks, Syrians, Jews, Gentiles, even the black and yellow races, were specifically mentioned in Zangwill's rhapsodic enumeration. And this pot patently was to boil in the great cities of America.

Thus around the turn of the century the melting-pot idea became embedded in the ideals of the age as one response to the immigrant receiving experience of the nation. Soon to be challenged by a new philosophy of group adjustment (to be discussed below) and always competing with the more pervasive adherence to Anglo-conformity, the melting-pot image, however, continued to draw a portion of the attention consciously directed toward this aspect of the American scene in the first half of the twentieth century. In the mid-1940s a sociologist who had carried out an investigation of intermarriage trends in New Haven, Connecticut, described a revised conception of the melting process in that city and suggested a basic modification of the theory of that process. In New Haven, Ruby Jo Reeves Kennedy[9] reported from a study of intermarriages from 1870 to 1940 that there was a distinct tendency for the British-Americans, Germans, and Scandinavians to marry among themselves—that is, with a Protestant "pool"; for the Irish, Italians, and Poles to marry among themselves—a Catholic "pool"; and for the Jews to marry other Jews. In other words, intermarriage was taking place across lines of nationality background, but there was a strong tendency for it to stay confined within one or the other of the three major religious groups. Protestants, Catholics, and Jews. Thus, declared Mrs. Kennedy, the picture in New Haven resembled a "triple melting pot" based on religious divisions, rather than a "single melting pot." Her study indicated, she stated, that "while strict endogamy is loosening, religious endogamy is persisting and the future cleavages will be along religious lines rather than along nationality lines as in the past. If this is the case, then the traditional 'single-melting-pot' idea must be abandoned, and a new conception, which we term the 'triple-melting-pot' theory of American assimilation, will take its place as the true expression of what is happening to the various nationality groups in the United States."[10] The triple melting-pot thesis was later taken up by the theologian, Will Herberg, and formed an important sociological frame of reference for his analysis of religious trends in American society, *Protestant-Catholic-Jew.*[11] But the triple melting-pot hypothesis patently takes us into the realm of a society pluralistically conceived. We turn now to the rise of an ideology which attempts to justify such a conception.

Cultural Pluralism

Probably all the non-English immigrants who came to American shores in any significant numbers from colonial times onward—settling either in the forbidding wilderness, the lonely prairie, or in some accessible urban slum— created ethnic enclaves and looked forward to the preservation of at least some of their native cultural patterns. Such a development, natural as breathing, was supported by the later accretion of friends, relatives, and countrymen seeking out oases of familiarity in a strange land, by the desire of the settlers to rebuild (necessarily in miniature) a society in which they could communicate in the familiar tongue and maintain familiar institutions, and finally, by the necessity to band together for mutual aid and mutual protection against the uncertainties of a strange and frequently hostile environment. This was as true of the "old" immigrants as of the "new." In fact, some of the liberal intellectuals who fled to America from an inhospitable political climate in Germany in the 1830s, 1840s, and 1850s looked forward to the creation of an all-German state within the union, or, even more hopefully, to the eventual formation of a separate German nation, as soon as the expected dissolution of the union under the impact of the slavery controversy should have taken place.[12] Oscar Handlin, writing of the sons of Erin in mid-nineteenth-century Boston, recent refugees from famine and economic degradation in their homeland, points out: "Unable to participate in the normal associational affairs of the community, the Irish felt obliged to erect a society within a society, to act together in their own way. In every contact therefore the group, acting apart from other sections of the community, became intensely aware of its peculiar and exclusive identity."[13] Thus cultural pluralism was a fact in American society before it became a theory—a theory with explicit relevance for the nation as a whole, and articulated and discussed in the English-speaking circles of American intellectual life. . . .

The classic statement of the cultural pluralist position, however, had been made over a year before. Early in 1915 there appeared in the pages of *The Nation* two articles under the title "Democracy *versus* the Melting-Pot." Their author was Horace Kallen, a Harvard-educated philosopher with a concern for the application of philosophy to societal affairs, and, as an American Jew, himself derivative of an ethnic background which was subject to the contemporary pressures for dissolution implicit in the "Americanization," or Anglo-conformity, and the melting-pot theories. In these articles Kallen vigorously rejected the usefulness of these theories as models of what was actually transpiring in American life or as ideals for the future. Rather he was impressed by the way in which the various ethnic groups in America were coincident with particular areas and regions, and with the tendency for each group to preserve its own language, religion, communal institutions, and ancestral culture. All the while, he pointed out, the immigrant has been learning to speak English as the language of general communication, and has participated in the over-all economic and political life of the nation. These developments in which "the United States are in the process of becoming a federal state not merely as a union of geographical and administrative unities, but also as a cooperation of cultural diversities, as a federation or commonwealth of national cultures,"[14] the author argued, far from constituting a violation of historic American political principles, as the "Americanizers" claimed, actually represented the inevitable consequences of democratic ideals, since individuals are implicated in groups, and since democracy for the individual must by extension also mean democracy for his group.

The processes just described, however, as Kallen develops his argument, are far from having been thoroughly realized. They are menaced by "Americanization" programs, assumptions of Anglo-Saxon superiority, and misguided attempts to promote "racial" amalgamation. Thus America stands at a kind of cultural crossroads. It can attempt to impose by force an artificial, Anglo-Saxon-oriented uniformity on its peoples, or it can consciously allow and encourage its ethnic groups to develop democratically, each emphasizing its particular cultural heritage. If the latter course is followed, as Kallen puts it at the close of his essay, then,[15]

> The outlines of a possible great and truly democratic commonwealth become discernible. Its forms would be that of the federal republic: its substance a democracy of nationalities, cooperating voluntarily and autonomously through common institutions in the enterprise of self-realization through the perfection of men according to their kind. The common language of the commonwealth, the language of its great tradition, would be English, but each nationality would have for its emotional and involuntary life its own peculiar dialect or speech, its own individual and inevitable esthetic and intellectual forms. The political and economic life of the commonwealth is a single unit and serves as the foundation and background for the realization of the distinctive individuality of each nation that composes it and of the pooling of these in a harmony above them all. Thus "American civilization" may come to mean the perfection of the cooperative harmonies of "European civilization"—the waste, the squalor and the distress of Europe being eliminated—a multiplicity in a unity, an orchestration of mankind.

Conclusions

In the remaining pages I can make only a few analytical comments which I shall apply in context to the American scene, historical and current. My view of the American situation will not be documented here, but may be considered as a series of hypotheses in which I shall attempt to outline the American assimilation process.

First of all, it must be realized that "assimilation" is a blanket term which in reality covers a multitude of subprocesses. The most crucial distinction is one often ignored—the distinction between what I have elsewhere called "behavioral assimilation" and "structural assimilation."[16] The first refers to the absorption of the cultural behavior patterns of the "host" society. (At the same time, there is frequently some modification of the cultural patterns of the immigrant-receiving country, as well.) There is a special term for this process of cultural modification or "behavioral assimilation"—namely, "acculturation." "Structural assimilation," on the other hand, refers to the entrance of the immigrants and their descendants into the social cliques, organizations, institutional activities, and general civic life of the receiving society. If this process takes place on a large enough scale, then a high frequency of intermarriage must result. A further distinction must be made between, on the one hand, those activities of the general civic life which involve earning a living, carrying out political responsibilities, and engaging in the instrumental affairs of the larger community, and, on the other hand, activities which create personal friendship patterns, frequent home intervisiting, communal worship, and communal recreation. The first type usually develops so-called "secondary relationships," which tend to be relatively impersonal and segmental; the latter type leads to "primary relationships," which are warm, intimate, and personal.

With these various distinctions in mind, we may then proceed.

Built on the base of the original immigrant "colony" but frequently extending into the life of successive generations, the characteristic ethnic group experience is this: within the ethnic group there develops a network of organizations and informal social relationships which permits and encourages the members of the ethnic group to remain within the confines of the group for all of their primary relationships and some of their secondary relationships throughout all the stages of the life cycle. From the cradle in the sectarian hospital to the child's play group, the social clique in high school, the fraternity and religious center in college, the dating group within which he searches for a spouse, the marriage partner, the neighborhood of his residence, the church affiliation and the church clubs, the men's and the women's social and service organizations, the adult clique of "marrieds," the vacation resort, and then, as the age cycle nears completion, the rest home for the elderly and, finally, the sectarian cemetery—in all these activities and relationships which are close to the core of personality and selfhood—the member of the ethnic group may if he wishes follow a path which never takes him across the boundaries of his ethnic structural network.

The picture is made more complex by the existence of social class divisions which cut across ethnic group lines just as they do those of the white Protestant population in America. As each ethnic group which has been here for the requisite time has developed second, third, or in some cases, succeeding generations, it has produced a college-educated group which composes an upper middle class (and sometimes upper class, as well) segment of the larger groups. Such class divisions tend to restrict primary group relations even further, for although the ethnic-group member feels a general sense of identification with all the bearers of his ethnic heritage, he feels comfortable in intimate social relations only with those who also share his own class background or attainment.

In short, my point is that, while *behavioral assimilation* or acculturation has taken place in America to a considerable degree, *structural assimilation,* with some important exceptions has not been extensive.[17] The exceptions are of two types. The first brings us back to the "triple-melting-pot" thesis of Ruby Jo Reeves Kennedy and Will Herberg. The "nationality" ethnic groups have tended to merge within each of the three major religious groups. This has been particularly true of the Protestant and Jewish communities. Those descendants of the "old" immigration of the nineteenth century, who were Protestant (many of the Germans and all the Scandinavians), have in considerable part gradually merged into the white Protestant "subsociety." Jews of Sephardic, German, and Eastern-European origins have similarly tended to come together in their communal life. The process of absorbing the various Catholic nationalities, such as the Italians, Poles, and French Canadians, into an American Catholic community hitherto dominated by the Irish has begun, although I do not believe that it is by any means close to completion. Racial and quasi-racial groups such as the Negroes, Indians, Mexican-Americans, and Puerto Ricans still retain their separate sociological structures. The outcome of all this in contemporary American life is thus pluralism—but it is more than "triple" and it is more accurately described as *structural pluralism* than as cultural pluralism, although some of the latter also remains.

NOTES

1. The phrase is the Coles'. See Stewart G. Cole and Mildred Wiese Cole, *Minorities and the American Promise* (New York, Harper & Brothers, 1954), ch. 6.
2. Maurice R. Davie, *World Immigration* (New York, Macmillan, 1936), p. 36, and (cited therein) "Letter of Benjamin Franklin to Peter Collinson, 9th May, 1753, on the condition and character of the Germans in Pennsylvania," in *The Works of Benjamin Franklin, with notes and a life of the author,* by Jared Sparks (Boston, 1828), vol. 7, pp. 71–73.
3. *The Writings of George Washington,* Collected by W. C. Ford (New York, G. P. Putnam's Sons, 1889), vol. 12, p. 489.
4. Thomas Jefferson, "Notes on Virginia, Query 8"; in *The Writings of Thomas Jefferson,* ed. A. E. Bergh (Washington, The Thomas Jefferson Memorial Association, 1907), vol. 2, p. 121.
5. *Niles' Weekly Register,* vol. 18, 29 April 1820, pp. 157–158; also, Marcus L. Hansen, *The Atlantic Migration,* 1607–1860, pp. 96–97.
6. Ellwood P. Cubberly, *Changing Conceptions of Education* (Boston, Houghton Mifflin, 1909), pp. 15–16.
7. J. Hector St. John Crèvecoeur, *Letters from an American Farmer* (New York, Albert and Charles Boni, 1925; reprinted from the 1st edn., London, 1782), pp. 54–55.
8. Israel Zangwill, *The Melting Pot* (New York, Macmillan, 1909), p. 37.
9. Ruby Jo Reeves Kennedy, "Single or Triple Melting-Pot? Intermarriage Trends in New Haven, 1870–1940," *American Journal of Sociology,* 1944, 49:331–339. See also her "Single or Triple Melting-Pot? Intermarriage in New Haven, 1870–1950," *ibid,* 1952, 58:56–59.
10. Kennedy, "Single or Triple Melting-Pot . . . 1870–1940," p. 332 (author's italics omitted).
11. Will Herberg, *Protestant-Catholic-Jew* (Garden City, Doubleday, 1955).

12. Nathan Glazer, "Ethnic Groups in America: From National Culture to Ideology," in Morroe Berger, Theodore Abel, and Charles H. Page, eds., *Freedom and Control in Modern Society* (New York, D. Van Nostrand, 1954), p. 161; Marcus Lee Hansen, *The Immigrant in American History* (Cambridge, Harvard University Press, 1940), pp. 129–140; John A. Hawgood, *The Tragedy of German-America* (New York, Putnam's, 1940), passim.

13. Oscar Handlin, *Boston's Immigrants* (Cambridge, Harvard University Press, 1959, rev. edn.), p. 176.

14. Horace M. Kallen, "Democracy *versus* the Melting-Pot," *The Nation,* 18 and 25 February 1915; reprinted in his *Culture and Democracy in the United States,* New York, Boni and Liveright, 1924; the quotation is on p. 116.

15. Kallen, op. cit., p. 124.

16. Milton M. Gordon, "Social Structure and Goals in Group Relations," p. 151.

17. See Erich Rosenthal, "Acculturation without Assimilation?" *American Journal of Sociology,* 1960, 66:275–288.

DISCUSSION QUESTIONS

1. Compare and contrast Anglo-conformity and cultural pluralism.
2. Do you agree with Gordon that "structural pluralism" typifies the American experience?

Article 25

Cognitive Styles and Multicultural Populations

JAMES A. ANDERSON

IN THE PAST TWO DECADES, minority students have gained limited access to many predominantly white colleges and universities. Because minority students historically have been drawn from isolated rural areas or depressed residential areas where educational resources are substandard, most of these students are inadequately prepared to compete favorably at the university level against better educated, more affluent students. Even though the percentage of blacks, for example, who complete high school has increased steadily since 1970, the percentage who go on to college has declined since 1980. And, among those who do attend, the retention rates reflect serious problems. Wilson (1984) suggests this decline will continue until 1990 unless there is an increase in the number of those attending universities and an increase in retention.

Through the early 1960s student retention received comparatively little attention in the professional literature. Even when it was discussed, it was largely an academic exercise but rarely resulted in program development. During the last few years a concern with retaining minority students has appeared in the academic literature and at institutions because minority students, especially blacks, represent an important resource. For predominantly white universities and colleges, the in-

From "Cognitive Styles and Multicultural Populations," by James A. Anderson, *Journal of Teacher Education,* Jan./Feb., 1988. Reprinted by permission of the publisher.

creased retention of minorities would satisfy two needs: (a) it would allow the institutions to meet federal guidelines, and (b) it would allow the institutions to fill classrooms left vacant by the disappearance of the applicant pool that had been created by the legacy of the baby boom. . . .

One of the major assumptions of most retention programs is that the incoming minority student should adapt to all facets of the program. Adherents to this perspective assume that the standard retention model can effectively meet the needs (academic and emotional) of minority students and can match up with their values/attitudes concerning achievements. The lack of success among retention programs over the past decade suggests that this assumption is incorrect.

Two critical factors underscore the minor success of retention programs. First, the programs themselves share the same model, one which emanates from basic educational learning theory and which reflects Anglo-European notions about cognitive functioning, learning, and achievement. A second critical factor is that these programs have almost never attempted to identify the cognitive assets and learning preferences of nonwhite students. What has precluded the identification of the cognitive/learning styles of minority students in retention programs is the ethnocentric assumption on the part of whites that minorities do not have a valid and substantive cognitive framework which may be somewhat different but equally effective for them.

It is very easy to ignore the ethnocentric dominance of the theory and practice that exists in higher education. Universities and colleges are run (with a few exceptions) by white males, as are the departments in those same institutions. Departmental curriculums and retention programs, in fact the basic models of learning and achieving, derive from a very narrow white male perspective. The issue which has surfaced among many scholars who study minorities concerns the affirmation of the cognitive/learning styles among multicultural populations. Moreover, these same scholars call for an incorporation of knowledge about this cultural and racial diversity into university programs and ultimately into the teaching styles of individual instructors.

When students of color enroll at predominantly white colleges and universities, they are expected to adapt to the milieu of that environment. In fact, their capacity to adapt may significantly underscore their ability to achieve academically. But the question which is seldom addressed and incorporated into the success equation of these students is, "to what degree does their cultural and/or racial diversity impact their perception of this (new) learning environment?" Such a question is difficult to address when little attention has been given to the varied nature of cultural differences among multicultural populations. . . .

Cultural Style and Classroom Learning

A pluralistic society is one which is populated by disparate ethnic groups and cultures. Social order is often a function of the tolerance level exhibited by the dominant group, and subgroups are often indirectly stymied as they attempt to gain access to mainstream society. In American society the educational system is recognized as a primary vehicle to success-achievement. But, this system is built upon the type of European world view which was alluded to earlier and tends to benefit whites whose cultural style is more attuned to it. It seems feasible to suggest that the test-measured differences between blacks and other groups of color and whites may be due to the fact that some minorities are not motivated towards optimal achievement within a Western educational setting. Cohen (1969) suggests that most school environments reflect a field-independent style, a style unfamiliar to Mexican-American, Puerto Rican, and black children. Work by McNeil (1968) and McNeil and Phillips (1969) suggests that the school setting which is oriented towards whites does not parallel the learning system of blacks. Even more important than the above suggestions would be an identification of the behavior patterns which possibly reflect differences in learning styles and which simultaneously contribute to differential academic performance.

Cohen (1969), Messick (1970), and Ramirez (1973) found that Mexican-American children tend to be field-dependent and do best on verbal tasks. They are also said to learn materials more easily which have humor, social content, and which are characterized by fantasy and humor; and are sensitive to the opinions of others. Anglo-American children do best on analytic tasks; learn material that is inanimate and impersonal more easily; and their performance is not greatly affected by the opinions of others. Kagan and Madsen (1971) studied the motivational styles of Mexican, Mexican-American, and Anglo-American children. They found that Anglo-American children were more competitive than either Mexican or Mexican-American children. The Mexican-American children also were more highly motivated in the cooperative setting than in the competitive. Ramirez and Price-Williams (1974a) also examined motivational style by utilizing the School Situation Picture Stories Technique (SSPST). They found that Anglo-American children scored higher on need achievement for self, in which the achiever is the primary beneficiary. In another study with the SSPST, Ramirez and Price-Williams (1974b) showed that Mexican-American children scored higher than Anglo-American children on need affiliation, and need succorance which refers to a need to be comforted.

In his book, *The Psychology of the Afro-American,* Adelbert Jenkins (1982) suggests that learning involves the application of one's meaningful framework to new situations in order to make sense of them. Learning becomes solidified when this mental reshaping becomes attached with some positive or negative affect. For example, one of the functions of language is the transmission of culture. The indications that language may be illustrative of cognitive style suggests that children internalize the cognitive style and perceptual views of their parents, along with the more overt aspects of cultural preference of the society. Cooper (1980a) suggests, for example, that as children hear and use holistic language features their preference for a holistic style is reinforced by most other contacts, both peer and adult, and if children are expected to behave in a particular way and in a particular situation where this behavior is reinforced, again, their preference for a particular style is reinforced.

In America, as white children leave the home and move on through the educational system and then into the work world, the development of cognitive and learning styles follows a linear, self-reinforcing course. Never are they asked to be bicultural, bidialectic, or bicognitive. On the other hand, for children of color, biculturality is not a free choice, but a prerequisite for successful participation and eventual success. Nonwhite children generally are expected to be bicultural, bidialectic, bicognitive; to measure their performance against a Euro-American yardstick; and to maintain the psychic energy to maintain this orientation. At the same time, they are being castigated whenever they attempt to express and validate their indigenous cultural and cognitive styles. Under such conditions cognitive conflict becomes the norm rather than the exception.

Cognitive Style and Cultural Groupings

Although the perception might be that cognitive styles are disparate entities, they actually operate along a continuum. Along this continuum, certain groups seem to cluster at one end or the other. There are many similarities in the world views and cognitive styles of certain groups of color that affect their fundamental perceptions of the world and how they choose to think about it and then interact with it. Table 25.1 categorizes some of the groups who share aspects of a world view; Table 25.2 identifies some of the cultural dimensions characteristic of each grouping.

As was alluded to earlier, the cognitive style of a group is strongly influenced by the cultural history of that group. There is no such thing as one style being "better than another," although in our country the Euro-American style is projected by most institutions as the one which is most valued. Cultural and cognitive conflict often occur when a group is asked to perform in a manner and setting which in someways is foreign to their style or does not capitalize on it. In many critical areas of human functioning and behavior, the world view of the dominant group is indifferent to or conflicts with the world view of other groups in that culture (Jenkins, 1982; Greenspan, 1983; Baldwin, 1985; Day, 1985). Table 25.3 labels and compares various styles as they might impact classroom learning.

TABLE 25.1 Cultural Groupings of World Views

Non-Western	Western
• American-Indians • Mexican-Americans • African-Americans • Vietnamese-Americans • Puerto Rican-Americans • Chinese-Americans • Japanese-Americans • Many Euro-American females	• Euro-Americans (primarily males) • Minorities with high degree of acculturation

TABLE 25.2 Some Fundamental Dimensions of Non-Western vs. Western World View

Non-Western	Western
• Emphasize group cooperation	• Emphasize individual competition
• Achievement as it reflects group	• Achievement for the individual
• Value harmony with nature	• Must master and control nature
• Time is relative	• Adhere to rigid time schedule
• Accept affective expression	• Limit affective expression
• Extended family	• Nuclear family
• Holistic thinking	• Dualistic thinking
• Religion permeates culture	• Religion distinct from other parts of culture
• Accept world views of other cultures	• Feel their world view is superior
• Socially oriented	• Task oriented

Multicultural Communication and Cognitive Style

According to Cooper (1981), a linguistics specialist at the University of the District of Columbia, almost no one has examined sufficiently the influence of cognitive style on the many aspects of speech (language) and writing. During the late 1960s and 1970s, sociolinguistic studies identified various nonstandard dialects, particularly black English, as valid language systems, and the validity of the dialects was generally accepted by the English profession. Grammatical and phonological aspects of dialects, however, cannot totally account for language differences among diverse populations. Because cognition and cognitive style directly influence the style and content of language (and vice versa), it is imperative that researchers examine cultural differences from this perspective.

TABLE 25.3 Cognitive Style Comparison

Field-dependent Relational/Holistic Affective	Field-independent Analytic Nonaffective
Characteristics	Characteristics
1. Perceive elements as a part of a total picture.	1. Perceive elements as discrete from their background.
2. Do best on verbal tasks.	2. Do best on analytic tasks.
3. Learn material which has a human social content and which is characterized by fantasy and humor.	3. Learn material that is inanimate and impersonal more easily.
4. Performance influenced by authorizing figure's expression of confidence or doubt.	4. Performance not greatly affected by the opinions of others.
5. Style conflicts with traditional school environment.	5. Style matches up with most school environments.

TABLE 25.4 Comparison of Features in the Writing Styles of Holistic vs. Analytical Thinkers

Holistic (Non-Western)	Analytical (Western)
1. Descriptive abstraction	**1.** Analytic abstraction
2. Word meaning based on content	**2.** Formal meanings for words
3. Use few synonyms	**3.** Use many synonyms
4. Use few comparisons	**4.** Use many forms of generalization comparison
5. Use relational and institutional classification	**5.** Use hierarchical modes of classification
6. Tend to use second person "you," reflects group identity; tends to pull reader in as part of the writing	**6.** Can easily adopt a third person viewpoint in writing and speaking, is objective, reflects separate identity from what is going on

Speech patterns that are developed by a group equip them for effective interaction within their own community first, and then the larger society second. These speech patterns also reflect the cognitive style of that group. Ultimately, the speech patterns fuse with other aspects of communication for that group to provide reciprocal reinforcement for what is most valued by the group.

The white American or standard English communication style is simply one of many. It was not the first and, objectively speaking, it is not the best. Simply, it is more functional for those with an Anglo-European frame of reference.

Generally speaking, nonwhite and rural white students with a minimal degree of acculturation exhibit a communication style that is at variance with the Western communication style. Table 25.4 compares some of the key features of speaking/writing that differentiate holistic vs. analytical thinkers. These features have been identified by several researchers (Cooper, 1980b; Vygotsky, 1978; Cohen, 1969).

Another aspect of the holistic (nonwestern) communication style that distinguishes it from the analytical involves the degree to which symbolic and concrete imagery are utilized as a communicative tool. For some ethnic groups the extended use of imagery represents one of the dominant ways of thinking, conceptualizing, writing, and speaking. This process seems to be more characteristic of those groups that emphasize the affective, holistic, relational style.

According to Matthews (1977), the concrete symbolic image is the tool of a cognitive style preferred by blacks (and other people of color) throughout the world. He states:

> In black use the thought is generated through the use of a picture concept (Visualization) rather than through the use of . . . theoretical statement . . . a picture of the thing as it really exists is put before the mind and imagination . . . one proceeds through visual as against nonvisual thinking. (p. 16)

TABLE 25.5 Comparison of Form and Function of Symbolic Imagery Between Disparate Cognitive Processes (Speech & Writing)

Non-Western	Western
1. Visual (pictorial thinking)	**1.** Notions or theoretical statements
2. Thought is perceived as . . . living thing, holistic thing, doing thing	**2.** Thought is . . . mentalistic, devitalized, static
3. Imagery is intensely affective with cultural base	**3.** Imagery minimizes affective associations
4. Extensive expression of concrete emotional words and heightened use of metaphors	**4.** De-emphasis on such unless in specialized disciplines or situation
5. Medium is the message	**5.** Medium communicates the message
6. Medium motivates and socializes	**6.** Things must be contemplated before they motivate
7. Introduces self into objective analysis of events	**7.** Removes self

Many cultures utilize symbolism, but European symbolism is empirical and abstract while that of holistic cultures is concrete and drawn from everyday life. Moreover, the latter communicates the affective aspects of that life. The Anglo-European style *does* often make use of symbolic imagery but selectively categorizes its usage under headings such as "poetry" and "literature." Table 25.5 represents a comparison of the stylistic difference in the utilization of symbolic imagery.

One of the most critical problems encountered by students of color is that secondary school teachers and college faculty are not equipped to identify, interpret, and respond to the variant styles of multicultural populations. A communication gap exists between their teaching style and the students' indigenous learning styles. Thus, the symbolic, affective, reality-based approach to learning of some students will not only be misconstrued but also branded as deficient. For example, the writing/speaking styles of Mexican-American, black-American, and Puerto Rican-American students are frequently viewed as "too flowery," too subjective, involving an excessive use of metaphors, utilizing the wrong tense of verbs, etc. What is a valuable and valid communication process under one cognitive style becomes a deformed example of cognitive/linguistic deficits under another.

Even more salient are the problems that students of color encounter when they attempt to adapt their styles to the theoretical, often abstract, reasoning process utilized in mathematics and the hard sciences. Most courses in both areas utilize a format in which the teaching of the theory (in an abstract sense) precedes any practical application or direct experience (like laboratory exercises). The implicit assumption is that this is the proper sequence of training because, historically speaking, this has always been the approach to mathematics and science instruction; and because this approach coincides with the Anglo-European cognitive style, especially that of males. The opposite approach, in which direct experience precedes discussion of formal concepts and laws, is not as valued and, hence, utilized as much by teachers. McDermott, Piternick, and Rosenquist (1980) found such an approach to be extremely successful in the development of a curriculum in physics and biology at the University of Washington. Brown (1986) at the University of San Diego discovered that the same approach worked in her mathematics lab. Successful programs which serve minority populations utilize other dimensions of the holistic/affective. For example, one of the most successful science/pre-med programs of the last decade has been the SOAR program at Xavier University in New Orleans. The program builds confidence and skill in its predominantly black population by creating an aura of family in which cooperation is highly valued, bonding between the students and faculty is encouraged, and a maintenance of positive ethnic identity is fostered. Learning occurs in a socially reinforcing environment. Incidentally, the director of the program is a white male. One does not have to be the same race/ethnicity to identify and capitalize upon the cultural/cognitive assets of minority populations. . . .

Conclusion

At the superficial level, cross-racial, cross-ethnic teaching, learning, and/or service delivery occurs when the persons interacting are of different racial or ethnic identities. When one adds to this equation the differences in degree of acculturation and type of cognitive/learning style, the examination and explanation of these differences becomes more complicated and the urgency to identify the critical dimensions associated with them more pronounced. Whereas it was once fashionable and sometimes academically rewarding to deny the existence of cultural assets and variations among nonwhite populations, social scientists and researchers now recognize that such traditional approaches have become anachronistic. The failure of retention programs, the ineffectiveness of service delivery to multiethnic populations, and the inability to produce effective communication between majority and minority members are glaring examples that new models and approaches must evolve which not only deal with debilitating misconceptions about minorities, but, more important, also operate within a framework of equal respect and appreciation for the similarities and differences among groups.

REFERENCES

Baldwin, J.A. (1985). Psychological aspects of European cosmology in American society. *Western Journal of Black Studies, 9* (4), 216–223.

Brown, M. (1986, November). *Calculus by the dozen: A retention program for undergraduate minority students in mathematics based majors.* A paper presented at the second annual Conference on Black Student Retention, Atlanta, GA.

Cohen, R.A. (1969). Conceptual styles, culture conflict and nonverbal tests of intelligence. *American Anthropologist, 71,* 828–856.

Cooper, G. (1980a). Different ways of thinking. *Minority Education, 2* (5), 1–4.

Cooper, G. (1980b). Everyone does not think alike. *English Journal, 60,* 45–50.
Cooper, G. (1981). Black language and holistic cognitive style. *Western Journal of Black Studies, 5,* 201–207.
Day, M.W. (1985). *The socio-cultural dimensions of mental health.* NY: Vantage.
Greenspan, M. (1983). *A new approach to women and therapy.* New York: McGraw-Hill.
Jenkins, A.H. (1982). *The psychology of the Afro-American.* Elmsford, NY: Permagon Press.
Kagan, S. and Madsen, M.C. (1971). Cooperation and competition of Mexican, Mexican-American, and Anglo-American children of two ages under four instruction sets. *Developmental Psychology, 5,* 32–39.
Matthews, B. (1977). Voice of Africa in the Diaspora. *New Directions, 4,* 16–19.
McDermott, L.C., Piternick, L.K., and Rosenquist, M.L. (1980). Helping minority students succeed in science. *Journal of College Student Teaching, 10* (1), 135–140.
McNeil, K. (1968). Semantic space as an indicator of socialization. *Journal of Educational Psychology, 59,* 325–327.
McNeil, K. and Phillips, B. (1969). Scholastic nature of responses to the environment in selected subcultures. *Journal of Educational Psychology, 60* (2), 79–85.
Messick, S. (1970). The criterion problem in the evaluation of instruction: Assessing possible, not just intended outcomes. In M.C. Wittrock & G.D.E. Wiley (eds.), *The evaluation of instruction: Issues and problems.* New York: Holt.
Ramirez, M. (1973). Cognitive styles and cultural democracy in education. *Social Science Quarterly, 53,* 895–904.
Ramirez, M. and Price-Williams, D.R. (1974a). Achievement motivation in Mexican-American children. Unpublished manuscript. Houston, TX: Rice University.
Ramirez, M. and Price-Williams, D.R. (1974b). Cognitive styles of children of three ethnic groups in the United States. *Journal of Cross-Cultural Psychology, 5* (2), 212–219.
Vygotsky, L.S. (1978). *Mind in society: The development of higher psychological processes.* Cambridge, MA: Harvard University Press.
Wilson, R. (1984, February). *Minority underrepresentation in post-secondary education.* Paper presented at the Illinois Committee on Black Concerns in Higher Education Workshop, Normal, IL.

DISCUSSION QUESTIONS

1. Compare and contrast non-Western holistic thinking with Western analytical thinking.
2. According to Anderson how can the needs of minorities be better served in American educational institutions?

Article 26

A New Pool of Talent

PHILLIP HOOSE

AFTER THE PLANE touched down at Cleveland Hopkins Airport, six young black athletes straightened their blue-and-gold team parkas and started toward the baggage claim area. As they strode through the corridor with their parents and coach, a black woman squinted from behind the Avis counter at the "PDR Swimming" insignia on their backs and hustled out to catch them. "You all *swimmers*?" she asked, her face bright. "So's my son. You here for the nationals? Well, all right. Lookin' good."

Throughout the following week, coaches, officials, fans and competitors attending the Junior National Championship meet in Cleveland last month took special notice of the black swimmers whose attire bore the letters PDR, for Philadelphia Department of Recreation. This was something new. While there have been a scattering of black individuals competing on a national level in the past, the PDR squad, coached by Jim Ellis, was by all accounts the largest contingent of black swimmers ever to appear at a national meet. To many, they are a harbinger of things to come.

One of those watching was Chris Martin, a tall, 30-year-old black man who coaches a predominantly white prep school team in New Jersey. To Martin, who as a youngster competed as the only black on a prep school squad, the presence of a team of inner-city black swimmers at an elite national meet was little short of revolutionary. "By the force of his will, Jim Ellis has turned swimming into a

From "A New Pool of Talent," by Phillip Hoose. *New York Times Magazine,* April 29, 1990, pp. 49–61.

normal experience for black kids in the city of Philadelphia," Martin said. "And he's 90 percent of the way to making it normal for the people watching them at this meet. You can see it. . . . Not 100 percent, but getting there."

Throughout the nation, black athletes from urban areas, many trained by black coaches like Ellis, are beginning to prove themselves as competitive swimmers. Last year, an Arkansas teen-ager named Matt Twillie, who, at 6-feet-3 and 195 pounds, gave up several sports for swimming, turned in the nation's fastest time in the 100-yard butterfly for the 15- to 16-year-old age group. In 1987, a Cleveland teen-ager named Byron Davis, another versatile athlete now at University of California, Los Angeles, recorded the fastest time in United States history for his age group in the 50-yard freestyle event.

The City of Atlanta Dolphins, a huge, publicly financed and almost entirely black squad, now features several of Georgia's top-ranked swimmers.

In Chicago, thousands of black kids from 87 park district teams compete in the summer. The Chicago South Swim Club includes four black swimmers who have posted times among the top 10 statewide for their events.

But best of all are the PDR swimmers from Philadelphia. Among the program's 175 swimmers are three—14-year-old breast-stroker Michael Norment, 12-year-old breast-stroker Atiba Wade and 15-year-old backstroker Jason Webb—whose times place them among the top six nationally in their events, as well as eight other swimmers who are regionally ranked in the top 10. In 1988, a boys' 10-year-and-under relay team from PDR set a national record. Behind these children are a host of 8-year-olds, who, Ellis claims, will make everyone forget about their elders. "I am blessed with talent in all age groups," Ellis says. "We haven't even scratched the surface here yet."

There is no sport, except perhaps for skiing, in which black Americans have been so rare at elite levels as swimming. United States Olympic teams have included black figure skaters, cyclists, gymnasts, wrestlers, judo wrestlers, volleyball players, weight lifters, fencers, even an oarswoman. But according to all available records, it took until 1984—nearly a century after the resumption of the modern Olympic Games—for the first black American swimmer even to reach the Olympic trials. And while black swimmers have competed from other nations—most notably Anthony Nesty, who won a gold medal for the tiny Republic of Suriname in the 1988 Games—no black swimmer has ever made the United States Olympic team.

Whites have long been content to explain the scarcity of black competitive swimmers by supposing Americans of African ancestry to be, as a race, engineered to drown. As the former Los Angeles Dodger executive Al Campanis put it in his now infamous 1987 appearance on ABC's "Nightline": "Why are black men or black people not good swimmers? Because they don't have the buoyancy."

Over the years, it has been said that blacks are aquatically limited by, among other supposed design flaws, heavy bones, dense muscles, hair that retains water, skin that repels it and pores that release carbon dioxide too slowly. "There was a theory that blacks had thicker skulls than whites and that was the problem," Buck Dawson, now executive director emeritus of the International Swimming Hall of

Fame, said two years ago. "There was a theory about ankles. It's not a flexible ankle. . . . Everyone called them 'sinkers.' "

Given the discouragement blacks have faced, the current crop is something of a miracle. Quality indoor pools in the inner city are scarce, as are swim teams in inner-city high schools. There are only a handful of black coaches with the technical expertise to work with champions, and virtually no role models on the order of a Michael Jordan. It is rare enough to find a black swimmer who grew up with swimmers in the family or whose parents even knew how to swim. "I never even thought of swimming," says Verner Webb, father of 15-year-old Jason Webb, who last year had the nation's fastest 100-meter backstroke for his age group. "I'm a typical black person. I can dog paddle but that's about it. I grew up in Arkansas and Chicago. The pools were segregated. When the coach said Jason had potential as a swimmer, I said, "What's a swimmer? I saw Mark Spitz on TV but that's about it."

For most of this century, whites sought desperately to avoid contact with blacks in swimming pools. Until the 1950's, and in some areas even through the mid-60's, municipalities maintained separate pools for blacks and whites, kept separate schedules for the races, or excluded blacks altogether. "What it was, really, was sexual taboos," says Andrew Young, the former Atlanta Mayor and an ex-Howard University freestyler whose administration last year spent $1.25 million in an effort to make swimming available to inner-city residents. "Swimming is the sport that you do with the least amount of clothes on. It's the sport where, especially in swimming pools, males and females are likely to come in the closest contact."

During the civil rights movement, leaders organized "Wade-ins" and "Swim-ins" to gain access to pools and beaches. One memorable incident occurred in 1964, when a racially mixed group of seven demonstrators leaped together into a white-owned motel pool in St. Augustine, Fla. Horrified, the owner poured gallons of muriatic acid, a chemical used to clean the pool, into the water. When the demonstrators remained, the police jumped in and forced them out.

When, gradually, pools became available, few blacks felt at home in them. "D.C. Parks and Recreation only had two pools before 1961," recalls Lorn Hill, chief of the Aquatics Division of the District of Columbia Department of Recreation and Parks. "But then in the next nine years we built 45 pools. I was a lifeguard then. We were pulling out 10 to 12 people every day. Nobody knew how to swim."

Through the years, blacks competed mainly on Y.M.C.A. and Y.W.C.A. teams—segregated throughout much of the century—or on city recreation department teams, in black colleges and in the armed services. A few excellent swimmers were recruited by predominantly white universities. But while black athletes began to break into other sports, the shabby facilities, intramural competition and scarcity of black coaches who could train international competitors kept black swimmers out of the Olympics. It was frustrating. "No colored swimmers in the last Olympic Games. None in the ones before that or before those," lamented The California Eagle, a black-owned newspaper in 1934. "Well isn't it high time we showed the world that we can swim as well as sprint, jump and box."

It took another half-century for the first black swimmer, Chris Silva, a freestyler, even to compete in the Olympic trials. The current inner-city blossoming has been spurred in part by Silva's highly visible bid for the 1984 and 1988 United States Olympic teams. The 1988 effort was financed in part by Silva's barnstorming, pass-the-hat clinics throughout the country. One group of inspired black Atlanta children organized The Silva Bullets Booster Club to help pay for his training expenses and to keep him on the road.

Now inner-city teams are sprouting up everywhere, many of them coached by the black pioneer swimmers of a generation ago, men and women who are determined to make competitive swimming available for everyone. One coach, a 39-year-old former backstroker named Clarence E. (Moby) McLeod, 3d, is now in his 20th year of coaching black boys and girls from downtown Cleveland. McLeod moonlights as an all-night tow-truck driver, and begins practice for his Cleveland Barracudas swim team only when the kids can bang loudly enough on the pool door to wake him up.

"Without someone besides their parents and grandparents to help them," he says, "I can see some of them not making it to their 18th birthday. Or the girls not making it to 21 without having children. If you can make it as a swimmer you can make it at anything."

Last February, more than 300 black swimmers from teams in eight cities gathered in Washington for the fourth annual Black History Invitation Swim Meet. It was a family affair, a Woodstock of black swimmers who usually swim against whites, and of coaches like McLeod who volunteer their time. They conceded that competitive swimming, still a sport with little black tradition and no professional tour, remains a hard sell in the inner city. As one T-shirt, seen at the Black History meet put it, "Bo May Know Weights . . . Bo May Know Football . . . But Bo Don't Know Swimming."

But for the increasing number who are stepping onto the blocks and beginning to taste success, the rewards are obvious. Vanessa Patterson, a lean, 14-year-old backstroker from the PDR team who qualified for the United States Junior National meet this year, spends 18 hours a week in a pool. Nine years of chlorine has given her hair a slightly reddish tint. She doesn't regret a minute of it. "At the lunch table my friends tell me about things they shouldn't be doing, like with their boyfriends," she says. "Going to swim practice does more for me than just sitting there with my boyfriend. I get to meet new people and see new places. I'm off the street. Once you start this commitment, you don't want to stop."

Every Tuesday and Thursday, when a morning workout is added to the daily afternoon regimen, 30 or so PDR parents get up and drive their children through the dawn to meet Jim Ellis at the Marcus Foster Recreational Center, a bleak, two-room building in a depressed section of central Philadelphia called Nicetown.

They rarely know what to expect when they get there. One morning they discovered a boy curled up and sleeping in the heating ducts. Two weeks later a custodian reported that all the steel parts to their filtration system had been removed overnight, presumably stolen and sold for scrap. For much of the winter there was no heat at all.

According to the United States Swimming Office, which regulates amateur swimming in this country, most Olympians come from one of the nation's approximately 2,500 competitive swim clubs. Typically, clubs are formed by an entrepreneurial coach who rents the local country club or college pool and who draws a salary by charging for lessons and collecting monthly dues from team parents.

One elite national club, Club Mission Bay, in Boca Raton, Fla., recruits top athletes by providing what its brochure describes as "a total life style" for the entire family. The Mission Bay Aquatic Center, home of the Mission Bay Makos swim team, is the centerpiece of a 565-acre development devoted to competitive swimming, which includes two adjacent 50-meter pools, a diving complex, two condominium parks, office buildings, a mall, a Montessori school and two Olympic team coaches.

Jim Ellis's situation is radically different. A junior high school math teacher by day, Ellis, 42, becomes an $18,000-a-year "Water-Safety Instructor II" at a neighborhood recreation center by night. This gives him morning and after-school access to a deteriorating 25-yard-long pool (less than half the distance of pools used in Olympic meets). He charges his 80 or so families annual dues of $100. They pay for expenses by holding pizza sales, swimathons and raffles. Having little, they scavenge materials and use them in innovative ways. Ellis has long taught his backstrokers the proper techniques of turning and spinning by placing them on a large scrap of slippery green matting that once lay beneath the artificial turf at Philadelphia's Veterans Stadium.

There are few seats for spectators at Marcus Foster, and the deck surrounding the pool is too narrow for anything more than dual meets. Sometimes they have to practice seven swimmers to a lane. But it's home. "This is my Mission Bay," Jim Ellis shouts above the churning water of a morning practice. "I got six lanes of fast water. And we *are* on a mission here. We want to go to the Olympic trials in 1992. Most exceptional black swimmers have been recruited by major white clubs. And they'll go, thinking there's not a black coach able to get them to a national level. I believe swimmers can come out of the urban community with a black coach. I have the key to this building. For now, that's enough."

Ellis recruited most of his swimmers by advertising free swimming lessons at day-care centers and elementary schools. He has known them since they were barely out of diapers. "I've had to grow my own team, starting with little children," he says. "Where was I going to find black kids in Philly who were going to walk in with technique?"

Ellis, who had been a freestyler at Westinghouse High School in Pittsburgh in the early 1960s, attended Cheyney State College and swam there his freshman year; then the coach quit when he was a sophomore and the team was dissolved. In 1971, still in school, he took a job as a water safety instructor at the Sayre Community Recreation Center in West Philadelphia. His first swimmers were proud if they could put their faces in the water and flail the 10 yards that earned them a Red Cross pin. He pitted them against one another, and goaded them to bring in their big brothers. Soon they wanted to race Ellis. "Everyone wanted to beat me," he recalls. "I told them to do that they'd have to be on a team."

Weeks later, the Sayre Sea Devils trundled off to a meet in Delaware for children 8 years and under. "My wife laughed at me all the way out the door," he recalls. "But I told her, 'We have to start somewhere.' We came home with one little brown ribbon, for 15th place."

From the start, he decided to pit his young athletes against strong competitors in the Philadelphia and Delaware suburbs. Seeing five or six Sea Devils approaching, locals would sometimes assume they were basketball players and point out the gym. The parents and officials he met told him constantly, as if the observation made his day, that the kids were exceptionally well behaved.

Some of the original Sayre Sea Devils families dropped out after a few excursions into the suburbs. "Some of them felt inferior, like they didn't belong," Ellis recalls. "We'd go on a trip, and the father would buy a bottle and stay in his room." But Ellis knew that for the children to feel genuinely comfortable in the white world of club swimming, a large number of parents would have to travel with the team. He could well remember his own experience as a teen-ager when a group of white swimmers surrounded and threatened him before a major indoor meet. The only other black person present that day, as usual, had been his mother.

In the mid-70's, one of Ellis's swimmers, an 8-year-old named Trevor Freeland, began to win regularly against stiff regional competition. At first, Ellis recalls, Freeland seemed hopelessly awkward, a churner with little innate feel for finding what Ellis calls "the good water" on a given stroke. What he did have, though, was an appetite for hard work and a hunger to excel.

Ellis saw in Freeland the national-caliber swimmer that could anchor a team, and the pursuit of training information became an obsession for the coach. "He was always asking, 'What are the things I need to know to move a swimmer up to the next level?'" recalls Mark Bernardino, head coach of the University of Virginia men's swimming team. "He raided our library. He met every great teacher and coach out there and grabbed their tricks and brought them back."

From George Haines, who coached four different United States Olympic teams, Ellis learned to shave the hair from his swimmers' bodies before a big meet. "Haines saw my swimmers at a meet one day and asked why I didn't shave them," Ellis recalls. "I told him, 'Hey, black people don't have a lot of body hair. Why shave off what little we have?' He sat me down and explained:

" 'Your kids come to a meet and everybody else is in there shaving, putting on linaments and getting rubdowns. And your kids aren't doing it. They're going to get up there on the blocks, thinking, "The others are doing something we didn't do.' " It stuck with me. So I started talking it up, saying, 'This is going to help you.' And they believed it. I could shave the kid and not do anything else different in training and he'd go faster."

Much of what he learned had to do with giving black children positive expectations, the sense that, even though they trained in a small neighborhood pool, they were limited only by their desire to excel. When it became obvious that the best swimmers lifted weights, they filled coffee cans with cement and devised a program. He gave them metric-conversion tables to carry in their wallets and purses so that they would begin to think internationally.

When Trevor Freeland began to establish national-caliber times, Ellis tore the local pool record off the wall, which he then papered with a listing of the best 100 times for each age group in United States history. Now his swimmers have six entries on that list.

With Freeland as a role model, more and more parents began to bring their children in for lessons. Many of the parents, Ellis observed, were teachers, disciplined by nature and holding high expectations for their children. They were, he thought, perfect.

In the mid-1980's, Ellis moved to the Marcus Foster center and changed the team's name simply to PDR. His swimmers begged him to let them be dolphins or sharks or swimming cobras but he told them that they were lucky PDR meant nothing. That way, he said, you have the chance to make it mean something.

Now the PDR swimmers convoy up and down the mid-Atlantic coast with a battalion of parents, friends, and alumni, often including several of the 25 swimmers for whom Ellis has found college scholarships. A regular attendee is Trevor Freeland, who, after an exceptional swimming career at the University of Virginia, last year won two events at the Corporate Superstars Swim meet, representing a D.C.-based engineering firm.

They arrive early and drape a blue-and-gold PDR banner in a conspicuous place. The parents sit front and center and Ellis assumes a command position on the deck. He huddles with each swimmer before a race, forcing him or her to visualize every component of the swim, every length, every turn, the start, the kick, the stroke and the finish. Then comes the standard benediction. "O.K.," he says. "It's show-time. Swim funky."

Success has brought changes in the way the PDR swimmers are regarded. Mostly, people seem amazed. "The swimmers say, 'I didn't know you could swim that good,'" says Vanessa Patterson. "I think it's just because we're black that they say that, to distract us." The parents agree that the question they hear most commonly from white onlookers now is "What do you feed those kids?" Nate Norment, Michael's father, usually says chitlins. Others say greens. "It depends on who's doing the asking," says Ellis. "If it seems like they're just trying to make us sound different, I tell them the truth: chlorine, three meals a day."

Beyond PDR, successful black swimmers in general—many of whom compete in short-distance races—are beginning to hear a different tune, not that they can't swim but that they had an advantage all along. The highly influential and recently retired Indiana University swimming coach James (Doc) Counsilman wrote in 1975: "The black athlete excels because he has more white muscle fibers, which are adapted for speed and power, than red fibers, which are adapted for endurance."

The first successful black American runners, more than a half century ago, were sprinters, and it was long accepted as gospel that black runners tired after a mile or so. Now that black African athletes, especially Kenyans, have come to the forefront as long-distance runners, theories have surfaced explaining that there have really been two kinds of black people all along: those of East African ancestry, whose muscle fibers are adapted for endurance, and those of West African ancestry, whose muscles contain fibers that deliver oxygen rapidly, producing explosive power.

The discussion baffles even some scientists. "We create, we imagine a physiology," Dr. David Pearson has said. Pearson is a longtime staff member at the Human Performance Laboratory at Ball State University in Muncie, Ind., which has conducted thousands of muscle biopsies on subjects of all races since 1966 and has found no differences in muscle fibers by race. "It's as if they're saying, 'Let's hide our myth deeper and deeper in science so that fewer and fewer people understand it.' "

Jim Ellis finds the discussion absurd. "The black sprinter is a stereotype," he says flatly. "I think the white world looks at us as sprinters. My first kids wanted to race fast all the time, like track. So I went with it, and we developed some great sprinters. I'm out to develop middle-distance and distance athletes as well. Now we are winning 200- and 400-meter races. We're just attacking the 1,000 this year."

His swimmers are hampered, he says, only by the shortness of the Marcus Foster pool, whose walls prematurely interrupt their strokes. PDR's best distance swimmer is Valerie Patterson, Vanessa's twin, who has won freestyle events in regional meets in distances up to 1,650 meters. Ellis works with Valerie on her pace, which he says is almost eerily consistent. "Ask her for a 32-second lap, and she'll give it to you, lap after lap," he says. "Take it down to 31, and she knows exactly where that is. Her potential is unlimited."

As Ellis's reputation grows, parents of black swimmers throughout the nation are beginning to find him. After observing the PDR team at an all-star meet in Buffalo, Nate Norment moved to Philadelphia from Long Island to give his son a chance to swim for PDR. Whites, too, are becoming interested. About a year ago, David Goodner, a physician who is the father of two well-known young swimmers around the Philadelphia area, passed over Team Fox catcher, a well-heeled private club that placed two swimmers on the 1988 United States Olympic team, and asked Ellis for a chance with PDR. "I'd go to these big meets and see Jim," Goodner recalls. "He so obviously loves kids. He treated them with respect and love. I wanted that for my kids." Both Goodner children, Blake, 15, and Alyson, 11, now swim for PDR.

After a recent article about the team in a Philadelphia newspaper, Ellis received five calls from other parents of white swimmers. An unanticipated byproduct of his success, it continues to cause him some thought. "It's something I have to deal with—as a coach, as a person, as a black man," he says.

As it turned out, the PDR delegation did not blow away the rest of America's young swimmers at the junior national meet. It was the first major national competition for five of the six swimmers, and the nervousness showed. Only Jason Webb, the lone veteran of national competition, finished in the top half of his field in an event. Jim Ellis noticed that his kids seemed to swim well in the straightaways, but lost ground when they thrust against the walls to change direction, a sign to him that they need more weight training.

But while most meets, like the junior nationals, offer lessons and disappointments, some moments shine through like beacons, vindicating all the dawn practices and the sacrifices the families have made. For Jim Wade, Atiba's father, such a moment came in the summer of 1988. On the recommendation of a coaching friend,

Jim Ellis had accepted an invitation for the team to swim at a major regional meet in Greensboro, N.C.

Like Ellis, Jim Wade did not know what to expect. It was their first meet ever in the South. He had grown up in Coosawhatchie, S.C., a town in which every public facility had been segregated. On the bus ride down, he spoke to the kids in small groups, telling them of his childhood. They listened politely.

When they got there, Jim Ellis, himself nervous, told the kids to walk confidently from the bus into the facility and take their rightful place in the practice pool. They did. Wade took a seat in the bleachers to watch, wondering if he and Ellis had perhaps made them overwrought. "They tore that meet up," Wade recalls, laughing. "Almost everybody swam their best time. People were *amazed.* But I'll tell you when I knew we were getting somewhere. It was in the 100-meter butterfly. One of our swimmers, Akida Stephens, was the only black swimmer in the race.

"When they got to the 50-meter mark, Akida and a white girl were neck and neck. I was sitting behind two white ladies. One turned to the other and said, 'My God, they're tied.' After 75 it was, 'My God, she's *ahead.*' When Akida won, it was as if that woman's view of the world had turned upside down in a 100 meters. For me, it was like a victory. I hadn't even been able to swim in the pool in my town. I said to myself, 'Thank God I have lived to see this moment.' "

DISCUSSION QUESTIONS

1. How has prejudice affected the athletic life of black swimmers?
2. What particular problems have black swimmers faced?

X

The Family

WHAT TO FOCUS ON:

1. What new forms of family life are emerging in contemporary America?
2. How has the role of women changed in the modern family?

SOCIOLOGISTS ARE IN AGREEMENT that the contemporary family is in a process of change and transition. The family in modern society has been particularly affected by changing demographic forces, gender roles, and sexual norms. Fewer people are marrying, an increasing number of marriages end in divorce, single parent families are on the increase and an ever larger number of people are opting to postpone marriage and children. The family, however, for all its strains and problems remains an important institution in American culture. Having a good relationship and a happy family life remain significant goals for most Americans.

In "The Shape of the American Family in the Year 2000," Andrew Cherlin and Frank Furstenberg Jr. discuss demographic trends and their future consequences. Their data show that while the conventional nuclear family will continue, new and diverse forms of the family will take on increasing importance. Given the data on divorce and remarriage, an increasing number of people will live in single parent families and in families of remarriage.

One of the newer forms of marital relations is the commuter marriage in which both spouses live in different geographical areas. Naomi Gersel and Harriet Gross in the selection "Commuter Marriages" report on their research with couples who live and work in different cities. They found that in spite of difficulties of separation many couples enjoyed their increased independence and time for professional activities. Gersel and Gross suggest that the commuter marriage may be a contemporary mode of combining commitment and independence.

John W. Conner's work focuses on Japanese women who, according to Conner's research, exhibit more strength and self-reliance in their roles as mothers than in their position as wives. Conner insightfully compares and contrasts husband and wife interaction in Japanese and American culture.

Article 27

The Shape of the American Family in the Year 2000

ANDREW CHERLIN AND FRANK F. FURSTENBERG, JR.

The Two Contrasting Views

- At current rates, half of all marriages begun in the early 1980s will end in divorce.
- The number of unmarried couples living together has more than tripled since 1970.
- One out of four children is not living with both parents.

THE LIST COULD go on and on. Teenage pregnancies: up. Adolescent suicides: up. The birth rate: down. Over the past decade, popular and scholarly commentators have cited a seemingly endless wave of grim statistics about the shape of the American family. The trends have caused a number of concerned Americans to wonder if the family, as we know it, will survive the twentieth century.

From "The Shape of the American Family in the Year 2000," by Andrew Cherlin and Frank F. Furstenberg, Jr., *The Tap Report,* American Council of Life Insurance, Washington, D.C., 1982. Reprinted by permission of publisher.

And yet, other observers ask us to consider more positive developments:

- Seventy-eight percent of all adults in a recent national survey said they get "a great deal" of satisfaction from their family lives; only 3% said "a little" or "none."
- Two-thirds of the married adults in the same survey said they were "very happy" with their marriages; only 3% said "not too happy."
- In another recent survey of parents of children in their middle years, 88% said that if they had to do it over, they would choose to have children again.
- Eighty-four percent described relations with their children as quite close. Only 9% said the children had been trouble to bring up.
- The vast majority of the children (71%) characterize their family life as "close and intimate."

Family ties are still important and strong, the optimists argue, and the predictions of the demise of the family are greatly exaggerated.

In this report, we will present our own view of the most probable future for the family in the period from the present to the year 2000. We will reject the arguments of both the dire pessimists who believe that the family is falling apart and the unbridled optimists who claim that the family has never been in better shape. We shall explain why we think that neither view provides an accurate picture of family life in the near future.

The Family Will Take on Diverse Forms

Several considerations lead us to expect a growing amount of diversity in family forms. Fewer Americans than was the case a generation ago will spend most of their life in a simple "nuclear" family consisting of husband, wife, and children. By the year 2000, three kinds of families will dominate the personal lives of most Americans: families of first marriages, single-parent families, and families of remarriages.

First-marriage Families. In these families, both spouses will be in a first marriage, frequently begun after living alone for a time or following a period of cohabitation. The desire to begin having children may be what causes many cohabitating couples to marry. Most of these couples will have one or two or, less frequently, three children. Still, a sizeable minority will remain childless. Demographer Charles F. Westoff predicts that about one-fourth of all women currently in their childbearing years will never bear children. If this is true, there will be a greater number of childless women than any time in our history. Even for the three-fourths who will have children, the period of childbearing and childrearing will be compressed, leaving a potentially longer "empty nest" stage of marriage after all of the children have left home. One other important shift: in a large majority of these families, both the husband and the wife will be employed outside the home. In 1940 only about one out of seven married women worked outside the home; today the proportion is one out of two. We expect this proportion to continue to rise, although not as fast as it did in the past decade or two. More and more families will be facing the problems common to two-earner couples: how to balance their work responsibilities and their family responsibilities. Today, most working mothers have two jobs: they work for pay and then come home to do most of the childcare and the house work. The strain these responsibilities place on working couples, and especially on working mothers, will likely make childcare and a more equitable sharing of housework into prominent issues in the 1980s and 1990s.

Single-parent Families. The second major type of family can be formed in two ways: most are formed in the aftermath of a marital separation, and the rest are formed by births to unmarried women. As mentioned above, about half of all marriages will end in divorce at current rates. And we doubt that the rates will fall substantially in the near future. Since divorces tend to occur early in a marriage, three-fifths of all divorces involve couples with children living at home.

When the couple is childless, the formerly married partners are likely to set up independent households, and resume life as singles. The high rate of divorce is one of the reasons why more men and women are living in single person households than ever before. In 1980, more than a fifth of all households consisted of persons living alone. Of course, only some of these persons are refugees from broken marriages, but the rise of single person households resulting from marital instability has been dramatic.

But as we said, divorce usually involves children. In at least nine out of ten cases, the wife retains custody of the children after a separation. Although joint custody has received a lot of attention in the press and in legal circles, national data show that it is still uncommon. Moreover, it is likely to remain the exception rather than the rule because most ex-spouses can't get along well enough to manage raising their children together. In fact, a national survey of children aged 11 to 16 conducted by one of the authors (Furstenberg) demonstrated that fathers have little contact with their children after a divorce: about half of the children whose parents had divorced hadn't seen their father in the last year; only one out of six had managed to see their father on the average of once a week.

Sharing childcare responsibilities after divorce does not necessarily imply a high level of collaboration between residential and nonresidential parents. The study just mentioned shows that even when nonresidential parents continue to see their children, very little, if any, communication takes place between the custodial and noncustodial parent. As divorce becomes even more common, rules of conduct may develop to help ex-spouses get along, but we expect that parenting apart will remain difficult for most couples.

The vast majority of single-parent families are headed by mothers, and we believe that this situation is unlikely to change markedly in the near future. We estimate that if the current rate of divorce persists, about half of all children will spend some time in a single-parent family before they reach 18. Much has been written about the psychological effects on children of living with one parent, but the literature has not yet conclusively proven that any lasting negative effects occur. One effect, however, does occur with regularity: women who head single-parent families typically experience a sharp decline in their income relative to their family income before their divorce. Husbands usually do not experience a decline. Many divorced women have difficulty reentering the job market after a long absence; others find that their low-paying clerical or service-worker jobs aren't adequate to support a family. Of course, absent fathers are supposed to make child-support payments, but only a minority do. In a 1979 Bureau of the Census survey, 43% of all divorced and separated women with children present reported receiving child support payments during the previous year, and the average annual payment was about $1,900. Thus, the most detrimental effect for children living in a single-parent family is not the lack of a male presence but the lack of a male income.

Families of Remarriages. The experience of living as a single parent is temporary for many divorced women, especially in the middle class. Three out of four divorced people remarry, and about half of these remarriages occur within three years of the divorce. The annual rate of remarriage has fallen over the past 15 years, but much of that decline merely reflects the greater tendency of divorced people to postpone remarrying for a brief period while they look more carefully for a partner or live with a potential spouse. At current rates, nearly half of all children who are living in single-parent families following a parental divorce will see their mothers remarry before they reach 18. Remarriage does much to solve the economic problems that single-parent families face because it typically adds a male income. Remarriage also relieves a single parent of the multiple burdens of running a household and supporting a household by herself. But remarriage also frequently involves blending together two families into one, a difficult process which is complicated by the absence of clearcut ground rules for how to accomplish the merger. There is some evidence, for example, that children of divorce, having adjusted to the loss of a parent, may have at least temporary difficulties adjusting to the presence of a stepparent. Families formed by remarriages can become quite complex, with children from either spouse's previous marriage or from the new marriage and with numerous sets of grandparents, step-grandparents and other kin and quasi-kin. The divorce rate for remarriages is modestly higher than for first marriages, perhaps reflecting the greater propensity of previously divorced persons to end an unsatisfactory marriage or the complexities that many remarried families face. Nevertheless, most couples and their children adjust successfully to their remarriage, and, when asked, consider their new marriage to be a big improvement over their previous one. Most studies have failed to find large differences in the well-being of either remarried adults when compared to people in their first marriages, or their children, when their offspring are compared to children in unbroken families.

The Life Course: A Scenario for the Next Two Decades

Because of the recent sharp changes in marriage and family life, changes which we argue are unlikely to be reversed substantially in the next 20 years, the life course of children and young adults today is likely to be far different from what a person growing up earlier in this century would have expected. It will not be uncommon, for instance, for children born in the 1980s to follow this sequence of living arrangements: *live with both parents for several years, live with their mothers after their parents divorce, then live with their mothers and stepfathers, live alone for a time when in their early twenties, live with someone of the opposite sex without marrying, get married, get divorced, live alone again, get remarried, and end up living alone once more following the death of their spouse.* Not everyone will have a family history this complex, but it is likely that a substantial minority of the population will. And many more will have family histories only slightly less complex. Overall, we estimate that about half of the young children alive today will spend some time in a single-parent family before they reach 18; about nine out of ten will eventually marry; about one out of two will marry and then divorce, and about one out of three will marry, divorce, and then remarry. In contrast, only about one out of six women born in the period 1910 to 1914 married and divorced, and only about one in eight married, divorced, and remarried. Without doubt, Americans today are living in a much larger number of family settings during their lives than was the case a few generations ago. The role of each of these settings in a person's life and responsibilities people owe to kin from different settings is sometimes unclear, as we will discuss below.

The life course changes have been even greater for women than for men because of the far greater likelihood of employment during the child-bearing years for middle-class women today compared to their mothers and grandmothers. Moreover, the increase in life expectancy has increased the difference between men's and women's family lives. Although the life expectancy of both men and women has increased during this century, the increases have been greater for women, perhaps due to a superior resistance among women to degenerative diseases. Thus, women tend to outlive men by a wide margin, a development that is new in this century. Consequently, many more women face a long period of living without a spouse at the end of their lives, either as a widow (sometimes from a second marriage) or as a divorced person who never remarried. Most of these women will live alone; fewer are sharing the household of a child or other relative than in earlier generations. Long-lived men, in contrast, often find that their position in the marriage market is excellent, and they are much more likely to remain married (or remarried) until they die.

Some Implications

Having sketched our view of the most probable future, we will consider some of the most important implications of the kind of future we see. There are a large number of developments that could be discussed. We shall, however, mention only three that we think will be of greatest interest.

Growing Up in Changing Families. Children growing up in the past two decades have faced a maelstrom of social change. As we have pointed out, family life is likely to become even more complex, diverse, and unpredictable in the next two decades. In many respects, children's lives are likely to be more similar to what they were a century ago, when mortality ravished the family, and economic uncertainty was a way of life for a large proportion of the population. Of course, the kinds of challenges children face in growing up are quite different today, when they must relate to parents living apart or manage relationships with more than two parents. Even children who grow up in stable family environments will probably have to get along with a lot less childcare from parents, mothers in particular, than was provided to children growing up early in this century.

Available evidence suggests that more and more families are resorting to childcare outside the home as a way of managing the conflicting obligations of work and parenthood. Ever since the 1950s, there has been a marked and continuous increase in the proportion of working mothers whose preschool children are cared for outside the home, rising from 31% in 1958 to 62% in 1977. The upward trend is, in our opinion, likely to continue until it becomes standard practice for very young children to receive care either in someone else's home or in a group setting. It is noteworthy that there has been a distinct drop in the care of children by relatives, as fewer aunts, grandmothers, or adult children are available to supplement the care provided by parents.

Although daycare options outside the home have been expanding, their growth is not nearly great enough to satisfy the demand created by the upsurge in dual working parent and single families. At present, there is little consideration of how current childcare arrangements affect the growth and development of children, and, accordingly, there is even less thought about what kinds of policies or programs might be designed to assist working parents.

Family Obligations. Many of the one out of three Americans who, we estimate, will enter a second marriage will do so after having children in a first marriage. Others may enter into a first marriage with a partner who has a family from a previous marriage. It is not clear in these families what obligations remain after divorce or are created after remarriage. For one thing, no clear set of norms exists specifying how people in remarriages are supposed to act toward each other: stepfathers don't know how much to discipline their stepchildren, second wives don't know what they're supposed to say when they meet their husband's first wives, stepchildren don't know what to call their absent father's new wife.

The ambiguity about family relations after divorce and remarriage also extends to the economic support that family members provide to each other. There are no clear-cut guidelines to tell adults how to balance the claims of children from previous marriages versus children from their current marriages. We know from national studies that many divorced men pay no child support and others pay very little. But suppose a divorced man who has been making fairly regular payments to support his two small children from a previous marriage marries a woman with children from her previous marriage. Suppose her husband isn't paying any child support. Suppose further that the remarried couple have a child of their own. Which children should have first claim on the husband's income? Legally, he is obligated to pay child support to his ex-wife, but in practice he is likely to feel that his primary obligation is to his stepchildren, whose father isn't helping, and to his own child from his remarriage. Our guess, supported by some preliminary evidence from national studies, is that remarriage will tend to further reduce the amount of child support that a man pays, particularly if the man's new family includes children from his new wife's previous marriage or from the remarriage. As we mentioned, a sizeable proportion of all absent fathers are involved with new families. What appears to be occurring in many cases is a form of "childswapping," with men exchanging an old set of children from a prior marriage for a new set from their new wife's prior marriage and from the remarriage. There are few generally accepted rules for how and to whom parents should provide support in these complex situations.

How are children responding to the shifting circumstances of family life today? Are we raising a generation of young people who, by virtue of their own family experiences, lack the desire and skill to raise the next generation? As we indicated earlier in our discussion of divorce and remarriage, existing evidence has not convincingly demonstrated that marital disruption creates lasting personality damage or instills a distinctly different set of values about family life. Similarly, a recent review on children of working mothers, conducted by the National Research Council of the National Academy of Sciences, concludes:

> If there is only one message that emerges from this study, it is that parental employment in and of itself—mothers' employment or fathers' or both parents'—is not necessarily good or bad for children.

Of course, this does not mean that some children do not suffer from inattention and develop problems relating to growing as a "latch-key child," but this study, and the evidence it reviews, indicates that the fact that both parents work *per se* does not adversely affect the well-being of children. It is possible that parents in the future may lower their standards of childcare in order to accommodate to economic demands, but we don't think so. Rather, we expect parents will continue to have relatively few children, give them a great deal of attention, but look outside the family for childcare assistance. Early educational programs for preschool children are growing and likely to continue to grow. Increasingly, the government at all levels will be pressured to provide more support for out-of-home daycare. Motherhood, as a full-time activity, is therefore likely to decline. It is not clear whether this decline will be offset by more active childrearing in times when mothers and children are together—"quality time" instead of "quantity time," in the popular jargon. Currently, most fathers whose wives are employed do little childcare. Pressure from a growing number of harried working wives could prod fathers to watch less television and change more diapers. But this change in fathers' roles is proceeding much more slowly than the recent spate of articles about the "new father" would lead one to expect.

Sociologist Lenore J. Weitzman provides a related example in her book *The Marriage Contract.* Suppose, she writes, a 58-year-old corporate vice president with two grown children divorces his wife to marry his young secretary. He agrees to adopt the secretary's two young children. If he dies of a heart attack the following year:

> . . . in most states, a third to half of his estate would go to his new wife, with the remainder divided among the four children (two from his last marriage, and his new wife's two children). His first wife will receive nothing—neither survivors' insurance nor a survivors' pension nor a share of the estate—and both she and his natural children are likely to feel that they have been treated unjustly (p. 162).

Since the rate of mid-life divorce has been increasing nearly as rapidly as that of divorce at younger ages, this type of financial problem will become increasingly common. It would seem likely that there will be substantial pressure for changes in family law and in income security systems to provide more to the ex-wife and natural children in circumstances such as this one. In general, these post-divorce family systems provide more possibilities for providing support to children but no clear assignment of the obligation to do so.

A similar lack of clarity about who should support whom may affect an increasing number of elderly persons. Let us consider the case of an elderly man who long ago divorced his first wife and, as is fairly typical, retained only sporadic contact with his children. If his health deteriorates in old age and he needs help, will his children provide it? In many cases it would seem that the relationship would be so distant that the children would not be willing to provide major amounts of assistance. To be sure, in most instances the elderly man would have remarried, possibly acquiring stepchildren, and it may be these stepchildren who feel the responsibility to provide assistance. Possibly the two sets of children may be called upon to cooperate in lending support, even when they have had little or no contact while growing up. Currently, there are no clear guidelines for assigning kinship responsibilities in this new type of extended family.

A Final Note

Were we to be transported suddenly to the year 2000, the families we would see would look very recognizable. There would be few unfamiliar forms: not many communes, group marriages, and probably not a large proportion of lifelong singles. Instead, families by and large would continue to center around the bonds between husbands and wives and between parents and children. One could say the same about today's families relative to the 1960s: the forms are not new. What is quite different, comparing the 1960s with the 1980s, or the 1980s with a hypothetical 2000, is the distribution of these forms. In the early 1960s there were far fewer single-parent families and families formed by remarriages after divorce than is the case today; and in the year 2000 there are likely to be far more single-parent families and families of remarriage than we see now. Moreover, in the early 1960s both spouses were employed in a much smaller percentage of two-parent families; in the year 2000 the percentage with two-earners will be greater still. Cohabitation before marriage existed in the 1960s, but it was a frowned-upon, bohemian style of life. Today it has become widely accepted; it will likely become more common in the future. Yet we have argued that cohabitation is less an alternative to marriage than a precursor to marriage, though we expect to see a modest rise in the number of people who never marry.

Because of these changes in the distribution of family forms, people's perceived needs for services could be quite different. We have noted that divorced mothers often experience a drastic drop in their standard of living after they separate; with one out of two marriages likely to end in divorce, the economic plight of divorced mothers and their children will become a major public issue, requiring legislative, legal, and social attention. We have noted that two-earner couples often have difficulty combining their work responsibilities with the raising of their children and the maintenance of their homes. We have noted that the obligations of family members to help one another are unclear when parents and children must balance the needs of kin from present and prior marriages.

Therefore the life events that can disrupt and complicate family life are different and more diverse than a few generations ago, when the death of a spouse or a parent was the major hazard a parent or child faced. Today and for the near future, parental divorce is a greater economic hazard for children than is the death of a parent. The services required to protect parents and children from economic hazards in the near future, correspondingly, may need to become more diverse. Just as no single form of the family will be dominant in the next two decades, no single form of economic security will suffice to protect family members from the hardships of marital disruption.

DISCUSSION QUESTIONS

1. Cherlin and Furstenberg argue that the family will take on new and diverse forms in the twenty-first century. Do you agree or disagree? Why?
2. Distinguish between "families of remarriage" and "first-marriage families."

Article 28

Commuter Marriage

NAOMI GERSEL AND HARRIET GROSS

RECENTLY, SOCIAL SCIENTISTS have begun to focus on the ways in which the intact nuclear family reduces the satisfaction of its individual members. Earlier formulations, depicting the nuclear family as an emotional haven, now seem little more than idealizations, not only misleading but also the source of impossible, even harmful expectations. Some feminist critics, in particular, identify the family as a key institution responsible for the subordination of women. As now structured, feminists argue, the family requires a full commitment to the needs of husband and children at the expense of women's own power, autonomy, and independence (Easton, 1979; Epstein, 1982; Hartmann, 1981). More recently, "male liberationists" have argued that men also suffer emotionally because of the asymmetrical responsibilities imposed on them as husbands (David & Brannon, 1976; Lewis, 1981; Pleck, 1982). Many other social scientists and therapists, without focusing on gender-linked difficulties, have argued that at the moment values promoting "personal growth" and "self-actualization" have surfaced, marriage, at least in its conventional form, "spells the end of self-development" (e.g., see Kammeyer, 1977).

A central theme runs through the discussions of all these writers—marriage is a mechanism of social control. But often it remains hidden *how* marriage becomes such a mechanism. What the comparison of commuter and conventional marriage reveals is how traditional marriage becomes such a mechanism. The analysis of commuter marriage suggests that it is shared physical space, coordinated schedules

From *Commuter Marriage: A Study of Work and Family,* by Naomi Gersel and Harriet Gross, New York, Guilford, 1984, pp. 114–123. Reprinted by permission.

and a division of labor that leads to social control. Commuter marriage—by reducing shared time and space—is a form of individuation and may be, at least, partially liberating. As a result, it may yield benefits for each spouse individually that are not realizable in most homes where family members are together every day. In this chapter, we look at how the "normal" American family—with its characteristic single residence and gender-typed division of labor—obstructs individual functioning. But we will do so by looking at what commuter spouses, who leave the conventional home situation, reap for themselves as *individuals.*

Simplification of Daily Lives and the Intensification of Professional Work

Most dual-career couples organize and routinize their lives in well-planned, tight schedules. With the demands of job and family pressing constantly, the spouses expend a great deal of energy compartmentalizing and coordinating both sets of responsibilities (Rapoport & Rapoport, 1976). But when they are alone—away from the immediate responsibilities of family—both husbands and wives experience new freedom in arranging their daily lives.

Commuters enjoy the simplification of their days apart. Away from their families, they avoid much of the detailed daily planning that characterized their lives together. As a result, they have much more time and energy to pursue individual desires. Many spoke of the pleasure in less structured lives:

> There is a great luxury in coming home whenever you want and then doing just what you want to do.

One woman spoke of the change in highly charged emotional terms:

> I was really unprepared for the fierce joy I have felt at being my own woman, being able to concentrate on my own activities, my own thoughts and my own desires. It's a completely selfish, self-centered existence. It's almost a religious experience when you're fifty years old and have never felt that before.

Simplification means selfishness, and selfishness means "fierce joy" for these individuals who had previously led coordinated, routinized, lives. Both men and women talk about the pleasures of eating when they want, of working late without worrying about the time, or reading or watching television late at night. Typical remarks were:

> I like to read and I can do that anytime. I don't need to be responsible to anyone but myself.

> If you want to listen to the radio late at night, you can, I can. If I want to sleep late, or go to bed late, I can. Just those little things, I'm free to do what *I* want when *I* want to do it.

Any time an individual is alone, there are fewer demands and fewer constraints. Certainly, not all demands are experienced as problems: a "demand" to talk or to relax with one's spouse may be quite welcome. But as the commuters' comments suggest, periodic release from such temptations (and obligations) is a type of freedom.

Interestingly, men and women do not value this simplification equally. Though a few men make such comments, almost all the women do, and it is women who celebrate the attendant joys. That women are more likely to express this sentiment should come as no surprise. In a shared residence, women are more likely to be responsible for a greater number of daily family demands. As a result, they are also more likely to experience separation as freedom because separation removes them from those demands.

That the simplification of daily life, and the concomitant release from family responsibilities, is far greater for women than men becomes particularly clear when we examine changes in their daily professional lives. Both men and women were asked if commuting led to an increase, decrease, or no change in the amount of work they did. Women were almost twice as likely as men to increase professional work involvement (76% vs. 43%). In contrast, men were almost twice as likely to say they experienced no change (34% vs. 20%). Moreover, about one quarter (23%) of the men decreased their professional work involvement as compared to only 4% of the women.

As these figures indicate, not even half of the men actually increase the amount of time they work. Most who do so are those who "help" around the family home or share equally in domestic chores while sharing a single residence. When alone, men, too, often let housework and cooking standards decline. They also do not have anyone with whom they can spend (or "waste") time.

Yet, for most men, the time saved and obligations avoided are not great enough to free significant time for work. In fact, many stated quite simply:

> It's had no effect on the amount of work that I do.
>
> I thought that I would spend more time working living apart, but I don't think that I do.

Some of their comments suggest that they had been working to capacity while sharing a single residence. As one man put it:

> I work hard together or apart. I can't work *all* the time.

Indeed, a surprising number of husbands claim that while alone they actually decrease the amount of time they work. Some of these men provide a simple explanation: without a wife to provide domestic services, household work impinges on professional work. In general, the husbands' professional roles set the parameters of their daily existences even when they shared a single home with their wives. For them, family life did not intrude, but instead supported their professional lives.

Others explicitly state that because living in a family unit relieves strain, it simultaneously promotes intense work involvement:

> I probably work less now. I think I spend more time moping around. Maybe a bit more drinking. Not excessive, but a bit more escapist.
>
> I might work less because, of course, when you are living with your family, you can, say do some work for the next day for an hour, then put the children to bed, get involved with the family and then go back and be re-energized to do some more work.

[Marriage] provides—especially for men—the sense of order that makes productive work possible. Without sharing time and space, some of these men are clearly disoriented for some of the time and, as a result, become less productive in their hours alone.

This inability to concentrate, to work productively in the absence of a spouse, is far less characteristic of commuter wives. As seen, the large majority of these women increase the amount of time spent on work when they live alone. They do so because the time they previously reserved for leisure companionship they can now direct to professional activities. These women also work more because, as we suggested in Chapter 4, they invest less time in household chores in a separate home. Almost all women said things like:

> Every night I bring work home. If he was here, I'd have to let it go. I would have prepared real meals. Made sure the house was neat. Had much more laundry to do. Oh, you know, the whole list. But being alone, it's just easy to work. I'm kind of lured into it.

Finally, wives also work more because their own schedules are no longer determined by their families' schedules or needs:

> I love my work and here apart I can really enjoy the freedom to put as much into it as I want to. If I were with him and wanted to put in extra time, I would run into real conflicts.
>
> I guess I have done more professionally. In some ways, I have more free time. I have one less person to contend with during the week. I am more of a night person and he is more of a day person.

As their comments suggest, these women are not only able to increase the amount of time they spend on work, but they can focus better, with fewer interruptions, when alone. For many of these women, then, living alone does not introduce the sense of disorder or strain that characterizes so many of their commuter husbands. Quite the reverse—without interruptions and conflicting obligations, commuter wives enjoy greater involvement in professional lives.

Women who leave children with their husbands note the reduction of responsibility and intensified professional involvement most emphatically. In all of these cases, the amount of time spent on work and the ability to concentrate increases dramatically. One woman, who left her young daughter with her husband, said:

> I can treat myself with all the luxury that a student can. Now I work when I would be with my little girl.

Another remarked, as did so many, on her sense of guilt and sense of release:

> I do feel guilty leaving my children behind. But I can concentrate on my work here with no interruptions. I can work 14, 16 hours a day. And I'm not torn between, say, going to a breakfast meeting because I have to make sure the children are off to school.

In contrast, the group least likely to increase their work output were these women's husbands: Those men left with the children. Here the benefits to the spouses are the most clearly asymmetrical. Women left with the children generally recognize some added domestic obligations, but typically were already used to heavier child-care responsibilities. The time they had previously spent with, and doing for, their husbands could now be used for their jobs. Thus, most women left with children are still able to get at least the same amount accomplished. But as we saw in Chapter 4, the men left with the children generally find themselves spending much more time helping, talking to, and playing with them than in the past. And, the effect on their work was negative:

> It necessarily reduces the amount of time available for work. I have to take both mine and my wife's responsibility for the children. Somebody has to have dinner with them, talk to them, and help them with their homework every night. You can reduce sleeping from 8 to 7 to 6 hours, but at some point, you can't handle that anymore.

For commuter husbands, housecleaning standards can be lowered and chores can be delegated to outsiders. But when the children are left with the husband, they require immediate and regular attention. When the wife, typically the major provider of child care, is absent, the husband has no choice but to fill the gap. Thus, in terms of professional involvement, the wife is the prime beneficiary.

Autonomy, Independence, and Self-Esteem

Not only does living apart reduce familial responsibilities and simplify the commuters' lives, it also provides these husbands and wives with a new and positive sense of themselves. Spouses are quick to discover the benefit of increased independence and autonomy when they enter a commuter marriage. This new-found self-esteem is especially apparent in activities traditionally done by either husband or wife. As discussed previously wives learn they are able to fix dripping faucets, change tires, or mow lawns. The men learn to vacuum or sew on buttons. Before commuting, many felt as though they had to ask for help in what was defined as the spouse's area of expertise. With separation, they learn to cope alone, thereby gaining a new sense of self-effectiveness.

Their increased sense of autonomy not only comes from the discovery of an ability to perform tasks generally done by their spouses, but also from the very fact of being able to live alone. Many of the commuters had never lived by themselves or had not done so for many years. Before commuting, they had been afraid to do so. Now, they discover, often to their own surprise and elation, that is is possible. As one woman commented:

> I've learned to live with myself, by myself, which I couldn't do before or at least was afraid I couldn't do. So many people can't be alone without feeling lonely. I've learned to enjoy that.

A man remarked:

> We've both discovered that we have some resources that we may not have used for a while. One of the things that worried me to begin with was that I was going to get uptight at the idea of being alone. I have proved to myself that I can be alone.

Sharing a residence assures spouses of the constant availability of one another and a sense of need grows from this habit. Before commuting, spouses were frightened at the prospect of "being all alone." After commuting for awhile, they reassess their own needs and discover that they can be "alone but not lonely." While a husband's or wife's presence may have been pleasant and comforting, it is not essential. They may miss one another, but they also find compensation in a new sense of self-sufficiency.

Some even translate this compensation into a desire they had never known or recognized: a desire for private space. Their discussion of "private space" is not metaphorical, as in popular usage, but instead quite literal. They discover, as Virginia Woolf did before them, a need for "a room of one's own." As one woman remarked:

> I never had a place of my own or a real space of my own. I didn't know it was what I wanted. That was a real discovery for me.

When asked about loneliness, another woman said:

> No, in fact, I would say that one of the problems with being married is that you don't have enough chance to be on your own. You don't have the same kind of privacy. And commuting has certainly changed that. You call it loneliness and I call it privacy. And I see it positively rather than negatively.

Perhaps most importantly, learning to live alone and discovering an ability to cope with varied tasks leads to a sense of independence. Certainly the fact that they were willing to set up a commuter marriage in the first place suggests that these couples are not overly dependent. But the discovery that they are able to provide so well for themselves often increases their self-confidence. That is, commuting not only affects how participants structure their daily lives but how they fashion their identities as well. Conventional marriage, with its elaborate, and often fixed, division of labor, shared space and coordinated schedules, brings a sense of dependence; commuting, in breaking down these connections, increases independence and competence.

However, this benefit is not experienced equally by women and men. Women, in particular, express the new sense of self in a variety of ways. Women learn to hammer nails or change tires, and they take some satisfaction, however slight, in these new-found abilities. Even more important, though, is that, for women, commuting allows full participation in the professional world. Because achievement in a career is so highly valued in our society, success in that realm provides a heightened sense of worth. A typical comment about the full professional involvement that commuting permits was:

> Last year, I was thinking to myself that I am all washed up and had nothing to offer. He was the one person who made our world. Now, I am much more secure. I regard myself up here having a job as a neater person.

Finally, in part from this fuller participation in their professions, and in part from living alone, women renew their sense of individual identity. Reflecting on their lives before commuting, some wives said they had felt invisible. This sense of dependence expressed itself in their relationship to others outside of marriage: These women felt that others perceived them solely as extensions of their husbands. They did not experience this as a benefit, as a "status rub-off," or as a vicarious achievement, but as a denial of identity.

In contrast, commuting provides a sense of visibility. As one woman, contrasting her commuting experience with her experience in the shared home, said:

> I guess the best way to explain it is that I am an individual in my own right. And partly because I am not playing the role of wife, I like the idea that other people will like me, or they don't like me, but for my own characteristics, not because I am my husband's wife.

Another woman said:

> I got something back that I lost when I was part of a team all the time. People know me as me and not as part of the team of which Harry [her husband] is the captain. And just being me, and reacted to as just me, for at least part of the time, that feels good.

Commuting has far fewer consequences for husbands' identities. A few do learn to do some household chores they had been unable to do before. And, to be sure, they do take some pride in these accomplishments. But none of the men talk about changes as fundamental to their sense of self as those cited by the wives. Because they had always participated in a professional world, none talk about a new sense of confidence deriving from participation in that world. Also, not a single husband mentioned that before commuting others had responded to him as an extension of his wife.

However, if the husbands do not benefit directly from a new sense of identity, many do benefit indirectly from their wives' higher self-esteem:

> I like having a professional wife. Someone I feel proud of and who feels proud of herself. Commuting made that possible.

> Having this job has restored her self-confidence. Sharpens her. It makes her better company. That's a bad expression. It makes her more interesting.

In this sense, the men benefit as individuals because their wives do.

At the same time, such individual benefits do have potential costs for the unity of the couple. Of these, commuters are keenly aware. In particular, they believe that a sense of independence could, ultimately, undermine the marriage itself. Some commuters speak of a delicate balance between independence and dependence. As one man remarked:

> You are freer for certain lengths of time and there is certainly some satisfaction in that. But I wouldn't push it too far. There is a certain point at which it could turn the other way. You become too free. I don't think it has happened yet, and I hope it won't, but I think it would be silly to think it would be impossible.

A woman spoke in very similar terms:

> I've learned I can function on my own, can face life on my own, even enjoy my independence. And obviously that has a potentially debilitating effect if you see it as something that would lead you not to be able to function in a close relationship. That hasn't happened. But I see that it could be a logical progression.

Periodically, then, the commuters worry that the very advantages they find as individuals could in the long run weaken their marriages. They enjoy their autonomy and freedom, but also value being married. Wanting both, they are afraid their desires are contradictory and that eventually growing independence may undermine their need, or their spouse's need, to remain married.

DISCUSSION QUESTIONS

1. Compare and contrast the responses of men and women to commuter marriage.
2. What are the advantages and disadvantages of commuter marriage?

Article 29

Differential Socialization and Role Stereotypes in Japanese Families

JOHN W. CONNER

IN THE AMERICAN MASS MEDIA and particularly the popular press, Japan is pictured as the final bastion of male supremacy. The Japanese female is depicted as being dependent, docile, deferent, shy, submissive, and subservient. Indeed, the stereotype of Madame Butterfly as a fragile blossom whose greatest joy lies in enhancing the male ego remains a potent image down to the present. The reality is quite different.[1]

A major source of difficulty lies in the confusion between the role and the self. As used here, role will refer to the dynamic aspect of status. That is, the behavior to be enacted on a particular occasion. Status may be defined as a position in society or a collection of rights and duties. The self refers to such things as internalized values and the more stable, enduring aspects of the personality; as for example such traits as persistence, a need for order, self-assertiveness, etc. The two are interrelated. The role affects the self, and the self affects the role. Thus the role perform-

From "Differential Socialization and Role Stereotypes in Japanese Families," by John W. Conner, *Journal of Psychoanalytic Anthropology,* Vol. 8, No. 1, Winter, 1985.

ance associated with the office of the presidency can vary considerably depending on certain inner traits of the individual occupying that status (Sarbin and Allen 1968: 488–496).

An additional source of difficulty lies in the fact that Japan still remains an age-graded society. In such a society youths more readily accept what to Americans would be low-paying menial jobs that require a high degree of deference to one's elders and superiors. These jobs are undertaken with the implicit assumption that, in time, one will advance in the system. Although women make up 40% of the workforce, it is assumed by many employers that women will naturally drop out of the workforce at a comparatively early age—say in their mid-twenties—to rear a family. In other words, the Japanese ultimately see the woman in the mother's role which has much greater valence than the wife's role in Japan. Americans, on the other hand, continue to perceive women as wives and mothers and do not conceive of the role of mother as being necessarily superior to that of wife or provider. Moreover, American youths find it difficult to accept low-paying menial jobs because there is no implicit assumption that they will automatically move up the ladder as they grow older.

With respect to the Japanese female, I submit that the confusion of the role of the Japanese female as "female" rather than "mother" is a major reason for the perpetuation of the stereotypes and a barrier to an understanding of the real nature of the relationship between the sexes. I further submit that an understanding of differential socialization and the development of a separate or more "individualistic" sense of self in the Japanese female will contribute greatly to an appreciation of the dynamics of male/female interaction in Japanese society.

In order to clarify the differences, it will be necessary to give some background on the differential socialization of the sexes. Although Article 9 of the post-war constitution of Japan is in some ways more assertive of equality between the sexes than in some of the states, the mores associated with traditional *samurai* type of family with its Confucian ethical base and its emphasis on inequality still permeate much of contemporary thought (DeVos 1973: 144–64). Ideally, this type of family was a patrilineal, patrilocal stem family with an emphasis on primogeniture, and one that extended through time. Following her arranged marriage, the bride came to live with the husband's family. Relations with the mother-in-law were often harsh.

Beardsley, Hall, and Ward (1959: 331), for example, record the behavior of one such mother-in-law. She sent three of the brides of her first son home and was about to send the fourth bride home when he moved out rather than have his marriage cancelled. His mother then disinherited him and passed the inheritance on to her next son. After she sent the second son's first two brides home, he solved the problem by moving out and building a new house nearby for his third bride.

The harsh treatment of the bride is so common and so anticipated that George DeVos (personal communication) recently mentioned that during his field research in Japan he stopped using the Japanese version of a TAT Card (Jl2F) depicting an older woman looking over the shoulder of a younger one. The reason, of course, was that every Japanese subject interpreted the picture as a mother-in-law, daughter-in-law confrontation. Indeed, the customary harsh relationship between the mother-in-law and daughter-in-law is so embedded in Japanese social structure that when Yukiko Kimura did a study of both European and Japanese war brides of second generation (*Nisei*) Japanese American veterans in the 1950s, she was surprised to find that there was less tension between the European war brides and their mothers-in-law than was the case with the Japanese brides. The immigrant (*Issei*) mothers-in-law were of rural farm backgrounds and knew their European daughters-in-law would be ignorant of Japanese customs, while they expected their Japanese-reared daughters-in-law to conform to traditional role relationships. The Japanese brides, on the other hand, were largely from major urban areas, and because of their marriage to an American thought of themselves as being more or less liberated in their attitudes toward marriage; the last thing they expected was a traditional mother-in-law (Kimura 1958:70–76). . . .

Differential Socialization

There is, however, considerable difference between the socialization of the male and female. While initially in early childhood both males and females are given about the same amount of gratification, at around the time they are four or five some major differences are introduced in the socialization practices. Girls are trained to have more self-control, and are given far more household duties than are boys. In rural Japan—usually in urban Japan as well—the boy was allowed to sleep with arms and legs all spread out so that he might resemble the character *dai* (大) ("large"). The girl, on the other hand, was expected to control her body so that even in sleep she would resemble the character *sho* (小) ("small"). Throughout childhood the girl was expected to be capable of more self-control and self-discipline than the boy (Sugimoto 1966). By way of personal observation, I recall, while once on a train, seeing a sleeping Japanese woman who would automatically reach to pull down her skirt every time she changed positions. . . .

Moreover, the girl is trained to perform all of the domestic chores, even to the extent of being a mother surrogate in carrying a younger sibling on her back when she went out to play. Indeed, frequently the mother would be very demanding and quite severe in the training of her daughter. Again, the rationale was two-fold: one, a well-trained daughter reflected favorably on her mother; two, it was anticipated that the relationship with her future mother-in-law would be quite strained and the daughter must be prepared.

The interviews that I conducted with urban-reared female college students in Japan in 1981 disclosed that the differential child rearing patterns depicted above are not confined to rural families. Indeed, many of those interviewed reported numerous themes not only of hostility toward the mother and elder brother because of the differential treatment, but also something of a feeling of disappointment in fathers who were not strong enough or were unable to oppose the mother.

Moreover, research among Japanese Americans (Caudill and DeVos 1956, Connor 1977) and among Japanese war brides (Connor 1976a) disclose that the tradition of being rather demanding and severe in the training of a daughter has been carried over into the second and third generations as well. A frequent source of tension and cause for complaint among the teen-age female offspring of the

Japanese-Americans and Japanese war brides is that maternal demands are too harsh, biased, and unreasonable. . . .

The end-result of female socialization with its early emphasis on severe self-discipline, prolonged responsibility, and the expectation of being on her own resources, results in the creation of a self that is marked by inner strength, a capacity for extreme self-discipline and an independence and self-reliance that frequently exceeds that of the male.

The males, on the other hand, continue to receive a great deal of gratification. They are frequently pampered and their wishes are deferred to. Even among third generation Japanese Americans a common complaint by the females was that the son would be given the use of the family car while the daughter would have to take the bus. He would be allowed to stay out very late at night while she was expected to be in early. And he would be sent to a prestigious university while she would have to go to a junior college (Connor 1977: 291). . . .

Discussion

Much has changed in contemporary Japan. In urban areas about one-half of all marriages are now love matches rather than arranged marriages, and some 80% of families are independent nuclear ones with the husband, wife, and children; still many traditional beliefs remain. In a survey conducted in 1972–73, sampling 20,000 women and 3,000 men, the question was asked: "Do you agree with the statement that the husband should work and make a living and the wife should stay home and take care of the family?" Fully 83% of both males and females answered yes (Tsurumi 1977: 5). Moreover, when females were asked to reply to the question: "What makes your life most meaningful?" "Children" came first (52.16%), "family" came second (13.3%), "one's occupation" came third (9%), "husband" ranked last (at 2.7%). In contrast, among men "one's occupation" ranked first (43.9%), "children" came second (28.8%), third was "hobbies" (15.9%), and "wife" ranked last at 4.8% (Tsurumi 1977: 5).

It can be seen, then, that the role requirements are quite different. The male is given considerable gratification and has strong dependency needs. Yet these are quite adaptive. As the individual who has the major responsibility for the family's status, much is expected of him. He is expected to pass the difficult entrance examinations and enter a major university. Later, it is expected that he will have an important position with a prestigious company. Without question the company absorbs a great deal of his time and energy. Most Japanese males work 40 to 60 hours a week, to say nothing of several hours each day they spend commuting to and from work.

The Japanese image of the family, then, is quite different from the American. The American ideal is one of sharing; the Japanese is more one of complementarity. The husband provides the income and status, and the wife and children are the supporting cast.

Although the American ideal of sharing has been growing in recent years in Japan, along with the increase of love marriages as opposed to the more traditional arranged marriage, the old ideal of complementarity remains strong. There are occasional outings by young couples with their small children on Sundays, but throughout the week—including half a day on Saturday, the husband's work group absorbs the greater part of his attention and energy. It is the work group that meets together for drinks and a meal after work to mull over the problems of the day and cement group ties while the wife usually remains at home to care for the children and engage in other activities such as flower arranging or sewing classes. Motherhood in Japan is complete and all-embracing. . . .

What must be kept clearly in mind—and what cannot be overstated—is that it is the status of mother rather than wife that gives the Japanese female an enormous amount of power. It is here that the effect of the role on behavior is clearly manifest; and it is here that the behavior of the Japanese male becomes quite different. When he is enacting the role of husband he can be—and often is—quite demanding, and it is the wife who is deferent and subservient. When, however, she is enacting the role of mother, it is not uncommon for the male as father to follow orders. . . .

Conclusion

In conclusion, it must be stressed that the levels of role performance in Japan are not only very high for both sexes, but there is also an equally strong demand for role reciprocity. Thus, if the other party is remiss in performing his or her role properly, the aggrieved person feels betrayed and can become quite demanding. It is here that the inner strength of the females becomes apparent. In the films of Naruse and Mizoguchi,[2] and in countless TV dramas, it is always the weak male who gets the family or himself into trouble, and it is always the strong female who saves the day. Indeed, in my own research on Japanese war brides, I was frequently amazed at both the flexibility and inner strength of the Japanese female. Even in those divorced there was often the capacity for extreme self-sacrifice for the sake of the children. One such case involved a son who had been unjustly accused of being a peeping tom by a neighbor. The boy had been in all evening and the mother knew it. When the sheriff's deputies arrived to investigate, the mother, who was ordinarily quite reserved and very deferent to all authority, became very angry and outspoken and actually had one deputy apologizing at the end. . . .

Finally, it must be mentioned that without question there is considerable discrimination against the advancement of women in the business and professional world. Although women make up 40 per cent of the work force, the average duration of work is only 5.4 years. At marriage, and especially pregnancy, they are expected to leave. Although the pay for both males and females is the same for those just out of high school, at age 25 females earn 10 per cent less; at age 30, 20 per cent less, and 50 per cent less at age 40. Japanese women hold only 5 per cent of managerial jobs as compared with 15 per cent in the United States. Similarly, one per cent of elementary principals are female, although they constitute 50 per cent of the teachers. It is a major goal of the women's movement in Japan to remove these inequalities (Bernard 1978: 61–71).

NOTES

1. Aside from the sources given, much of the impetus for the paper is based upon the author's five years of residence in Japan and his 31-year marriage to a native Japanese.

2. See Mellon (1976: 252–289) for a clear explication of the films of Mizoguchi and Naruse.

REFERENCES

Beardsley, R., J. Hall, and R. E. Ward. 1959. *Village Japan.* Chicago: University of Chicago Press.

Bernard, Kyoko. 1978. Women in Japan: Roles, Rules and Restrictions. PHP (Peace, Happiness and Prosperity) Vol. 9:2, pp. 61–71.

Caudill, William and George DeVos. 1956. Achievement, Culture and Personality: The Case of the Japanese Americans. *American Anthropologist* 58:1102–1126.

Connor, John W. 1976a. *A Study of the Marital Adjustment of Japanese War Brides.* San Francisco: R. and E. Research Associates.

———. 1977. *Tradition and Change in Three Generations of Japanese Americans.* Chicago: Nelson-Hall Company.

DeVos, George. 1973. *Socialization for Achievement: Essays on the Cultural Psychology of the Japanese.* Berkeley and Los Angeles: University of California Press.

Kimura, Yukiko. 1958. War Brides in Hawaii and Their In-Laws. *American Journal of Sociology* 63:70–76.

Mellon, Joan. 1976. *The Waves at Genji's Door.* New York: Pantheon Books.

Sarbin, Theodore R., and Vernon L. Allen. 1968. Role Theory. In *Handbook of Social Psychology,* ed. by Gardner Linzey and Elliot Aronson. Reading, Mass.: Addison-Wesley Publishing Company, Vol. I, pp. 488–567.

Sugimoto, Etsu Imagaki. 1966. *A Daughter of the Samurai.* Rutland Vt. and Tokyo, Reprint of 1927 edition.

Tsurumi, Kazuko. 1977. Women in Japan: A Paradox in Modernization. *The Japan Foundation Newsletter* Vol. V:I, pp. 2–7.

DISCUSSION QUESTIONS

1. Do Japanese women exhibit greater power in their role as wife or mother? Why?
2. How does the Japanese view of family life and husband/wife relationships differ from the American pattern?

XI
Religion

WHAT TO FOCUS ON:

1. What possible functions does the institution of religion fulfill in the organization of human society?
2. Is America, basically, a secular or religious society?

FROM THE SOCIOLOGICAL point of view, the institution of religion occupies a central place in human societies. Religion as a social institution provides meanings for and legitimizes established social patterns. Although there are disagreements between functionalists and conflict theorists regarding the precise functions of religion, the institution of religion remains an enduring part of the social order.

Robert Wuthnow in the selection, "Divided We Fall: America's Two Civil Religions" continues the consideration of how religion functions in his discussion of the different versions of America's civil religion. Wuthnow demonstrates that in spite of widespread secularism, Americans remain a deeply religious people. The content of this religious faith may not be entirely acceptable to all branches of Christianity but civil religion provides a sense of ultimate purpose and destiny to American civilization. Wuthnow shows how the fracture of this integrating world-view into conservative and liberal versions threatens the integrating features of civil religion.

Some sociologists suggest that while religion had important functions in pre-modern societies, contemporary cultures have been so secularized that religion no longer plays a significant role. The family, the state, and economy, it is argued, all operate in contemporary society without any necessary religious interpretations or legitimations. Rodney Stark and William Sims Bainbridge in the selection, "Secularization, Revival, and Cult Formation," reject this thesis. In a bold and innovative approach, they argue that secularization—usually viewed as signaling the decline of religion—is but a stage in religious transformation. Secularization in a particular religious setting represents the decline of one religion but is, itself, the generator for newer and emerging religious forms.

Article 30

Divided We Fall

America's Two Civil Religions

ROBERT WUTHNOW

AMERICANS HAVE always created public myths about our identity as a people. These myths locate us in the world and in history. In election years they provide resources for political rhetoric and they guide us in choosing our candidates.

Robert Bellah has written that America legitimates itself with a dynamic of sacred and secular myths. On the one hand, our civil religion links us to the biblical tradition; on the other hand, the moral and political philosophies of the Enlightenment instill in us a deeply utilitarian orientation. Civil religion portrays a divine order of things, giving us a sense of worth and direction in relation to ultimate purposes. Utilitarianism provides us with proper governmental procedure, legitimates our economic system and underwrites the importance of life, liberty, and the pursuit of happiness.

Together, these cultural traditions have promoted great national crusades. They have joined forces against the worst excesses of raw political expediency, exposing

Excerpts from *The Restructuring of American Religion: Society and Faith Since W.W. II,* by Robert Wuthnow, Princeton University Press, 1988.

our short-term policies in the harsh light of more enduring values. The two have also contended with one another for political supremacy.

A decade ago social scientists predicted the demise of civil religion at the hands of the seemingly more aggressive individualistic and materialistic orientations supported by utilitarianism. The "Me Decade," a wave of narcissism and the rise of yuppie-style hedonism seemed to signal the ultimate triumph of secular materialism.

But this was only part of the story. For all our secularism we have remained a deeply religious people. And civil religion continues to play a prominent role in our culture. In recent election campaigns political candidates have often stumbled over one another in their haste to demonstrate loyalty to some branch of the Judeo-Christian tradition. Political speeches, now as in the past, pay ritual obeisance to the divine judge. Prayers at all major political functions invoke God's presence and blessing. Despite constitutional restrictions, much mixing of religious and political practice continues. We are, our civil religion assures us, a God-fearing people, the champions of religious liberty, and in many ways a nation that God has chosen to carry out a special mission in the world.

The civil religion to which we so blithely pay homage has, however, become deeply divided. Like the fractured communities found in our churches, our civil religion no longer unites us around common ideals. Instead of giving voice to a clear image of who we should be, it has become a confusion of tongues. It speaks from competing traditions and offers partial visions of America's future. Religious conservatives offer one version of our divine calling; religious liberals articulate one that is radically different.

On the conservative side, religious leaders argue that America's vitality rests on a distinct, historic relation to God. According to this interpretation, our form of government enjoys lasting legitimacy because it was created by Founding Fathers who were deeply influenced by Judeo-Christian values. Although in their personal convictions they may have strayed occasionally from this standard, Washington, Franklin, Witherspoon and Adams knew the human heart from a biblical perspective and thus understood what kind of government would function best. As the late Francis A. Schaeffer, a popular evangelical author, asserted in *A Christian Manifesto:*

> These men truly understood what they were doing. They knew they were building on the Supreme Being who was the Creator, the final reality. And they knew that without that foundation everything in the Declaration of Independence and all that followed would be sheer unadulterated nonsense. These were brilliant men who understood exactly what was involved.[1]

This view has deep roots in conservative thinking. In the 19th century a close relation between America and God was often heralded in millennialist language. America not only was called of God, but existed as a chosen people, brought into being for the final fulfillment of God's purposes on earth. Herman Melville's much-read novel *White-Jacket,* for example, described Americans as "the Israel of our time" and the nation as a "political Messiah" sent as an advance guard to "bear the ark of the liberties of the world." Walt Whitman's epic poem "Passage to India" drew an even more direct connection between the nation's wonders and God's purposes.

In the 20th century, war and economic depressions dampened much of this millennial enthusiasm. Yet as America increasingly found itself in the forefront of world military and economic affairs, some of the traditional zeal continued to be voiced.

A favorite theme was the slogan, "One Nation Under God," which signaled not only that America was a unified nation but also an "only," "best," "leading," or "special" nation under God. Norman Vincent Peale, in a book with this slogan as its title, argued that America, at the beginning of its history, had received a unique calling from God which continued to be expressed in a special zeal and spiritual quality of its people. In another book by the same title, evangelical writer Rus Walton arrived at the conclusion that even the U.S. Constitution had been "divinely inspired."

During the 1960s and '70s, as the nation's military involvement in Vietnam inspired a mood of questioning and cynicism, defenders of U.S. policy seemed to become even more explicit in their efforts to find divine legitimacy in American history. Edward Elson, writing in *Decision* magazine, asserted that America could not be understood except as a "spiritual movement" with God as its source and the Holy Spirit guiding its development. Christian businessman George Otis, echoing the same theme, wrote: "God's hand was in the founding of this country, and the fiber of Christ is in the very fabric of America."[2] With similar conviction, entertainer Dale Evans Rogers contended that America "was in the mind of God before it became earthly reality" and that it was still "a part of His purpose for mankind."[3]

These arguments remain an important feature of contemporary political rhetoric. A recent fund-raising letter from the "Robertson in 88" campaign, for example, asserts that the ten commandments are the "bedrock of America." Then, step-by-step it links each commandment with a political theme (for instance, as Moses received the first commandment, God also "inspired our Founding Fathers to say that all men are *created* equal"). The letter also asserts that the essential truth on which Pat Robertson's campaign was based is the conviction that "we must never forget—and always remind those who will forget—that we are *one nation under God.*"

In emphasizing the close historical connection between America and God, evangelicals and fundamentalists assert the importance of religious values which they themselves still uphold. Their version of American history points to a time when such values were evidently taken quite seriously.

To be sure, the distinction between personal convictions and the religious story of the nation remains sufficiently sharp in evangelical teachings that militant religious nationalism is the exception rather than the rule. Priorities generally focus on personal salvation, spiritual growth, biblical knowledge and the affairs of local religious communities instead of God's providence in American history. Even Jerry Falwell alludes only occasionally in his books and sermons to America's collective relation to God. He also asserts flatly that "America is not the kingdom of God."[4]

Yet conservative civil religion does grant America a special place in the divine order. Falwell goes on to say, for example, that "the United States is not a perfect nation, but it is without doubt the greatest and most influential nation in the world. We have the people and the resources to evangelize the world in our generation." Writer-evangelist Tim LaHaye, head of the American Coalition for Traditional Values, makes the same point negatively: were it not for America, he asserts, "our contemporary world would have completely lost the battle for the mind and would doubtless live in a totalitarian, one-world, humanistic state."[5]

America evangelizing the world is, of course, a much-emphasized theme in conservative civil religion. God wants America to use its advantaged position to preach Christianity to all nations—a task which in some evangelical eschatologies represents the final work that will hasten Christ's second coming. America's wealth and power are regarded both as the divinely given resources for carrying out this important task and the token of God's good faith to those willing to shoulder the task. This view is particularly prominent among conservative Christians who have a strong missionary emphasis.

Conservative civil religion also voices strong arguments about the propriety of the American economic system. These arguments grant capitalism absolute legitimacy by drawing certain parallels between capitalist principles and biblical teachings. Economist George Gilder, who identifies himself as an evangelical Christian, has argued, " 'Give and you'll be given unto' is the fundamental practical principle of the Christian life, and when there's no private property you can't give it because you don't own it. . . . Socialism is inherently hostile to Christianity and capitalism is simply the essential mode of human life that corresponds to religious truth" (reported in Rodney Clapp, "Where Capitalism and Christianity Meet").[6] Elsewhere he remarks, drawing a calculated reference to the Apostle Paul's teaching on love, "the deepest truths of capitalism are faith, hope, and love."[7]

Falwell has also been an outspoken apologist for American capitalism. "I believe in capitalism and the free enterprise system and private property ownership. . . . people should have the right to own property, to work hard, to achieve, to earn, and to win." For Falwell, this is not simply an assertion of personal opinion, but a position that has divine sanction: "God is in favor of freedom, property ownership, competition, diligence, work, and acquisition. All of this is taught in the Word of God in both the Old and New Testaments."[8]

Other spokespersons for conservative civil religion also connect Christian doctrines to American capitalism. Ronald H. Nash, arguing against liberation theology, for instance, suggests that capitalism is the preferred system because it is impossible to have "spiritual freedom" without "economic freedom."[9] Pat Robertson draws directly on Gilder's work to arrive at the conclusion that "free enterprise is the economic system most nearly meeting humanity's God-given need for freedom."[10]

The liberal version of American civil religion draws on a different set of religious values and portrays the nation in a very different light. Few spokespersons for the liberal version make explicit reference to the religious views of the founding fathers or suggest that America is God's chosen nation. Indeed, the idea of one nation under God is often rejected because of its particularistic connotations and, more generally, because of the way it has been interpreted by conservatives.

A recent letter from Clergy and Laity Concerned, for instance, argues that "this is no longer 'one nation under God' " Instead, the letter proclaims, there are now two very different views of America: "One based on arrogance and a false sense of superiority. The other based on ethical, biblical principles."

References to America's wealth or power as God's means of evangelizing the world are also rare among liberals, and religious apologetics for capitalism are virtually taboo.

The liberal view of America focuses less on the nation as such, and more on humanity in general. In this view, America has a vital role to play in world affairs not because it is the home of a chosen people but because it has vast resources, has caused many of the problems currently facing the world, and simply as part of the community of nations has a responsibility to help alleviate the world's problems. Rather than drawing attention to the distinctiveness of the Judeo-Christian tradition, liberal civil religion is much more likely to include arguments about basic human rights and common human problems. Issues like nuclear disarmament, human rights, world hunger, peace and justice receive special emphasis.

The importance attached to these issues is generally not legitimated with reference to any particular sacred mandate, but simply on the assumption that these are matters of life and death. Nevertheless, religious faith often plays a prominent part in the discussion, differentiating liberal civil religion from purely secular or humanist beliefs.

Faith provides a motivating element, supplying strength to keep going against what often appear to be insuperable odds. The biblical prophets, who spoke out for peace and justice, are often cited as sources of strength and hope. And universal appeals are couched in explicitly religious language. As the Clergy and Laity Concerned letter explains, its goal is "to establish social and economic justice for all of God's children."

Because of its awesome destructive potential, the problem of nuclear arms occupies an especially prominent place in liberal civil religion. Liberal clergy have so often taken the lead in seeking solutions to the arms race that the peace movement has come to be identified in many circles as a religious issue. In a survey of Presbyterian laity, for example, two-thirds agreed strongly with the statement that "peacemaking is not simply 'another political issue' but is a basic aspect of the Christian faith."[11]

Other crusades in the liberal version of American civil religion include civil rights, international justice, and ecology. Liberal religious periodicals have kept these issues in the forefront of readers' attention. For example, a count of headlines in this journal during one six-month period revealed a total of 136 articles on topics such as nuclear weapons, social issues, economic issues and peace, compared with only 22 articles on the Bible, nine on evangelism, and nine on prayer.

A survey of Presbyterian clergy further illustrates the priority given such causes. When asked to rate various goals for the nation, respondents gave top priority to having America serve as an example of liberty and justice to all nations. Also ranked near the top were conserving the world's scarce resources and reducing disparities between poor and wealthy nations. Spreading American capitalism ranked at the bottom of the list. The survey also showed that eight of every ten pastors saw national pride as a hindrance to the work of the Christian church in the world, while fewer than a third thought America was currently a blessing to humankind throughout the world.[12]

The rhetoric of liberal religious leaders, unlike that of their conservative counterparts, has often questioned the value of America's distinctive cultural traditions. Father John Langan of the Woodstock Theological Center, for example, suggests that we make a "clear delineation of the moral claims of the solidarity that binds us together as human beings sharing a common destiny under God." A delineation of this kind, he argues, "necessarily involves a critique of individualism and self-reliance in our national culture."[13]

A critique of this sort was a prominent feature of the Catholic bishops' "Pastoral Letter on Catholic Social Teaching and the U.S. Economy." Calling both Catholics and non-Catholics to a greater commitment to alleviating the suffering of the poor, the bishops were openly critical of America's practices in relation to their understanding of the Christian tradition. "We live in one of the most affluent cultures in history where many of the values of an increasingly materialistic society stand in direct conflict with the gospel vision," they charged. "Our contemporary prosperity exists alongside the poverty of many both at home and abroad, and the image of disciples who 'left all' to follow Jesus is difficult to reconcile with a contemporary ethos that encourages amassing as much as possible."

The liberal version of American civil religion, it should be noted, taps into a relatively deep reservoir of sentiment in the popular culture about the desirability of peace and justice. Recent public opinion polls, for instance, have shown that more than 90% of Americans would like to see "a sharp decline in the number of people who suffer from hunger," "a decline in terrorism and violence," "a real easing of tension between the U.S. and the Soviet Union," "a decline in racial and religious prejudice," and "an end to the production, storage, and testing of nuclear weapons by all countries on earth."[14]

Surveys also indicate, however, that most Americans have little confidence in these goals' being realized in the foreseeable future. "The problem," concluded the authors of the study cited above, "is not so much a lack of motivation by the people of this country, but the inability of those vested with power and responsibility to fulfill the hopes and aspirations of the people."

In the face of such difficulties, liberal religious leaders have often presented themselves as a small prophetic remnant, despite the public's support for their causes. This rhetorical stance, critics suggest, may be useful for building solidarity among the faithful, but it can also lead to an isolated mentality in which rituals of solidarity replace more effective appeals.

Both the liberal and the conservative wings of American religion have a vision of where the U.S. should be heading. But the two visions are fundamentally at odds. The conservative vision seems to embody what Max Weber termed the "priestly" function of religion, while the liberal vision expresses religion's "prophetic" function. The conservative vision offers divine sanction to America, legitimates its form of government and economy, explains its privileged place in the world, and justifies a uniquely American standard of luxury and morality. The liberal vision raises questions about the American way of life, scrutinizes its political and economic policies in light of transcendent concerns, and challenges Americans to act on behalf of all humanity rather than their own interests alone. Each side inevitably sees itself as the champion of higher principles and the critic of current conditions.

The two versions of American civil religion appear to have divided along a fracture line long apparent in discussions of civil religion. That line is the inherent tension between symbols that express the unique identity of a nation and those that associate the nation with a broader vision of humanity. As Bellah noted in his initial essay on the subject, civil religion in America seems to function best when it apprehends "transcendent religious reality . . . as revealed through the experience of the American people"; yet the growing interdependence of America with the world order appears to "necessitate the incorporation of vital international symbolism into our civil religion."[15]

The two civil religions correspond in a general way with the ambivalent character of the state in American society. On the one hand, the long period during which the nation enjoyed virtual isolation from the rest of the world resulted in a state oriented toward nationalistic concerns. On the other hand, America's rise to global power in this century has forced the state to act not only on behalf of narrow U.S. interests but also as a potential contributor to the common good in global terms.

These dual functions have sometimes been sufficiently different that particular agencies have identified with one or the other. More commonly, policy proposals have vacillated between the two orientations. Under these circumstances, both versions of American civil religion have found proponents within the state who have been willing to exploit them for purely political purposes.

In consequence, the two visions of America have been the subject of disagreement and polarization more than of consensus and mutual understanding. A few leaders have borrowed ideals from both sides, but that is the exception rather than the rule. It is more common for the two camps to take up openly hostile positions.

Given this hostility, neither side can claim to speak for consensual values. Each side only represents a constituency. Since any claim one side makes is likely to be disputed by the other, the public is left to doubt the credibility of both.

Religion, therefore, becomes (as it has often been characterized in the press) a sectarian concern rather than a basis of unity. And in a society that is not only deeply religious but decidedly secular, other values and assumptions stand as ready alternatives to the civil religion. Faced with conflicting interpretations based on religious premises, national leaders can readily turn to other arguments on which there is greater consensus.

As the conflict between religious liberals and conservatives has intensified, the different versions of American civil religion have continued to energize specific policies and programs. But in the eyes of many middle-of-the-roaders, both sets of arguments have lost plausibility by virtue of being too much disputed. Much room has been left for secular ideologies—not the least of which are the creeds of material success, radical individual freedom, and an amoral pragmatism.

NOTES

1. Schaeffer, Francis A., *A Christian Manifesto,* Crossway Books, West Chester, Illinois, 1981, p. 33.
2. Otis, George, *The Solution to Crisis America,* Revell, Old Tappan, N.J., 1972, p. 53.
3. Rogers, Dale Evans, *Let Freedom Ring,* Revell, Old Tappan, N.J., 1975, pp. 19–20.
4. Falwell, Jerry, *The Fundamentalist Phenomena,* Doubleday and Company, Inc., New York, 1981, p. 212.
5. LaHaye, Tim, *The Battle for the World,* Revell, Old Tappan, N.J., 1980, p. 35.
6. Clapp, Rodney, "Where Capitalism and Christianity Meet," Christianity Today, February 4, 1983.
7. Gilder, George, "Moral Sources of Capitalism," Society, Sept/Oct, 1981.
8. Falwell, Jerry, *Wisdom for Living,* Victor, Wheaton, Illinois, 1984, pp. 131, 102.
9. Nash, Ronald H., "The Christian Choice Between Capitalism and Socialism," in *Liberation Theology,* Mott Media, Milford, Michigan, 1984.
10. Robertson, Pat, *The Secret Kingdom: A Promise of Hope and Freedom in a World of Turmoil,* Thomas Nelson, Nashville, 1982, p. 151.
11. Research Division of the Support Agency, Presbyterian Panel, January, 1982.
12. Hoge, Dean R., "Theological Views of America Among Protestants," Sociological Analysis, Summer, 1976.
13. Langdon, John, "The Bishops and the Bottom Line," Commonweal, Nov. 2–16, 1984.
14. The Harris Survey, December 22, 1983, No. 104.
15. Bellah, Robert, *Beyond Belief,* Harper and Row, Inc., New York, 1970, pp. 179, 186.

DISCUSSION QUESTIONS

1. What role does civil religion play in American society?
2. Compare and contrast liberal and conservative versions of American civil religion.

Article 31

Secularization, Revival, and Cult Formation

RODNEY STARK AND WILLIAM SIMS BAINBRIDGE

FOR AT LEAST A CENTURY, one theme has dominated scholarly assessments of religious trends: *secularization* (Wilson, 1979). According to Webster, the term secular means "of or belonging to the world and worldly things as distinguished from the church and religious affairs." Undoubtedly, over the past several centuries, and at an accelerating pace, the major religious organizations of industrial societies (and, perhaps, throughout most societies) have been becoming more worldly.

More specifically, by *secularization* we mean the *erosion of belief in the supernatural.* For generations, now, explanations based on supernatural assumptions have been giving way to science: other-worldly explanations have been replaced by worldly ones. This process can be seen at two levels. First, industrial societies in general have become more secularized. Smaller proportions of their populations accept traditional teachings about an active supernatural, and religion has been excised from many aspects of life (American public schools, for example). Secondly, the leading religious organizations within these societies have become more secularized. They no longer project an image of a god so near at hand, interested, and active in human affairs (Stark and Glock, 1968; Wilson, 1966, 1975, 1976, 1979; Fenn, 1978; Martin, 1978).

From "Secularization, Revival, and Cult Formation," by Rodney Stark and William Sims Bainbridge, *Journal for the Scientific Study of Religion,* Vol. 4, 1980. Reprinted by permission of the author.

Many observers have assumed that present trends towards secularization will not cease until religion has all but vanished. Some predict that in another century religion will linger only in cultural backwaters or among isolated groups—that religion rapidly is becoming "only an interesting historical memory" (Wallace, 1966:265).

Yet, for all these predictions of its sudden demise, religion displays few terminal symptoms. Despite decades of repression, religion remains a vital force in the USSR. China now talks of religious freedom for its *persistent* Christian communities. Millions greeted the Pope during a visit to officially atheist Poland. And, in America, while the most secularized denominations show grave signs of weakness—and apathetic membership and a disaffected clergy—the more orthodox groups appear very vigorous (Stark and Glock, 1968; Kelley, 1972). Recently, 34% of Americans claimed to be "born-again" Christians (Gallup, 1976). New cults and sects abound. Public interest in the mystical is rising. Are these signs of life merely one last dying spasm?

In this paper we argue that *both* the trend towards secularization *and* the trend towards religious renewal are real. In our view this does not represent a paradox. Rather, we conclude that secularization is the *primary cause* of the current religious fervor. Indeed, we shall argue that *secularization is a self-limiting phenomenon that prompts religious revival over the short run, and religious innovation over the longer term.* We conclude that predictions of the death of religion are faulty because they have mistakenly identified *dominant* religious traditions in modern societies with the phenomenon of *religion in general.* Critics correctly have noted the crumbling of major Christian-Judaic organizations, but have failed to see or appreciate the growing vigor of religion in less 'respectable' quarters. . . .

The Process of Secularization

Religions that arise prior to the development of organized science will tend to include a good deal of magic in their offerings. That is, they will not only deal in very general compensators (which are not subject to empirical evaluation), but will also offer quite specific compensators that are subject to empirical evaluation.

Science is simply the name for the development of systematic procedures for evaluating explanations. The process of evaluation will always tend to drive out empirically testable explanations that are false or at least less efficient than some other explanation. In consequence, as science is more widely practiced it will tend to drive out magic. This is no more than an application of Malinowski's famous middle-range proposition about magic, which, as deduced in our theory takes the form: *People will not exchange with the gods when a cheaper and/or more efficient alternative is known and available.* This simply means that magical explanations about how to gain a desired reward (or avoid a damaging cost) will tend to be discredited by scientific test and to be discarded in favor of scientifically verified explanations.

This tendency has serious consequences for religions that include a significant magical component. Consider the case of the lightning rod (White, 1896). For centuries the Christian church held that lightning was the palpable manifestation of divine wrath and that safety against lightning could only be gained by conforming to divine will. Since the bell towers of churches and cathedrals tended to be the only tall structures, they were the most common targets of lightning. Following damage or destruction of a bell tower by lightning, campaigns were launched to stamp out local wickedness and to raise funds to repair the tower. Ben Franklin's invention of the lightning rod caused a crisis for the church. The rod demonstrably worked. The laity began to demand its installation on church towers—backing their demands with a threat to withhold funds to restore the tower should lightning strike it. The church had either to admit that Ben Franklin had the power to thwart divine retribution, or that lightning was merely a natural phenomenon. Of course they chose the latter. But in so doing they surrendered a well-known and dramatic magical claim about the nature of the supernatural. Such admissions *call into question other claims* made by a religion, including even those that are eternally immune from empirical disconfirmation.

Thus the rise of science meant a retreat by religions that, originating in prescientific ages, contained significant elements of magic. In this way these religions became increasingly secularized—they made progressively fewer claims about the powers of the supernatural and the extent to which the supernatural was active in the empirical world. Because humans have memory, these retreats were noted and recorded for posterity. . . .

Revival

In response to an unmet demand for more efficacious compensators movements will arise to restore the potency of the conventional religious traditions. This pattern is typified by the vigor of evangelical Protestantism and the growth of the Catholic charismatic movement in contemporary America. The tactic involved is simply to reassert the validity of the general compensators of traditional faith since these in fact have not been invalidated by scientific discovery (and cannot be).

However, such a reassertion raises the problems that led to the extreme secularization of the major denominations in the first place. Many traditional elements of the Christian-Judaic tradition have in fact been disconfirmed by science. Not merely lightning, but the literal interpretation of creation and of the flood, indeed, the underlying astronomical and geological assumptions of the Bible clearly are discrepant with secular knowledge: the sun does not go around the earth and it seems incredible that it was ever stationary in the sky no matter what God wanted to signal to His people. Thus the trouble with revival is that it is *heir to a whole cultural history* and this history is replete with defeats of doctrine by science. Moreover, as soon as this problem is dealt with by picking and choosing those parts of the tradition that remain invulnerable to disproof, secularization has been reintroduced as legitimate—that science will dictate what doctrines can be accepted. Thus, revival seems to be chronically vulnerable to secularization and to lack long-term staying power, especially if there is an alternative. Such alternatives are created by the rise of new religious traditions.

Innovation

The dominant faiths of today arose a very long time ago and offered desired explanations unavailable from science. That is, they were well-suited to the culture in which they arose—they did not make claims that were obviously false at that time. In consequence, the dominant faiths suffer from an ineradicable history of defeat because they were *not designed for our present culture.* But this is not necessarily so for new faiths—faiths that arise to meet the circumstances of *this* culture. A new faith can offer a set of general compensators invulnerable to secularization. Such a faith will have no history of futile holding actions and past defeats by science. It will not have to admit to picking and choosing among its tenets, for it has none at risk. Put another way, new faiths can be fully in harmony with the culture without having to be in any way subservient to it.

A case in point is Mormonism. Although it claims to be merely the next unfolding of the Christian-Judaic tradition, it appeared in the nineteenth century and was fully compatible with scientific knowledge of that time. Indeed, a major denunciation of the *Book of Mormon* made by nineteenth century Christian theologians was its modernity. Unlike the *Bible,* which posits a tiny earth and seems to regard the Mediterranean as the whole of the oceans, the *Book of Mormon,* while claiming to be of ancient origins, bases its accounts on the existence of a large world and on knowledge of all the continents and oceans. Indeed, its primary setting is in the New World and thus it is aware of the existence of the western hemisphere and of details of the cultures and peoples to be found there. "Unfair," charged the Christian clergy. "How easy to prophesy of the past or of the present time!" wrote Alexander Campbell (1832: 13).

As a new faith, Mormonism is much less vulnerable to empirical disconfirmation (although too great reliance on empirical arguments rooted in nineteenth century anthropology may be a source of trouble). And, more recent faiths may entirely eschew empirically vulnerable claims and thus be wholly accommodated to potential secularization.

This does not mean that a new faith must accommodate itself to prevailing *moral* norms. To the contrary it would probably be strengthened if it fostered a stricter morality—faiths can lose credibility by being too inexpensive.

Thus, *new* faiths would appear to have much better long-run chances than do old faiths for maintaining highly efficacious compensators in the midst of a culture that is corrosive to magic. Of course, our predictions depend upon the continuing social influence of organized science. But while a new Dark Age might restore traditional Christianity to its former throne (Miller, 1960), a collapse of civilization could as easily establish contemporary cults as the dominant churches (Sorokin, 1941).

The argument we have developed thus far is incompatible with the dominant view of the relationship between secularization and religious innovation. The prevailing wisdom, best expressed by Wilson (1975) and by Fenn (1978), is that the prevalence of cults or "new religions" in the modern world is part and parcel of the process of secularization *as such.* Thus Wilson argues that the modern world produces "a supermarket of faiths; received, jazzed-up, homespun, restored, imported and exotic. But all of them co-exist only because the wider society is so secular, because they are relatively unimportant consumer items" (1975: 80). Wilson's evaluation of new religions as superficial and inauthentic is echoed by many others (Fenn, 1978; Truzzi, 1970; Luckman, 1967).

This evaluation of cults is rooted in Christian-Judaic parochialism. Since cults fall outside the dominant, respectable, religious traditions of western civilization, this is taken as *prima facie* evidence of their fundamental inferiority. The fact that in the first century Christianity was both deviant and unimpressive is ignored. New faiths are dismissed as inauthentic because they are new.

We suggest that anyone with a serious interest in empirically testing the worth of this judgment spend some time in one of the highly respectable denominations (Episcopalians, for example) and then spend some time with the Mormons or Moonies. Then, make a comparative judgment about the depth of commitment and the authenticity of these religious groups. It will be patent that Mormonism and the Unification Church are not "relatively unimportant consumer items." Furthermore, if we can demonstrate that cult movements are serving as alternatives to conventional faiths, what grounds remain for calling the one authentic and the other superficial? However, as we point out below, many modern cults do seem in many ways to be ill-conceived and implausible. We expect that many of these will be short-lived and insignificant. But it only takes a *few* effective cults to serve as the vehicle for a massive religious renewal. Indeed, it might only take one.

In any event, simply to equate cults with religious trivia and to make them a *symptom* of secularization, is to miss the opportunity to investigate the link between secularization and religious innovation. Surely it is to deprive the concept of secularization of coherent meaning if we describe persons deeply engrossed in supernatural belief and worship as secularized. We therefore propose to examine cult formation as *religious reaction* to secularization, and to suggest that simply because some faiths retain little religious content is no reason to suppose *all* faiths have been emptied of the power to satisfy fundamental human needs.

Another problem with the view that cults reflect secularization *per se* has been the failure to distinguish among cultic social phenomena. As we have pointed out elsewhere, not all cults are full-fledged religions (Stark and Bainbridge, 1979). We have suggested that only *cult movements* are religions. *Client cults* deal primarily in magic, not religion, and consequently cannot bind their clients into stable organizations. *Audience cults* deal primarily in myth and entertainment. Because they function primarily through the mass media, audience cults attract considerable attention and may well be the basis for judgment of all cults as "unimportant consumer items." But, surely such a blanket judgment is absurd in light of the deaths of 917 members of the Jim Jones cult. People do not commit mass suicide on behalf of unimportant consumer items.

Given our line of analysis it follows that the weaker the established religions become, the more religious innovation that ought to occur. Hence, our primary hypothesis:

Cults will abound where conventional churches are weakest.

To follow the logic of the dominant view of secularization leads to a quite contrary prediction. Secularization is seen as an unstoppable trend. If we mean by secularization a decline in the credibility of all systems of thought that postulate the existence of the supernatural, then it follows that secularization produces people who resist supernatural explanations. To the extent that occurs there will not exist a clientele for *religion,* whether new or old, or for magic. This leads to a hypothesis wholly opposite to the one we have advanced:

Cults will be weakest where conventional churches are weakest.

This second hypothesis simply argues that one sells religion to the religious, just as one sells books to readers. People who have turned their backs on the rich variety available within the Christian-Judaic tradition are unlikely to take up with exotic cults. . . .

Conclusion

We have tried to explain in this paper why current social science conceptions that secularization spells the eventual end of religion are erroneous. Many prominent religious organizations may be in their last days. But religion is a much more general phenomenon than some specific set of denominations. We have argued that secularization is in fact a self-limiting phenomenon that generates new religions. The data available for analysis offered support for this point of view.

To conclude this paper we must confess that we cannot point to a religion that is ready to contend for the dominant position so long enjoyed by Christianity. In part this is because we suspect that religious pluralism is the natural state of the religious market, except when the coercive powers of the state are utilized to attempt to create a monopoly for one faith. Hence, it may be that no one faith ever again will assume so wholly dominant a position. But we must also admit that when we examine the many cults in America, most do not conform to our expectations of what a really successful faith for our times would look like.

Many current cults, such as the various witchcraft and pagan groups, have reacted to secularization by a headlong plunge back into magic. They reject the whole scientific culture as well as Christian-Judaic religious traditions. They succeed in gathering a few members because they claim to offer extremely efficacious compensators. They unblushingly promise to give the individual the power to harness supernatural powers to manipulate the natural world. In our judgment these cults are reactionary and have little future. They are utterly vulnerable to the same forces of secularization that have corroded much better organized and accommodated faiths. They will not thrive unless the modern world itself were to collapse.

Other current cults have reacted to secularization by adopting a scientific facade. Indeed, Scientology is in the curious position of defining itself as a science posing as a religion in order to evade the law. Actually, it is a religion posing as a science. The trouble with this approach is that the "science" of such groups is highly vulnerable to empirical evaluation and, most likely, will be exposed as magic when such evaluations are made. Indeed, Scientology, est, and other new therapy-based cults can only sustain their position so long as they prevent outside evaluation of their therapeutic value (Bainbridge and Stark, in press). But in so doing they face social encapsulation and an inability to continue to grow.

In our judgment, faiths suited to our time will contain no magic, only religion. When we examine the current cult scene, all current cults seem to contain too much magic to become really successful mass movements. But simply because we cannot point to an apt example does not mean there is no suitable cult out there or that one will not be born tomorrow.

All religions begin as cults and all arise in obscurity. Looked at in its very early days, no new religion appears very promising. Had a sociologist conducted a field observation study of a new messiah and his band of followers in Israel about A.D. 32, the result would have been just another monograph describing an obscure and ephemeral cult. Today, of course, we would have discovered countless portents of vast potential in such a monograph on the first days of Christianity. But those portents would have escaped contemporary readers. Hence, merely because no signs are apparent to us now does not mean that new, major world faiths are not going through their infancy in our midst.

REFERENCES

Bainbridge, William Sims and Stark, Rodney, 1979. Cult formation: Three compatible models. *Sociological Analysis.*

———, In press. Client and audience cults in America.

Campbell, Alexander, 1832. *An Analysis of the Book of Mormon.* Boston: Benjamin H. Greene.

Fenn, Richard K., 1978. *Toward a Theory of Secularization.* Ellington, Conn.: Society for the Scientific Study of Religion.

Gallup, George H. (ed.), 1976. *The Gallup International Public Opinion Polls: Great Britain 1937–1975.* New York: Random House.

Kelley, Dean, 1972. *Why the Conservative Churches are Growing.* New York: Harper and Row.

Luckman, Thomas, 1967. *The Invisible Religion.* New York: Macmillan.

Martin, David, 1978. *A General Theory of Secularization.* New York: Harper and Row.

Miller, Walter M., Jr., 1960. *A Canticle for Leibowitz.* Philadelphia: Lippincott.

Sorokin, Pitirim A., 1941. *The Crisis of Our Age.* New York: Dutton.

Stark, Rodney and Bainbridge, William Sims, 1979. Of Churches, sects, and cults: Preliminary concepts for a theory of religious movements. *Journal of the Scientific Study of Religion* 18.

Stark, Rodney and Glock, Charles Y., 1968. *American Piety.* Berkeley: University of California Press.

Truzzi, Marcello, 1970. The occult revival as popular culture: Some random observations on the old and nouveau witch. *Sociological Quarterly* 13: 16–36.

Wallace, Anthony F. C., 1966. *Religion: An Anthropological View.* New York: Random House.

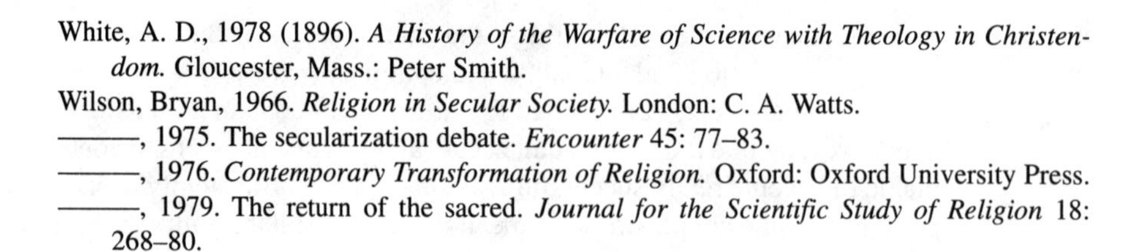

White, A. D., 1978 (1896). *A History of the Warfare of Science with Theology in Christendom.* Gloucester, Mass.: Peter Smith.

Wilson, Bryan, 1966. *Religion in Secular Society.* London: C. A. Watts.

———, 1975. The secularization debate. *Encounter* 45: 77–83.

———, 1976. *Contemporary Transformation of Religion.* Oxford: Oxford University Press.

———, 1979. The return of the sacred. *Journal for the Scientific Study of Religion* 18: 268–80.

DISCUSSION QUESTIONS

1. Stark and Bainbridge argue that secularization leads to the rise of "new religions." Do you agree? Why or why not?
2. How do the authors distinguish between "client cults" and "audience cults?"

XII

Organizations and Economic Life

WHAT TO FOCUS ON:

1. How is the organization of work influenced by its technological base?
2. Should formal organizations have ethical responsibility?

THIS CHAPTER BRINGS together the notion that in modern societies economic activities take place within highly organized and rationalized contexts. Most work takes place in the white-collar bureaucracies of governments and private corporations. However, the smaller workplace also has an organization to its existence and performance. Therefore, economic life—small or large, public or private—has organizational features that need to be explored and understood. After all, for most students, you will spend a great deal of your future within the context of organized economic activities. From a business standpoint most people will be concerned with whether the organization makes a profit. However, from a sociological position, much concern centers on the relationship between the individual and the organization as a whole. Do organizations exist and act as separate entities or are they the collective action of individuals? Can we hold organizations to the same ethical codes we hold individuals? Who, or what, is responsible for the results of organizational activity? How much control does the individual worker have over the organization's output? The sociological study of organizations and economic life have led to some classic statements about social life, i.e. Durkheim's mechanical and organic solidarity via the study of the organization of divisions of labor; and Weber's conceptualizations of modernity as a "cold iron cage". It should be noted that sociologists are not interested in whether an economic organization turns a profit, but rather they are concerned with the social consequences of the organization of economic activities. The articles in this chapter provide interesting insights on these activities.

The Shoshana Zuboff work on "New Worlds of Computer-Mediated Work," demonstrates how the increasing use of computers on the job is not only changing the nature of work but also its social relations. Computer work becomes more rule-bound and structured, there is little room for negotiation. One cannot argue with a computer. While this new technology may be more efficient, it may be affecting work in ways we may not like.

By analyzing the organization of a funeral home as a work system, Salomone focuses on how death in modern societies has become a formalized and secularly controlled ritual. Beginning from the moment of death and ending with the final interment, the funeral home has become the center of social activity in our expression of grief and our attitudes toward death. Salomone provides a detailed examination of the inside life of the funeral home. We see a well organized system of specialized actors with different levels of training and secular certification. We are also witness to specialized tasks and a stratified order of importance to the tasks and actors. In short, death and interment has become a highly organized social process.

Was the Challenger shuttle disaster the result of a fluke of chance, the failure of an individual worker or engineer, or the fault of NASA's organizational design? Boisjoly, et al. examine the internal workings of NASA. They provide great detail on the flow of information and the decision-making process utilized by NASA. The authors explore questions that are at the cutting-edge of organizational research in sociology. Are organizations responsible for their actions? Should organizations be held accountable for the impact of their results or is this an issue for the individual worker or executive? Is it proper to think of organizations acting according to ethical codes?

Article 32

New Worlds of Computer-Mediated Work

SHOSHANA ZUBOFF

WHEN INFORMATION TECHNOLOGY reorganizes a job, it fundamentally alters the individual's relation to the task. I call the new relationship "computer mediated." Usually, this means that a person accomplishes a task through the medium of the information system, rather than through direct physical contact with the object of the task.

Computer mediation can be contrasted to other forms of task relationships in terms of the way in which one *knows* about the object of the task. The potter who turns a pot with his or her own hands has a direct experience of the task's object through a continual series of sights and tactile sensations. These sensations form the basis for moment-by-moment judgments regarding the success of the process and any alterations that the potter should make. Machines, such as a press or a welding torch, usually remove the worker as the direct source of energy for the labor process, but leave the task's object within sensuous range. Those who work with paper and pencil usually feel "in touch" with the objects of their tasks through the activity of writing because they are the sources of what they write.

From excerpts from "New Worlds of Computer-Mediated Work," by Shoshana Zuboff, *Harvard Business Review,* Sept/Oct 1982.

With computer-mediated work, employees get feedback about the task object only as symbols through the medium of the information system. Very often, from the point of view of the worker, the object of the task seems to have disappeared "behind the screen" and into the information system.

The distinction in feedback is what separates the linotype machine operator from the clerical worker who inputs cold type, the engineer who works with computer-aided design from one who directly handles materials, the continuous process operator who reads information from a visual display unit from one who actually checks vat levels, and even the bill collector who works with an on-line, real-time system from a predecessor who handled accounts cards. The distinctiveness of computer-mediated work becomes more clear when one contrasts it against the classic image of work from the nineteenth century in which labor was considered to be the transformation of nature by human muscle. Computer-mediated work is the electronic manipulation of symbols. Instead of a sensual activity, it is an abstract one.

Many employees I spoke to reported feeling frustrated because in losing a direct experience of their task it becomes more difficult to exercise judgment over it. In routine jobs, judgment often becomes lodged in the system itself. As one bill collector said:

"In our old system, come the end of the month, you knew what you were faced with. With the automated system, you don't know how to get in there to get certain accounts out. You have to work the way the system wants you to."

People in even more complex jobs can also lose direct experience of their tasks. The comptroller of a bank that was introducing information systems to a variety of functions commented:

"People become more technical and sophisticated, but they have an inferior understanding of the banking business. New people become like systems people and can program instructions that don't necessarily reflect the spirit of the operation."

The auditor at one bank is working with a new information system that frees him from traveling to regional branches. The branches feed financial data directly into the information system that he can access in real time. He described his job this way:

"The job of auditing is very different now. More imagination is required. I am receiving data on-line. I don't go to the branches if I don't want to. I don't see any books. What do I audit in this situation? I always have to be thinking about what is in the system. I may be auditing, but it doesn't feel like it."

The auditor now has access to a new level of complexity in his data. He has the possibility of comparing branches according to criteria of his choice and searching out new relationships in the data. But in order to do this, he must now develop a theory of the auditing process. He needs to have a conceptual framework that can guide him through the mass of available information. Theoretical insight and imagination will be the keys to his effectiveness on the job.

By creating a medium of work where imagination instead of experience-based judgments is important, information technology challenges old procedures. Judging a given task in the light of experience thus becomes less important than imagining how the task can be reorganized based on new technical capabilities. In the banking industry, for example, planners are not automating the old, but inventing the new.

While working through information systems seems to require a more challenging form of mental effort, it can also induce feelings of frustration and loss of control.

A collections supervisor described the difference between the manual and computer systems:

"If you work with a manual system and you want to see an account on a given day, you have a paper file and you simply go to that particular section and pull out the file. When you're on the computer system, in a sense all your accounts are kind of floating around in space. You can't get your hands on them."

Some people cope with this frustration by creating physical analogues for their tasks. In one branch, an on-line system had been installed to update information on current accounts. Instead of making out tickets that would be sent to a data center for overnight keypunching, operators enter data directly into terminals; the system continuously maintains account information. Despite senior management's efforts to persuade them to change, the branch manager and his staff continued to fill out the tickets. When asked why, they first mentioned the need for a backup system. The real reason came out when the branch manager made the following comment: "You need something you can put your hands on. How else can we be sure of what we are doing?"

People are accustomed to thinking of jobs that require employees to use their brains as the most challenging and rewarding. But instead, the computer mediation of simple jobs can create tasks that are routine and unchallenging, while demanding focused attention and abstract comprehension. Nevertheless, the human brain is organized for action. Abstract work on a mass scale seems likely to create conditions that are peculiar if not stressful to many people. While it does seem that those who shift from conventional procedures to computer-mediated work feel this stress most acutely, it's impossible to forecast what adaptation to the abstraction of work will do to people over the long term.

Social Interaction Is Affected

Doubtless, once information technology reorganizes a set of jobs, new patterns of communication and interaction become possible. In time, these patterns are likely to alter the social structure of an organization.

When resources are centered in the information system, the terminal itself can become employees' primary focus of interaction. This focus can lead people to feel isolated in an impersonal situation. For example, because functional operations in the back office of one bank have been reorganized, a clerical worker can complete an entire operation at his or her "professional" work station, rather than repeat a single procedure of it before passing the item on to someone else. Although employees I talked to were split in their attitudes toward the new back-office system, most of them agreed that it created an uncomfortable isolation. Because they had a few remaining reasons to interact with co-workers, the local social network was fragmented.

Decades of research have established the importance of social communities in the workplace and the lengths to which people will go to establish and maintain them. Since people will not easily give up the pleasures of the workplace community, they tend to see themselves at odds with the new technology that transforms the quality of work life. The comments of one employee illustrate this point.

> I never thought I would feel this way, but I really do not like the computer. If a person makes a mistake, dealing with the computer to try and get that mistake corrected is so much red tape. And it's just taken a lot of feeling out of it. You should have people working with people because they are going to give you what you want, and you're going to get a better job all around.

In a very different kind of application, professionals and managers in the R&D organization of a large consumer goods company find the range of their interaction greatly extended with computer conferencing. While there is some evidence of reduced face-to-face interaction, the technology makes it relatively easy to initiate dialogues and form coalitions with people in other parts of the corporation. Clearly, information technology can offset social life in a variety of ways. It is important to realize, however, that this technology has powerful consequences for the structure and function of communication and social behavior in an organization.

New Possibilities for Supervision and Control

The dream of the industrial engineer to create a perfectly timed and rationalized set of activities has never been perfectly realized. Because face-to-face supervision can be carried on only on a partial basis, employees usually find ways to pace their own activities to meet standards at a reasonable rate. Thus, traditionally, supervision depended on the quality of the relationship between supervisor and worker. If the relationship is a positive one, employees are likely to produce quality work without constant monitoring. If the relationship is adversarial, the monitoring will be continual.

But because work accomplished through the medium of video terminals or other intelligent equipment can be recorded on a second-by-second basis, the industrial engineer's presence can be built into all real-time activities. With immediate access to how much employees are producing through printouts or other visual displays, supervisors and managers can increase surveillance without depending on face-to-face supervision. Thus the interpersonal relationship can become less important to supervision than access to information on the quality and quantity of employee output. One bank supervisor described this new capability: "Instead of going to someone's desk and physically pulling out files, you have the ability to review peoples' work without their knowledge. So I think it keeps them on their toes."

Another variant of remote supervision involves controls that are automatically built into systems operations, as in the collections system described earlier. These rules are substitutes for a certain amount of supervisory effort. Because the system determines what accounts the collector should work on and in what order, a supervisor does not have to monitor collectors' judgments on these issues. Managers also see automatic control as the organization's defense against the potentially massive pollution of data that can occur through access by many people to an on-line real-time system.

Remote supervision, automatic control, and greater access to subordinates' information all become possible with computer-mediated work. In some cases, these capabilities are an explicit objective, but too often management employs them without sufficiently considering the potential human and organizational consequences.

With remote supervision, many employees limit their own risk-taking behavior, such as spotting an error in the data and correcting it, developing a more effective approach to the work than the procedures established by the information system, or trying to achieve quality at the expense of keeping up with new production standards.

One reason the initiative to design a custom-made approach to a particular task has become too risky is that many people have difficulty articulating why their approach might be superior to other alternatives. Usually, management has developed a clearly articulated model of the particular task in order to automate it, and if employees cannot identify their own models with equal clarity, they have little hope of having their views legitimated.

Another reason for decreased employee initiative is that the more an information system can control the details of the job, the less even relatively trivial risk-taking opportunities are available. Finally, the monitoring capabilities increase the likelihood that a supervisor will notice a deviation from standard practice. As one bank employee noted:

"Sometimes I have a gut feeling I would rather do something another way. But, because it is all going to be in the computer, it changes your mind. If somebody wouldn't listen to the reason why you did it that way, well, it could cause you quite a problem."

Another frequent response to the new relationships of supervision and control involves perceptions of authority in the workplace. Employees can tend to see technology less as an instrument of authority than as a source of it. For instance, one group of bank employees with an especially easygoing manager described the work pace on their computer-mediated jobs as hard-driving, intense, and at times unfair, but thought the manager was friendly, relaxed, and fair-minded.

One collector told about the difference in her attitudes toward her work under the manual system and under the automated system:

"When I worked with the account cards, I knew how to handle my responsibilities. I felt, 'Hey! I can handle this!' Now I come in every day with a defeatist attitude, because I'm dealing with the tube every day. I can't beat it. People like to feel not that they are necessarily ahead of the game, but they have a chance. With the tube I don't have a chance." . . .

The Nature of Organization and Management

With information technology, managers will do a variety of tasks that others once did for them. Because of this, we are likely to see a gradual shift in the overall shape of the organization from a pyramid to something closer to a diamond-shape with a diminishing clerical support staff, swelling numbers of professionals and middle managers, and a continually more remote, elite, policy-making group of senior managers.

While these considerations should be of central importance to management policy in the coming years, as a society we are sure to see a continuing challenge to the salience of work and the workplace in our daily lives. The traditional importance of occupational distinctiveness may be further eroded as what it means to "accomplish a task" undergoes a fundamental change. When a person's primary work consists of monitoring or interacting with a video screen, it may become more difficult to answer the questions, "Who am I?" and "What do I do?" Identification with an occupational role may diminish, while the transferability of on-the-job skills increases. Will this have implications for individual commitment to an organization and for the relative importance of work and nonwork activities?

Information technology is also likely to introduce new forms of collective behavior. When the means of production becomes dependent on electronic technology and information flows, it is no longer inevitable that, as in the case of the weavers, work be either collective or synchronous. As long as a terminal and communications links are available, people will be able to perform work in neighborhood centers, at home, or on the road. At the same time, electronic technology is altering the traditional structure and function of communication within the organization. Who interacts with whom in the organization? Can the neat chain of command hierarchy be maintained? Should it be? What does it take to lead or influence others when communication itself becomes computer mediated? Finally, who is likely to gain or lose as we make the transition to this environment?

These developments make it necessary to rethink basic conceptions of the nature of organization and management. What is an organization if people do not have to come face to face in order to accomplish their work? Does the organization itself become an abstraction? What happens to the shared purpose and commitment of members if their face-to-face interaction is reduced? Similarly, how should an "abstract" organization be managed?

If information technology is to live up to its promise for greater productivity, managers need to consider its consequences for human beings and the qualities of their work environment.

DISCUSSION QUESTIONS

1. How do computers change social relations on the job?
2. How does the changing nature of work, brought about by computers, affect workers' ability to make a commitment to the company or organization?

—Article 33—

The Funeral Home as a Work System

A Sociological Analysis

JEROME J. SALOMONE

THIS ESSAY IS ABOUT DEATH, which ranks in importance with birth as one of the two greatest and most significant facts of all existence. These enormously important existential conditions have given rise, according to Herbert Spencer, to pervasive and timeless fears—the fear of living which becomes the basis of political institutions, and the fear of death which becomes the basis of religious institutions.[1] Indeed, birth and death are thought to be so critical throughout the world that everywhere religious belief systems support the notion that these events are in fact sacred phenomena. . . .[2]

In general, it can be observed that the less advanced technologically the society, the more consonant the beliefs and rites regarding death within the society. This means, for example, that in agricultural societies both the beliefs and rites related to death and the disposition of the dead tend to be predominantly, if not exclusively, sacred or religious in nature, with the shaman or priest clearly in unchallenged control over the funeralization process. By contrast, in more technologically advanced industrial societies the beliefs tend to remain sacred while the rites assume a more secular or materialistic aura, with the funeral director substituting for the clergyman in managing the funeral ceremonies. In fact, the funeralization process

From "The Funeral Home as a Work System: A Sociological Analysis," by Jerome Salomone. Originally published in Clifton Bryant (ed.) *The Social Dimensions of Work*, Prentice-Hall, Englewood Cliffs, NJ, 1972, pp. 164–176. Reprinted by permission.

in contemporary America has come under heavy criticism recently because of the alleged commercialization and materialization of what historically has been, and should remain, according to the argument, an entirely religious process.[3]

The elaboration of the procedures and rituals associated with the disposition of the dead has reached the point where it requires, for its efficient performance, a coterie of occupational specialists who operate as a coordinated team and whose overall goal is to process the corpse from death to the grave. . . .

The Internal System

Funeral Director

Just as the handling of illness is rapidly becoming an institutional matter, with the hospital rather than the family caring for the sick, so also is the funeral home replacing the family as the agent in handling the dead. This transformation is virtually complete in large urban centers where overwhelmingly the home has given way to the funeral home as the environmental setting for the ceremonies accompanying the disposition of the dead.

As a consequence, the funeral home has become a rather elaborate work system with its own peculiar occupational subculture. At the heart of this activity is the modern American funeral director, who is in overall operational charge of the activities associated with processing the dead. As such, he is a central figure in a fascinating, if not unique, work culture.

The funeral director is the organizational representative who is the go-between linking the funeral home with the family of the dead person. As the person in managerial control of the ceremonies, he plays a public relations role in the funeralization process.[4] Future funerals are sold on the basis of how past and current funerals are conducted. One of the main means of advertising in the industry is the production of the funeral itself. Adverse criticism, therefore, must be kept to a minimum, as its deleterious affects would be difficult to overcome. Indeed, price advertising is altogether prohibited by an industry-wide code of ethics, and advertising in general is allowed for informational purposes only. Competitive advertising is disallowed through the application of strong internal negative sanctions. Violation of these expectations or norms constitutes grounds for the possible dismissal of a funeral director from the several professional associations in the industry.

The funeral director receives the call from the bereaved family announcing the death. Subsequently it is he who interviews the survivors charged by the family with making the arrangements for the funeral. The funeral director's supervisory role includes managerial responsibility over the following lengthy list of disparate activities:

Attend to the immediate needs of the bereaved.

Notify the family's clergyman.

Call the coroner if this is deemed necessary.

Notify the relatives and friends of the deceased. Send necessary wires.

Secure death certificates, burial permit, and release.

Remove remains from home, hospital, or depot.

Bathe, shampoo, shave, and manicure the body.

Perform necessary dermasurgery.

Prepare, restore, and preserve the body.

Consult with the family for vital information and details.

Notify local and distant newspapers for printing of obituary and funeral notices.

Contact cemetery for grave opening—arrange for use of cemetery equipment.

Meet trains and airplanes bringing out-of-town relatives and friends.

Arrange for family's flowers.

Contact pallbearers and vocalist.

Contact military and fraternal organizations.

Receive, arrange, and remove flowers; retain flower cards.

Provide acknowledgment, mass cards, memorial folders, and similar items.

Provide visitor's registration book.

Provide equipment for various religious and lodge services.

Provide seating, special lighting, and casket carriage.

Making shipping and other arrangements if the deceased is to be interred at a distant point.

Arrange for transportation for the family, if needed.

Arrange appropriate music for service.

Advance the honorarium for the clergy, soloist, cemetery, florist, transportation, and other cash items . . . as an added convenience for the family.

Provide casket coach, sedan passenger car, transportation for the clergy and the floral tributes.

Provide parking space and personnel.

Direct and supervise funeral service according to particular religious, national, and local customs.

Arrange for church or home service.

Arrange auto cortege.

Notify family attorney, bank, and insurance agent.

Assist in securing Social Security and Veterans' Benefits as well as insurance claims.

Provide Notary Public service.

Advise as to any other benefits which will be due to the family.

Assist with any personal problems that fall within his province.[5]

Funeral directors must be licensed according to state law. In general, they must be high school graduates, or, increasingly, college graduates with one or two years' experience as an apprentice director. Licensed embalmers are also eligible to become funeral directors. Historically, the practice was that embalmers and funeral directors were one-in-the-same person. In time, the jobs split. When that first happened, the usual career line followed by practitioners in the industry was from embalmer to funeral director. But current practice is different, as will be explained in a later section.

The Embalmer

There are state licensing requirements[6] for embalmers which include graduation from an accredited college of embalming. Additionally, every state has established certain minimum academic educational prerequisites which must be met before matriculating in an embalming college. Since these academic standards are set on the state level, as might be anticipated, they vary considerably from one state to another. Prospective student embalmers are required to complete high school or its approved equivalent (for example, the high school equivalent examination given in the Armed Forces), or to complete one or two years of academic college before admittance to an embalming college.

Approximately one-third of the states now require two years of college prior to admittance to a college of mortuary science and the trend is in the direction of more and more emphasis on academic educational prerequisites.

There is also a period of apprenticeship during which the embalming student receives on-the-job training under the tutelage of a licensed embalmer. The length of the apprentice or interne training program varies from twelve to thirty-six months. The various states are about equally divided between twelve and twenty-four months' apprenticeship requirements, with only two states having a thirty-six months' practicum. The internship is variously administered across the country. Some require its completion before enrollment in embalming college; some after graduation; and some split the internship, requiring that it be completed partly before and partly after completion of the embalming curriculum.

The embalmer is caught in the middle insofar as his career aspirations are concerned. The funeral industry is moving from a small family owned and operated business to a large corporate enterprise. In the process, managerial entrepreneurs are emerging within its bureaucratic framework. These funeral management specialists are recruited from college campuses more and more, in contradistinction to what was found historically, where one moved up from an embalmer in the preparation room (embalming room) to a funeral director in charge of directing the drama that is the modern funeral service.

> The emergence of new types of funeral management executives has had the effect of reducing the status of the embalmer to that of "technician." The result of this has been to curtail the supply of qualified embalmers. Schools of mortuary science have been reporting shortages in applicants, and several schools have closed. The future of the embalmer seems dim. Capital outlay for the business is large and the corporate structure is more and more in evidence in funeral service. This means that

> only a limited number of embalmers and funeral directors can be expected to be in positions of ownership; the embalmer appears to be more and more relegated to the role of hard working, poorly paid employee. The advent of unionization in some of the larger cities reflects this trend.[7]

The trend toward more stringent educational prerequisites prior to matriculating is accompanied by increased educational demands on the student when he enters embalming college. Once there, his curriculum includes study in the basic sciences of anatomy, physiology, and chemistry; in the public health sciences of microbiology, hygiene, and pathology; in the mortuary arts and sciences, including the elementary and advanced principles of embalming, and the application of embalming principles in the restorative arts (i.e., modeling); in funeral management, such as business and mortuary law, accounting, psychology, and the principles of funeral directing and management.[8]

There is no mystery as to why educational requirements are becoming more demanding. Funeral educators are, like everyone else, intent on professionalizing the industry. Their conviction that this should be done precisely at a time when opportunities for upward mobility for embalmers are diminishing introduces into the industry an occupational incongruity of the greatest magnitude.

The embalmer's training is intended to prepare him eventually for a managerial position in the funeral industry, though the future holds dim prospects that he will ever get out of the embalming room. As this realization becomes more widespread, embalmers come to view themselves as "locked into" their jobs. As of this writing, funeral educational curricula have not adjusted to this industry-wide trend. They still require training in areas outside the purely technical skills required for preparing the dead for viewing.

Two types of skills are central to the embalmer: dermasurgical skills and cosmetological skills. Dermasurgery refers to skills required to restore, through surgery, any deformities or abnormalities associated with a corpse. Especially important are certain parts of the anatomy, like the face and hands, which are exposed during viewing. Sometimes great skill and artistry are required to remake a face deformed in an accident or to rebuild a countenance emaciated through some prolonged terminal illness.

Cosmetology refers to the application of cosmetics in preparing the body for viewing. For example, where beauticians are not subcontracted, embalmers do the actual facial make-up, using rouge, lipstick, etc., in the preparation of the body.

Dermasurgery and cosmetology are collectively considered the skills that comprise, what is called in the industry, the *restorative arts.* The restoration of the body to a lifelike resemblance of the dead person is considered of the utmost importance since, according to the funeral industry, it is in this way the family experiences the benefits of *grief therapy.*

The Social Psychology of Death

Proper grief therapy, it is believed, is obtained through the restorative arts by returning the dead person to a natural and lifelike resemblance of his former self. Through proper restoration of the corpse the bereaved survivors experience an indelible "memory picture" of the dead person which is said to have positive psychological consequences.

This entire philosophy of viewing is heavily dependent on embalming skills, and as such is determined by the level of sophistication of the technological tools available in the industry and known to the embalmer. Since the embalmer is the *technical expert* responsible for preparation of the corpse, it is quite logical that his occupational skills are crucially important in the over-all funeralization process.

But grief therapy is not entirely dependent on the memory picture and the preparation of the dead person. The funeral director must also be expert in *social relational skills.* The proper application by him of psychological and sociological principles in handling the funeral ceremonies contributes to a gestaltist perception on the part of the bereaved that the funeralization process is a worthwhile and valuable experience. It should be clear, then, that the funeral director takes over or enters where the embalmer leaves off or exits. The two occupational encumbents, together, constitute a team—with the embalmer and his technical expertise behind the scenes and the funeral director and his expertise in social relationships on the scene in the drama of the funeral.

Although the other employees who assist in funeralizing the dead are not the central figures in these activities, they nevertheless make a major contribution toward achieving the overall desired effect of leaving all the participants—bereaved and sympathizers—with a wholesome image of the ceremonies. They accomplish this goal primarily in *the manner in which certain services are provided.*

The receptionist at the funeral home, the driver of the hearse and limousines, and the funeral director's assistants are expected to perform their assigned tasks with a solemnity, courtesy, kindness, promptitude, and conviction characteristic of people who sincerely want to please those they serve. This occupational attitude on the part of the entire funeral home staff contributes to the memory picture and feeling the participants have toward the mortuary establishment itself. Their roles, therefore, complement those of the embalmer and funeral director, in guiding the bereaved, through grief therapy, toward a satisfactory post-funeral psychological adjustment.

Funeralizing the dead, it is believed, satisfies certain needs of the bereaved; it is therefore considered a necessary process that provides a friendly environment within which the grief-stricken can work through their feelings of loss, emptiness, or void occasioned by death. As such, funerals are thought to be therapeutic in eight ways.

> The bereaved experiences an emotional catharsis through the *therapy of direct expression.*
>
> When the grief-stricken "talks to himself" or communicates with others he benefits from the *therapy of language.*
>
> Emotional, physical, and financial support received by the next of kin constitutes the *therapy of sharing.*
>
> Survivors are "forced" out of their immobility and are required by custom to participate in the funeral rituals; this is considered the *therapy of activity.*

> The memory picture of a lifelike, but sleeping corpse together with the comfort, quiet, and beauty of the funeral home (in America) constitutes the *therapy of aesthetics.*
>
> Seeing the "remains" itself makes up the *therapy of viewing.*
>
> The *therapy of ceremony* is an ennobling and glorifying experience from which the grievers benefit.
>
> Guilt feelings and our reactions to them during funeralization constitute the *therapy of self-denial and suffering.*[9]

The External System

Clergymen

The funeral director's responsibilities involve him in a network of institutional relationships with representatives of other community organizations and agencies. Foremost among these external contacts is the funeral director's association with clergymen.

Fulton reported that "criticism of the funeral director and of funeral practices by the clergy is both intensive and extensive in America." The principle complaints of American ministers, he found, revolve around three themes. First, the clergy object to what they consider an overemphasis on the body with the subsequent diminution of attention to the spiritual meaning of the funeral. Second, clergymen throughout the nation have negative attitudes toward the funeral director because the funeral director is involved in the dual role of businessman and professional man. As a businessman he is involved in the commercial end of the funeral; as a professional man he is seen by the clergy as identifying with the sacred aspects of the funeral. Thus, the ambivalence of the funeral director's professional role gives rise to an attitudinal ambivalence on the part of the clergy toward the funeral director. Third, Fulton says:

> For the individual clergyman, the funeral is one of the most significant ceremonies in his church. Moreover, by the very nature of faith he believes that his church's particular rites, ceremonies and beliefs command what has been called a "priority of sanctity" over all other churches. There is as a consequence, a fear of taint that is evidenced sometimes when a clergyman or relative requests or insists that the funeral director by of the same faith as the deceased. It seems that when the funeral director makes his services available to people of different faiths, or relates all funerals past and present to an apparent effort to establish the claim of equal sanctity for all of them, he leaves himself open to the charge of paganism from clergymen of different persuasions.[10]

Another point at which funeral directors and clergymen are apt to differ relates to the preparation of the body. Clergymen feel that the purpose of preparation of the body is to improve appearance, while the funeral director favors preparation designed to create the illusion of life.[11]

Still another source of difficulty between these two occupational practitioners has to do with relative emphases between the wake and the funeral service. The wake is primarily a secular ceremony over which the funeral director has complete charge. It is customarily scheduled in the evening hours when it is more convenient for accommodating sympathizers. The funeral service, on the other hand, is by tradition a sacred rite, conducted by a clergyman and is held prior to interment, the morning after the wake, when people are working and are consequently less likely to be able to attend. The greater attendance at the wake over the funeral service results in a shift in the emphasis of the supervisory roles of the funeral director and the clergyman, with the funeral director emerging in the ascendant position.

Finally, the modern funeral director, guided by contemporary social science, is expected to supervise the funeral ceremonies in such a manner that they do not play harshly on the emotions. He rejects the previous crude emphasis on sorrow, guilt, and fear encouraged by some clergymen of a previous era. Clergymen agree with funeral directors in that they believe the entire funeralization process contributes to the amelioration of grief among the survivors. But, clergymen feel, of the three elements comprising the funeral ceremonies (the wake, the funeral service, and the interment service), the wake plays a relatively insignificant role in the social-psychological adjustments of the bereaved to a world devoid of a recently lost love object. The funeral director, by contrast, emphasizes the therapeutic role of the wake in aiding the bereaved survivors.

But the controversial relationship between clergymen and funeral directors is more latent than manifest, more private than public, and more institutional than personal. From all outward signs they work harmoniously and cooperatively together, as the clergyman offers prayers and comfort to the survivors at the wake, and as he conducts his religious ceremonies during the funeral and interment service—all the while, of course, with the funeral director inconspicuously standing by orchestrating the whole process.

Government Personnel

Besides the clergyman, the funeral director is continuously in close liaison with the cemeterians and governmental officials. His relationship with both classes of worker is purely administrative. The cemeterian must work with the funeral director to insure that the cemetery is prepared to receive the encasketed remains upon the arrival of the funeral cortege. In this regard timing is of the utmost importance. Any disjunction between the plans of the funeral director and those of the cemeterian would result in confusion and delay at a time when emotions are running high. Teamwork and coordination between the two are therefore held as inviolate virtues to be compromised under no circumstances.

The connections between funeral directors and governmental officials have been summarized by Bowman, who observes:

> Advice is given to clients in the matter of benefits and proceedings of which they may not have been aware. These include old age insurance for surviving spouses and children under eighteen years of age, old age assistance, veterans' rights, and local welfare benefits. Advice is given also on matters in which government

agencies may be involved, such as procedures in respect to wills, laws of inheritance, and settling estates. The advice that is given involves only a limited knowledge of social security, welfare, and law; but, coming at the time it does, it is important.[12]

Summary

This descriptive essay highlighted selected characteristics of the funeral home as an environmental setting within which is located a special occupational subculture. Of particular concern were the internal and external dimensions of the funeral home as a work system. The funeral director and the embalmer were considered the central occupational characters involved as a team in processing the dead. The funeral director was defined as the social relations expert who, in addition to this role, also was in overall supervisory charge of the funeralization process. In carrying out these responsibilities, the funeral director is, in fact, also serving in a public relations capacity for his firm and the entire industry.

The technical expert charged with preparing the dead person for viewing is the embalmer, who, together with the funeral director, is responsible for cultivating among the bereaved survivors a wholesome image of the dead person known as a memory picture, which presumably will aid the bereaved in working through their grief.

The funeral director is the link between the funeral home and persons and/or institutions connected with, but external to, the funeral industry. In this regard, the funeral director is in close outward cooperative contact with the clergyman, who nevertheless harbors certain latent critical reservations concerning the funeral director. Whatever differences exist between them are the result of two considerations: (1) the gradual usurpation by the funeral director of the supervisory functions of the funeral, which were formerly monopolized by the clergy, and (2) relative secular orientation of the funeral director as opposed to the sacred orientation of the clergyman. Finally, an administrative connection between the funeral director and the cemeterian and representatives of government was mentioned, with special emphasis on the critical importance of timing in coordinating the activities of everyone concerned, so as to minimize the probability of disruption and confusion that would disturb the bereaved and distort their memory picture.

NOTES

1. Herbert Spencer, *The Principles of Sociology,* Vol. 1, reprinted in Robert Bierstedt (ed.), *The Making of Society* (New York: Random House, 1959), 255.

2. See Emile Durkheim, *The Elementary Forms of the Religious Life,* especially the Introduction and Book I, entitled "Preliminary Questions on the Connection Among Values, Belief, and Religion" (London: George Allen and Unwin, Ltd., 1915), pp. 1–64.

3. The most vocal and perhaps antagonistic contemporary critic is Jessica Mitford, *The American Way of Death* (Greenwich: Fawcett Publications, Inc., 1964).

4. The entire funeralization process is understood to include the wake, the funeral service, and the interment service.

The term "wake" is an Anglo-Saxon word which literally means "to watch a corpse." It is a custom of unknown origin and antiquity, although waking the dead almost certainly was invented before the advent of civilization and is found all over the world. It used to be an uninterrupted vigil of relatives and friends over the human remains from death until committal of the body; this custom, relatively unmodified by time, still exists in many societies around the world as well as among many Americans, especially among those of African, Irish, and Italian descent. See William S. Walsh, *Curiosities of Popular Customs* (Philadelphia: J.B. Lippincott Company, 1925), pp. 790–92. By wake we understand that period when the dead person is exposed for public viewing sometime between death and disposition. It might be an all night affair, determined by the family of the dead person and/or the funeral director handling the funeral.

By the funeral service is meant a ceremony, usually religious, held in a church or, increasingly, in a special room in the funeral home called a funeral chapel, and which ordinarily is held immediately before the interment service.

The interment service refers to the final ceremony of the dead at which time the body is committed to the ground.

5. John T. Arends, "The Great Controversy Relating to Funerals" (printed brochure, Decatur, Illinois, n.d.), pp. 17–19. This brochure is part of the funeral industry's public relations program of public education. Its contents, therefore, must be evaluated in that light.

6. Information in the following three paragraphs is synthesized from *Design for Learning,* College Catalogue of the Cincinnati College of Embalming, School of Art and Science (n.d.).

7. This quotation taken from William H. Porter, "Some Sociological Notes on a Century of Change in the Funeral Business," unpublished paper presented at the Meetings of the Southern Sociological Society, March-April, 1967, Atlanta, Georgia. A revised version of this paper has subsequently been presented in *Sociological Symposium,* No. 1 (Fall 1968), 36–46.

8. *Design for Learning, op. cit.,* pp. 29–39.

9. Robert W. Habenstein and W.M. Lamers, *Funeral Customs the World Over* (Milwaukee: Bulfin Printers, Inc., 1960), pp. 763–70.

10. Robert L. Fulton, "The Clergyman and the Funeral Director: A Study in Role Conflict," *Social Forces,* XXXIX (May 1961), 317–23.

11. Paul E. Irion, *The Funeral: Vestige or Value?* (Nashville, Tennessee: Abingdon Press, 1966), pp. 47–51.

12. Leroy Bowman, *The American Funeral* (New York: Public Affairs Press, 1964), pp. 62–63.

DISCUSSION QUESTIONS

1. What is the role of the funeral home director in death?
2. How is the funeral home similar to other forms of secular work activities?

Article 34
Ethical Dimensions of the Challenger Disaster

RUSSELL BOISJOLY, ELLEN FOSTER CURTIS AND EUGENE MELLICAN

ON JANUARY 28, 1986, the space shuttle Challenger exploded 73 seconds into its flight, killing the seven astronauts aboard. As the nation mourned the tragic loss of the crew members, the Rogers Commission was formed to investigate the causes of the disaster. The Commission concluded that the explosion occurred due to seal failure in one of the solid rocket booster joints. Testimony given by Roger Boisjoly, Senior Scientist and acknowledged rocket seal expert, indicated that top management at NASA and Morton Thiokol had been aware of problems with the O-ring seals, but agreed to launch against the recommendations of Boisjoly and other engineers. Boisjoly had alerted management to problems with the O-rings as early as January, 1985, yet several shuttle launches prior to the Challenger had been approved without correcting the hazards. This suggests that the management practice of NASA and Morton Thiokol had created an environment which altered the framework for decision making, leading to a breakdown in communication between technical experts and their supervisors, and top level management, and to the acceptance of risks that both organizations had historically viewed as unacceptable.

From "Roger Boisjoly and the Challenger Disaster: The Ethical Dimensions." *Journal of Business Ethics* 8, pp. 217–30.

With human lives and the national interest at stake, serious ethical concerns are embedded in this dramatic change in management practice.

In fact, one of the most important aspects of the Challenger disaster—both in terms of the causal sequence that led to it and the lessons to be learned from it—is its ethical dimension. Ethical issues are woven throughout the tangled web of decisions, events, practices, and organizational structures that resulted in the loss of the Challenger and its seven astronauts. Therefore, an ethical analysis of this tragedy is essential for a full understanding of the event itself and for the implications it has for any endeavor where public policy, corporate practice, and individual decisions intersect.

The significance of an ethical analysis of the Challenger disaster is indicated by the fact that it immediately presents one of the most urgent, but difficult, issues in the examination of corporate and individual behavior today, i.e., whether existing ethical theories adequately address the problems posed by new technologies, new forms of organization, and evolving social systems. At the heart of this issue is the concept of responsibility. No ethical concept has been more affected by the impact of these changing realities. Modern technology has so transformed the context and scale of human action that not only do the traditional parameters of responsibility seem inadequate to contain the full range of human acts and their consequences, but even more fundamentally, it is no longer the individual that is the primary locus of power and responsibility, but public and private institutions. Thus, it would seem, it is no longer the character and virtues of individuals that determine the standards of moral conduct, it is the policies and structures of the institutional settings within which they live and work.

Many moral conflicts facing individuals within institutional settings do arise from matters pertaining to organizational structure or questions of public policy. As such, they are resolvable only at a level above the responsibilities of the individual. Therefore, some writers argue that the ethical responsibilities of the engineer or manager in a large corporation have as much to do with the organization as with the individual. Instead of expecting individual engineers or managers to be moral heroes, emphasis should be on the creation of organizational structures conducive to ethical behavior among all agents under their aegis. It would be futile to attempt to establish a sense of ethical responsibility in engineers and management personnel and ignore the fact that such persons work within a social-technical environment which increasingly undermines the notion of individual, responsible moral agency (Boling and Dempsey, 1981; DeGeorge, 1981).

Yet, others argue that precisely because of these organizational realities individual accountability must be re-emphasized to counteract the diffusion of responsibility within large organizations and to prevent its evasion under the rubric of collective responsibility. Undoubtedly institutions do take on a kind of collective life of their own, but they do not exist, or act, independently of the individuals that constitute them, whatever the theoretical and practical complexities of delineating the precise relationships involved. Far from diminishing individuals' obligations, the reality of organizational life increases them because the consequences of decisions and acts are extended and amplified through the reach and power of that reality. Since there are pervasive and inexorable connections between ethical standards and behavior of individuals within an organization and its structure and operation, "the sensitizing of professionals to ethical considerations should be increased so that institutional structures will reflect enhanced ethical sensitivities as trained professionals move up the organizational ladder to positions of leadership" (Mankin, 1981, p. 17).

By reason of the courageous activities and testimony of individuals like Roger Boisjoly, the Challenger disaster provides a fascinating illustration of the dynamic tension between organizational and individual responsibility. By focusing on this central issue, this article seeks to accomplish two objectives: first, to demonstrate the extent to which the Challenger disaster not only gives concrete expression to the ethical ambiguity that permeates the relationship between organizational and individual responsibility, but also, in fact, is a result of it; second, to reclaim the meaning and importance of individual responsibility within the diluting context of large organizations. . . .

Preview for Disaster

On January 24, 1985, Roger Boisjoly, Senior Scientist at Morton Thiokol, watched the launch of Flight 51-C of the space shuttle program. He was at Cape Canaveral to inspect the solid rocket boosters from Flight 51-C following their recovery in the Atlantic Ocean and to conduct a training session at Kennedy Space Center (KSC) on the proper methods of inspecting the booster joints. While watching the launch, he noted that the temperature that day was much cooler than recorded at other launches, but was still warmer than the 18 degree temperature encountered three days earlier when he arrived in Orlando. The unseasonably cold weather of the past several days had produced the worst citrus crop failures in Florida history.

When he inspected the solid rocket boosters several days later, Boisjoly discovered evidence that the primary O-ring seals on two field joints had been compromised by hot combustion gases (i.e., hot gas blow-by had occurred) which had also eroded part of the primary O-ring. This was the first time that a primary seal on a field joint had been penetrated. When he discovered the large amount of blackened grease between the primary and secondary seals, his concern heightened. The blackened grease was discovered over 80 degree and 110 degree arcs, respectively, on two of the seals, with the larger arc indicating greater hot gas blow-by. Post-flight calculations indicated that the ambient temperature of the field joints at launch time was 53 degrees. This evidence, coupled with his recollection of the low temperature the day of the launch and the citrus crop damage caused by the cold spell, led to his conclusion that the severe hot gas blow-by may have been caused by, and related to, low temperature. After reporting these findings to his superiors, Boisjoly presented them to engineers and management at NASA's Marshall Space Flight Center (MSFC). As a result of his presentation at MSFC, Roger Boisjoly was asked to participate in the Flight Readiness Review (FRR) on February 12, 1985 for Flight 51-E which was scheduled for launch in April, 1985. This FRR represents the first association of low temperature with blow-by on a field joint, a condition that was considered an "acceptable risk" by Larry Mulloy, NASA's Manager for the Booster Project, and other NASA officials. . . .

The tough questioning he received at the February 12th FRR convinced Boisjoly of the need for further evidence linking low temperature and hot gas blow-by. He worked closely with Arnie Thompson, Supervisor of Rocket Motor Cases, who conducted subscale laboratory tests in March, 1985, to further test the effects of temperature on O-ring resiliency. The bench tests that were performed provided powerful evidence to support Boisjoly's and Thompson's theory: Low temperatures greatly and adversely affected the ability of O-rings to create a seal on solid rocket booster joints. If the temperature was too low (and they did not know what the threshold temperature would be), it was possible that neither the primary or secondary O-rings would seal!

One month later the post-flight inspection of Flight 51-B revealed that the primary seal of a booster nozzle joint did not make contact during its two minute flight. If this damage had occurred in a field joint, the secondary O-ring may have failed to seal, causing the loss of the flight. As a result, Boisjoly and his colleagues became increasingly concerned about shuttle safety. This evidence from the inspection of Flight 51-B was presented at the FRR for Flight 51-F on July 1, 1985; the key engineers and managers of NASA and Morton Thiokol were now aware of the critical O-ring problems and the influence of low temperature on the performance of the joint seals.

During July, 1985, Boisjoly and his associates voiced their desire to devote more effort and resources to solving the problems of O-ring erosion. In his activity reports dated July 22 and 29, 1985, Boisjoly expressed considerable frustration with the lack of progress in this area, despite the fact that a Seal Erosion Task Force had been informally appointed on July 19th. Finally, Boisjoly wrote the following memo, labelled "Company Private," to R. K. (Bob) Lund, Vice President of Engineering for Morton Thiokol, to express the extreme urgency of his concerns. Here are some excerpts from that memo:

> This letter is written to insure that management is fully aware of the seriousness of the current O-ring erosion problems. . . . The mistakenly accepted position on the joint problem was to fly without fear of failure . . . is now drastically changed as a result of the SRM 16A nozzle joint erosion which eroded a secondary O-ring with the primary O-ring never sealing. If the same scenario should occur in a field joint (and it could), then it is a jump ball as to the success or failure of the joint. . . . The result would be a catastrophe of the highest order—loss of human life . . .
>
> It is my honest and real fear that if we do not take immediate action to dedicate a team to solve the problem, with the field joint having the number one priority, then we stand in jeopardy of losing a flight along with all the launch pad facilities (Boisjoly, July, 1985a).

On August 20, 1985, R. K. Lund formally announced the formation of the Seal Erosion Task Team. The team consisted of only five full-time engineers from the 2500 employed by Morton Thiokol on the Space Shuttle Program. The events of the next five months would demonstrate that management had not provided the resources necessary to carry out the enormous task of solving the seal erosion problem.

On October 3, 1985, the Seal Erosion Task Force met with Joe Kilminster to discuss the problems they were having in gaining organizational support necessary to solve the O-ring problems. Boisjoly later stated that Kilminster summarized the meeting as a "good bullshit session." Once again frustrated by bureaucratic inertia, Boisjoly wrote in his activity report dated October 4th:

> NASA is sending an engineering representative to stay with us starting Oct. 14th. We feel that this is a direct result of their feeling that we (MTI) are not responding quickly enough to the seal problem . . . upper management apparently feels that the SRM program is ours for sure and the customer be damned (Boisjoly, October, 1985b).

Boisjoly was not alone in his expression of frustration. Bob Ebeling, Department Manager, Solid Rocket Motor Igniter and Final Assembly, and a member of the Seal Erosion Task Force, wrote in a memo to Allan McDonald, Manager of the Solid Rocket Motor Project, "HELP! The seal task force is constantly being delayed by every possible means. . . . We wish we could get action by verbal request, but such is not the case. This is a red flag" (McConnell, 1987).

At the Society of Automotive Engineers (SAE) conference on October 7, 1985, Boisjoly presented a six-page overview of the joints and the seal configuration to approximately 130 technical experts in hope of soliciting suggestions for remedying the O-ring problems. Although MSFC had requested the presentation, NASA gave strict instructions not to express the critical urgency of fixing the joints, but merely to ask for suggestions for improvement. Although no help was forthcoming, the conference was a milestone in that it was the first time that NASA allowed information on the O-ring difficulties to be expressed in a public forum. That NASA also recognized that the O-ring problems were not receiving appropriate attention and manpower considerations from Morton Thiokol management is further evidenced by Boisjoly's October 24 log entry, "Jerry Peoples (NASA) has informed his people that our group needs more authority and people to do the job. Jim Smith (NASA) will corner Al McDonald today to attempt to implement this direction."

The October 30 launch of Flight 61-A of the Challenger provided the most convincing, and yet to some the most contestable, evidence to date that low temperature was directly related to hot gas blow-by. The left booster experienced hot gas blow-by in the center and aft field joints without any seal erosion. The ambient temperature of the field joints was estimated to be 75 degrees at launch time based on post-flight calculations. Inspection of the booster joints revealed that the blow-by was less severe than that found on Flight 51-C because the seal grease was a grayish black color, rather than the jet black hue of Flight 51-C. The evidence was now consistent with the bench tests for joint resiliency conducted in March. That is, at 75 degrees the O-ring lost contact with its sealing surface for 2.4 seconds, whereas at 50 degrees the O-ring lost contact for 10 minutes. The actual flight data revealed greater hot gas blow-by for the O-rings on Flight 51-C which had an ambient temperature of 53 degrees than for Flight 61-A which had an ambient temperature of 75 degrees. Those who rejected this line of reasoning concluded that temperature must be irrelevant since hot gas blow-by had occurred even at room temperature (75 degrees). This difference in interpretation would receive further attention on January 27, 1986.

During the next two and one-half months, little progress was made in obtaining a solution to the O-ring problems. Roger Boisjoly made the following entry into his log on January 13, 1986, "O-ring resiliency tests that were requested on September 24, 1985 are now scheduled for January 15, 1986."

The Day Before the Disaster

At 10 a.m. on January 27, 1986, Arnie Thompson received a phone call from Boyd Brinton, Thiokol's Manager of Project Engineering at MSFC, relaying the concerns of NASA's Larry Wear, also at MSFC, about the 18 degree temperature forecast for the launch of Flight 51-L, the Challenger, scheduled for the next day. This phone call precipitated a series of meetings within Morton Thiokol at the Marshall Space Flight Center, and at the Kennedy Space Center that culminated in a three-way telecon involving three teams of engineers and managers, that began at 8:15 p.m. E.S.T.

Joe Kilminster, Vice President, Space Booster Programs, of Morton Thiokol began the telecon by turning the presentation of the engineering charts over to Roger Boisjoly and Arnie Thompson. They presented thirteen charts which resulted in a recommendation against the launch of the Challenger. Boisjoly demonstrated their concerns with the performance of the O-rings in the field joints during the initial phases of Challenger's flight with charts showing the effects of primary O-ring erosion, and its timing, on the ability to maintain a reliable secondary seal. The tremendous pressure and release of power from the rocket boosters create rotation in the joint such that the metal moves away from the O-rings so that they cannot maintain contact with the metal surfaces. If, at the same time, erosion occurs in the primary O-ring for any reason, then there is a reduced probability of maintaining a secondary seal. It is highly probable that as the ambient temperature drops, the primary O-ring will not seal; that there will be hot gas blow-by and erosion of the primary O-ring; and that a catastrophe will occur when the secondary O-ring fails to seal.

Bob Lund presented the final chart that included the Morton Thiokol recommendations that the ambient temperature including wind must be such that the seal temperature would be greater than 53 degrees to proceed with the launch. Since the overnight low was predicted to be 18 degrees, Bob Lund recommended against launch on January 28, 1986 or until the seal temperature exceeded 53 degrees.

NASA's Larry Mulloy bypassed Bob Lund and directly asked Joe Kilminster for his reaction. Kilminster stated that he supported the position of his engineers and he would not recommend launch below 53 degrees.

George Hardy, Deputy Director of Science and Engineering at MSFC, said he was "appalled at that recommendation," according to Allan McDonald's testimony before the Rogers Commission. Nevertheless, Hardy would not recommend to launch if the contractor was against it. After Hardy's reaction, Stanley Reinartz, Manager of Shuttle Project Office at MSFC, objected by pointing out that the solid rocket motors were qualified to operate between 40 and 90 degrees Fahrenheit.

Larry Mulloy, citing the data from Flight 61-A, which indicated to him that temperature was not a factor, strenuously objected to Morton Thiokol's recommendation. He suggested that Thiokol was attempting to establish new Launch Commit Criteria at 53 degrees and that they couldn't do that the night before a launch. In exasperation Mulloy asked, "My God, Thiokol, when do you want me to launch? Next April?" (McConnell, 1987). Although other NASA officials also objected to the association of temperature with O-ring erosion and hot gas blow-by, Roger Boisjoly was able to hold his ground and demonstrate with the use of his charts and pictures that there was indeed a relationship. The lower the temperature the higher the probability of erosion and blow-by and the greater the likelihood of an accident. Finally, Joe Kilminster asked for a five minute caucus off-net.

According to Boisjoly's testimony before the Rogers Commission, Jerry Mason, Senior Vice President of Wasatch Operations, began the caucus by saying that "a management decision was necessary." Sensing that an attempt would be made to overturn the no-launch decision, Boisjoly and Thompson attempted to review the material previously presented to NASA for the executives in the room. Thompson took a pad of paper and tried to sketch out the problem with the joint, while Boisjoly laid out the photos of the compromised joints from Flights 51-C and 61-A. When they became convinced that no one was listening, they ceased their efforts. As Boisjoly would later testify, "There was not one positive pro-launch statement ever made by anybody" (Report of the Presidential Commission, 1986, IV, p. 792, hereafter abbreviated as R.C.).

According to Boisjoly, after he and Thompson made their last attempts to stop the launch, Jerry Mason asked rhetorically, "Am I the only one who wants to fly?" Mason turned to Bob Lund and asked him to "take off his engineering hat and put on his management hat." The four managers held a brief discussion and voted unanimously to recommend Challenger's launch. . . .

Aside from the four senior Morton Thiokol executives present at the teleconference, all others were excluded from the final decision. The process represented a radical shift from previous NASA policy. Until that moment, the burden of proof had always been on the engineers to prove beyond a doubt that it was safe to launch. NASA, with their objections to the original Thiokol recommendation against the launch, and Mason, with his request for a "management decision" shifted the burden of proof in the opposite direction. Morton Thiokol was expected to prove that launching Challenger would not be safe (R.C., IV, p. 793).

The change in the decision so deeply upset Boisjoly that he returned to his office and made the following journal entry:

> I sincerely hope this launch does not result in a catastrophe. I personally do not agree with some of the statements made in Joe Kilminster's written summary stating that SRM-25 is okay to fly (Boisjoly, 1987).

The Disaster and Its Aftermath

On January 28, 1986, a reluctant Roger Boisjoly watched the launch of the Challenger. As the vehicle cleared the tower, Bob Ebeling whispered, "we've just dodged a bullet." (The engineers who opposed the launch assumed that O-ring failure would result in an explosion almost immediately after engine ignition.) To continue in Boisjoly's words, "At approximately T + 60 seconds Bob told me he had just completed a prayer of thanks to the Lord for a successful launch. Just thirteen seconds later we both saw the horror of the destruction as the vehicle exploded" (Boisjoly, 1987).

Morton Thiokol formed a failure investigation team on January 31, 1986 to study the Challenger explosion. Roger Boisjoly and Arnie Thompson were part of the team that was sent to MSFC in Huntsville, Alabama. Boisjoly's first inkling of a division between himself and management came on February 13 when he was informed at the last minute that he was to testify before the Rogers Commission the next day. He had very little time to prepare for his testimony. Five days later, two Commission members held a closed session with Kilminster, Boisjoly, and Thompson. During the interview Boisjoly gave his memos and activity reports to the Commissioners. After that meeting, Kilminster chastised Thompson and Boisjoly for correcting his interpretation of the technical data. Their response was that they would continue to correct his version if it was technically incorrect.

Boisjoly's February 25 testimony before the Commission, rebutting the general manager's statement that the initial decision against the launch was not unanimous, drove a wedge further between him and Morton Thiokol management. Boisjoly was flown to MSFC before he could hear the NASA testimony about the pre-flight telecon. The next day, he was removed from the failure investigation team and returned to Utah.

Beginning in April, Boisjoly began to believe that for the previous month he had been used solely for public relations purposes. Although given the title of Seal Coordinator for the redesign effort, he was isolated from NASA and the seal redesign effort. His design information had been changed without his knowledge and presented without his feedback. On May 1, 1986, in a briefing preceding closed sessions before the Rogers Commission, Ed Garrison, President of Aerospace Operations for Morton Thiokol, chastised Boisjoly for "airing the company's dirty laundry" with the memos he had given the Commission. The next day, Boisjoly testified about the change in his job assignment. Commission Chairman Rogers criticized Thiokol management, "if it appears that you're punishing the two people or at least two of the people who are right about the decision and objected to the launch which ultimately resulted in criticism of Thiokol and then they're demoted or feel that they are being retaliated against, that is a very serious matter. It would seem to me, just speaking for myself, they should be promoted, not demoted or pushed aside" (R.C., V, p. 1586).

Boisjoly now sensed a major rift developing within the corporation. Some co-workers perceived that his testimony was damaging the company image. In an effort to clear the air, he and McDonald requested a private meeting with the company's three top executives, which was held on May 16, 1986. According to

Boisjoly, management was unreceptive throughout the meeting. The CEO told McDonald and Boisjoly that the company "was doing just fine until Al and I testified about our job reassignments" (Boisjoly, 1987). McDonald and Boisjoly were nominally restored to their former assignments, but Boisjoly's position became untenable as time passed. On July 21, 1986, Roger Boisjoly requested an extended sick leave from Morton Thiokol.

Ethical Analysis

It is clear from this case study that Roger Boisjoly's experiences before and after the Challenger disaster raise numerous ethical questions that are integral to any explanation of the disaster and applicable to other management situations, especially those involving highly complex technologies. The difficulties and uncertainties involved in the management of these technologies exacerbate the kind of bureaucratic syndromes that generate ethical conflicts in the first place. In fact, Boisjoly's experiences could well serve as a paradigmatic case study for such ethical problems, ranging from accountability to corporate loyalty and whistle-blowing. Underlying all these issues, however, is the problematic relationship between individual and organizational responsibility. Boisjoly's experiences graphically portray the tensions inherent in this relationship in a manner that discloses its importance in the causal sequence leading to the Challenger disaster. The following analysis explicates this and the implications it has for other organizational settings.

By focusing on the problematic relationship between individual and organizational responsibility, this analysis reveals that the organizational structure governing the space shuttle program became the locus of responsibility in such a way that not only did it undermine the responsibilities of individual decision makers within the process, but it also became a means of avoiding real, effective responsibility throughout the entire management system. The first clue to this was clearly articulated as early as 1973 by the board of inquiry that was formed to investigate the accident which occurred during the launch of Skylab I:

> The management system developed by NASA for manned space flight places large emphasis on rigor, detail, and thoroughness. In hand with this emphasis comes formalism, extensive documentation, and visibility in detail to senior management. While nearly perfect, such a system can submerge the concerned individual and depress the role of the intuitive engineer or analyst. It may not allow full play for the intuitive judgment or past experience of the individual. An emphasis on management systems can, in itself, serve to separate the people engaged in the program from the real world of hardware (Quoted in Christiansen, 1987, p. 23).

To examine the prescient statement in ethical terms is to see at another level the serious consequences inherent in the situation it describes. For example, it points to a dual meaning of responsibility. One meaning emphasizes carrying out an authoritatively prescribed review process, while the second stresses the cognitive independence and input of every individual down the entire chain of authority. The first sense of responsibility shifts the ethical center of gravity precipitously away from individual moral agency onto the review process in such a way that what was originally set up to guarantee flight readiness with the professional and personal integrity of the responsible individuals, instead becomes a means of evading personal responsibility for decisions made in the review process.

A crucial, and telling, example of this involves the important question asked by the Rogers Commission as to why the concerns raised by the Morton Thiokol engineers about the effects of cold weather on the O-rings during the teleconference the night before the launch were not passed up from Level III to Levels II or I in the preflight review process. The NASA launch procedure clearly demands that decisions and objections methodically follow a prescribed path up all levels. Yet, Lawrence Mulloy, operating at Level III as the Solid Rocket Booster Project Manager at MSFC, did not transmit the Morton Thiokol concerns upward (through his immediate superior, Stanley Reinartz) to Level II. When asked by Chairman Rogers to explain why, Mr. Mulloy testified:

> At that time, and I still consider today, that was a Level III issue, Level III being a SRB element or an external tank element or Space Shuttle main engine element or an Orbiter. There was no violation of Launch Commit Criteria. There was no waiver required in my judgment at that time and still today (R.C., I, p. 98).

In examining this response in terms of shifting responsibility onto the review process itself, there are two things that are particularly striking in Mr. Mulloy's statement. The first is his emphasis that this was a "Level III issue." In a formal sense, Mr. Mulloy is correct. However, those on Level III also had the authority—and, one would think, especially in this instance given the heated discussion on the effects of cold on the O-rings, the motivation—to pass objections and concerns on to Levels II and I. But here the second important point in Mr. Mulloy's testimony comes into play when he states, "there was no violation of Launch Commit Criteria." In other words, since there was no Launch Commit Criteria for joint temperature, concerns about joint temperature did not officially fall under the purview of the review process. Therefore, the ultimate justification for Mr. Mulloy's position rests on the formal process itself. He was just following the rules by staying within the already established scope of the review process.

This underscores the moral imperative executives must exercise by creating and maintaining organizational systems that do not separate the authority of decision makers from the responsibility they bear for decisions, or insulate them from the consequences of their actions or omissions.

Certainly, there can be no more vivid example than the shuttle program to verify that, in fact, "an emphasis on management systems can, in itself, serve to separate the people engaged in the program from the real world of hardware." Time and time again the lack of communication that lay at the heart of the Rogers Commission finding that "there was a serious flaw in the decision making process leading up to the launch of flight 51-L" (R.C., I, p. 104) was explained by the NASA officials or managers at Morton Thiokol with such statements as, "that is not my reporting channel," or "he is not in the launch decision chain," or "I didn't meet with Mr. Boisjoly, I met with Don Ketner, who is the task team leader" (R.C., IV, p. 821, testimony of Mr. Lund). Even those managers who had direct responsibility for line engineers and workmen depended on formalized memo writing procedures for communication to the point that some "never talked to them directly" (Feynman, 1988, p. 33).

Within the atmosphere of such an ambiguity of responsibility, when a life threatening conflict arose within the management system and individuals (such as Roger Boisjoly and his engineering associates at Morton Thiokol) tried to reassert the full weight of their individual judgments and attendant responsibilities, the very purpose of the flight readiness review process, i.e., to arrive at the "technical" truth of the situation, which includes the recognition of the uncertainties involved as much as the findings, became subverted into an adversary confrontation in which "adversary" truth, with its suppression of uncertainties, became operative (Wilmotte, 1970).

What is particularly significant in this radical transformation of the review process, in which the Morton Thiokol engineers were forced into "the position of having to prove that it was unsafe instead of the other way around" (R.C., IV, p. 822; see also p. 793), is that what made the suppression of technical uncertainties possible is precisely that mode of thinking which, in being challenged by independent professional judgments, gave rise to the adversarial setting in the first place: groupthink. No more accurate description for what transpired the night before the launch of the Challenger can be given than the definition of groupthink as:

> a mode of thinking that people engage in when they are deeply involved in a cohesive in-group, when the members' strivings for unanimity override their motivation to realistically appraise alternative courses of action. . . . Groupthink refers to the deterioration of mental efficiency, reality testing, and moral judgment that results from in-group pressures (Janis, 1972, p. 9).

From this perspective, the full import of Mr. Mason's telling Mr. Lund to "take off his engineering hat and put on his management hat" is revealed. He did not want another technical, reality-based judgment of an independent professional engineer. As he had already implied when he opened the caucus by stating "a management decision was necessary," he wanted a group decision, specifically one that would, in the words of the Rogers Commission, "accommodate a major customer" (R.C., I, p. 104). With a group decision the objections of the engineers could be mitigated, the risks shared, fears allayed, and the attendant responsibility diffused.[1]

This analysis is not meant to imply that groupthink was a pervasive or continuous mode of thinking at either NASA or Morton Thiokol. What is suggested is a causal relationship between this instance of groupthink and the ambiguity of responsibility found within the space shuttle program. Whenever a management system, such as NASA's generates "a mindset of 'collective responsibility' " by leading "individuals to defer to the anonymity of the process and not focus closely enough on their individual responsibilities in the decision chain," (N.R.C. Report, 1988, p.

68) and there is a confluence of the kind of pressures that came to bear on the decision making process the night before the launch, the conditions are in place for groupthink to prevail.

A disturbing feature of so many of the analyses and commentaries on the Challenger disaster is the reinforcement, and implicit acceptance, of this shift away from individual moral agency with an almost exclusive focus on the flaws in the management system, organizational structures and/or decision making process. Beginning with the findings of the Rogers Commission investigation, one could practically conclude that no one had any responsibility whatsoever for the disaster. The Commission concluded that "there was a serious flaw in the decision making process leading up to the launch of flight 51-L. A well structured and managed system emphasizing safety would have flagged the rising doubts about the Solid Rocket Booster joint seal." Then the Commission report immediately states, "Had these matters been clearly stated and emphasized in the flight readiness process in terms reflecting the views of most of the Thiokol engineers and at least some of the Marshall engineers, it seems likely that the launch of 51-L might not have occurred when it did" (R.C., I, p. 104). But the gathering and passing on of such information was the responsibility of specifically designated individuals, known by name and position in the highly structured review process. Throughout this process there had been required "a series of formal, legally binding certifications, the equivalent of airworthiness inspections in the aviation industry. In effect the myriad contractor and NASA personnel involved were guaranteeing Challenger's flight readiness with their professional and personal integrity" (McConnell, 1987, p. 17).

When the Commission states in its next finding that "waiving of launch constraints appears to have been at the expense of flight safety," the immediate and obvious question would seem to be: Who approved the waivers and assumed this enormous risk? And why? This is a serious matter! A launch constraint is only issued because there is a safety problem serious enough to justify a decision not to launch. However, the Commission again deflects the problem onto the system by stating, "There was no system which made it imperative that launch constraints and waivers of launch constraints be considered by all levels of management" (R.C., 1986, I, p. 104).

There are two puzzling aspects to this Commission finding. First, the formal system already contained the requirement that project offices inform at least Level II of launch constraints. The Commission addressed the explicit violation of this requirement in the case of a July 1985 launch constraint that had been imposed on the Solid Rocket Booster because of O-ring erosion on the nozzle:

> NASA Levels I and II apparently did not realize Marshall had assigned a launch constraint within the Problem Assessment System. This communication failure was contrary to the requirement, contained in the NASA Problem Reporting and Corrective Action Requirements System, that launch constraints were to be taken to Level II (R.C., 1986, I, pp. 138–139; see also p. 159).

Second, the Commission clearly established that the individual at Marshall who both imposed and waived the launch constraint was Lawrence Mulloy, SRB Project

Manager. Then why blame the management system, especially in such a crucial area as that of launch constraints, when procedures of that system were not followed? Is that approach going to increase the accountability of individuals within the system for future Flights?

Even such an independent minded and probing Commission member as Richard Feynman, in an interview a year after the disaster, agreed with the avoidance of determining individual accountability for specific actions and decisions. He is quoted as saying, "I don't think it's correct to try to find out which particular guy happened to do what particular thing. It's the question of how the atmosphere could get to such a circumstance that such things were possible without anybody catching on." Yet, at the same time Feynman admitted that he was not confident that any restructuring of the management system will ensure that the kinds of problems that resulted in the Challenger disaster—"danger signs not seen and warnings not heeded"—do not recur. He said, "I'm really not sure that any kind of simple mechanism can cure stupidity and dullness. You can make up all the rules about how things should be, and they'll go wrong if the spirit is different, if the attitudes are different over time and as personnel change" (Chandler, 1987, p. 50).

The approach of the Rogers Commission and that of most of the analyses of the Challenger disaster is consistent with the growing tendency to deny any specific responsibility to individual persons within corporate or other institutional settings when things go wrong. Although there are obviously many social changes in modern life that justify the shift in focus from individuals to organizational structures as bearers of responsibility, this shift is reinforced and exaggerated by the way people think about and accept those changes. One of the most pernicious problems of modern times is the almost universally held belief that the individual is powerless, especially within the context of large organizations where one may perceive oneself, and be viewed, as a very small, and replaceable, cog. It is in the very nature of this situation that responsibility may seem to become so diffused that no one person IS responsible. As the National Research Council committee, in following up on the Rogers Commission, concluded about the space shuttle program:

> Given the pervasive reliance on teams and boards to consider the key questions affecting safety, 'group democracy' can easily prevail . . . in the end all decisions become collective ones (N.R.C. Report, pp. 68 and 70).

The problem with this emphasis on management systems and collective responsibility is that it fosters a vicious circle that further and further erodes and obscures individual responsibility. This leads to a paradoxical—and untenable—situation (such as in the space shuttle program) in which decisions are made and actions are performed by individuals or groups of individuals but not attributed to them. It thus reinforces the tendency to avoid accountability for what anyone does by attributing the consequences to the organization or decision making process. Again, shared, rather than individual, risk-taking and responsibility become operative. The end result can be a cancerous attitude that so permeates an organization or management system that it metastasizes into decisions and acts of life-threatening irresponsibility.

In sharp contrast to this prevalent emphasis on organizational structures, one of the most fascinating aspects of the extensive and exhaustive investigations into the Challenger disaster is that they provide a rare opportunity to re-affirm the sense and importance of individual responsibility. With the inside look into the space shuttle program these investigations detail, one can identify many instances where personal responsibility, carefully interpreted, can properly be imputed to NASA officials and to its contractors. By so doing, one can preserve, if only in a fragmentary way, the essentials of the traditional concept of individual responsibility within the diluting context of organizational life. This effort is intended to make explicit the kind of causal links that are operative between the actions of individuals and the structures of organizations.

The criteria commonly employed for holding individuals responsible for an outcome are two: (1) their acts or omissions are in some way a cause of it; and (2) these acts or omissions are not done in ignorance or under coercion (Thompson, 1987, p. 47). Although there are difficult theoretical and practical questions associated with both criteria, especially within organizational settings, nevertheless, even a general application of them to the sequence of events leading up to the Challenger disaster reveals those places where the principle of individual responsibility must be factored in if our understanding of it is to be complete, its lessons learned, and its repetition avoided.

The Rogers Commission has been criticized—and rightly so—for looking at the disaster "from the bottom up but not from the top down," with the result that it gives a clearer picture of what transpired at the lower levels of the Challenger's flight review process than at its upper levels (Cook, 1986). Nevertheless, in doing so, the Commission report provides powerful testimony that however elaborately structured and far reaching an undertaking such as the space shuttle program may be, individuals at the bottom of the organizational structure can still play a crucial, if not deciding, role in the outcome. For in the final analysis, whatever the defects in the Challenger's launch decision chain were that kept the upper levels from being duly informed about the objections of the engineers at Morton Thiokol, the fact remains that the strenuous objections of these engineers so forced the decision process at their level that the four middle managers at Morton Thiokol had the full responsibility for the launch in their hands. This is made clear in the startling testimony of Mr. Mason, when Chairman Rogers asked him: "Did you realize, and particularly in view of Mr. Hardy's (Deputy Director of Science and Engineering at MSFC) point that they wouldn't launch unless you agreed, did you fully realize that in effect, you were making a decision to launch, you and your colleagues?" Mr. Mason replied, "Yes, sir" (R.C., 1986, IV, p. 770).

If these four men had just said no, the launch of the Challenger would not have taken place the next day. Could there have been any doubt about what was at stake in their decision, or about the degree of risk involved? Not in view of the follow up testimony of Brian Russell, another Thiokol engineer present at the teleconference. Mr. Russell was asked by Mr. Acheson to give his recollection of the thought process followed in his mind "in the change of position between the view presented in the telecon that Thiokol was opposed to the launch, and the subsequent conclusion of the caucus within the company" (R.C., 1986, IV, p. 821). In the course of his response, Mr. Russell stated:

> But I felt in my mind that once we had done our very best to explain why we were concerned, and we meaning those in the camp who really felt strongly about the recommendation of 53 degrees, the decision was to be made, and a poll was then taken. And I remember distinctly at the time wondering whether I would have the courage, if asked, and I thought I might be, what I would do and whether I would be alone. I didn't think I would be alone, but I was wondering if I would have the courage, I remember that distinctly, to stand up and say no . . . I was nervous . . . there was a nervousness there that we were increasing the risk, and I believe all of us knew that if it were increased to the level of O-ring burnthrough, what the consequences would be. And I don't think there's any question in anyone's mind about that (R.C., 1986, IV, pp. 822–823).

Some pertinent observations that have direct implications for managers in any organization must be made about where the principle of individual responsibility intersects with the structural flaws and organizational deterioration that have been attributed such a prominent role in the Challenger disaster. While it is on the basis of these flaws that the Rogers Commission absolved NASA officials of any direct responsibility for the disaster, it must nevertheless be pointed out that such officials "act in the context of a continuing institution, not an isolated incident, and they or other officials therefore may be culpable for creating the structural faults of the organization, or for neglecting to notice them, or for making inadequate efforts to correct them" (Thompson, 1987, p. 46). While it is true that attributing responsibility demands precision in determining the consequences of acts as much as in identifying the agents, this specificity of outcomes "does not preclude responsibility for patterns of decision and decision making" (Thompson, 1987, p. 48). Therefore, among the outcomes for which managers are held responsible, the continuing practices, standards, and structures of their organizations should be included.

Of all the descriptions of the flaws, break downs, and deterioration of NASA's managerial system, none point to any failures that fall outside the well-documented pathologies of bureaucratic behavior (e.g., lack of communication, distortion of information as it passes up the hierarchy, jealousy of existing lines of authority, bias in favor of the status quo, bureaucratic turf protection, power games, inclination to view the public interest through the distorted lens of vested interests, the "think positive" or "can-do" syndrome), and, as such, they can be anticipated. That bureaucratic routines "have a life of their own, often roaming beyond their original purpose, is a fact of organizational behavior that officials should be expected to appreciate. The more the consequences of a decision fit such bureaucratic patterns, the less an official can plausibly invoke the excuse from ignorance" (Thompson, 1987, p. 61).

So much has been made of NASA's top officials not being fully informed of the extent of the problems with the O-rings, and specifically of the Thiokol engineers' objections to the Challenger launch in cold weather, that an analysis of the disaster in *Fortune* magazine had as its title, "NASA's Challenge: Ending Isolation at the Top" (Brody, 1986). The actual extent of their isolation has been questioned, and even the Rogers Commission is not consistent on this issue. In its findings for Chapter V, the Commission states, "A well structured and managed system emphasizing safety would have flagged the rising doubts about the Solid Rocket Booster joint seal." Nevertheless, it concludes in the next chapter that "the O-ring erosion history presented to Level I at NASA headquarters in August 1985 was sufficiently detailed to require corrective action prior to the next flight" (R.C., 1986, I, pp. 104 and 148).

Whatever the extent of their ignorance, an important principle comes into play in determining the degree of individual responsibility. It is implied in Richard Feynman's position where he drew the line in not ascribing accountability for the Challenger disaster to specific individuals. Referring to Jesse Moore, Associate Administrator for Space Flight, the Level I manager with whom final approval for launch rested, Feynman maintained, "the guy at the top never should have an excuse that nobody told him. It seemed to me he ought to go out and find out what's going on" (Chandler, 1987, p. 50). The moral principle underlying Feynman's position here and which must be considered in tracing the boundaries of individual responsibility *vis-à-vis* the question of ignorance is the principle of "indirect responsibility."

As applied to the issue of ignorance, this principle confronts anyone in an organization with the inherent expectations of his or her position of power and level of expertise. The contours of indirect responsibility follow in the wake of these expectations because the standards against which to measure a claim of ignorance are precisely the standards of a given position and requisite knowledge. Therefore, to reject an excuse from ignorance it is sufficient to say: You are indirectly responsible for what has transpired because, given your position and professional experience, if you didn't know, you should have (Rosenblatt, 1983).

Although this principle operates in a gray area where the difference between indirect responsibility and pardonable ignorance can be marginal, a tragic, complex event like the Challenger disaster demands its application. Like the law, ethical thought must not be willing to accept ignorance as a sufficient excuse when it can be reasonably established that those in the causal sequence or in positions of authority should have known, or found out before acting or rendering decisions. This is especially true for managers who become instruments of their own ignorance whenever they prevent the free and complete flow of information to themselves, either directly by their acts, or indirectly through the subtle messages they convey to their subordinates, in their management style, or by the organizational climate they help create (Thompson, 1987, pp. 60–61).

Although fragmentary and tentative in its formulation, this set of considerations points toward the conclusion that however complex and sophisticated an organization may be, and no matter how large and remote the institutional network needed to manage it may be, an active and creative tension of responsibility must be maintained at every level of the operation. Given the size and complexity of such endeavors, the only way to ensure that tension of attentive and effective responsibility is to give the primacy of responsibility to that ultimate principle of all moral conduct: the human individual—even if this does necessitate, in too many instances under present circumstances, that individuals such as Roger Boisjoly, when they attempt to exercise their responsibility, must step forward as moral heroes. In so doing, these individuals do not just bear witness to the desperate need for a system of full accountability in the face of the immense power and reach of modern technology and institutions. They also give expression to the very essence of what constitutes the moral life. As Roger Boisjoly has stated in reflecting on his own experience, "I have been asked by some if I would testify again if I knew in advance of the potential consequences to me and my career. My answer is always an immediate 'yes.' I couldn't live with any self-respect if I tailored my actions based upon the personal consequences" (Boisjoly, 1987).

NOTES

1. A contrasting interpretation of the meeting the night before the launch given by Howard Schwartz, is that NASA began to view itself as the ideal organization that did not make mistakes. According to Schwartz, "The organization ideal is an image of perfection. It is, so to speak, an idea of God. God does not make mistakes. Having adopted the idea of NASA as the organization ideal it follows that the individual will believe that, if NASA has made a decision, that decision will be correct" (Schwartz, 1987).

In his testimony before the Rogers Commission, Roger Boisjoly indicated the extent to which NASA procedure had changed: "This was a meeting (the night before the launch) where the determination was to launch, and it was up to us to prove beyond the shadow of a doubt that it was not safe to do so. This is the total reverse to what the position usually is in a preflight conversation or a flight readiness review" (Boisjoly, 1986).

As Schwartz indicates: "If it was a human decision, engineering standards of risk should prevail in determining whether it was safe to launch. On the other hand, if the decision was a NASA decision, it is simply safe to launch, since NASA does not make mistakes" (Schwartz, 1987).

REFERENCES

Boisjoly, Roger M. 1985a. Applied Mechanics Memorandum to Robert K. Lund, Vice President, Engineering, Wasatch Division, Morton Thiokol, Inc., July 31.

Boisjoly, Roger M. 1985b. Activity Report, SRM Seal Erosion Task Team Status, October 4.

Boisjoly, Roger M. 1987. Ethical Decisions: Morton Thiokol and the Shuttle Disaster. Speech given at Massachusetts Institute of Technology, January 7.

Boling, T. Edwin and Dempsey, John. 1981. "Ethical dilemmas in government: Designing an organizational response," *Public Personnel Management Journal* 10, 11–18.

Brody, Michael. 1986. "NASA's challenge: Ending isolation at the top." *Fortune* 113 (May 12), pp. 26–32.

Chandler, David. 1987. "Astronauts gain clout in 'revitalized' NASA," *Boston Globe* 1 (January 26), 50.

Christiansen, Donald. 1987. "A system gone awry," *IEEE Spectrum* 24 (3), 23.

Cook, Richard C. 1986. "The Rogers commission failed," *The Washington Monthly* 18 (9), 13–21.

DeGeorge, Richard T. 1981. "Ethical responsibilities of engineers in large organizations: The Pinto Case," *Business and Professional Ethics Journal* 1, 1–14.

Feynman, Richard P. 1988. "An outsider's view of the Challenger inquiry," *Physics Today* 41 (2) 26–37.

Janis, Irving L. 1972. *Victims of Groupthink,* Boston, MA: Houghton Mifflin Company.

Kilminster, J. C. 1985. Memorandum (E000-FY86-003) to Robert Lund, Vice President, Engineering, Wasatch Division, Morton Thiokol, Inc., July 5.

McConnell, Malcolm. 1987. *Challenger, A Major Malfunction: A True Story of Politics, Greed, and the Wrong Stuff,* Garden City, N.J.: Doubleday and Company, Inc.

Mankin, Hart T. "Commentary on 'Ethical responsibilities of engineers in large organizations: The Pinto Case.' " *Business and Professional Ethics Journal* 1, 15–17.

National Research Council. 1988. *Post-Challenger Evaluation of Space Shuttle Risk Assessment and Management,* Washington, D.C.: National Academy Press.

Report of the Presidential Commission on the Space Shuttle Challenger Accident. 1986. Washington, D.C.: U.S. Government Printing Office.

Rosenblatt, Roger. 1983. "The commission report: The law of the mind." *Time* 126 (February 21), 39–40.

Schwartz, Howard S. 1987. "On the psychodynamics of organizational disaster: The case of the Space Shuttle Challenger," *The Columbia Journal of World Business,* Spring.

Thompson, Dennis F. 1987. *Political Ethics and Public Office,* Cambridge, MA: Harvard University Press.

Wilmotte, Raymond M. 1970. "Engineering truth in competitive environments," *IEEE Spectrum* 7 (5), 45–49.

DISCUSSION QUESTIONS

1. What moral conflicts existed within NASA in deciding whether to launch the shuttle?
2. How could the individual engineer affect the organization in the launch decision-making?

XIII
Education

WHAT TO FOCUS ON:

1. What is the proper role of education? Should educational programs place more emphasis on vocational preparation or intellectual curiosity and growth?
2. Does involvement in big-time college sports enhance or detract from the educational experience of student athletes?

IN MODERN TECHNOLOGICAL SOCIETIES formal education has had an increasingly pervasive impact on peoples' lives. Knowledge has become an important source of power. However, formal education on a mass scale is a relatively recent historical phenomenon. In the past, formal education was not necessary because a child learned everything he or she needed to know from his family or from religious authorities. Basically, education is an extension of the process of socialization. General education refers to the transmission of culture and the acquisition of the knowledge, skills, and values necessary to participate in one's society. In a hunting and gathering society, a child learns the skills necessary for survival by observing his parents and other community members. As the knowledge base and technology of a social system expands and becomes more complex, the need for formal, specialized education increases. In a highly technological society, the rapid explosion of knowledge often requires a constant re-education of its members. Due to increased specialization and the expanding knowledge base of modern societies, formal education has come to serve a gatekeeping function. Rather than assess people by their personal characteristics and life experiences, we focus on external signs of legitimation—degrees, resumés, and vitaes. We have increasingly become a credential-oriented system.

Although we place great emphasis and faith on formal education in contemporary life, there has been an ongoing controversy concerning the proper functions and goals of education. One viewpoint is that education should serve a utilitarian and practical function. The purpose of education is to provide an individual with the specialized skills necessary for the job market. Others argue that this perspective is too narrow and focused and results in limiting rather than expanding the potential of individuals.

In the first selection, "Democratic Faith and Education," John Dewey provides a classic statement on the importance of "liberal arts" education. Although Dewey wrote this essay during the height of World War II, his message is relevant to current issues in education. Dewey points out that one of the problems with specialized or vocational education is that "it is not presented in connection with the ways in which it actually enters every aspect and phase of present human life." Education and science do not have a life of their own and should not be isolated from "man's serious moral concerns." For Dewey, the task of education is to "humanize science." Dewey is also concerned about inequality and its relationship to educational processes. Dewey contends that the denial of liberal arts education results "in a denial of democracy." An issue in education and society is the social placement of individuals in educational structures. Rather than serving as an agent of upward social mobility, education may function to restrict one's mobility.

One of the editors of this volume, Charles Selengut, picks up on this theme. In the second article, "Should Social Background Count," Selengut focuses on the role of community colleges as educational gatekeepers. What is the proper role and mission of community colleges? Should community colleges serve the needs of local industry and business by training its students for low-entry positions? Are some community colleges shortchanging their students both "vocationally and intellectually" by lack of exposure to the humanities and social sciences? Is higher education resulting in the "denial of democracy"?

Big-time sports is a major part of the life of many colleges and universities. A successful team puts the school in the national spotlight, pays the bills, and solidifies the emotional and financial support of alumni. A major problem in higher education is the tension between the integrity of academic standards and the lure of the marketplace. In the third selection, Peter Adler and Patricia A. Adler discuss their sociological study of a big-time basketball program at a midwestern university. They trace the increasing alienation of student-athletes from academics and college life in general. Who is using whom? Is the athlete using the school or is the school using the athlete?

In the past, educational managers have placed great emphasis on one's IQ test score. This magic number could be used to sort students into different tracks or groups in order to prepare them for jobs or careers that corresponded with their IQ potential. In the final article, Jerome Kagan offers some refreshing insight on the IQ controversy. He points out that the cultural bias that exists in IQ tests provides the white middle class with a distinct advantage over other ethnic, racial, and social class groups. Kagan provides some clarity on the social and political implications of the concept of intelligence.

Article 35

Democratic Faith and Education

JOHN DEWEY

THE ORGANIZED ATTACK now being made against science and against technology as inherently materialistic and as usurping the place properly held by abstract moral precepts—abstract because divorcing ends from the means by which they must be realized—defines the issue we now have to face. Shall we go backwards or shall we go ahead to discover and put into practice the means by which science and technology shall be made fundamental in the promotion of human welfare? The failure to use scientific methods in creating understanding of human relationships and interests and in planning measures and policies that correspond in human affairs to the technologies in physical use is easily explained in historical terms. The new science began with things at the furthest remove from human affairs, namely with the stars of the heavens. From astronomy the new methods went on to win their victories in physics and chemistry. Still later science was applied in physiological and biological subject-matter. At every stage, the advance met determined resistance from the representatives of established institutions who felt their prestige was bound up with maintenance of old beliefs and found their class-control of others being threatened. In consequence, many workers in science found that the easiest way in which to procure an opportunity to carry on their inquiries was to adopt an attitude

From "Democratic Faith and Education," by John Dewey, *The Antioch Review,* Vol. 4, No. 2, Summer 1944. Reprinted by permission of the publisher.

of extreme specialization. The effect was equivalent to the position that their methods and conclusions were not and could not be "dangerous," since they had no point of contact with man's serious moral concerns. This position in turn served to perpetuate and confirm the older separation of man as man from the rest of nature and to intensify the split between the "material" and the moral and "ideal."

Thus it has come about that when scientific inquiry began to move from its virtually complete victories in astronomy and physics and its partial victory in the field of living things over into the field of human affairs and concerns, the interests and institutions that offered resistance to its earlier advance are gathering themselves together for a final attack upon that aspect of science which in truth constitutes its supreme and culminating significance. On the principle that offense is the best defense, respect for science and loyalty to its outlook are attacked as the chief source of all our present social ills. One may read, for example, in current literature such a condescending concession as marks the following passage: "Of course, the scientific attitude, though often leading to such a catastrophe, is not to be condemned," the immediate context showing that the particular "catastrophe" in mind consists of "errors leading to war . . . derived from an incorrect theory of truth." Since these errors are produced by belief in the applicability of scientific method to human as well as physical facts, the remedy, according to this writer is to abandon "the erroneous application of the methods and results of natural science to the problems of human life."

In three respects the passage is typical of the organized campaign now in active operation. There is first the assertion that such catastrophes as that of the present war are the result of devotion to scientific method and conclusions. The denunciation of "natural" science as applied to human affairs carries, in the second place, the implication that man is outside of and above nature, and the consequent necessity of returning to the medieval prescientific doctrine of a supernatural foundation and outlook in all social and moral subjects. Then thirdly there is the assumption, directly contrary to fact, that the scientific method has at the present time been seriously and systematically applied to the problems of human life.

I dignify the passage quoted by this reference to it because it serves quite as well as a multitude of other passages from reactionaries would to convey a sense of the present issue. It is true that the *results* of natural science have had a large share, for evil as well as for good, in bringing the world to its present pass. But it is equally true that "natural" science has been identified with *physical* science in a sense in which the physical is set over against the human. It is true that the interests and institutions which are now attacking science are just the forces which in behalf of a supernatural center of gravity are those that strive to maintain this tragic split in human affairs. Now the issue, as is becoming clearer every day, is whether we shall go backward or whether we shall go forward toward recognition in theory and practice of the indissoluble unity of the humanistic and the naturalistic.

What has all this to do with education? The answer to this question may be gathered from the fact that those who are engaged in assault upon science center their attacks upon the increased attention given by our schools to science and to its application in vocational training. In a world which is largely what it is today because of science and technology they propose that education should turn its back upon even the degree of recognition science and technology have received. They propose we turn our face to the medievalism in which so-called "liberal" arts were identified with literary arts: a course natural to adopt in an age innocent of knowledge of nature, an age in which the literary arts were the readiest means of rising above barbarism through acquaintance with the achievements of Greek-Roman culture. Their proposal is so remote from the facts of the present world, it involves such a bland ignoring of actualities, that there is a temptation to dismiss it as idle vaporing. But it would be a tragic mistake to take the reactionary assaults so lightly. For they are an expression of just the forces that keep science penned up in a compartment labelled "materialistic and anti-human." They strengthen all the habits and institutions which render that which is morally "ideal" impotent in action and which leave the "material" to operate without humane direction.

Let me return for the moment to my initial statement that the basic error of social idealists was the assumption that something called "natural law" could be trusted, with only incidental cooperation by human beings, to bring about the desired ends. The lesson to be learned is that human attitudes and efforts are the strategic center for promotion of the generous aims of peace among nations; promotion of economic security; the use of political means in order to advance freedom and equality; and the worldwide cause of democratic institutions. Anyone who starts from this premise is bound to see that it carries with it the basic importance of education in creating the habits and the outlook that are able and eager to secure the ends of peace, democracy, and economic stability.

When this is seen, it will also be seen how little has actually been done in our schools to render science and technology active agencies in creating the attitudes and dispositions and in securing the kinds of knowledge that are capable of coping with the problems of men and women today. Externally a great modification has taken place in subjects taught and in methods of teaching them. But when the changes are critically examined it is found that they consist largely in emergency concessions and accommodation to the urgent conditions and issues of the contemporary world. The standards and the controlling methods in education are still mainly those of a prescientific and pretechnological age. This statement will seem to many persons to be exaggerated. But consider the purposes which as a rule still govern instruction in just those subjects that are taken to be decisively "modern," namely science and vocational preparation. Science is taught upon the whole as a body of readymade information and technical skills. It is not taught as furnishing in its method the pattern for all effective intelligence conduct. It is taught upon the whole not with respect to the way in which it actually enters into human life, and hence as a supremely humanistic subject, but as if it had to do with a world which is "external" to human concerns. It is not presented in connection with the ways in which it actually enters into every aspect and phase of present human life. And it is hardly necessary to add that still less is it taught in connection with what scientific knowledge of human affairs might do in overcoming sheer drift. Scientific method and conclusions will not have gained a fundamentally important place in education until they are seen and treated as supreme agencies in giving direction to collective and cooperative human behavior.

The same sort of thing is to be said about the kind of use now made in education of practical and vocational subjects, so called. The reactionary critics are busy urging that the latter subjects be taught to the masses—who are said to be incapable of rising to the plane of the "intellectual" but who do the useful work which somebody has to do, and who may be taught by vocational education to do it more effectively. This view is of course an open and avowed attempt to return to that dualistic separation of ideas and action, of the "intellectual" and the "practical," of the liberal and servile arts, that marked the feudal age. And this reactionary move in perpetuation of the split from which the world is suffering is offered as a cure, a panacea, not as the social and moral quackery it actually is. As is the case with science, the thing supremely needful is to go forward. And the forward movement in the case of technology as in the case of science is to do away with the chasm which ancient and medieval educational practice and theory set up between the liberal and the vocational, not to treat the void, the hold, constituted by this chasm, as if it were a foundation for the creation of free society.

There is nothing whatever inherent in the occupations that are socially necessary and useful to divide them into those which are "learned" professions and those which are menial, servile, and illiberal. As far as such a separation exists in fact it is an inheritance from the earlier class structure of human relations. It is a denial of democracy. At the very time when an important, perhaps *the* important, problem in education is to fill education having an occupational direction with a genuinely liberal content, we have, believe it or not, a movement to cut vocational training off from any contact with what is liberating by relegating it to special schools devoted to inculcation of technical skills. Inspiring vocational education with a liberal spirit and filling it with a liberal content is not a utopian dream. It is a demonstrated possibility in schools here and there in which subjects usually labelled "practically useful" are taught charged with scientific understanding and with a sense of the social-moral applications they potentially possess.

If little is said in the foregoing remarks specifically upon the topic of democratic faith, it is because their bearing upon a democratic outlook largely appears upon their very face. Conditions in this country when the democratic philosophy of life and democratic institutions were taking shape were such as to encourage a belief that the latter were so natural to man; so appropriate to his very being, that if they were once established they would tend to maintain themselves. I cannot rehearse here the list of events that have given this naive faith a shock. They are contained in every deliberate attack upon democracy and in every expression of cynicism about its past failures and pessimism about its future—attacks and expressions which have to be taken seriously if they are looked at as signs of trying to establish democracy as an end in separation from the concrete means upon which the end depends.

Democracy is not an easy road to take and follow. On the contrary, it is as far as its realization is concerned in the complex conditions of the contemporary world a supremely difficult one. Upon the whole we are entitled to take courage from the fact that it has worked as well as it has done. But to this courage we must add, if our courage is to be intelligent rather than blind, the fact that successful maintenance of democracy demands the utmost in use of the best available methods to procure a social knowledge that is reasonably commensurate with our physical knowledge, and the invention and use of forms of social engineering reasonably commensurate with our technological abilities in physical affairs.

This then is the task indicated. It is, if we employ large terms, to humanize science. This task in the concrete cannot be accomplished save as the fruit of science, which is named technology, is also humanized. And the task can be executed in the concrete only as it is broken up into vital applications of intelligence in a multitude of fields to a vast diversity of problems so that science and technology may be rendered servants of the democratic hope and faith. The cause is capable of inspiring loyalty in thought and deed. But there has to be joined to aspiration and effort the formation of free, wide-ranging, trained attitudes of observation and understanding such as incorporate within themselves, as a matter so habitual as to be unconscious, the vital principles of scientific method. In this achievement science, education, and the democratic cause meet as one. May we be equal to the occasion. For it is our human problem and if a solution is found it will be through the medium of human desire, human understanding, and human endeavor.

DISCUSSION QUESTIONS

1. According to Dewey, what is the major task of education? How can education function to "humanize" science?
2. What does Dewey mean by the "denial of democracy"? In what ways are educational systems undemocratic?

Article 36

Should Social Background Count?

CHARLES SELENGUT

IN AN ARTICLE, "Thinking About the Aims of Education," (Mid-Career Fellowship Program, Princeton University, *Bulletin,* Winter 1984), Donald Schmeltekopf suggests that "we educators tacitly comply with the materialistic outlook of the present generation when we sacrifice our legitimate authority as educators to the interests of the marketplace, the polity, and current student desires for occupational preparation." Schmeltekopf acknowledges the rightful place of vocational and professional training in higher education but calls upon the nation's colleges to assert their traditional role in providing liberal education. Schmeltekopf's essay brings into clear focus a continuing dilemma regarding the community college curriculum, the tension between vocational training and humanistic learning.

I think the issues Schmeltekopf raises require continued attention and further analysis. In the last decade, according to most observers, the curriculum in community colleges has moved far in the direction of increased vocational training. David Breneman of the Brookings Institution described the situation quite accurately when he wrote that "community college leaders pride themselves on being responsive to the needs and wishes of the community and if people want technical training

From "Should Social Background Count?", by Charles Selengut, *The Community College Humanist,* Spring, 1984. Reprinted by permission of the Community College Humanities Association, Community College of Philadelphia.

uncluttered with general education, that is what they will get" (*AAHE Bulletin,* June 1980). Consequently, many community colleges have ignored or de-emphasized their liberal arts offerings. In attempts to cater to this or that development in computer-hardware production, business education or advanced high-technology, colleges have allocated scarce institutional resources to these areas leaving the humanities and social sciences woefully understaffed and underbudgeted. The much-used phrase "serving the community" has become quite frequently narrowly defined as serving the interests of local business and industry. The distinct needs of humanities programs have remained at the periphery of institutional concerns. While it is true that many colleges offer an array of courses in the liberal arts, the financial and administrative support for these programs have remained less than those provided to the more fashionable job-training and technology programs.

How is this state of higher education in America to be understood? Why have colleges—particularly community colleges but non-elite baccalaureate institutions as well—so quickly and with such seeming self-confidence jumped on the bandwagon of vocational education and preparation? Community college administrations tend to offer two main reasons for the emphasis on vocational training. First, many say the state's mandate to community colleges is to provide vocational training. This is what state legislators intended when, primarily in the 1960s, the major systems were set into place. Second, many hold that the typical community college student is not attending school for "disinterested learning" or the cultivation, in Veblen's term, of "idle curiosity," but for the distinctly utilitarian goal of preparing for a decently paying job. The students at community colleges, it is said, are practical minded, down-to-earth, not given to philosophical reflection or literary and sociological imagination.

I am less than sanguine about this view and believe the current emphasis on job training is problematic on several grounds. The focus on the acquisition of vocational "skills" for a specific job ignores the massive structural transformations now occuring in the workplace. Increasingly, in this age of rapid technological change, the most highly valued skills are not job specific. More valued is the ability to think clearly and critically in adapting general knowledge to concrete situations—true now for the factory as for the office. And it is precisely at this historical moment that the humanities and social sciences have much to offer. Sensitivity to cultural nuances, knowledge of international affairs, fluency in foreign languages, and the ability to apply logic and reason to changing work conditions are not superfluous talents but skills central to career success and mobility in the contemporary marketplace. No less important to an individual's present and future is the contribution of the humanities to the formation of a critical imagination. To contemplate the great books, masterpieces of art, or distant utopias is to transcend, at least for a time, the iron cages of culture and biography. Indeed, in more than a decade of community college teaching, I have found students demonstrating enormous "idle curiosity" and intellectual delight in their encounters with the humanities and social sciences.

Why then the denial of the rightful place of the humanities in the college curriculum? To understand the current situation, I believe, one needs to ask the classical sociological question, "in whose interest"? That is, in whose interest is it to remove attention, concern, and resources from the humanities? Clearly not in the interest of students enrolled in programs with little or no significant exposure to humanistic learning. Nor can we say that it is in the interest of a college community to operate without the lively interplay between the humanities and other branches of human endeavor. One must therefore consider whether the current situation is not more a function of cultural and class bias on the part of educational managers than on the supposed lack of student interest or vocational utility. Community college students are frequently drawn from a lower-status sector of the population and are consequently often labeled—in my view erroneously—as not interested in "higher learning," philosophical reflection, or critical thinking. This labeling process often results in stigmatization and self-fulfilling prophecy whereby persons so labeled take on the characteristics of the negative stereotype. The ethos, curriculum, and counseling at community colleges often reinforce the stereotype of the student as "vocationally minded." He/she is viewed as a person not interested in esthetic sensibility or scholarly insight but as one content to attain limited marketable skills.

Cultural elites, as the Italian sociologist Vilfredo Pareto pointed out, seek to maintain their hegemony through power or manipulation. Might the current emphasis on limited vocational training in community colleges represent an attempt to restrict access to the "higher" professions, banking, and the corporate world? The narrow focus on work-related education in community colleges provides, as has been pointed out before, a "cooling out process." Students are provided higher education but community college education cannot deliver what more elite institutions can, namely, access to the great humanistic traditions which results in the acquisition of skills, insights, and sensibilities necessary for career advancement.

Put another way, the lack of learning in the humanities and social sciences shortchanges students both vocationally and intellectually. We fail as educators when we prejudge student abilities and aspirations on the basis of social background. College educators should recognize that while students pursue vocational training, such activity does not entail the totality of their goals and educational needs. We do a disservice to students when we do not address in our curriculum their intellectual curiosity and search for meaning. Indeed, as Schmeltekopf puts it so well, "we sacrifice our legitimate authority" when we accept almost without question the prevailing values and assumptions of the marketplace. Courageous leadership is now needed which will recognize the continuing validity of humanistic studies for both vocational effectiveness and personal growth.

What is suggested here is no conspiracy view of American society. I am not saying that any elite has planned vocational education as an attempt to keep community college students "in their place." I do, however, maintain that as the system now operates—particularly in the unequal allocation of funds and resources to the humanities and the social sciences—community college students have unequal access to an authentic experience of humanistic learning. Vocational education without a thorough cultivation of the critical faculties of thinking, writing, and expression is a ticket to occupational and social-class stagnation. For community colleges to authentically serve the community, what is now required is a refocusing of direction and a redistribution of funds and personnel in realization of the centrality of humanistic learning in the post-modern age. I hope the community college movement born in progressive optimism will be in step with the realities of our time and the full aspirations of our students.

DISCUSSION QUESTIONS

1. In what ways does a college curriculum reflect the tensions between vocational training and humanistic learning?
2. According to Selengut, how does the lack of exposure to the humanities and social sciences limit a student both vocationally and intellectually?

Article 37

From Idealism to Pragmatic Detachment

The Academic Performance of College Athletes

PETER ADLER AND PATRICIA A. ADLER

IN RECENT YEARS, the relationship between the athletic participation and academic performance of college athletes has become a topic of scholarly concern. The sociological literature in this area, however, has been inconsistent in its findings. Some studies have cited a weak positive relationship, claiming that although most college athletes had poor academic records in high school, they have higher GPAs, lower attrition rates, and a greater likelihood of graduating than nonathletes because they receive extra tutoring, more attention, and special "breaks" (Hanks and Eckland, 1976; Henschen and Fry, 1984; Michener, 1976; Shapiro, 1984). But most studies of college athletes have found a negative relationship between athletic participation and academic performance. These studies conclude that athletes are unprepared for and uninterested in academics, that they come to college to advance their athletic careers rather than their academic careers; therefore, they have lower GPAs, higher attrition rates, and lower chances of graduating than other students

From "From Idealism to Pragmatic Detachment: The Academic Performance of College Athletes," by Peter Adler and Patricia A. Adler, *Sociology of Education,* Vol. 58, Oct. 1985, pp. 241–249.

(Cross, 1973; Edwards, 1984; Harrison, 1976; Nyquist, 1979; Purdy, Eitzen, and Hufnagel, 1982; Sack and Thiel, 1979; Spivey and Jones, 1975; Webb, 1968).

Our research, which also finds a negative relationship, extends previous studies in several ways. First, we show that although most college athletes ultimately become disillusioned with and detached from academics, many begin their college careers idealistically, caring about academics and intending to graduate. Second, we show that the structure of college athletics fosters the academic deindividuation of athletes. We trace the stages through which athletes progress as they become socialized to their position in the university environment and learn its structural characteristics. We describe how their academic goals and behavior become increasingly influenced by their athletic involvement. The initial academic aspirations of freshman athletes are considerably varied, but these various individual ideals gradually give way under the force of the structural conditions athletes encounter. Thus, by the time athletes complete their eligibility requirements, their academic attitudes and goals closely resemble each other's. This process, which reduces individual differences between athletes, is accompanied by collective academic detachment and diminished academic performance. Third, using a longitudinal analysis of process and change, made possible by our method of data collection, we show the influence of interconnecting factors on athletes' progression through college. This is the first systematic participant-observation study of college athletics. Such an in-depth, ethnographic investigation of this area (suggested by Coakley, 1982; Fine, 1979; Loy, McPherson, and Kenyon, 1978; Purdy et al., 1982) is useful for two reasons: (1) it enables us to determine whether athletic participation hinders or enhances academic performance, and (2) it reveals the factors and processes that produce this relationship. . . .

Methods and Setting

The Research. Over a four-year period (1980–1984), we conducted a participant-observation study of a major college basketball team. We used team field research strategies (Douglas, 1976) and differentiated, multiperspectival roles to enhance our data gathering and analysis. I (first author) was initially granted access to the team because the coaches became interested in our earlier works on the sociology of sport (Adler and Adler, 1978; Adler, 1981). After reading these and talking with me, they perceived me as an expert who could provide valuable counsel on interpersonal, organizational, and academic matters. Although college and professional sports settings are generally characterized by secrecy and an extreme sensitivity to the insider-outsider distinction (see Jonassohn, Turowetz, and Gruneau, 1981), I gradually gained the trust of significant gatekeepers, particularly the head coach, and was granted the status and privileges of an assistant coach. As the "team sociologist," my primary duty was to informally counsel players on social, academic, and personal matters and help them make the adjustment to college life and athletics. This role allowed me to become especially close to the athletes, who came to me with their problems, worries, or disgruntlements. Becoming an active member (Adler and

Adler, 1987) and interacting with other members on a daily basis was also the only way I could penetrate the inner sanctum and achieve the type of rapport and trust necessary for the study.[1]

The second author assumed the outsider role, "debriefing" me when I returned from the setting, looking for sociological patterns in the data, and ensuring that I retained a sociological perspective on my involvement. She helped me conduct a series of intensive, taped interviews with 7 of the coaches and with the 38 basketball players who passed through the program during the four years.[2] She also helped construct the final analysis and written reports.

The Setting. The research was conducted at a medium-size (6,000 students) private university (hereafter referred to as "the University") in the mid-south-central portion of the United States. Most of the students were white, suburban, and middle class. The University, which was striving to become one of the finer private universities in the region, had fairly rigorous academic standards. . . . Players were generally recruited from the surrounding region. Most of them came from the lower and middle classes, and 70% of them were black. In general, the basketball program represented what Coakley (1982) and Frey (1982) have termed big-time college athletics. Although it could not compare to the upper echelon of established basketball dynasties or to the really large athletic programs that wield enormous recruiting and operating budgets, its recent success has compensated for its small size and lack of historical tradition. The University's basketball program could best be described as up-and-coming. Because the basketball team (along with other teams in the athletic department) was ranked nationally and sent graduating members into the professional leagues, the entire athletic milieu was imbued with a sense of seriousness and purpose.

Academic Expectations

Contrary to the recent negative thought, noted earlier, most of the athletes we observed entered the University feeling idealistic about their impending academic experience and optimistic about their likelihood of graduating. Their idealistic orientation and aspirations derived from several sources. First, they had received numerous cultural messages that a college education would enhance their ability to be successful in our society (cf. Semyonov and Yuchtman-Yaar, 1981). These messages were reinforced by their families, their most outspoken significant others. One sophomore described his family's involvement in his academic career: "When my mom calls she always asks me, first, 'How you feelin,' second, 'How you doin' in school?' She won't even let me talk 'bout basketball 'til she hear I'm doin' okay in school. She always be thinkin' 'bout my future and wantin' me to get that degree." College coaches also reinforced these messages. During recruitment, the coaches stressed the positive aspects of a college education and the importance of graduating (cf. Cross, 1973). The athletes accepted the rhetoric of these sports personnel (what Tannenbaum and Noah [1959] called "sportuguese"), but they never really considered what a higher education entailed. Thus, a third factor fostering their optimism about academics was their naive assumption that after attending college for four years they would automatically get a degree. They never anticipated the amount or kind of academic work they would have to do to earn that degree. Many of them had not taken a sequence of college preparatory courses in high school.[3] . . .

In their first few months on campus, athletes' early idealism was strengthened. During these summer months, the coaches repeatedly stressed the importance of "getting that piece of paper." Once the school year began, freshman athletes attended required study halls nightly, were told how to get tutors, and were constantly reminded by the coach to go to class. One freshman, interviewed during the preseason, indicated his acceptance of the coaches' rhetoric: "If I can use my basketball ability to open up the door to get an education, hopefully I can use my degree to open up the door to get a good job. . . . I think that's really important to Coach, too, 'cause in practice he always be mentioning how important the degree is an' everything."

Although these athletes unquestionably cared more about their athletic and social lives than their academic performance, getting through school, at least in the abstract, was still important to them. For most, this period of early idealism lasted until the end of their freshman year. After this time, their naive, early idealism gradually became replaced by disappointment and growing cynicism as they realized how difficult it was to keep up with their schoolwork. They encountered unexpected problems in the articulation of the athletic, social, and academic spheres of the University.

Athletic Experiences

A major difference athletes encountered in moving from high school to college lay in the size of the athletic sphere. In high school, athletics was primary to their self-identities; but in college, it played an even more central role in their lives. It dominated all facets of their existence, including their academic involvement and performance.

A primary change in their athletic involvement was rooted in the *professionalization* of the sport. Upon entering college, freshman athletes immediately noticed its commercialization (cf Coakley, 1982; Eitzen, 1979; Hoch, 1972; Sack, 1977; Underwood, 1980). They were no longer playing for enjoyment. This was big business ("there's a lotta money ridin' on us"). As a result, basketball changed from a recreation to an occupation (cf. Ingham, 1975). The occupational dimensions of the sport and their desire to perform well intensified the pressure to win (cf. Odenkirk, 1981; Underwood, 1980). A senior described this emphasis on winning: "In college the coaches be a lot more concerned on winning and the money comin' in. If they don't win, they may get the boot, and so they pass that pressure on to us athletes. I go to bed every night and I be thinkin' 'bout basketball. That's what college athletics do to you. It take over you mind."

Professionalization also brought with it the fame and glamour of media attention. During the season, athletes were regularly in the newspaper and on television and were greeted as celebrities whenever they ventured off campus. Overall, then, the professionalization of college athletics drew athletes' focus to this arena and riveted it there. . . .

Athletes' academic performance was also affected by *coaches intervention* in their academic lives. Assistant coaches handled academic matters for the athletes, declaring their majors, registering them for courses, adjusting their schedules, and periodically contacting their professors (to monitor their progress). Athletes, therefore, were largely uninvolved in academic decision-making and did not interact directly with professors, academic counselors, or academic administrators. As a result, they failed to develop the knowledge, initiative, or, in many cases, the interest to handle these academic matters themselves. As one sophomore stated, "The day before class you go up to the office and they hand you a card that got your schedule all filled out on it. You don't say nothin' or think nothin' 'bout it, you just go. And it kinda make you feel like you not involved in it, 'cause you don't have nothin' to do with it. Like it's they's job, not yours."

Because the coaches managed these administrative matters, the athletes developed a false sense of security, a feeling that someone was looking out for them academically and would make sure that they were given another chance, a feeling that they could foul up and not have to pay the consequences. They believed that their coaches dominated their professors and the administrators, that they would be "taken care of" academically, and that they need not involve themselves in this arena. This also led them to distance themselves from their academics and to diminish their effort.

Having formed this belief, many athletes were surprised to discover, usually sometime during their sophomore or junior year, that this overseeing and management extended to administrative areas only. Coaches placed them in their courses, but they could not guarantee them special breaks. Athletes then realized, often too late, that they were responsible for attending classes and completing their assignments on their own and that they had to do the same work that other students did to pass their courses. Many athletes were shepherded through high school; therefore, they were ill-equipped to assume responsibilities in college and often failed to fulfill them.

Finally, the athletes received greater *reinforcement* for athletic performance than for academic performance. No one closely monitored their academic behavior, but they were carefully watched at games, practices, booster functions, and on road trips. The celebrity and social status they derived from the media, boosters, and fans brought them immediate gratification, which the academic realm, with its emphasis on future rewards, could not offer.

With a few exceptions, athletes' experiences within the academic realm brought neither close contact nor positive reinforcement. Like many other college students, athletes generally found their professors aloof and uninterested. One freshman gave his impressions of college professors:

> At my high school back home, the teachers would make sure everyone done the reading before we went on to the next subject. The teachers really cared if the students got behind, so sometimes they would teach individually. But here, by the

> next time the class meets, they ask if anyone has any questions, and if no one says anything, then most of them would give a pop quiz. I cannot really say the teachers care here, because if you get behind it's your problem, not theirs.

Given the paucity of contact with the faculty, the lack of reinforcement within the academic realm, and the omnipresence of the coaches, media, fans, and boosters, who provided both positive and negative feedback on daily athletic performance, it became easier for athletes to turn away from academics and concentrate their efforts on sport.

Social Experiences

The athletes' social experiences also affected their academic performance. Their social lives at the University were dominated by their relationships with other athletes. They had initially expected to derive both friendship and status recognition from a wide variety of students, both athletes and nonathletes, as they had in high school (cf. Coleman, 1961; Cusick, 1973; Eitzen, 1975; Rehberg and Schafer, 1968; Spady, 1970). But instead of being socially integrated, they found themselves isolated (cf. Antonelli, 1970). They were isolated geographically because they were housed in the athletes' dorm in a remote part of campus. They were cut off temporally by the demands of their practices, games, study halls, and booster functions. They were isolated culturally by their racial and socioeconomic differences from the rest of the student body. They were isolated physically by their size and build, which many students, especially women, found intimidating. A freshman described his feelings of social alienation:

> This school is nothing like I thought it would be when I left home. The social life is very different and I have to adjust to it. A main problem for me are the white people. Where I grew up, all my friends were black, so I really don't know how to act toward whites. Here, when I speak to some of them, they just give me a fake smile. I really can't understand the people here because this is college and everyone should have a good time socially.

Since they had few opportunities to interact with nonathletes, they formed extremely strong social bonds among themselves. Housed together in a dorm reserved almost exclusively for male athletes (primarily football and basketball players), they were bonded together into a reference group and peer subculture. Relations within this group were especially cohesive because they lived, played, and travelled together.

Within the dorm, athletes exchanged information about various individuals and how to handle certain situations. This helped them form common attitudes and beliefs about their athletic, social, and academic experiences. The peer subculture thus provided them with a set of norms and values that guided their interpretations and behavior within these three realms.

One of the most predominant influences of the peer subculture was its anti-intellectual and anti-academic character (cf. Coleman, 1960; Sack, 1977). Typically, dorm conversation centered on the athletic or social dimensions of the athletes' lives; little reference was made to academic, cultural, or intellectual pursuits (cf. Meggysey, 1971; Shaw, 1972). As one junior remarked, "If a athlete was living in the dorm with just ordinary people, what do you think they'll be talkin' about? Ordinary things. But you got all athletes here. What are they goin' be talkin' about? It won't be Reaganomics, believe me. It'll definitely be *Sports Illustrated.*" Separating athletes from other students thus made their athletic reality dominant and distanced them from any academic inclinations they may have had. . . .

Classroom Experiences

Athletes' attitudes toward academics and their effort and performance were also affected by the difficulties and disillusionments they encountered in the classroom. Athletes believed that many professors labeled them as jocks because they looked different from most of the other students, they were surrounded in their classes by other athletes, and they were identified by coaches early in the semester to the professors as athletes. They perceived, then, that professors treated them differently from the general student body. On the one hand, because of the widely held subcultural lore that as college athletes they would have special privileges and because of the important and visible role they played at the University, they commonly thought that professors would accord them greater tolerance—i.e., extra tutoring sessions, relaxed deadlines, relaxed academic standards (cf. Raney, Knapp, and Small, 1983). This perception was fostered by their placement, especially in their freshman year, in courses taught by sympathetic faculty members who tried to give them extra attention or assistance. Because of these placements, athletes often began college thinking that academics would not be a major concern. On the other hand, athletes also encountered a number of less sympathetic professors who they thought stereotyped them as dumb jocks or cocky athletes. In these cases they "rejected the rejectors" (Sykes and Matza, 1957), using persecution as a rationale for disengaging from academics. One player discussed his experiences with professors:

> Some are goin' help you, if they can, and you can always tell who they are 'cause you got a bunch o' athletes in your class. Some try to make it harder on you. They're out to get you 'cause they feel like you living like a king and it shouldn't be that way. With those jerks, it don't matter how hard you try. They gonna flunk you just 'cause you a athlete.

This differential treatment served to reinforce the perceptions that they were athletes more than students. Therefore, when they returned to their dorm rooms at night, exhausted and sore from practicing, it became easier for them to rationalize, procrastinate, and "fritter" (Bernstein, 1978) their time away instead of studying.

Athletes also became uninterested in academics because of the *content* of their classes. Many individuals placed in physical education or recreation courses, even those who were fairly uninterested in academics from the beginning, felt that their courses lacked academic or practical merit and were either comical, demeaning, or both. One sophomore articulated the commonly held view: "How could I get into this stuff? They got me takin' nutrition, mental retardation, square dancing, and camp counseling. I thought I was goin' learn something here. It's a bunch o' b.s."

When athletes enrolled in more advanced or demanding courses to fulfill their requirements, they often found themselves unequipped for the type of work expected. Because of their inadequate academic backgrounds, poor study habits, tight schedules, peer distractions, and waning motivation, the athletes often became frustrated and bored. Their anticipated positive feedback from academics was replaced by a series of disappointments from low grades and failed classes. One player described how his failures made him feel inadequate and uncertain: "When I first came here I thought I'd be goin' to class all the time and I'd study and that be it. But I sure didn't think it meant studyin' all the time. Back in high school you just be memorizin' things, but that's not what they want here. Back in high school I thought I be a pretty good student, but now I don't know. . . . "

Academic Adjustments

As college athletes progressed through school, they changed their perspectives and priorities, re-evaluating the feasibility of their original optimistic, albeit casually formed, academic goals. This caused them to effect a series of *pragmatic adjustments* in their academic attitudes, efforts, and goals.

First, whenever possible, athletes externalized the blame for their academic failures. Failures, for instance, were not caused by their own inadequacies or lack of effort but by boring professors, stupid courses, exhaustion, the coaches' demands, or injury. This allowed them to accept the frequent signs of failure more easily and served as an important neutralizing mechanism for their competitiveness.

More important, athletes re-examined their academic goals. Because of their initially optimistic expectations, some athletes had declared majors based on career choices that sounded good to them or their parents (e.g., doctor, teacher, engineer, or businessman). About one-fourth of the individuals who began in preprofessional majors stayed in these majors all the way through college and graduated.[4] Nevertheless, these individuals generally expended less effort and had less success than they had initially anticipated. Though they graduated in their original major, their academic performance was largely characterized by an attitude of getting by; in most cases, they achieved only the minimum GPA and took the minimum number of hours required for eligibility. One junior described how his attitude toward academics had changed during his years at college: "If I was a student like most other students I could do well, but when you play the calibre of ball we do, you just can't be an above-average student. What I strive for now is just to be an average student. My best GPA was 2.75. You just don't find the time to do all the reading."

More commonly, athletes in preprofessional majors found that a more concrete adjustment was necessary. The remaining three-quarters of this group dropped out of preprofessional programs and enrolled in more manageable majors. This shift indicated that they had abandoned both their academic idealism and their earlier career goals. Nevertheless, they still maintained the goal of graduating, regardless of the major. As one player commented, "Look at George [a former player]. He was a rec major, but now he's got a great job in sales, working for some booster. It don't matter what you major in as long as you keep your nose clean and get that piece of paper."

Athletes who began their college careers with lower academic aspirations, majoring in physical education or recreation, made corresponding adjustments. Approximately one-fifth of these athletes held onto their initial goal and graduated in one of these fields. But like the professional majors, they did not perform as well as they had planned. The other four-fifths realized, usually relatively late, that their chances of graduating from college were slight. This genuinely distressed them, because getting a degree had become both a hope and an expectation. They shifted their orientation, then, toward maintaining their athletic eligibility. A junior's remarks illustrate how this shift affected his attitude toward academics:

> I used to done thought I was goin' to school, but now I know it's not for real. . . . I don't have no academic goals no more. A player a coach is counting on, that's all he think about is ball. That's what he signed to do. So what you gotta do is show up, show your smilin' face, try as hard as you can. Don't just lay over in the room. That's all the coach can ask. Or else you may not find yourself playing next year.

By their senior year, when they had completed their final eligibility requirements, many members of this last group entirely abandoned their concern with their academic performance.[5] As one senior put it, "I just be waitin', man. I be waitin' for my shot at the NBA. I be thinking about that all the time. Once the season is over, I be splittin'. I don't see no reason to go to classes no more."

As a result of their experiences at the University, athletes grew increasingly cynical about and uninterested in academics. They accepted their marginal status and lowered their academic interest, effort, and goals. They progressively detached themselves from caring about or identifying themselves with this sphere. . . .

Discussion

The transformation athletes undergo corresponds to Goffman's (1959) conception of occupational role progression, in which the attitudes of persons socialized to a new social status (here, college athlete) evolve from belief to disbelief. This process begins with the learning and internalization of charter values. For college athletes, this occurs during the final year of high school and the freshman year of college, when they form moderately high aspirations and expectations about their academic futures. A period of desocialization then ensues, in which athletes progressively realize the structural constraints framing their situation. They become unable to accommodate the myriad, often conflicting, expectations and demands confronting them. As a result, they make choices and establish priorities that compromise their early idealism. Expediency thus supplants a concern for academics (Ingham and Smith, 1974), leading them to engage in role-distancing and to forge pragmatic adaptations that undermine their academic performance.

This in-depth investigation confirms the findings and interpretations of those studies positing a negative relationship between athletic participation and academic performance at universities with big-time athletic programs. We extend these analyses by showing that college athletes' academic performance is multifaceted and is determined less by demographic characteristics and high school experiences than by the structure of their college experiences. Athletes progress through a pattern of experiences, which first raises their hopes and then diminishes their opportunities for attaining the professed goals of the educational system.

Given the revenue that athletic programs generate, it may be unrealistic to expect this structure to change dramatically. However, there are several policy implications that can be derived from this research. First, athletes should be sheltered, as much as possible, from the enticing whirlwind of celebrity. This can best be accomplished by reinstituting the ban on freshman eligibility. Second, athletic dorms should be abolished and athletes should be better integrated into the larger university culture. In these ways we can begin to transform college athletes from strangers into neighbors. Third, athletes should be provided with more academic role models and advisors. The current arrangement, in which athletic personnel masquerade as academic advisors, functions counterproductively to the academic goals of the university. Only after these changes are made can college athletes begin to meet the goals of the educational system.

NOTES

1. For a more detailed discussion of the methodological issues involved in this research, see Adler (1984).

2. Some individuals were interviewed several times, at various stages of their socialization process.

3. Several sociological studies have noted that the admission standards for athletes are lower than those for the general student body, leading to the admission of academically marginal, ill-prepared students (Edwards, 1984; Purdy et al., 1982; Sack, 1977; Shapiro, 1984; Spady, 1970).

4. These figures represent rough estimates based on the number of individuals who graduated, the number of individuals who used up their eligibility, and projections for individuals still in the program. They are intended to be suggestive rather than exact.

5. Ironically, however, even the marginal players never abandoned their dreams of making it in the NBA.

REFERENCES

Adler, P., *Momentum: A Theory of Social Action,* Beverly Hills, CA: Sage, 1981.

Adler, P., "The sociologist as celebrity: The role of the media in field research." *Qualitative Sociology* (1984) 7:310–26.

Adler, P. and P. A. Adler, "The role of momentum in sport." *Urban Life* (1978) 7:153–76.

Adler, P. A. and P. Adler, *Joining the Crowd: Membership Roles in Field Research.* Beverly Hills, CA: Sage.

Antonelli, F., "Psychological problems of top-level athletes." *International Journal of Sport Psychology* (1970) 1:34–39.

Bernstein, S., "Getting it done: Notes on student fritters." Pp. 17–23 in J. Lofland (ed.), *Interaction in Everyday Life.* Beverly Hills, CA: Sage, 1978.

Coakley, J. J., *Sport in Society.* 2nd ed. St. Louis: Mosby, 1982.

Coleman, J. S., "Adolescent subculture and academic achievement." *American Journal of Sociology* (1960) 65:337–47.

Coleman, J. S., *The Adolescent Society.* New York: Free Press, 1961.

Cross, H. M., "The college athlete and the institution." *Law and Contemporary Problems* (1973) 38:151–71.

Cusick, P. A., *Inside High School.* New York: Holt, Rinehart and Winston, 1973.

Douglas, J. D., *Investigative Social Research.* Beverly Hills, CA: Sage, 1976.

Edwards, H., "The collegiate arms race: Origins and implications of the 'Rule 48' controversy." *Journal of Sport and Social Issues* (1984) 8:4–22.

Eitzen, D. S., "Athletics in the status system of male adolescents: A replication of Coleman's 'The Adolescent Society'." *Adolescence* (1975) 10:268–76.

Eitzen, D. S., "Sport and deviance." Pp. 73–89 in D. S. Eitzen (ed.), *Sport in Contemporary Society.* New York: St. Martin's, 1979.

Fine, G. A., "Preadolescent socialization through organized athletics: The construction of moral meanings in little league baseball." Pp. 79–105 in M. Krotee (ed.), Dimensions of Sport Sociology. Corning, NY: Leisure Press, 1979.

Frey, J. H., "Boosterism, scarce resources and institutional control: The future of American intercollegiate athletics." *International Review of Sport Sociology* (1982) 17:53–70.

Goffman, E., *The Presentation of Self in Everyday Life.* Garden City, NY: Anchor Doubleday, 1959.

Hanks, M. P. and B. K. Eckland, "Athletics and social participation in the educational attainment process," *Sociology of Education* (1976) 49:271–94.

Harrison, J. H., "Intercollegiate football participation and academic achievement." Paper presented at the Annual Meeting of the Southwestern Sociological Association, Dallas, 1976.

Henschen, K. P. and D. Fry, "An archival study of the relationship of intercollegiate athletic participation and graduation." *Sociology of Sport Journal* (1984) 1:52–56.

Hoch, P., *Rip Off the Big Game.* New York: Doubleday, 1972.

Ingham, A. G., "Occupational subcultures in the work world of sport." Pp. 337–89 in D. W. Ball and J. W. Loy (eds.), *Sport and Social Order: Contributions to the Sociology of Sport.* Reading, MA: Addison-Wesley, 1975.

Ingham, A. G. and M. D. Smith, "The social implications of the interaction between spectators and athletes." Pp. 189–224 in J. Wilmore (ed.), *Exercise and Sport Science Reviews.* Vol. 2. New York: Academic Press, 1974.

Jonassohn, K., A. Turowetz, and R. Gruneau, "Research methods in the sociology of sport." *Qualitative Sociology* (1981) 4:179–97.

Loy, J. W., B. D. McPherson, and G. Kenyon, *Sport and Social Systems.* Reading, MA: Addison-Wesley, 1978.

Meggysey, D., *Out of Their League.* Berkeley, CA: Ramparts, 1971.

Michener, J. A., *Sports in America.* New York: Random House, 1976.

Nyquist, E. B., "Wine, women, and money: College athletics today and tomorrow." *Educational Review* (1979) 60:376–93.

Odenkirk, J. E., "Intercollegiate athletics: Big business or sport?" *Academe* (1981) 67:62–66.
Purdy, D. A., D. S. Eitzen, and R. Hufnagel, "Are athletes also students? The educational attainment of college athletes." *Social Problems* (1982) 29:439–48.
Raney, J., T. Knapp, and M. Small, "Pass one for the gipper: Student athletes and university coursework." *Arena Review* (1983) 7:53–59.
Rehberg, R. A. and W. E. Schafer, "Participation in interscholastic athletics and college expectations." *American Journal of Sociology* (1968) 73:732–40.
Sack, A. L., "Big time college football. Whose free ride?" *Quest* (1977) 27:87–97.
Sack, A. L. and R. Thiel, "College football and social mobility: A case study of Notre Dame football players." *Sociology of Education* (1979) 52:60–66.
Semyonov, M. and E. Yuchtman-Yaar, "Professional sports as an alternative channel of social mobility." *Sociological Inquiry* (1981) 1:47–53.
Shapiro, B., "Intercollegiate athletic participation and academic achievement: A case study of Michigan State University student-athletes." *Sociology of Sport Journal* (1984) 1:46–51.
Shaw, G., *Meat on the Hoof.* New York: St. Martin's, 1972.
Spady, W. G., "Lament for the letterman: Effects of peer status and extra-curricular activities on goals and achievements." *American Journal of Sociology* (1970) 75:680–702.
Spivey, D. and T. A. Jones, "Intercollegiate athletic servitude: A case study of the black Illinois student-athletes, 1931–1967." *Social Science Quarterly* (1975) 55:939–47.
Sykes, G. M. and D. Matza, "Techniques of neutralization." *American Sociological Review* (1957) 22:664–70.
Tannenbaum, P. M. and J. E. Noah, "Sportuguese: A study of sports page communication." *Journalism Quarterly* (1959) 36:163–70.
Underwood, J., "The writing is on the wall." *Sports Illustrated* (1980) 52, 21:36–71.
Webb, H., "Social backgrounds of college athletes." Paper presented at the Annual Meeting of the American Alliance for Health, Physical Education, and Recreation, St. Louis, 1968.

DISCUSSION QUESTIONS

1. In what ways does the structure of college athletics influence the academic deindividuation of college athletes?
2. According to Adler and Adler, how does the transformation of college athletes relate to Goffman's conception of occupation progression? How and why do many college athletes progress from idealism to cynicism concerning their college experiences?

Article 38

The Case Against IQ Tests

The Concept of Intelligence

JEROME KAGAN

THE CONCEPT OF INTELLIGENCE is among the most confused in our repertoire of ideas. Ambiguity surrounds its definition, etiology, and social significance. A central issue is to what degree scores on standard intelligence tests reflect a generalized quality of memory and reasoning that is not limited to a particular cultural setting. In my view, a person's score on a contemporary IQ test has a poor relation to his ability to think logically and coherently. Moreover, the psychological trait "intelligence"—now unfortunately equated with the IQ score—has become a primary explanation for the unequal access to power in our society.

To state my own view briefly: The white, middle-class Western community, like any moderately isolated social group, has created over the years a specialized vocabulary, reservoir of information, and style of problem-solving summarized under the concept "intelligence." Since possession of these skills is a rite of passage to positions of power and wealth in the society, many have been easily seduced into concluding that those without power or wealth are of fundamentally different intellectual competence. This view ignores the fact that children's access to the experiences necessary to acquire the valued intellectual skills differs enormously by social classes. But our society has been doing this for so long that the faulty logic

From "The Case Against IQ Tests: The Concept of Intelligence," by Jerome Kagan, *The Humanist,* Jan/Feb 1972, pp. 295–298.

has gone unnoticed. We are much like the Bushman mothers who believe that a child will not walk unless he is placed erect in sand from the earliest weeks of life. Since no Bushman mother bothers to test this hypothesis, and all children walk by 18 months, the false idea continues to live.

Let me state the issue in kernel form: Every society, or large cohesive group within a society, recognizes that in order to maintain stability a small group must possess some power over the much larger citizenry. This power can be inherited, awarded, attained, or seized. In actual practice, this lean and rather raw description is usually disguised by a clever strategy—much like a magician's wrist movement—that makes select psychological traits symbolic of highly valued, status-conferring attributes. Those who possess these traits are inevitably those to whom power is given.

At other times and in other places, sexual abstinence, sexual potency, hunting skill, a capacity for silent meditation, good soldiering, or efficient farming have been the basis for ranking men and dividing them into unequal groups. Tenth-century Europe awarded power to those who were assumed to be more religious than their brothers. The presumption of a capacity for more intense religiosity provided a rationale for the fact that a privileged few were permitted entry into marble halls, and allowed the larger society to accept it. Contemporary American society uses intelligence as one of the bases for ranking its members. We celebrate intelligence the way the Islamic Moroccans celebrate the warrior-saint.

Moreover, the cultural similarity extends to our explanations of the unequal distribution of either intelligence or saintliness. The majority of Americans believe that children are born with differing intellectual capacities and that as a result some are destined to assume positions of status and responsibility. A much smaller group believes that this psychological capacity has to be attained through the right combination of early experience and will. These opposing hypotheses are identical in substance to the two interpretations of differential "capacity for religiosity" held by Muslims in Morocco and Indonesia. The Moroccans believe that some are born with a greater capacity for strong and intense religious experience. The Javanese believe it is attained following long periods of meditation. And they, like we, discover the small proportion of their population that fit the description of the pure and allow them ascent.

We are not contesting the obvious fact that individuals really do differ in regard to the psychological traits valued by our society. But we lack sufficient information about the causes of these differences.

Let me try to support this rather strong statement by partially analyzing what an intelligence test is made of. The widely publicized announcement that 80% of intelligence is inherited and 20% environmentally determined is based on information from two similarly constructed standardized IQ tests invented by Caucasian middle-class Western men, at the request of Caucasian middle-class Western men, for Caucasian middle-class Western men to use for ranking everyone in the society.

The most important set of test questions (important because scores on this set have the highest correlation with the total IQ) asks the testee to define words of increasing rarity. Rarity is a relative quality, depending always on the language community one selects as referent. "Shilling" is a rare word for the American child, but so is "joint." The test constructors decided that rarity would be defined with respect to the middle-class Caucasian experience. And a child reared in a middle-class home is more likely to learn the meaning of "shilling" than the meaning of "joint." If contemporary black psychologists had accepted the assignment of constructing the first part of the intelligence test, they probably would have made a different choice.

A second set of questions poses the child some everyday problem and asks him what he would do in that situation. For example, one question asks a 7-year-old, "What should you do if you were sent to buy a loaf of bread and the grocer said he didn't have any more?" Clearly, this question assumes a middle-class urban or suburban environment with more than one grocery store within safe walking distance of the home, for, believe it or not, the only answer for which maximum credit is given is, "I would go to another store." It is not surprising that rural and ghetto children are less likely to offer that answer. I recently examined a set of protocols on poor black children living in a large Eastern city and found that many of them answered, "Go home"—a perfectly reasonable and even intelligent answer for which they were not given credit. One task that does not favor middle-class white children asks the testee to remember a list of four or five numbers read at the rate of one per second. This test usually yields minimal differences among class and ethnic groups in the United States.

These biases in the selection of questions comprise only part of the problem. There is also a serious source of error in the administration of the test. White middle-class examiners usually administer the tests to children of different linguistic backgrounds. The test protocols of the black children mentioned above, gathered by well-intentioned, well-trained examiners, indicated that the children often misunderstood the examiner's pronunciation. When asked to define the word "fur" some said, "That's what happens when you light a match." Clearly, the child had understood the word to be "fire," but he received no credit. Similarly, when requested to define "hat," some children said, "When you get burned," indicating that they perceived the word as "hot." Again, they received no credit.

Many other sources of error could be documented, but even these few examples suggest that the IQ test, the basis for Arthur Jensen's argument and for the statement that 80% of IQ is inherited, is a seriously biased instrument. It almost guarantees that middle-class white children will obtain higher scores than any other group of children in the country, and that the more similar the experiences of two people, the more similar their scores should be.

Most citizens, however, are unaware both of the fundamental faults in the IQ test and of the multiple bases for differences in tested intelligence. But like the Greeks, Islamic Moroccans, and medieval Christians, we too need a rational basis for the awarding of power and prizes. Intelligence is our modern substitute for saintliness, religiosity, courage, or moral intensity, and, of course, it works. It works so well that when we construct an intervention project, be it a major effort like Head

Start or a small study run by a university scientist, we usually evaluate the effect of the intervention by administering a standard intelligence test or one very similar to it, a practice reflecting the unconscious bias that a child's IQ must be the essential dimension we wish to change.

What implications are to be drawn from this acerbic analysis of the IQ? The first may seem paradoxical, considering our apparently hostile critique of the IQ test. Despite the injustice inherent in awarding privilege, status, and self-esteem to those who possess more of some attribute the society happens to value, this practice seems to be universal, perhaps because it is necessary. Power—and we mean here benevolent power—probably has to be held unequally. Therefore the community must invent a complex yet reasonable rationale that will both permit and explain the limited distribution of this prized resource. Knowledge of Western language, history, and customs is one partial basis. But let us be honest about the bases for this arbitrary decision and rid ourselves of the delusion that those who temporarily possess power are biologically more fit for this role because their brains are better organized. Sir Robert Filmer made this argument in 1680 to rationalize the right of kings to govern, and John Locke's political philosophy was shaped on a brilliant critique of Filmer's thesis.

We do not deny that biological differences, many of them inherited, exist between and within ethnic and racial groups. But we do not think that inherited characteristics like eye color or tendency to perspire entitle anyone to special favor. Similarly, we should reflect on the wisdom of using 15-point differences on a culturally biased test—regardless of the magnitude of the genetic contribution to the IQ—to sort some children into stereotyped categories, thus impairing their ability to become mayors, teachers, or lawyers. It is possible to defend the heretical suggestion that for many contemporary occupations—note that I did not say all—IQ should not be the primary attribute by which a candidate is judged. Of course, biological factors determine a person's muscle mass, brain size, and adrenalin secretion under stress. But let us not unfairly exploit these hard-won facts to rationalize the distribution of secular power, which is a political and sociological dimension. That is using fair science for dark deeds that she is ill-prepared to carry out.

Those who insist that IQ is inherited base their conclusion on a mathematical model of heritability which assumes that the statistical variation in IQ scores is additive, some of it due to genetic and some to environmental factors. That assumption is questionable and has been criticized by many psychologists and mathematicians. Hence, all one can say at the moment is that the genetic contribution to IQ is still unknown. A second fact has also led some to conclude that intelligence is controlled in a major way by genetic factors: American blacks, who are of a different gene pool than whites, have lower IQ scores. We have argued that the point average difference between American blacks and whites is likely to be due to the strong cultural biases in the IQ test. Hence, given the current knowledge no one can be sure of the determinants of variation in IQ score, a conclusion that is even more true of intelligence itself.

DISCUSSION QUESTIONS

1. What are some of the ambiguities surrounding the concept of intelligence?
2. What do IQ tests really measure? Do IQ tests objectively measure intelligence or do they largely measure cultural experience?

XIV
Politics and Power

WHAT TO FOCUS ON:

1. Does power lie solely with individuals or political organizations?
2. How were physicians used as political symbols in Nazi Germany?

POLITICS, AS DEFINED by Harold Lasswell, refers to a decision-making process that determines who gets what, when, where and how. This process can be institutionalized in the form of government, or can refer to any collectively sponsored decision-making activity. In the Weberian sense, power is the ability to influence others, even in an adversarial relationship. Power exists in political systems as individuals and groups attempt to influence the outcome of decision-making. One could say that politics regulates the exercise of power. Sociologists are interested in the patterns of this exercise of power. In what ways is power exercised and what are the consequences? When is power coercive and when is it persuasive? Identifying who controls power and the patterns to its exercise allows sociologists to see who controls social institutions and other aspects of group life. It is important to understand that politics is not synonymous with democracy, politics is a decision-making system whether many people are involved or only a select few, as in totalitarian systems.

Studying who controls power is only one aspect of understanding the relationship between power and politics. The dynamic qualities of cultural values, historical precedent, social environmental conditions, and ideological orientation all play a part in making decisions. The articles in this section provide some insight to understanding power relations.

The lead article in this chapter by Robert Bierstedt is a provocative discussion of what power is and what it is not. The discussion involves a comparison of power in the social and physical sciences, as well as demonstrating the difficulties found in defining power. In addition, Bierstedt examines power in relation to prestige, influence, dominance, and authority. This becomes an important introduction to understanding the complexities of power and how they can be related to the government and economic spheres of life.

Lifton examines the broader rationale utilized by the Nazi Party to enact and enforce a program of genocide. Jews were portrayed as an illness in the socio-political body of Germany. Removal of the illness was similar to the surgical removal of a cancerous tumor. This powerful socio-biological vision and ideology created the imagery of illness coupled with the need to develop a purer and more healthy race of people—the Aryans. Lifton argues that such an ideological vision of the past, present, and future of Germany made the mass killing more respectable—the killing was therapeutic. Having physicians preside over the mass genocide was a strong symbolism of the Nazi program.

Barlett and Steel ask the question, "What went wrong in America?" As the later part of this century witnessed the end of the American dream, as the middle class was being devastated by lay-offs and company closings, the authors sought to understand how this could occur in a country committed to economic success. They trace the answers to a change in the economic order: to a shift in power. The authors relate the ability of corporations to take-over others and the government tax policies that encouraged such corporate cannibalism. They examine the inability of middle-class workers and entrepreneurs to keep pace. The authors argue that an economic order quite different from that existing in the beginning of the twentieth century is in place. Additionally the article gives a view of the human consequences of this shift.

Article 39
On Power

ROBERT BIERSTEDT

SOCIOLOGICAL INQUIRY provides few problems as perplexing as the problem of power. It is as perplexing in its way as the problem of electricity in physics. As a matter of fact, social power is like electrical power. We see the effects and manifestations of both but not the phenomenon itself. Social power is transformed into order, force, and authority; electrical power into light, heat, and motion. The misapplication of both, to be macabre for a moment, can result in death. But the essence of these phenomena is elusive. Not even the dictionary can give us a satisfactory definition of electricity and indeed can only call it "a fundamental entity of nature." We can similarly—and truthfully—say that power is "a fundamental entity of society," but with an awareness that we are not saying very much, if indeed we are saying anything at all. Our relative ignorance of the nature of power is itself a curious phenomenon. The word has been in our vocabularies for as long as we can remember and we frequently use it. But we find ourselves unable to define it. We here confront the dilemma of St. Augustine who confessed that he knew perfectly well what time was—until someone asked him. *(Si non rogas, intelligo.)*

Power and Society

The power structure of society is not an insignificant problem. In any realistic sense it is both a sociological (i.e., a scientific) and a moral (i.e., a social) problem. It has

From *The Social Order,* by Robert Bierstedt, 4th ed., McGraw-Hill, Inc., New York, 1974, pp. 350–355, 357–359. Reprinted by permission of the publisher.

traditionally been a problem in political philosophy. Like so many other problems of a political character, however, it has roots that lie deeper than the *polis* and reach into the community itself. Its primitive basis and ultimate locus are to be sought in society, and not only in government, because in government it is already institutionalized. It is apparent, furthermore, that not all power is political power and that political power—like economic, financial, industrial, and military power—is only one of several and various kinds of social power. Wall Street, for example, can compete with the government of the United States in exercising power over foreign trade and in affecting the exchange rate of foreign currencies.

Society, in fact, is shot through with power relations—the power a father exercises over his child, a master over his slave, a teacher over his pupils, the victor over the vanquished, the blackmailer over his victim, the warden over his prisoners, the judge over the convicted defendant, an employer over his employee, a general over his lieutenants, a captain over his crew, a creditor over a debtor, and so on through an impressively large number of social relationships. Some of these are examples of authority. But all of them are examples of power because authority is a species of power. It is worth an incidental note that not all these examples of power enjoy the support of the state. To some of them the state is indifferent, to others it is opposed.

Power, in short, is a universal phenomenon in human societies. It is seldom absent in social interaction (including courtship[1]) except in the ideal family, where personal identification is complete; in sincere friendship, where, unlike love, sexuality, jealousy, and exaltation give way to service, candor, and contentment; and those social relations in the narrower sense that the sociologist Georg Simmel called relations of "polite acquaintance," the kind of interaction, for example, that appears at cocktail parties and at wedding receptions. Most other social relations contain elements of power. What, then, is this phenomenon? In trying to answer the question we shall first distinguish it from other phenomena with which it has often been associated and often confused.

Power and Prestige

Social power has variously been identified with prestige, influence, eminence, competence, dominance, rights, strength, force, and authority, and it was the distinguished Lord Chancellor of England, Francis Bacon, who identified it with knowledge. Since the intension of a term varies, if at all, inversely with its extension—i.e., the more things a term can be applied to the less precise its meaning—it is necessary to distinguish power from most of these other phenomena. Let us begin by separating power from prestige.

A close association between power and prestige was made by the American sociologist E. A. Ross in his classic work on social control. "The immediate cause of the location of power," he said, "is prestige." And further, "The class that has the most prestige will have the most power."[2] Now prestige may certainly be construed as something that is sometimes related to power, in the sense that powerful groups tend to be prestigious and prestigious groups powerful. Prestige clearly separates man from man and group from group and it has, as one of its consequences, one kind of stratification that appears in human societies. But we can always escape confusion if we can find, no matter how close the relationship, one phenomenon in the absence of the other. We can do this with respect to power and prestige and consequently the two phenomena are not identical. They are in fact independent variables. Prestige is frequently unaccompanied by power, as in the case of scholars elected to membership in the American Academy of Arts and Sciences, and power may similarly be unassociated with prestige, as in the case of a group of gangsters preying upon the small independent stores in the Bronx in New York City. Physicists, in our world, have great prestige, but not much power. Policemen, on the other hand, have significant power but—except perhaps in London—little prestige. The Phi Beta Kappa Society has high prestige in American academic circles, but no power. Prestige, in short, does not suffice to create power, and the two phenomena, both sociologically important, are not identical and may or may not appear together.

Similar observations may be made about the relationship of knowledge, eminence, skill, and competence to power. All four of these may contribute to prestige, but they may be quite unaccompanied by power. When power does accompany them the association is incidental rather than necessary. Thus the most erudite archaeologist, the most famous sculptor, the most talented pianist, and the most competent automobile mechanic in the world might all four be devoid of power. Knowledge, eminence, skill, and competence, although they may accompany it, have nothing intrinsically to do with power.

Power and Influence

When we turn to the relationship between power and influence we find a more intimate connection, but once again it is necessary to make a distinction. It is necessary because influence is persuasive whereas power is coercive. We submit voluntarily to influence but power requires our submission. The mistress of a king may influence the destiny of a nation, but only because her paramour permits himself to be swayed by her designs. In any ultimate reckoning her influence may be more important than his power, but it is inefficacious unless it is transformed into power. The power a teacher exercises over his pupils stems not from his superior knowledge (this is competence rather than power) and not from his opinions (this is influence rather than power), but from his ability to apply the sanction of failure to the student who does not fulfill his requirements and meet his standards. The competence may be unappreciated, and the influence may be ineffective, but the power may not be gainsaid.[3]

Furthermore, power and influence can occur in isolation from each other and so they also are independent variables. We should say, for example, that Karl Marx exerted an incalculable influence upon the twentieth century, but this poverty-stricken exile who spent so many of his hours in the British Museum was hardly a man of power. Even the assertion that he was a man of influence is an ellipsis. It is the ideas that were—and continue to be—influential. The Soviet dictator Stalin, on the other hand, was a man of power, but he had few if any influential ideas.

Influence does not require power, and power may dispense with influence. Influence may convert a friend, but power coerces friend and foe alike. Influence attaches to an idea, a doctrine, or a creed, and has its locus in the ideological sphere. Power attaches to a person, a group, or an association, and has its locus in the sociological sphere. Plato, Aristotle, St. Thomas, Shakespeare, Galileo, Newton, and Kant were men of influence, but none of them exercised any noticeable power. One need only compare Aristotle, for example, with his famous pupil, Alexander the Great. Napoleon Bonaparte and Abraham Lincoln were men of both power and influence. Genghis Khan and Adolf Hitler were men of power. Archimedes was a man of influence, but the soldier who slew him at the gates of Syracuse had more power.

When we speak, therefore, of the power of an idea or when we are tempted to say that ideas are weapons or when we assert, with the above-mentioned Napoleon, that the pen is mightier than the sword, we are using figurative language, speaking truly as it were, but metaphorically and with synecdoche.[4] Ideas are influential, they can change the course of history, but for the sake of logical and sociological clarity it is preferable to deny to them the attribute of power. Influence in this sense, of course, presents quite as serious and as complex a problem as power, but it is not the problem we are now discussing.[5]

Power and Dominance

It is relatively easy to distinguish power from dominance. Power is a sociological, dominance a psychological phenomenon. The locus of power is in both persons and groups, and in almost all of the important cases it is in the latter. The locus of dominance, on the contrary, is only in individuals. Power is a function and resource of the organization and opposition of associations, of the arrangement and juxtaposition of groups, including classes, and of the structure of society itself. Dominance, on the other hand, is a function of personality or of temperament. It is a personal trait. A timid robber, who flaunts his gun, has more power than his unarmed victim, however dominant or aggressive the latter may be in his normal social relationships. Furthermore, and one of the most interesting facets of this distinction, dominant individuals play roles in powerless groups and submissive individuals play roles in powerful ones. Some groups indeed acquire an impressive power in society, especially political power, because there are so many submissive individuals who are persuaded to join them and who meekly agree to the norms and ideologies that membership imposes. A clear example of this is the growth of the National Socialist Party in Germany in the 1930s. We can easily see, therefore, that dominance is a problem in social psychology, power a problem in sociology.

This distinction, among others, illustrates once more the impropriety of associating sociology too closely with psychology, or even social psychology. Individual and group phenomena are fundamentally different in character. The subjective factors that motivate an individual to participate in social action, the ends he seeks and the means he employs to achieve them, have little to do with the objective social consequences of the action. A man may join the army, for example, for any number of reasons—to achieve financial independence, to earn early retirement, to conform with the law, to escape a delicate domestic situation, to withdraw from an embarrassing emotional commitment, to see the world, to escape the pressure of mortgage payments, to fight for a cause in which he believes, to wear a uniform, to do what his friends are doing, or to do what he believes is right. None of these motivations will affect very much the power of the army that he joins. Similarly, people do not have children because they wish to increase the birthrate, to raise the classification of the municipal post office, or to contribute to the military strength of the state. The births, however, may have all three of these consequences, and many more besides. And finally, to return to our subject, a dominant personality does not confer power upon the man who possesses it. Power, in short, is one thing, dominance quite another. . . .

Power, Force, and Authority

It is the concepts of force and authority that give us a solution to our problem. Power is not force and power is not authority, but it is intimately related to both. We want, therefore, to propose three definitions and then examine their implications: (1) power is latent force; (2) force is manifest power, and (3) authority is institutionalized power. The first two of these propositions may be considered together. They look like circular definitions and, as a matter of fact, they are. If an independent meaning can be found for one of these concepts, however, the other may be defined in terms of it and the circularity will disappear.[6]

We may therefore suggest an independent definition of the concept of force. Force in sociology is remarkably similar to force in physics and here we have an interesting linkage between nature and society. In both cases force means the production of an effect, an alteration in movement or action that overcomes resistance. It is an interference with a body at rest or in motion that changes its state or direction, an interference with a person that changes what he is doing or intends to do. In the sociological sense, where it is synonymous with coercion it compels a change in the course of action of an individual or a group against the wishes of the individual or the group. It means the application of sanctions when they are not willingly received. It means, further, the reduction or limitation or closure or even total elimination of alternatives to the social action of one person or group by another person or group. "Your money or your life" is a threat that, when acted upon, becomes a situation of naked force, the reduction of alternatives to two.[7] The blackmailer who exacts his tribute from his victim as the price of silence is again limiting alternatives—pay or be exposed. The bouncer who throws an obstreperous patron out of a bar or nightclub is depriving him of the alternative of staying for another round of drinks. The execution of a sentence to hang represents the total elimination of alternatives. One army progressively limits the social action of its enemy until only two alternatives remain for the unsuccessful contender—to surrender or die.[8]

Now all of these are situations of manifest power. Power itself is the predisposition or prior capacity that makes the use of force possible. Only groups that have power can threaten to use force and the threat itself is power. Power is the ability to employ force, not its actual employment, the ability to apply sanctions, not their actual application. Power is the ability to introduce force into a social situation; it is stance, not action; it is a presentation of the probability of force. Unlike force, incidentally, power is always successful; when it is not successful it was not, or ceases to be, power. The bankrupt corporation and the vanquished army are both powerless. Power symbolizes the force that may be applied in any social situation and supports the authority that *is* applied. Power is thus neither force nor authority but it makes both force and authority possible. Without power there would be no force and without power there would be no authority.

NOTES

1. On this subject, and on power in general, see Peter M. Blau, *Exchange and Power in Social Life,* John Wiley & Sons. New York, 1964, pp. 76–85.

2. *Social Control.* The Macmillan Company. New York, 1916, p. 78. Dennis Wrong is most enlightening on the relationship between power and social control. See his "Some Problems in Defining Social Power." *The American Journal of Sociology,* vol. 73, no. 6, May, 1968, pp. 673–681.

3. In this case, however, as shown in the preceding chapter, the power is transformed into authority.

4. We frequently speak of the power of the press. The President of the United States, for example to say nothing of the Cabinet, the Congress, and even the Court, listens intently to the voice of *The New York Times,* and *The Times* of London is not known as "The Thunderer" for nothing. But neither newspaper can elect a single candidate to political office, and neither editor nor columnist, however influential, can issue an order that will alter a governmental policy or force a change in one. To revert to our earlier analogy, power is lightning, not thunder.

5. For sophisticated treatments of influence, see William A. Gamson, *Power and Discontent.* The Dorsey Press, Homewood, Illinois, 1968; Talcott Parsons, "On the Concept of Influence," *Public Opinion Quarterly,* Vol. 27, Spring, 1963, pp. 37–62; James S. Coleman. "Comment on 'On the Concept of Influence.' " *Ibid,* pp. 63–82; and Parsons' rejoinder to Coleman. *Ibid,* pp. 87–92. For an unusually clear and correct use of the concepts of influence, leadership, power, and authority in the study of a United States congressman, in this case the Chairman of the Ways and Means Committee of the House of Representatives, see John F. Manley. "Wilbur D. Mills: A Study in Congressional Influences," *The American Political Science Review,* vol. LXIII, no. 2, June, 1969. pp. 442–464.

6. As a matter of purely technical interest, it may be observed that all definitions are ultimately circular. Every system of inference contains undefined or "primitive" terms in its initial propositions because, if it were necessary to define every term before using it, it would be impossible ever to talk or write or reason. There would be no word with which to begin. An undefined term in one system, however, may be defined in another. Although we may still perhaps have a logical deficiency here, it is not necessarily a practical deficiency if the circle, so to speak, is not too small. When we find an independent meaning for one of the terms in a couplet of circular definitions we are, in effect, enlarging the circle. The problem involved

here has engaged some of the best minds in the history of logic, including Whitehead and Russell, who discuss it in the Introduction to *Principia Mathematica.*

7. The holdup man expresses his disjunction dramatically but incorrectly. What he really means is "Your money, or your life and your money."

8. There is a further distinction to be made between force and violence. We should be inclined to say, although a continuum and not a dichotomy is involved, that violence is uncontrolled force, undisciplined force. A mob engaged in shooting, looting, and arson, as in the riots that occur in cities, is an expression of violence. The police that restrain, subdue, and finally control it are an expression of force. Unfortunately, as in the student demonstrations that have occurred in universities in the world's major cities, the police too have often become undisciplined—"lost their cool" as the slang phrase so aptly puts it—and have themselves indulged in violence. War, although fought by disciplined force on both sides, is always violent at the points where the opposing armies clash. Political assassination is always an act of violence and so, more generally, is the act of murder. In these cases it is the destruction of life, rather than the absence of discipline, that becomes the governing criterion. Violence is force used not to maintain or to restore order, but to destroy. It thus has a moral connotation whereas the concepts of power, force, and authority are morally neutral.

DISCUSSION QUESTIONS

1. What are the problems in defining power and what is Bierstedt's solution?
2. How is power related to prestige and dominance, and why are these concepts inadequate in defining power?

Article 40
Medicalized Killing

ROBERT JAY LIFTON

Medicalized Killing

IN NAZI MASS MURDER, we can say that a barrier was removed, a boundary crossed: that boundary between violent imagery and periodic killing of victims (as of Jews in pogroms) on the one hand, and systematic genocide in Auschwitz and elsewhere on the other. My argument in this study is that the medicalization of killing—the imagery of killing in the name of healing—was crucial to that terrible step. At the heart of the Nazi enterprise, then, is the destruction of the boundary between healing and killing.

Early descriptions of Auschwitz and other death camps focused on the sadism and viciousness of Nazi guards, officers, and physicians. But subsequent students of the process realized that sadism and viciousness alone could not account for the killing of millions of people. The emphasis then shifted to the bureaucracy of killing: the faceless, detached bureaucratic function originally described by Max Weber, now applied to mass murder.[1] This focus on numbed violence is enormously important, and is consistent with what we shall observe to be the routinization of all Auschwitz function.

Yet these emphases are not sufficient in themselves. They must be seen in relation to the visionary motivations associated with ideology, along with the specific individual-psychological mechanisms enabling people to kill. What I call "medicalized killing" addresses these motivational principles and psychological mechanisms, and permits us to understand the Auschwitz victimizers—notably Nazi doctors—both as part of a bureaucracy of killing and as individual participants whose attitudes and behavior can be examined.

Medicalized killing can be understood in two wider perspectives. The first is the "surgical" method of killing large numbers of people by means of a controlled technology making use of highly poisonous gas; the method employed became a means of maintaining distance between killers and victims. This distancing had considerable importance for the Nazis in alleviating the psychological problems experienced (as attested over and over by Nazi documents) by the *Einsatzgruppen* troops who carried out face-to-face shooting of Jews in Eastern Europe—problems that did not prevent those troops from murdering 1,400,000 Jews.[2]

I was able to obtain direct evidence on this matter during an interview with a former *Wehrmacht* neuropsychiatrist who had treated large numbers of *Einsatzgruppen* personnel for psychological disorders. He told me that these disorders resembled combat reactions of ordinary troops: severe anxiety, nightmares, tremors, and numerous bodily complaints. But in these "killer troops," as he called them, the symptoms tended to last longer and to be more severe. He estimated that 20 percent of those doing the actual killing experienced these symptoms of psychological decompensation. About half of that 20 percent associated their symptoms mainly with the "unpleasantness" of what they had to do, while the other half seemed to have moral questions about shooting people in that way. The men had greatest psychological difficulty concerning shooting women and children, especially children. Many experienced a sense of guilt in their dreams, which could include various forms of punishment or retribution. Such psychological difficulty led the Nazis to seek a more "surgical" method of killing.

But there is another perspective on medicalized killing that I believe to be insufficiently recognized: *killing as a therapeutic imperative.* That kind of motivation was revealed in the words of a Nazi doctor quoted by the distinguished survivor physician Dr. Ella Lingens-Reiner. Pointing to the chimneys in the distance, she asked a Nazi doctor, Fritz Klein, "How can you reconcile that with your [Hippocratic] oath as a doctor?" His answer was, "Of course I am a doctor and I want to preserve life. And out of respect for human life, I would remove a gangrenous appendix from a diseased body. The Jew is the gangrenous appendix in the body of mankind."[3]

The medical imagery was still broader. Just as Turkey during the nineteenth century (because of the extreme decline of the Ottoman empire) was known as the "sick man of Europe," so did pre-Hitler ideologues and Hitler himself interpret Germany's post-First World War chaos and demoralization as an "illness," especially of the Aryan race. Hitler wrote in *Mein Kampf,* in the mid-1920s, that *"anyone who wants to cure this era, which is inwardly sick and rotten, must first of all summon up the courage to make clear the causes of this disease."*[4] The diagnosis was racial. The only genuine "culture-creating" race, the Aryans, had permitted themselves to be weakened to the point of endangered survival by the "destroyers of culture," characterized as "the Jew." The Jews were agents of "racial pollution" and "racial tuberculosis," as well as parasites and bacteria causing sickness, deterioration, and death in the host peoples they infested. They were the "eternal bloodsucker," "vampire," "germ carrier," "peoples' parasite," and "maggot in a rotting corpse."[5] The cure had to be radical: that is (as one scholar put it), by "cutting out the 'canker of decay,' propagating the worthwhile elements and letting the less valuable wither away, . . . [and] 'the extirpation of all those categories of people considered to be worthless or dangerous.' "[6]

Medical metaphor blended with concrete biomedical ideology in the Nazi sequence from coercive sterilization to direct medical killing to the death camps. The unifying principle of the biomedical ideology was that of a deadly racial disease, the sickness of the Aryan race; the cure, the killing of all Jews.

Thus, for Hans Frank, jurist and General Governor of Poland during the Nazi occupation, "the Jews were a lower species of life, a kind of vermin, which upon contact infected the German people with deadly diseases." When the Jews in the area he ruled had been killed, he declared that "now a sick Europe would become healthy again."[7] It was a religion of the will—the will as "an all-encompassing metaphysical principle";[8] and what the Nazis "willed" was nothing less than total control over life and death. While this view is often referred to as "social Darwinism," the term applies only loosely, mostly to the Nazi stress on natural "struggle" and on "survival of the fittest." The regime actually rejected much of Darwinism; since evolutionary theory is more or less democratic in its assumption of a common beginning for all races, it is therefore at odds with the Nazi principle of inherent Aryan racial virtue.[9]

Even more specific to the biomedical vision was the crude genetic imagery, combined with still cruder eugenic visions. Here Heinrich Himmler, as high priest, spoke of the leadership's task as being "like the plant-breeding specialist who, when he wants to breed a pure new strain from a well-tried species that has been exhausted by too much cross-breeding, first goes over the field to cull the unwanted plants."[10]

The Nazi project, then, was not so much Darwinian or social Darwinist as a vision of absolute control over the evolutionary process, over the biological human future. Making widespread use of the Darwinian term "selection," the Nazis sought to take over the functions of nature (natural selection) and God (the Lord giveth and the Lord taketh away) in orchestrating their own "selections," their own version of human evolution.

In these visions the Nazis embraced not only versions of medieval mystical anti-Semitism but also a newer (nineteenth- and twentieth-century) claim to "scientific racism." Dangerous Jewish characteristics could be linked with alleged data of scientific disciplines, so that a "mainstream of racism" formed from "the fusion of anthropology, eugenics, and social thought."[11] The resulting "racial and social biology" could make vicious forms of anti-Semitism seem intellectually respectable to learned men and women.

One can speak of the Nazi state as a "biocracy." The model here is a theocracy, a system of rule by priests of a sacred order under the claim of divine prerogative. In the case of the Nazi biocracy, the divine prerogative was that of cure through purification and revitalization of the Aryan race: "From a dead mechanism which only lays claim to existence for its own sake, there must be formed a living organism with the exclusive aim of serving a higher idea." Just as in a theocracy, the state itself is no more than a vehicle for the divine purpose, so in the Nazi biocracy was the state no more than a means to achieve *"a mission of the German people on earth":* that of *"assembling and preserving the most valuable stocks of basic racial elements in this* [Aryan] *people . . .* [and] *. . . raising them to a dominant position."*[12] The Nazi biocracy differed from a classical theocracy in that the biological priests did not actually rule. The clear rulers were Adolf Hitler and his circle, not biological theorists and certainly not the doctors. (The difference, however, is far from absolute: even in a theocracy, highly politicized rulers may make varying claims to priestly authority.) In any case, Nazi ruling authority was maintained in the name of the higher biological principle.

Among the biological authorities called forth to articulate and implement "scientific racism"—including physical anthropologists, geneticists, and racial theorists of every variety—doctors inevitably found a unique place. It is they who work at the border of life and death, who are most associated with the awesome, death-defying, and sometimes death-dealing aura of the primitive shaman and medicine man. As bearers of this shamanistic legacy and contemporary practitioners of mysterious healing arts, it is they who are likely to be called upon to become biological activists.

I have mentioned my primary interest in Nazi doctors' participation in medicalized or biologized killing. We shall view their human experiments as related to the killing process and to the overall Nazi biomedical vision. At Nuremberg, doctors were tried only limitedly for their involvement in killing, partly because its full significance was not yet understood.[13]

In Auschwitz, Nazi doctors presided over the murder of most of the one million victims of that camp. Doctors performed selections—both on the ramp among arriving transports of prisoners and later in the camps and on the medical blocks. Doctors supervised the killing in the gas chambers and decided when the victims were dead. Doctors conducted a murderous epidemiology, sending to the gas chamber groups of people with contagious diseases and sometimes including everyone else who might be on the medical block. Doctors ordered and supervised, and at times carried out, direct killing of debilitated patients on the medical blocks by means of phenol injections into the bloodstream or the heart. In connection with all of these killings, doctors kept up a pretense of medical legitimacy: for deaths of Auschwitz prisoners and of outsiders brought there to be killed, they signed false death certificates listing spurious illnesses. Doctors consulted actively on how best to keep selections running smoothly; on how many people to permit to remain alive to fill the slave labor requirements of the I.G. Farben enterprise at Auschwitz; and on how to burn the enormous numbers of bodies that strained the facilities of the crematoria.

In sum, we may say that doctors were given much of the responsibility for the murderous ecology of Auschwitz—the choosing of victims, the carrying through of the physical and psychological mechanics of killing, and the balancing of killing and work functions in the camp. While doctors by no means ran Auschwitz, they did lend it a perverse medical aura. As one survivor who closely observed the process put the matter, "Auschwitz was like a medical operation," and "the killing program was led by doctors from beginning to end."

We may say that the doctor standing at the ramp represented a kind of omega point, a mythical gatekeeper between the worlds of the dead and the living, a final common pathway of the Nazi vision of therapy via mass murder.

NOTES

1. See Raul Hilberg, *The Destruction of the European Jews* (Chicago: Quadrangle, 1967); Richard L. Rubenstein, *The Cunning of History: Mass Death and the American Future* (New York: Harper & Row, 1975); Hannah Arendt, *Eichmann in Jerusalem: A Report on the Banality of Evil* (New York: Viking, 1961). Hilberg's expanded edition of his classic work was too recent to consult fully for this book; see *The Destruction of the European Jews,* 3 vols., rev. and definitive ed. (New York: Holmes & Meier, 1985).

2. Hilberg, *Destruction,* p. 256.

3. A slightly different, published version is found in Ella Lingens-Reiner, *Prisoners of Fear* (London: Gollancz, 1948), pp. 1–2.

4. Adolf Hitler, *Mein Kampf* (Boston: Houghton Mifflin, 1943), p. 435.

5. Ibid., pp. 150, 300–308, 312–13. For scholarly treatments of Hitler's (and earlier) metaphors for the Jews, see Eberhard Jäckel, *Hitler's Weltanschauung: A Blueprint for Power* (Middletown, Conn.: Wesleyan University Press, 1972); Rudolph Binion, *Hitler Among the Germans* (New York: Elsevier, 1976); Lucy S. Dawidowicz, *The War Against the Jews, 1933–1945* (New York: Holt, Rinehart & Winston, 1975), pp. 19–21, 55–56; Uriel Tal, *Christians and Jews in Germany: Religion, Politics and Ideology in the Second Reich, 1870–1914* (Ithaca: Cornell University Press, 1975), pp. 259–89.

6. Hans Buchheim, quoted in Helmut Krausnick, "The Persecution of the Jews," in Krausnick et al., *Anatomy of the SS State* (New York: Walker, 1968), p. 15.

7. Hilberg, *Destruction,* p. 12.

8. J. P. Stern, *Hitler: The Führer and the People* (Glasgow: Fontana/Collins, 1971), p. 70. The celebration of that religious impulse was epitomized by the gigantic Nuremberg rally of 1934, whose theme, "The Triumph of the Will," became the title of Leni Riefenstahl's noted film. Riefenstahl, in an interview with an assistant of mine, made clear that Hitler himself provided that slogan.

9. George L. Mosse, *The Crisis of German Ideology: Intellectual Origins of the Third Reich* (New York: Grosset & Dunlap, 1964), p. 103.

10. Himmler, quoted in Krausnick, "Persecution," p. 14.

11. George L. Mosse, *Toward the Final Solution: A History of European Racism* (New York: Fertig, 1978), p. 77.

12. Hitler, *Mein Kampf,* pp. 397–98.

13. *Nuremberg Medical Case,* especially vol. I, pp. 8–17 (the indictment) and 27–74 (opening statement by Chief Prosecutor Telford Taylor, 9 December 1946); personal interview with James M. McHaney, prosecutor of the Medical Case.

DISCUSSION QUESTIONS

1. Why were physicians important to the Nazi program of Jewish genocide?
2. Through what processes could the German people come to accept the need for the mass killings?

Article 41

America: What Went Wrong?

DONALD L. BARLETT AND JAMES B. STEEL

Casualties of the New Economic Order

LARRY WEIKEL AND BELINDA SCHELL know all about the future. For them, it arrived in 1990 when they paid the price for Wall Street's excesses—and Congress's failure to curb those excesses.

Weikel is forty-seven years old and lives with his wife in Boyertown, Pennsylvania. Their children are grown. Schell is thirty-three and lives with her husband and three children, two teenagers and a seven-year-old, in Royersford, Pennsylvania.

Both worked at the old Diamond Glass Company plant that had been a fixture in downtown Royersford for all of this century. Until, that is, the takeover craze of the 1980s led to its closing, to the elimination of their jobs and the jobs of 500 co-workers—and to profits of tens of millions of dollars for those behind it all.

Their stories are the stories of middle-class jobholders everywhere. In interviews across America, the authors heard a constant refrain. It was a litany sounded in city after city, from Hagerstown, Maryland, to South Bend, Indiana; from Hermann, Missouri, to Martell, California. Over and over, blue-collar and white-collar workers, midlevel managers—middle class all—talked of businesses that once

From *America: What Went Wrong?*, by Donald L. Barlett and James B. Steel, Kansas City, Missouri, Andrews and McMeel, 1992, pp. 12–17. Reprinted by permission.

were, but are no more. Sometimes the business was glass-making. Sometimes it was printing. Or timber. Or shoe-making. Or meat-packing. But always the words were the same.

They talked about owners and managers who had known the employees by name, who had known their families, who had known the equipment on the floor, who had walked through the plants and offices and stopped to chat. They talked about working with—and for—people who were members of an extended corporate family. And, finally, they talked—some with a sense of bewilderment, some with sadness, some with bitterness—of the takeovers, of the new owners and the new managers who replaced the old.

Sometimes those new managers knew the workers' names, but never the people behind the names. The new managers had only a nodding acquaintance with the equipment. And they were obsessed with meeting ever-rising production quotas.

Listen to Larry Weikel, who grew up in Spring City, Pennsylvania, went to Springford High School, joined the air force, spent four years in the service, returned home and, in 1966, went to work at the Diamond Glass Company, a family-owned business that dated from 1874: "Everybody knew everybody. Everybody was friendly. The supervisors were all nice. The owner would come in and talk to you. It was just a nice place to work. It was a nice family, you know . . . I loved to go to work."

Belinda Schell, born in Keyser, West Virginia, the daughter of a glassmaker, remembers how difficult it was to get a job at Diamond. Everyone, it seemed, wanted to work there. "It took me about two years to get into the plant," she said. That was in 1984.

But already the plant was operating under the new economic rules. The company embarked on a course that thousands of other businesses had embarked on and would follow—because the rules by which the American economy operates actually encourage it.

That course went something like this: Take the company public, borrow a lot of money to expand by acquiring other glass companies, run up the price of the stock and sell it off at a nice profit.

At first, the process moved slowly. The company, which had changed its name to Diamond-Bathurst, Inc., following a management buyout, picked up a second glassmaking plant in Vienna, West Virginia, from a bankrupt producer in 1981. Two years later, in 1983, it went public. Then, in April 1985, Diamond-Bathurst purchased Container General Corporation, a Chattanooga, Tennessee, glass manufacturer with twelve plants. And in July 1985, the company purchased most of the assets of Thatcher Glass Company of Greenwich, Connecticut, a manufacturer with six plants that was operating under the protection of a United States bankruptcy court.

Thatcher, like so many companies in the 1980s, had gone through a leveraged buyout in which managers and investors purchased the company with mostly borrowed money. So much borrowed money that the company eventually was forced into the bankruptcy court. That same month, Diamond-Bathurst moved from the drab second-floor offices above the aging Royersford plant into a modern office complex built into a hillside in the wooded and rolling countryside in Malvern, Pennsylvania. As Frank B. Foster 3d, the company's president and chief executive officer, put it at the time: "We became in three short months one of the largest glass-container manufacturers in the United States, with projected annualized sales of $550 million." To finance it all, Diamond-Bathurst borrowed big. Its debt rocketed 700 percent, going from $13 million in 1984 to $104 million in 1985.

Wall Street loved it. The stock shot up from a low of $6 a share to a high of $29. Later, it split. Sales climbed from $62 million to $408 million. Profits went from $2 million to $11 million.

The *Philadelphia Inquirer* in July 1985 quoted a First Boston Corporation securities analyst, Cornelius W. Thornton, as saying: "There's a whole lot of synergism in this deal. I don't think the question is can Diamond pull it off. I think they've done it." They hadn't. But Wall Street has a short attention span and many investors already had made a killing.

It soon became clear that Diamond-Bathurst would be unable to make the interest payments on its mountain of debt. The debt was made possible by a Congress that, at the time, was working on a tax bill that would eliminate the deductibility of most forms of consumer interest but retain the interest deduction for corporations.

Without that deduction, much of the corporate restructuring that took place in the 1980s, and the job loss that followed, might never have occurred, since the deals depended on the tax advantage. The use of debt to buy and dismantle companies—instead of to build them—was exploding. Congress, in hammering out the Tax Reform Act of 1986, chose to ignore that phenomenon.

In any event, Diamond-Bathurst posted a $6.2 million loss for 1986 rather than the profit that had been forecast by stockbrokers and company management. In June 1987, Moody's lowered the credit rating on Diamond-Bathurst's bonds. Company executives had already closed one manufacturing plant after another—in Indianapolis; Wharton, New Jersey; Mount Vernon, Ohio; Vienna, West Virginia; and Knox, Pennsylvania—abolishing the jobs of several thousands of workers.

It was not enough. In August 1987, a heavily indebted Diamond-Bathurst was acquired by a competitor, the new corporate headquarters in Malvern was closed and more than 250 salaried workers were dismissed. The buyer was Anchor Glass Container Corporation of Tampa, Florida, a descendant of a leveraged buyout.

When the new owners arrived in Royersford, Larry Weikel, by then a shift foreman; Belinda Schell, a clerk; and other workers noticed an immediate change. "It just became so competitive," Weikel said, "and things just started getting nasty and out of hand. It just seemed like they didn't care what you did to get the numbers. . . . They'd expect you to get on somebody about a problem that wasn't their fault to start with."

Schell said Anchor Glass sent in managers from its plants in other parts of the country, and they issued conflicting orders. Jobs were eliminated and the remaining employees were pressured to increase output. But there was no investment in more modern equipment or new technology. The final day of production came in August 1990. Weikel, Schell, and the remaining 275 or so employees were out of work.

Once again, their stories were much like the stories the authors heard in scores of interviews across the country. With few exceptions, the former Anchor Glass workers have moved into jobs that pay lower wages and offer reduced health-care benefits. Weikel works part time at a marine-supply store run by his brother-in-law. His wife works in a sewing factory, earning about $6 an hour. When he lost his job, he refinanced the mortgage on the family home and has been draining their savings. Jobs that pay the $15 an hour he earned at Anchor Glass do not exist.

Said Weikel: "That's all I ever did in my life, work in a glass plant. I went to work there when I came out of the service and, you know, I really never learned anything because all I did was make bottles, and there's not much call for that. I could reeducate myself, I guess, but I don't want to get into another mess like that. I could get a job anywhere, I mean making $5, $6 an hour. But that's not worth my time. . . . I would do it if I was starving. But I'm not. My kids are grown and I'm not worrying about it that much anymore. I spent twenty-three years worrying about it. . . . All I really have to do is make enough money to feed my wife and myself."

Belinda Schell, with a growing family, had no choice but to go back to work. At Anchor Glass, she earned more than $10 an hour. At her new job, as a nursing home aide, she earns considerably less. It is an occupation that the federal government touts as a growth industry that will provide many jobs—mostly low-paying—as the aged population continues to grow.

Belinda Schell's husband, who like Weikel earned $15 an hour at Anchor Glass, found a job in another manufacturing plant in King of Prussia, Pennsylvania. He, too, earns less than he did.

Mrs. Schell said her brother-in-law encountered another obstacle when he sought a job at lower pay than he had made: "They would tell him he made too much money and he wouldn't be satisfied. He was making $16 at Anchor Glass and they said he wouldn't be satisfied making $8. But people like that don't know what it's like going through a plant closing when you have a mortgage and children to feed. He has two children. He had just bought a new home the year before." She said her brother-in-law finally found other work, but at lower pay than he made at the glass plant. As for other co-workers, she said, "some of them that are working are only making $5 to $7 an hour, which doesn't compare with what we were making at Anchor. . . . I don't know anybody that is making what they made at Anchor Glass."

For Larry Weikel, the experience was disheartening: "You know what hurts me, that I was liked there at that plant at one time. And then for this to happen. . . . Twenty-three years in there, you know, and everything was great. And then an outfit comes in like this and destroys you.

"It seems like I prostituted my whole young life to that company and then they turn me out to pasture. . . . I spent Saturdays and Sundays down there. I didn't do anything with the kids. I didn't go to ball games. I didn't do that. I was always working. And then they turn around and do something like that to you."

Weikel, Schell and the other Diamond Glass employees were working under America's old economic rules that, for many, provided a job and good salary and health care and a pension for life in exchange for a commitment to the company.

The new rules were quite different, and the owners of the Anchor Glass company that bought Diamond Glass knew them intimately. In fact, you might even say that one of Anchor Glass's original owners helped to write those rules. He was former United States Treasury Secretary William E. Simon, who catapulted himself onto the *Forbes* magazine directory of the 400 richest Americans (his worth is estimated at $300 million) by taking advantage of the tax deduction for corporate debt.

Anchor Glass Container Corporation was itself the product of a leveraged buyout. It was formed in April 1983 by Wesray Corporation and executives of the glass-container division of the Anchor Hocking Corporation, one of the country's glass-making institutions. Wesray was an investment-banking firm founded by Simon along with Raymond G. Chambers, an accountant. It was one of the first of what would be many leveraged-buyout firms that acquired companies with mostly borrowed money.

After making cosmetic changes that often included job cutbacks and other short-term cost-reduction measures, the companies would be sold, in whole or in part, at a substantial profit—or taken public, another form of sale.

Newspapers and financial publications regaled readers with Simon successes during the 1980s—among them Anchor Glass. In an article published in October 1988, the *Los Angeles Times* reported that after Simon helped engineer the Anchor Glass buyout, "managers cut the work force, slashed expenses and made a successful acquisition." Simon, the *Times* said, "made more than 100 times his money."

When Anchor Glass purchased the old glass-container division of Anchor Hocking, the transaction was financed with the patented Simon debt formula: $76 million in borrowed money and $1 million investment by Wesray and others. You might think of that kind of arrangement this way: Let's say you want to buy a house for $100,000. You visit your friendly neighborhood bank and offer to put $1,500 down. That is not the kind of deal you can get.

But Simon and his associates got a much better one when they organized Anchor Glass. After Anchor Glass borrowed the $76 million, according to documents filed with the United States Securities and Exchange Commission (SEC), $48.5 million of that sum was reloaned to Simon and friends. They, in turn, used $24 million of that money to buy the land and buildings of various glass plants. Then they leased the land and buildings back to their new company, Anchor Glass, for twenty years.

In other words, the new owner of the glass plants, Anchor Glass, would pay rent on the land and buildings to Simon and the other investors.

There was still more. Simon and his associates bought the furnaces and other glass-making equipment in the various plants in exchange for a note promising to pay $43.6 million. Then they leased the glass-making equipment back to Anchor Glass.

Several years later, Anchor Glass, in a report filed with the SEC, said the transactions were too generous to Simon and the other investors: "These arrangements were entered into when the company was privately owned, were not the result of arm's-length bargaining and on the whole were not as favorable to the company as could have been obtained from unrelated third parties."

There were other deals. Wesray picked up investment-banking fees for handling the purchase of the glass-container properties and the acquisition of Midland Glass Company. Anchor Glass purchased its casualty and liability insurance, and its employee health and benefit insurance, from two brokerage firms in which Simon and his colleagues also held interest. That was worth more millions of dollars in fees. And finally, there was the Anchor Glass corporate headquarters in Tampa. It, too, was owned by Simon and associates, who leased the building to the company.

In March 1986, Anchor Glass, which had been a private company, offered stock for sale to the public. By February 1988, according to an SEC report, Simon had sold his holdings. His total profits from the deals are unknown. But they run into the tens of millions of dollars.

One more note: In October 1989, Anchor Glass was sold. The buyer was Vitro, S.A., a Mexican glass company that ships products into the United States, competing with American-owned companies. Vitro is part of the corporate empire of Mexico's Sada family, which is ranked by *Forbes* among the world's billionaire families. The Mexican company's first moves included a decision to close the glass plant in Royersford. And another plant in Vernon, California. And another plant in Gulfport, Mississippi. And another plant in San Leandro, California.

DISCUSSION QUESTIONS

1. Who benefits from the corporate buy-outs?
2. Compared with the old, where does the power lie in the new economic rules?

XV

Population and Health

WHAT TO FOCUS ON:

1. In what ways can the field of epidemiology contribute to the understanding and control of AIDS?
2. How do greeting cards reflect changing demographic trends?

IN THIS CHAPTER we examine population and health as related topics. The study of population and health shares a focus as evidenced by the fields of demography and epidemiology. The scientific study of human population is called demography. Demographers examine both structural and dynamic components of human population. Structural components refer to population characteristics such as size, density, distribution, and composition (sex, age, race). Dynamic components refer to population processes such as fertility and mortality rates, occupational trends, and migration rates. Demographic studies are essential for assessing the challenges and potential issues related to population characteristics and trends in our society and throughout the world. In the previous chapter, the focus on the "baby-boom" generation and the gradual aging of our population illustrates the significance of demography.

Sociologists are interested in examining patterns of health and illness in social systems. Epidemiology is a field that studies both the occurrence and distribution of disease in a given population. It examines the rates of disease within given groups and studies the factors that may be related to those rates. Basically, epidemiology focuses on who gets sick and why. Epidemiologists function as medical detectives investigating the broad range of factors that may be involved in any disease.

Epidemiology views health and disease from a multicausal perspective. Health and disease may be linked to one's biological makeup and vulnerability, one's psychological state, and social and cultural factors. Sociological studies in epidemiology have investigated the incidence and prevalence of disease and its relationship to lifestyle, stress, and social change. Social epidemiologists have discovered protective folkways that function to sustain health as well as lifestyles that pose potential health risks. The field of epidemiology was probably first brought into the public eye due to the perplexing outbreak of the Legionnaires' disease in Philadelphia in 1976. Currently, epidemiologists have an essential role in combating the AIDS crisis.

In the first article, Jeffrey P. Rosenfeld and Susan Rodin examine the greeting card industry and its relationship to demographic trends and popular lifestyles. The greeting card market reflects a more diverse set of themes in order to stay in tune with demographic changes. Like television, greeting cards function as a looking glass of our culture.

In the second article, Peter Conrad presents an excellent analysis of the social and cultural meanings of AIDS. He puts a human face on the AIDS crisis. People with AIDS, and often their families, must cope not only with the ravaging effects of a deadly disease, but also with the stigma of having AIDS. The societal response to AIDS victims generally has been marked by a lack of regard and compassion. Conrad offers some timely suggestions for reducing both the stigma and hysteria surrounding the disease.

Article 42

Lifestyle: It's in the Cards

JEFFREY P. ROSENFELD AND SUSAN RODIN

THE MESSAGE IS INTIMATE. The demographics are mind-boggling. Americans bought 7 billion greeting cards in 1983, a card for everything from birthdays to barbecues.

Greeting cards were half the personal mail sent last year, a total of 2.3 billion names on our cumulative Christmas list, 1.5 billion birthday greetings amounting to 6.3 cards for each of us, and 900 million hearts on Valentine's Day, 1983. The remainder announced events private and public, secret desires and personal woes—a $1.88 billion industry based on what Hallmark's Nancy Matheny calls our "communication needs."

Greeting cards also tell about demographics, because card sales are linked to population trends and life-styles. No wonder we usually find what we need when we visit the local card shop. The companies that specialize in greetings can satisfy us because they are in sync with demographics.

Tracking Trends

No two companies have the same markets. But most of the 400 and more greeting card manufacturers, from Puffin in Seattle to the fledgling Heart Deco in New York City, know something about demographics.

From "Lifestyle: It's in the Cards," by Jeffrey Rosenfeld and Susan Rodin, *American Demographics,* Dec., 1984, pp. 311–333, 337. Reprinted by permission.

At Alfred Mainzer, Inc., with card copy in 22 languages, the goal is to anticipate ethnic migration and settlement patterns. The company needs to know these trends because they reflect cultural differences that affect card sales. Recently, for example, New York's Mott Street district— once mainly Italian—became heavily Chinese. Apart from the obvious language difference is the fact that Italians are big Christmas card senders while the Chinese are not. Even when the language is similar—as in the case of the Spanish spoken by Mexicans, Cubans, and Puerto Ricans—there can be subtle differences in dialect and phrasing that affect card sales. This is why some card companies follow migration data with such interest.

Labor force statistics are another source of ideas for the greeting card industry. Bert Hobrath, of American Greetings, explains that his company may produce more cards for working women, because more than half of women today are in the labor force. If so, this company will join Hallmark, Recycled Paper, and other manufacturers now selling feminine business greetings.

There are important demographic trends behind the success of feminine business greetings and ethnic greetings. They meet the communication needs of our changing society. Card companies, large and small, adapt to these needs by following the behavior of a so-called model buyer.

Statistically speaking, she is in her late 40s, married, suburban, and traditional. Apparently she keeps the cash registers humming too. Hallmark and American Greetings, two companies that track her card-buying habits, together sell half of all cards purchased in the U.S. every year. These industry giants work on the assumption that women buy 85 percent of all greeting cards. Other companies disagree, however.

Bert Murrie attributes the success of such companies as Paper Moon, Recycled Paper, Rock Shots, and his own California Dreamers to an alternate card market. The demographics of this alternate market are anything but traditional, suburban, and female. Says Murrie, an estimated 35 percent of people buying Paper Moon, Rock Shots, and California Dreamers are men living in gentrifying urban areas. In general, "alternate" card buyers are better educated, less traditional, and more cosmopolitan than card-buyers from Hallmark country.

Whatever the market, greeting card companies are following five trends with gusto. The aging of the population is first on everyone's list of trends, followed by working women, divorce, cohabitation, and the ethnic market.

You're 40

The industry divides card-buyers into two markets based on aging. The first is the older American—the 25 million people aged 65 or older. The other is the age-conscious people aged 35 to 64.

Card shops are stocking greater numbers of cards for older Americans, because there are more four-generation families, and more social situations involving older people. Cards intended for older people include the expected ones to commemorate birthdays, anniversaries, and retirements. New additions include grandparent announcements for older people to send, and birthday wishes for great-grandchildren.

Hallmark created variety packs of cards for older people—packages of cards for different occasions—after learning that older Americans wanted to minimize their trips to the stationery store.

Cards for and about grandparenting make good demographic sense because 75 percent of older Americans have living children; and 90 percent of these have grandchildren. The best comment on increased longevity is Hallmark's *To My Grandchild On His/Her Wedding Anniversary.* Older Americans live to witness more family events than ever before.

The greeting cards older Americans give and get are respectful and friendly in tone. They reconfirm traditional roles and celebrate the part that older people play in American family life. This celebration of old age is different from greeting cards that deal with aging—cards pitched at a younger market.

There have always been greeting cards to remind us—and none too gently—that we are getting older. What's different about today's versions is that they start at an earlier age and continue to taunt us well into our 60s. Recycled Paper Products shrewdly appeals to a common anxiety in a card that reads, *You're 30 . . . And I'm Not.* The card is also available for 40-, 50-, and 60-year-olds. The gift-wrapped bottle of Milk of Magnesia featured on another card makes the same point. Abrasive as they are, these cards sell briskly. Nobody can avoid getting old, something the greeting card industry uses to its advantage.

Women's Business

The cover shows an overworked middle-manager, her desk piled high with work due yesterday. She is saying to herself, *There's No Place Like Home.* Inside is a picture of the same woman at home, up to her elbows in dirty dishes and piles of laundry. *There's No Place Like The Office,* she says.*

The greeting card industry—with a large female work force of its own—has been giving special attention to women. It has successfully capitalized on the subject of work, and also on the fact that working women want to save time. Greeting cards are a quick fix.

Cards for working women can be serious, sarcastic, or just plain nice. They are rarely floral or frilly. American Greetings has avoided the floral look in promoting Kathy for working women, as has Hallmark in its cards, including the Modern Woman line. Working women enjoy the humor, but shy away from the frills.

Jim and Barbara Dale struck a responsive chord in the card-buying public with their slogan, *Behind Every Successful Woman Is An Enormous Pile Of Unwashed Laundry.* The Dales have a following because they use humor to describe the overloaded lives of so many working women.

Housework, child care, and job obligations are not easy to juggle. Hallmark understands that working women can overlook dirty laundry now and then, but will never compromise on child care. As a result, working women now have cards that

*Elizabeth W. Stanley and Jan Graveline Eliot for The Maine Line Company.

read, *Thanks For All Your Help;* or *You Have Such A Way With Children;* and *Can't Thank You Enough For Doing So Much.*

Working women are more likely than working men to send cards to the people who work for them. They also send more cards to co-workers and supervisors. Examples of women's business greetings include, *Congratulations On Your Promotion,* and *Good Luck In Your New Job,* as well as a simple *Thanks For A Good Job.*

My Father's Wife

Greeting cards confirm what so many of us know from thumbing through our personal address books: relationships are changeable and complex. This fact only increases the opportunities for greeting card manufacturers, who see new relationships and remarriages as a way to sell more cards.

Divorce is still a sensitive subject, but is socially acceptable enough for Hallmark to be marketing a number of cards for divorced people, including Hallmark's *Thinking Of You As You're Starting Over.* Hallmark also helps the recently divorced with packaged divorce announcements.

The greeting card industry appreciates children whose parents are divorced or remarried—a delicate topic. An estimated 8 percent of American households are single-parent households, which is why American Greetings will offer a card that reads, *Because You Do The Work Of Two People, You're Appreciated Twice As Much.*

There are greeting cards for the live-in lover or new spouse. Gone are the days of the wicked step-mother, especially since 1,300 new step-families are created each day. This is why Drawing Board Greeting Cards in Dallas now markets greetings *To My Dad And His Wife,* and *To My Other Mother.* Carolyn Walters of Drawing Board says the company also has cards for the step-grandparents that any divorce and remarriage will generate. An estimated 65 percent of grandparents will be step-grandparents by the year 2000—a legacy of all the divorcing and remarrying their children have done. American Greetings is pleased with sales figures on cards *For Someone Who Is Like A Father To Me.* Hallmark is satisfied with how tactful greetings *To A Very Special Person* are doing. The only issue left to be communicated is who gets custody of these cards if the new relationship breaks up.

There are currently 1.9 million couples living together unmarried, more than triple the 1970 figure. Cohabitants are a prime market for greeting card manufacturers. Paper Moon's display rack in one Manhattan card shop on the Upper West Side has more slots for Friends/Lovers cards than for Wedding or Anniversary Greetings.

Cards for cohabitants are based on the relationship itself, and not on the milestones that a married couple celebrates. Hallmark's line of New Relationships cards explores such themes as coping, support, and friendship. *Happy Anniversary On Your Special Day* is a Hallmark card that sells briskly, according to Debbie Reed Scarfino of Hallmark, because the card never specifies what the special day is.

New relationships have their ups and downs, as card designers know. Heart Deco, a young New York company, has developed a card for the friend/lover who catches the other in a lie. *Admit It,* says the copy in this card.

There are now greeting cards for people of all social and sexual persuasions; cards as prim as the Just Desserts line with its sundae-shaped greetings, and cards as naughty as those from Rock Shots. *A Poem For Your Birthday* reads the front of one card by The Maine Line Company. *Hip Hip Hooray! I'm Glad You're Gay!,* says the inside. No one can accuse greeting cards of not keeping up-to-date.

Future Stock

Like any other profit-oriented industry, greeting card companies can't afford to be locked into today's ideas. Two trends are already emerging that show signs of reshaping the industry in years to come.

The first is a growing health consciousness. Daniel Yankelovich, a public opinion researcher who has studied this trend, says interest in health and fitness will intensify, and with it will come more self-expression. Even now this is translating into subjects and occasions for card-sending. Everything from weight-loss to good wishes on an upcoming marathon shows up in greeting cards.

Ironically, there will also be an increased demand for get-well cards in the coming age of health and fitness. But their function will change.

Cards saying *Get Well Soon* cannot sell in a population of chronically ill people. The shift from acute to chronic illness that has already reshaped American health care will soon affect the greeting card industry. Along with *Get Well Soon* wishes for acutely ill people will be *Feel Better* cards for the chronically ill.

Ethnic cards will become big sellers, especially for Hispanics, who now number 16 million. Cards for Asian Americans—particularly Chinese, Japanese and Koreans—will become more visible, at least in some cities. Asians' educational and income levels make them prime greeting card consumers.

Whatever demographic changes lie ahead, the industry that was once based on eternal verities like love and marriage will continue to adapt. Roses may still be red and violets blue, but greeting cards, more than ever, will reflect you.

DISCUSSION QUESTIONS

1. What are the five major trends that the greeting card market has recently focused on?
2. How is the greeting card industry related to demographic trends and lifestyles? In what ways do greeting cards reflect changes in cultural norms and values?

Article 43

The Social Meaning of AIDS

PETER CONRAD

DISEASE AND ILLNESS can be examined on different levels. Disease is understood best as a biophysiological phenomenon, a process or state that affects the body. Illness, by contrast, has more to do with the social and psychological phenomena that surround the disease. The world of illness is the subjective world of meaning and interpretation; how a culture defines an illness and how individuals experience their disorder.

In this article I am going to examine the social and cultural meanings of Acquired Immune Deficiency Syndrome or AIDS as it is manifested in late-20th-century America and relate these meanings to the social reaction that it has engendered. When I talk about the social meaning of AIDS, I am including what Susan Sontag has termed the metaphorical aspects of illness: those meanings of diseases that are used to reflect back on some morally suspect element of society.[1] As Sontag suggests, metaphorical aspects of illness are especially prevalent with dread diseases that have great unknowns about them. We need to look at AIDS not only as a biomedical entity, but as an illness that has a socially constructed image and engages particular attitudes. The social meanings of AIDS are simultaneously alarmingly

From "The Social Meaning of AIDS," by Peter Conrad, *Social Policy,* Summer, 1986, pp. 51–56.

simple and bafflingly complex, but are key to understanding the social reaction to AIDS.

The Social Reaction to AIDS

The medical reality of AIDS, as we know it, remains puzzling but is becoming clearer. AIDS is a disease caused by a virus that breaks down the immune system and leaves the body unprotected against "opportunistic infections" that nearly invariably lead to death. The number of AIDS cases is growing dramatically and AIDS is considered an epidemic in the society. Over 19,000 cases have been diagnosed, with four or five times that many people having a chronic disorder called AIDS-Related Complex (ARC) and perhaps over a million individuals having an antibody-positive response to HTLV-III, the virus believed to cause AIDS. It is estimated that 5 to 20% of this exposed group will contract AIDS, but no one knows who they will be.

Over 90% of AIDS victims come from two risk groups: homosexual or bisexual men and intravenous drug users. (Hemophiliacs and others requiring frequent blood transfusions and infants born to mothers with AIDS are also considered risk groups.) The evidence is clear that the AIDS virus is transmitted through the direct exchange of bodily fluids, semen and blood; the most common mode of transmission is anal intercourse among male homosexuals and unsterile needle-sharing among intravenous drug users. There is virtually *no* evidence that the virus can be transmitted by everyday "casual contact," including kissing or shaking hands, or exposure to food, air, water, or whatever.[2] With the exception of very specific modes of semen or blood-related transmission it does not appear that the AIDS virus is very easy to "catch."

Yet the public reaction to AIDS has bordered on hysteria. Below are a few examples of the reactions to AIDS or AIDS victims.

> 11,000 children were kept out of school in Queens, New York, as parents protested the decision to allow a 7-year-old girl with AIDS to attend second grade (despite no evidence of transmission by school children).
>
> Hospital workers in San Francisco refused to enter the room of an AIDS patient. When ordered to attend the patient, they appeared wearing masks, gowns, and goggles.
>
> A Baltimore policeman refused to enter the office of a patient with AIDS to investigate a death threat and donned rubber gloves to handle the evidence.
>
> In New York, undertakers refused to embalm AIDS victims, householders fired their Haitian help, and subway riders wore gloves, all from fear of contracting AIDS.
>
> One child, hospitalized with AIDS, had a "do not touch" sign on her bed and was isolated from all physical contact with her parents.
>
> In a Boston corporation, employees threatened to quit en masse if the company forced them to work with an AIDS patient.

> Dade County, Florida, voted to require the county's 80,000 food workers to carry cards certifying they are free of communicable diseases, including AIDS, despite no known cases of AIDS transmitted through food and even though public health officials opposed this policy.
>
> The U.S. military is beginning to screen all new recruits for AIDS antibodies, with the likely result of declaring those who test seropositive ineligible for service.
>
> Several major life insurance companies are requiring certain applicants (young, single, male, living in certain areas) to undergo an HTLV-III antibody test.

The list could go on. There is clearly a great fear engendered by the spectre of AIDS, a fear that has led to an overreaction to the actual problem. This is in no way to say that AIDS is not a terrible and devastating disease—it is—or to infer that it is not a serious public health concern. What we are seeing is an overblown, often irrational, and pointless reaction to AIDS that makes the disease more difficult for those who have it and diverts attention from the real public health concerns.

The Social and Cultural Meanings of AIDS

To better understand the reaction to AIDS, it is necessary to examine particular social features of the disease: (1) the effect of marginal and stigmatized "risk groups"; (2) sexually-related transmission; (3) the role of contagion; and (4) the deadly nature of the disease.

The effect of marginal and stigmatized "risk groups." There are some illnesses that carry with them a certain moral devaluation, a stigma. Leprosy, epilepsy, mental disorder, venereal disease, and by some accounts, cancer, all reflect moral shame on the individuals who had the ill luck to contract them. Stigmatized illnesses are usually diseases that in some fashion are connected to deviant behavior: either they are deemed to produce it as with epilepsy or are produced by it, as in the case of VD.

The effect of the early connection of AIDS to homosexual conduct cannot be underestimated in examining its stigmatized image. The early designation of the disorder was Gay Related Immune Deficiency Syndrome (GRID) and was publicly proclaimed as a "gay plague." It was first thought to be caused by the use of "poppers" (amylnitrate) and later by promiscuity.[3] Something those fast-track gays were doing was breaking down their immune system. However, AIDS is not and never was specifically related to homosexual conditions; viruses don't know homosexuals from heterosexuals.

Within a short time, other "risk" groups were identified for what was now called AIDS—intravenous drug users, Haitians, and hemophiliacs. With the exception of hemophiliacs (who made up less than two percent of the cases), AIDS' image in the public eye was intimately connected with marginal populations. It was a disease of "those deviants," considered by some a deserved punishment for their activities. In 1983 Patrick J. Buchanan, who later became a White House staffer, wrote: "Those poor homosexuals. They have declared war on nature, and nature is exacting an awful retribution."[4] It is certain that fear of AIDS was amplified by the widespread and deeply rooted "homophobia" in American society.

Sexually-related transmission. The dominant vector of transmission of AIDS is through sexual activity, particularly anal intercourse of male homosexuals. Although scientifically AIDS is better seen as a "blood disease" (since contact with blood is necessary for transmission), this common form of transmission has contributed to its image as a sexually transmitted disease.

Venereal diseases are by nature also stigmatized. They are deemed to be the fault of the victims and would not occur had people behaved better. As Allen Brandt points out, venereal diseases have become a symbol of pollution and contamination: "Venereal disease, the palpable evidence of unrestrained sexuality became a symbol for social disorder and moral decay—a metaphor of evil."[5]

AIDS, with its connection to multiple sex encounters and once-forbidden "sodomy," touches deep Puritanical concerns and revives alarms of promiscuity and "sexual permissiveness" that have become more muted in recent decades. The connection of AIDS to "sexual irresponsibility" has been made repeatedly.

Now that it appears AIDS can be transmitted through heterosexual intercourse as well, although apparently not as efficiently and rapidly, there is increasing concern among sexually active people that they may be betrayed in their most intimate moments. This connection with intimacy and sexuality amplifies our anxieties and creates fears that one sexual act may bring a lifetime of pollution and ultimately death.

The role of contagion. We have almost come to believe that large-scale deadly epidemics were a thing of the past. The polio panics of the early 1950s have receded far into our collective memory, and the wrath of tuberculosis, cholera, or diphtheria have become, in American society at least, artifacts of the past. Everyday models for contagion are more limited to the likes of herpes, chicken pox, and hepatitis. When we encounter AIDS, which is contagious but apparently in a very specific way, our fear of contagion erupts almost without limits. When little is known about a disease's transmission, one could expect widespread apprehensions about contagion. But a great deal is known about AIDS' transmission—it appears only to be transmitted through the exchange of bodily fluids and in *no* cases through any type of casual contact. In fact, compared to other contagious diseases it has a relatively low infectivity. Yet the fear of contagion fuels the reaction to AIDS.

Given our extant medical knowledge, what are the sources of fear? We live in a society where medicine is expected to protect us from deadly contagious diseases, if not by vaccine, then by public health intervention. And when medicine does not do this, we feel we must rely on our own devices to protect ourselves and our loved ones. Contagion, even of minor disorders, can engender irrational responses. Several months ago my 5-year-old daughter was exposed to a playmate who came down with chicken pox. A good friend of mine, who happens to be a pediatrician, did not want his 4-year-old to ride in the car with my daughter to gymnastics class, even though he knew medically that she could not yet be infectious. He just did not want to take any chances. And so it is with us, our reactions to contagion are not always rational.

With AIDS, of course, the situation is much worse. When we read in the newspapers that the AIDS virus has been found in saliva or tears, though only occasionally, we imagine in our commonsense germ-theory models of contagion that we could "catch AIDS" in this manner. Reports that no transmission has ever occurred in this fashion become secondary. The public attitudes seem to be that exposure to the AIDS virus condemns one to the disease.

While AIDS is contagious, so is the fear and stigma. The fear of AIDS has outstripped the actual social impact of the disease. But, more importantly for families of people who suffer from AIDS, the stigma of AIDS becomes contagious. They develop what Erving Goffman has called a courtesy stigma, a taint that has spread from the stigmatized to his or her close connections.[6] Family members of people with AIDS are shunned and isolated by former friends and colleagues, for fear that they too might bring contagion.

A deadly disease. AIDS is a devastating and deadly disease. It is virtually 100% lethal: 75% of people with AIDS die within two years. There are few other diseases that, like AIDS, attack and kill people who are just reaching the prime of their lives. Currently, AIDS is incurable; since there are no treatments for it, to contract AIDS in the 1990s is to be served with a death warrant. Many sufferers waste away from Kaposi's sarcoma or some rare form of chronic pneumonia.

As various researchers have shown, caretakers and family alike tend to distance themselves from sufferers who are terminally ill with diseases that waste away their bodies.[7] The pain of suffering and the pollution of dying are difficult for many people to encounter directly in a society that has largely removed and isolated death from everyday life.

Taken together, these features form a cultural image of AIDS that is socially as well as medically devastating. It might even be said that AIDS is an illness with a triple stigma: it is connected to stigmatized groups (homosexuals and drug users); it is sexually transmitted; and, like cancer, it is a terminal, wasting disease. It would be difficult to imagine a scenario for a more stigmatizing disease, short of one that also makes those infected obviously visible.

The Effects of AIDS

The social meaning affects the consequences of AIDS, especially for AIDS sufferers and their families and the gay community but also for medicine and the public as well.

The greatest consequences of AIDS are of course for AIDS sufferers. They must contend with a ravaging disease and the stigmatized social response that can only make coping with it more difficult. In a time when social support is most needed, it may become least available. And in the context of the paucity of available medical treatments, those with AIDS must face the prospect of early death with little hope of survival.

People with ARC or those who test antibody-positive must live with the uncertainty of not knowing what the progression of their disorder will be. And living with this uncertainty, they must also live with the fear and stigma produced by the social meanings of AIDS. This may mean subtle disenfranchisement, overt discrimination, outright exclusion, or even total shunning. The talk of quarantine raises the anxiety of "why me?" Those symptomless seropositive individuals, who experts suggest have a 5 to 20% chance of developing full-blown AIDS, must live with the inner conflict of whom to tell or not to tell, of how to manage their sexual and work lives, and the question of whether and how they might infect others. The social meanings of AIDS make this burden more difficult.

Families and lovers of people with AIDS, ARC, or an antibody-positive test are placed in an uncomfortable limbo status. Many live in constant fear that they might contract the AIDS virus, and thus limit their contact with the infected individual. Others wonder whether they too might be or become infectious. As mentioned earlier, families often share the AIDS stigma, as others see them as tainted, cease visiting their home, or even sever all contact with them. In one recent study of screening for AIDS among blood donors, the researchers noted they "have interviewed people in the pilot phase of [their] notification program who have been left by their spouses or significant others after telling them about their blood test results."[8]

The gay community has been profoundly affected by AIDS. The late 1960s and 1970s were an exciting and positive period of the American gay community. Thousands of gay men and women came "out of the closet" and proclaimed in a variety of ways that "gay is good." Many laws forbidding gay sexual activity were removed from the books. Gay people developed their own community institutions and more openly experimented and practiced alternative lifestyles. Although the celebration of anonymous sex among some gay males resulted in high rates of sexually-transmitted diseases and hepatitis B, the social atmosphere in the gay community remained overwhelmingly positive. While the attitudes toward homosexuality never became totally accepting, public moral opprobrium toward gays was perceptibly reduced.[9]

And along came AIDS. With its image as a "gay disease" related to a fast-track gay male lifestyle, the fear of AIDS tapped into a reservoir of existing moral fear of homosexuals. It was a catalyst to the reemergence of a latent "homophobia" that had never really disappeared. Now there was a new reason to discriminate against gays. Thus AIDS has led to a restigmatization of homosexuality. Every avowed male homosexual is a suspected carrier of AIDS and deemed potentially dangerous. This, of course, has pushed many gay men back into the closet, living their lives with new fears and anxieties. It is clear that AIDS threatens two decades of social advances for the gay community.

Concern about AIDS has also become the overriding social and political concern of the gay community, consuming energy that previously went toward other types of social and political work. The gay community was the first to bring the AIDS problem into the public arena and to urge the media, medicine, and government to take action. Action groups in the gay community have engaged in extensive

AIDS educational campaigns. This was done out of concern, but not without a fear of government surveillance and invasion of privacy. There was also apprehension that the images of "bad blood" and depictions of gays as health risks might lead to new exclusions of gays.[10]

The scourge of AIDS in the gay community has led, on the one hand, to divisions among gays (e.g., should bath houses be closed) and, on the other, to unprecedented changes in sexual behavior (e.g., witness the dramatic drop in the number of sex partners and types of sexual encounters reported in several studies and indexed by the large decrease in new cases of rectal gonorrhea).[11]

There is also a great emotional toll from the AIDS epidemic in the gay community. Nearly everyone in the community has friends or acquaintances who have died from the disease. As one gay activist recently put it, many people in the gay community were suffering a "grief-overload" as a result of the losses from AIDS.[12]

The social image of AIDS has affected medical care and scientific research as well. In general, the medical voice concerning AIDS, at least in terms of describing it to the public and outlining its perils, has on the whole been cautious and even-handed. The tenor of information has been factual and not unduly emotional. The Center for Disease Control (CDC) has again and again declared that AIDS is not transmitted by casual contact and, although it is a major epidemic and a public health threat, it is one with specific risk groups.

However, some medical scientists have placed the dangers of AIDS in a highly negative light either to raise the public's concern or to elicit private or governmental research funds. For example, "Dr. Alvin Friedman-Kein, an AIDS researcher who saw the first cases, said that AIDS will probably be the plague of the century."[13] Dr. Mathilde Krim was quoted in *The New York Post* last September as saying that "it is only a matter of time before it afflicts heterosexuals on a large scale" while presenting no evidence or data to support the claim.[14] The media, of course, picks up these assertions, often highlighting them in headlines, which reinforces the public fear. . . .

Finally, stigmatized attitudes toward a disease can constrain medical progress. As Allen Brandt points out, the negative social meanings attached to VD actually obstructed medical efforts. He noted that research funding was somewhat limited because the issue was thought to be best dealt with behaviorally. Among many VD researchers the discovery of penicillin was treated with ambivalence, since they were afraid a cure of syphilis would promote promiscuity.[15]

While medical scientists have recently gained a great deal of knowledge about AIDS, including isolating the virus, describing the modes of transmission, and developing a test for screening HTLV-III antibodies in blood (although it is imperfect for screening people)[16], the stigma AIDS presents has probably limited public funding for AIDS research and deterred some types of community research on AIDS natural history. Several commentators have noted that federal funding for research and prevention of AIDS was slow in emerging because AIDS was seen as a "gay disease." It was only when it threatened blood transfusions and blood products that public consciousness was aroused and federal support was forthcoming. Unfortunately, this increased support for research and education was "misinterpreted as an indicator that AIDS was a universal threat destined to work its way inexorably through all segments of society."[17]

One of the most striking aspects about the social reaction to AIDS is how fear and stigma have led to a resistance to information about AIDS. While at times the media has sensationalized AIDS, there has also been a great deal of information communicated concerning AIDS, its characteristics, and its modes of transmission. Yet study after study finds a small but substantial and consistent proportion of the population that exhibits profound misinformation about AIDS. . . . In a study of adolescents in Ohio, fully 60% believed that touching or coming near a person with AIDS might transmit the disease.[18] These authors contend that low knowledge of AIDS is correlated with high perceived susceptibility.

In a survey in San Francisco, New York, and London, the researchers found that "more knowledge was significantly negatively correlated with general fear of AIDS and with anti-gay attitudes among risk groups."[19] It appears that rather than low knowledge creating fear, the social meaning of AIDS creates resistance and barriers to taking in accurate information about AIDS.

Such misinformation is also prevalent among health-care providers. In a Massachusetts study of the effect of AIDS educational programs on health-care providers, the researchers reported that before the program, "20.5% of providers thought AIDS could be transmitted by shaking hands and 17.2% thought it could be acquired simply by being in the same room with a patient."[20] Many of these beliefs seem resistant to change. In the Massachusetts study, "after the [educational] programs, 15% of the providers still thought AIDS could be transmitted by sneezing or coughing, and 11.3% thought it could be transmitted by shaking hands. [In addition] after the . . . programs, the majority (66.2%) still thought that gowns were always necessary and a substantial minority (46.3%) still considered quarantine necessary."[21] While the educational programs affected some change in knowledge about AIDS, the researchers found a strong resistance to changing knowledge and attitudes among a substantial minority of health-care providers. Such misinformation among health-care providers can only have negative effects on AIDS patients.

One of the social tragedies of the fear and stigma is that it has constrained compassion for AIDS sufferers. In our culture, we generally show caring and compassion for severely and terminally ill patients. The social meaning of AIDS mutes this compassion in families, among health-care providers, and with the public at large. It is a shame that a victim of any disease in our society must suffer the plight of Robert Doyle of Baltimore. After discovering he had pneumonia brought on by AIDS, no nursing home or hospice would take him. His family rejected him and his lover demanded that he move out of the apartment. With only months to live, he had no support, resources, or place to die. He finally rented a room in a run-down hotel, where the staff refused to enter the room and left food for him in the hallway. After a newspaper story, a stranger took him into her home, only to ask him to leave in a few days; next an elderly couple took him in, until threatening telephone calls and vandalism forced him to move again. He finally found a home with three other adults, one also an AIDS victim. Soon he was returned to the hospital where he died.[22] The fear of AIDS turned this sick and dying man into a social outcast.

Conclusion

The social meaning of AIDS has added to the victim-blaming response common to sexually and behaviorally-related diseases a powerful victim-fearing component. This has engendered an overreaction to the perils of AIDS and fueled the public fears of the disease. Some dangers and threats are, of course, very real, but the triple stigma of AIDS presents a frightening picture to the public, which leads to misguided attempts at "protection" and to resistance to contrary information. This only makes managing life more difficult for the sufferers and does not make the world "safer" from AIDS.

Since a medical cure or prevention for AIDS in the near future is unlikely, it is important that efforts be made to reduce the "hysteria" and overreaction surrounding this disease. We need to redouble our efforts to diffuse the unwarranted aspects of the fear of AIDS and to reduce its stigma. There are several strategies for attempting to accomplish this.

AIDS appears to be "out of control." If some type of medical intervention emerged that could limit the spread and/or symptoms of the disease, this sense of lack of control might be decreased and the public expectations of medicine's protective function might be somewhat restored. But given the historical examples of epilepsy and syphilis, available and efficacious medical treatments do not in themselves alter the image of a disorder. The stigma of these diseases, while perhaps reduced, are still prevalent in our society.

Activists, policymakers, and medical personnel must directly attempt to change the image of the disease. Sometimes a disease's stigmatized image is reinforced by incorrect information. A classic example is the notion that leprosy was highly contagious and sufferers needed to be placed in isolated colonies. We know now that leprosy is not easily communicable. With epilepsy, myths developed that both emerged from and sustained the stigma, including notions like epilepsy is an inherited disease or it causes crime. These myths often gained professional support and led to misguided public policies such as forbidding marriage or immigration.[23] Such incorrect information and mythology must be unmasked and not be allowed to become the basis for social policies.

Another strategy to reduce stigma is to "normalize" the illness; that is, to demonstrate that not only "deviants" get the disease. It is important to show that conventional people can suffer the disease and, to the extent possible, lead normal lives. For example, Rock Hudson's belated public disclosure of his AIDS was an important symbol. He was identified as a solid, clean-cut American man, almost an ideal. He was also a movie hero with whom many people had made some kind of vicarious relationship. To a certain extent Rock Hudson helped bring AIDS out of the closet. An important public policy strategy should be to "normalize" AIDS as much as possible—to present exemplars of people who still can live relatively normal, if difficult, lives, with positive antibodies, ARC, or even AIDS. The media has done this to a degree with children—depicted as innocent victims of the disease—but we need to bring other AIDS sufferers back into our world and recreate our compassion for them.

We need to develop policies that focus on changing the image of AIDS and confront directly the stigma, resistance to information, and the unnecessary fears of the disease. Given the social meaning of AIDS, this won't be easy. While studies have shown us how difficult it is to change public attitudes toward illnesses,[24] images of diseases like leprosy (Hanson's disease) and, to a lesser degree, epilepsy have changed. We must develop the professional and public resolve to change the social meanings and response to AIDS and make this a high priority, along with the control, treatment, and eventual eradication of the disease. It is incumbent upon us to reduce the social as well as the physical suffering from AIDS.

NOTES

1. Susan Sontag, *Illness as Metaphor* (New York: Farrar, Straus and Giroux, 1978).
2. Merle A. Sande, "The Transmission of AIDS: The Case Against Casual Contagion," *New England Journal of Medicine,* vol. 314 (1986), pp. 380–82. See also, June E. Osborn, "The AIDS Epidemic: An Overview of the Science," *Issues in Science and Technology* (Winter, 1986), pp. 40–55.
3. Jacques Liebowitch, *A Strange Virus of Unknown Origin* (New York: Ballantine, 1985), pp. 3–4.
4. Cited in Matt Clark et al., "AIDS," *Newsweek* (October 12, 1984), pp. 20–24, 26–27.
5. Allen M. Brandt, *No Magic Bullet* (New York: Oxford University Press, 1985), p. 92.
6. Erving Goffman, *Stigma* (Englewood Cliffs, NJ: Prentice-Hall, 1968), pp. 30–31.
7. Sontag, 1978. op. cit. See also, Anselm Strauss and Barney Glaser, *Awareness of Dying* (Chicago: Aldine, 1965).
8. Paul D. Cleary et al., "Theoretical Issues in Health Education about AIDS Risk." Unpublished paper. Department of Social Medicine and Health Policy, Harvard Medical School, 1986.
9. Peter Conrad and Joseph W. Schneider, *Deviance and Medicalization: From Badness to Sickness* (St. Louis: C. V. Mosby, 1980).
10. Ronald Bayer, "AIDS and The Gay Community: Between the Specter and the Promise of Medicine," *Social Research* (Autumn, 1985), pp. 581–606.
11. Donald E. Riesenberg, "AIDS-Prompted Behavior Changes Reported," *Journal of the American Medical Association* (January 10, 1986), pp. 171–72; Ronald Stall, "The Behavioral Epidemiology of AIDS: A Call for Anthropological Contributions," *Medical Anthropology Quarterly* (February, 1986), pp. 36–37; Jonathan Lieberson, "The Reality of AIDS," *New York Review of Books* (January 16, 1986), p. 47.
12. Christopher Collins, "Homosexuals and AIDS: An Inside View." Paper presented to the American Society of Law and Medicine conference on "AIDS: A Modern Plague?" Boston, April, 1986.
13. Lieberson, 1986, p. 45.
14. Ibid., p. 46.
15. Brandt, 1985, p. 137.

16. Carol Levine and Ronald Bayer, "Screening Blood: Public Health and Medical Uncertainty," *Hastings Center Report* (August, 1985), pp. 8–11.

17. George F. Grady, "A Practitioner's Guide to AIDS," *Massachusetts Medicine* (January/February, 1986), pp. 44–50. See also, Kenneth W. Payne and Stephen J. Risch, "The Politics of AIDS," *Science for the People* (September October, 1984), pp. 17–24.

18. Ralph J. DiClemente, Jim Zorn, and Lydia Temoshok, "A Large-Scale Survey of Adolescents' Knowledge, Attitudes, and Beliefs About AIDS in San Francisco: A Needs Assessment." Paper presented at the meetings of the Society for Behavioral Medicine, March, 1986, p. 4.

19. Lydia Temoshok, David M. Sweet, and Jane Zich, "A Cross-Cultural Analysis of Reactions to the AIDS Epidemic." Paper presented at the meetings of the Society for Behavioral Medicine, March, 1986.

20. Dorothy C. Wertz et al., "Research on the Educational Programs of the AIDS Action Committee of the Fenway Community Health Center: Final Report." Submitted to the Massachusetts Department of Public Health, AIDS Research Program, 1985, p. 11.

21. Ibid, p. 12.

22. Jean Seligman and Nikki Fink Greenberg, "Only Months to Live and No Place to Die," *Newsweek* (August 12, 1985), p. 26.

23. Joseph W. Schneider and Peter Conrad, *Having Epilepsy: The Experience and Control of Illness* (Philadelphia: Temple University Press, 1983), pp. 22–46.

24. Elaine Cumming and John Cumming, *Closed Ranks* (Cambridge: Harvard University Press, 1957).

DISCUSSION QUESTIONS

1. What are some of the myths about AIDS? Discuss the triple stigma of AIDS.
2. What strategies need to be implemented to reduce the hysteria surrounding AIDS?

XVI
Community and Urban Life

WHAT TO FOCUS ON:

1. Does the process of urbanization enhance or impede the development of a human community?
2. What can be done to reduce the plight of the homeless?

COMMUNITY AND URBAN life refers to both physical and social contexts. Physically, they reflect varying spatial and territorial landscapes. Socially, they reflect the social organization and structure of space. Sociology has a long tradition of exploring the different social contexts of community life. Töennies examined *gemeinschaft* and *gesellschaft*. Durkheim focused on mechanical and organic solidarity. Redfield examined folk societies. Cooley examined primary groups. For sociologists, communities are more than geographic locations. Rather they are human structures in which people interact, play various roles, and are involved in numerous social groups and activities.

Sociologists have focused on three basic types of community life: rural, suburban, and urban. The classic views, however, examined only the contrasts between rural and urban life. Analysis of suburban life is a relatively recent phenomenon in sociology. The basic distinctions between rural and urban life reflect the differences of both community composition and structure. The inhabitants of rural communities tend to be homogeneous in terms of background, cultural characteristics, and lifestyle. The social structure of rural life is less diversified and there tends to be a predominance of primary relationships. Urban areas tend to be socially heterogeneous and reflect a myriad of differences in terms of cultural characteristics. In regard to social structure, urban areas exhibit greater degrees of role specialization and relationships often tend to be more functional and impersonal. Suburban communities appear to have elements of both rural and urban life. Suburban areas often strive to recapture the image of small-town life. Designers of planned suburban communities place great emphasis on grass, trees, and community shopping centers. However, the social structure of suburbia tends to be diversified, and many relationships tend to be impersonal reflecting the transitory nature of many suburban communities.

Generally, American society is characterized by the gradual process of urbanization. Urbanization entails both a physical and cultural process. Physically, it involves the migration of people from rural to urban areas. Culturally, it involves the diffusion of urban culture to rural and suburban areas. Gradually, our social space is becoming increasingly urbanized.

In a classic sociological work, Ferdinand Töennies examines two different types of communities, the Gemeinschaft and the Gesellschaft. These types of communities reflect contrasts in social organization, social order, and quality of life. Töennies raises some important sociological questions about changes in culture as a community is transformed from a body-social based upon a consensus of wills "ennobled by folkways, mores, and religion" to a state based upon social contract and political legislation.

During the last decade there has been an alarming increase of the antithesis of community life—the homeless. Who are the homeless? In a nation of riches and overabundance, why does America have an increasing number of homeless? Kim Hopper presents a penetrating analysis of this issue and offers some thoughtful and workable suggestions for its solution.

Article 44

Community and Society

FERDINAND TÖENNIES

1. Order—Law—Mores

THERE IS A CONTRAST between a social order which—being based upon consensus of wills—rests on harmony and is developed and ennobled by folkways, mores, and religion, and an order which—being based upon a union of rational wills—rests on convention and agreement, is safeguarded by political legislation, and finds its ideological justification in public opinion.

There is, further, in the first instance a common and binding system of positive law, of enforcible norms regulating the interrelation of wills. It has its roots in family life and is based on land ownership. Its forms are in the main determined by the code of the folkways and mores. Religion consecrates and glorifies these forms of the divine will, i.e., as interpreted by the will of wise and ruling men. This system of norms is in direct contrast to a similar positive law which upholds the separate identity of the individual rational wills in all their interrelations and entanglements. The latter derives from the conventional order of trade and similar relations but attains validity and binding force only through the sovereign will and power of the state. Thus, it becomes one of the most important instruments of policy; it sustains, impedes, or furthers social trends; it is defended or contested publicly by doctrines and opinions and thus is changed, becoming more strict or more lenient.

There is, further, the dual concept of morality as a purely ideal or mental system of norms for community life. In the first case, it is mainly an expression and organ

From *Community and Society,* by Ferdinand Töennies, Translation by Charles Loomis, East Lansing, Michigan State University, 1957, pp. 223–231. Reprinted by permission.

of religious beliefs and forces, by necessity intertwined with the conditions and realities of family spirit and the folkways and mores. In the second case, it is entirely a product and instrument of public opinion, which encompasses all relations arising out of contractual sociableness, contacts, and political intentions.

Order is natural law, law as such = positive law, mores = ideal law. Law as the meaning of what may or ought to be, of what is ordained or permitted, constitutes an object of social will. Even the natural law, in order to attain validity and reality, has to be recognized as positive and binding. But it is positive in a more general or less definite way. It is general in comparison with special laws. It is simple compared to complex and developed law.

2. Dissolution

The substance of the body social and the social will consists of concord, folkways, mores, and religion, the manifold forms of which develop under favorable conditions during its lifetime. Thus, each individual receives his share from this common center, which is manifest in his own sphere, i.e., in his sentiment, in his mind and heart, and in his conscience as well as in his environment, his possessions, and his activities. This is also true of each group. It is in this center that the individual's strength is rooted, and his rights derive, in the last instance, from the one original law which, in its divine and natural character, encompasses and sustains him, just as it made him and will carry him away. But under certain conditions and in some relationships, man appears as a free agent (person) in his self-determined activities and has to be conceived of as an independent person. The substance of the common spirit has become so weak or the link connecting him with the others worn so thin that it has to be excluded from consideration. In contrast to the family and co-operative relationship, this is true of all relations among separate individuals where there is no common understanding, and no time-honored custom or belief creates a common bond. This means war and the unrestricted freedom of all to destroy and subjugate one another, or, being aware of possible greater advantage, to conclude agreements and foster new ties. To the extent that such a relationship exists between closed groups or communities or between their individuals or between members and nonmembers of a community, it does not come within the scope of this study. In this connection we see a community organization and social conditions in which the individuals remain in isolation and veiled hostility toward each other so that only fear of clever retaliation restrains them from attacking one another, and, therefore, even peaceful and neighborly relations are in reality based upon a warlike situation. This is, according to our concepts, the condition of Gesellschaft-like civilization, in which peace and commerce are maintained through conventions and the underlying mutual fear. The state protects this civilization through legislation and politics. To a certain extent science and public opinion, attempting to conceive it as necessary and eternal, glorify it as progress toward perfection.

But it is in the organization and order of the Gemeinschaft that folk life and folk culture persist. The state, which represents and embodies Gesellschaft, is opposed to these in veiled hatred and contempt, the more so the further the state has moved away from and become estranged from these forms of community life. Thus, also in the social and historical life of mankind there is partly close interrelation, partly juxtaposition and opposition of natural and rational will.

3. The People (Volkstum) and the State (Staatstum)

In the same way as the individual natural will evolves into pure thinking and rational will, which tends to dissolve and subjugate its predecessors, the original collective forms of Gemeinschaft have developed into Gesellschaft and the rational will of the Gesellschaft. In the course of history, folk culture has given rise to the civilization of the state.

The main features of this process can be described in the following way. The anonymous mass of the people is the original and dominating power which creates the houses, the villages, and the towns of the country. From it, too, spring the powerful and self-determined individuals of many different kinds: princes, feudal lords, knights, as well as priests, artists, scholars. As long as their economic condition is determined by the people as a whole, all their social control is conditioned by the will and power of the people. Their union on a national scale, which alone could make them dominant as a group, is dependent on economic conditions. And their real and essential control is economic control, which before them and with them and partly against them the merchants attain by harnessing the labor force of the nation. Such economic control is achieved in many forms, the highest of which is planned capitalist production or large-scale industry. It is through the merchants that the technical conditions for the national union of independent individuals and for capitalistic production are created. This merchant class is by nature, and mostly also by origin, international as well as national and urban, i.e., it belongs to Gesellschaft, not Gemeinschaft. Later all social groups and dignitaries and, at least in tendency, the whole people acquire the characteristics of the Gesellschaft.

Men change their temperaments with the place and conditions of their daily life, which becomes hasty and changeable through restless striving. Simultaneously, along with this revolution in the social order, there takes place a gradual change of the law, in meaning as well as in form. The contract as such becomes the basis of the entire system, and rational will of Gesellschaft, formed by its interests, combines with authoritative will of the state to create, maintain and change the legal system. According to this conception, the law can and may completely change the Gesellschaft in line with its own discrimination and purpose; changes which, however, will be in the interest of the Gesellschaft, making for usefulness and efficiency. The state frees itself more and more from the traditions and customs of the past and the belief in their importance. Thus, the forms of law change from a product of the folkways and mores and the law of custom into a purely legalistic law, a product of policy. The state and its departments and the individuals are the only remaining agents, instead of numerous and manifold fellowships, communities, and commonwealths which have grown up organically. The characters of the people, which were influenced and determined by these previously existing institutions, undergo new changes in adaptation to new and arbitrary legal constructions. These earlier institutions lose the firm hold which folkways, mores, and the conviction of their infallibility gave to them.

Finally, as a consequence of these changes and in turn reacting upon them, a complete reversal of intellectual life takes place. While originally rooted entirely in the imagination, it now becomes dependent upon thinking. Previously, all was centered around the belief in invisible beings, spirits and gods; now it is focalized on the insight into visible nature. Religion, which is rooted in folk life or at least closely related to it, must cede supremacy to science, which derives from and corresponds to consciousness. Such consciousness is a product of learning and culture and, therefore, remote from the people. Religion has an immediate contact and is moral in its nature because it is most deeply related to the physical-spiritual link which connects the generations of men. Science receives its moral meaning only from an observation of the laws of social life, which leads it to derive rules for an arbitrary and reasonable order of social organization. The intellectual attitude of the individual becomes gradually less and less influenced by religion and more and more influenced by science. Utilizing the research findings accumulated by the preceding industrious generation, we shall investigate the tremendous contrasts which the opposite poles of this dichotomy and these fluctuations entail. For this presentation, however, the following few remarks may suffice to outline the underlying principles.

4. Types of Real Community Life

The exterior forms of community life as represented by natural will and Gemeinschaft were distinguished as house, village, and town. These are the lasting types of real and historical life. In a developed Gesellschaft, as in the earlier and middle stages, people live together in these different ways. The town is the highest, viz., the most complex, form of social life. Its local character, in common with that of the village, contrasts with the family character of the house. Both village and town retain many characteristics of the family; the village retains more, the town less. Only when the town develops into the city are these characteristics almost entirely lost. Individuals or families are separate identities, and their common locale is only an accidental or deliberately chosen place in which to live. But as the town lives on within the city, elements of life in the Gemeinschaft, as the only real form of life, persist within the Gesellschaft, although lingering and decaying. On the other hand, the more general the condition of Gesellschaft becomes in the nation or a group of nations, the more this entire "country" or the entire "world" begins to resemble one large city. However, in the city and therefore where general conditions characteristic of the Gesellschaft prevail, only the upper strata, the rich and the cultured, are really active and alive. They set up the standards to which the lower strata have to conform. These lower classes conform partly to supersede the others, partly in imitation of them in order to attain for themselves social power and independence. The city consists, for both groups (just as in the case of the "nation" and the "world"), of free persons who stand in contact with each other, exchange with each other and co-operate without any Gemeinschaft or will thereto developing among them except as such might develop sporadically or as a leftover from former conditions. On the contrary, these numerous external contacts, contracts, and contractual relations only cover up as many inner hostilities and antagonistic interests. This is especially true of the antagonism between the rich or the so-called cultured class and the poor or the servant class, which try to obstruct and destroy each other. It is this contrast which, according to Plato, gives the "city" its dual character and makes it divide in itself. This itself, according to our concept, constitutes the city, but the same contrast is also manifest in every large-scale relationship between capital and labor. The common town life remains within the Gemeinschaft of family and rural life; it is devoted to some agricultural pursuits but concerns itself especially with art and handicraft which evolve from these natural needs and habits. City life, however, is sharply distinguished from that; these basis activities are used only as means and tools for the special purposes of the city.

The city is typical of Gesellschaft in general. It is essentially a commercial town and, in so far as commerce dominates its productive labor, a factory town. Its wealth is capital wealth, which, in the form of trade, usury, or industrial capital, is used and multiplies. Capital is the means for the appropriation of products of labor or for the exploitation of workers. The city is also the center of science and culture, which always go hand in hand with commerce and industry. Here the arts must make a living; they are exploited in a capitalistic way. Thoughts spread and change with astonishing rapidity. Speeches and books through mass distribution become stimuli of far-reaching importance.

The city is to be distinguished from the national capital, which, as residence of the court or center of government, manifests the features of the city in many respects although its population and other conditions have not yet reached that level. In the synthesis of city and capital, the highest form of this kind is achieved: the metropolis. It is the essence not only of a national Gesellschaft, but contains representatives from a whole group of nations, i.e., of the world. In the metropolis, money and capital are unlimited and almighty. It is able to produce and supply goods and science for the entire earth as well as laws and public opinion for all nations. It represents the world market and world traffic; in it world industries are concentrated. Its newspapers are world papers, its people come from all corners of the earth, being curious and hungry for money and pleasure.

5. Counterpart of Gemeinschaft

Family life is the general basis of life in the Gemeinschaft. It subsists in village and town life. The village community and the town themselves can be considered as large families, the various clans and houses representing the elementary organisms of its body; guilds, corporations, and offices, the tissues and organs of the town. Here original kinship and inherited status remain an essential, or at least the most important, condition of participating fully in common property and other rights. Strangers may be accepted and protected as serving-members or guests either temporarily or permanently. Thus, they can belong to the Gemeinschaft as objects, but not easily as agents and representatives of the Gemeinschaft. Children are, during minority, dependent members of the family, but according to Roman custom they are called free because it is anticipated that under possible and normal conditions they will certainly be masters, their own heirs. This is true neither of guests nor of servants, either in the house or in the community. But honored guests can approach the position of children. If they are adopted or civic rights are granted to them, they fully acquire this position with the right to inherit. Servants can be esteemed or treated as guests or even, because of the value of their functions, take part as members in the activities of the group. It also happens sometimes that they become natural or appointed heirs. In reality there are many gradations, lower or higher, which are not exactly met by legal formulas. All these relationships can, under special circumstances, be transformed into merely interested and dissolvable interchange between independent contracting parties. In the city such change, at least with regard to all relations of servitude, is only natural and becomes more and more widespread with its development. The difference between natives and strangers becomes irrelevant. Everyone is what he is, through his personal freedom, through his wealth and his contracts. He is a servant only in so far as he has granted certain services to someone else, master in so far as he receives such services. Wealth is, indeed, the only effective and original differentiating characteristic; whereas in Gemeinschaften property it is considered as participation in the common ownership and as a specific legal concept is entirely the consequence and result of freedom or ingenuity, either original or acquired. Therefore, wealth, to the extent that this is possible, corresponds to the degree of freedom possessed.

In the city as well as in the capital, and especially in the metropolis, family life is decaying. The more and the longer their influence prevails, the more the residuals of family life acquire a purely accidental character. For there are only few who will confine their energies within such a narrow circle; all are attracted outside by business, interests, and pleasures, and thus separated from one another. The great and mighty, feeling free and independent, have always felt a strong inclination to break through the barriers of the folkways and mores. They know that they can do as they please. They have the power to bring about changes in their favor, and this is positive proof of individual arbitrary power. The mechanism of money, under usual conditions and if working under high pressure, is means to overcome all resistance, to obtain everything wanted and desired, to eliminate all dangers and to cure all evil. This does not hold always. Even if all controls of the Gemeinschaft are eliminated, there are nevertheless controls in the Gesellschaft to which the free and independent individuals are subject. For Gesellschaft (in the narrower sense), convention takes to a large degree the place of the folkways, mores, and religion. It forbids much as detrimental to the common interest which the folkways, mores, and religion had condemned as evil in and of itself.

The will of the state plays the same role through law courts and police, although within narrower limits. The laws of the state apply equally to everyone; only children and lunatics are not held responsible to them. Convention maintains at least the appearance of morality; it is still related to the folkways, mores, and religious and aesthetic feeling, although this feeling tends to become arbitrary and formal.

The state is hardly directly concerned with morality. It has only to suppress and punish hostile actions which are detrimental to the common weal or seemingly dangerous for itself and society. For as the state has to administer the common weal, it must be able to define this as it pleases. In the end it will probably realize that no increase in knowledge and culture alone will make people kinder, less egotistic, and more content and that dead folkways, mores, and religions cannot be revived by coercion and teaching. The state will then arrive at the conclusion that in order to create moral forces and moral beings it must prepare the ground and fulfill the necessary conditions, or at least it must eliminate counteracting forces. The state, as the reason of Gesellschaft, should decide to destroy Gesellschaft or at least to reform or renew it. The success of such attempts is highly improbable.

6. The Real State

Public opinion, which brings the morality of Gesellschaft into rules and formulas and can rise above the state, has nevertheless decided tendencies to urge the state to use its irresistible power to force everyone to do what is useful and to leave undone what is damaging. Extension of the penal code and the police power seems the right means to curb the evil impulses of the masses. Public opinion passes easily from the demand for freedom (for the upper classes) to that of despotism (against the lower classes). The makeshift, convention, has but little influence over the masses. In their striving for pleasure and entertainment they are limited only by the scarcity of the means which the capitalists furnish them as price for their labor, which condition is as general as it is natural in a world where the interests of the capitalists and merchants anticipate all possible needs and in mutual competition incite to the most varied expenditures of money. Only through fear of discovery and punishment, that is, through fear of the state, is a special and large group, which encompasses far more people than the professional criminals, restrained in its desire to obtain the key to all necessary and unnecessary pleasures. The state is their enemy. The state, to them, is an alien and unfriendly power; although seemingly authorized by them and embodying their own will, it is nevertheless opposed to all their needs and desires, protecting property which they do not possess, forcing them into military service for a country which offers them hearth and altar only in the form of a heated room on the upper floor or gives them, for native soil, city streets where they may stare at the glitter and luxury in lighted windows forever beyond their reach! Their own life is nothing but a constant alternative between work and leisure, which are both distorted into factory routine and the low pleasure of the saloons. City life and Gesellschaft down the common people to decay and death; in vain they struggle to attain power through their own multitude, and it seems to them that they can use their power only for a revolution if they want to free themselves from their fate. The masses become conscious of this social position through the education in schools and through newspapers. They proceed from class consciousness to class struggle. This class struggle may destroy society and the state which it is its purpose to reform. The entire culture has been transformed into a civilization of state and

Gesellschaft, and this transformation means the doom of culture itself if none of its scattered seeds remain alive and again bring forth the essence and idea of Gemeinschaft, thus secretly fostering a new culture amidst the decaying one.

DISCUSSION QUESTIONS

1. What are some of the differences between Gemeinschaft and Gesellschaft?
2. According to Töennies, the Gemeinschaft is centered upon a common belief in folkways and mores while the Gesellschaft is based upon social contract and legalistic law. Explain how the nature of social order and control changes as societies evolve from Gemeinschaft to Gesellschaft.

Article 45

Homelessness

Reducing the Distance

KIM HOPPER

A CROWD ASSEMBLED on the steps of the National Capitol in Washington to hear what was billed as the "People's State of the Union" address. There were some 300 women, men, and children of all ages and colors: workers out of work; families on public assistance and families too proud to apply; people who run soup kitchens and shelters, and people who survive because of them; litigators and agitators; researchers and street philosophers; even an odd bureaucrat or two. They had all come this cold blustery day to hear a man named Roosevelt, who lives in one of the abandoned school buildings recently pressed into service as a public shelter.

What he had to say was painfully simple—something is wrong, grievously so, with the state of this nation. Millions of its citizens are homeless. They crisscross the country in a futile search for work, scavenge food from dumpsters, tie scrap

From "Homelessness: Reducing the Distance," by Kim Hopper, *New England Journal of Human Services,* Fall 1983. Reprinted by permission of the publisher.

Note: This article has been excerpted from *1933/1983—Never Again,* a report to the National Governor's Association Task Force on the Homeless presented by Mario M. Cuomo, governor of the State of New York.

The author would like to thank the scores of homeless folks who made this report possible. Their grace, courage, and willingness to share parts of their lives with a virtual stranger were little short of daunting. Thanks, too, to the shelter workers and advocates in New York City, Chicago, Pittsburgh, Boston, San Francisco, Houston, and Phoenix who provided contacts and guidance. Special thanks for hospitality to Karen Singer, Phil Pappas, Carol Bower Johnson, Sara Colm, and Shad Dabaghi; for companionship, to Paul Selden; and for research assistance which bordered on the preternatural, to Dan Salerno.

lumber and cardboard together for shelter. Millions more totter just this side of abject poverty, getting by with the help of friends, private charity, and food pantries. They are not asking to be put on the dole. What these people want, what they need, are three things: food, shelter, jobs. On that gray day in January, those three words rang out, a defiant counterpoint to the nostrums delivered six hours later in the official State of the Union Address.

Roosevelt was no idle alarmist. Nationwide, estimates of the legions of American homeless have run as high as 2.5 million.[1] In the last two years, their plight has assumed the dimensions of a national disgrace. It has been the object of congressional hearings, sustained media attention at home and abroad, and a proliferation of studies and reports the like of which has not been seen since the discovery of "the other America" in the early 1960s. Few can profess ignorance of the problem. But the numbers and the surge of awareness tell only part of the story. There is a disquiet in the streets, not the muted desperation Thoreau lamented, but an angry, ashamed, indignant, uncomprehending one. Why, in this land of conspicuous bounty, should Americans go hungry and homeless? . . .

Homelessness

Estimates of those living on the streets, in jerry-rigged structures, or in emergency shelters are more difficult to come by. In some measure, this is a definitional problem. In addition to those in shelters, or literally without a roof over their heads, there is good reason to believe that large numbers of citizens are making do with quarters that are temporary and makeshift, sleeping on the floors of friends' or family's apartments, tolerating substandard accommodations, or getting by on a day-to-day basis in flophouses, turning to public or private shelters only on those occasions when they lack sufficient funds to pay for a night's lodging. To their numbers must be added those who are institutionalized on a time-limited basis in hospitals, and jails, who, upon release or discharge, will be without a residence. . . .

The states have generally adopted more restrictive definitions. This version is fairly representative: "Persons or families who, on one particular day or night, have neither friends, family, nor sufficient funds which will provide for certain elementary resources they need to survive."[2] At the other end of the continuum is that of New York: "An undomiciled person who is unable to secure permanent and stable housing without special assistance."[3]

Even if, for the sake of simplicity, one restricts the category of "homeless" to people who are in shelters or on the street, difficulties abound in securing good estimates of their numbers. They are especially acute for those living in other than officially sanctioned refuges, many of whom have a legitimate interest in not being discovered. Then, too, the pride and fear of street dwellers make an admission of homelessness on their part to an interviewer who is, in many instances, a virtual stranger, a less than straightforward affair. Finally, the various homeless populations themselves may be subject to fluctuations in season, economic activity, and the frequency of such crises as mass displacement from sites of usual residence.

For these reasons, estimates of the homeless population in cities across the country are bound to be rough. In many instances, they are little more than guesswork. Such "guesstimates" have ranged from 60,000 people in New York City, 30,000 in Los Angeles, and 22,000 in Houston through 8,000 in Philadelphia, 4,000 in Seattle, and 2,000 in Boston to less than 1,000 in Salt Lake City, Jacksonville, and Anchorage, Alaska.

There are other measures, though indirect, that are more reliable. In the last few years, public shelter capacity has increased markedly in New York, Boston, Seattle, and Washington, D.C. Phoenix, Chicago, Detroit, Salt Lake City, San Francisco, and Milwaukee have been forced either to open public facilities or to fund private shelters, some for the first time in their histories. Atlanta, Las Vegas, Denver, Tulsa, Houston, Cleveland, Savannah, Birmingham, and Miami are relying upon private charities and religious organizations to meet the need. The results of the recent infusion of emergency jobs bill funds to the shelters and voluntary agencies should make a more complete picture possible by the end of the year.

At any rate, few would dispute the claim that, in the course of the last few years, homelessness in the United States has quietly taken on crisis proportions. . . .

Causes of Homelessness Today

Although data are scanty, and the longitudinal studies necessary to establish causality nonexistent, observers generally agree that there are four major forces responsible for mass displacement throughout the 1970s and into the 1980s: unemployment, scarcity of affordable housing, deinstitutionalization of the mentally disabled, and social service cutbacks and the culling of disability rolls.

It is often remarked that the new forces of dislocation have conspired to create a novel breed of homeless poor—novel at least for this past half century—those dubbed the "new poor." But in reviewing the contemporary causes of homelessness, it is important to realize that the effects of these factors may well outlast the period of their operation. Dislocation may assume its own momentum, spiraling downward in a self-destructive gyre. The tactics of survival learned on the streets (be it a consciously cultivated foul odor or techniques of vigilance and concealment) serve to further isolate and alienate. What is adaptive behavior on the streets may be ill-suited to resuming a settled mode of living. . . .

Unemployment. Although the link between unemployment and displacement seems obvious today, this was not always the case. Historically, the association between unemployment and vagrancy has received mixed interpretations. Deep runs the fear of the man without ties, and no man has shed more ties than the vagrant.[4] Despite what, in retrospect, would appear to have been repeated evidence to the contrary, reformers of the nineteenth century remained transfixed by their suspicion of the tramp and blamed the influx of immigrants, availability of indiscriminate relief, or ravages of demon rum for the rise in vagrancy that followed each of four major depressions.[5] Idleness was viewed as a moral, not economic, evil, the result of character defects. Poverty was considered the lot of the miscreant; few crimes were held "more reprehensible than inability to make a living."[6] It was not until after the panics of 1893 and 1907—each attended by widespread violence and vast recruitments into the armies of the homeless—that attitudes began to shift. Both the sheer numbers and closer scrutiny of their ranks finally persuaded reformers that vagrancy might be the result of unemployment rather than the other way around.

Still, however cruel an equalizer the loss of a job had been shown to be, postwar prosperity dimmed the memory and dampened its threat. Except under extraordinary circumstances, it was the sort of thing that was confined to the margins of the work force, people used to fluctuations in demand for their labor. A mere year and a half ago, it almost sufficed to note simply that unemployment showed a decided preference for the already vulnerable, striking, as Elliot Liebow of the National Institute of Mental Health phrased it, "first, hardest and repeatedly at those who can least withstand it, especially the poor, the young and the minorities."[7]

One still sees the truth of this observation reflected in the faces and statistics of the public shelters in New York City.[8] The average age of new applicants is 34, with 7% under 21; they are predominantly black or Hispanic; at least half have never finished high school; and fully a quarter of them wind up at the shelter owing to the loss of a job. Among the longer term (over two months) residents at one of the city's largest shelters, many of whom were far better educated than the average shelter client, nearly 40% reported that they were homeless because they had lost a job. Nor is this picture restricted to New York. Where figures are available, the story is similar: the average age of single homeless and/or sheltered populations surveyed in San Francisco, Boston, and Phoenix is well under forty.

But unemployment has been striking in a widening compass of late and its effect has been to transform the composition of the dispossessed.[9] Everywhere one turns, one hears the same refrain: "From the people who man the missions where the drifters eat and sleep, from the police on the beat who keep them in line, comes the word that the recession has changed the caliber of their clientele."[10] Police sergeant Ken Ersland of Corpus Christi, Texas, puts it simply: "The majority of the transients now are looking for work."[11]. . .

The Shortage of Low-Income Housing

> You don't have to be clairvoyant . . . to understand the relationship between housing cuts and an old woman out there on the street. You can talk to her and find out that she just got squeezed out of her apartment as it went up in rent, [or] was converted into a cooperative or condominium of some kind.[12]

Over the grim statistics on homelessness looms the shadow of a housing crisis that may well be unexampled in this century. Current estimates by the National Housing Law Project place the number of people who are involuntarily displaced from their homes each year at 2.5 million—casualties of "revitalization" projects, eviction, economic development schemes, and rent inflation. At the same time, half a million units of low-rent dwellings are lost each year through the combined forces of conversion, abandonment, inflation, arson, and demolition.[13] When one realizes that the major victims of mass displacement are the poor, those with the fewest resources to absorb new hardship or to recover in its wake, it is no mystery that the ranks of the homeless continue to swell.

A number of studies have shown how loss of housing can be the immediate precipitating cause of homelessness. Typically, this takes one of three forms: eviction or threat of eviction, intolerable conditions in one's prior residence, or rent increases that outstrip one's capacity to pay. And so to the dwindling supply of housing stock must be added the diminished capacity of people to pay for what stock remains. . . .

It isn't just rental housing that is affected. The Mortgage Bankers Association reports that 130,000 Americans lost their homes due to foreclosure in 1982. Farming regions were especially hard hit: the rate of foreclosure was 1.6% in Illinois, 1.41% in Ohio, 1.36% in South Dakota, and 1.1% in Indiana. The national average for the last four months of 1982 was 0.67%. In Illinois, foreclosures have risen 25–30% in the last fifteen months, reflecting the state's long-standing high rate of unemployment. The newest victims are those who have exhausted their unemployment benefits.[14] In Wisconsin, farm foreclosures are at their highest level since the Great Depression. Of 9,000 farmers on the lending rolls of the Farmers Home Administration, 231 have filed for bankruptcy.[15] In Illinois, 20% of all FMHA loans were delinquent in 1982, three times the 1970 level. Among FMHA borrowers nationwide, there were 1,245 bankruptcies, 5,908 liquidations and 844 foreclosures.[16]

Families are often the first line of resort once homes have been lost. The Census Bureau's Annual Survey of Housing found that in 1982, the number of households with two or more related families sharing space jumped from 1.2 million units to 1.9 million units—an increase of 58%, the first significant such increase since 1950.[17] Fully 17,000 people in public housing in New York are thought to be "doubling up" in this manner with all its attendant strains.[18]

Those who have lost homes are only the most desperate of those experiencing housing distress. Figures for New York City and the state are especially telling. Nearly half of all tenants in the city currently spend at least 30% of their gross income for rent and utilities. In 1981, 31% of all renters spent more than 40% of their income for rent— an increase of 83% since 1968. Among households receiving public assistance (excluding SSI), the figure is 72%; among the occupants of dilapidated housing (which accounts for 4.2% of all renter-occupied units), it is 45%. Fully 38% of all renters with incomes under $6,500 live in dilapidated or severely deteriorated housing.

Nor is this problem restricted to large cities. A review of housing needs in North Carolina—where 5.2% of the homes, compared with 2.7% nationwide, lack plumbing facilities—concluded that: "The most severe housing problems for low- and moderate-income families and elderly persons are the short supply of affordable housing and the widespread existence of lower cost housing which is neither safe nor sanitary."[19] One-third of the state's poor households live in substandard housing.[20]

The Failure of Community Psychiatry. The history of this movement is well known. The shift in mental health policy from institutional to community-based care resulted in a dramatic decline in the censuses of public mental hospitals—from 559,000 in 1955, to 505,000 in 1963, to 216,000 in 1974, to approximately 146,000 in 1979. Despite its popular depiction as a deinstitutionalization movement, it is more accurately considered one of reinstitutionalization. Many of the chronically mentally disabled adults in the United States, estimated to number between 1.7 and 2.4 million, are still institutionalized—in nursing homes and public mental hospitals. Moreover, most of those who remain in public hospitals have been found not to require inpatient care; they could be living in less costly and less restrictive settings in the community were such residences available.

Similarly, most of the chronically mentally ill in nursing homes are inappropriately placed; they are there owing to the lack of other suitable residential alternatives. While the numbers of chronically mentally ill persons in community settings are especially difficult to gauge, nationwide the range is 800,000 to 1.5 million. Among these people, some are cared for by families, while others—300,000 to 400,000 nationwide—are consigned to unsafe or substandard board and care homes. Increasing numbers of the mentally disabled are found confined within the criminal justice system. In urban centers, many thousands still live in single-room-occupancy hotels although, as noted earlier, the supply of such dwellings is shrinking dramatically. Thousands of others are simply left to fend for themselves on the streets, searching for food and warmth and doing slow damage to their mental and physical well-being.

No aspect of contemporary homelessness is more riddled with myths and misunderstandings than its perceived association with chronic mental disability. Admittedly, the linkage is there, but it is neither so common nor so determinant a factor as is often thought. As Philip O'Connor has suggested, at least some portion of the readiness to label the homeless as mad is a way of quelling the uneasiness the presence of such individuals provokes.[21] If homelessness were simply a matter of personal eccentricity or pathology, the unstated argument goes, then it cannot be indicative of any larger societal failure; it calls nothing in question—except perhaps the wisdom of psychiatric committment policies. The following passage, taken from a series on deinstitutionalization in the *Philadelphia Inquirer,* is evidence that this attitude persists: "Walk America's streets and you can see them: disheveled men and women rummaging in trash cans, curled up on steam grates, cowering in subway tunnels. They are insane."[22]

Lest there be any misunderstanding: the bulk of research to date indicates that (1) the majority of the homeless poor are not seriously mentally disabled, and that (2) even for those with severe disabilities, preferable alternatives to rehospitalization exist, although in far too short a supply. Moreover, it is often not a simple matter to judge to what degree an observed disorder should be considered a cause, and to what degree a consequence, of street living.

Nevertheless, that large numbers of psychiatric patients were discharged with insufficient consideration of their residential placement outside the hospital and that many of them subsequently wound up on the streets is undeniable. In addition, owing to restrictive admitting criteria put into effect over the last fifteen years, many persons who formerly would have been hospitalized are now turned away. Prominent among this latter group are the so-called "young adult chronics."[23] In the absence of alternative sources of housing and clinical attention, some of these individuals, too, wind up on the street.[24]...

Reductions in Disability Benefits. In the past two years, a fourth factor has entered the picture: intensified review procedures, initiated at the federal level, of disability aid recipients has resulted in many qualified claimants losing their benefits. In September 1982, the Congressional Quarterly Weekly Report estimated that "about 158,000 persons have been taken off the rolls since the stepped-up reviews began last year, causing a flood of horror stories and complaints to congressional offices."[25] By June 7, 1983, that number had risen to more than 350,000.[26]

Evidence compiled from seven different regions by the Mental Health Law Project in March, 1982, indicates that most often the loss of benefits is due to a severely checked ability on the part of the recipient to challenge the ruling, not to a legitimate winnowing from relief rolls of those who have recovered. Equally noteworthy, mental disability is overrepresented in successful review cases (those that are discontinued) by a factor of three: roughly 11% of all disability checks go to the mentally disabled, but nearly a third of the discontinued cases are psychiatrically impaired. The word given to local review offices was direct and simple, according to the Wisconsin head of the state disability review agency: "Deny, deny, deny."[27]

The rationale behind such cuts is apparent. The federal government expected to save some $11 billion between 1981 and 1984, by culling the disability rolls by almost 700,000 of the currently 4.3 million, and by continuing to enforce stricter approval procedures for first-time applicants. But the savings are offset by the administrative costs of the appeals process and of reinstatement—60% of such appeals are successful. They are also offset by new costs incurred through higher rates of institutional reimbursement for those discontinued cases who return to nursing homes or hospitals. The net effect is projected to be both a marked reduction in cost savings to the federal government and a transfer of costs—conservatively estimated at $3 billion—to the states.[28]

In February 1983, the state and city of New York sued the federal government, charging capricious and harmful treatment of the mentally disabled under the intensified review. One case described is that of Richard Roe, a 36-year-old man diagnosed as paranoid schizophrenic and currently residing in a city shelter after living for a while in Central Park. Mr. Roe is subject to hallucinations, talks to himself and, owing to his disability, has not worked for six years. His application for SSI was denied because it was determined that although he cannot return to his "usual" job, "there are 'many other jobs' that he can do."[29]...

Conclusion

When the streets and emergency shelters become rough homes for millions of Americans, the specter of skid row—traditionally seen as the lot of those lacking the fortitude or fiber to hold a steady job—takes on a farcical character. What good does it do to further disgrace people whose lives have already been subject to the insults of a failing economy, a heartless bureaucracy, broken families, and private shame? Hardship and humiliation have their limits as disciplinary prods. What good does it do to continue to insist that the down-and-out rehabilitate themselves if, once physically and morally retooled (presuming they need it), there are no jobs, no housing, no future but the same dreary round of "two hots and a cot"?

There are, assuredly, signs that hope is something other than a fool's errand. Public attitudes have swung in a noticeably more sympathetic arc of late. Local and state governments in many regions are devoting resources and attention to the problem, and the homeless poor in some areas like San Francisco have begun to organize themselves into effective constituencies of demand. Moreover, a number of states, local governments, and voluntary associations have begun to construct networks of residences and services for the growing numbers of homeless individuals. Several states have initiated specialized medical, mental health, and addiction control services for the homeless. However, we have not done nearly enough and the situation is worsening.

Emergency food and shelter programs are essential in the short term to meet the most immediate life-threatening needs of people with nowhere to go. But these shelters must be open around the clock throughout the year. They must offer refuge tailored to the special circumstances of the homeless. They must provide food, personal hygiene facilities, and transportation as needed. Just as important, they must be designed as *temporary* stops on the way to a more stable way of life for homeless individuals and families. Referral and access to job training and placement, and income maintenance services are essential aspects of a shelter program that offers hope for the future. In that regard, it would be helpful if the administration in Washington would provide flexibility in the existing emergency assistance program and recognize that it cannot be a one-time-only commitment.

Emergency food and shelter are essential, but they do not deal with the fundamental causes of homelessness. Longer term solutions are needed, including a careful review of a variety of public and private policies which contribute, sometimes indirectly, to the creation and perpetuation of homelessness. Each state should establish a mechanism—similar to the task forces already in effect in several states—to subject existing policies to close scrutiny. Specifically, the following areas are in need of review, and, if found wanting, revamping:

1. Adequacy of the number and quality of emergency shelters for single men and women, families, victims of domestic violence, and youth
2. Adequacy of existing regulations and enforcement procedures to ensure minimal levels of decency in such facilities
3. Adequacy of discharge planning and aftercare—including appropriate residential placement—in psychiatric facilities
4. Adequacy and fairness of shelter and basic living allowances for those on public assistance
5. Adequacy and fairness of general relief regulations, especially as they affect the single, able-bodied man or woman

6. Adequacy and fairness of current housing policies, especially as they affect low-income individuals
7. Adequacy and effectiveness of monitoring and review procedures to ensure that government does not lose touch with the people affected by its policies

At the federal level, a national commission, similar to the task forces established at the state level, is needed to identify existing problems and possible solutions. At the same time, we must do more than simply study the problem. There are actions that must be taken as soon as possible.

First, we need jobs. In many of our major cities, thousands of people who want to work cannot find jobs and have been out of work for long periods of time. Despite the recent upturn, the unemployment rate in our cities and rural areas continues at double-digit rates. We need a massive federal jobs program—providing work for those with the necessary skills and training for those whose job skills are obsolete or nonexistent.

Second, we must establish a national housing program for low-income individuals and families. This should be two-pronged: a program to fund the construction of permanent housing and a rent-subsidy program similar to Section 8. While such a program will be expensive, it is certainly as affordable and more sensible than the MX missile or the B-1 bomber.

Third, for those people who cannot work or who, in the absence of public works programs, cannot find work, we must provide income assistance sufficient to obtain decent, stable housing. It makes no sense to provide emergency shelter to remedy the problems of the existing homeless if we take no action to prevent future additions to their ranks.

Fourth, the agencies involved in assisting the mentally ill must work together to address the basic living and clinical needs of the psychiatrically disabled. Specifically, we must make the concept of supportive residences a workable, growing reality.

Finally, the problems of the homeless cannot be solved by one level of government or indeed government alone. Rather, we will need the cooperative efforts of not only every level of government but also voluntary and nonprofit organizations, religious groups, and individual volunteers.

Our own capacity to care as a society is on trial. The burden of this article has been to recover the familiarity of the homeless poor, in the strict sense of the term, as extended family. There can be no excuse for ignoring the plea of kinsfolk.

NOTES

1. *Homelessness in America,* Hearing before the subcommittee on Housing and Community Development of the Committee on Banking, Finance and Urban Affairs, House of Representatives, 97th Congress, December 15, 1982 (Washington, D.C.: U.S. Government Printing Office, 1983).

2. As adopted by the Governor's Advisory Committee on the Homeless, Boston, Massachusetts, January 1983.

3. New York State, Chapter 61, Laws of 1983. Homeless Housing and Assistance Program. Note that other definitions are currently in effect, among them: Missouri includes those in public or private shelters or in subsidized motel accommodations, as well as those "requiring separate housing as opposed to congregate shelter"—the latter including abused spouses and those displaced as a result of housing code enforcement. North Dakota refers to "adult men, women and families who have no identifiable *personal unshared* place of residence" (emphasis in original)—while noting that "the 'homeless' are mainly housed in the homes of friends or relatives and, to a lesser extent, in private facilities such as hotels/motels." Most states responding agreed with the definition offered by the survey form: "adult men, women and families who have no identifiable place of residence" which, notably, excludes homeless youth.

4. H. Bahr, *Skid Row: An Introduction to Disaffiliation* (New York: Oxford University Press, 1973), p. 41–42, 119–20.

5. P. T. Ringenbach, *Tramps and Reformers, 1873–1916* Westport, Conn.: Greenwood Press, 1973.

6. R. M. Bremmer, *From the Depths,* 1950, p. 71, as quoted by Ringenbach, *Tramps and Reformers,* p. 19.

7. E. Liebow, "The Urban Unemployed," *San Diego Union,* December 6, 1981, p. C-7.

8. Human Resources Administration of New York City, *New Arrivals: First-Time Shelter Clients,* June 1982; and *Chronic and Situational Dependency: Long-Term Residents in a Shelter for Men,* May 1982.

9. Among states responding to the NGA survey as of mid-May 1983, the median rate of increase in the unemployment rate over the past three years was 49%.

10. *Corpus Christi Caller-Times,* March 4, 1983.

11. Quoted in ibid.

12. *Homelessness in America,* p. 65.

13. C. Hartman, D. Leating, and R. LeGates, *Displacement: How to Fight It* (Berkeley: National Housing Law Project, 1982), p. 3.

14. *Chicago Sun-Times,* March 20, 1983.

15. *Iowa City Press-Citizen,* May 6, 1983.

16. *Illinois Action,* March-April, 1983.

17. *New York Times,* February 24, 1983.

18. *New York Times,* April 1983.

19. The Commission to Study Housing Programs in North Carolina, *The House We Live In,* January 1983, pp. 37–38.

20. Office of Economic Opportunity, North Carolina Department of Natural Resources and Community Development, *The Changing Face of Poverty,* Raleigh, N.C., March 1983, p. 5.

21. P. O'Connor, *Britain in the Sixties: Vagrancy* (London: Penguin, 1963).

22. *Philadelphia Inquirer,* "The Foresaken," July 18, 1982.

23. B. Pepper and H. Ryglewicz, "The Young Adult Chronic Patient," *New Directions for Mental Health Services* 14, June 1982.

24. S. Segal and J. Baumohl, "Engaging the Disengaged: Proposals on Madness and Vagrancy," *Social Work* 25 (1980): 358–65.

25. September 11, 1982, p. 2,242.

26. *New York Times,* June 8, 1983.

27. *New York Times,* May 9, 1982.
28. W. C. Copeland, "Current Administration of Social Security Disability Programs" (New York: Study Group on Social Security, May 28, 1982).
29. *New York Times,* February 19, 1983.

DISCUSSION QUESTIONS

1. Who are the homeless? Do states have varying definitions of the homeless?
2. According to Hopper, what are the four major forces contributing to the existence of homelessness? What steps can be taken to remedy the plight of the homeless?

XVII
Collective Behavior

WHAT TO FOCUS ON:

1. How are cultural symbols and rumors responsible for one's involvement in collective behavior?
2. What characterizes collective behavior compared to institutional behavior?

COLLECTIVE BEHAVIOR refers to action taken by groups of people that lacks conformity to established norms. Collective behavior studies human action that appears to be irrational, such as mass hysteria: Riots, crowd response to rumor, or fights at sporting events, seem to indicate that people have lost their sanity. Such action is not perceived as institutional behavior that has a structure of roles and norms. Nor is it seen as behavior that has a devised plan and goal. For most people, collective behavior looks like a group of individuals acting without organization. Sociologists are interested in this form of behavior: Are there observable patterns or are they random spontaneous events? What do these actions say about social order and institutional behavior? Are crowds incited or is there a rationality to their response? There are common elements found in its actions. Momentary and emergent norms, roles, and rationalities exist. The behavior responds to external conditions and incidents. Short-term goals exist for the collectivity. Finally, the group membership, itself, is temporary and transient. As such, collective behavior offers a wonderful comparison to the structured and institutional behavior we exhibit in the family, work, and education.

Gustave LeBon's work on "The Crowd" is a classic description of the unity that can exist in this type of group. He explores the conditions under which the crowd develops a "collective mind" that motivates the individuals to act as a single entity. While LeBon's position has become the source of controversial debates, it represents the first attempt to analyze this form of behavior. As such, it is an important starting point for understanding collective action.

In the Best and Horiuchi piece we look at the phenomena of tainted Halloween treats. Razor blades and cyanide-laced candy appear to be material of concern for parents and public safety officials. Why would sociologists be interested? Best and Horiuchi disclose that the reports of anonymous sadistic persons tampering with Halloween goodies are over-exaggerated. The authors argue that the stories are, in actuality, urban legends. Such legends are passed by word-of-mouth and reflect the perceived dangerousness and social tension that exist in modern society. Can it be that the conception of wide-spread Halloween tragedies are social constructions and not actual occurrences?

In the Bil Gilbert and Lisa Twyman work, "Violence: Out of Hand in the Stands," the topic of fights and disorderly behavior at sporting events is explored. What causes a fan, who may have spent large sums of money to attend the competition, to physically assault another fan? Is this simply intense loyalty to the team or a sports figure? How much is related to alcohol consumption, the physical structure of the arena, or the game itself? What role do the owners, television, and security guards play in promoting and controlling the violence? These are some of the questions examined in this section.

Article 46

The Crowd

GUSTAVE LEBON

IT BEING IMPOSSIBLE to study here all the successive degrees of organization of crowds, we shall concern ourselves more especially with such crowds as have attained to the phase of complete organization. In this way we shall see what crowds may become, but not what they invariably are. It is only in this advanced phase of organization that certain new and special characteristics are superposed on the unvarying and dominant character of the race; then takes place that turning already alluded to of all the feelings and thoughts of the collectivity in an identical direction. It is only under such circumstances, too, that what I call above the *psychological law of the mental unity of crowds* comes into play.

Among the psychological characteristics of crowds there are some that they may present in common with isolated individuals, and others, on the contrary, which are absolutely peculiar to them and are only to be met with in collectivities. It is these special characteristics that we shall study, first of all, in order to show their importance.

The most striking peculiarity presented by a psychological crowd is the following: Whoever be the individuals that compose it, however like or unlike be their mode of life, their occupations, their character, or their intelligence, the fact that they have been transformed into a crowd puts them in possession of a sort of collective mind which makes them feel, think, and act in a manner quite different from that in which each individual of them would feel, think, and act were he in a

From *The Crowd,* by Gustave LeBon, Ernest Benn, Ltd., London, 1896, pp. 5–6, 9, 13–14. Reprinted by permission of the publisher.

state of isolation. There are certain ideas and feelings which do not come into being, or do not transform themselves into acts except in the case of individuals forming a crowd. The psychological crowd is a provisional being formed of heterogeneous elements, which for a moment are combined, exactly as the cells which constitute a living body form by their reunion a new being which displays characteristics very different from those possessed by each of the cells singly. . . .

Different causes determine the appearance of these characteristics peculiar to crowds, and not possessed by isolated individuals. The first is that the individual forming part of a crowd acquires, solely from numerical considerations, a sentiment of invincible power which allows him to yield to instincts which, had he been alone, he would perforce have kept under restraint. He will be the less disposed to check himself from the consideration that, a crowd being anonymous, and in consequence irresponsible, the sentiment of responsibility which always controls individuals disappears entirely.

The second cause, which is contagion, also intervenes to determine the manifestation in crowds of their special characteristics, and at the same time the trend they are to take. Contagion is a phenomenon of which it is easy to establish the presence, but that it is not easy to explain. It must be classed among those phenomena of a hypnotic order, which we shall shortly study. In a crowd every sentiment and act is contagious, and contagious to such a degree that an individual readily sacrifices his personal interest to the collective interest. This is an aptitude very contrary to his nature, and of which a man is scarcely capable, except when he makes part of a crowd.

A third cause, and by far the most important, determines in the individuals of a crowd special characteristics which are quite contrary at times to those presented by the isolated individual. I allude to that suggestibility of which, moreover, the contagion mentioned above is neither more nor less than an effect. . . .

It is for these reasons that juries are seen to deliver verdicts of which each individual juror would disapprove, that parliamentary assemblies adopt laws and measures of which each of their members would disapprove in his own person. Taken separately, the men of the Convention were enlightened citizens of peaceful habits. United in a crowd, they did not hesitate to give their adhesion to the most savage proposals, to guillotine individuals most clearly innocent, and, contrary to their interests, to renounce their inviolability and to decimate themselves.

It is not only by his acts that the individual in a crowd differs essentially from himself. Even before he has entirely lost his independence, his ideas and feelings have undergone a transformation, and the transformation is so profound as to change the miser into a spendthrift, the sceptic into a believer, the honest man into a criminal, and the coward into a hero.

The conclusion to be drawn from what precedes is, that the crowd is always intellectually inferior to the isolated individual, but that, from the point of view of feelings and of the acts these feelings provoke, the crowd may, according to circumstances, be better or worse than the individual. All depends on the nature of the suggestion to which the crowd is exposed.

DISCUSSION QUESTIONS

1. What causes a crowd to develop a "collective mind"?
2. As LeBon describes it, what is the "collective mind" and how does it cause a group to act as a single entity?

Article 47

The Razor Blade in the Apple

The Social Construction of Urban Legends

JOEL BEST AND GERALD T. HORIUCHI

THE 1970s WITNESSED THE discovery of a frightening new deviant—the Halloween sadist, who gave dangerous, adulterated treats to children. Each year, Halloween's approach brought warnings to parents:

> . . . that plump red apple that Junior gets from a kindly old woman down the block . . . may have a razor blade hidden inside (*New York Times,* 1970).

> If this year's Halloween follows form, a few children will return home with something more than an upset tummy: in recent years, several children have died and hundreds have narrowly escaped injury from razor blades, sewing needles and shards of glass purposefully put into their goodies by adults (*Newsweek,* 1975).

From "The Razor Blade in the Apple: The Social Construction of Urban Legends," by Joel Best and Gerald Horiuchi, *Social Problems,* Vol. 32, No. 5, June, 1985, pp. 488–497.

> It's Halloween again and time to remind you that. . . . [s]omebody's child will become violently ill or die after eating poisoned candy or an apple containing a razor blade (Van Buren, 1983).

Various authorities responded to the threat: legislatures in California (1971) and New Jersey (1982) passed laws against Halloween sadism; schools trained children to inspect their treats for signs of tampering; and some communities tried to ban trick-or-treating (Trubo, 1974). According to press reports, many parents restricted their children's trick-or-treating, examined their treats, or arranged parties or other indoor celebrations (*New York Times,* 1972; *Los Angeles Times,* 1982). By 1984, the threat of Halloween sadists was apparently taken for granted. Doubts about the threat's reality rarely appeared in print. Several Oregon third graders wrote letters to a newspaper: "I wish people wouldn't put poison in our Halloween treats" (*Times,* 1984). Adults questioned for an Illinois newspaper's "Sidewalk Interview" column (*DeKalb Daily Chronicle,* 1984) expressed concern: " . . . part of it is checking to make sure you know your neighbors and checking the candy. I think it's terrible that people are doing this and I guess people's morals have to be examined." "Dear Abby" printed a letter describing a North Carolina hospital's program to X-ray treats (Van Buren, 1984); radiologists at a Hanford, California hospital checked 500 bags of treats (*Fresno Bee,* 1984). In 1985, 327 students at California State University, Fresno wrote essays for an upper-division writing examination, advocating the abolition of some holiday. Nearly a third (105 students) wrote about Halloween, and 90 percent of those essays mentioned the threat of Halloween sadism.

Halloween sadism is thought to involve random, vicious, unprovoked attacks against small children. The attacks seem irrational, and the attackers are routinely described as disturbed or insane. These "child-haters" are theorized to "have had a really deprived childhood" having been "abused as children," they are now "frustrated and filled with resentment against the world in general" (Isaacs and Royeton, 1982:69; *New York Times,* 1970; Trubo, 1974:28). Law enforcement officials and the media reaffirm that the threat is real, urging parents to protect their children against sadistic attacks.

Although Halloween sadism is widely regarded as a serious threat, it has received little scholarly attention. In this paper, we examine the phenomenon from a sociological perspective, addressing three issues. First, we try to assess the incidence of Halloween sadism in order to demonstrate that the threat has been greatly exaggerated. Second, we draw upon a concept from folklore studies to argue that the belief in Halloween sadism is best viewed as an "urban legend." Finally, we suggest that urban legends can be understood as unconstructed social problems. Like collective hysteria and organized claims-making efforts, urban legends are a product of social strain and of the social organization of the response to that strain.

A Holiday for Sadists?

There are no reliable official statistics on Halloween sadism. Minor incidents, particularly those that do not involve injuries, may never be reported to the police.

Cases that are reported may be classified under a wide range of offenses, and there is no centralized effort to compile cases from different jurisdictions. Moreover, the circumstances of the crime—the young victim, the unfamiliar assailant, the difficulty in remembering which treats came from which houses—make it unlikely that offenders will be arrested.

While the true incidence of Halloween sadism cannot be measured, newspaper reports reveal changes in public reaction to the threat. Therefore, we examined the coverage of Halloween sadism in four daily newspapers between 1959 and 1984. For the *New York Times,* we checked all entries under "Halloween" in the paper's annual indexes for information about Halloween sadism. The *New York Times Index* proved to be unusually complete, listing even short items of a sentence or two.[1] The published indexes for two other major regional newspapers, the *Chicago Tribune* and the *Los Angeles Times,* were less thorough, so for each year, we read both papers' issues for the first three days in November. Finally, we examined all Halloween stories in the files of the *Fresno Bee.* Our search found stories about 76 alleged incidents of Halloween sadism, which included at least the community where the incident occurred and the nature of the attack.[2] Table 1 shows the number of incidents reported in each year.

Obviously, the 76 incidents identified through this procedure do not form a complete list of cases of Halloween sadism. However, there are several reasons why it is unlikely that many serious incidents—involving deaths or serious injuries—were overlooked. First, the papers' coverage was national. The 76 reported incidents came from 15 states and two Canadian provinces; while each of the four newspapers concentrated on incidents in its own region, all reported cases from other regions. All four included at least one case from the South—the only major region without a newspaper in the sample. Second, the 76 reported cases were

TABLE 47-1 Reported Incidents of Halloween Sadism, 1958–84

Year	Number of Incidents	Year	Number of Incidents
1958	0	1972	1
1959	1	1973	4
1960	0	1974	1
1961	0	1975	2
1962	1	1976	2
1963	1	1977	0
1964	3	1978	0
1965	1	1979	3
1966	5	1980	0
1967	4	1981	0
1968	3	1982	12
1969	7	1983	1
1970	10	1984	0
1971	14		

generally not serious. Injuries were reported in only 20 cases, and only two of these involved deaths. It seems unlikely that newspapers would choose to print accounts of minor incidents, while ignoring more serious crimes. This impression is bolstered further by the frequent appearance of stories—often from different states—about other Halloween tragedies: children struck by cars and other accidental deaths; people murdered when they opened their doors, expecting trick-or-treaters; racial disturbances; vandalism; and so on. At least two of the newspapers carried reports on each of the two deaths attributed to Halloween sadists. It is therefore unlikely that the list of 76 incidents excludes any fatal instances of Halloween sadism.

Table 1 reveals two peaks in the pattern of reporting. Thirty-one of the 76 incidents occurred in the three years from 1969 to 1971. This wave of reports encouraged recognition of Halloween sadism as a threat. As a holiday when millions of children venture out at night, Halloween has a long history of tragic accidents. Routinely, newspapers and magazines print lists of safety tips, warning parents against flammable costumes, masks that obscure the wearer's vision, and the like. A systematic review of such lists found no mention of the danger posed by sadists before 1972; but, from that year on, lists of safety tips almost invariably warned parents to inspect their children's treats for signs of tampering. At the same time that these warnings spread, reports of Halloween sadism fell to a few per year until 1982, when there was a dramatic increase. Of course, this reflected the fear caused by the Tylenol murders. A month before Halloween, seven people died after swallowing poisoned Extra-Strength Tylenol capsules. In the weeks that followed, there were hundreds of reports of "copycats" adulterating food, over-the-counter medications, and other household products. As Halloween approached, the media repeatedly warned parents that trick-or-treaters would be in danger. After raising the specter of Halloween sadism, the press naturally covered the incidents that were reported. A year later, however, coverage fell to pre-Tylenol levels.

Examining the reports of the 76 incidents leads to three conclusions. First, the threat of Halloween sadism has been greatly exaggerated. There is simply no basis for *Newsweek*'s (1975) claim that "several children have died." The newspapers attributed only two deaths to Halloween sadists, and neither case fit the image of a maniacal killer randomly attacking children. In 1970, five-year-old Kevin Toston died after eating heroin supposedly hidden in his Halloween candy. While this story received considerable publicity, newspapers gave less coverage to the follow-up report that Kevin had found the heroin in his uncle's home, not his treats (*San Francisco Chronicle,* 1970). The second death is more notorious. In 1974, eight-year-old Timothy O'Bryan died after eating Halloween candy contaminated with cyanide. Investigators concluded that his father had contaminated the treat (Grider, 1982). Thus, both boys' deaths were caused by family members, rather than by anonymous sadists.[3] Similarly, while the newspaper reports rarely gave detailed information about the remaining 18 cases in which injuries were reported, most of the victims were not seriously hurt. Several incidents involved minor cuts and puncture wounds; what was apparently the most serious wound required 11 stitches. In short, there were no reports where an anonymous sadist caused death or a life-threatening injury; there is no justification for the claim that Halloween sadism stands as a major threat to U.S. children.[4]

A second conclusion is that many, if not most, reports of Halloween sadism are of questionable authenticity. Children who go trick-or-treating know about Halloween sadism; they have been warned by their parents, teachers, and friends. A child who "discovers" an adulterated treat stands to be rewarded with the concerned attention of parents and, perhaps, police officers and reporters. Such a hoax is consistent with Halloween traditions of trickery, just as the fear of sadists resembles the more traditional dread of ghosts and witches (Santino, 1983). The 76 reported incidents included two cases that were identified as hoaxes at the time, and it seems likely that other cases involved undiscovered fraud. After all, it is remarkable that three-quarters of the children who reported receiving contaminated treats had no injuries. Efforts to systematically follow up reports of Halloween sadism have concluded that the vast majority were fabrications. After Halloween 1972, *Editor and Publisher* (1973)—the trade magazine of the newspaper industry—examined several papers' efforts to trace all local reports of Halloween sadism; it concluded that virtually all the reports were hoaxes. Ten years later, in the wake of the Tylenol scare, the confectionary industry tried to reassure potential customers in a "white paper" on Halloween candy tampering in 1982 (National Confectioners Association et al., n.d.). The report noted that "more than 95 percent of the 270 potential Halloween 1982 candy adulterations analyzed by the Food and Drug Administration have shown no tampering, which has led one FDA official to characterize the period as one of 'psychosomatic mass hysteria.' " Further, a confectionary industry survey of police departments in "24 of the nation's largest cities, as well as smaller towns in which highly-publicized incidents were alleged to have occurred, found two reports of injuries—neither requiring medical treatment—from among the hundreds of claims of candy tampering."[5] Thus, not only does a survey of press coverage reveal fewer reports of Halloween sadism than might be expected, but there is good reason to suspect that many of the reports are unfounded.

Third, the press should not be held responsible for the widespread belief that Halloween sadism poses a serious threat. While the news media can manufacture "crime waves" by suddenly focusing on previously ignored offenses (Fishman, 1978), the press has given Halloween sadism relatively little publicity. Many of the 76 reported incidents received minimal coverage, in news stories of only two or three sentences. Often the reports were embedded in larger stories, such as a wire service summary of Halloween news from around the country. Nor did popular magazines highlight Halloween sadism; before 1982, only two short articles focused on the problem. The absence of authentic cases of serious injuries caused by Halloween sadism undoubtedly explains this limited coverage. While the publication of annual warnings to parents to inspect their children's treats, as well as occasional short items reporting minor incidents, may help keep the fear of Halloween sadism alive, the media do not seem to be the principal channel by which people learn of the danger. Rather, knowledge of Halloween sadism apparently spreads by word of mouth.

Roots of an Urban Legend

The belief in Halloween sadism as a serious threat can be understood using a concept developed by folklorists: Halloween sadism is an *urban legend* (Grider, 1982). Urban legends are contemporary, orally transmitted tales that "often depict a clash between modern conditions and some aspect of a traditional life-style" (Brunvand, 1981:189). Whereas traditional legends often feature supernatural themes, most urban legends "are grounded in human baseness . . . " (Fine, 1980:227). They describe criminal attacks, contaminated consumer goods, and other risks of modern life.[6] Halloween sadism combines two themes found in several other urban legends: danger to children (e.g., the babysitter who cooks an infant in a microwave oven; the child kidnapped from a department store or an amusement park); and contamination of food (e.g., the mouse in the soft-drink bottle; the Kentucky Fried Rat) (Brunvand, 1981, 1984; Fine, 1979, 1980, 1985). These legends, like that of the Halloween sadist, are typically told as true stories. They "gratify our desire to know about and to try to understand bizarre, frightening, and potentially dangerous or embarrassing events that *may* have happened" (Brunvand, 1981:12). Urban legends may even have a factual basis; soft-drink manufacturers have been sued by people claiming to have found mice in their drinks (Fine, 1979). Whether a legend begins with a real incident or as a fictional tale, it is told and retold, often evolving as it spreads. On occasion, urban legends appear in newspaper stories, reinforcing the tale's credibility (Brunvand, 1981, 1984). The belief in Halloween sadism is maintained through orally transmitted warnings about the dangers contemporary society poses for the traditional custom of trick-or-treating. These warnings, which greatly exaggerate the threat, are an urban legend. That some incidents of Halloween sadism have occurred, and that the media have reported such incidents, does not disqualify the warnings as legends.

Viewing Halloween sadism as an urban legend helps explain why the belief became widespread when it did. News reports of Halloween sadism are not new (cf., *New York Times,* 1950).[7] But the general perception that Halloween sadism is a serious threat can be dated to the early 1970s. This was the period when the press began reporting more incidents and warning parents to inspect treats, and legislatures began passing laws against Halloween sadism. In general, urban legends are products of social tension or strain. They express fears that the complexities of modern society threaten the traditional social order (Fine, 1980, 1985). Urban life requires contact with strangers who—the legends suggest—may be homicidal maniacs, unscrupulous merchants, voyeurs, or otherwise threatening. By repeating urban legends, people can respond to social strain, expressing their doubts about the modern world.

While it is obviously impossible to establish a causal link between particular social tensions and the spread of a particular urban legend, folklorists typically examine a legend's elements for clues about its roots (Brunvand, 1981, 1984; Fine, 1980). Some legends feature a transparent message, but others are more difficult to interpret. In the case of Halloween sadism, a plausible argument can be made that the legend's flowering in the early 1970s was tied to the heightened social strains of that period. The late 1960s and early 1970s were years of unparalleled divisiveness in post-World War II America (Carroll, 1982; O'Neill, 1971). The media exposed several serious crises to the public, including an increasingly unpopular war, ghetto riots, student demonstrations, and increased drug use. It was a period of intense social strain. Three forms of strain that emerged or grew during these years seem related to the growing fear of Halloween sadism.

Threats to Children

The form of strain that seems most clearly linked to a belief in Halloween sadism was the growing sense that children were no longer safe in the United States. During the 1960s and early 1970s, physicians and social workers promoted child abuse as a major social problem; the popular press responded with dozens of dramatic stories about children who had been cruelly treated by their parents (Pfohl, 1977). The rhetoric of this campaign emphasized that all children were potential victims, that child abuse occurred in all sectors of society. But even parents who remained confident that their children would never be abused could worry about losing their children to other threats. Older children adopted radical political views and experimented with illegal drugs.[8] Other parents found their grown children facing a less symbolic threat—death in Vietnam. The social conflicts that marked America during these years must have left many parents wondering if their hopes for the next generation would be fulfilled.

Since the emergence of the belief in Halloween sadism, the generation gap seems to have narrowed, but threats to children remain visible. The movement against child abuse continues to spread, receiving still more publicity. And, during the late 1970s and early 1980s, emerging campaigns against incest, child pornography, child molesting, and abortion may have contributed to a larger sense of children in jeopardy. Perhaps the clearest link between threats to children and the fear of Halloween sadism appeared during the series of murders of Atlanta schoolchildren. In 1980, STOP, an organization of the victims' parents, argued that "the city should organize Halloween night events that will minimize dangers to the children" (*New York Times,* 1980).[9]

Fear of Crime

Other forms of strain involved more general threats. Survey data reveal that the fear of crime grew substantially between the mid-1960s and the early 1970s (Erskine, 1974; Stinchcombe et al., 1980). Although violent crimes often involve offenders and victims who are acquainted, the fear of crime focuses on the threat of an anonymous attacker.[10] The threat of an unpredictable, unprovoked criminal attack parallels the Halloween sadist menace.

Mistrust of Others

Survey data also reveal rising expressions of general mistrust during the early 1970s. The proportion of Americans who agreed that ". . . you can't be too careful in dealing with people" rose from 45.6 percent in 1966, to 50.0 percent in 1971, to 54.3 percent in 1973 (Converse et al., 1980:28). Studies of urban dwellers in the 1970s found high levels of mistrust for strangers (Fischer, 1982; Merry, 1981; Suttles, 1972). While warnings about the collapse of the neighborhood in the anonymous modern city have proven exaggerated, the belief that people now live in greater isolation remains widespread. The social conflicts of the 1960s and early 1970s may have encouraged doubts about the trustworthiness of other people. Such doubts provided another form of strain during the period when the belief in Halloween sadism spread.

These sources of strain—threats to children, fear of crime, and mistrust of others—provided a context within which the concern about Halloween sadism could flourish. The Halloween sadist emerged as a symbolic expression of this strain: the sadist, like other dangers, attacks children—society's most vulnerable members; the sadist, like the stereotypical criminal, is an anonymous, unprovoked assailant; and the sadist, like other strangers, must be met by doubt, rather than trust.[11] Placed in the context of the late 1960s and early 1970s, the spread of Halloween sadism is easily understood.

If these sources of strain account for the belief's spread, what explains its persistence? The extraordinary social conflicts of the early 1970s have moderated, yet the belief in Halloween sadism remains. Why? First, some of the same sources of strain continue to exist: the media still publicize threats to children (e.g., child abuse), and the fear of crime and strangers remains high.

Second, and more important, Halloween sadism is an established urban legend; it can remain as a taken-for-granted, if dormant, part of American culture. The survey of newspaper stories found only five reports of Halloween sadism from 1976 to 1981—less than one per year.[12] However, warnings about sadists continued to appear during these years and, of course, the Tylenol poisonings in 1982 led to both predictions and reports of Halloween sadism.

Third, folklorists have traced the evolution of some legends over centuries (Brunvand, 1984). Legends seem most likely to persist when they have a general, underlying message (for instance, warnings about trusting outsiders) which can be tailored to fit new situations. Thus, the dangers of eating commercially prepared food were detailed in nineteenth-century stories about cat meat in baked pies and, more recently, in tales about rats sold at fried-chicken franchises (Fine, 1980; Simpson, 1983). Like other urban legends about homicidal maniacs, the Halloween sadist legend expresses fears about criminal attacks. Given the general nature of this threat, the legend may persist as long as the custom of trick-or-treating.

Urban Legends as Unconstructed Social Problems

Where do urban legends fit within the broader framework of sociological theory? The case of Halloween sadism suggests (1) that urban legends may be viewed as a form of unconstructed social problem, (2) that collective hysteria, urban legends, and social problems construction offer alternative responses to social strain, and (3) that the emergence of a particular response to strain reflects social organization.

At first glance, the fear of Halloween sadists resembles some of the instances of collective hysteria in the collective behavior literature. The Halloween sadist can stand beside the "phantom anesthetist" of Mattoon (Johnson, 1945), the "phantom slasher" of Taipei (Jacobs, 1965), the "June bug epidemic" in a Southern textile plant (Kerckhoff and Back, 1968), and the windshield pitting in Seattle (Medalia and Larsen, 1958) as a focus of exaggerated fears. Studies of collective hysteria usually account for the emergence of hysterical beliefs as a response to social strain: the Mattoon episode occurred during wartime; the workers in the textile plant were putting in heavy overtime, and so on. In response to this strain, there emerges a belief in some threat, "an ambiguous element in the environment with a generalized power to threaten or destroy" (Smelser, 1962:82). This threat is credible, frightening, and difficult to protect oneself against:

> Instead of simply having a feeling that something is awry, the belief in a tangible threat makes it possible to *explain* and *justify* one's sense of discomfort—instead of anxiety, one experiences fear, and it is then possible to act in some meaningful way with respect to this tangible threat rather than just feeling frustrated and anxious. (Kerckhoff and Back, 1968:160–61—emphasis in original)

However, some of this model's key features do not fit the emergence of the belief in Halloween sadism and other urban legends. Collective hysteria is bounded in time and space. Hysterical beliefs are short-lived; they typically emerge, spread, and die within the space of a few days or weeks. Further, they are typically confined to a restricted locality—a single region, town, or facility (Lofland, 1981). In contrast, the belief in Halloween sadists appears to have spread more slowly, over a period of years, and to have become an established, taken-for-granted part of the culture. Nor has the belief observed the normal geographic limits of collective hysteria—reports of Halloween sadism have come from throughout the country, suggesting that the belief is nationwide. If the Halloween sadist resembles the threats identified in instances of collective hysteria, the dynamics of the belief's spread do not fit the hysterical pattern.

The process of social problems construction offers an alternative perspective for understanding the fear of Halloween sadism. Blumer (1971) and Spector and Kitsuse (1973, 1977) defined social problems as products of claims-making activities, in which people call others' attention to social conditions. Thus, the emergence of a social problem is a political process: ". . . recognition by a society of its social problems is a highly selective process, with many harmful social conditions and arrangements not even making a bid for attention and with others falling by the wayside in what is frequently a fierce competitive struggle" (Blumer, 1971:302). Case studies of claims-making focus on the role of social movements (Tierney, 1982), professionals (Pfohl, 1977), the press (Schoenfeld et al., 1979), and other interested parties in constructing social problems. While these studies demonstrate how some claims-making campaigns succeeded, they do not explain why other social conditions, with the potential to be defined as social problems, never reach this status. Emergent or unconstructed social problems are less often studied (Troyer and Markle, 1983, 1984). Urban legends, such as the Halloween sadist, may be seen in these terms.

While the belief in Halloween sadism is widespread, it has not led to effective claims-making activities. Halloween sadism has, for brief occasions, occupied the attention of legislators, city officials, journalists, and PTA associations, but the belief spread largely outside institutionalized channels.[13] The press never reported more than a handful of incidents in a given year, and most of these reports were very short; the belief spread informally, by word-of-mouth. Similarly, there was no especially visible response to the threat. By the mid-1970s, the press reported a few organized attempts to thwart sadists—hospitals offering to X-ray treats, communities organizing alternative celebrations, and municipalities passing ordinances against trick-or-treating.[14] But most of these efforts remained localized; they received little publicity and did not lead to a broader, organized response to Halloween sadism. (Similarly, organized campaigns by the confectionary industry to expose fabricated reports of Halloween sadism also failed to attract widespread recognition [*Editor and Publisher,* 1973; National Confectioners Association et al., n.d.].) While it is possible to trace the claims-making activities by which many social problems are constructed, this is not true for Halloween sadism. Although the belief spread widely, it moved largely through informal channels, and the principal reaction—parents restricting their children's trick-or-treating—was equally informal.

This analysis suggests that collective hysteria, urban legends, and social problems construction are alternative responses to social strain, alternatives in which strain is translated into different forms of threat that are spread through different forms of social organization. Strain—discomfort caused by existing social conditions—is made manifest in a perceived threat to the collectivity.[15] This threat may be genuine or false. Commonly, genuine threats are a more symbolic expression of strain (e.g., a "June bug" attacks people under a heavy work load). The identification of genuine threats often suggests a solution—something that can be done to reduce or eliminate the threat—while false threats are frequently amorphous and difficult or impossible to manage. In general, collective hysteria and urban legends respond to strain through the identification of false threats, while social problems construction deals with genuine threats. Social organization affects the spread of perceptions of threat. In compact, homogeneous collectivities, collective hysteria can spread quickly. In larger, more diffuse collectivities, it takes longer to attract attention to the threat and to mobilize concerned individuals. Typically, in social problems construction, some individuals take the lead in organizing claims-making activities, while urban legends spread through informal contacts.

The example of Halloween sadism suggests some specific factors that may affect the response to social strain. The reports of Halloween sadism did not lead to collective hysteria for two reasons. First, the belief spread throughout the country, rather than within a compact collectivity. Second, this spread could occur relatively slowly, given the limited nature of the threat. Reports of sadistic incidents posed no threat to other children for another year. There was no urgency to the news; the tale could be disseminated slowly, through informal channels. Although a few organizations began claims-making activities directed at Halloween sadism, little came of their efforts. In part, this may have been caused by the absence of serious, documented sadistic incidents; without genuine atrocities to demonstrate the need for action, claims-makers had trouble making a convincing case. Further, potential social movements aimed at Halloween sadism lacked a well-organized natural constituency; while no one approved of Halloween sadism, no group found it in its interest to mount a sustained campaign against the threat. Again, the fact that the danger was limited to one evening a year may have inhibited the construction of Halloween sadism as a social problem. Nor was it clear how collective action might stop Halloween sadism; parents who worried about the threat found the best protection in individually curtailing their children's trick-or-treating or inspecting their treats. Thus, the diffuse collectivity, the infrequency of the reported attacks, the absence of convincing evidence, the lack of interested individuals willing to commit extensive time to the cause, and the difficulty of devising solutions meant that Halloween sadism became the focus of neither collective hysteria nor successful claims-making. Yet, retaining considerable symbolic power as an expression of social strain, Halloween sadism endured as an urban legend.

Implications: "Halloween and the Mass Child" Revisited

Holiday celebrations reflect the larger culture. The events celebrated, as well as the customary ways of celebrating, reveal the society's values and structure. And, as society changes, its holidays often take on new meanings, consistent with the altered culture. Where earlier American celebrations were communal, ceremonial, and often religious or patriotic, contemporary observances tend to be individualistic, materialistic, secular occasions, marked largely by unstructured leisure time (Caplow, 1982; Caplow and Williamson, 1980; Hatch, 1978).[16]

Gregory P. Stone's (1959) "Halloween and the Mass Child" developed this thesis. Stone traced the evolution of Halloween activities in his lifetime, from the elaborate pranks of adolescents in the 1930s, to the playful trick-or-treating of young children in the 1950s. He found the 1950s children did not understand the extortionate premise of "trick or treat;" for them, Halloween was merely an occasion to receive candy. Stone interpreted this shift as consistent with the changes in American values described in Riesman's (1950) *The Lonely Crowd:*

> . . . Riesman's character type of "other-direction" may, indeed, be a *prototype* of American character and not some strange mutation in the northeast. Consumption, tolerance, and conformity were recognizable in the Halloween masquerade of a near-southern town. Production, indignation, and autonomy were not. (Stone, 1959:378—emphasis in original)

Twenty-five years after Stone's analysis, the fear of Halloween sadism has further altered the meaning of Halloween. While Stone saw trick-or-treating as a part of the emerging culture of consumption, folklorists view Halloween as among the least commercialized of modern holidays (Grider, 1982; Santino, 1983). But this informality has been labeled dangerous by those who warn against Halloween sadists. Children are urged to refuse homemade treats and accept only coupons or mass-produced candy with intact wrappings, as though commercialism offers protection.[17] Long celebrated through vandalism and extortion, Halloween has been a symbolic expression of disorder. Today, the Halloween sadist has become an annual reminder of the fragility of the social bond—an expression of growing doubts about the safety of children, the trustworthiness of strangers, and the strength of the modern urban community.

Examining the fear of Halloween sadists reveals topics that deserve further sociological attention. First, urban legends merit more analysis as expressions of social strain. Second, theories of social problems construction need to address the processes by which topics become the focus of claims-making activities. Most existing case studies describe relatively successful claims-making efforts, taking for granted the appropriateness of those efforts. But a complete theory of social problems construction would also examine the earliest stages in the process, asking why some social conditions fail to become the focus for claims-making, how strain, social organization, and other social conditions generate claims-making, and why some strain is translated into collective hysteria or urban legends, rather than claims-making. To define social problems in terms of claims-making without identifying the roots of that process begs the question of why some phenomena become social problems.

NOTES

1. On the reliability of this index, see Troyer and Markle (1983:141–42).

2. In addition, all entries under "Halloween" in the *Reader's Guide to Periodical Literature* and MEDLINE—the computerized medical data base—were checked. Neither popular magazines nor the medical literature described any additional cases of Halloween sadism. Every case was included if the news report treated it as an instance of Halloween sadism. As noted below, some of the cases included were of questionable authenticity.

3. The particulars of these cases are sometimes forgotten, so that the deaths continue to be used as proof that Halloween sadists pose a real threat. Trubo (1974:28) describes Toston as "the victim of a sadistic prankster." Similarly, an anonymous reviewer of an earlier draft of this paper recalled the O'Bryan case but did not mention that it was the boy's father who was convicted.

4. Certainly other elements of everyday life, while not receiving as much attention, are far more hazardous. In 1980–81, according to the U.S. Consumer Product Safety Commission (1982), 60 children under age five died in "product associated deaths" involving nursery equipment and supplies; another 13 deaths involved toys.

5. In one apparent hoax:

. . . a youth claimed to have ingested an insecticide-saturated candy bar. . . . Testing showed no traces of any chemicals in the youth's blood. . . . although there was insecticide on one end of the bar, the side of the candy bar that had been bitten into was insecticide-free. (National Confectioners Association et al., n.d.)

Similarly, over 80% of the reports of so-called "copycat" poisonings that followed the Tylenol deaths were apparently fabricated (*Time,* 1982). Some were anonymous pranks, but others involved publicity-seekers or schemes to collect insurance settlements from manufacturers. As in the case of Halloween sadism, the threat was exaggerated; Congressional hearings denounced "a new kind of thug that is stalking the American communities" (U.S. Congress: House of Representatives, 1982:2), while psychiatrists speculated that "copycat criminals may have weak ego structures and 'have difficulty running their lives' " (*New York Times,* 1982).

6. The term "urban legend" is generally used by folklorists to distinguish modern folk tales from those told in traditional societies; it ignores the differences between contemporary urban and rural communities. Some familiar urban legends include: "The Hook"—a maniac who terrorizes a couple parked in a lover's lane; the black widow spider that nests in a beehive hairdo; the deep-fried rat sold at a fried-chicken franchise; and "The Choking Doberman," that swallows a burglar's fingers. Brunvand's (1981, 1984) books present several dozen such tales.

7. This case involved giving children pennies heated on a skillet. Apparently this was an early image of Halloween sadism; Grider (1982) recalls a heated pennies legend circulating among Texas children in the 1940s. Of course, the fear of Halloween sadism also seems linked to traditional warnings about accepting candy from strangers.

8. The possibility that their children might adopt disapproved values may have suggested betrayal to some parents, creating another source of strain—ambivalence toward one's children. This ambivalence is nicely revealed in a popular cultural genre which regained popularity during the late 1960s and early 1970s. In popular novels and films (e.g., *The Exorcist* and *Rosemary's Baby*), the horror tale—traditionally associated with Halloween—took on a new emphasis: stories about children with demonic powers.

The concern with growing drug use may have been especially important in fostering the initial fear of Halloween sadism. Although only one of the 76 newspaper reports involved "hippies" giving drugs to children, early oral versions of contaminated-treat tales often took this form. (On a related, early 1970s legend—that LSD was being distributed on pictures of Mickey Mouse, which children might mistake for a lick-on tattoo—see Brunvand, 1984:162–69.) Only later did the razor blade in the apple become the standard image for Halloween sadism. Six of the 12 incidents reported before 1967 involved over-the-counter or prescription drugs; only one involved a sharp object. In contrast, 49 of the 64 reports after 1966 involved razors or other sharp objects, while only four involved drugs. Of course, razor blades, pins, and so on are readily available equipment, which would make it easy to carry out hoaxes.

9. Similarly, the Tylenol poisonings raised the prospect of attacks via product contamination. Like the Atlanta murders, these real crimes by an anonymous sadist led to warnings about Halloween sadists.

10. This fear also found expression in a popular culture horror genre—the "mad slasher" films in which a maniac stalks and kills a series of high school or college students. Interestingly, the first of these films was *Halloween* (1979).

11. Grider (1982:6) agrees: "The Razor Blades Syndrome expresses a deep-rooted fear of strangers, a distrust of old customs and traditions, an acknowledgement of child abuse and infanticide, and an ambivalence toward random, wanton violence."

12. Presumably, incidents continued to be reported during this period. The decline in press coverage may have reflected journalists' doubts about the authenticity of the reports (*Editor and Publisher,* 1973), as well as their recognition that the reported incidents were minor and, given the well-established nature of the legend, no longer newsworthy.

13. Medical professionals, for instance, paid minimal attention to Halloween sadism. MEDLINE listed no articles on the subject from 1966 to 1983.

14. While the press routinely interpreted these actions as responses to Halloween sadism, many attempts to restrict trick-or-treating were, in fact, prompted by more traditional Halloween problems, e.g., vandalism or children struck by cars (cf. Trubo, 1974).

15. Social constructionist theorists attack the notion that strain or other objective social conditions offer a sufficient explanation for social problems; they argue that claims-making activities must occur (Blumer, 1971; Spector and Kitsuse, 1977). Troyer and Markle (1983), however, suggest that strain usually, if not always, precedes claims-making.

16. When they are inconsistent with modern practices, earlier forms of celebrating may be forgotten. On the drunken, riotous Christmas customs of the nineteenth-century working class, see Davis (1982).

17. The intense reaction to the Tylenol murders reflected consumers' dependence on mass-produced food and medications. "The revolt of the product is the ultimate nightmare for a society like ours" (Spiro, 1982:11). However, new standards for tamper-resistant packaging apparently reestablished confidence in product safety.

REFERENCES

Blumer, Herbert (1971) "Social problems as collective behavior." Social Problems 18:298–306.

Brunvand, Jan Harold (1981) The Vanishing Hitchhiker. New York: Norton.

_____ (1984) The Choking Doberman. New York: Norton.

Caplow, Theodore (1982) "Christmas gifts and kin networks." American Sociological Review 47:383–92.

Caplow, Theodore and Margaret Holmes Williamson (1980) "Decoding Middletown's Easter Bunny." Semiotica 32:221–32.

Carroll, Peter N. (1982) It Seemed Like Nothing Happened. New York: Holt, Rinehart, & Winston.

Converse, Philip E., Jean D. Dotson, Wendy J. Hoag and William H. McGee III (1980) American Social Attitudes Data Sourcebook. Cambridge: Harvard University Press.

Davis, Susan G. (1982) " 'Making the night hideous.' " American Quarterly 34:185–99.

DeKalb Daily Chronicle (1984) "Sidewalk interview." October 28:10.

Editor and Publisher (1973) "Press finds Halloween sadism rare but warns of danger." 106 (March 3):22.

Erskine, Hazel (1974) "The polls: fear of crime and violence." Public Opinion Quarterly 38:131–45.

Fine, Gary Alan (1979) "Cokelore and coke law." Journal of American Folklore 92:477–82.

_____ (1980) "The Kentucky fried rat." Journal of the Folklore Institute 17:222–43.

_____ (1985) "The Goliath effect." Journal of American Folklore 98:63–84.

Fischer, Claude S. (1982) To Dwell Among Friends. Chicago: University of Chicago Press.

Fishman, Mark (1978) "Crime waves as ideology." Social Problems 25:531–43.

Fresno Bee (1984) "No tricks found in Fresno treats." November 1:B1.

Grider, Sylvia (1982) "The razor blades in the apples syndrome." Unpublished paper.

Hatch, Jane M. (ed.) (1978) The American Book of Days. Third edition. New York: Wilson.

Isaacs, Susan and Robert Royeton (1982) "Witches, goblins, ghosts." Parents Magazine 57 (October):66–9.

Jacobs, Norman (1965) "The phantom slasher of Taipei." Social Problems 12:318–28.

Johnson, Donald M. (1945) "The 'phantom anesthetist' of Mattoon." Journal of Abnormal and Social Psychology 40:175–86.

Kerckhoff, Alan C. and Kurt W. Back (1968) The June Bug. New York: Appleton-Century-Crofts.

Lofland, John (1981) "Collective behavior." Pp. 441–46 in Morris Rosenberg and Ralph H. Turner (eds.), Social Psychology. New York: Basic Books.

Los Angeles Times (1982) "Trick or treat subdued amid poisoning scares." November 1:1,28.

Medalia, Nahum Z. and Otto N. Larsen (1958) "Diffusion and belief in a collective delusion." American Sociological Review 23:180–86.

Merry, Sally Engle (1981) Urban Danger. Philadelphia: Temple University Press.

National Confectioners Association, Chocolate Manufacturers Association, and National Candy Wholesalers Association n.d. "Halloween/1982: an overview." Unpublished paper.

New York Times (1950) "Punish Halloween 'witch,' angry parents demand." November 3:52.

_____ (1970) "Those treats may be tricks." October 28:56.

_____ (1972) "Trick-or-treating till stroke of 7." November 1:30.

_____ (1980) "Atlanta and Miami curbing Halloween." October 31:A14.

_____ (1982) "Experts theorize about 'copycat syndrome.' " October 30:6.

Newsweek (1975) "The goblins will getcha. . . . " 86 (November 3):28.

O'Neill, William L. (1971) Coming Apart. Chicago: Quadrangle.

Pfohl, Stephen J. (1977) "The 'discovery' of child abuse." Social Problems 24:310–23.

Riesman, David (1950) The Lonely Crowd. New Haven: Yale University Press.

San Francisco Chronicle (1970) "Capsule caused Halloween death." November 10:3.

Santino, Jack (1983) "Halloween in America." Western Folklore 42:1–20.

Schoenfeld, A. Clay, Robert F. Meier and Robert J. Griffin (1979) "Constructing a social problem." Social Problems 27:38–61.

Simpson, Jacqueline (1983) "Urban legends in *The Pickwick Papers.*" Journal of American Folklore 96:462–70.

Smelser, Neil J. (1962) Theory of Collective Behavior. New York: Free Press.

Spector, Malcolm and John I. Kitsuse (1973) "Social problems." Social Problems 21:145–59.

_____ (1977) Constructing Social Problems. Menlo Park, CA: Cummings.

Spiro, Peter (1982) "Chaos by the capsule." New Republic 187 (December 6):10–1.

Stinchcombe, Arthur L., Rebecca Adams, Carol A. Heimer, Kim Lane Scheppele, Tom W. Smith and D. Garth Taylor (1980) Crime and Punishment. San Francisco: Jossey-Bass.

Stone, Gregory P. (1959) "Halloween and the mass child." American Quarterly 11:372–79.

Suttles, Gerald D. (1972) The Social Construction of Communities. Chicago: University of Chicago Press.

Tierney, Kathleen J. (1982) "The battered woman movement and the creation of the wife beating problem." Social Problems 29:207–20.

Time (1982) "Copycats on the prowl." 120 (November 8):27.

Times (Beaverton, OR) (1984) "Letters." October 25:36.

Troyer, Ronald J. and Gerald E. Markle (1983) Cigarettes. New Brunswick, NJ: Rutgers University Press.

_____ (1984) "Coffee drinking." Social Problems 31:403–16.

Trubo, Richard (1974) "Holiday for sadists." PTA Magazine 69:28–9.

U.S. Congress: House of Representatives (1982) Hearing on Tamper-Resistant Packaging for Over-the-Counter Drugs. Committee on Energy and Commerce, Subcommittee on Health and the Environment. 96th Congress, 2nd session. Washington: U.S. Government Printing Office.

U.S. Consumer Product Safety Commission (1982) Annual Report. Washington: U.S. Government Printing Office.

Van Buren, Abigail (1983) "Dear Abby." Fresno Bee (October 31):D2.

_____ (1984) "Dear Abby." Fresno Bee (September 30):C4.

DISCUSSION QUESTIONS

1. Why are most of the reports of Halloween sadism found in the early 1970's?
2. What are the urban conditions that produce urban legends?

Article 48

Violence

Out of Hand in the Stands

BIL GILBERT AND LISA TWYMAN

PERHAPS BECAUSE we're so heavily bombarded with dire news and doomsday prophecies, there's a temptation for those concerned with a problem—whether it be viral skin disorders, reading deficiencies of youth or the drying up of swamps—to call attention to it by stridently suggesting that if it isn't immediately solved the Republic will crumble. This is an especially suspect and ludicrous practice when applied to sports. The difficulties of junky jocks, sneaky coaches or greedy promoters are seldom related in any significant way to the substantial ills of society. This should be kept in mind as we consider the subject of this report, fan violence.

Through the ages sporting spectators have been notorious for hooliganism. The original Olympics were suspended because of belligerent crowd behavior. In one three-day period in 532 B.C., during the reign of the Emperor Justinian, 30,000 Romans died in riots at the chariot races. In year 1314 Edward II of England banned "that dreadful game, football," because it touched off such bloody brawls among 14th-century fans. The worst recent outburst of this sort occurred in Lima, Peru, where at a soccer match in 1964, 300 people were killed and 500 injured. There have always been incidents of this kind, but their number and seriousness fluctuate, reflecting, some theorize, disorders in the real world. (The hypothesis that behavior at sports events may serve as a barometer for measuring pressures and tension in society is probably the most thought-provoking aspect of this phenomenon.)

Currently, nearly all knowledgeable sources think there is a rising level of fan violence in the U.S. The consensus is that, in comparison to 20 or even 10 years ago, it's more difficult and expensive to control sports crowds; that they cause more personal injury and property damage and are uglier in manner and mood. Now, this is bad news for sport, but it hardly constitutes a grave threat to public order, health and morals. In any general discussion of violence, that which occurs at sports events is little more than an aside. During the past year, on any number of days in the Middle East or Central America there was more violence than has occurred in all of modern sports history. Spending an evening at Yankee Stadium now may be more risky than going to the zoo or staying at home, but it's still safer than walking for three hours in the neighborhood around Yankee Stadium. What fan violence amounts to may be suggested by the following sampler of happenings in recent years:

> After the WBC California State Junior Lightweight Boxing Championship in Sacramento last summer, a brawl broke out and eventually involved, police estimated, 75 to 100 fans. Before it was over, seven spectators had been stabbed, four requiring hospitalization.
>
> At a Friday night of boxing in Madison Square Garden in 1978, two men were stabbed, another man was shot (by an off-duty corrections officer) and a woman was treated for a severe head laceration after being struck by a bottle. While the police were carrying the gunshot victim from the Garden, someone lobbed an exploding cherry bomb at them.
>
> At New York's Shea Stadium during a 1978 Jets-Steelers game, spectators overpowered a security guard and dropped him over a railing to a concrete walkway 15 feet below. He suffered a fractured skull, along with a concussion and various neck injuries.
>
> At a 1981 Rams-Bears game in Chicago's Soldier Field there were 31 arrests, the principal charges being battery, disorderly conduct and possession of drugs. Two security men and several ushers were attacked by fans, one of whom dropped his pants and shot a moon for the benefit of the Honey Bears, the Chicago cheerleaders, and the ABC television cameras.
>
> In 1980 the Detroit Tigers temporarily closed the bleacher section in their stadium to retake it, so to speak, from chronically violent spectators. For the same reason, in May, 1981 the Cincinnati Reds asked their players and the opposing players, the Pittsburgh Pirates, to leave the field at Riverfront Stadium until the rowdy crowd could be brought under control.
>
> During a 1981 American League playoff game at Yankee Stadium, a fan carrying a blackjack ran onto the field and charged and knocked down the third-base umpire, who was saved from injury by the quick intervention of the Yankees' Graig Nettles and Dave Winfield.
>
> Pittsburgh Outfielder Dave Parker claims to be the No. 1 target of fan violence in America because he's black, highly paid, hasn't performed well the last couple of seasons and is proud, perhaps even a bit arrogant. He has been pelted with apple cores, hundreds of paper beer cups, jawbreakers, transistor-radio batteries and bullets (thrown not fired), as well as obscenities and racial slurs. "You ain't nothin' but a stinkin', lousy nigger" is a printable example of the latter. Once, in his hotel

room in Philadelphia, Parker received a telephone call from a man who informed him that if he came down to the lobby he would be killed. Parker did and wasn't. He's among the growing number of sports figures who have received death threats during the past five years.

The list of such happenings isn't endless, but it's very long. Beyond those that draw public attention there are innumerable violent acts that go unreported. It's fair to say that on game day in every major sporting facility there are a few fights and several minor assaults and a dozen or so spectators are ejected because of bad conduct.

"This crowd violence thing has been in the dark for so long," says David M. Schaffer, director of park operations (including security) for the Chicago White Sox, a team that has made notable efforts to face up to its problems. "Hell, just go anywhere and there will be a fight of one kind or another."

Traditionally, the sporting establishment has been mum on the subject, believing that a certain amount of crowd misbehavior is part of the game and one which, like the legs of a Victorian lady, gentlemen speak of euphemistically; that talking about violence would focus attention on it and stimulate others to commit it; that the subject is bad for business. "We prefer to talk about crowd involvement rather than violence," said a Philadelphia Flyers official several years ago. "Violence has such an ugly connotation."

However, the fact that buying a ticket to a game markedly increases a customer's chances of getting a punch in the snoot, doused with beer, an earful of X-rated language or a vandalized car makes it difficult to sustain former traditions and illusions. By their actions, if not their words, most sports executives indicate that they regard fan violence as a large problem, one that's going to get larger, more expensive, and more embarrassing if something isn't done about it soon. As never before, leagues and teams are trying to find out why their fans have grown so difficult to handle, and in making such assessments, sports executives are calling in "violence experts," a new breed of consultant.

Some of the observations, theories and conclusions of these violence experts are:

Sports crowds generally follow some vague rules of order—for example, people don't usually stand and block the view of other spectators—but can become unstable, erratic, and edgy human organizations. Within a crowd there are many low-level sources of tension—close, involuntary contact with strangers, abnormal physical discomforts, competition for territory, goods, services and information—that frustrate individuals and make them more irritable and belligerent than they are when alone or in smaller groups. Crowds provide anonymity and encourage miscreants to act more irresponsibly than they might in situations where they can be easily identified and punished. Simple, primitive emotions, such as elation, anger, panic and vengeance, are contagious within a crowd and create so-called mass hysteria. Sports events regularly draw the largest crowds of any public events, but sports facilities, compared to those offered to other crowds, are often among the most inefficient, uncomfortable, and unattractive. If the environment were as grim and aggravating at art galleries, lecture halls, and movie theaters as it is at Schaefer Stadium, there probably would be more disturbances at those places.

Sports events are exhibitions of skill, grace, strength, coordination, and other attractive human properties. They're also contrived, dramatic charades, of which violence is an intrinsic element or, at least, violence is not too far below the surface. In some sports, such as boxing, football, and hockey, the scripts are explicitly violent. Even in those sports where the participants are not called upon to push, shove, and beat each other the action is confrontational with one individual or team trying to demolish, as the scribes say, an opponent—or crush, roll over, thump, trample, pulverize, stick it to, and kill him, as they also say. The underlying themes of competitive games are strikingly similar to those of war, and the language of the two activities has become almost identical.

Our newspapers, magazines, books, TV shows, movies, theater, music, and advertisements testify to our fascination with violence, that it rates not far behind sex in its vicarious attraction. One explanation for this is that many people would like to be more violent than they are. They find the idea of taking arms against their enemies—or people who merely frustrate or cause them trouble—and flattening them, so to speak, by direct physical action to be very appealing. Most people don't act on such impulses because of the law, ethics, or the fear of getting hurt. Stymied by reality, they take deep satisfaction in watching and identifying with others who seem to be acting in this bold way. As a group, athletes are encouraged and rewarded for being violent while on-stage, and sport has become one of our most successful devices for providing fantasy relief.

Sports crowds are encouraged to respond freely to the action of the game. Cheering, booing, hissing, stamping feet, waving fists, and screaming criticisms and threats are considered normal at games, though those activities would be treated as aberrant and unruly in other circumstances. As tragedies can bring their audiences to tears and comedies can provoke laughter, sport can make its crowds a bit more violent. And as in other forms of show business, the assumption is that the more powerful the production the more pronounced the reaction of the audience.

Michael Smith, a former football and hockey player and hockey coach, is a Canadian sociologist interested in such matters. He says, "I believe that violence in sport contributes to violence in the crowd, as opposed to the notion of catharsis, that viewing violent acts results in draining away feelings of violence. I have looked at newspaper accounts of 68 episodes of collective violence or riots among spectators during or after sporting events, and in three-quarters of those the precipitating event was violence in the game. Yet for decades and decades eminent scholars wrote without a shred of evidence that acts of violence in sport are cathartic or therapeutic for spectators." Indeed, the catharsis theory is still advanced occasionally but, as Smith suggests, has been largely discredited by social scientists simply because nobody can find cases where this saltpeter-like effect has been produced.

The association between sport and violence isn't aberrant. However, it's supposedly understood by everyone involved that what's going on is just a game, a staged conflict. That this is frequently forgotten is testimony to the power of sports. Even participants who have long rehearsals and the rules of the game and referees to remind them that they are actors in a play get carried away by the make-believe battle. Losing one's grip on reality happens more often in the stands. Spectators have few restraints on their behavior, and it isn't surprising that some of them give vent to their own fantasies by responding physically to the fictitious battle being played out by the athletes. "The crowd is going crazy" is an instructive sporting cliché.

Dr. John Cheffers, a former Australian football player and international track athlete and coach, is a professor of education at Boston University. For a decade he has been professionally interested in fan violence and now offers his services to sports organizations, among them the New England Patriots. For some time Cheffers and an associate, a sociologist named Dr. Jay Meehan, have been using video equipment and graduate students to observe spectators at football, hockey, soccer, and baseball games in order to identify types and causes of what they call "incongruous behavior."

Cheffers and Meehan have been investigating whether "unwarranted" actions by athletes, i.e., fights, elicit exceptional responses from fans. Here their findings have been surprising. In soccer, fights among the players have triggered violence in the stands in 57% of the cases the researchers have observed. For football and baseball the percentages are 49 and 34, respectively. However, in hockey only 8.5% of the on-ice fights touched off acts of fan violence. Cheffers speculates that hockey customers see so many fights that they have become a bit blasé about them. He suggests that hockey may be moving in the direction of what he calls the "giggle sports," professional wrestling, and Roller Derby. At these attractions, ostensibly illegal and violent acts by the participants are so common and highly stylized that they are largely regarded as phony and have lost much of their impact.

Such information as Cheffers and a few others have collected tends to confirm the commonsense observation that the rougher the game the rougher the crowd. Cheffers believes that "if it [violence] is on the field it will be in the stands." Contact sports provide most of the examples of fan violence, while in golf, tennis, and track they are rare. But if this is the rule, there are many exceptions and anomalies. Outside the U.S., soccer, not a contact sport, has the most dangerous and destructive fans. This may be because of social and economic factors. There's a strong tradition in Europe, and particularly in the British Isles, that soccer is a workingman's game, and the rowdyism of the spectators may be, Cheffers speculates, a kind of class statement, a means of showing contempt for polite society and cocking a snoot at the well-behaved gentry.

Boxing is the most violent of all sports, but its crowds are not exceptionally disorderly. However, when something does stir them, they often become more vicious than other fans. In the U.S. during the past 10 years, *all* of the disturbances in which spectators have had at each other with knives and guns, with the intent to kill and maim, have occurred in boxing crowds. Apparently, the nature of the sport enables its fans to deal sanely with a lot of violence, but when they lose control, it's with great ferocity. Baseball may demonstrate the opposite side of the hockey-boxing coin. Small, fairly tame acts of violence on a baseball field may appear to be much worse than they really are because the game generally lacks physical contact.

Also at the heart of baseball is one of the most explicitly warlike charades in all sport: the repeated and possibly fatal confrontation between pitcher and batter.

In many cases the players' unwarranted (illegal, according to the rules) acts, which Cheffers finds are likely to stir up fans, are unintentional or accidental. When an athlete makes mistakes in judgment—say, commits a dumb foul—he sometimes becomes so aroused that he begins fighting or throwing a tantrum. In other cases such displays are a matter of design and are performed for inspirational reasons or in the hope of achieving competitive advantage. Baiting umpires is a traditional baseball tactic that also incites spectators, whose calls of "kill the ump" or "throw the bum out" are often followed by fisticuffs in the stands and objects thrown out of them. Jack Dunn III, the vice-president for stadium operations of the Baltimore Orioles, says that the most fights he ever saw in the stands occurred on a day when former Oriole Manager Earl Weaver argued with an umpire and was ejected from the game. Last summer Sam Rutigliano, coach of the Cleveland Browns, in effect came down on the side of unnecessary roughness in the NFL. He said that while officials might still penalize his players for such infractions of league rules, he wasn't going to reinforce the refs' authority by fining, as he had the year before, Browns who drew unnecessary roughness calls. He said that he thought worrying about being assessed such fines might interfere with the concentration of his players and lower their morale.

Perhaps more regularly than any other sporting figures, basketball coaches attempt to incite and exploit crowd reaction by means of histrionic displays. "There's no question about it," says Shelby Metcalf, the basketball coach at Texas A&M. "Some coaches—we have a couple here in the Southwest Conference—try to get their home crowds fired up and use them to intimidate opposing players and officials. I think it works less often than these coaches and the press think it does because the players and officials are more sophisticated than they used to be. But it works often enough that there are coaches who continue to use the technique to try to get an edge. It is a danger and a disgrace to the game. We ought to be doing more than we are to stop it."

Metcalf is an unusual and unusually well-qualified authority on fan violence. In addition to having coached the Aggies for 19 seasons, he has a Ph.D. from A&M in philosophy. For his doctoral dissertation on crowd behavior and control, Metcalf selected 84 variables, ranging from the deportment of cheerleaders to the size of arena, that he thought might influence crowd actions. His list was sent to the Southwest Conference office. After each of the 112 basketball games used in the survey, referees, coaches, and sports information directors on the scene were asked to check the factors that seemed to have most influenced the fans. Tabulating the results, Metcalf found, again to the surprise of no one, that the behavior of coaches, players, and officials had the most effect, good and bad, on the spectators. Commenting tangentially, Metcalf says, "It's sad but true. If there's a good fight, one that gets a lot of attention in the press, attendance is going to be up for two or three weeks afterward for games of the teams involved."

Though sports entrepreneurs may not deliberately set out to pump up their customers to the point of belting each other or trashing stadiums, many team officials are inclined to stimulate frenzy and emphasize the wilder aspects of the entertainment being offered. Touting mayhem has been the principal promotional thrust of wrestling and Roller Derby. There are chronic suspicions that hockey moguls, despite repeated pious protests to the contrary, are inclined to regard brawls as good for business. The late and unlamented professional box-lacrosse league advertised itself as putting on happenings that Attila the Hun and anybody with a taste for blood and battle would love.

There are a good many sporting hypes—provocative cheerleaders, drums, horns, organs, posters, cartoons, effigy burnings, pep rallies, exploding and smart-aleck scoreboards—that have become so common that nobody thinks much about their subliminal messages and influence anymore. For example, like many other major league baseball teams, the Baltimore Orioles have an official mascot, in this case a guy in bird drag who hops around Memorial Stadium to entertain and exhort the home crowd. Among other stunts of the Baltimore bird: Between innings he dons boxing gloves and goes a few rounds with someone dressed to represent the opponents, say the Detroit Tigers, before scoring a KO, to the delight of the fans. . . .

Many other sports officials have made the same observation. Buffalo's Don Guenther, the manager of Rich Stadium, home of the Bills, says he thinks 99% of the arrests at games are related to alcohol.

Dick Vertlieb now is an entertainment and financial consultant in Seattle but in the past has been the general manager of three NBA teams, the Warriors, Pacers, and Sonics, and of baseball's Seattle Mariners. "The problem," says Vertlieb, speaking of fan violence, is the "goddamn beer. All the teams do is push beer and push beer, and then when someone gets out of line, they send the cops after the guy. When I was with the Sonics there was no beer in the Coliseum and it was a family event. Now it's difficult even to take your wife. It's an outrage."

The connection between guzzling and fan violence needs very little explanation. Nobody has ever suggested that a good way to calm down a crowd is to fill it to the gills with strong drink. To a greater degree than at any other assemblies, except perhaps stag conventions, alcohol is made available to sports spectators, and they are encouraged to use it freely. There are 63 stadiums and arenas in the U.S. that serve major pro teams. Beer is sold in 61 of them and hard liquor in 24. (Only a handful of colleges sell beer at their games. This is almost universally accepted as a principal reason why collegiate crowds, despite their youth and exuberance, present fewer serious security problems than do professional ones.)

Why beer and booze, despite being named by many executives as a main cause of fan violence, are so readily available is also fairly obvious. They are profitable. How profitable can't be determined, because teams and concessionaires don't routinely divulge sales figures. However, it seems likely that where beer is sold it accounts for about half of the overall concession take. This would work out to about $500,000 a season generated by a team such as the Sonics.

Beyond the retail income, the alcohol business is profitable for sports organizations in many other ways. Radio and TV broadcasts of virtually every major league game are sponsored in whole or part by breweries. According to a 1982 survey conducted by Simmons Market Research Bureau, the heavy beer-drinker is a sports lover. Male heavy beer-drinkers represent 30% of the total beer-drinking public and are responsible for nearly 80% of the total volume of beer sales.

The relationship of beer and booze to sports is so profitable that managerial types are loath to finger in-park sales as a contributing cause of fan violence. Invariably, they say the real problem is with contraband stuff, i.e., alcohol that's brought to the ball park by fans in coolers, brown bags, or their bloodstreams.

Joe McDermott, the Boston Red Sox executive in charge of security at Fenway Park, says that most of the Sox spectator trouble occurs in the first few innings of a game and is caused by people who were soused on arrival. "Let's face it," says McDermott, his righteous instincts overcoming his commercial caution, "it's pretty hard to get loaded on the beer sold here—it's mostly froth." Like many other teams, the Red Sox have and exercise the right to search incoming customers, confiscate containers, and refuse entry to those who seem likely to make trouble.

Though, again, it's not much talked about for obvious reasons, spectator use of drugs, notably marijuana, cocaine, and Quaaludes, seems to be increasing more rapidly than alcohol consumption. "Get yourself a Coke with whatever you smoke," chants a Schaefer Stadium soft-drink vendor. "Get your hot pretzels, ludes, and joints," responds a mocking fan. In many arenas particular ramps and rest rooms are favored by the heads and dealers. The dangers and morality of drug use can be debated elsewhere, but there's no reason to believe that numbers of people with rolling eyeballs or runny noses make a constructive contribution to the good behavior of sports crowds.

To improve crowd control in 1976, the Red Sox began employing 20 football players from local colleges. During games they roam Fenway with the aim of soothing potentially troublesome fans or unobtrusively giving the heave-ho to those—sometimes 30 a game—who are beyond pacifying. Sox management has been pleased with the footballers, whose size gives them respect as well as clout and whose youth gives them rapport with the sort of spectators most likely to be difficult. Security people everywhere single out 20- to 30-year-old males as the most likely to create disturbances. The general opinion is that they are especially vulnerable to macho fantasies and to acting them out when stirred up by sporting events.

Wayne Thornton, a 6'3", 230-pound Holy Cross graduate, was a member of the Fenway patrol one summer and says of his routine activities, "We look for drunks, of course, and very loud belligerent types. Every couple of innings we check out some of the restrooms and ramps for people smoking and snorting dope. Also, we watch for guys who aren't paying much attention to the game, just waiting around and hanging out."

It's perhaps arbitrary to say that hangers-out come to an event with the intention of being violent. But there's reason to believe that the possibility of bashing heads is on their minds and an attraction in itself. Dr. Arnold R. Beisser, a Los Angeles psychiatrist with an interest in sports, has commented, "We're seeing a new use of violence. It's being used not as a means to an end but for recreational purposes, for pleasure. It's an end in itself." . . .

"I believe the incidences of violence are way up," says Dr. Irving Goldaber, a sociologist who is the director and founder of the Center for Study of Crowd and

Spectator Behavior, a Miami-based research and consulting firm. "My file of current incidents gets larger and larger every year. Where about 10 years ago I had one folder, now every year I do another file drawer."

Goldaber, who has advised the NFL, major league baseball, and the International Association of Chiefs of Police, among others, is perhaps the country's best-known expert on fan violence. He says that five years ago he was receiving about three requests a year to appear as an expert witness in court actions having to do with incidents involving sporting crowds. Now he's getting about one every two weeks.

During the 1950s and '60s, Goldaber, who says, "Human conflict was always my field," instructed law-enforcement groups in dealing with street disturbances, protesters, terrorists and hostage takers. In the mid-'70s, he says, he detected the emergence of a new form of violence in this country. He terms it "violence for vicarious power" and finds it's most openly manifested in sporting crowds, whose behavior is now one of his principal professional interests. Like many other experts Goldaber believes that the problems of sport reflect larger ones in society. Specifically, he says, "More and more people aren't making it. You work hard, you exist, but you haven't got much to show for it. There are increasing numbers of people who are deeply frustrated because they feel they have very little power over their lives. They come to sporting events to experience, vicariously, a sense of power."

In a stadium, the power trippers are even more vulnerable to ordinary crowd stimuli and irritations than more traditional fans. "They respond to the violence on the field," says Goldaber. "They respond to the hype and hoopla of the event, to the beer, cheerleaders, scoreboards, and bands. When you have a crowd that is anticipating a physical experience, it will have a physical experience."

Goldaber believes that several characteristics distinguish the vicarious power-seekers. They're very prone to overidentify with a team or individuals. "They're dressed in the numbers and the letters and the names and the colors, with the jackets, the sweaters, the scarves, and the pennants," he says. "They're part of the team and they're in the game." They aren't particularly concerned or knowledgeable about how games are played and take little pleasure in stylish athletic performances. "The reason they come to sporting events isn't so much to watch the game as to be in the game and especially to experience winning through their team or hero. In this world, where so many individuals are diminished, it's pretty important to matter, to win, to be No. 1. When their team wins, they have a sense of being important: 'I won.'

"Because they overidentify and think they're in the game, they feel they have a right to affect the outcome of the game, in the old ways by cheering and booing, but also with new violent forms of threatening and intimidating action. Because winning, being No. 1, is everything, they're likely to be very ferocious if they—their team—are thwarted and they vent their frustrations physically against players, officials, or other spectators. That's the nub of the problem."

Goldaber feels that a vicious cycle has been created. Sensing the obsessive mood, sports management has tended to pander to it, overpromoting fan identification. Goldaber has developed this theme perhaps more fully than others, but that there's a connection between fan violence and win-at-all-cost attitudes has occurred to many. Lennie Wirtz, a veteran basketball referee who has had visions of an enraged spectator coming at him with an ice pick, says he thinks the most important reason for the worsening of behavior of coaches and players—and because of them, crowds—is the enormous pressure to win that's now at work on the participants.

Bill Veeck, a shrewd and iconoclastic baseball entrepreneur and observer for more than half a century, agrees with Wirtz. "Unfortunately, like Dr. Frankenstein, people in baseball have created a monster," Veeck says. "They think only a winning club is any good. People forget that we're in the entertainment business. Look what you get then, a George Steinbrenner. What more horrible fate could possibly happen, unless you get two?"

Many authorities say there's evidence that things could get worse. Based on information provided by police departments from around the nation, Goldaber makes the ominous estimate that in any large pro sports crowd somewhere between 0.5% and 2% of the spectators are now carrying concealed weapons. This works out to 250 to 1,000 fans packing guns, lethal knives, or Wirtz's ice pick in a crowd of 50,000. Goldaber believes it's likely that we will shortly have a sports assassination, carried out by a demented fan who will rise up with, say, a 30-30 and take out a quarterback or power forward. "And when it happens once," he says, "there will be enormous publicity and this will trigger more of it. Years ago, if somebody said that we would have weapons checks before boarding airplanes it would have been thought absurd, but that's normal now and may well become normal at sporting events. Hostage-seizing at games is also a possibility. In a sense, we have already had it. Death threats are really hostage situations in which an athlete is told not to play in a certain way or be killed."

Neither Goldaber's facts nor predictions much surprise other crowd-control professionals. As to the 30-30 scenario, Cheffers remarks, "Actually, it's surprising it hasn't happened. In this country athletes are at least as celebrated as rock stars or politicians. There are a lot of Hinckleys out there who have strong feelings about sport."

Cheffers finds it easy to imagine that because of such a disaster, or in an attempt to prevent one, high-security measures might alter sport as drastically as the violence itself. "We could reach a point where major sporting events are staged in shielded areas before 5,000 or so spectators who pay several hundred dollars each for safe, luxurious accommodations," Cheffers says. "Attending live sporting events could disappear as a popular entertainment."

All of this is prophesy, but events that have occurred suggest that such possibilities should be taken seriously. The almost reflexive response of sports promoters to bad crowd situations is to lay on more cops of one sort or another. Following an ugly Monday-night football game, Sullivan said that to prevent further outbursts he would "bring in the National Guard if we have to to make things safe." Attack dogs were used for crowd control in a 1980 World Series game in Philadelphia and in 1982 in St. Louis. This prompted Goldaber to quip, "If dogs aren't effective [he thinks they are], maybe they'll bring out attack lions next." Both the Patriots and Red Sox are converting sections of their stands into posh, heavily guarded apartment-like boxes that lease for $20,000 to $36,000 a year. Most other stadiums have, or are planning, similar facilities. Elsewhere, the ultimate crowd-control technique has already been employed. Because of reasonable fears about the conduct of supporters of rival teams, soccer games in England and American high school football and basketball games have been played in facilities from which all fans have been barred. . . .

The most commonly recommended measure is to improve facilities to lessen environmental irritations in crowd situations. Places that are clean, comfortable and convenient tend to promote good behavior. Even the illusion that management is concerned with the amenities seems to have a good effect. Goldaber advises clients, not entirely facetiously, that if they have only $50 for crowd-control innovations, they should employ two men, dress them in immaculate white coats, give them brooms and set them to furiously and conspicuously sweeping. Whether they sweep up any dirt is beside the point.

Last fall, Cheffers attended a Monday-night Patriots game at Schaefer Stadium. He's a big, beefy man, but even so found himself uneasy in the midst of bands of drunken, truculent, orgiastic fans roaming about in shadowy parking lots, reeking corridors, and grimy stands. Following his field trip he submitted a detailed report to the Patriots, with suggestions for improvements. He thought "animalistic behavior" could be reduced if the joint—he called the parking lot Grub City—was cleaned up, smelled sweeter, and was better lit. He felt there was great need to improve access to the parking and concession areas to cut down on jostling and long, frustrating lines. Hundreds of fans gathered hours before the game in parking lot "wastelands," where they had little to do but mill about, drink, and start trouble. He thought that prettifying the lots, putting in some picnic and play areas, with room to throw Frisbees and balls around, might be worth a try. Among other things, Cheffers is very big on flowers as crowd controllers. "We will jump over ropes, knock down barricades, tear up lawns," he says, "but it takes a lot to make us walk through a flower bed." Cheffers believes that judiciously planted hardy annuals can do much to keep crowds where they are wanted and subliminally to remind them of their manners.

The Patriots, with the benefit of advice from both Cheffers and Goldaber, are now in the process of spending $5.8 million to upgrade Schaefer Stadium. "Generally, we want to make it an attractive place. We want good fans," says Sullivan. "Security and crowd control are not the only factors, but they are important ones."

Today, the idea of staging a major sporting event without dozens of law-and-order officers on hand is unthinkable. (On game day at Schaefer Stadium the security force, in or out of uniform, numbers more than 250.) However, security forces are often part of the fan-violence problem, not the solution to it. By tradition there is a certain anti-authoritarian spirit in sporting crowds, and this can be inflamed by rude, belligerent, or even overly conspicuous cops. "When a guard ejects a fan, *who* is getting booed?" Goldaber asks. "Invariably, it's the guard." Goldaber thinks there's a need, not necessarily for larger security forces, but those that are better trained and more inclined to calm spectators by means other than busting them. Employing the 20 unarmed, ununiformed, fairly cool football players to patrol Fenway is seen as a step in the right direction.

Like everyone else, unruly spectators buy tickets, and promoters not wanting to offend them are inclined to tolerate behavior that wouldn't be permitted outside the stadium. Cheffers feels this is shortsighted. He thinks crowd controllers should be trained to spot troublemakers before they reach the explosive stage and to remove them quickly. Fans who are repeat offenders should be suspended for misconduct, as players are, and barred from attending games for a period of time. He agrees that the ejection should be accomplished as gently and unobtrusively as possible so as not to rile other spectators, but that the policy should be publicized and firmly carried out. Some customers might be lost, he admits, but their loss would be more than compensated for because new and better fans would be attracted by the improved conditions.

The link between hooliganism and alcohol consumption is as obvious as the reasons that sporting entrepreneurs have been loath to face up to this problem. Perhaps one of the best indications of serious concern about fan misbehavior is the new willingness to cut down on the beer and booze trade. In the last several years a dozen or so major stadiums and arenas have taken steps to halt sales before the latter part of a game and to restrict sales in certain particularly rowdy sections or the amounts individual fans can buy. There's even occasional talk of eliminating beer concessions entirely. For example, Sullivan says the Patriots "had considered" such a drastic move at Schaefer Stadium, even though it's named for a brewery, which reportedly paid a million dollars for the honor.

Perhaps the boldest action of this sort has been taken by the Chicago White Sox. According to Schaffer, the Comiskey Park security chief, when new ownership acquired the Sox in 1981, it was alarmed at the amount of violence in the park and Comiskey's steadily deteriorating reputation. In an effort to improve things, all hard-liquor sales were banned inside the stadium. The Sox estimate this cost them about $100,000 but that it has had a calming effect on crowd behavior and made security enforcement, for which the White Sox now pay about $300,000 a season, much easier.

Sports have been successful in developing techniques that move spectators toward rather than away from explosive states. Again, nobody wants them actually to blow up, just to come close to the exhilarating flash point. "It's good business for the teams to psych up a crowd," says Goldaber. "We talk about killer instincts, rivalries. You give the wrong guy a rivalry, give him people around him who are raucous, contributing to the steam-up, and you may well have a dangerous problem."

The statement of the problem more or less indicates the solution. What Goldaber calls the hype and hoopla needs to be toned down, and reality—that these are games, not genuine confrontations of world-shaking significance— must be emphasized. The participants, from management to coaches to players, are in the best position to deliver this message and make it believable in the stands. "Unwarranted behaviors"—such as on-the-field fights, tantrums and the like, which Cheffers has found are so likely to incite spectators—need to be eliminated, not just mildly rebuked or penalized. Goldaber also believes players should be instructed and encouraged to display pacific behavior and to make more gestures of what used to be referred to as sportsmanship—pregame handshakes, etc.

"When a lineman hits the quarterback," says Goldaber, "the crowd is going to yell for a roughing-the-passer call. But if the lineman reaches down and yanks up the guy he just hit and pats him on the back, and they both run back to their huddles, that's something I call a sociological signal to the crowd that this is just a game. Those fans who feel they're in a war will be calmed by the gesture."

Cheffers also feels that efforts must be made to educate or reeducate fans. "I care about this," he says, "because I'm one of those who think that sport can and should have a very constructive influence on society. I would say that the greatest value of sporting competition is that it teaches us how to handle winning and losing without becoming antisocial. When what's achieved predominates over how it's achieved, then a disrespect for the entire game, the entire sport, ensues. Violence follows disrespect. The fearful thing is that what we are now being taught to respect is violence. Sport is making it fashionable."

DISCUSSION QUESTIONS

1. As identified by Gilbert and Twyman, what are some of the reasons for fan violence?
2. What are some suggested policies for controlling fan violence? Do you feel that they will work? Why or why not?

XVIII

Social Change

WHAT TO FOCUS ON:

1. How is social change affecting the economic and social organization of American society?
2. What are some of the social conditions that influence political and economic change?

SOCIAL CHANGE is an ongoing process in all human societies. Although sociology tends to focus upon collectivities and systems at a particular point in time, the study of change is an essential part of the sociological tradition. Sociologists seek to report, interpret, analyze and, on occasion, offer predictions as to the nature of emerging societal and cultural patterns. Social change takes place both behaviorally—established behaviors are replaced by new forms—and on the level of social values whereby new moral interpretations are given to emerging normative patterns.

George Ritzer, in the selection, "The McDonaldization of Society," shows how the process of rationalization—the emphasis on rationality and calculability—has affected all areas of contemporary society. Taking fast food restaurants as a case study of a larger social process, Ritzer demonstrates the significance of this process in the areas of work, family, and education. Ritzer's work is particularly revealing in showing the social psychological consequences of rationalization.

The most powerful recent example of massive social change is probably the breaking apart of the Soviet Union. In "The Soviet Upheaval and Western Sovietology," Bruce Parrott analyzes why scholars were apparently unaware of the cataclysmic changes going on in the Soviet Union. Parrott explains that much scholarship assumes things will remain static and does not pay enough attention to the constant flux of modern societies, including non-democratic ones. Parrott shows how the basic outlook of Sovietology will now have to be itself transformed to keep pace with changing political and cultural realities.

Harold Lasswell identifies the class basis for the phenomena of Hitlerism as it existed in Germany during the 1930s. Lasswell focuses in particular on the psychological aspects, rather than the material side of class. From our historical vantage point, the German acceptance of Nazism seems incomprehensible. However, Lasswell argued that the nationalism and anti-Semitism were well-fitted to the psychological threats felt between the German classes.

— Article 49 —

The McDonaldization of Society

GEORGE RITZER

A WIDE-RANGING PROCESS of *rationalization* is occurring across American society and is having an increasingly powerful impact in many other parts of the world. It encompasses such disparate phenomena as fast-food restaurants, TV dinners, packaged tours, industrial robots, plea bargaining, and open-heart surgery on an assembly-line basis. As widespread and as important as these developments are, it is clear that we have barely begun a process that promises even more extraordinary changes (e.g., genetic engineering) in the years to come. We can think of rationalization as a historical process and rationality as the end result of that development. As an historical process, rationalization has distinctive roots in the western world. Writing in the late 19th and early 20th centuries, the great German sociologist Max Weber saw his society as the center of the ongoing process of rationalization and the bureaucracy as its paradigm case. The model of rationalization, at least in contemporary America, is no longer the bureaucracy, but might be better thought of as the fast-food restaurant. As a result, our concern here is with what might be termed the "McDonaldization of Society." While the fast-food restaurant is not the ultimate expression of rationality, it is the current exemplar for future developments in rationalization.

From "The McDonaldization of Society," by George Ritzer, *Journal of American Culture,* pp. 100–107. Reprinted by permission of the publisher.

A society characterized by rationality is one which emphasizes *efficiency, predictability, calculability, substitution of nonhuman for human technology,* and *control over uncertainty.* In discussing the various dimensions of rationalization, we will be little concerned with the gains already made, and yet to be realized, by greater rationalization. These advantages are widely discussed in schools and in the mass media. In fact, we are in danger of being seduced by the innumerable advantages already offered, and promised in the future, by rationalization. The glitter of these accomplishments and promises has served to distract most people from the grave dangers posed by progressive rationalization. In other words, we are ultimately concerned here with the irrational consequences that often flow from rational systems. Thus, the second major theme of this essay might be termed "the irrationality of rationality." . . .

Efficiency

The process of rationalization leads to a society in which a great deal of emphasis is placed on finding the best or optimum means to any given end. Whatever a group of people define as an end, and everything they so define, is to be pursued by attempting to find the best means to achieve the end. Thus, in the Germany of Weber's day, the bureaucracy was seen as the most efficient means of handling a wide array of administrative tasks. Somewhat later, the Nazis came to develop the concentration camp, its ovens, and other devices as the optimum method of collecting and murdering millions of Jews and other people. The efficiency that Weber described in turn-of-the-century Germany, and which later came to characterize many Nazi activities, has become a basic principle of life in virtually every sector of a rational society.

The modern American family, often with two wage-earners, has little time to prepare elaborate meals. For the relatively few who still cook such meals, there is likely to be great reliance on cookbooks that make cooking from scratch much more efficient. However, such cooking is relatively rare today. Most families take as their objective quickly and easily prepared meals. To this end, much use is made of prepackaged meals and frozen TV dinners.

For many modern families, the TV dinner is no longer efficient enough. To many people, eating out, particularly in a fast-food restaurant, is a far more efficient way of obtaining their meals. Fast-food restaurants capitalize on this by being organized so that dinners are fed as efficiently as possible. They offer a limited, simple menu that can be cooked and served in an assembly-line fashion. The latest development in fast-food restaurants, the addition of drive-through windows, constitutes an effort to increase still further the efficiency of the dining experience. The family now can simply drive through, pick up its order, and eat it while driving to the next, undoubtedly efficiently organized, activity. The success of the fast-food restaurant has come full circle with frozen food manufacturers now touting products for the home modeled after those served in fast-food restaurants.

Increasingly, efficiently organized food production and distribution systems lie at the base of the ability of people to eat their food efficiently at home, in the fast-food restaurant, or in their cars. Farms, groves, ranches, slaughterhouses, warehouses, transportation systems, and retailers are all oriented toward increasing efficiency. A notable example is chicken production where they are mass-bred, force-fed (often with many chemicals), slaughtered on an assembly line, iced or fast frozen, and shipped to all parts of the country. Some may argue that such chickens do not taste as good as the fresh-killed, local variety, but their complaints are likely to be drowned in a flood of mass-produced chickens. Then there is bacon which is more efficiently shipped, stored, and sold when it is preserved by sodium nitrate, a chemical which is unfortunately thought by many to be carcinogenic. Whatever one may say about the quality or the danger of the products, the fact remains that they are all shaped by the drive for efficiency. . . .

One of the most interesting and important aspects of efficiency is that it often comes to be not a means but an end in itself. This "displacement of goals" is a major problem in a rationalizing society. We have, for example, the bureaucrats who slavishly follow the rules even though their inflexibility negatively affects the organization's ability to achieve its goals. Then there are the bureaucrats who are so concerned with efficiency that they lose sight of the ultimate goals the means are designed to achieve. A good example was the Nazi concentration camp officers who, in devoting so much attention to maximizing the efficiency of the camps' operation, lost sight of the fact that the ultimate purpose of the camps was the murder of millions of people.

Predictability

A second component of rationalization involves the effort to ensure predictability from one place to another. In a rational society, people want to know what to expect when they enter a given setting or acquire some sort of commodity. They neither want nor expect surprises. They want to know that if they journey to another locale, the setting they enter or the commodity they buy will be essentially the same as the setting they entered or product they purchased earlier. Furthermore, people want to be sure that what they encounter is much like what they encountered at earlier times. In order to ensure predictability over time and place a rational society must emphasize such things as discipline, order, systemization, formalization, routine, consistency and methodical operation.

One of the attractions of TV dinners for modern families is that they are highly predictable. The TV dinner composed of fried chicken, mashed potatoes, green peas, and peach cobbler is exactly the same from one time to another and one city to another. Home cooking from scratch is, conversely, a notoriously unpredictable enterprise with little assurance that dishes will taste the same time after time. However, the cookbook cannot eliminate all unpredictability. There are often simply too many ingredients and other variables involved. Thus the cookbook dish is far less predictable than the TV dinner or a wide array of other prepared dishes.

Fast-food restaurants rank very high on the dimension of predictability. In order to help ensure consistency, the fast-food restaurant offers only a limited menu. Predictable end-products are made possible by the use of similar raw materials, technologies, and preparation and serving techniques. Not only the food is predictable; the physical structures, the logo, the "ambience," and even the personnel are as well.

The food that is shipped to our homes and our fast-food restaurants is itself affected by the process of increasing predictability. Thus our favorite white bread is indistinguishable from one place to another. In fact, food producers have made great efforts to ensure such predictability.

On packaged tours travelers can be fairly sure that the people they travel with will be much like themselves. The planes, buses, hotel accommodations, restaurants, and at least the way in which the sites are visited are very similar from one location to another. Many people go on packaged tours *because* they are far more predictable than travel undertaken on an individual basis.

Amusement parks used to be highly unpredictable affairs. People could never be sure, from one park to another, precisely what sorts of rides, events, foods, visitors, and employees they would encounter. All of that has changed in the era of the theme parks inspired by Disneyland. Such parks seek to ensure predictability in various ways. For example, a specific type of young person is hired in these parks, and they are all trained in much the same way, so that they have a robot-like predictability.

Other leisure-time activities have grown similarly predictable. Camping in the wild is loaded with uncertainties—bugs, bears, rain, cold and the like. To make camping more predictable, organized grounds have sprung up around the country. Gone are many of the elements of unpredictability replaced by RVs, paved-over parking lots, sanitized campsites, fences and enclosed camp centers that provide laundry and food services, recreational activities, television, and video games. Sporting events, too, have in a variety of ways been made more predictable. The use of artificial turf in baseball makes for a more predictable bounce of a ball. . . .

Calculability or Quantity Rather than Quality

It could easily be argued that the emphasis on quantifiable measures, on things that can be counted, is *the* most defining characteristic of a rational society. Quality is notoriously difficult to evaluate. How do we assess the quality of a hamburger, or a physician, or a student? Instead of even trying, in an increasing number of cases, a rational society seeks to develop a series of quantifiable measures that it takes as surrogates for quality. This urge to quantify has given great impetus to the development of the computer and has, in turn, been spurred by the widespread use and increasing sophistication of the computer.

The fact is that many aspects of modern rational society, especially as far as calculable issues are concerned, are made possible and more widespread by the computer. We need not belabor the ability of the computer to handle large numbers of virtually anything, but somewhat less obvious is the use of the computer to give the illusion of personal attention in a world made increasingly impersonal in large part because of the computer's capacity to turn virtually everything into quantifiable dimensions. We have all now had many experiences where we open a letter personally addressed to us only to find a computer letter. We are aware that the names and addresses of millions of people have been stored on tape and that with the aid of a number of word processors a form letter has been sent to every name on the list. Although the computer is able to give a sense of personal attention, most people are nothing more than an item on a huge mailing list.

Our main concern here, though, is not with the computer, but with the emphasis on quantity rather than quality that it has helped foster. One of the most obvious examples in the university is the emphasis given to grades and cumulative grade point averages. With less and less contact between professor and student, there is little real effort to assess the quality of what students know, let alone the quality of their overall abilities. Instead, the sole measure of the quality of most college students is their grade in a given course and their grade point averages. Another blatant example is the emphasis on a variety of uniform exams such as SATs and GREs in which the essence of an applicant is reduced to a few simple scores and percentiles.

Within the educational institution, the importance of grades is well known, but somewhat less known is the way quantifiable factors have become an essential part of the process of evaluating college professors. For example, teaching ability is very hard to evaluate. Administrators have difficulty assessing teaching quality and thus substitute quantitative scores. Of course each score involves qualitative judgments, but this is conveniently ignored. Student opinion polls are taken and the scores are summed, averaged, and compared. Those who score well are deemed good teachers while those who don't are seen as poor teachers. There are many problems involved in relying on these scores such as the fact that easy teachers in "gut" courses may well obtain high ratings while rigorous teachers of difficult courses are likely to score poorly. . . .

In the workworld we find many examples of the effort to substitute quantity for quality. Scientific management was heavily oriented to turning everything work-related into quantifiable dimensions. Instead of relying on the "rule of thumb" of the operator, scientific management sought to develop precise measures of how much work was to be done by each and every motion of the worker. Everything that could be was reduced to numbers and all these numbers were then analyzable using a variety of mathematical formulae. The assembly line is similarly oriented to a variety of quantifiable dimensions such as optimizing the speed of the line, minimizing time for each task, lowering the price of the finished product, increasing sales and ultimately increasing profits. The divisional system pioneered by General Motors and thought to be one of the major reasons for its past success was oriented to the reduction of the performance of each division to a few, bottom-line numbers. By monitoring and comparing these numbers, General Motors was able to exercise control over the results without getting involved in the day-to-day activities of each division. . . .

Thus, the third dimension of rationalization, calculability or the emphasis on quantity rather than quality, has wide applicability to the social world. It is truly central, if not the central, component of a rationalizing society. To return to our favorite example, it is the case that McDonald's expends far more effort telling us how many billions of hamburgers it has sold than it does in telling us about the quality of those burgers. Relatedly, it touts the size of its product (the "Big Mac") more than the quality of the product (it is not the "Good Mac"). The bottom line in many settings is the number of customers processed, the speed with which they are processed, and the profits produced. Quality is secondary, if indeed there is any concern at all for it.

Substitution of Nonhuman Technology

In spite of Herculean efforts, there are important limits to the ability to rationalize what human beings think and do. Seemingly no matter what one does, people still retain at least the ultimate capacity to think and act in a variety of unanticipated ways. Thus, in spite of great efforts to make human behavior more efficient, more predictable, more calculable, people continue to act in unforeseen ways. People continue to make home-cooked meals from scratch, to camp in tents in the wild, to eat in old-fashioned diners, and to sabotage the assembly lines. Because of these realities, there is great interest among those who foster increasing rationality in using rational technologies to limit individual independence and ultimately to replace human beings with machines and other technologies that lack the ability to think and act in unpredictable ways.

McDonald's does not yet have robots to serve us food, but it does have teenagers whose ability to act autonomously is almost completely eliminated by techniques, procedures, routines, and machines. There are numerous examples of this including rules which prescribe all the things a counterperson should do in dealing with a customer as well as a large variety of technologies which determine the actions of workers such as drink dispensers which shut themselves off when the cup is full; buzzers, lights, and bells which indicate when food (e.g., french fries) is done; and cash registers which have the prices of each item programmed in. One of the latest attempts to constrain individual action is Denny's use of pre-measured packages of dehydrated food that are "cooked" simply by putting them under the hot water tap. Because of such tools and machines, as well as the elaborate rules dictating worker behavior, people often feel like they are dealing with human robots when they relate to the personnel of a fast-food restaurant. When human robots are found, mechanical robots cannot be far behind. Once people are reduced to a few robot-like actions, it is a relatively easy step to replace them with mechanical robots. Thus Burgerworld is reportedly opening a prototypical restaurant in which mechanical robots serve the food.

Much of the recent history of work, especially manual work, is a history of efforts to replace human technology with nonhuman technology. Scientific management was oriented to the development of an elaborate and rigid set of rules about how jobs were to be done. The workers were to blindly and obediently follow those rules and not to do the work the way they saw fit. The various skills needed to perform a task were carefully delineated and broken down into a series of routine steps that could be taught to all workers. The skills, in other words, were built into the routines rather than belonging to skilled craftspersons. Similar points can be made about the assembly line which is basically a set of nonhuman technologies that have the needed steps and skills built into them. The human worker is reduced to performing a limited number of simple, repetitive operations. However, the control of this technology over the individual worker is so great and omnipresent that individual workers have reacted negatively manifesting such things as tardiness, absenteeism, turnover, and even sabotage. We are now witnessing a new stage in this technological development with automated processes now totally replacing many workers with robots. With the coming of robots we have reached the ultimate stage in the replacement of human with nonhuman technology.

Even religion and religious crusades have not been unaffected by the spread of nonhuman technologies. The growth of large religious organizations, the use of Madison Avenue techniques, and even drive-in churches all reflect the incursion of modern technology. But it is in the electronic church, religion through the TV screens, that replacement of human by nonhuman technology in religion is most visible and has its most important manifestation. . . .

Control

This leads us to the fifth major dimension of rationalization-control. Rational systems are oriented toward, and structured to expedite, control in a variety of senses. At the most general level, we can say that rational systems are set up to allow for greater control over the uncertainties of life—birth, death, food production and distribution, housing, religious salvation and many, many others. More specifically, rational systems are oriented to gaining greater control over the major source of uncertainty in social life—other people. Among other things, this means control over subordinates by superiors and control of clients and customers by workers.

There are many examples of rationalization oriented toward gaining greater control over the uncertainties of life. The burgeoning of the genetic engineering movement can be seen as being aimed at gaining better control over the production of life itself. Similarly, amniocentesis can be seen as a technique which will allow the parents to determine the kind of child they will have. The efforts to rationalize food production and distribution can be seen as being aimed at gaining greater control over the problems of hunger and starvation. A steady and regular supply of food can make life itself more certain for large numbers of people who today live under the threat of death from starvation.

At a more specific level, the rationalization of food preparation and serving at McDonald's gives it great control over its employees. The automobile assembly line has a similar impact. In fact, the vast majority of the structures of a rational society exert extraordinary control over the people who labor in them. But because of the limits that still exist on the degree of control that rational structures can exercise over individuals, many rationalizing employers are driven to seek to more fully rationalize their operations and totally eliminate the worker. The result is an automated, robot-like technology over which, barring some *2001* rebellion, there is almost total control.

In addition to control over employees, rational systems are also interested in controlling the customer/clients they serve. For example, the fast-food restaurant with its counter, the absence of waiters and waitresses, the limited seating, and the drive-through windows all tend to lead customers to do certain things and not to do others.

Irrationality of Rationality

Although not an inherent part of rationalization, the *irrationality of rationality* is a seemingly inevitable byproduct of the process. We can think of the irrationality of rationality in several ways. At the most general level it can simply be seen as an overarching label for all the negative effects of rationalization. More specifically, it can be seen as the opposite of rationality, at least in some of its senses. For example, there are the inefficiencies and unpredictabilities that are often produced by seemingly rational systems. Thus, although bureaucracies are constructed to bring about greater efficiency in organizational work, the fact is that there are notorious inefficiences such as the "red tape" associated with the operation of most bureaucracies. Or, take the example of the arms race in which a focus on quantifiable aspects of nuclear weapons may well have made the occurrence of nuclear war more, rather than less, unpredictable.

Of greatest importance, however, is the variety of negative effects that rational systems have on the individuals who live, work, and are served by them. We might say that *rational systems are not reasonable systems.* As we've already discussed, rationality brings with it great dehumanization as people are reduced to acting like robots. Among the dehumanizing aspects of a rational society are large lecture classes, computer letters, pray TV, work on the automobile assembly line, and dining at a fast-food restaurant. Rationalization also tends to bring with it disenchantment leaving much of our lives without any mystery or excitement. Production by a hand craftsman is far more mysterious than an assembly-line technology where each worker does a single, very limited operation. Camping in an RV tends to suffer in comparison to the joys to be derived from camping in the wild. Overall a fully rational society would be a very bleak and uninteresting place.

Conclusions

Rationalization, with McDonald's as the paradigm case, is occurring throughout America, and, increasingly, other societies. In virtually every sector of society more and more emphasis is placed on efficiency, predictability, calculability, replacement of human by nonhuman technology, and control over uncertainty. Although progressive rationalization has brought with it innumerable advantages, it has also created a number of problems, the various irrationalities of rationality, which threaten to accelerate in the years to come. These problems, and their acceleration should not be taken as a case for the return to a less rational form of society. Such a return is not only impossible but also undesirable. What is needed is not a less rational society, but greater control over the process of rationalization involving, among other things, efforts to ameliorate its irrational consequences.

DISCUSSION QUESTIONS

1. What is meant by rationalization?
2. Ritzer argues that educational institutions are undergoing a process of rationalization. Do you agree? Why or why not?

Article 50

The Soviet Upheaval and Western Sovietology

BRUCE PARROTT

DURING THE PAST FIVE YEARS Western specialists on the Soviet Union have received some stunning surprises. Many of the things most Sovietologists said could never happen have happened. A country that was ruled by an iron-fisted dictatorship has abolished the legal monopoly of the Communist Party and introduced multicandidate elections. A population once afraid to hint at any disagreement with the government has begun to demand full-fledged democracy. Official praise of central economic planning has been replaced with calls for the introduction of free markets, and a regime long hostile to Western countries has sought a lasting political and cultural accommodation with its former Western rivals. In short, we are witnessing a new Soviet revolution that may negate almost the entire legacy of the Russian Revolution of 1917.

The new revolution has put heavy demands on the Western analysts who study the Soviet Union. For Sovietologists of all ages there are many new truths to learn and many old truths to discard. In these circumstances we have understandably become preoccupied with what is happening today in the Soviet Union and with what may happen tomorrow. As a profession, however, we must try to gain a broader perspective on these startling events. Sovietologists need to look back and ponder

From "The Soviet Upheaval and Western Sovietology," by Bruce Parrott, *Sociology: A Global Perspective,* Joan Ferrante (Ed.). Belmont, California, Wadsworth, 1992, pp. 464–472.

why so few of us in the early 1980s had any sense of what was coming. That we were so surprised says something about the country we study and something about the way we have traditionally studied it.

To understand why the new revolution surprised most Sovietologists, we need to examine the issue of what scholars can know and how they can know it. When I was a college student, I believed that a professor somewhere had written a book about almost every significant subject and that there was a single, "correct" way of understanding almost everything. Writing my doctoral dissertation opened my eyes to a far more complex reality. When I looked for books that would provide vital background for my dissertation, I often found that they didn't exist. Moreover, I discovered that even after I had done the research for a chapter of the dissertation, I was still unsure what all the evidence meant. What did those stacks of note cards add up to, besides lots of paper? Figuring that out required me to make intellectual choices—choices about which evidence to emphasize and which evidence to minimize or ignore as insignificant. Because I was working with Soviet political material written in an obscure ideological "code," I sometimes found that publications that seemed insignificant on first reading assumed great importance when I reread them, sometimes months later, with a different question in mind.

Being a sort of academic detective, I often enjoyed "decoding" Soviet political statements, but when the work got tedious, I consoled myself with the thought that life was easier for Sovietologists than for natural scientists. Delving into the sociology of science as background for my dissertation research, I learned how quickly the intellectual content of the natural sciences changes. Often, particle physicists and molecular biologists have to assimilate new information and theories that revise or invalidate many ideas they believed to be true earlier in their careers. Reading about the professional and personal problems this causes for natural scientists, I thought how lucky I was to be in a field of scholarship that changes relatively slowly. In the pre-Gorbachev era, doing research on Soviet politics required plowing through piles of books and articles written in a political language meant to obscure their real point. Brezhnev's speeches and articles alone filled nine fat volumes! But at least when I discovered something important, I could add it to the existing stock of scholarly knowledge with some confidence that it would last.

Then the new Soviet revolution struck. Today I remember my earlier comparison between Sovietology and the natural sciences with a sense of irony and a certain nostalgia. The Soviet upheaval of the past five years has produced an explosion of new information that Western scholars are struggling to digest—for example, the results of burgeoning public opinion polls asking Soviet citizens about everything from their sexual behavior and Gorbachev's political standing to the desirability of Soviet intervention in the Persian Gulf and the permissibility of using military force at home. We are being swamped with detailed information about parts of the system we couldn't study before, and so many of the parts are in flux that it's difficult to know what to concentrate on. Moreover, the upheaval in the Soviet Union has radically altered the relative professional status of various subfields—and the relative professional status of the people who specialize in them—within Sovietology. The elevation of the study of non-Russian parts of the Soviet empire, such as

Lithuania, and the declining importance of studying Soviet military programs exemplify these dramatic shifts. The changes suggest that natural scientists do have an advantage after all: at least the things they study don't metamorphose from one month to the next.

Another way of putting this is to say that the Soviet upheaval has forced specialists on the Soviet Union to rethink the paradigms that guide our work. By paradigm I mean an informal set of ideas concerning what is known about a particular academic subject, what new questions should be asked about the subject, and what kinds of evidence will answer those questions. All academic fields and subfields have their own paradigms. Within a particular field of learning, paradigms are debated, passed on from one generation of scholars to another, and modified by the accumulation of research findings. In devising paradigms social scientists must always make some assumptions about their subject that haven't been proved empirically but that appear plausible. Otherwise, we could never construct a picture that aims to describe the behavior and development of whole countries such as the Soviet Union.

In trying to redefine our paradigms, Western analysts of the Soviet Union have always faced several intertwined problems. One is the political immediacy of our subject. For virtually the whole period since World War II, relations with the Soviet Union have been at the center of American foreign policy, and an international ideological competition has raged between the advocates of communism and the proponents of Western democracy. This means that Western experts on the Soviet Union have worked on topics that were often at the center of American political controversies and that were vulnerable to serious ideological distortions—frequently from the Soviet side, but sometimes from the American side as well. These conditions made it especially difficult for experts to reach balanced judgments and to develop paradigms that accurately captured the behavior and development of the Soviet system.

Developing useful paradigms was made even more problematic by the traditional secretiveness of the Soviet regime. The assumptions built into such intellectual models can have an especially misleading effect when essential empirical evidence about the subject is missing. For decades the Soviet government tried to shore up its image among Soviet citizens and foreign audiences by falsifying or suppressing vital information about the country. The Communist Party faked "democratic" elections and lied about the killing of millions of Soviet citizens during the 1930s. It prohibited the organization of public opinion surveys that might reveal what the public really wanted, and it blocked the collection and release of statistics that might undermine its claim that the Soviet system was the best in the world. As a result, Western experts had to try to strike an intellectual balance between Soviet official claims and fragmentary evidence that pointed toward radically different conclusions. This task was made all the more difficult because the evidence of official crimes in the 1930s and 1940s led some Western advocates of liberal democracy to argue that the Soviet system had not changed significantly since then—even though mass terror, the key feature of Stalinism, disappeared when Stalin died in 1953.

The paradigms that we derived from studying Soviet history hampered our ability to foresee the revolution of the 1980s in several ways. As someone with a vested interest in these matters, I may not be completely objective, but I think three major blind spots kept us as a profession from sensing what was coming. Not all of us had the same blind spots, however. Thanks to different intellectual perspectives and political values, liberal and conservative analysts each were sensitive to particular pressures for change that were building up inside the Soviet Union. But almost all of us, liberal or conservative, suffered from some distinctive combination of blind spots that kept us from grasping the enormity of the impending upheaval.

First, in the early 1980s many Western analysts underestimated the depth of the socioeconomic crisis simmering under the calm surface of Soviet officialdom's optimistic pronouncements. Liberal Western analysts were more likely than conservative analysts to make this mistake, because in the atmosphere of U.S.–Soviet confrontation under President Reagan, we thought that Americans who proclaimed the "crisis of communism" were engaged in wishful thinking—just as Soviet spokesmen had long engaged in wishful thinking about a "general crisis of capitalism" that was supposed to produce socialist revolutions in the industrial West but never did. In retrospect, it's clear that as a group, conservative experts were much closer to the truth about the Soviet domestic crisis than liberal analysts were.

On the other hand, liberal analysts were less susceptible than conservatives to a second professional blind spot—the assumption that *all* members of the Soviet leadership were so preoccupied with their own power that they would avoid embarking on risky reforms. In this respect liberal scholars came closer to the truth, because we believed that the party leadership contained not only reactionaries but reformers with a deep desire to improve the country economically and socially. Conservative experts, who were dubious about the existence of serious policy differences inside the Soviet elite, had trouble imagining that some Communist Party leaders might introduce drastic reforms. Instead, conservative experts tended to expect that the internal crisis would simply cause the Soviet Union to deteriorate further and further without serious attempts at reform from above.

A third professional blind spot was that most of us failed to understand how long-term changes in Soviet social groups and values could gradually undermine the dictatorship of the party-state bureaucratic apparatus. The academic study of Soviet politics has always focused primarily on decision making at the top of the system—on "Kremlinology," as it is sometimes called—and has given much less attention to politics and social currents at lower levels. This focus resulted partly from the totalitarian paradigm we derived from studying the Stalin years, when the party-state structure seemed to achieve the total domination of society by means of mass terror. Our neglect of society's long-term influence on the political structure was also prompted in part by a shortage of reliable sociological information. Consistent with their claim that Marxism-Leninism had already revealed the "laws of social development," Soviet leaders before Gorbachev vigorously opposed the emergence of empirical sociology as an independent academic discipline, and the scarcity of data kept the number of Western sociologists who studied the Soviet Union extremely small. Thus the combination of our preconceptions and inadequate information prevented us from grasping a subtle shift in the interaction between the party-state apparatus and Soviet society as a whole. Yet it was this shift that made the new revolution possible.

Western specialists are still groping for new paradigms to replace those destroyed by the Soviet upheaval. But even as we grope, we must make provisional assumptions, either explicit or implicit, in order to interpret events. Today we often must make such assumptions not because we have too little concrete information, as in the past, but because the explosion of available information and the pace of change exceed our ability to assimilate them. For example, has the Soviet populace developed an enduring commitment to democracy that will help sustain the process of domestic reform, or is the populace still under the influence of an authoritarian political legacy that will cause it to turn away from liberalization as economic hardships worsen? Assumptions on this point—and on many others—have a powerful effect on Western experts' thinking about what kind of Soviet system is most likely to emerge in the future. The American public and governmental officials want answers to such pressing questions, yet until the huge influx of new information can be sorted out, we can answer only on the basis of our hunches. Obviously, Sovietology is still no closer to being an ivory-tower discipline divorced from current political concerns than it was in previous decades.

Sovietologists are obligated to try to answer the public's questions about the future as best we can. At the same time, however, we must vigorously emphasize the limits of our capacity to predict the future. Moreover, we must not become so engrossed with forecasting the future that we neglect to study the past—both the distant and the recent past. If we permit today's headlines to divert us from careful empirical analysis of what happened in the past month, the past year, or the past decade, we will have allowed the enormous excitement of the present to keep us from performing the one task that can genuinely contribute to better Western understanding of the Soviet Union in the coming years.

DISCUSSION QUESTIONS

1. Why were Soviet experts unable to predict the breaking apart of the Soviet Union?
2. What does the author mean by his call for "new paradigms"?

Article 51

The Psychology of Hitlerism

HAROLD LASSWELL

SINCE A POLITICAL ORDER which fails to coincide with an era of international prestige and domestic prosperity is endangered by the accumulating animosities of the community, it need occasion little surprise that a mass movement of protest swept aside some of the conventionalities of orderly government in Germany. Smarting under the humiliation of defeat, burdened by the discriminatory aftermath of Versailles, racked by the slow tortures of economic adversity, ruled in the name of political patterns devoid of sanctifying tradition, the German mentality has been ripening for an upsurge of the masses.

It is less the broad fact of mass action than the specific direction of discharge that demands explanation. The lower middle classes have become active factors in the struggle against the "proletarian" and the "Marxist" on behalf of an order of society in which the "profits system" though excoriated is none the less protected. Powerful trades unions have been demoralized as potent instruments in maintaining wage scales; "Marxist" bureaucrats in public offices and private unions have given way to loyal National Socialists from the bourgeoisie; restless young men, usually sons of the impoverished middle classes, have been inducted into the violence department of the state; Jews have suffered personal outrage and economic boycott.

From *The Political Quarterly,* Vol. 4, October/December 1933, pp. 373–384. Reprinted by permission of Basil Blackwell, Ltd.

The torrents of inflammatory rhetoric against the foreign enemies of Germany have culminated in no impulsive martyrdom in the Rhineland, or in Silesia, or along the "Corridor"; it is obvious that the re-armament of Germany has not gone far enough to repel the French. The separately manufactured parts of heavy artillery and tanks require from six weeks to two months to assemble, and French arms could devastate the West at once. Most of those who were in material want before Hitler are in material want today, though many of the materially cramped have been emotionally rejuvenated by the crusade to regenerate the German nation. New meaning has come to life, symbols are welcome substitutes for bread, and a lowered standard of living is but a sacrifice to the cause of national resurrection. The vast discrepancy between promise and performance in high politics and emergency economics is worthy of attention, for it reveals the peculiar dependence of Hitlerism on abracadabra.

Insofar as Hitlerism is a desperation reaction of the lower middle classes it continues a movement which began during the closing years of the nineteenth century. Materially speaking, it is not necessary to assume that the small shopkeepers, teachers, preachers, lawyers, doctors, farmers and craftsmen were worse off at the end than they had been in the middle of the century. Psychologically speaking, however, the lower middle class was increasingly overshadowed by the workers and the upper bourgeoisie, whose unions, cartels and parties took the center of the stage. The psychological impoverishment of the lower middle class precipitated emotional insecurities within the personalities of its members, thus fertilizing the ground for the various movements of mass protest through which the middle class might revenge themselves.

The insecurities of the class were reflected in the small bourgeois youth who furnished the basis of the German youth movement during its formative years. One of the first significant political expressions of the lower bourgeoisie was the Pan-German movement among German-speaking subjects of the Hapsburg monarchy. Pan-Germanism and Christian Socialism profoundly influenced Adolf Hitler during his years in Vienna; later he was able to adapt the nationalistic, socialistic and anti-Semitic features of these agitations to his own uses.

Nationalism and anti-Semitism were peculiarly fitted to the emotional necessities of the lower bourgeoisie. Rebuffed by a world which accorded them diminished deference, limited in the opportunities afforded by economic reality, the members of this class needed new objects of devotion and new targets of aggression. The rising cult of nationalism furnished a substitute for the fading appeal of institutionalized religion in a secularizing world. Anti-Semitism provided a target for the discharge of the resentments arising from damaged self-esteem; and since the scapegoat was connected with the older Christian tradition, guilt feelings arising from lack of personal piety could be expiated by attacking the Jew.

Anti-Semitism gave a plausible alternative to the uncompromising indictment of capitalism circulated by proletarian socialists. The proletarian doctrines offended the middle classes less by denouncing the extremes of wealth fostered by capitalism than by praising the "workers" and insulting the "bourgeoisie." The chief aspiration of the thrifty little bourgeois was to differentiate himself from the manual worker;

his self-esteem was openly wounded by the taunts, jibes and sneers of the proletarian agitators. He was often alienated from the political parties which were conspicuously identified with the older aristocracy and the new plutocracy, yet he could not endure the humiliation of associating with the "proletariat." He drifted uncertainly toward the democratic parties of the middle, but democratic republicanism coincided with want and humiliation in the post-war years. The lure of anti-Semitism lay partly in the opportunity which it provided for discharging animosity against the rich and successful without espousing proletarian socialism. It was not capitalism but Jewish profiteering which was the root of modern evils. The international character of finance, with which the Jews were so conspicuously connected, was apparently irreconcilable with fervent nationalism, and the crusade against the Jew became a legitimate act of devotion to the idols of Germanism.

The prominence of the Jew in proletarian socialism enabled the lower bourgeoisie to rationalize its hostility to the wage earners as resentment against the Jew. This paved the way for a political alliance with those wage earners who were sufficiently "Germanic" to renounce Jewish doctrine, which could be distinguished from "socialism" by naming it "Marxism." Thus by hating "Marxists" middle class elements were able to discharge enough hatred of the wage earning class as a whole to permit limited cooperation with wage earners who would espouse a truly "national" form of "socialism." By adopting the word "socialism" in a vague, emasculated sense, the lower bourgeoisie directed some of its hatred against the blood suckers who ran chain stores and exacted high profits, without being constrained to join with the most insolent spokesmen of the wage earners. And it was evident that some flirting with the "Left" could improve bargaining relations with the "Right."

The growth of anti-Semitism also favored political collaboration of the lower middle classes with the landed aristocracy, despite conflicting economic interests. The aristocracy cherished the old fashioned hatred of money-making by the use of mobile capital. The hatred of modern capitalism by the aristocracy would be rationalized as hatred of the Jew, the money-lender of tradition; by hating Jewish capitalism the aristocracy is enabled to work off its hostility to capitalism as a whole, and to collaborate with some capitalistic elements. When the petty bourgeoisie utilized the Jew as a scapegoat, a common hatred favored political association with the aristocracy. By flocking into a separate party, the lower bourgeoisie emancipated itself to some extent from the tutelage of the old order, but remained able to cooperate with it on the basis of common loyalty to "Germanism" and common hatred of "Semites."

In some measure the use of the Jewish scapegoat is an incident in the struggle for survival within the intellectual class, which includes many members of the bourgeoisie. The growth of the vast material environment in modern society has been paralleled by the unprecedented expansion of specialized symbolic activity. Medicine, engineering and physical science have proliferated into a thousand specialties for the control of specific aspects of the material world. Those who master the necessary symbol equipment are part of the intellectual class whose "capital" is knowledge, not muscle. There is a sub-division of the intellectual workers, the "intellectuals" in the narrow sense, who specialize in the symbols connected with political life. The growing complexity of modern civilization has created a vast net of reporters, interpreters, pedagogues, advertisers, agitators, propagandists, legal dialecticians, historians and social scientists who compete among themselves and with all other classes and sub-classes for deference, safety and material income. These specialists in the invention and transmission of political symbols can reminisce about history, argue about morals, law, philosophy and expediency, inculcate myths and legends, or exemplify rituals and ceremonies. Lenin dismissed the "intellectuals" as classless prostitutes hired out to the highest bidder. It is evident that a "brain trust"—to use a current American expression employed to describe President Roosevelt's expert advisers—is a useful form of political armament on all sides, but the tremendous growth of symbol specialists in The Great Society suggests that we have to do with the emergence of a potent social formation with objective interests of its own, some of which can be fostered, paradoxically enough, by encouraging symbolic warfare among its members.

During times of economic adversity the symbol specialists suffer deflation like the rest of the community, and if colleges, universities, and other agencies for transmitting skill are not proportionately curtailed, the difficulties of the "intellectuals" are accentuated. Post-war Germany abolished many limitations upon university training, and German universities pumped an increasing volume of trained talent into an overstocked market. The prominence of the Jew in law, medicine, acting, literature, journalism (indeed, in all branches of the intellectual arts) contributed to his vulnerability as an object of mass attack led by rival intellectuals, with or without the aid of other social classes.

The position of the Jew in German society has been further weakened by the frequency with which he has appeared as an enemy of the *mores*. His activity as an intellectual of necessity brought him into conflict with the conventional patterns of German bourgeois life. A Jewish physician in Vienna invented psychoanalysis, which scandalized, even as it fascinated, the middle classes. A Jewish physician in Berlin attained celebrity by identifying himself with the cause of the homosexuals. Jewish writers and actors have produced plays which horrified the provincial conscience. Indeed, one of the avenues to money, prestige and heightened self-importance which is open to the intellectual is sensationalism, which usually involves some defiance of accepted taboos. The Jew was relatively free from the parochial loyalties of gentile Germans, who were often bound to the sentiments of the separate cultural islands throughout the German-speaking territories. Less entangled by local tradition, the Jews were able to seize the opportunity to cater to the whole German market, and to many of the symbols which were capable of appealing to all Germans everywhere.

Modern urban culture is fatal to the simple prescriptions of the rural and provincial conscience; to the moralists of the hinterland the cities defy the laws of god and man. The middle-class code of sexual abstinence, thrift, work and piety crumbles before the blandishments and the concealments of the city. The vulnerability of the conventional code provokes heroic acts in its defense. Today the resentments of the threatened provincial conscience have been adroitly turned against "cultural Bolshevism," which means the urban, intellectual, Marxist, syndicated Jew.

Hitlerism is a concession to cultural fundamentalism in a far deeper sense than that it defends property from communist expropriation. Hitler has come to stand for the re-affirmation of the cardinal moral virtues whose neglect has weakened the whole fiber of the German nation. Putrid literature, putrid drama, putrid practices are imputed to the foul Jew who desecrated the homeland whose hospitality he so long enjoyed. The stress of battle, undernourishment, inflation, and unemployment during these recent eventful years has exposed many men and women to "temptations" which they could not resist, and the accumulated weight of guilt arising from these irregularities drives many of them into acts of expiation. In some measure the "awakening of Germany" is a cleansing gesture of aspiration for a feeling of moral worth, and the Jew is the sacrificial ram.

Such is the meaning of the emphasis in Hitler's public personality upon abstinence from wine, women and excess; this is the clue to the appeal of the humorless gravity which is one of his most obvious traits. The irreverent urbanities of Berlin find Hitler dull, and his appearances have been relatively infrequent and as ceremonial as possible. The biting Goebbels is the darling of the city; the sober Hitler is the lion of the provinces. This pious deacon with the silver tongue is the articulate conscience of the petty bourgeoisie.

Hitler's appeal to the conservative mothers of Germany derives from their resentment against all the slogans which have been associated with a world in which their sons have been killed or demoralized since 1914. Through Hitler comes revenge against the immoral monsters who have defied the immutable principles of human decency and divine order. Through Hitler comes the hope of rescue for sons, who may learn discipline and self-respect in the uniform, the exercises, and even the dangers of the National Socialist movement. The sons of German mothers who were sacrificed in vain, betrayed by the alien Jewish cankers in our midst, are to be avenged. The traitors shall not go unpunished. The dawning day of resurrection is nigh. The organized might of German manhood shall rise to purify the state and to recover the honor of Germany on the field of battle. Our blood shall not have been shed in vain. The flesh of our flesh shall not decay; it shall live in the glories of immortal Germany.

There is a profound sense in which Hitler himself plays a maternal role for certain classes in German society. His incessant moralizing is that of the anxious mother who is totally preoccupied with the physical, intellectual and ethical development of her children. He discourses in public, as he has written in his autobiography, on all manner of pedagogical problems, from the best form of history teaching to the ways of reducing the ravages of social disease. His constant preoccupation with "purity" is consistent with these interests; he alludes constantly to the "purity of the racial stock" and often to the code of personal abstinence or moderation. This master of modern Galahadism uses the language of Protestant puritanism and of Catholic reverence of the institution of family life. The conscience for which he stands is full of obsessional doubts, repetitive affirmations, resounding negations and stern compulsions. It is essentially the bundle of "don'ts" of the nurse-maid conscience.[1]

In yet another way Hitler has performed a maternal function in German life. The disaster of defeat in war left the middle classes of German society shocked, dazed and humiliated. The "we" symbol which meant so much was damaged, and they were left shorn of means of revenging themselves upon their enemies. When an individual is suddenly deprived of his customary mode of externalizing loves and aggressions the resulting emotional crisis is severe. In extreme cases, the aggressive impulses which were formerly directed against the outside world are turned back against the personality itself, and suicide, melancholia, and other mental disorders ensue. Most thwarted people are protected from such extreme reactions by finding new objects of devotion and self-assertion. Emotional insecurities are reduced by hating scapegoats and adoring heroes, and insofar as politics provides the formulae and the activities which satisfy these requirements, politics is a form of social therapy for potential suicides.

Hitler was able to say, in effect, "You are not to blame for the disaster to your personality involved in the loss of the war. You were betrayed by alien enemies in our midst who were susceptible to the duplicity of our enemies. Germany must awaken to the necessity of destroying the alien at home in order to prepare to dispose of the enemy abroad." The self-accusations which signify that aggressive impulses are turned against the self are thus no longer necessary; not the "sacred ego," but the Jews are to blame. By projecting blame from the self upon the outside world, inner emotional insecurities are reduced. By directing symbolic and overt attacks against the enemy in our midst, Hitler has alleviated the anxieties of millions of his fellow Germans (at the expense of others). He has also provided fantasies of ultimate victory over the French and the Poles, and arranged marches and special demonstrations as symbolic acts of attack upon the outer as well as the inner enemies of Germany. Hitler has offered himself as the hero and Germanism as the legitimizing symbol of adoration. These partially overt but principally magical acts have provided many distraught Germans with renewed self-confidence either to ignore or to face the rough deprivations of daily life. From one point of view, Hitler's role resembles that of the nurse who tells her crying charge that the neighbor boy was very naughty to hit him; but Hitler's reassurances stir up trouble within the household by diverting animosity against the Jewish fellow-national.

When realities do not facilitate the discharge of aggressive tendencies against the outer group, these impulses are often turned back against subgroups within one's own community. This is one aspect of the larger proposition stated before that impulses which are denied expression in the outside world rebound against symbols more closely associated with the personality. Germany, though gaining in fighting power, is as yet too weak for war, and the heightening tensions since the economic collapse of 1929 have therefore been discharged in civil persecution and not in war.

As aggressive impulses are turned against the self, those aspects of the personality are chosen which are deplored as particularly weak or immoral. Germans have long lamented the absence of a unified German nation, attributing this weakness in part to the dogmatic pride of opinion which is so deeply rooted in German pride of mind. Unity has been partially attained by the superficial co-ordination of external motions; "the German national dance step is the goose step." Beneath the facade of external harmony survive the legacies of disunion. Since the Germans hate most in themselves, as a collective unit, cultural diversity and intellectual virtuosity (qualities which they simultaneously admire), it is scarcely surprising to discover that they have turned upon the Jew as the most typical exponent of their own limitations. German devotion to the symbols of uncompromising nationalism is constantly threatened by contrasting loyalties and intellectual scruples. In the Jew, the eternal scapegoat, they can expiate their own sins against the collective god.

In the hope of contributing to the consolidation of the German nation many elements of German society have condoned the "excesses" of the National Socialists, and welcomed the vigorous centralization and inspired fervor of the movement. Accustomed to submissiveness within the hierarchy of home, army, bureaucracy and party, Germans have assumed the yoke of Hitlerism in the name of freedom, socialism and nationalism.

The appeal from the politics of discussion to the arbitrament of violence and dictatorship came readily in Germany. The symbols and practices associated with the Weimar Republic have meant comparatively little to anybody. The failure to liquidate the symbols of the old régime is shown in the battle over the national colors, and in the persistence of the older personnel in the universities, in the schools, and in the principal organs of administration. Civic training on behalf of the Republic has been formal and uninspired; for some time after the inauguration of the Republic, the schools continued to use the old Imperialist textbooks. Perhaps no amount of skill and ingenuity could have built up a body of myths capable of sustaining the Republic under the unfavorable conditions of the post-war era, but in some measure the battle of Weimar was lost by default.

Just as the influential Jews failed to see the handwriting on the wall and lulled themselves into a false sense of safety, the nominal heads of the Republic neglected to intervene boldly and aggressively in the unfolding situation. The fear of the Communists by the bureaucrats of the Social Democratic party and the trades unions drove them into collaboration with their class enemies. Socialist and union officialdom denounced Communist workers to the employers; the Communists were frequently weeded out and superseded by National Socialists. The bureaucratizing tendency of the labor movement in Germany has long been notorious; a job in the union or in the party transformed the fervent agitator into a model bourgeois, anxious to keep his job by preserving discipline among the masses.

That the bourgeoisie of Northern Germany has never fought and bled for republican institutions is connected with the belated industrialization of the country. The English middle classes and the French struggled for responsible government, but the rising Prussian bourgeoisie first connected democratic internationalism with the French invasion; later they began to fear the proletariat as the menace on the

"Left," which drove them steadily to the "Right." Thus national parliamentarism is not deeply enshrined in the loyalties of the classes most closely associated with it in the West.

The future of the middle classes in Germany depends on the success of the new ruling régime in improving their material prospects and psychological rewards. Unless this problem is solved, enthusiasm for the new symbols will gradually die away, and the resulting disillusionment will gradually transform the middle classes into mere passive supporters of the reigning order of society. They will then conform more closely to the role which the older revolutionists expected the middle classes to play in the class struggle. Recent events in Italy and in Germany have given rise to the reflection that the political activism of the middle classes has been grossly underestimated, for they contributed sons to supply the sinews, money to defray the cost, and ballots to sustain the candidates, of potent alternatives to proletarianism.

The abandonment of so many of the forms of democratic government has corroborated the communist teaching that such trifles will be cast away whenever the class struggle seems to render it imperative for the protection of the profits principle. This convincing demonstration may be expected to dissolve much of the "democratic romanticism" which enabled the tiny bureaucrats of the older labor movement to drift and not to fight.

Communism may supply the symbol in whose name mass hostilities will ultimately discharge themselves against bourgeoisie and aristocracy. No doubt this is improbable, short of military defeat in war, or long-protracted war, when foreign war may be transformed into civil war. In the meanwhile, it is sound tactics to preserve the integrity of the term "Communist" by refusing to associate it with its near rivals. Small disciplined revolutionaries may one day use the uncontaminated symbol and the technique of the *coup d'état* to ride the waves of mass discontent to the seats of power.

It is worthy of comment that the lower middle classes, stung from political passivity into political action, have been able to furnish their own crusading leadership. Hitler, the self-made semi-intellectual, son of a small customs official in the service of the Hapsburgs, stirs his own class to an unwonted spurt of political aggressiveness. Other social groups, like the wage earners, have so often been led by men who were social renegades from the older social strata that this self-sufficiency of the bourgeoisie inspires respectful interest.

Influential elements of the upper bourgeoisie of Germany have partially financed the Hitler movement to break up the collective bargaining system which was sustained by the powerful German trades unions. This was impossible in the name of the older parties of the "Right," who were too intimately connected with the plutocracy and the aristocracy. Only a movement thoroughly nationalistic and demagogic could stir the lower bourgeoisie to enthusiastic action, and make substantial inroads in the more passive elements of the wage earning class. In general, the symbols of Hitlerism have assuaged the emotional conflicts of the lower bourgeoisie, while the acts of Hitlerism have lowered the labor costs of the upper bourgeoisie.

NOTE

1. This analysis of Hitler's public role among middle-class conservatives carries no implications concerning his private life.

DISCUSSION QUESTIONS

1. Why was Hitlerism a desperate reaction of the lower middle class?
2. What elements of "nationalism" and "anti-Semitism" allowed the lower middle class to form political alliances with Germany's aristocracy?

References

Adler, P. & Adler, P. A. (1985). From idealism to pragmatic detachment: The adademic performance of college athletes. *Sociology of Education, 58,* 241–249.

Anderson, J. A., (1988). Cognitive styles and multicultural populations. *Journal of Teacher Education,* 2–9.

Bartlett, D. L. & Steel, J. B. (1992). *America, what went wrong?* Kansas City, Missouri: Andrews and McMeel, 12–17.

Berger, P. L. (1963). *Invitation to sociology.* New York: Doubleday and Co., 1–4.

Best, J. & Horiuchi, G. T. (1985). The razor blade in the apple: The social construction of urban legends. *Social Problems, 32,* 488–497.

Bierstedt, R. (1974). On power. *The Social Order* (4th ed.). New York: McGraw-Hill, 350–355, 357–359.

Boisjoly, R., Curtis, E. F. & Mellican, E. (1989). Ethical dimensions of the challenger disaster. *Journal of Business Ethics, 8,* 217–230.

Butler, R. N. (1988). A generation at risk: When the baby-boomers reach golden pond. *The Conference Board.*

Cherlin, A. & Furstenberg, F. F., Jr. (1982). The shape of the american family in the year 2000. *The Tap Report.* Washington, D.C.: American Council of Life Insurance.

Conner, J. W. (1985). Differential socialization and role stereotypes in japanese families. *Journal of Psychological Anthropology, 8,* 29–31, 33–36.

Conrad, P. (1986). The social meaning of AIDS. *Social Policy,* 51–56.

Davis, K. & Moore, W. E. (1945). Principles of social stratification. *American Sociological Review, 10,* 242–249.

Devereux, E. (1977). Backyard versus little league baseball: The impoverishment of children's games. *Social Problems in Athletes.* Champaign: University of Illinois Press, 38–41, 43–46, 52–54.

Dewey, J. (1944). Democratic faith and education. *The Antioch Review, 4,* 278–283.

Ehrenreich, B. & English, D. (1989). Blowing the whistle on the "mommy track." *Ms Magazine, 18,* 56–58.

Erikson, K. (1962). Notes on the sociology of deviance. *Social Problems, 9,* 307–314.

Fromm, E. (1966). Karl marx's theory of alienation. *Marx's Concept of Man.* New York: Ungar.

Gersel, N. & Gross H. (1984). *Commuter Marriage.* New York: Guilford, 114–123.

Gerth, H. & Mills, C. W. (1953). Institutions and social roles. *Character and Social Structure: The Psychology of Social Structure.* New York: Harcourt Brace Jovanovich, 10–14.

Gilbert, B. & Twyman, L. (1983, Jan. 31). Violence: Out of hand in the stands. *Sports Illustrated.*

Goffman, E. (1959). Presentation of self in everyday life. New York: Doubleday and Co., 17–19, 22–24, 30–33, 35–36, 55–56, 249–255.

Gordon, M. M. (1961). Assimilation in america: Theory and reality. *Daedalus, 90,* 263–280.

Hall, E. & Hall, M. H. (1971, June). The sounds of silence. *Playboy,* 95–102.

Hoose, P. (1990, April 29). A new pool of talent. *New York Times Magazine,* 49–61.

Hopper, K. (1983). Homelessness: Reducing the distance. *New England Journal of Human Services,* 30–31, 33–34, 36–40, 42–43, 45–47.

Hunt, J. (1985, Jan.). Police accounts of normal force. *Urban Life, 13.*

Jewell, D. P. (1952). A case of a psychotic navaho indian male. *Human Organization, 11,* 32–36.

Kagan, J. (1975). The case against i.q. tests: The concept of intelligence. In R. J. Antonio & G. Ritzer (eds.), *Social Problems: Values and Interests in Conflict.* Boston: Allyn and Bacon, 295–298.

Kluckhohn, C. (1949). Queer customs. *Mirror for Man.* New York: McGraw-Hill, 103–107.

Kusha, H. R. (1992). Iran's white revolution and its outcome for iranian women. *Sociology: A Global Perspective,* Joan Ferrante (ed.). Belmont, CA: Wadsworth.

Lasswell, H. D. (1933). The psychology of hitlerism. *The Political Quarterly, 4,* 373–384.

LeBon, G. (1896). *The crowd.* London: Ernest Benn, Ltd., 5–6, 13–14.

Lifton, R. J. (1986). Medicalized killing. *The Nazi Doctors: Medical Killing and the Psychology of Genocide.* New York: Basic, 14–18.

Meltzer, B. N. (1964). *The social psychology of george herbert mead.* Center for Sociological Research: Western Michigan University, 10–31.

Mills, C. W. (1959). *The sociological imagination.* New York: Oxford University Press.

Parrott, B. (1992). The soviet upheaval and western sovietology. *Sociology: A Global Perspective,* Joan Ferrante (ed.). Belmont, CA: Wadsworth.

Persell, C. H. & Cookson, P. W. (1985). Chartering and bartering: Elite education and social reproduction, *Social Problems, 33,* 114–126.

Ritzer, G. (1984). The mcdonaldization of society. *Journal of American Culture,* 100–107.

Rosenfeld, J. & Rodin, S. (1984, Dec.). Lifestyle: It's in the cards. *American Demographics,* 311–333, 337.

Rosenhan, L. (1973). On being sane in insane places. *Science, 179,* 250–258.

Scully, D. (1990). *Understanding sexual violence.* New York: Unwin Hyman, 103–112.

Selengut, C. (1984/Spring). Should social background count? *The Community College Humanist.* Philadelphia: Community College of Philadelphia.

Salomone, J. J. (1972). The funeral home as a work system. *The Social Dimensions of Work.* Clifton Bryant (ed.). Englewood Cliffs: New Jersey, 164–177.

Stark, R. & Bainbridge, W. S. (1980). Secularization, revival, and cult formation. *Journal for the Scientific Study of Religion, 4.*

Tobias, S. (1989, Sept.). Tracked to fail. *Psychology Today,* 54–60.

Töennies, F. (1957). *Community and society* (translated by Loomis, C.), East Lansing: Michigan State University Press, 223–231.

Turner, J. (1985). Knowing about things. *Sociology: A Student Handbook.* New York: Random House, 20–24.

Wade, N. (1976). I.Q. and heredity: Suspicion of fraud beclouds classic experiment. *Science, 194,* 916–918.

Weinberg, M. S. (1976). The nudist management of respectability. *Sex Research: Studies from the Kinsey Institute.* New York: Oxford University Press, 217–232.

Wuthnow, R. (1988). Divided we fall: America's two civil religions. *The Restructuring of American Religion: Society and Faith Since W.W. II.* Princeton, NJ: Princeton University Press, 395–399.

Zuboff, S. (1982, Sept.). New worlds of computer-mediated work. *Harvard Business Review.*